EDRA TWO

**COMMUNITY DEVELOPMENT
SERIES**

Series Editor: Richard P. Dober, AIP

Volumes Published and in Preparation

CDS/21

EDRA TWO

**Proceedings of the Second Annual
Environmental Design Research
Association Conference
October 1970
Pittsburgh, Pennsylvania**

Edited by

John Archea and Charles Eastman
Carnegie–Mellon University

Dowden, Hutchinson
& Ross, Inc.
STROUDSBURG, PENNSYLVANIA

Distributed by
HALSTED   A division of
PRESS   John Wiley & Sons, Inc.

Library of Congress Cataloging in Publication Data

Exclusive Distributor: **Halsted Press**
A Division of John Wiley & Sons, Inc.

EDRA Steering Committee

Co-Chairmen:

Sidney Cohn
Henry Sanoff

Members:

Daniel Carson
Robert Frew
Richard Krauss
Gary Moore
Stuart Silverstone

Ex-Officio:

John Archea
Charles Eastman
Thomas Thomson
Gary Winkel

Conference Planning

Co-Chairmen:

John Archea
Charles Eastman

Planning Team:

Daniel Carson
Imre Cohn
Asher Derman
John Grason
Reinhart Lai
Thomas Moran
Leonard Olsen
Alton Penz
Richard Pohlman
Wolfgang Preiser
Paul Shaffer
Raymond Studer
Christos Yessios

PREFACE

The Environmental Design Research Association was formed in 1968 to promote research and communication among those working to gain new knowledge or develop new techniques for solving environmental problems. Since its inception, EDRA has included geographer, psychologists, sociologists, computer scientists and operations researchers, as well as the design professions of architecture and planning. As such, EDRA represents one effort directed toward the breaking down of boundaries between traditional academic fields and between researcher and professional.

The EDRA currently consists of subscribers to three journals whose focus is environmental design research: Environment and Behavior, Man Environment Systems, and Design Methods Group Newsletter. The first conference of the organization was held in Chapel Hill, North Carolina in June, 1969. The emphasis of this first meeting was the bringing together of different groups working on environmental problem solving. The emphasis was on communication and the development of a forum for exchanging information among researchers. With over two hundred attendees, the organizational and communication goals of the first conference were clearly achieved.

As a young field whose focus is a problem domain, environmental design research has drawn from experimental and analytical techniques from a mixture of other fields. As in many other newly recognized problem domains, much of the early work has emphasized the fervor of commitment over the actual gain in knowledge. Research in this field occasionally reflects ignorance of experimental controls, of logical inference, and of the existence of better methods for achieving the same end. It was considered an appropriate focus of this second conference to be the presentation of research in environmental design which, by the quality of the research formulation, execution and interpretation, have provided an outstanding contribution to the field. In this way it is hoped that the quality of future environmental design research will be far superior to that which is available today. We hope that this volume may provide a model for students of the area.

The resulting collection of papers, presented on the following pages, speak for themselves. From over one hundred submissions, the following forty plus papers were considered outstanding by the paper's referees. Hopefully, future conferences will continue to advance the knowledge and technique available to environmental design.

Charles M. Eastman

Referees of Submitted Papers

Richard Alden
Irwin Altman
Shirley Angrist
John Archea
Mary Arnold
Richard Barrow
Alfred Blumstein
Joseph Britton
Charles Burnette
David Canter
Daniel Carson
Richard Chase
John Christian
Weldon Clark
Harry Coblentz
Sidney Cohn
John Collins
Kenneth Craik
Alton DeLong
Asher Derman
Roger Downs
Charles Eastman
Aristide Esser
John Grason
Edward Krokowsky
Samuel Leadly

Samuel Leinhardt
Stan Lembeck
Gordon Lewis
John Liu
David Lowenthal
Stuart Mann
Peter Manning
Peter Meyer
Gary Moore
Thomas Moran
Theodore Myer
Leonard Olson
Wolfgang Preiser
David Sandahl
Peggy Sanday
Henry Sanoff
Robert Shellow
Leonard Singer
David Stea
Conrad Strack
Raymond Studer
Charles Taylor
Robert Taylor
Jan Wilking
Joahim Wohlwill
Christos Yessios

CONTENTS

NOTE: The final version of papers denoted with an asterisk (*) were not received in time to be
      included in the Proceedings.

Invited Paper:

Style in Design

by Herbert A. Simon
Carnegie-Mellon University

Abstract

A style is some one way of doing things, chosen from a number of alternative ways. Since design problems generally do not have unique optimal solutions, style may enter in choosing any one of many satisfactory solutions. Components of style can arise from three sources: direct specification of the final object, the processes used to manufacture it, and the processes used to design it. This paper examines the dynamic aspects of style, and particularly those aspects that arise from the design process itself. The analysis suggests a new interpretation of the esthetic significance of functionalism.

The following passage from E. H. Gombrich's remarkable book, ART AND ILLUSION (page 21), will serve as my thesis:

"The history of taste and fashion
is the history of preferences, of
various acts of choice between
given alternatives . . . [But]
an act of choice is only of symptomatic significance, is expres-
sive of something only if we can
really want to treat styles as
symptomatic of something else,
. . . , we cannot do without
some theory of the alternatives."

A style, in this view, is some one way of doing things, chosen from a number of alterna- tive ways. If Frederick Taylor had been cor- rect in insisting that there is "one right way of doing anything," there would be an inevita- ble clash between function and style--we could exercise stylistic freedom only by sacrificing function. One purpose of this paper is to argue that we are not in fact faced with this particular dilemma--that design problems gen- erally do not have unique optimal solutions, hence that we may choose any one of many satisfactory solutions.

Styles are generally identified by fea- tures of the objects designed. We may char- acterize (not very profoundly) the Gothic style in architecture by its pointed arches, and the Romanesque style by its round arches. Sometimes, however, at one step removed from the objects themselves, we connect styles in objects with the particular manufacturing pro- cesses that produced them. Thus, observing different styles of flint arrowheads, we may distinguish between those produced by percus- sion and those produced by pressure. Or we may distinguish pottery made on the wheel from coiled pottery.

At one further remove from the final ob- ject, styles may also arise from differences in the process of design. Buildings designed primarily from the inside out, are different from those designed primarily from the outside in. Thus, components of style can arise from at least three sources: the direct specifica- tions of the final object, the nature of the processes used to manufacture it, and the na- ture of the processes used to design it. Of course, the latter two sources--manufacturing and design processes--also manifest themselves in features of the final object, but only in- directly as a consequence of the interplay of dynamic forces. It is the second purpose of this paper to examine the dynamic aspects of style, and particularly those aspects that a- rise from the design process itself.

Satisficing and the One Right Way

There is a proverb to the effect that the best is enemy of the good. A little reflec- tion shows that the proverb can be read in two diametrically opposed ways, and that it is not clear which reading is intended--or is the more defensible. By one interpretation, the proverb means that if we are willing to settle for the good enough--to satisfice--we will never attain the best. By the other interpre- tation, it means that our striving to reach an unattainable best may prevent us from reaching an achievable good-enough. It is this latter interpretation that describes the stern real- ities of the design process in the world we know--in any world, for that matter, that is even moderately complex.

Since I have made the satisficing argu- ment at length elsewhere, I will review it only briefly here, and then apply it specifical- ly to the problem of design (1). Most problem solving can be represented as a search through a large space of possibilities. For real-world problems, the spaces are not merely large, but immense, and there is not the slightest chance for either man or computer to search them exhaustively for the solution that is absolutely best.

Best solutions are therefore only attainable in those situations where there exist some systematic procedures, or algorithms, for going more or less directly to the optimum with only a moderate amount of highly selective search, or, in favorable instances with no search at all. Thus, to find the local maxima of a real-valued, continuous and differentiable function of a variable defined on a closed interval, simply execute the algorithm for finding the first derivative of the function, set the first derivative equal to zero, and solve for the unknown. That the function consists of a non-denumerable infinity of points causes no trouble, for only a small finite set of these is ever examined, and the algorithm leads us directly to them.

In other kinds of problem spaces, the available algorithms are not powerful enough to eliminate entirely the need for search, but are sufficiently selective to reduce search to tolerable proportions. An important class of examples are the situations that can be formulated as linear programming problems. The available algorithms for seeking the optimum in a linear programming problem--for example, the simplex algorithm--search only certain boundary points of the space, are guaranteed to climb monotonically toward the optimum, and reach that optimum after a finite number of steps. Although it is easy to find real-life problems that demand more computation in a linear programming formulation than man or computer can provide, a good many problems become manageable when stated in linear programming terms.

Where optimizing algorithms are unavailable, or are impractical for problems of the size we must solve, settling for a satisfactory solution instead of seeking the best one is generally an excellent way out. Techniques for satisficing are often called "heuristic programming techniques."

Satisficing is sometimes dismissed as obvious and not very interesting common sense: "If you can't do the best, do the best you can." Alternatively, economists sometimes argue that satisficing is simply optimizing under a constraint on the resources available for search. The optimizing rule, in this view, is: Continue searching until the expected improvement in the solution from investment of additional search effort is just worth that effort; then halt.

Because they overlook two important points, the arguments from common sense and economics underestimate the importance of taking a satisficing viewpoint. First of all, when no selective optimizing algorithm is available, the cost of a search to find the best tends to increase at least linearly with the size of the space searched. In contrast, the cost of a search to find a satisfactory solution depends only on the density of distribution of solutions of varying quality through the space, and is more or less independent of the size of the total space. The familiar needle-in-haystack problem illustrates the point. In a haystack throughout which needles of varying sharpness are distributed randomly, finding the sharpest needle requires a search of the entire stack. Finding a needle sharp enough to sew with requires a search of a pile of hay big enough to contain one such needle--a pile whose size does not depend at all on the size of the whole stack. For most practical purposes, the real world is an infinite haystack, hence a place where we are well advised to satisfice.

The second point often ignored by optimizers is that, if the general magnitude of the available search effort is known in advance, then following an optimizing procedure until the marginal cost of additional search exceeds the expected gain is <u>not</u> equivalent to employing the best satisficing procedure. <u>Given</u> a resource limit, there may exist many satisficing procedures that will, on average, find better solutions than a truncated optimizing procedure. This proposition can again, of course, be translated into optimizing terms, but as a practical matter, it has often been overlooked by optimizers, who have consequently invested too little of their effort in the search for powerful heuristic procedures. Some of us would argue that this has resulted, in the past two decades, in a serious imbalance between the amount of research devoted to improving the kit of optimizing tools and the amount devoted to improving the kit of satisficing tools; and a consequent imbalance in the kits themselves. But pursuing this point would take me away from my main topic, which is style. What has the distinction between satisficing and optimizing to do with style?

Optimizing techniques generally produce unique solutions or small sets of similar solutions. Although one can construct all sorts of more or less pathological counterexamples to this generalization, they have little relevance to the real world. Hence, an optimizer faces no question of style, but simply a question of finding the best solution. If we insist on according the optimizer a style, we can only equate it with an extreme functionalism, in which function determines form, utterly and completely. Few designers who subscribe to the functionalist view would feel comfortable with the doctrine that they exercise no choice and that no questions of style enter their design. But that is certainly where an attempt to combine functionalism with optimizing leads us.

For the satisficer, the unique solution is the exception rather than the rule. Mushrooms can be found in many places in the forest, and the time it takes us to fill a sack

with them may not depend much on the direction
we wander. We may feel free, then, to exercise some choice of path, and even to introduce additional choice criteria (for example,
the pleasantness of the walk or the avoidance
of wet places) over and above the pragmatic
one of bringing back a full sack.

There are really two cases to be distinguished here. In the one case, two distinct
search paths may be generated by two different
heuristic procedures each of which is designed
only to find mushrooms. In the other case,
two distinct search paths may be generated by
two different heuristic procedures because one
of them incorporates criteria beyond the
basic one of finding mushrooms--or both incorporate auxiliary criteria, but different ones.
In the former case, the choice of one or the
other of the heuristic procedures is a choice
of style; in the latter case, the choice of
auxiliary criteria is a choice of style. In
both cases, it is the non-uniqueness of satisfactory solutions that permits us the choice.
Hence, in a world where the best is the enemy
of the good, there is almost unlimited room
for the expression of preferences in style
even for the functionalist.

Criteria and Constraints

The requirements for a design or problem solution are usually expressed by some
combination of criteria and constraints. In
a typical linear programming problem, for example, the criterion is a function that is to
be maximized or minimized, and the constraints
are bounds on the magnitude of certain of the
variables: e.g., minimize the cost of the basket of food (criterion) that contains at least
2,000 calories (constraint) and not less than
a_1, a_2, a_3, ... milligrams of vitamins and
minerals 1, 2, 3, ... (constraints).

Notice that in this example the distinction between criterion and constraints is not
the distinction we commonly make between the
goals of an action and the side conditions it
must satisfy. For the goal of buying a basket
of food is not to save money, but to meet
nutritional requirements. Here the goal is a
set of constraints, while a side condition is
the criterion--the minimization of cost. The
distinction in linear programming between
criterion and constraints is a technical distinction between the variables that are to be
subjected to an optimizing procedure and those
that are to be held within bounds. Either may
be goal; either may be side condition. In the
problem of maximizing the return on an investment portfolio, subject to limits on risk, the
main goal and the criterion function become
identical.

When heuristic techniques are used for
satisficing, the asymmetry between criteria
and constraints disappears. The task is to
find an object that satisfies all of a (possibly large) set of constraints. On the
borderline between optimizing and satisficing

lie hybrid procedures that satisfy a set of
constraints, with one or more variables left
undetermined, then optimize some function of
the remaining free variables. Whether we regard these as optimizing or satisficing procedures depends on two things: how severely
the satisfaction of the constraints restricts
the solutions that remain; and whether the
function to be optimized corresponds to a central goal of the design or to a relatively unimportant side condition.

If the constraints do most of the work
of determining the solution, while the optimization only modifies it marginally, we often
speak of "suboptimization." Suboptimizing is
most profitably viewed as satisficing, for
this view calls our attention to the all-impor-
tant constraints rather than to the relatively
uninfluential criteria. Suboptimizing reminds
one of the joke about the household in which
the husband made all the important decisions
(about international affairs) and the wife all
the unimportant ones (about the family budget).
In many suboptimizing procedures, the constraints make the really important selections.

In the remainder of this paper, I shall
be concerned with situations where the goals
and side conditions of the design are all expressed as constraints to be satisfied. Sym-
metrizing the design requirements in this way
has the further advantage that it allows us to
treat identically both the requirements that
are imposed by the designer and his client
and the requirements that are imposed by nature.
For example, the compressive strength of concrete can be introduced into the design problem as a constraint of the same form as the
minimum dimensions of a room.

Generators and Tests

Having put all constraints on an equal
footing, we now discriminate among them along
a new dimension--we distinguish between constraints imbedded in generators and constraints
expressed by tests. The simplest paradigm for
a design process contains two subprocesses.
The first of these generates, sequentially,
certain objects that are candidate solutions
or components of solutions. The second process
tests whether a candidate satisfies a set of
constraints. Any object generated that then
satisfies the test process is guaranteed to
satisfy all the design requirements (2).

Most commonly, in a generate-and-test
process the design is assembled component by
component. Each component generated is added
to the previous assembly, and the new structure then tested. If the test succeeds, the
process continues; if it fails, the new component is discarded and another generated.
Here the design process involves not just a
cycle of generating and testing, but a whole
sequence of such cycles.

The monkeys in the British Museum who
were trying to reproduce the works of Shakespeare on their typewriters employed the most

primitive form of a generate-and-test process, simply typing random sequences of letters until a sequence should emerge that duplicated Shakespeare's. Generate-and-test processes of practical interest proceed more subtly and selectively than this. They are constructed so that any object they generate is already guaranteed to satisfy a certain subset of the design requirements.

The distribution of design constraints between generators and tests is well illustrated by theorem-proving programs (3). The proof of a theorem in some branch of mathematics is a sequence of well-formed expressions, (1) the final one of which is the theorem to be proved, and (2) each one of which either (a) is directly derivable by definite and simple operations from one or two of the expressions that precede it in the sequence or (b) is an axiom or previously-proved theorem. Consider now a theorem prover that works backward from the theorem to expressions from which it can be derived, and from these expressions to others, until connection is made with the axioms and previously-proved theorems. The generator in such a program is guaranteed to produce only well-formed expressions. Moreover, it is guaranteed that in the tree of expressions that is generated, the later members are all directly derivable in one or more ways from earlier members. Hence, all that remains for the test process is to determine when expressions produced by the generator belong to the axioms and previously-proved theorems.

Other divisions of labor between the generator and the test process of a theorem prover are conceivable. For example, the generator might produce expressions that are not guaranteed to be well formed, but grammaticality of these expressions could be determined by a test, and the ungrammatical ones weeded out. An analogue to this can be found on certain chess-playing programs that generate moves not guaranteed to be legal, and then test the moves for legality if they have other desirable properties.

The division of labor between generators and tests is pragmatic. It depends in considerable measure upon what constraints are easily embedded in generators and what ones are not. The theorem-prover example suggests that when the generator is producing a continually growing assembly of potential design components, "local" constraints--that is, relations among neighboring components--are easily incorporated in generators, while more global constraints may have to be left for tests.

J. Grason's (1970) program for laying out floor plans provides another example of a division of labor between generators and tests. The program employs a planar graph representation of the room layout problem, thereby guaranteeing that any arrangements generated will lie in the plane. Satisfaction of specified size constraints for the rooms, however, is guaranteed by tests applied to proposed layouts. The generator, in this case, guarantees satisfaction of certain topological constraints; the tests deal with other topological constraints and with metrical properties.

The Creation of Design Alternatives

Up to this point, I have made no distinction between design and any other kind of problem-solving activity. In ordinary language, however, we apply the term "design" only to problem solving that aims at synthesizing new objects. If the problem is simply to choose among a given set of alternatives--to choose the location or site for a plant, say--we do not usually call it a design problem, even if the set of available alternatives is quite large, or possibly infinite.

The algorithm for finding the maximum of a function by setting its first derivative equal to zero selects a solution from a non-denumerable infinity of possibilities. However large this set of possibilities, it is, in a certain sense, given in advance by the definition of the function and the range of its independent variable. If we don't call the maximizing algorithm a design algorithm (and we certainly don't), our terminological decision has nothing to do with the number of alternatives, but possibly with their "givenness." But what it means for an alternative to be given requires further discussion.

An architect seeking to produce the room layout for a house would ordinarily be thought to be engaged in design. But the number of alternative floor plans that can be drawn on a sheet of paper is exactly the same non-denumerable infinity--the infinity of the continuum--as the number of points on a continuous function, neither more nor less. If the possible solutions of the maximum problem are given, why not the possible solutions of the architectural problem?

The difference between these two situations cannot be divorced from the availability of solution processes. There are two reasons, one negative and one positive, why we call the layout problem, but not the maximizing problem, a design problem. The negative reason is that we do not have a simple finite algorithm for going directly to a solution of the layout problem. The positive reason is that the processes we do have for attacking it involve synthesizing the solution from component decisions that are selective, cumulative and tentative.

The possible alternatives for solving a design or synthesis problem are also given in a certain sense. Synthesis does not make things out of whole cloth, but assembles them from components. What is given in the case of synthesis are a set of elementary components and a grammar defining the admissible ways of combining components into larger structures. In the layout problem, the components are possible walls, each of which can be defined by the four coordinates of its two endpoints.

(For simplicity, I am denying the architect the privilege of curving his walls, but the generalization to permit this would not change the argument.) The basic grammatical rule is that walls may not overlap--that the entire set of walls must constitute a planar graph.

Why do we think the architect is synthesizing, or even "creating" when he makes the layout? Because he solves his problem by moving through a large combinatorial space in which he adds one element after another to his design--of course, sometimes revising or even deleting those that are already in it. In this respect, his process is not different from that of a chemist who is trying to synthesize a complex molecule having certain desirable properties (for example, a broad-band, biodegradable insecticide to replace DDT). To be sure, the chemist starts with only a finite number of building blocks--the 92 natural elements, say--while the architect starts with a four-parameter non-denumerable infinity of possible straight lines. The chemist, we might think, has far fewer alternatives open to him than the architect.

But we have already seen that number of alternatives is a misleading criterion. "Large" and "small" mean one thing in mathematics, but something quite different in the empirical world. For the problem solver, any number of alternatives is immense (and, for practical purposes, equal to any other immense number) if it is too large to be enumerated and examined exhaustively within a reasonable time. In design, 1,000 is an immense number, for designs must generally be produced by examination of fewer than 1,000 alternatives.

The richness of the combinatorial space in which the problem solver moves, then, rather than the number of elementary components he has at his disposal, is the hallmark of design activity. By virtue of this richness the designer must search selectively; for among all the immense--and possibly infinite--number of combinations potentially available to him, he can examine only a tiny number. The designer exercises choice, hence introduces style into his design.

Notice that the problem space through which the designer searches is not a space of designs, but a space of design components and partially-completed designs. Even this is a simplified picture, for the designer may operate sometimes in the space of design components, sometimes in one or another abstract planning space that represents only certain aspects of the entire problem. In all events, in the course of the design process very few complete designs are generated, compared and evaluated-- in the typical case, only one. The generator guarantees that a number of the constraints will be satisfied automatically at each stage of the design, and the tests guarantee that partial designs violating the remaining constraints will be rejected or modified as the search proceeds.

We can illustrate the process by reference again to theorem proving, which is not usually thought of as design, but whose processes do not differ from design processes in any significant way. There are two ways of viewing theorem proving. It can be thought of as search for the theorem through a space of theorems, in which each step involves application of the rules of inference to points of the space previously visited. (This is a description of forward search; with a little generalization, backward search can be brought within the paradigm.) But it can also be thought of as a process for generating an object called a proof--that is, a sequence of theorems having the properties we mentioned earlier. At each stage in the search, one or more partially completed proofs are augmented or modified until a proof of the desired theorem has been found.

Now selectivity in this design process is derived from several sources. First, the generator produces only legitimate proof steps. Second, the system incorporates a number of intermediate tests that guide the generation, by measuring progress toward the desired proof. For example, the final expression in the partial sequence can be compared with the theorem to be proved, and the differences between them used to determine the next step of generation. (This is the procedure, incorporated in the General Problem Solver, known as means-ends analysis.)

Hence, we should not conceive of the design generator as a process that spews out in a fixed sequence possible designs that are accepted or rejected by final tests. The generator is itself a parametrized process whose output at any given moment is determined both by its structure and by the information it obtains from its previous output. The testing processes include both tests for conformity with the problem constraints and tests for measuring progress toward satisfying those constraints.

Each of the partially completed designs generated during search corresponds, of course, to a whole class of final designs. The tests that are applied during the design process do not merely weed out unsatisfactory designs, but instead, they choose promising classes of designs for further particularization.

The Emergence of Style

The satisficing process we have been discussing can be described, slightly simplified, as follows:

The design program consists of one or more generators and a number of tests. When the program is furnished a set of constraints-- that is, a set of criteria for determining when a satisfactory solution to a design problem has been obtained--it proceeds to generate elements for consideration as components in the design. After each proposed addition to the design, two kinds of tests are applied.

Tests of the first kind determine whether the proposed addition satisfies certain of the design constraints--if so, it is added to the design. Tests of the second kind inform the generator whether progress is being made and what constraints remain unsatisfied, and thereby modify the next stage of generation.

The relation between the constraints defining a particular design problem and the design program is not simple. Not all of the constraints are incorporated in test routines for, as we have already noted, the generator may be, and usually will be, so constructed as to satisfy certain of the constraints automatically. Moreover, not all of the tests that are applied by the program come from the problem constraints. We need to distinguish, therefore, those characteristics of the generator that simply guarantee satisfaction of design constraints from its other characteristics--let us call them autonomous--which are not implied by the initial problem requirements. Similarly, we need to distinguish autonomous tests from tests that simply apply design constraints. Both generators and tests of the design program will generally contain both problem-determined and autonomous components.

One of the simplest, and most obvious, autonomous components of a design generator is the set of processes that determines the order in which elements will be considered. Seldom do the specifications of the object to be designed place restrictions on this order. Thus, for example, the architect's generator is free to begin work on a problem from the outside in or from the inside out. But in a satisficing process, seeking the first object that will satisfy a specified set of constraints, the order in which possibilities are examined may have a major influence on which solution is discovered. Hence, autonomous characteristics of the generator that determine the order of search are an important aspect of style.

A second set of autonomous elements in most design programs are "prefabricated" solutions to subproblems that arise repeatedly in different contexts. By using such assemblies as components in the design instead of synthesizing it from simpler elements, the program is able to operate at a more aggregate level and reduce its search effort. Since, again, the prefabricated assemblies are not uniquely determined, they provide a second source of idiosyncratic style.

The design program may add to the specification of a design problem yet another set of autonomous constraints. If the program resides in the head of a human designer, these additional specifications may simply represent characteristics the designer would like to see included in the object, over and above those mentioned in the problem specifications. It is frequently suspected by the clients of architects that the constraints actually applied by the architect's design program derive much more from the architect's store of criteria than from those provided by the client.

To view the matter in a little different light, there are of course strong positive reasons for incorporating in design programs both prefabricated assemblies and autonomous constraints. The former are a matter of efficiency--they make design less costly--but they are more than that. A subproblem solution that is to be used repeatedly as a component in the solution of larger problems can be brought to a level of high "polish"--that is, can be designed to severe constraints--beyond what would be justified if it were to be used only in a single design.

Autonomous constraints in design programs may also be highly desirable features. If the designer is a professional expert, serving a lay client, then the client may want the expert to take care of all the considerations that will become important to him in his actual use of the object designed, but which he is unable to anticipate in advance.

In conceptualizing a design program that makes use of prefabricated subproblem solutions and supplementary autonomous constraints, it is useful to distinguish between the program proper (the generators and test processes) and a memory in which the autonomous supplements are stored. Only a small subset of the latter may come into active use in the course of designing any single object. They will be evoked by particular situations that arise in the course of the design, retrieved from memory, and applied. Obviously, the contents of this memory will make an important contribution to the style of the design program having access to it.

In summary, we can speak of the distinctive style of a design program because the constraints that define design problems for it are never so limiting as to point to a unique solution. All of these characteristics of the program that determine which of the many possible satisfactory designs will actually be created define the program's style. Among the most important of these autonomous, style-determining characteristics are (1) the processes that determine the order of search, (2) stored prefabricated solutions to recurrent subproblems, and (3) stored autonomous constraints to be added to the explicitly given problem constraints.

In ordinary discourse, style is predicated both of objects and of persons who create them. We speak of a building as Gothic in style, but we also speak of Mozart's style of music. In the former case, a collection of objects possessing certain common characteristics is set off and labelled as belonging to a particular style. In the later case, the collection is defined by the design program from which the objects issued (4).

Mozart, in a celebrated letter, puzzled about the connection between design process and product: "Now, how does it happen, that, while I am at work, my compositions assume the form or the style which characterize Mozart and are not like anybody else's? Just as it happens that my nose is big and hooked, Mozart's nose and not another man's. I do not aim at originality and I should be much at a loss to describe my style. It is quite natural that people who really have something particular about them should be different from each other on the outside as well as on the inside."

To determine whether an object belongs to a particular style, we may test whether certain constraints, obvious or subtle, apply to it. If its arches are pointed, we say, "That's Gothic," if round, "That's Romanesque." Or we may reject the former classification on discovering that the arches do not bear the weight of the vault, but hide a steel frame. Whatever the criteria, obvious or subtle, tests applied to the characteristics of the object tell us whether or not it belongs to the style in question.

We determine whether a particular object was produced by a particular design program in exactly the same way--by applying tests to characteristics of the object. One reason we do this is because we ordinarily do not have direct access to the program, hence can identify it only by its products. We cannot (yet) look inside Mozart to determine what it is about his program that makes his music Mozart's. But the cues we detect in the design to identify its source may also be obvious or subtle, superficial or essential.

Some painters employ obvious trademarks-- the usually conspicuous X, for example, that can be found on Stuart Davis's canvases. The trademark is an explicit and conscious symbol of the author's identity, almost a signature. The tests range from these very obvious ones to others that are difficult or impossible to verbalize. As an exercise for the reader, I propose that he try to write a characterization of the paintings of Cezanne that would permit someone who had never seen one to identify them.

A more sophisticated approach to characterizing the style of a design program is to define it by statistical measures. This approach has been farthest developed in the identification of literary style from the statistics of vocabulary and syntax, and the identification of music from the statistics of tonal or chordal sequences (5). The technique is sometimes successful, and undoubtedly can be developed further, but in some important sense we find it artificial. The identifying statistics are clearly symptoms, not causes. They are the accidental byproducts of the working out of the underlying characteristics of the design program, and we should expect to find no direct one-to-one relation between the statistics and the program characteristics.

One important episode in the history of modern science illustrates dramatically these two ways of characterizing style--by features of the object, and by features of the program that designed it, respectively. In this case the designer was Nature. Kepler discovered a beautifully succinct characterization of the style of the planets; by determining that each moved in an ellipsoidal orbit, with the Sun at one focus of the ellipse. But Newton showed that the style could be characterized even more fundamentally by a gravitational process that accelerated each planet toward the Sun in inverse ratio to the square of its distance. The style of the process described by Newton implied the style of the orbits generated by that process.

Style from the Dynamics of Design

In the remainder of this paper, I should like to give particular attention to aspects of style that reveal characteristics of the design process. In doing this, I shall have to stray perilously close to realms of esthetics in which I have only amateur status, and to draw examples from painting, music, and architecture. If my examples do no more than irritate professionals into correcting or improving them, they will have served their purpose.

The Kepler-Newton example given above illustrates the central esthetic premise from which I shall proceed. Kepler found pattern in the planetary orbits, but Newton disclosed the deeper pattern by demonstrating that it was not a brute fact of Nature, but followed inexorably from the working of a simple generator. The Newtonian explanation gave us the more parsimonious characterization of the pattern.

Functionalism in design offers the same kind of parsimony. When we notice that some feature of a design follows from the function the design is supposed to serve, that feature no longer requires its own independent constraint--its special fiat--but derives from conditions central to the design problem itself. Functional design is parsimonious of constraints, producing objects that are more than the additive outcomes of multitudes of detailed design specifications.

At one time or another, both obedience to function and simplicity have been erected into basic esthetic principles. What our analysis suggests, instead, is that the key term is parsimony, and that we value functionalism and classicism precisely when they disclose economy of pattern. Functionalism becomes an important source of parsimonious design precisely because Nature is cleverer than Man in devising dynamic principles that have rich sets of consequences for the objects they generate. Simplicity warns us against multiplying constraints as a cheap source of superficial richness in pattern. It urges us to omit detail when that detail is arbitrary and not derivable from constraints or components of the design process that are already present and expressed in other ways. It urges us, also, to be sparing of detail when that detail would make it difficult to perceive the dynamic sources of pattern.

Let me leave these general principles before I strain them beyond credibility, and turn to some examples of how style emerges from (and can be characterized by) dynamic features of the design process.

A crude architectural example was already suggested earlier in this paper. The fenestration of a building can be entered into the design at an early stage, or it can be postponed until many aspects of the internal layout have been determined. If we see a building with a symmetric facade, we can be reasonably sure that that facade was generated at an early point in the design. If, on the other hand, we see one with many asymmetries, we will conjecture with some confidence that these asymmetries are external expressions of decisions about how to meet internal requirements.

This does not mean, of course, that asymmetry cannot be introduced deliberately as one of the design constraints. A designer can introduce any constraint that whimsy or esthetic sensibilities suggest, provided it does not interact too strongly and contrarily with the other constraints already present. When he does so, he generally succeeds in producing something that the viewer finds "quaint" or "ornamental." He does not produce a Mont-St-Michel, whose wonderful forms are almost by-products of the demands of site and history, but which, far from appearing accidental or adventitious, are integral expressions of those fundamental demands.

This is not simply another way of saying that the forms are functional. However, difficult it is for us to imagine it now, the rock of Mont-St-Michel might have been crowned by many other masses of masonry performing the same function. Perhaps some of these alternatives would have excited as much wonder over the years as the particular one that emerged. But each of them would have a style reflecting not just the demands of the site and its use (identical for all), but also the process for generating possible ways of meeting those demands.

Of course an element of style that arises in this way—from interaction between design requirements and design processes—may become so valued that it is incorporated directly into the design constraints. A modern Gothic or Gothicized church, built on a steel frame, deliberately satisfies visual requirements that in no way follow from other design constraints or processes, but are simply ornamental. The objection to such ornamentation is not its lack of functionality, but its failure to communicate something about the design process.

I will return later to the topic of ornamentation. Before I do so, I should like to look to music for other illustrations of the basic thesis. Music has a complex structure built on the dimensions of rhythm, melodic line, harmony, tonal quality, and others. Composition cannot proceed simultaneously with all these dimensions, but must take one, or a small number as the point of departure, with consequences for the style of the completed work.

Roger Sessions (THE MUSICAL EXPERIENCE, Princeton University Press, Princeton, N. J., 1950, pp. 46-47) has given a description of the process of composition that accords well with this view of style.

"I would say that a musical idea is simply that fragment of music which forms the composer's point of departure, either for a whole composition or for an episode or even a single aspect of a composition. I say 'fragment' knowing full well that it can get me into difficulties. For in my experience, in which I include observation and analysis as well as composition, a 'musical idea'—the starting point of a vital musical 'train of thought'—can be virtually anything which strikes a composer's imagination. It may, certainly, be a motif, a small but rhythmically self-sufficient fragment of melody or of harmony; but I am fairly certain that by no means all motifs can be called 'musical ideas'. On the other hand, I could cite many examples where the most essential musical ideas, the elements that give the music its real character, consist not in motifs at all, but in chords, in sonorities, in rhythmic figures, or even in single notes of a particularly striking context. Sometimes—and this occurs, I think, more often though not always in works of composers of great maturity, in 'late works,' as we call them—one of the most important musical ideas, in a fundamental and motivating sense, may be not even a thematic fragment at all but some feature of the large design, such as a recurring relationship between two harmonies or keys, or even a linear relationship embodied in different aspects of the music at different moments."

The differences among the major styles of classical Western music further illustrate the dependence of style upon process. The composition of homophonic music, with its emphasis on a prominent melodic line harmonized by the other parts, proceeds in quite different ways from the composition of polyphonic music, with its interweaving of independent voices. Viewed from a harmonic standpoint, polyphonic music exhibits many unusual chords or even dissonances (e.g., of passing tones) that are simply byproducts of the working out of contrapuntal problems; and these harmonies and dissonances are an important element of polyphonic style as experienced by the listener. But polyphonic music is not written by introducing dissonances.

Perhaps the clearest expressions of this notion of the sources of style come from the exponents and practitioners of composition with twelve tones--the idea of Arnold Schoenberg that underlies so much Twentieth Century music. (See, e.g., Joseph Rufer, Composition with Twelve Notes. London: Barne and Rockliff, revised edition, 1961.) The twelve-tone procedure may be summarized crudely as follows: The chromatic scale contains twelve tones in each octave (corresponding to the twelve keys per octave of the piano keyboard). The composer selects, on the basis of some set of criteria, a particular tone row, a permutation of the twelve tones of the chromatic scale. He then proceeds to design a composition, using this ordering of the tones to define both the vertical (harmonic) and horizontal (melodic) relations. There are many ways in which this can be done, and correspondingly many sub-styles that are all covered by the broad label of "twelve-tone music." But all twelve-tone music receives a strong stylistic imprint from its method of generation--from taking the tone row as the initial input to the generator.

The quotation from Gombrich with which I introduced this paper equates style with choice, but the choices of which Gombrich speaks pertain mainly to perception rather than to design process. Gombrich's choice is a choice among the many perceptual cues that are available for representing, or creating the illusion of, the external reality. The painter chooses a small subset of these cues as the basis of his style and omits or de-emphasizes the rest. The artist cannot meet the totality of demands that an attempt to reproduce nature literally would impose on him, hence selects out as his design constraints just a few of these demands.

In actual fact, perceptual selection and selection of design process are not at all independent. For example, the choice between a linear and a painterly mode of representation carries with it all sorts of commitments as to how the painting shall proceed. Witness Leonardo's prescription for (linear) painting in Chapter IV of his ART OF PAINTING:

> "Painting is divided into two principal parts. The first is the figure, that is, the lines which distinguish the forms of bodies, and their component parts. The second is the colour contained within those limits."

In some modes of modern non-representational painting, the role of the process in forming the style is especially clear. Here, the painter may put an initial design upon the canvas for its suggestive value as to what he might do next. Such painting becomes--even more than painting with other methods--a feedback process of interaction between painter and partially completed canvas.

Duane Palyka has used the computer as instrument to create visual compositions with the aid of this kind of feedback. His composing program employed a number of separate subroutines. The initial subroutines produced a simple composition that was then stored in memory--generated some points, for example, that then served as centers for circles of varying diameters; or generated points that served as vanishing points for subsequently-generated sets of lines. Other subroutines then examined and modified the stored initial compositions, distorting figures, shading them, sharpening or blurring boundaries, and so on. In principle, there was no limit to the number of stages in the composing process, but in practice, two or three stages sufficed to produce compositions of substantial esthetic interest.

Function, Process, Ornament

If the designer's task is to choose and select, then he must have some basis for choosing what he does. In worlds having immense numbers of alternative possibilities, it would seem that he would need a great many criteria in order to narrow down these possibilities to a single design. He would be confronted with combinatorics in the space of possible criteria almost as fearsome as the combinatorics in the space of possible designs, and his design activity would have to be preceded by a pre-design activity to select the criteria.

However, the design process synthesizes only one (or a few) objects rather than a large number, and proceeds iteratively to build the object cumulatively from an initial kernel. Under these circumstances, a few constraints embedded in the structure of the design process itself, together with a few design requirements applied again and again at each stage of the cumulation, may suffice to determine the final design. To the extent that they do, the object designed will exhibit deep unity in all its aspects, which express the working out in interaction of a small number of processes and parameters.

Designers are most fortunate when nature and technique impose severe constraints upon them. If we did not understand it, we might view the cathedral at Rheims as highly decorated and decorative. But with any feel for the Gothic designer's problem, we see the flying buttresses and their pinnacles as functional means for turning the great sideward thrusts of the vault downward and conducting them safely to the ground. The elaborateness of the structure is acceptable because it arises from applying a few basic processes to an equally few imperative constraints.

When a set of initial design constraints is too easily satisfied, the design process will present us with solutions too easily. We will obtain more than one solution, and will feel constrained to choice among them-- that is, to impose new constraints that bear no particular relation to the initial set. Since these will frequently be constraints on characteristics of the final design, rather than on its suitability to function or on the search process, they will lead us to superficiality and mannerism.

An alternative is to retain the initial constraints but set more severe acceptance levels for them. Again, the Gothic cathedral is a case in point. As long as the designers made extravagant demands on the structure to admit as much light as possible and, as a means to doing this, sought to raise the height of the vault, all of their ingenuity was spent in finding a way to achieve their goal. There was great need for elaboration, but little room for irrelevant elaboration.

Conclusion

My main purpose here, however, is not to preach a particular esthetic doctrine. Rather, I have sought to show that those differences among designs that we call "style" arise from a variety of sources, and that the design process is one of the most important of these. The imprints of design process upon style are fundamental in the same sense that the imprints of function, of material, and of manufacturing process are.

We have now entered an era where, for the first time in history, the design process itself is becoming directly accessible to examination and description. Increasingly, we are able to characterize the method of creating explicitly, instead of being forced to indicate it indirectly, in descriptions of the things created. Already, this new capability is being reflected in novel forms of artistic activity, in which the human artist's task is to create a design process that will, in turn, create objects of esthetic value. I have cited above the example of Palyka's program for producing non-representational "prints" (I don't know what else to call them); and many of you are familiar with computer-composed music like Lejaren Hiller's ILLIAC SUITE and COMPUTER CANTATA (6).

This shift in attention from the work of art to the design process is bound to have consequences for style and design as significant as the transformation from Kepler's kinematic pattern descriptions to Newton's dynamic ones.

Notes

* This work was supported by Public Health Service Research Grant MH-07722, from the National Institute of Mental Health. The ideas set forth here began to urge themselves on me when I was preparing my Karl Taylor Compton Lectures, now published as The Sciences of the Artificial (M.I.T. Press, 1969). For a discussion of design, see Chapter 3 of that volume, and for a brief statement of its relation to style, p. 75.

1. The reader wishing to pursue this point will find a fuller discussion in my Models of Man (Wiley, 1957), particularly the introduction to Part IV, and Chapters 14, "A Behavioral Model of Rational Choice," and 15, "Rational Choice and the Environment."

2. The organization of problem solving systems is discussed more fully in Newell, A., & Simon, H. A., Human Problem Solving (Prentice-Hall, forthcoming, 1971), especially Chapters 4 and 14.

3. Newell, A., & Simon, H. A. (1971), Chapter 4.

4. Defining the boundaries of a style by a period in time and a geographical location really amounts to the same thing, for such boundaries only make sense if there are communalities among the design programs that operated inside them.

5. See the extensive discussion of these matters in Hiller & Isaacson, Experimental Music (McGraw-Hill, 1959), Chapters 5 and 7.

6. See Hiller & Isaacson, 1959.

Session One:

Performance Appraisal

Chairmen: David Canter
Faculty of Education, Tokyo University

Thomas Markus
Building Performance Research Unit, University of Strathclyde

After a great deal of talk in the last twenty years about the need for designers to obtain feedback information on the quality of their products, at long last techniques for doing this are being developed and this session covers many of them. The papers raise, and to some extent answer, some fundamental questions.

1. What is the real difference between a building and a representation of it? My own paper argues for similarities. Lau's paper exposes some of the problems associated with visual simulations used for lighting judgments; problems that research workers in lighting have often glossed over and problems which designers need to understand and solve if they are to have any faith either in their own or in their clients' judgments based on models.

2. What is the design process like and especially how does the introspective act which we call appraisal take place? Dean Hawkes in his paper puts forward a technique for continuous and rapid output of performance measures on the basis of which a designer can evaluate and change his strategy. Thomas Davis puts forward a model which attempts to explain the nature of this activity both during design and after completion.

3. The key question--if it is peoples' efficiency and above all their feelings, relationships and personal responses which are to be the main criterion of success, how do we measure these?, and how can we predict them? My colleague, David Canter, puts forward a theoretical framework into which these various types of response fit and illustrates them with examples. Davis and Roizen used some of these techniques in a college hall of residence and artinian in Canadian schools. Davis also refers to questionaire and interview techniques and methods of scoring and scaling.

The relationship between the papers inevitably is loose and many questions remain not only unanswered but even unasked. Amongst the former is the question as to how concepts about buildings and environment fit mental maps and human experience in general. Some, but not all the authors, at long last have given up talking about "building users" as some peculiar human species different from all other types of people. An area which no doubt psychologists will be exploring more thoroughly is the way in which a child's development of the concept of place and space happens. Cross-cultural studies by anthropologists in this area are also required. The effect of changes with time in social groups and in individuals as a separate issue from personality development also remains to be tackled.

The unification of environmental measures into a form where public discussion and argument is possible seems as yet an immence task. Costs and values, as used in cost-benefit studies, may be one answer and the limited usefulness of such studies should not be a cause for disparagement today but rather for an effort to improve their complexity and their realism in treatment of value judgment. To fall back on a distinction between objective measures and subjective evaluation shelves the problem but does not solve it.

David V. Canter - Thomas Markus

The Elementary School Classroom:

A Study of Built Environment

by Vrej-Armen Artinian

M. Arch., School of Architecture, McGill University, Montreal

Abstract

This study, based upon the responses of 800 students and 400 teachers in the region of Greater Montreal, analyses the physical environment of the classrooms. The spatial thermal, luminous and aural factors are considered. Many correlations have been found between them and the attitudes of the respondents. Correlations have also been found between the foregoing and cultural, social and other factors. It is concluded that the school populations are under many environmental influences. Further research is required to make quantitative recommendations.

Introduction

This study is an attempt to explore various factors which, in one way or another, can affect man's perception and appreciation of his physical environment, and can influence his behavior therein.

Although many scholars have pointed out the importance of the effects of the man-made surroundings in such buildings as schools, a general unawareness of these effects persists among architects and educators alike. Moreover existing research has always dealt with individual factors, but almost never with the totality of the environment.

This study, showing the complexity of the problem, does not provide answers, but it raises many questions. The reader is urged to consider the findings hypothetical.

Methodology

This study is based upon a survey of 32 elementary schools built between 1950-1968 in the region of Greater Montreal. They belonged in equal numbers to the French & English-Canadians & were spread over lower, lower-middle, middle and upper income level districts, and urban, semi-urban and suburban localities.

Architects and principals have been interviewed. Half a day was spent in each school to visit the premises and to attend a regular class of the highest grade (11-13 years old).

800 students and 400 teachers have filled-in questionnaires concerning the various physical aspects of their schools.

The thesis made use of a portion of the collected material, namely, that part which pertained to the classroom.

Part One - The Spatial Environment

1. The Environmental Factors

Area is the first environmental factor to be studied, and no classroom (CR) can be evaluated as "big" or "small" without taking into consideration the number of children in the CR, the type of activity therein, as well as psychological and anthropological factors. The actual dimensions of the room seem to be less significant compared to the above factors.

The 32 CR's ranged between 650 and 860 square feet, with an average of 725. These CR's included 26 completely enclosed rooms, 3 with operable partitions and 3 without partitions. It was found in general that the more densely populated CR's were the larger rather than the smaller rooms, the latter providing 1.5 times greater surface area per student than the former.

Enrollments ranged between 16 and 35 students, with an average of 28, while per capita area ranged between 41 and 19 square feet, with an average of 26.

Dissatisfaction with the CR area seemed to be general feeling on all levels of the school population. Thus 53% of students required larger area, 2% smaller area. 49% of teachers deemed their CR area barely adequate or inadequate. As to the principals, 20 out of 32 were dissatisfied with the area one way or another.

Although there were large demands by the students for "bigger" CR's in schools which did not have either the smallest CR's or the biggest CR enrollments, in general the greatest satisfaction occurred in CRs with smaller enrollments

(25.75 students, average), and larger percapita areas (27.75 square feet, average) as compared to the CRs which caused the least satisfactions (29.5 students, 25.75 square feet/student, average).

No. of students/CR	16-26	27-30	31-35
Ave. area, Sq.ft.	715	715	750
Ave. area/ST Sq.ft.	30	25	23
% of Students satisfied with area	54	45	34

Note ST = student

TABLE 1 Spatial Environment - (Students)

The shape of the CR is another important factor which seems to affect children's appreciation of the CR area. The higher satisfactions are evoked in square rooms, where for the majority of the students sightlines have equal length. As sightlines increase in long-rectangular rooms satisfactions decrease, while they become lowest in wide-rectangular rooms where sightlines are excessively shortened.

Another spatial factor which seems to affect children's satisfaction with the CR area is their orientation. They are less satisfied when they face the wall opposite the windows, than when they are in any other position which enables them to see outdoors.

Teachers too, as it was mentioned, are dissatisfied with the CR area (51% rate it "adequate"), as well as with the storage space (only 42% rate it "adequate"). However, a higher proportion (63%) of them is satisfied with the number of students in the CR. Very strong relationships are found between these 3 factors, i.e., as satisfactions increase with any one of these, they do so with the other two factors too.

Percentage of teachers rating "adequate"	No. of ST per CR	Storage area
8 Schools with max. (84.5%) "adequate" responses to area	78	61.5
8 Schools with min. (19 %) "adequate" responses to area	43.75	25.5

TABLE 2 Spatial Environment - (Teachers)

When comparing the responses of the students and the teachers, the most striking evidence is that a greater proportion of the latter are satisfied with their CR area. Are children more sensitive to the confinement of the physical environment than their elders? One wonders.

2. The Attitudes

Students' attitudes were examined through the two following questions:
- Do you like being in your CR?
- If asked to remain longer in school, would you be glad, would you not mind, or would you be sad?

It is interesting to note that the first question roused much more positive responses than the second. Moreover, a very strong relationship is found between the two questions. Positive attitudes in one are accompanied with positive attitudes in the other.

Keeping always in mind that these attitudes are conditioned by a multitude of factors, specially non-environmental ones, which are outside the scope of our study, we observe certain mutual effects between the spatial factors and the attitudes.

Thus, the CR area and the students' attitudes are in inverse proportions. The more positive attitudes are found in smaller CR's, the least in larger ones, and conversely, the smallest CR's evoke more positive attitudes than the largest ones. This is in line with the fact that the smaller CRs provide larger per capita space. Also, children are happier in less congested CRs than in more congested ones. In addition, a very strong and direct relationship exists between attitudes and satisfaction with CR area.

Being in the CR	"remain" & "glad"	ave. area sq. ft.	ave. no. of ST/ CR	ave. area /ST sq.ft	% satisfied with area
9 CRs with max. "like" resp's (87 %)	22.5	700	25	28.5	52.5
9 CRs with min. "like" resp's (40.75%)	8	760	30	25.5	36.75

TABLE 3 Attitudes: Spatial Env. - (Students)

Teachers were consulted about the adequacy of their CRs vis-a-vis their teaching method (TM), the physical health of their students(PH) and their mental health (MH).

We notice that teachers are most critical of the first question and least critical of the last one.

As it was observed in the case of the student responses, when teachers' opinions about one of these 3 issues become more or less favorable, then their opinions about the other two vary in the same way.

And again direct and strong relationships are found between the above opinions and the responses to the environmental factors. The more the teachers are satisfied, say with the CR area, the more they consider the CR adequate for TM, etc., & vice versa, i.e., the higher the "adequate" responses to "TM", etc., the more the satisfaction with area.

Teaching Method	% of Teachers Rating "adequate"				
	PH	MH	Area	No.of ST	Store.
			Note: SC = school		
8 SC's w/max. "adeq."resp's (87 %)	80.75	92.50	76.75	79.00	54.50
7 SC's w/min. "adeq."resp's (30.5%)	50.25	67.75	29.50	48.50	30.50

TABLE 4 Attitudes: Spatial Env.-(Teachers)

These are clear indications that our opinions about the general adequacy of our physical environment, can be strongly affected by the way we evaluate its different components.

3. Cultural and Other Factors

Several factors such as the socio-economic background, the location of the schools, the age of the children, etc., were considered. Significant results were obtained however only from "Language" and "Age of the School Building".

a) Language

The population of Montreal is basically composed of 60% French-Canadians and 40% of English-Speaking Canadians (English, Scottish, Irish, etc.). In the region of Greater Montreal the proportion of French-Canadians is greater. Big masses of French-Canadians live in the East End of the Island in less favorable socio-economic conditions than the English who mostly dwell in the West End. The upper middle income districts (the suburbs specially) have as much French as English-Canadian residents.

The educational system is based upon religious denomination, with Catholic School Commissions (mainly the Montreal Commission) taking care of the educational needs of almost all the French-Speaking community, and the Protestant School Boards (mainly the Montreal Board), of almost all the English-Speaking community, including most of the non-catholic minorities.

The results of the analyses show that there is a marked difference between the responses of English-Canadians and French-Canadians. Children in French-Speaking schools are more inclined to be satisfied with their CR area, than those in English-speaking schools.

	English	French
Ave. area sq.ft.	750	700
Ave. no.of ST /CR	28.5	27.5
Ave. area/ST sq.ft.	26.5	25.5
ST's,% satisfied	38	50

TABLE 5 Language: Spatial Env. - (Students)

It has been observed already that smaller CR's evoked more satisfaction than larger ones, but this was significant as larger CR's were more densely congested. From this table we see that, although, housing on the average one student less per CR than the English schools, the French CR's provide less area per student, but result in higher satisfaction. It can be hypothesized that French students would feel at ease in smaller areas than would be required by the English students. This could have some bearing with the fact that the French usually live in bigger families and more congested dwellings.

Examining the teachers' responses, we again find that the French are more satisfied with their CR area than their English counterparts.

Teachers, % rating "Adeq."	English	French
CR area	38	64
No. of students/CR	60	66
Storage area	38	47

TABLE 6 Language: Spatial Env. - (Teachers)

One explanation for this difference in the teachers' evaluation of the spatial environment of their CR's would be the fact that at the time of the study activist methods were implemented more in English rather than French schools, and would hence necessitate larger space which was lacking. However, when comparing the activist schools in both groups we find 58% of teachers in French schools approving the CR area, against 34% in English schools.

One should bear in mind that both the students' attitudes, and the teachers' opinions about the adequacy of their CR's vis-à-vis their TM, the PH and the MH of their students, are more positive in French rather than in English schools.

b) The Age of the School Building

Between 1950 and 1968 the educational evolution in Montreal has caused many changes in the planning of school buildings. The conventional corridor type has given way to cluster-type and later to open-plan types, and square CR's or teaching areas have replaced the long-rectangular rooms. Building and finishing materials have remained essentially the same, except that carpets are used nowadays in the open-plan schools. At the same time the total surface of windows have been reduced to a minimum, and is not eliminated altogether only for psychological reasons. These factors are to be borne in mind when the effects of the age of building are considered. This study, however, does not analyse the responses in relation to all those variables.

It was found that newer schools evoke higher student satisfaction than old schools. Teachers' opinions, however, do not seem to be influenced by the novelty of the buildings; sometimes their satisfaction is even higher in the older buildings.

	ave. area sq.ft.	ave. no.of ST/CR	ave. area/ ST	ST % satisf of area	Teachers % rating"adeq." A	B	C
1951-56	755	29	26	37	43	64	39
1957-62	750	26	29	39	75	80	66
1963-68	700	28.5	24.5	49	50	59	39

A: area B:No.of students C:storage
TABLE 7 Age of Building:the Spatial Env.

Many observations can be founded on the foregoing table:
First, CR areas have been considerably reduced during the past 18 years, the largest reduction being effected in the most recent schools,built after 1966. This reduction may reflect the decrease of the birth rate in Montreal in recent years. The average enrollment per CR seems to be uniform in all categories of schools, and is very close to the norm set by the Department of Education, which is 27. This uniform enrollment gives the older schools an advantage over the new ones, providing larger per capita area.
This fact, however, affects only the teachers' opinionsas they give more positive responses in the 5 schools (built between 1957-62)where the CR enrollment is the lowest.
Second,the attraction of novelty is very strong for the students, even though new schools have less area per student in the CR's.
The same remarks are true in the case of the students' atti tudes and the teachers' opinions about the adequacy of the CR's.
If results in old and new schools based upon language differences are compared, the following is observed:
Older English schools rouse in the students much less satisfaction with the CR area than newer English schools.
Older English schools cause less satisfaction than older French schools.
In some cases older French schools evoke more satisfaction than new French schools.
Finally, new French schools almost always cause higher satisfaction with area than new English schools.
Moreover, student attitudes are more positive in the newer than in the older schools.

Part Two - The Thermal Environment

1. The Environmental Factors
The average dry bulb temperature, as recorded during the visits in the 32 CR's, was 73°F (between 67°F-80°F). The average humidity was found to be 54.5% (30-65%). The effective temperature resulting would be 69°F (64 - 74°F).

About two thirds of all students were satisfied with the thermal atmosphere of their CR's. The rest were equally divided in asking warmer and cooler temperatures.
No consistent relationship was found between the recorded temperatures and the students' satisfaction with the thermal atmosphere.
However, other very interesting relationships were noticed between the thermal satisfaction and the spatial characteristics of the CR's, as well as between the thermal and the spatial satisfactions.

Therm.Atm. students	ave. area sq.ft.	ave. No.of ST/CR	ave. area/ ST	% satisf. of area
8 CR's w/ max. satisfaction(85%)	700	24.25	28.50	55.00
8 CR's w/ min. satisfaction(47%)	760	30.50	25.25	42.50

TABLE 8 Thermal Env.: Spatial Env.-(Students)

It is obvious that, as in the case of satisfaction with the CR area, students' contentment with the thermal atmosphere is inversely proportional with the CR area and the number of children therein, and directly proportional with the area per capita. It is also directly related with the satisfaction with the area.
The converse of these relationships are found to be true too. For example, when comparing the largest and the smallest CR's we have found that satisfaction with the temperature is higher in the latter than in the former,and so on.

The teachers were given a set of two questions, one concerning the adequacy of the temperature and the other, that of the ventilation in the CR. A little less than two thirds of them, on the average found both factors adequate. It was perceived that "adequate" responses to one of the questions almost inevitably was accompanied with "adequate" responses for the other.
While the teachers' opinions about the adequacy of the CR area do not seem to affect their opinions about the thermal atmosphere,the latter seem to be influenced, however, by the ratings of the number of students per CR.
Also, satisfaction with the CR windows concurs with the satisfaction with the ventilation.

| Ventilation | % rating "adequate" | | |
Teachers	Temp.	No.of STs	Windows
8 schools w/ max. satisf.(88.5%)	81	71	80
7 schools w/ min. satisf.(26.5)	38	62.5	68.5

TABLE 9 Thermal Env.: Spatial Env. (Teachers)

2. The Attitudes

Students' satisfaction with thermal environment had little bearing on their attitudes. Indeed, there is a certain parallel between the two, but it is too insignificant.

In the teachers' case however, it is different. When they are most satisfied with the temperature, their ratings of the adequacy of the CR vis-à-vis their TM, the PH and the MH of the students run very high, and they decrease when their satisfaction with the temperature decreases. Ventilation, on the other hand, seems to affect the above opinions about the adequacy of the CR with respect to PH.

| Thermal Atm. | % rating "adequate" | |
Teachers	TM	PH
8 schools w/ max. satisfaction(88.25%)	68	72.5
6 schools w/ min. satisfaction (33%)	53	57

TABLE 10 Attitudes: Thermal Env.-(Teachers)

3. Cultural and Other Factors

Students' responses do not show any significant variations when compared on the basis of either language or the age of the school building.

Teachers, however, show very interesting differences. English teachers are more satisfied, than French teachers, with both the thermal atmosphere and the ventilation. Now, though the CR's in French schools were warmer than in English schools, it was the French who required still warmer temperature.

The age of the building seems to affect teachers' opinions about the thermal atmosphere very slightly and this in favour of older buildings.

Par Three - The Luminous Environment

1. The Environmental Factors

Gross inequalities were found to exist in the intensity of lighting from one CR to another.

Ft-Cndles on		sunny days	hazy days	cloudy days	general ave.
Desks	max.	275	255	160	275
	ave.	100	166	97	109
	min.	40	65	50	40
Chalk-Boards	max.	230	130	100	230
	ave.	70	92	45	62.5
	min.	15	30	20	15

TABLE 11 Luminous Environment

We observe that there is a big difference between the maximums on sunny and cloudy days, but the minimums are almost equal (even a little higher on cloudy days). Sunny days gave lower readings than hazy days, which may be explained by the fact that the shades or the curtains were nearly always drawn to keep out the sun. More important, however, are the big ranges found between the maximums and the minimums in the same categories.

However, other factors such as the altitude and the type of luminaires, the amount of window surfaces and their being shaded or not, the CR orientation, etc., may be the cause of the large differences in light intensities. For example, fluorescent fixtures with acrylic cover produced an ave. of 133 ft-cndles on desks and 80 on boards, while louvered ones gave 91,5 and 48 respectively. The light produced by incandescent luminaires was considerably less.

One thing is certain: children have been able to adapt themselves to work in luminous environments of greatly varying characteristics.

| Students | % requiring the light | | |
	more	as it is	less
On the desks	27	49	8
On the boards	20	44	14
In the CR	20	61	9

TABLE 12 Luminous Env.-(students)

This leads us to the next point: are these percentages proportional to the light readings taken in the CR's? Yes indeed! Generally higher satisfactions with the existing conditions are found in CR's with higher light intensities.

However, it is also observed that in 10 CR's with the highest demand for more light n the desks the average reading is 104.5 ft-cndles, while in 8 CR's with the highest demand for less light the reading is 118. This, once more, indicated that there are no optimum limits to lighting conditions, or more correctly, these limits are very far apart, with a very big range of "comfort".

Students' satisfactions with both the luminous environment and the spatial environment show mutual influences. Thus, the higher the satisfaction with the lights, the higher that of the area and vice versa.

Students	Area % satisfied
9 CR's w/ max. satisfaction w/ lights on desks (72%)	55
8 CR's w/ min. satisfaction w/ lights on desks (27.25%)	43
8 CR's w/ max. satisfaction w/ lights on boards (67.5%)	54
8 CR's w/ min. satisfaction w/ light on boards (24%)	37
9 CR's with max. satisfaction with lights in CR (77.5%)	56.5
8 CR's with min. satisfaction with lights in CR (42.75%)	33

TABLE 13 Luminous Env.: Spatial Env. (students)

It has also been found that satisfaction with the CR area is higher in CR's with high light intensities than in CR's with low light intensities.

"Lighting" was considered "adequate" by almost all teachers (89%).

A certain direct relationship was found between satisfaction with the lighting and with the windows in the CR.

79% of the teachers rated the CR colours adequate.

2. Attitudes

The most positive responses to the question "do you like being in the CR" have occured in those CR's with stronger light and with higher satisfaction with that light.

Students	ft-cndles on		% satisf.w/ light		
	desks	brds	on desks	on brds	in CR
9 CR's w/ max. "like" resp's (87%)	117	78	52.5	47	66.25
9 CR's w/ min. "like" resp's (40.75%)	88	50.5	43	40	55

TABLE 14 Attitudes : Lum. Env.-(Students)

Since the vast majority of the teachers are satisfied with the lights in the CR's, their satisfaction does not show any effect on their opinions about the adequacy of the CR's. On the other hand a slight direct influence of the satisfaction with the CR colours is noted to exist.

3. Cultural and Other Factors

Surprisingly enough English students are more satisfied with the lights in the CR's than French students, and this, despite the existence of much higher luminous intensities in French than in English CR's.

Another paradox is that the French are more satisfied with the CR area than the English, but it was previously mentioned that, generally, satisfactions with area and with lighting were interrelated.

Students	ft-cndles on		% satisfied w/ light		
	desks	brds	on desks	on brds	in CR
English	76	34	63	60	71
French	141.5	88.5	55	54	64

TABLE 15 Language: Lum. Env.-(Students)

Colour preferences too have been differentiated according to language. The colour the English like most is light blue, while that of the French is white. The colour disliked most by the two groups is dark red.

Teachers show no differentiation due to ethnicity in their appreciation of the luminous environment.

As to the influence of the age of the school building, a slight difference is recorded in favour of the newer buildings both in the case of students and the teachers.

Part Four - The Aural Environment

1. The Environmental Factors

No qualitative measurements of sound transmission were taken: the only observation that was recorded was about the kind of noises produced inside and outside the CR's. Generally these noises did not disturb the classes, specially the activist groups since children's own voices and movements would cover all other noises.

The students' satisfactions with the aural environment are given below:

% of students replying	what the teachers say	what the others say	TV	Music
very well	71	34	29	47
fairly well	22	43	17	19
not well	4	11	14	14

TABLE 16 Aural Env.- (Students)

We notice that "what the teachers say" is claimed to be the best heard as compared to "what the others say", etc.. This, however, would not mean that the CR's were not suited for hearing the other factors as in Table 16 . The teachers' voices are the most common source of sounds that are listened to, and in most cases children sit such as to concentrate on the teacher's station. It would be natural that in such arrangements one could not hear his fellow classmates as well as his teachers. TV and music on the other hand, may be lacking in many schools, and that can be very good explanation for the low ratings given to these two sound sources.

Some very interesting relationships were found between responses to hearing and responses to other environmental factors. Satisfactions were found to go parallel with respect to "hearing", "area" and "lights"

Students: Do you hear what the teachers say	Area,% satisf.	Lights in the CR,% satisf.
8 CR's with max. "very well" resp's (90%)	51	75.5
8 CR's with min. "very well" resp's (43.75%)	36.5	48.5

TABLE 17 Aural Env. Lum. Env.: Spatial Env.
(Students)

Conversely, in those CR's where children are most satisfied with the area or the lights, they also show higher satisfaction with the acoustics than in the CR's with least satisfactions with the other factors.

Teachers are generally more satisfied with acoustics (80%) and noise reduction (65%) of their CR's. As expected, when they rate highly one, they do the same to the other factor too.
The responses to "acoustics" and to "noise reduction" are influenced by and themselves influenced the responses to "area" and to "no. of students".

Teachers Area	Acoustics % "adequate"	Noise reduction % "adequate"
8 schools w/ max. "adeq" resp's (84.5%)	93	81
8 schools w/ min. "adeq" resp's (19%)	68	47.5

TABLE 18 Aural Env.: Spatial Env. (Teachers)

"Thermal atmosphere" shows a certain direct relationship with "acoustics", while ventilation is inversely proportional to "noise reduction", when teachers satisfactions of all these factors are concerned.

A slight direct relationship is observed between the satisfaction with acoustics or noise reduction and with that of lighting in the CR by the teachers.

2. The Attitudes

Very significantly, as their satisfaction with the acoustics of the CR's increases, students exhibit more positive attitudes, and vice versa.

Students Being in the CR	Hear Teachers % "very well"
9 CR's w/ max. "like" responses (87%)	78.5
9 CR's w/ min. "like" responses (40.75%)	57

TABLE 19 Attitudes:Aural Env.-(Students)

Similarly, when teachers are highly satisfied with the acoustics and noise reduction of their CR's, they also rate the adequacy of their CR's very highly for their TM, the PH and MH of their students.

Teachers	% 'adequate'		
	TM	PH	MH
11 schools w/ max. "adeq." responses to "acoustics" (100%)	71	75	81
8 schools w/ min. "adeq." responses to "acoustics" (44.75%)	52	68.5	69
8 schools w/ max. "adeq." responses to "noise reduction" (95%)	69.5	69.5	81
8 schools w/ min. "adeq." responses to "noise reduction" (31%)	45.5	57	62

TABLE 20 Attitudes: Aural Env.-(Teachers)

3. Cultural and Other Factors

No differences resulting from ethnic-language variations have been found between students' or teachers' responses to the aural environment.
While students are more satisfied in older schools than the new ones, teachers do not show any such variations due to the age of the building with respect to the aural environment.

Summation

1. Environmental Factors

Man's judgement of his physical environment is the result of not only the actual conditions of that environment, but also of his experiences and his background.

Students' satisfaction with the CR area is found to be in inverse proportion with the no. of students in the CR, and in direct proportion with the per capita area. Their appreciation of the luminous environment is similarly directly related to the amount of light in the CR. The shape of the CR too affects the responses to the spatial environment.

Moreover, students' satisfactions with the spatial environment are related to their contentment with the thermal, luminous and aural environments. The responses they give to the "thermal environment" are also in inverse proportion with the no. of students, and in direct proportion with the per capita area. Also, aural and luminous environments evoke parallel satisfactions from the students.

Students are most satisfied with the aural then the thermal environments, less with the luminous and least with the spatial environment.

Teachers' satisfactions with the area, the no. of students and the storage area of the CR's run parallel. Similarly do satisfactions with the thermal atmosphere and ventilation, also those with acoustics and noise reduction.

As in the case of the students, direct relationships have been found between responses to the spatial, thermal, luminous and aural environments. Teachers are most satisfied with the luminous then the aural environments, and least with the spatial environment.

Teachers and students alike feel that lack of space is the biggest inconvenience. Both groups seem to be satisfied with a very wide range of luminous intensities. Generally in the same schools teachers and students have, more or less, same proportion of satisfaction as compared with other schools.

Finally, students are more critical towards their physical environment than their teachers.

2. The Attitudes

A much bigger number of students have replied positively to the question "do you like being in your CR?" than to "if asked to remain longer in school, would you be glad, not mind, or be sad?".

Both attitudes are more positive when students are highly satisfied with various environmental factors, than when they are less so. The strongest effect is that of the aural environment, the weakest that of the thermal.

Teachers are most critical when they judge the adequacy of the CR for their teaching method, less critical vis-à-vis the physical health of the students and least critical for their mental health.

The judgements concerning these three factors are directly interrelated.

The responses to the environmental factors affect and are affected by the opinions about the adequacy of the CR for the three above mentioned purposes. The most influential is the spatial environment, the least the luminous one

3. Cultural and Other Factors

a) Language

There are differences between the English and the French in the appreciation of the CR area. The French students are more satisfied than the English, so are the French teachers, despite their having smaller classrooms.

English teachers find the thermal environment of their CR's more adequate than do the French teachers.

Although they have generally lower light intensities in their CR's the English students are more satisfied with the lights, than the French.

There are also different colour preferences between English and French students. The former like light blue the most while the latter like white.

Both French students and teachers have more positive attitudes than their English counterparts.

b) Opening Year

Students' responses are more positive in the new schools than in the old schools towards the spatial and the luminous environments, and less positive towards the aural environment. The thermal environment makes no difference. Also the student attitudes are more positive in the newer schools.

The age of the school building does not seem to exert such clear influence on the teachers' responses.

Conclusions

The first fact which this thesis puts forward is that environmental factors do not affect us in separate or independent ways, but rather in a combined manner. Our reactions to one factor, say area are indeed unconscious reactions to all the other factors too, like sound light etc..

Moreover, our satisfaction with any factor depends upon our own experiences more than upon that factor itself. Any given area is large or small because we are used to consider it so and our perception of it is coloured by our habits and idiosyncrasies.

Attitudes and environmental satisfaction not only go parallel but directly affect each other so that one has difficulty to tell which one is more decisive.

Other social-cultural factors also exert certain influences on our appreciation of the physical environment. The ethnic origin is one such factor and the differences found between English and French respondents might be attributed to the inherent proxemic variations due to their origin. Another factor affecting responses to the physical environment is the age of the building which creates that environment.

It is desirable that teachers become aware of the 'good' or 'bad' effects the school environment can have on their and students' performance, in order to be able to critisize the physical surroundings and fully describe its characteristics required for their educational purposes.

Finally, this study is just an initial attempt to find a method of measuring user satisfactions in correlation with the existing conditions of the school physical environment. For a thorough evaluation of the latter, however, coordinated studies should be undertaken on a much wider basis and they should include, along-side the architect , specialists in the physiological, psychological, social, educational and other sciences.

The Place of Architectural Psychology: A Consideration of Some Findings

by David V. Canter

BA, PhD, Research Fellow, Building Performance Research Unit, Strathclyde University

1   Facts without Theories

It is often believed that new instruments for research do of themselves produce great increases in knowledge. Even if this view is rarely stated explicitly it underlies much of the thinking about methods of categorising spaces such as that by Thiel (1961) or the listing of techniques for research (Craik 1970, Sanoff 1968, Canter and Wools 1970). When startling insights do not come tumbling out from the latest technique, the research workers show some puzzlement.

They should not be surprised because an instrument can be no better than the theory upon which it is based and the data collected from an instrument are of no more value than the hypothesis they help to support. As Brecht illustrates the emissaries from the Pope refused to look through Galileo's telescope because the data it presented were irrelevant to their understanding of the universe. This is not to dismiss technology or empirical data in the development of science. The results of doing so would be sterile theorising and the production of concepts which are inapplicable to the real everyday world.

The implications for design of facts without theories are possibly even greater than they are for psychology, for if these facts are to be used by a designer they must be couched in spatial terms. They therefore inevitably present the designer with a pre-digested design solution. In other words, the research worker takes upon himself that task for which the architect is particularly suited; the manipulation of space. If the architect is not to modify, manipulate or create spatial forms, what is he to do?

It is assumed that given the right techniques we shall eventually produce a complete list of human needs and will learn what aspect of the environment will satisfy each. The asides in the human needs literature belie this basic concept of people consisting of a set of distinct, static needs each of which can be separately satisfied.

What then is the place of architectural psychology? If collecting data on the specific architectural requirements of building users is going to lead to unimaginative architecture and is based on a doubtful psychological premise, what is the contribution to be made?

The answer is not simple and is not likely to be readily accepted by the present generation of architects. It can be briefly stated by saying that the contribution of psychology should be to study the processes of interaction between buildings and their users with the aim of making architects understand more clearly the psychological impact of the built environment. This will influence their designs by changing their attitudes towards architecture. This approach is unlikely to produce any design solutions, but architects themselves are the experts in the production of design solutions and assistance at that level from psychologists or sociologists is neither necessary nor desirable.

2   Towards a Theory

What is really being suggested is that more effort should be put into the development of a theory that will explain the facts we have at present and which will guide us in the facts we are to look for in the future.

Before entering into the dangerous waters of theory building, two warnings from the Dalandhui conference should be borne in mind. Stringer (1970) suggests if an understanding of the relationship between architecture and psychology is to be achieved, we must deal with the process of architecture and the process of psychology in the same terms. This means that our explanation of how people interact with their physical environment should also contribute to an understanding of how buildings are designed. The second warning (Canter 1970) is that the subjective experience of a building and the objective observation of others using it must both be taken into account if we are to gain anything like a complete picture of the process of building/user interaction. If such all-embracing warnings are to be dealt with we must start from some simple fundamental observations. Such observations can be made all around us. The most common fact of the interaction of people with buildings is that in the great majority of cases behaviour and the places in which it is carried out seem appropriate to one another. It is generally accepted that people sleep in bedrooms, sit in sitting rooms, do clerical work in offices, and so on. So far research workers have come up with few surprises with regard to where people do things. This fact of appropriateness deals with the first warnings because it can be seen that it is precisely because architects are aware of the patterns of appropriateness which exist that they are able to produce usable buildings, and it is because most people are also aware of these same patterns that they are able to use these productions. The second warning is also heeded if we start from this point. The experience of appropriateness and the observation of appropriate behaviour are both amenable to study and complement each other.

3   The Search for Appropriateness

However, if patterns of appropriateness are considered only as a state which does or does not exist then much of the reality of human behaviour will be lost and many research findings will remain unexplained; rather they should be considered a goal towards which people aim.

Two examples from research at Strathclyde will serve to illustrate some of the potentials of this approach for the interpretation of findings.

In a study of the effect of office size on clerical performance (Canter 1968), office workers doing similar jobs in the same department but working in rooms of different sizes were given clerical aptitude tests. When the subjects were tested in the offices where they normally worked, a marked decrease in ability was found as office size increased, but a control group tested in other rooms showed no such relationship with room size. Any approach which deals only with the direct effect of the physical environment on behaviour would have difficulty explaining these results. On the other hand, some approach which considers the possibility of clerical workers searching (consciously or not) for an appropriate or suitable working environment can easily explain the fact that the more able workers tended to work in surroundings generally accepted by clerical workers as more acceptable; that is, smaller offices.

The second example (Canter 1970) was an investigation of seating preferences in seminars among undergraduates. It was found that the distance of the lecturer from the front row of chairs did not affect seating behaviour when the chairs were arranged in semi-circular form. When, however, the chairs were laid out in a rectangular block the closer the lecturer stood to the front row, the further back the undergraduates sat. It seems plausible that the form of the physical environment gives rise to expectations about what activities will be carried out, and people adjust their behaviour in accordance with these expectations. Semi-circular seating is probably perceived as informal, but rectangular seating is perceived as formal, and these students did not wish to become too deeply involved in a formal activity so they sat further back.

In other words, what is being suggested is that taking the accepted (or appropriate) behaviour for a particular seating arrangement as a starting point they modified their own behaviour to fit into that pattern in a way they felt would be satisfactory.

4   Categories

Before this notion of patterns of appropriateness can contribute in any detail to architectural understanding, it is necessary to understand the mechanisms by which they develop and change and the way in which they are organised. The ideas which Lee

(1970) put forward can be seen as central to this. He suggests that during the process of growing up objects and activities are mentally coded, not only in terms of what they are but also in terms of where they are. This coding leads to the formation of schemata or mental maps which relate things and activities to places. As Lee shows, much observable behaviour is consistent with the existence of these schemata and apparent inconsistencies in behaviour can be explained as maintaining consistent schema.

These mental maps can be thought of as containing summaries of a person's experience of the relationships between things, activities and places; summaries, that is, of patterns of appropriateness. However, in order to summarise these patterns or relationships it is necessary to codify or at least describe the constituent parts in some way. It must be possible to say what type of place it is and what type of thing or activity and then to examine the appropriateness of one for the other in terms of existing mental maps. This categorising of the constituent parts is a complex process and it seems likely that categories can exist at many levels of abstractness and be formed from many viewpoints or along many dimensions.

The studies carried out in order to explore the ways in which people think about physical environments, such as those reported by Vielhauer (1965), Hershberger (1968) and Collins (1969), are esentially examinations of the coding systems people use. Our own work at Strathclyde (Canter 1969a), looking at a number of buildings and dealing with representations as well as actual buildings, do help to support a general pattern found in the American studies. Four general dimensions can be discerned all dealing with what appear to be different aspects of what might be called emotional response. Any naming of these dimensions must be to some extent arbitrary but the four central concepts may be called 'pleasantness', 'comfort', 'friendliness', and 'coherence'. It would be found that the judgements of many different kinds of people, including architects, could conveniently be described in these terms, those of architects differing mainly in their distinguishing more clearly between the different factors (Canter 1969b). Further studies of this type are necessary, particularly with regard to eliciting the underlying dimensions of activities,

things, people from the viewpoint of the places to which they are appropriate. Such studies are now in process at Strathclyde, being carried out by Stephen Tagg and John Firth. Once the results of these studies are available then it will be possible to start drawing up an overall picture of the patterns of appropriateness which exist in the building context. Already it can be seen that the picture might not be nearly as complicated as was originally thought. The work we have carried out relating aspects of building to the friendliness dimension (Wools and Canter 1970, Canter and Wools 1970, Wools 1970) has shown that in general the furnishings account for 43%, the roof height and angle 33% and the window size and shape about 11% of the variance in the friendliness scores. The residual variance of 13% remaining unaccounted for suggests that at least when using drawings and photographs of models we are dealing with a significant proportion of the actual psychological variance involved.

5   Interaction and Adaption

It is apparent all around that people do interact with buildings and, as was mentioned earlier, there is evidence of a positive search for appropriateness. If the dimensions and relationships between them grow out of an interaction between the people and buildings then it is likely that the building itself has some influence on the particular dimensions people use. Evidence for this is shown by a factor analysis of answers to questions about the physical environment in two different schools. This showed that in one building daylighting, a view and sunshine were closely associated, but answers to questions about 'lighting' were taken to refer purely to electric lighting, while heating and ventilating were thought of as distinct from either of the other two categories. In the second building daylight and electric light plus view formed one factor, sunlight and ventilation a second and heating alone a third. The first school was of relatively compact plan with a central courtyard, the second more of a 'finger plan'. The reasons for the groupings is obvious from consideration of the plans but had the answers to questionnaires been taken purely at their face value in a study of, for instance, the 'need for daylight' they would have been very misleading. Pursuing the implications of this finding it might be suggested that people think about different kinds of buildings in different ways. It seems that this might give us a clue as to why some buildings are thought as 'works of architecture' and others merely as buildings; for some reason different ways of thinking of the buildings are used, different criteria are applied in assessing them.

The same phenomenom can be seen occurring with regard to spaces within buildings. In a recent study at Strathclyde, Ann Telford found that the relationship between the privacy dimension and the pleasantness dimension differed depending on which room of the house was being examined.

It can thus be seen that measurable relationships do exist between the different categories of our spatial coding system but these relationships are modified by the particular building involved. One of the most likely reasons for this modification is that the categories and relationships develop from an interaction with the particular environment. If this were so, then a range of other relationships should be found. The most likely one is that between time and satisfaction with a building for, as the interaction with building continues, so the assessment of that interaction, or satisfaction, would be modified. The direction of this relationship might well be the best overall estimate of the quality of a building that we can obtain. If it is highly negative then the building is a poor one as increased knowedge of it and interaction with it is leading to increasing dissatisfaction. In other words, a good building is one which 'withstands the test of time'. In our studies of school buildings (Canter 1970b) we have found a consistently negative relationship between various aspects of satisfaction and the age of a school building. The curve seems to level off after about 10 years and the relationship cannot be explained by differences in the age or make-up of the staff or the length of time they have been in the building, rather the relationship seems to be between the school organisation as a whole and the building in general.

One other finding from our schools study has been the relationship between expressed satisfaction with the size of classrooms and the space within them and the number of modifications of the building which could be observed on a visit to the school. Interestingly, the relationship is such that the more modifications made the more satisfied the teachers.

This lends support again to our active model of interaction, that the teachers positively benefit from the modification rather than it just keeping them up to a minimum level.

6   Complexity and Appropriateness

If this notion of a positive search for appropriate patterns of interaction with the environment is to contribute to the development of architecture besides discovering what the patterns are which exist, we need to know a lot more about the underlying mechanisms which contribute to causing any given relationship to be accepted or considered appropriate. It seems likely that many things will contribute to the particular level of appropriateness expected or accepted in a particular situation. The example given by Hill (1970) serves to illustrate this. Hill showed that the balance between amount of inward and outward vision selected as desirable by people was influenced by the type of room in which they assumed they were and their personality characteristics. The balance of inward to outward vision which was appropriate for some rooms in a house was not appropriate for others. In other words the level of appropriateness of any particular balance varied from condition to condition.

In this work Hill was concentrating on the variation of a relatively small and specific aspect of the environment, the view in and out, and that it was partly because he was attending to such a small part that variations in appropriateness were so subtle. If he had explored all the phenomena which might vary the picture that emerged would probably have been very complex indeed. What is needed, therefore, is to isolate those key aspects of the environment whose changes are critical in determining the appropriateness of that environment for a given activity. Ideally, these aspects would relate to the ways in which people think about buildings (the classification system upon which they build up their mental maps) and as a consequence should help to indicate the ways in which people differ in dealing with their environment. One such aspect of the environment might well be its complexity; the number of different things going on within it, the variety or intensity of information available from it.

Exactly how to measure complexity in a given situation is as yet difficult to determine but it does not seem too great a leap to suggest that, other things being equal, more complex environments will produce a higher level of physiological arousal in the users of those environments. This is, of course, an hypothesis open to investigation but it is plausible that the measures of arousal described by Payne (1970) and Griffiths (1970) might well be considered as estimates of the psychological complexity of the environment studied.

This concept of complexity would help to explain some of the relationships referred to earlier, such as the reduction in satisfaction over time being due to a reduction in psychological complexity. Relationships between aspects of the physical environment and friendliness such as those referred to earlier in the studies carried out by Wools (1970) might well benefit from examination in terms of the complexity of the stimulus material.

One further possibility that stems from this idea of patterns of appropriateness being developed to meet various levels of environmental arousal is that of relating environmental effects directly to variations between individuals. This can be done because of the known differences between individuals in terms of their cognitive complexity (the number of cognitive dimensions they have for handling any particular judgement). Briefly, it has been found (Canter 1970c) that there are definite relationships between satisfaction (which for the present we may take as an estimate of the degree to which an environment provides an appropriate setting for a range of activities) and the cognitive complexity of an individual. In the school situation this is usually such that the more complex the individual the less satisfied he is with the school building.

The implications of this direction of inquiry can be drawn from some very recent studies not yet written up. Wools has found that dealing with simple and complex stimuli and judgements of friendliness made by simple and complex people there is a clear interaction between type of person and type of stimuli in influencing judgements. Furthermore, Firth has found some relationship between the complexity of the stimulus effects and the age of schoolchildren. In other words, as the children get older so the aspects of the environment which influence their judgement get more complex. Might the development of this latter approach not eventually give us some rationale for school design?

References

Canter, D.V. (1968), Office Size: An example of psychological research in architecture, Architects' Journal, 24th April, 881-888.

Canter, D.V. (1969a), The Measurement of Appropriateness in Buildings, Transactions of the Bartlett Society, 6, 40-60.

Canter, D.V. (1969b), An Intergroup Comparison of Connotative Dimensions in Architecture, Environment and Behaviour, 1, 1, 38-48.

Canter, D.V. (1970a), Should we treat building users as subjects or objects? in Canter (1970d).

Canter, D.V. (1970b), Architectural Psychology and School Design, Scottish Educational Studies (in press).

Canter, D.V. (1970c), Individual differences in response to the physical environment, Paper presented to BPS Annual Conference, Southampton, April 1970.

Canter, D.V. (1970d), Architectural Psychology, RIBA Publications: London.

Canter, D.V. and Wools, R.M. (1970) A verbal measure for buildings Building, 19 June 218, 6631, 73-76.

Collins, J.B. (1969) Perceptual Dimensions of Architectural Space validated against behavioural criteria PhD thesis, University of Utah.

Craik, K.H. (1970) Environmental Psychology, in Newcomb J.M. New Directions in Psychology 4, Holt, Rinehart and Winston: New York, 1-121.

Griffiths, I.D. (1970) Thermal Comfort: A behavioural approach in Canter (1970d).

Hershberger, R.G. (1968) A study of meaning in Architecture Man and his environment, 1, 6, 6-7.

Hill, A. (1970) Visibility and Privacy in Canter (1970d).

Lee, T.R. (1970) Do we need a theory? in Canter (1970d).

Payne, I. (1970) Pupillary response to architectural stimuli in Canter (1970d).

Sanoff, H. (1968) Techniques of Evaluation for Designers Raleigh: Design Research Laboratory, School of Design, North Carolina State University.

Stringer, P. (1970) Architecture, Psychology: whatever the name, the game's the same in Canter (1970d).

Thiel, P. (1961) A sequence-experience notation for architectural and urban space Town Planning Review 32, 33-52.

Wools, R.M. (1970) The assessment of room friendliness in Canter (1970d).

Wools, R.M. and Canter, D.V. (1970) The effect of the meaning of buildings on behaviour Applied Ergonomics, 1, 3, 144-150.

Vielhauer, J.A. (1965) The development of a semantic scale for the description of the physical environment PhD thesis: Louisiana State University.

Architectural Determinants of Student Satisfaction in College Residence Halls

by Gerald Davis

President of TEAG,
Lecturer at Stanford University, Department of Architecture

and Ron Roizen

Abstract

The overall satisfaction of college students with their residence hall facilities was found to be relatively independent of their level of satisfaction about specific architectural features of their residence halls, such as the size of the room, or temperature control. Instead, the general type of residence hall, as perceived by the students, becomes the strongest determinant of satisfaction. Conventional long-corridor residence halls generated the least satisfaction, while halls that were perceived as experimental and not institutional were perceived as most satisfactory, with apartments close to the top of the scale.

Author's Note: The work described in this paper was supported in part by a grant from the U. S. Department of Health, Education, and Welfare, Office of Education, Bureau of Research. This grant was awarded to the University of California, San Diego under the direction of Mary C. Avery, Assistant to the Chancellor, Muir College, and in cooperation with TEAG-The Environmental Analysis Group, Pier 35, San Francisco, California, with Gerald Davis, President, as Principal Investigator. Mary C. Avery investigated and selected the campuses and individual residence halls to be sampled. Ron Roizen, Research Associate, with the assistance of Chuck Weesner, Associate, designed and arranged the distribution of the questionnaire, the primary research instrument of the study, and was responsible for the programming and analysis of the data received.

Summary

This is a study of the relationships between the architecture of college residence halls and the satisfaction of students living in them. We wanted to find out about those environmental characteristics which influence student satisfaction and which can be altered or affected by architectural design.

A questionnaire was designed which measured overall student satisfaction, as well as satisfaction with 25 specific environmental variables. The object was to evaluate the need for various architectural features in residence hall design by comparing satisfaction with the individual architectural feature with overall satisfaction with the total living environment. Additional data gathered permitted control for the effects of non-architectural variables which might have intervened to modify overall satisfaction. The questionnaire was completed by 950 students living in 43 residence halls on eight campuses. Several different types of residence halls were sampled: conventional dorms, apartments, suites and irregular or unconventionally designed residence halls.

The results indicated that student satisfaction or dissatisfaction with a particular architectural feature had little affect on overall satisfaction with the total housing environment very much. The architectural variables did correlate with student satisfaction, but the correlations were mild and the range of differences between correlations was small. Therefore, the architectural variables could not be ordered according to their relative importance to student satisfaction. No one architectural variable or group of variables stood out as being the principal cause of overall student satisfaction or dissatisfaction with their housing.

These findings do not demonstrate that architectural factors have no effect on student satisfaction. They do indicate, however, that if an architect tries to satisfy student gripes and complaints about specific architectural features, he may not be solving the real architectural or other problems that underly this dissatisfaction.

The best predictor of overall student satisfaction turned out to be residence hall types. Only nine percent of the students living in conventional dorms were highly satisfied overall compared to forty-eight percent living at the University of Guelph housing complex which was considered unconventional by its student residents. It seems that students who do not really consider their residence hall to be a dorm at all are the most satisfied. The overall impression that a student has of his housing is more important than his satisfaction with the individual environmental characteristics. What the building symbolizes to him is the deciding factor, not the complaints or gripes about specific detailed parts of his living experience.

Introduction

The administrators of the University of California, San Diego, (UCSD) were interested in establishing design criteria for the construction of college housing which would effectively meet student needs. This study was undertaken to gather information about the relationship of the architectural features of residence halls to student satisfaction.

Previous literature, research and design of student housing is based on the assumption that students will be generally satisfied with the housing their institution provides for them if the buildings are designed to meet their needs for privacy, quiet, control of temperature, and a number of other architectural qualities. If the paradigm is true, the problem for the architect in designing a residence hall is to allocate

his construction budget so as to achieve a good balance between spending on room size, on acoustical installation, on making it possible for the student to personalize his room, and on a host of other features. This study was designed to measure various aspects of this paradigm and to test its validity.

The progress of this research can be divided into three phases:

1) A preliminary investigation into the nature and scope of the problem which was conducted by TEAG-The Environmental Analysis Group and a separate academic investigation undertaken by Gerald Davis while teaching at Stanford University.

2) A research project in which Mary Avery and Gerald Davis conducted a series of focused group interviews and observed at a number of campuses across the United States. Gerald Davis prepared a report analyzing the preliminary findings with the participation of Charles Weesner as Project Manager for TEAG.

3) The research project on which this report is based developed out of the knowledge gained in phases one and two, and from a series of working sessions with George Murphy, the Dean of Students and now Vice Chancellor at UCSD; Alan Batchelder, Director of Residence Living at UCSD; Mary Avery; and members of staff of TEAG- The Environmental Analysis Group. A number of other experts, such as Harold Riker were also consulted. The object of the study was to determine if student satisfaction with the individual architectural features affected overall satisfaction with the living environment. We wanted to measure student needs as they relate to building design and to determine, if possible, a set of priorities architects designing college residence halls should take into consideration.

Methods and Procedures

In measuring people's responses to their living environment, there are three sets of variables we need to deal with. First we must identify and measure the aspects of the architectural environment we want to study. Then we must measure the responses of the users of that architectural environment. And finally, we must control the unwanted variables, in this case, the non-architectural aspects of college living.

We used a survey research approach to determine the relationship between the architecture of college residence halls and the satisfaction of students living in them. An individual's response to his environment is very subjective. We, therefore, wanted to examine the opinions of a large number of respondents to find out what general agreement there was about what people did and did not like about residence hall living. By using a standard set of questions, we were able to measure the student's response to the architectural environment, and to manipulate, test and control a set of environmental variables.

This did impose comparability upon the sample, in some cases where it did not exist. The comparability of responses, however, was essential to delving into the mechanics of student satisfaction. We did not want to end up with an array of anecdotes from each sample residence hall. This information would have been, we believe, only marginally useful to people involved in providing student housing.

Our sample consisted of 43 housing units on eight campuses in the USA and in Canada selected to provide a range of environmental conditions. The individual students to be questioned were selected at random from lists of the residents of the sample dorms. Approximately 70 percent (950) of the students selected actually completed usable questionnaires.

To compare and measure the differences between buildings, we had to identify and select specific attributes of the buildings for study. We could not cope with the whole potentially infinite range of similarities/ differences between buildings, and really

only some limited number of aspects are, in fact, of interest. We wanted to study those characteristics of a college housing unit which can be affected by architectural design decisions. We subdivided these characteristics into large scale and small scale differences in the environment. A variety of representative types (based on differences in size, design, sponsorship and type of student) of campuses and residence halls were surveyed. Included were new and interesting design approaches to the problems of student housing. We wanted to vary the environments as much as possible and look for the consequences in terms of student satisfaction. The large scale differences were differences in overall dorm design. The sample, therefore, consisted of a variety of housing units on eight campuses which were grouped into five types of residence halls: conventional long corridor dorms, suites, apartments and two housing complexes, one at St. Olaf and one at Guelph, which could best be termed irregular. A brief description of each type follows:

University of Guelph, Housing Complex B (Called Residence Hall Type A)

Complex B at Guelph, Ontario, Canada, (near Toronto) is an innovative residence hall design. It houses 1662 men and women students, approximately 70 percent in single rooms and 30 percent in doubles. The study-bedrooms, lounges, dining halls, and social spaces are distributed along an interior pedestrian street which serves as the spine of the grid patterned scheme. The basis for the design is the grouping of four single rooms and a double into a defined unit around a landing and sharing a washroom. Two of these groups combine vertically to share a lounge and kitchenette one half level between each group of bedrooms. Additional bedrooms, originally intended as work spaces for non-resident students, are located along secondary corridors. Each of the resulting towers of four to six students per floor is six stories high. The towers are grouped in threes along one side of the V-shaped connecting structure. The six floors of bedrooms and activity spaces within the V-shaped unit make one residence. Each residence is entered through an enclosed bridge from a dining hall and common room complex. The dining and common rooms are for the use of residents and non-residents alike.

Apartments (Called Residence Hall Type B)

Four University owned on-campus apartment buildings on three different campuses were studied. Individual apartment units accommodated from two to four students in single and double bedrooms. Each apartment had kitchen, bath, study and living facilities. All were new buildings having been built since 1966, and were high rise ranging from 8 to 14 stories. They were all open to upperclassmen only and the residents were responsible for upkeep of the apartment and were subject to a minimum of university regulations.

St. Olaf College Tower Dormitories, Northfield, Minnesota (Called Residence Hall Type C)

Larson and Mohn halls on the St. Olaf campus are two high rise residence halls of a somewhat unique architectural design. One is a twelve story hall for 292 women and the other a ten story hall for 296 men. The non-rectangular and varied shape of the two man study bedrooms is the unusual aspect of these buildings. Each of the 12-15 double rooms on a floor is a different shape. The study-bedrooms are large, averaging a net 230 sq/ft. There is one central washroom, laundry room and sound insulated study on each floor.

Suites (Called Residence Hall Type D)

Two types of suite arrangements from three residence halls on two campuses were included in the study. A suite was defined as a small cluster of sleep-study rooms sharing a joint use facility. In one case, the suite was four rooms accommodating six students around a common bath facility. In the other, it was eight students in four sleep-study rooms around a common bath and small lounge area. The three buildings were new (built since 1966) and were no more than three stories high.

Conventional Dorms (Called Residence Hall Type E)

Included in the sample were seventeen conventional dorms from seven different campuses. To be classified as conventional,

the dorm must have long, straight central corridors with single and double sleep-study rooms opening directly off each side. The building envelope was essentially rectangular and unvaried. The population of the individual dorms ranged from 72 to 488 and they all were open to students from each year in school. Some were open only to men, some to women only and one was coeducational. The year of construction of the individual dorms ranged from 1937 to 1966.

Architectural Variables

The micro-aspects of residence hall design we measured were the independent, discrete characteristics, such as quiet and comfort control. First we asked the respondent to draw a picture of his quarters. The sketch was a freehand, plan-view including the positions of beds, desks, shelves, doors, closets, dressers and so forth. Estimates of the room dimensions were included. Next, he was asked to describe his quarters as he would describe them to "...a close friend... who had never seen his quarters, (but) was thinking about moving into a room or rooms identical to (it)".

We then selected twenty-five variables out of the almost infinite possible range of micro-aspects that we could have studied, on the basis of one and/or the other of two criteria. Either the variable was an important practical factor in the architect's design, or from the interviewing and observation of the previous phase of the study, we had learned that the variable was probably a significant factor in the student's satisfaction. The twenty-five variables we came up with were hominess, privacy, storage space, size, flexibility, quietness, suitability for studying, suitability for sleeping, individuality, sociability, lighting, book storage space, desk top space, windows, seclusion, suitability for relaxation, modern-ness, aesthetic appeal, effort required for cleaning, adequacy of cooling and heating, freedom to alter appearance of room, opportunity to develop friends, comfort control, academic influence, bathroom facilities and ventilation.

We measured the micro-variables in two ways as perceived by the student. First we asked him the extent to which he had the quality or characteristic or achitectural feature present in his quarters. He was given a five-unit scale from minimum to maximum, on which to indicate his subjective evaluation of what he <u>had</u>. Immediately thereafter, we asked him to indicate, on the same five-unit scale, how much of the same characteristics he thought his quarters <u>should have</u>. This permitted us to measure the difference between what the student had and what he felt he should have had. This difference told us how satisfied he was with that aspect of his quarters.

To measure the students' overall satisfaction with his living environment we created a satisfaction index based on the responses to four questionnaire items concerning general feelings about the residence hall. Students were divided into three groups on the basis of their responses: high satisfaction, medium satisfaction and low satisfaction. These groups, of course, are only relative. Low satisfaction students are not necessarily desperate to get out. The index provides us with a simple divider. We are relatively sure that, most of the time, high satisfaction students like the place they live better than do low satisfaction students.

To be categorized a "high satisfaction" student, the student had to indicate:

1) that he was "very satisfied" with his quarters in his residence hall (question 24, answer 1).

2) that he thought his residence hall was "well designed" (question 25A, answer "yes" to "well designed").

3) that his present residence hall set up was better than living in an apartment, a fraternity or sorority, a rooming house, or another residence hall (question 18, rank "1" to "d").

4) that he was usually a little proud of his quarters when friends and or relatives came to visit him (question 25a-i, answer "agree").

If a student answered all four of these questions in the ways described above he was put in the high satisfaction group.

The "medium satisfaction" students failed to be so consistent in their praise of the environment, but at the same time, they did not indicate negative feelings about it. Students were included in the medium satisfaction category, if they were very satisfied with their environment (Q24, A1), but did not go on to complete the requirements of being highly satisfied; or if the student did not choose to use any of the critical or negative responses to any of the above four questions (for example, checking "no" to "well designed").

"Low satisfaction" students replied negatively to at least one of the four index questions. They indicated that they were "somewhat" or "very" dissatisfied with their quarters, they indicated that their hall was not "well designed", they ranked their hall low in comparison with other places to live, or they were not proud of their quarters.

Several items in the questionnaire dealt with the extraneous variables we wanted to control. We asked how much the student personally contributed to the cost of his room and board, where he had lived for the previous two academic years, his age, his family's income, whether he had a part-time job, his academic level, his major field of study, and several other items. Satisfaction with each of these variables were compared with overall satisfaction to determine any possible relationships.

Results and Conclusions

The results indicated that a majority of the students from all of the housing types registered at least some complaint about almost all of the variables that we supplied in the questionnaire. Students estimated the amount of each quality, say "quiet", for example, that they would like to have, and then the amount they actually felt that they had. Discrepancies ranged from 1-point to 4-points for each of the items that we scaled. Chart A is a profile of the proportion of students complaining about dorm factors. Within each residence hall type we collapsed the range of discrepancies into one group-- those who expressed any dissatisfaction.

These complaints carry implications for the decisions that a designer will make in coming up with a new college residence hall. A herioc effort to cut noise may lead the designer to incorporate low ceilings, carpeting, acoustical tiles, small social modules, or any of a number of architectural tactics. Complaints about size may move him to provide bigger rooms, just as complaints about privacy may suggest the importance of single quarters. The problem, of course, is that such decisions are locked in the economy of scarce resources. The designer, in most cases, must sacrifice something for something else. Therefore, we were especially interested in determining the relative importance of these variables. That is, how do these variables (qualities of the environment) relate to overall student satisfaction with their living environment and are some variables more important to student satisfaction than others? Are gripes, in fact, accurate indicators of student satisfaction?

By measuring overall satisfaction independently of satisfaction with the individual variables, we could test the validity of these common complaints and determine if a set of priorities could be established. In this way, we could compare satisfaction with any variable to overall satisfaction and determine if any relationship existed.

If satisfaction or dissatisfaction with a variable does not affect overall satisfaction, then although complaints about this variable may be a vehicle by which the failure of the environment is communicated, it is not really the source of discontent.

Table A illustrates the relationship of low satisfaction, medium satisfaction and high satisfaction with each variable to overall satisfaction. To test the relative strength of the relationship between satisfaction with a variable and overall satisfaction, we subtracted the percentage of students who were very dissatisfied with the variable but highly satisfied with the variable and with the overall environment. The difference between the percentage of students who are dissatisfied with a variable and those who are highly satisfied with it is the strength of the relationship of this variable to overall student satisfaction. We called this measure the association between two variables "e". If "e" approaches 100 percentage points, the relationship between the two variables

approaches units.

If an individual variable has a strong effect on student satisfaction, we would expect a greater percentage of students who were satisfied with a variable to have high overall satisfaction than students who complained about this variable. For example, 36 percent of the students who were highly satisfied with comfort control were highly satisfied overall, whereas 7 percent of the students who were dissatisfied with comfort control were highly satisfied overall. This is an "e" of 29. (See Chart A)

The "e's" ranged from 3 to 30, but most were close to the median 23. From this data a hierarchy of complaints could not be established. Because of the limited range of differences, none of the variables stood out as being most important to student satisfaction. The "e's" were not large enough to give us a very clear picture of the effect of these variables on student satisfaction.

We next looked at the data to determine the proportion of students who were highly satisfied, moderately satisfied and dissatisfied within each residence hall type, as shown in Table B.

The proportion of highly satisfied students by residence hall type varies as follows:

Residence hall type A (Guelph) contained the highest percentage of highly satisfied students (48 percent). This hall was very unconventional in its image as perceived by its Canadian student occupants. Residence hall type B (apartments) was perceived as highly satisfying by 33 percent of its residents, a difference of 15 percent. Residence hall type C (St. Olaf) which has some unique architectural features, but was recognizably a standard "dorm" in most other respects, was highly satisfying to 28 percent of its residents, a difference of 5 percent from Type B and 20 percent from Type A. Residence hall type D (suites) was highly satisfying to 26 percent of the student residents. This is a difference of only 2 percent from Type C, but a difference of 7 percent from Type B and 22 percent from Type A. Conventional dorms, Type E, had by far the lowest percentage of highly satisfied students, 9 percent. That is a difference of 17 percent from residence hall Type D, 19 percent from Type C, 24 percent from Type B and 39 percent from Type A.

The difference in overall student satis-faction between residence hall types is quite large. We now had to determine if this difference in overall satisfaction was due to the effect of the invironmental variables we were measuring. Residence hall types did differ in terms of how much each variable was complained about. In conventional dorms, 85 percent of those questioned complained about quiet, which led the list. Two-thirds or more complained about size, privacy, individuality, aesthetic appeal, flexibility, comfort control, and study-ability. On only one dimension did conventional dorms come off well: the opportunity to develop many new friendships. Almost 70 percent of the resi-dents of apartments complained about this factor. It led the list of apartment com-plaints; then came size, quiet, aesthetics, privacy, flexibility, individuality, and study-ability and comfort control. In suites, quiet once again led the list, followed by comfort control, study-ability, individuality, opportunity for friends, privacy and aes-thetics. The same kinds of permutations could be observed in the complaint lists for St. Olaf and Guelph. Quiet turned out to be the only consistently high variable: its rank never dropped below a third, regardless of the residence hall type. (See Chart B).

If a complaint is common among resi-dence hall occupants, then one would expect that a student within a residence hall who did not voice that complaint would be more satisfied than students who indicated that they were dissatisfied in this respect. Let us look, then at the increase in highly satisfied residents when we consider those who are satisfied with a quality of their environment. (See Chart C).

The increase in the percentage of students who are highly satisfied overall indicates the strength of the relationship between satisfaction with an individual variable and overall satisfaction.

Chart C indicates that in four of the dorm types satisfaction with quiet is asso-ciated with an increase of from 12 to 24 percent in the proportion of highly satisfied students. At Guelph, however, being satis-fied with the "quiet" causes a drop in satis-faction of approximately 10 percent.

This is especially curious because quiet was the most frequently complained about characteristic at Guelph.

A similar problem occurs with respect to the variable "opportunity to develop many friendships". In apartments this was the most frequently cited complaint, almost seven of ten residents indicated it; yet satisfaction with this variable or dissatis-faction with it did not affect general satisfaction.

These findings suggest some rather interesting hypotheses. First of all, quiet at Guelph and "friends" in apartment dorms appear to be phantom variables. Most students complain about them, but they did not appear to affect satisfaction. We might posit the existence of four kinds of variables:

1) Variables that students think are impor-tant and demonstrate a strong relation-ship to satisfaction.
2) Variables that students think are important, but do not demonstrate a strong relationship to satisfaction.
3) Variables that students do not think are important, yet demonstrate a strong relationship to satisfaction.
4) Variables that students do not think are important and do not demonstrate a strong relationship to satisfaction.

There is no hard and fast method for operationalizing the terms in the above typology. We submit the following possible definitions:

1) Let "variables that students think are important" be taken to mean variables that more than half of the students in a particular residence hall type com-plained about.

2) Let "variables that demonstrate a strong relationship" be taken to mean variables that produced an effect on student satisfaction that was stronger than the median variables effect. That is, a variable is "strong" if the dot it produced on Chart C is among the right-most dots on the chart. An e=18 cutoff point becomes the operational point; approximately half of the dorm type variables produced an effect greater than e=18.

Conventional dorms contained the highest percentage of dissatisfied students. Twelve of the thirteen variables that we scaled were complained about by more than 50 percent of the students in conventional dorms, but by our standard of a "strong" variables, none of these proved to be very important to student satisfaction. All twelve, therefore, can be considered Class 2 variables, or variables that students complain about, but that do not bear much relationship to satisfaction.

The conclusions that can be drawn from these data are: (1) satisfaction with a particular variable did not lead to much more general satisfaction and (2) the number of people voicing a complaint about a variable is not a very good indicator of its strength. It seems that if a basic threshold of user needs is met, individual architectural features are not the determinants of overall satisfaction. Looking for misfits and asking people what they would do better next time will not necessarily result in a residence hall that is more pleasing to its residents.

If this is the case, it might appear that the environment is not important to student satisfaction. This conclusion is not verified if we look at the effect of residence hall type on student satisfaction (Table B). The difference in student satisfaction among residence hall types is striking, especially when we compare conventional dorms with those at Guelph. The relationship of the residence hall types to overall satisfaction is not disturbed when satisfaction or dissatisfaction with individual variables is controlled. For example, students who were dissatisfied with quiet in Type A were still more highly satisfied overall than students in Type E who were dissatisfied with quiet; likewise, students who were satisfied with quiet in Type A are more satisfied than students in Type E who were satisfied with quiet.

Thus, it appears that the single best predictor of overall satisfaction is residence hall type. It appears to have a consistent effect on student satisfaction. No single variable influences overall satisfaction very much and some exert no influence at all. It seems from our study that student feelings about a residence hall come from his general image of the building, from his overall ideas about its character, mood, ethos. Specific features are to gripe about. The overall design and "feel" is to like or dislike. Gripes about specific features are quite independent of overall satisfaction.

It is possible that the apparent relationship between student satisfaction and residence hall type could be due to non-physical environmental factors or differences in the student populations of the various dorms. Suppose that some students are predisposed to like residence halls while others are not. The differences in student satisfaction we observed in different residence halls might be attributable to different proportions of dorm-liking and dorm-disliking students. Likewise, some residence halls may impose unreasonable restrictions on their student occupants. If so, the differences in student satisfaction in residence halls might be attributable to differences in the restrictiveness of residence hall rules. We built into the study a thorough investigation and analysis of non-physical environmental factors, so that we would be able to evaluate reliably the importance of the physical environment.

One of the most frequently cited complaints about college residence halls is the number of restrictions that they impose on their residents. It is possible that the differences in satisfaction in different residence halls are due to differences in the restrictiveness of the residence halls. Three questionnaire items can shed some light on the issue. Students were asked to indicate whether or not their hall had "far too many restrictions" (question 25A-a); elsewhere in the questionnaire, they were asked to indicate whether or not their hall had "too many restrictions" (question 25A-o), and they were asked to indicate whether or not their hall was "well managed" (question 25A-n). The responses to these items are reported in Table C.

Table C indicates that restrictions are not much of a problem in residence hall types A and B; neither are they particularly burdensome to most students in residence hall types D and E. Only in residence hall type C (St. Olaf) does a majority of the respondents complain about restrictions. The variable "well managed" does not generate significant differences among the residence halls. If restrictions were the most important determinant of student satisfaction, we might have expected that the residence halls would have lined up in the same order vis a vis restrictiveness as they did vis a vis satisfaction. They did not.

But Table C does not adequately indicate whether or not the differences among the residence halls in terms of satisfaction are in fact due to the variable of restrictiveness. To find this out, we can use the same method we devised to test the influence of individual environmental factors in overall satisfaction. If restrictiveness were to account for the differences in satisfaction that we observed in Table B, we would expect that students who saw their residence hall as having too many restrictions would be less satisfied, as a group, than students who did not see their residence hall as having too many restrictions. More importantly, we would expect that the differences among the residence halls in terms of student satisfaction would significantly diminish or disappear, once the variable of restrictiveness was controlled. If both of the above conditions are met, we could attribute the differences in satisfaction in each of the sample residence halls to the variable of restriction.

Table D indicates that "unrestricted" students are generally more satisfied than "restricted" students. The differences among satisfaction levels among the various dorms, however, persist. "Restricted" students in residence hall type A are still more highly satisfied than "restricted" students in type E; likewise, "unrestricted" students in type A are more satisfied than "unrestricted" students in type E. The indication is that residence hall type remains a significant determinant of student satisfaction.

We can conclude that the association we have observed between residence hall type and satisfaction is not in fact due to restrictiveness . Restrictiveness is also associated with satisfaction, but this relationship exists independently of the relationship between residence hall type and satisfaction.

A second potential non-physical source of differential satisfaction is a consequence of our sample design. As mentioned earlier, we sampled (in most cases) a conventional dorm and an experimental residence hall on each campus. We were concerned that the relatively low satisfaction of students living in conven-

tional dorms may have been the effect of their knowledge of another, "nicer", residence hall, (namely, the experimental one) on campus. That is, the differences in satisfaction between control and experimental residence halls would be more the consequence of a student's sense of relative deprivation rather than the direct consequence of design factors.

Question 13 read: "All things considered how does your residence hall compare with others on your campus?" In conventional halls, 19 percent of those sampled indicated that "other halls are better than mine"; the proportion dropped in the experimental halls. If we remove the students who felt relatively deprived from the sample, we are left with those students who feel no relative deprivation -- this in a way is the equivalent of removing the "nicer" experimental residence hall from the campus. We see from this that the relationship between residence hall type and satisfaction remains as strong as it was before.

More than 80 percent of the students in conventional dorms did not feel relatively deprived (Table F). If we analytically remove the influence of "a better residence hall on campus", the proportion of highly satisfied students in conventional dorms does not greatly increase and the degree of difference among the residence hall types with respect to satisfaction does not diminish.

There are not enough cases of relative deprivation in the experimental residence halls to test the relationship between residence hall type and satisfaction among the total set of relatively deprived students. Tables E and F suggest, however, that relative deprivation does not account for the differences in satisfaction in the sample residence halls.

Similar methods were used to test the importance of the other non-physical variables to overall satisfaction by dorm types, and similar results were obtained. The formal report on this study includes tables on "Satisfaction by residence hall type controlled by attitude toward dormies status on campus"; "Satisfaction by residence hall type controlled by compatibility with roommate among students with roommates";

Satisfaction by residence hall type among students who were not required to live in a residence hall"; and "Satisfaction by selected background characteristics", including sex, age, year in school, parents annual income, level of self-support. These and other tables indicate that non-physical environmental factors and differences in student populations in the dorm types do not account for the differences in student satisfaction that we have observed.

In all, approximately 3000 tables from the data were analyzed. Throughout, the same general pattern appeared. Overall satisfaction was strongly correlated with residence hall type, poorly correlated with specific architectural features, and little affected by the potential intervening variables.

Implications and Directions

We would like to suggest, based on the data, what an important determinant of user satisfaction might be. If, as our results indicate, "residence hall type" is the essential factor in student satisfaction with their living environment, then it may be the whole complex system of symbols and cues that form one's impression or image of a residence hall that is directly related to satisfaction or dissatisfaction.

Traditional "dorms" contained the smallest number of highly satisfied students, whereas the Guelph complex, which was perceived as unconventional by its occupants, contained the highest percentage of satisfied students. (This was true despite the fact that it was quite traditional in some respects). The specific unconventional features of Guelph are not as important as the fact that they were different and created a different overall effect.

It appears that the conventional "dorm" image has a negative symbolic value for most students. If this negative symbolism can be disrupted by changing the image perceived by the students, satisfaction is increased.

If increasing satisfaction with an environment is not a problem of allocating resources according to a set of variables, but rather involves understanding the way a building is perceived symbolically by its potential users, how can the architect approach this problem?

The architect must consider the symbolic value of a building as it exists on two broad levels or planes:

1) The cultural-social context, which is the general framework implied by the building plan (suites vs. apartments) and scale (multiple vs. single unit dwellings). These are the cues which make it obvious to us that a structure is an office or an apartment and enables us to talk about such things in the abstract. The ways behavioral patterns are controlled by physical arrangement are also cues.

2) The aesthetic-cultural context, which is the environment as an art form. This is the way a building symbolizes a users' perception of himself. This kind of symbolism changes with time according to the current aesthetic and cultural value system which determines such dimensions as beautiful-ugly. In this way, a building or building style may come in and out of fashion and its desirability to users may change, causing a change in satisfaction. Whether or not a building is perceived as appropriate to time and place may be important to user satisfaction.

The second level is the important one to consider here, because it affects residence hall image and, thus, student satisfaction. The residence halls at Guelph and St. Olaf are both unconventional architecturally in some respects, yet Guelph's Complex B had a higher percentage of highly satisfied students (48 percent) than the towers at St. Olaf (28 percent). The crucial difference seems to be that residence halls at Guelph are unconventional in mood and style, aspects related to aesthetics, while those at St. Olaf are unconventional in form, but not aesthetically. They are, therefore, still perceived as "dorms" in the traditional sense.

The role of aesthetics in affecting satisfaction is in the way in which it breaks up negative conventional cues. At Guelph the negative conventional cues are not sent out because aesthetically, Complex B is different. Thus, we can conclude that if a building type symbolizes something negative, as a conventional dorm seems to, then a building whose aesthetic nature breaks up this negative symbolism is more satisfying to its users.

We hypothesize from our study that the way to design a residence hall that will satisfy many students today is to create an environment avoiding a regimented, institutional, "dormitory" image. The goal should be instead to give the students the feeling that they are able to be "themselves", to be individuals, to be free from an inhibiting sense of regimentation and molding. If the architect can achieve this intangible feeling, then the students will not be put off even if they feel the buildings, and their own quarters, have many specific design or construction faults.

Complaints about specific physical features of student housing appear to be part of the gestalt of residence hall living. Dissatisfactions of this type cannot be treated as the basis for a cost/benefit calculation. If an architect apportions the inevitably limited budget for a residence hall, for instance, so that he budgets relatively more construction funds to correct the problems students complain about most loudly, and less for other aspects of the building, his efforts may have little or no effect on overall student satisfaction. Once he has provided basic "threshold value" requirements, so that the building is reasonably functional, he may well be using his budget unwisely. Indeed, experience suggests that if an attempt to satisfy student complaints leads him away from the design direction proposed above, his efforts may actually be self-defeating.

Our data does not prove the new hypothesis, but the hypothesis provides a workable explanation for the data. We also were not able to prove a related hypothesis...that there is no one best or ideal housing type that will please most students...rather, our data is better explained by the hypothesis that students come with a wide range of housing needs, and that a range of housing types on campus will satisfy more students than any one type, however ideal.

These findings are particularly striking because we set out to test and define an old paradigm, not to develop a new hypothesis. Our research plan, and our survey instrument, could, therefore, only take us a limited way into the understanding of our new hypothesis, and into the establishment of a new paradigm.

Further research is needed to build on our findings in this present study. A separate research project we have now in the field at Washington State University will, we hope, provide some further clarification of the new hypothesis.

These findings do suggest, however, the need for the use of behavioral science in an architectural context. The previous approach, which consisted of asking people in their present environment what they would do better next time, is a useful way of identifying gripes, but it is not relevant to studying symbolic context and requirements. The behavioral scientist has techniques for studying human perception and behavior which are much more effective than relying on the responses of a sample of individuals who voice their likes and dislikes.

The combination of architecture and behavioral science allows architectural forms to respond to behavior. In this way, the architect is able to control environmental factors which affect human behavior and, therefore, can more accurately satisfy user needs. The behavioral scientist can help the architect to understand the psychological and sociological meaning of what he builds for the people who will use it.

CHART A

PROPORTION OF STUDENTS COMPLAINING
ABOUT ARCHITECTURAL FACTORS BY RESIDENCE HALL TYPE

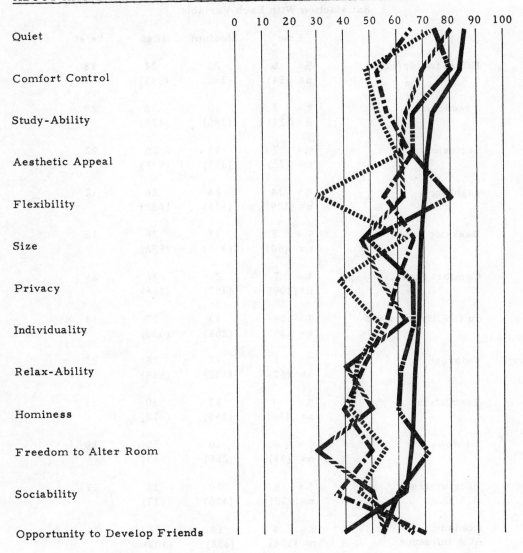

Quiet

Comfort Control

Study-Ability

Aesthetic Appeal

Flexibility

Size

Privacy

Individuality

Relax-Ability

Hominess

Freedom to Alter Room

Sociability

Opportunity to Develop Friends

0   10   20   30   40   50   60   70   80   90   100

Residence Hall Type A - Guelph
Residence Hall Type B - Apartments
Residence Hall Type C - St. Olaf
Residence Hall Type D - Suites
Residence Hall Type E - Conventional

TABLE A

THE PERCENTAGE OF HIGHLY SATISFIED STUDENTS

Grouped According to Low, Medium or High
Satisfaction With Each Variable

	Low	Medium	High	"e's"
Effort to tidy/clean	%= 6	22	24	18
	n= (54)	(348)	(547)	
Freedom	%= 3	18	32	29
	n = (123)	(386)	(428)	
Seclusion	%= 7	15	29	22
	n= (72)	(319)	(535)	
Lighting	%= 14	24	26	12
	n= (229)	(425)	(282)	
Desk-top space	%= 8	17	26	18
	n= (50)	(302)	(572)	
Comfort Contr.	%= 7	21	36	29
	n= (209)	(457)	(266)	
Suitability for sleep	%= 14	13	27	13
	n= (35)	(264)	(630)	
Bathroom	%= 5	18	28	23
	n= (87)	(302)	(548)	
Ventilation	%= 7	17	30	23
	n= (116)	(230)	(478)	
Windows	%= 8	20	26	18
	n= (91)	(265)	(547)	
Book storage B.S.D.	%= 5	20	32	27
	n= (178)	(336)	(411)	
Academic ACA influence	%= 8	19	32	24
	n= (134)	(482)	(303)	
Privacy	%= 3	20	31	28
	n= (128)	(424)	(374)	
Hominess	%= 2	16	32	30
	n= (92)	(404)	(428)	
Storage space	%= 8	20	30	22
	n= (132)	(405)	(384)	

		Low	Medium	High	"e's"
Flexibility	%=	8	19	33	25
	n=	(171)	(411)	(348)	
Size	%=	4	18	34	30
	n=	(120)	(459)	(350)	
Quiet	%=	9	23	34	30
	n=	(212)	(510)	(203)	
Suitability for study	%=	7	20	30	23
	n=	(137)	(472)	(319)	
Individuality	%=	8	17	33	25
	n=	(133)	(427)	(356)	
Sociability	%=	7	18	30	23
	n=	(97)	(358)	(453)	
Modern-ness	%=	2	14	29	27
	n=	(60)	(312)	(568)	
Aesthetic appeal	%=	4	20	34	30
	n=	(153)	(459)	(311)	
Opportunity to develop friends	%=	20	22	23	3
	n=	(82)	(378)	(462)	
Suitability for relaxation	%=	6	12	35	29
	n=	(62)	(430)	(427)	

TABLE B: STUDENT SATISFACTION BY RESIDENCE HALL TYPE

Residence Hall Types	Satisfaction Level			Total
	High	Medium	Low	
Residence Hall Type A (Guelph)	48%	38	13	99% (N=112)
Residence Hall Type B (Apartments)	33%	56	11	100% (N=141)
Residence Hall Type C (St. Olaf)	28%	34	38	100% (N= 96)
Residence Hall Type D (Suites)	26%	48	26	100% (N=167)
Residence Hall Type E (Conventional)	9%	42	48	99% (N=407)

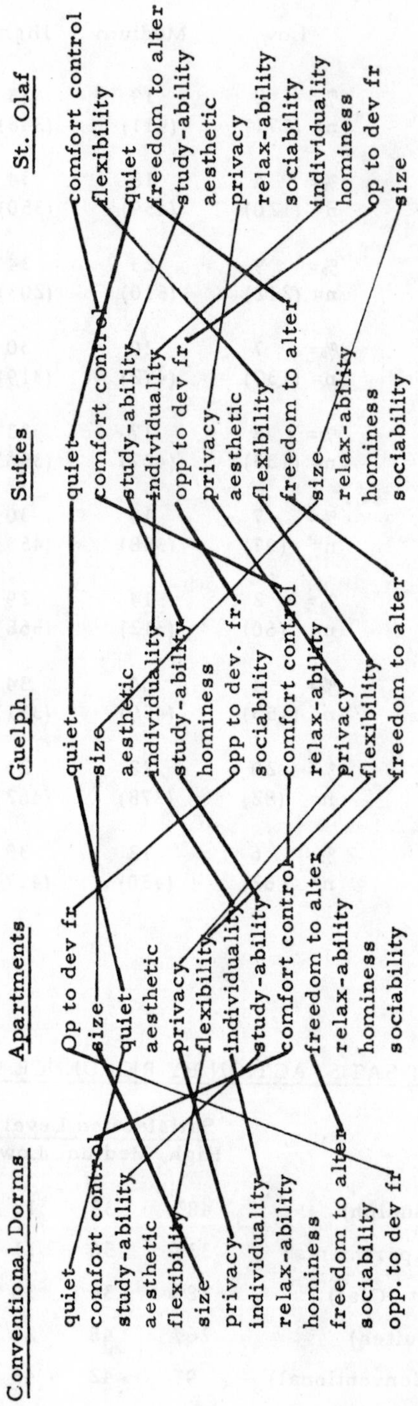

CHART B: RANKING OF COMPLAINTS BY RESIDENCE HALL

CHART C

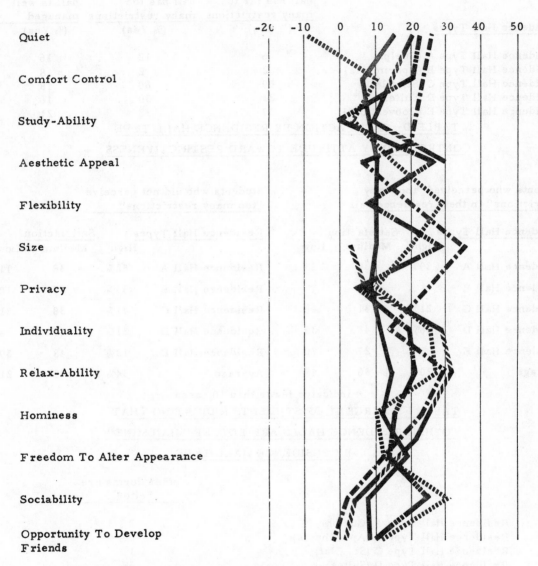

Quiet

Comfort Control

Study-Ability

Aesthetic Appeal

Flexibility

Size

Privacy

Individuality

Relax-Ability

Hominess

Freedom To Alter Appearance

Sociability

Opportunity To Develop
Friends

-20   -10   0   10   20   30   40   50

C: INCREASE IN PERCENTAGE OF HIGHLY SATISFIED STUDENTS

AMOUNG THOSE WHO ARE SATISFIED WITH A VARIABLE (e's)

.... Guelph
▪ ▬ ▪ ▬ ▪ Apartments
▬▬ ▮▮▮ ▬▬ St. Olaf
////// Suites
▬▬▬▬▬ Conventional

TABLE C: RESTRICTIVENESS OF THE RESIDENCE HALLS

BY RESIDENCE HALL TYPE

Residence Hall Types	my residence hall has far too many restrictions (% Yes)	my residence hall has too many restrictions (% Yes)	my residence hall is well managed (% Yes)
Residence Hall Type A (Guelph)	6	12	16
Residence Hall Type B (Apartments)	2	2	8
Residence Hall Type C (St. Olaf)	59	60	18
Residence Hall Type D (Suites)	23	30	16
Residence Hall Type E (Conventional)	27	32	21

TABLE D: SATISFACTION BY RESIDENCE HALL TYPE

CONTROLLED BY ATTITUDE TOWARD RESTRICTIVENESS

Students who perceived "too many restrictions" in their residence hall

Residence Hall Types	Satisfaction High	Medium	Low
Residence Hall A	39%	39	23
Residence Hall B	*	*	*
Residence Hall C	21%	31	48
Residence Hall D	16%	48	36
Residence Hall E	3%	27	70
Average	20%	36	44

Students who did not perceive "too many restrictions"

Residence Hall Types	Satisfaction High	Medium	Low
Residence Hall A	52%	38	11
Residence Hall B	33%	57	10
Residence Hall C	41%	38	21
Residence Hall D	31%	45	24
Residence Hall E	13%	48	39
Average	34%	45	21

* indicates fewer than 10 cases

TABLE E: PERCENT OF STUDENTS INDICATING THAT

"OTHER RESIDENCE HALLS ARE BETTER THAN MINE"

BY RESIDENCE HALL TYPE

	other dorms are better...
Residence Hall Type A (Guelph)	2%
Residence Hall Type B (Apartments)	0%
Residence Hall Type C (St. Olaf)	1%
Residence Hall Type D (Suites)	5%
Residence Hall Type E (Conventional)	19%

TABLE F: SATISFACTION BY RESIDENCE HALL TYPE AMONG STUDENTS

WHO DID NOT FEEL RELATIVELY DEPRIVED

	Satisfaction High	Medium	Low	
Residence Hall A (Guelph)	49%	39%	12%	(110)
Residence Hall B (Apartments)	33%	56%	11%	(141)
Residence Hall C (St. Olaf)	28%	35%	37%	(95)
Residence Hall D (Suites)	27%	48%	25%	(159)
Residence Hall E (Conventional)	11%	47%	41%	(331)

Evaluating for Environmental Measures

by Thomas A. Davis

Associate for Facilities Research, State University of New York, Albany

Abstract
The fit between a building and its users can be expressed as environmental measures. The measures have both environmental referents and human satisfaction referents. An evaluation field research procedure is hypothesized to correlate these referents and develop environmental measures as probability inductions. Assumptions are made about both the evaluation method and the environments in which it is to be used. Ten field comparisons are structured to show the kinds of arguments and warrants that must be used to link environmental referents to human satisfaction referents; i.e., to begin developing a body of theory about environmental measures.

1.0 ENVIRONMENTAL MEASURES

1.1 Design Fit

When a building "fits" a person, it effectively and attractively shelters, warms, cools, etc., his body in a manner that is efficient in terms of cost to build, operate and maintain. One way of operationally hypothesizing the chain of events leading to the design of buildings is as follows:

- PEOPLE express their physical needs in terms of their activities as individuals and groups, plus
- ENVIRONMENTAL MEASURES which describe the environment that occupants perceive: how much space an individual needs, how warm it should be, the light he needs, etc., for his activities; plus how many of what kinds of spaces an organization needs, their arrangement, convertibility, flexibility, etc., for organizational activities.
- The architect DESIGNS a FIT, using:
- CONSTRUCTIONAL MEASURES which describe various structural and materials possibilities in terms of strengths, hardness, insulation values, etc., that will provide the owner with a
- BUILDING that can be efficiently built, maintained and operated; and (hopefully) effectively used.

The designed linkages can be diagrammed as in Figure 1.

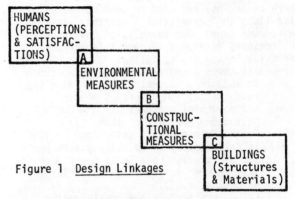

Figure 1 Design Linkages

1.2 The Symbolizing Problem

We can analyze the difficulties the designer faces in this model by looking at the linkages we have labled A, B and C. There are few problems at solid linkage "C" between building materials and the constructional measures, because an explicit set of categoricals have been developed for concepts such as lengths, weights, and volumes. In addition, object-referents and physical laws have been developed and are maintained to warrant (see Section 3.3) the continuous accuracy of the categoricals. The designer can use the categoricals and warrants with confidence in their continuing applicability.

The solid linkage at "B" is the "design fit" between constructional measures and environmental measures. Again, there are few problems at this linkage because the environmental referent of environmental measures have had categoricals and warrants developed for them using physical terms that are consistant with constructional measure terms. The designer, for example, can with confidence logically entail, from the need to maintain a room temperature of approximately 72° in a concrete and steel structure, the amount of heat that must be provided to the room.

The dotted linkage at "A" is between the environmental referent and the human satisfaction referent, and it is here that major problems exist. No sets of categoricals and warrants have been developed and maintained with which to represent enduring human satisfaction needs for comfort and utility. Since the "art and science of human perception and response" is still in the pioneering stages, several different kinds of referents are used in ad hoc ways to provide the needed linkages.

1.3 Seven Kinds of Links

In the absence of categoricals and warrants as links between environmental referents and human satisfaction referents, researchers have used words, verbal statements, graphics, and models as links. We will briefly discuss some of these approaches as background to the approach we call the evaluation.

The traditional approach (for the past three centuries) has been to develop quantitative links in "scientific" laboratory experiments over time. Two examples of environmental measures developed through this approach and still in use are as follows:

- Air temperature ranges were established in 1923 in a laboratory correlating the responses of 130 "average" people to environmental measures which satisfied just under one-half of them. (1)
- Fresh air needs were determined in 1936 in a laboratory correlating the responses of "average" people to environmental measures in rooms for 3, 5, 15 and 47 occupants. (2)

A second approach to the development of quantitative links is through the use of valuing techniques with groups of qualitative experts such as "wine tasters". Using the development of the Glare Index to show the approach, subjective comfort criteria were stated in descriptive terms wherein one unit on the scale constituted a difference that was just noticeable to the "experts". Under experimental conditions which included multiple sources, general lighting, and positional changes, the physical factors which cause glare, (such as brightness and size of the glaring source), were adjusted to accord with the stated criteria. Photometric and geometric factors were recorded, and the whole mass of data fed into a computer for correlation to the "expert's" judgments. Index Values were then computed that could be measured with standard equipment. The final step was to make field studies of varous types of interior rooms, noting the Glare Index from the table, with the "experts" judging whether the lighting did or didn't result in acceptable glare, all other factors considered. This resulted in Standards of Glare Index for each kind of room examined, which architects can use in the design process without the necessary involvement of their subjectivity in the procedure (3).

A third approach has been to develop graphic links. Ramsey and Sleeper's Architectural Graphics Standards (4) is an example of this approach for "floor area" environmental measures. A recent attempt by Bednar (5) to use graphic representations as a link between floor area and user satisfactions for research laboratories resulted in his conclusion that, if graphics were used, perhaps "the basic premise that users can evaluate is fallacious".

A fourth approach is the use of physical models as links. A full-scale manipulable model was used by Gassman and Green (6) to experiment with and develop both environmental and constructional measures for lecture halls. And scaled-down models of designs for new construction are often used to obtain the owners advance approval on environmental measures such as scale, form and arrangements.

A fifth, and more direct way that an individual's satisfactions may be quantified in the future is through the measure of concommitant physiological changes as a person is exposed to valued objects or statements about values. Two examples will suffice to show the approach:

- The opening of the pupils of the eye have been found experimentally to vary uncontrollably as an indication of whether the observer finds an object interesting or not.
- Muscular tension has been found experimentally to vary uncontrollably as an indication of whether a person feels he has enough light or not.

It remains to measure in each case what the physiological gaussain curve is as a function of people's feelings. Using the curve as referent, it should be possible to examine an individual's placement on it by scaling his physiological state at the moment. It would then be possible to state specific human values in numerical terms relating to pupil diameter, muscular tension, etc.

A sixth approach is the development of word symbols as links. Cantor (7) has proposed a theoretical model for development of environmental measures which he calls "psychological appraisal tools". He adopts Osgood's semantic differential to develop curves expressing the relationship between "physical correlates" and "psychological appraisals" of them. He recommends the same kind of approach used in the development of I.Q. tests. He would thus develop a standardized test for each human activity which would show environmental measure satisfaction ranges for a given percentage of people at a given activity. Barowsky (8) uses intensive group problem-solving techniques to develop what he calls "environmental characteristics", which are then ranked according to their importance to people for whom a new facility is to be designed. He is thus attempting to develop new subjective referents to which he can later assign objective referents.

The seventh approach is to develop verbal statements linking the environmental referent to the human satisfaction referent in the form of probability inductions. It is the approach for which the balance of this discussion sets forth a theoretical structure. In section 2, we hypothesize what we call an evaluation approach to the development of environmental measures. In Section 3, we define the content of probability inductions useful as environmental measures, and show what kinds of data are needed from which to make the inductions. Section 4 sets forth assumptions about the role of environments in human affairs, about human activity measurements, about opinions questionnaires, and about cultural meanings. In Section 5, ten comparisons are structured to show the kinds of arguments and warrants that must be used to begin building a body of theory of environmental measures.

2.0   THE EVALUATION APPROACH

2.1   Evaluations in the Natural Sciences

One approach to developing probability inductions as links between environments and the people who use them is the evaluation. It is the only investigation procedure that was known until about three centuries ago, and is the basic laboratory method of the applied sciences. The engineer often conducts extensive trial-and-error experiments to search for the best combination among a set of parameters. In so doing, he gathers data for comparison and tests and re-tests his findings to be sure this solution will be efficient and effective. This feedback kind of data-collection-via-testing process we are calling an evaluative procedure when human values are included as data.

2.2   Evaluations in the Social Sciences

The most informal and widely-used evaluation is the survey and synthesis approach by which, for example, building design and use criteria have been developed. Criteria such as square feet allowances per occupant, utilization goals for classrooms and laboratories, and acceptable reverberation times within rooms, have been developed by observing, counting and measuring actual situations experienced in the field, and comparing the results with data from other similar situations. As an end result of a survey such as this, a synthesis is induced, and a criterion is stated that is used predictively to guide the use of existing buildings and to plan and design future buildings.

2.3   Using Evaluations to Develop Probability Inductions

We propose in 2.4 a formal evaluation methodology to develop environmental measures in the form of probability inductions. It starts with the standards now being used, and compares appropriate measures and counts of built environments for congruence. In addition, the occupants' activities are observed and reported, and in questionnaires and interviews the occupants are asked if, in their opinion, the built environments which the measures describe are good, adequate, poor, etc. Measures and counts, and user's opinions are then correlated, and further interviews held to find

out exactly what the users were referring to in responding to questionnaires. The results of such investigations, gathered over time, season, geographic areas, room orientations, generic groups of people, kinds of construction, user activities, etc., and in parallel with all other known contributing factors, would yield a data bank of information from which probability patterns of successful ranges might be induced for all combinations of specific conditions.

2.4   The "Evaluating for Environmental Measures" Hypothesis

It is hypothesized that appropriate data can be developed through evaluations to express human-activity satisfaction (comfort and utility) needs in the form of environmental measures, where:

"Appropriate data" includes physical measures and counts of environments, activities of the people using them, and their opinions about the environments;

"Humans" includes people as individuals, and as groups or organizations;

"Activities" includes physical behavior, plus mental activity when appropriate;

"Satisfaction needs" means to develop, for each kind of activity, relationships showing ranges of measures for each environmental measure as a function of the percentage of people who will be satisfied.

"Environmental measures" are statements in the form of probability inductions which express probable human satisfaction needs in the built environments, in physical measure terms consistent with constructional measures; and

"Evaluations" as a research approach includes:

- accepting social realities as a condition, and studying objective realities as design hypotheses;
- gathering object and environment data through field observation and measurement;
- gathering human activity and satisfaction data through field observations and measures, interviews and questionnaires;
- searching for cultural meanings through user interviews and reporting the data from the user's point of view;
- stating environmental measures as probability inductions of human-activity satisfaction ranges, and the probable percentage of people who will be satisfied.

A minimum of four conditions must be met in order to accept the hypothesis:

1. Identification of "fits" and "misfits" between human activity satisfaction needs (as individuals and as organizations) and built environments, which

can be expressed as environmental measures;

2. Establishment of ranges of satisfaction and probable percentages of people satisfied for specific environments and for specific kinds of human activities;

3. Showing in what ways environmental measures interact with each other, and their combined affects on humans;

4. Development of new environmental measures.

2.5 Method as Theory

One condition to be kept in mind in using the evaluation approach to develop anything is that the method itself actually becomes indistinguishable from the theory. This is in contrast to the "scientific" laboratory experiment over time, where a formal structure with rigid conditions must be followed in order to give credence to the findings. The structure guarantees replicability of the experiment, to prove the validity of the findings. But it is entirely separate from the theory being tested or the findings which result. The method provides the structure of all such experiments, and the theory being tested provides the content.

In using the evaluation approach, however, the method which is used actually determines what data will be collected. Thus, the method is also the theory being tested, and any change in method is a change in the theory. This means that in using the evaluation approach, both the theory of environmental measures and the method to develop them must be developed together. And this also means that a complete set of assumptions must be made explicit about both the methods used, and the things observed and measured. These assumptions are set forth as far as possible (at this time) in Section 4.

2.6 Stating a Composite Theory

A composite theory of environmental measures must show in what ways the measures act and interact, for individuals and for organizations, for all kinds of activities, and under the influence of all kinds of natural environmental conditions. To cite two obvious examples, the climatic environmental measure could show in what ways the individual's needs for comfort and utility may change as he moves between polar positions such as, for example:

- hot, dry vs. cold, wet conditions,
- south (sun) orientation vs. a north orientation,
- large vs. small spaces,
- location next to wall vs. in center of space,
- physically active vs. sedentary activities, etc.

And space-time environmental measures for college would show in what ways their needs change as they move between polar positions such as:

- rural-residential vs. urban-commuter conditions,

- two-year college vs. the "multiversity",
- academic vs. professional orientations,
- large groups vs. individualized instruction,
- personal vs. automated instruction, etc.

Finally, to complete our two examples, a composite theory of environmental measures would also have to show when, and in what ways climatic measures for individuals interact with space-time measures for organizations.

3.0 EVALUATING FOR ENVIRONMENTAL MEASURES

We have shown the need to develop the "human satisfaction" component of environmental measures, and described seven kinds of links which have been used. We have hypothesized an evaluation approach to developing probability inductions as environmental measures and in this section will show what the inductions are, and what kinds of data are needed to make them.

3.1 Environmental Measure Inductions

From observations, measures and user-opinion data, second-level generalizations in the form of probability inductions can be stated. At least two kinds of inductions are useful:

1. Inferences of descriptive probable causality between humans (as individuals and in organizations) and their environments; (e.g. The fact that there are several independent evidences, each of which makes it probable that an air temperature below 68°F is uncomfortable for students seated in a lecture hall, makes it probable that the lower temperature is responsible for the discomfort (9).

2. Inferences of environmental measures ranges of satisfaction (comfort and utility) for individuals and organizations (e.g. The fact that 75% of the observed students seated in a lecture hall are uncomfortable when the temperature is below 68°F makes it probable that 75% of all students would be uncomfortable (10). This induction relates three things: a percentage of users; a level of their comfort, and a measure of an environment. One way to show this diagramatically is in Figure 2.

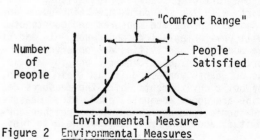

Figure 2   Environmental Measures

Within any culture, these inductions may be generalized: 1. as the commonly re-occuring patterns of a minor input to a total situation (e.g., the built environment input to a sitting-observing situation); 2. on the basis of specific (age, etc.) groups of people performing generic classes of human activities (e.g., sitting-observing); 3. on the basis of constructional measures (e.g., a given insulation value for an exterior wall can be provided by many different materials of combinations thereof); and 4. on the basis of organizational activities, methods, etc.

3.2 First-Level Statements

These probability inductions are second-level statements which combine or aggregate first-level data. First level data can be simply reports of observations of measures or counts. Or it can take one of three (11) forms depending on the degree to which the environment is contributant to user activities:

1. Cause-effect: This means that the environment is necessary and sufficient for the affect to be produced. Only observations can be reported in this form:
   - The environment, or a characteristic of it was demonstrated by the (user or observer) to be necessary and sufficient for the user's satisfaction (comfort or utility): a) for a user's activity; b) for the achievement of planning goals; or c) to result in changed conditions after its use.
2. Producer-product: This means that the environment is necessary but not sufficient for the affect to be produced. Both observations and opinions can be reported in this form:
   - The environment, or a characteristic of it was demonstrated by an observer or reported in the user's opinion to be necessary (but not sufficient) for user satisfaction (comfort or utility): a) for a user activity; b) for the achievement of planning goals, or; c) to result in changed conditions after its use.

   Note that although opinions can be structured in this form, the content of the opinions refers only to the specific case reported, not to an invariant empirical reality and has no validity per se for purposes of generalizing.
3. Correlation: No causality can be shown in this kind of relationship. It simply means that a concommitant variation has been observed. Both observations and opinions can also be reported in this form:
   - The environment, or a characteristic of it was demonstrated by an observer, or reported by a user to correlate with user satisfactions (comfort or utility): a) for a user activity; b)

for the achievement of planning goals; or c) to result in changed conditions after its use.
4. Preferred Value Statements: This is a composite of the user's opinions, attitudes and beliefs (again, not an invariant empirical reality), representing his preferences for each characteristic of the environment for his activities:
   - A characteristic of the environment is ranked by the user to be of more value than some and of less value than others for his activities.

3.3 Warranting the Data

Data on observations, or measures or counts of objects and environments, are gathered according to the rules of the natural sciences. Thus, both categoricals (standards of lengths, volumes, weights, etc.) and warrants (objective referents and physical laws) are supported by logic or evidence which guarantees predictability. However, data which reports on user satisfactions, opinions, attitudes or beliefs, have as yet no universal categoricals, or warrants for their use. All each finding normally has to support it is the method of collection used: the rules of the controlled experiment over time; or the rules of data analysis and statistical manipulation. In using the evaluation approach, probability inductions will be developed which can be used as "physical law probability" referents. Thus, there is need to warrant any of the four kinds of statements set forth in 3.2 above. The warrant represents the authority for the statement, and must be either the logic with which it entails from our assumptions, or a mass of experimental evidence. For example, one of the warrants we use in Section 5.2 is that "the user knows best". When inductions are based on a warrant like this, the reporter must be prepared to also substantiate the logic or the evidence of the warrant.

4.0 RESEARCH ASSUMPTIONS

In section 2.4 we showed that the evaluation method that is used actually becomes the theory of environmental measures, and that therefore, a complete set of assumptions must be made explicit before beginning any research. This section outlines some preliminary assumptions for this purpose, about the environment, user activities, user opinions, user attitudes and beliefs, and data manipulations.

4.1 Environmental Assumptions

The following environmental assumptions are patterned after Klapper's (12) "emerging generalizations" about mass communications, and provide a structure for the milieu "out there".

1. The effectiveness of a built environment can be stated in physical categorical measures that can be correlated to

human perceptions of satisfaction (comfort and utility).

The second assumption states that there are maximums and minimums for each environmental measure above and below which the environment will be perceived as unsatisfactory for human use:

2. There are extreme conditions (too much or too little) in which the built environment can be a direct cause for human discomfort or disfunction.

The next two assumptions state that the built environment is only one of many factors which make up a total environment, and that it interacts with the others toward a steady (predictable) state:

3. The built environment does not ordinarily serve as a necessary and sufficient cause for human comfort and utility, but instead, acts among and through a complex of mediating factors (influences) that make up the total environment.

4. These mediating factors are such that they typically render the built environment a contributory agent, but not the sole cause, in a process of reinforcing existing conditions (rather than changing them).

The next assumption states that when the built environment does contribute to change, either the other factors won't be acting, or there will be a "snowballing" effect.

5. When the built environment does function as an agent of perceived change, one of two conditions (is likely to) obtain: Either: a) the mediating factors to that perception will have been rendered inoperative by the agent of change; or b) the mediating factors will also be impelling toward change.

The last assumption states that the parts of the built environment are independent variables which interact with each other.

6. The role of the built environment (either as a contributory agent or direct affect on human comfort and utility) is influenced by the interactions between its independent environments (sonic, luminous, climatal, spatial, stability, time and esthetic environments).

Each independent environment of the total environment is thus described as working independently among several other independent variables acting on an individual at any one time: it may be a cause for unsatisfactory affects in extreme situations, but it normally acts only as a necessary but not sufficient contributant to human satisfactions.

It must be noted that we are not concerned in these assumptions with how the built environment may motivate a person, except to modify it to his needs. In other words, we are interested only in how it performs passively for his comfort and utility. There is a school of thought which emphasizes environmental factors as basic motivation forces. Wheeler (13) con-

cluded that "A building must be seen as a primary shaper and conditioner of our behavior". This is an interesting idea, but it is a step beyond our present concern with environmental measures for human comfort and utility.

4.2 User Activity Assumptions

Environmental measures are to be developed for different kinds or levels of human activities, so assumptions must be made about grouping them. Scientists and engineers in the natural sciences have been able to partition "objective" reality into equivalent sets (groups, categories, etc.) and to develop number notations and algebraic relations that can be considered literal translations of the groupings they represent. Floor area in a building, for example, can be partitioned into "square feet", and based on the criteria that they are contained "in the same building", assigned equivalence notations. To be equivalent means that each square foot in the building is related to (e.g. is not unequal to) itself by definition (the relexive property), that each square foot has the same relation to each of the other square feet in the building that they have to it (the symmetric property), and that any square foot has the same relationship to a second that the second has to a third and that therefore the first and third have the same relationship (the transitive property). Based on these equivalencies, the numbers assigned to the square feet of reality can be said to be a literal representation of the reality, because the reality is partitioned in such a way that the relationships between the partitions conform to the same rules as the numbering system.

However, when the same approach is used to partition and number an individual's activities (sitting, walking, etc.) or events (birthdays, etc.) or the activities and events of groups or organizations, the equivalency rules may not hold. For example, three equivalency problems that must be considered in partitioning social reality (both events and activities) are: social reality is compound in the sense that it does not contain identical elements (people); it is temporal in the sense that it changes (people learn) over time; and it has both an observable external behavior and a private meaning internal to each person involved (14). Euclidean and Boolean algebra, for example, can't easily accomodate all of these equivalency-conditions, and unless they are dealt with explicitly, and the researcher's assumptions stated to include them, the partitioning of social reality to conform to the rules for inert objects will distort social reality in ways which result in the reporting of invalid data. Thus, the only assumption we can make prior to gathering data is that the validity of social measurement data may be increased by inducing the rules of our algebraic and numbering systems from the social evaluation data that we collect. We shouldn't be

surprised if this results in new symbols, because, to put it another way, it assumes that
the properties of measurement systems must be
developed from rather than imposed upon the
structure of the realities the quantity.

4.3 User Opinion Assumptions

The measuring of human values (expressed
verbally as opinions) are different from those
of measuring and counting objects or environments:
- There is no ratio scale, as the object
  being valued is compared with another
  object or with verbal descriptive statements.
- The object may be universally the same,
  but it may also be another infinitely
  variable human being.
- The environment includes human valuers
  and thus cannot be held constant or
  varied at will.

Therefore, instead of the subject being directly estimated, the process is one of intellec-
tualizing a degree of satisfaction, interest,
desire or aversion, or some other mental aspect of human mentality (15). In other words,
a mental dimension of the valuer is the thing
that is estimated, as it views and interprets
reality in the context of its experience and
ideals. Furthermore, since a) each valuer has
unique capabilities and aggregate experiences,
and b) the mental dimension can include rational and emotional aspects in various combinations, and c) the very act of valuing has
the potential of changing the valuer's value
structure, it is concluded that:
- The valuing act can never be exactly
  replicated; in other words, cause and
  effect relationships cannot be generalized and used to make predictions about
  the future behavior of individuals, except as probability generalizations
  about groups of which he is a member.

Whether or not something is described as good
today by a particular person or group of people will not tell us how the same person or
group will describe it tomorrow. In valuing
facilities, some aspect of the facility is
compared: a) for preference, to the same aspect in a similar or dissimilar situation; or
b) for adequacy, to the valuer's own beliefs
as to what is comfort, etc. In a) valuing
preference, valid satisfaction information can
be developed about existing reality, such as,
for example, the relative comfort of a chair
in one room as compared to a different one in
another room. In this situation, where only
one person is involved, and at a single point
in time, the warrant that "the user knows best"
is sufficient to make valid preferred-value
statements which express nominal differences
between several items.

In b) valuing adequacy, the users are
asked to rate the environment on such things
as temperature, humidity, etc. as a check on
the objective measures for the same values; or

they are asked to rate sight-lines, feelings
of scale, etc., as a check on theoretical design criteria. If the architect anticipated
well, the facility will be valued highly. The
valuers are judging on the basis of their beliefs of what ought to be. Since these ideals
may be both narrow and fixed because they are
necessarily a product of their experience and
psychology, they may not include the myriad of
alternate choices that are actually available
in any situation. Thus, the only information
that can be developed in the valuing of adequacy by users is how well the architect's design anticipated the values of those who are
using the facilities. In other words, it's
the valuer's ideals of what ought to be that
the architect has designed. However, since we
can make use of this conclusion by combining
it with four further assumptions:
1. That relevant questions about human perceptions of environments can be communicated to the users;
2. That a substantial percentage of the
   users can and will respond with opinions
   (the verbal expression of their values)
   that represent their perception of their
   environment for their activities;
3. That the building design represents the
   architect's solution to the user's needs;
   and
4. That one goal of the architect is to
   provide a comfortable and utilitarian
   environment for the user-occupant.

Based on these assumptions, it follows
that useful user statements can be made from
their interview or questionnaire responses to
represent their perceived adequacy of an environment for their activities. However, no
claim can be made that they refer to actual
differences in the objective reality that is
perceived by different people, or by the same
people at two different times. The differences
refer to differences in user-occupant opinions,
not to objective reality, and must be correlated to all known commonalities in the total
situation in order to provide referents for the
words and validity for the statements of relationships. In working toward these correlations, and subsequent probability inductions,
we can avoid the "questionnaire development"
approach.

It wasn't included in Section 1.3, for
reasons that will become evident, but another
kind of human satisfaction referent that could
possibly be attempted is the questionnaire.
The development of the I.Q. test is an example.
The approach has been to start with the normal
curve - the graphic symbolization of the dispersion of measures in the social sciences,
and to work to make instruments (questionnaires
or tests) that will result in responses that
form a normal distribution when administered
to a selected sample of a population. When researchers get such a distribution, it is
claimed that a single characteristic has been
isolated and measured, and that the data is a

"valid" representation of the variable. When it can also be demonstrated that the repeated use of the instrument places an individual in about the same position on the normal curve, it is claimed that the procedure is "reliable" (16). Thus in this approach the researcher works to refine both his stimuli and his populations in ways which show his information to be dispersed in a normal curve (at which point he has actually "made" his curve), so that he can label his information as "data" representing a "valid" set of observations. In other words, he appears to define "culturally meaningful data" as "those questionnaire responses which can be shown to form a normal curve when elicited from a random sample of a population". Note that in using this approach, it must be assumed that the user doesn't possess all the information that is requested, and that the tester does. Thus the tester can construct a scale from 0 to 100%. Note that as a result, the intelligence which is defined grows out of the testing instrument, not out of any psychological or sociological theory about intelligence.

When the same approach is used on questionnaires such as those which may be designed to obtain opinions in environmental evaluation studies, we are seeking information about how users experience their environments. And if we are asking the users, we've got to remember that we don't have the "right" answers, (there are none) and that we are assuming that the users can provide us with some. This assumption is the reverse of the test-design situation, and there's no possibility of constructing a scale of intervals, or even of more or less, because we aren't testing anything. What we're trying to do is to correlate user responses (to our questions about their environments) to actual environmental conditions. And under all but the most extreme conditions the users answers can be expected to form a binomial distribution (17).

4.4 Cultural Meanings Assumptions
In other words, in studying normal conditions, the user's opinions about an environment or an activity can be expected to vary between extremes, and to cluster predominantly about a center position. And it is these variances that are so interesting to the evaluator. Because instead of the spread being an "error" of a "measure" it can actually represent differences in one or more of at least three possibilities: 1. environmental objects or other people "out there"; 2. individual perceptual or physiological equipment; and/or 3. the attitudes and beliefs of the users which help to determine the meanings they assign to our descriptions of objects, events and activities, and to the responses they make to our questions. All three are present in the response curves, and it's the shape of the curves, the extremes (ranges) of the responses, and what the users believe they were actually using

as referents that may enable us to construct theoretical models of people and of their environments that will reveal in what ways and why they interact.

Thus it is premature at this time to attempt to develop "reliable" questionnaire instruments and procedures via anonymous questionnaires and random sample populations. Instead, the evaluator must work to increase the validity of his data by searching for the complete meanings of words, in order to make explicit the common-sense assumptions he finds operative. He can then accept the users in all their diversity and changeability, and work to develop expressions that show in what ways they are different and changeable, and in what ways their environments can be made to fit these differences and changeabilities. He must begin with questionnaires and interviews of purposive samples of users, and go beyond the answers to search for their "cultural meanings" - i.e. their object referents plus those physiological conditions, and the attitudes and beliefs which also contributed to their responses.

Some techniques for this kind of data search are available, and Cantor's and Barowsky's approaches are mentioned in Section 1.3. Interviews also contributed meaningful data to the studies previously cited by Bednar. Other kinds of techniques that might be adopted include "T" groups or sensitivity training sessions. In using this data in combination with other data, the researcher can begin to explain behavior in terms of its meaningfulness to the social actor, and to develop a body of theory containing warrants and arguments that grow out of social empirical data rather than out of test instrument development procedures. In so doing, he will avoid biasing his data, as all social scientists must in making parametric studies, by assuming: 1. that the people being studied share his cultural meanings; or 2. that social meanings can be explained in terms of factors external to the actor, discarding as irrelevant those cases that don't appear to conform with the researcher's theory (18). These twin biases can be avoided in evaluations by using questionnaire data as "signal" probes, and going beyond to search for deeper meanings, particularly those meanings that don't conform with the preponderance of evidence.

4.5 Data Manipulation Assumptions
Studies of social meanings often involve the use of analytic techniques such as factor or regression analysis (19) to reveal patterns of association between man and his environment. Based on our discussion above, these correlations of socio-economic, etc., data are only a part of the story, and can only be fully understood by going on the show from "cultural meanings" studies what each factor "means" to, and in what ways it affects, the person(s) being studied. In working toward increasingly valid

data, we assume that face validity tests can be used with other data to seek user-referents for the words we use; interview - face validity correlations can be used to define the shape and size of the curve which represents the users responses; and percentage analysis correlations can be used to compare actual environmental measures to the curve of the responses. With enough of this kind of data in hand, we can work to refine our generalizations and assumptions (our body of theory) about the interactions of humans with their environments. And it is then that we can begin to construct "reliable" instruments which entail from our theory, and which can be used to test the human-environmental hypotheses which appear to be worth pursuing.

5.0   EVALUATION COMPARISONS

We have developed the concept of environmental measures as probability inductions, hypothesized an evaluation method with which to gather data, and made basic assumptions for a field study. This final section isolates five realities which bear on environmental measures sufficiently to be profitably compared, and is included exclusively to show the structure of the comparisons and the kinds of warranted arguments which must be used to begin developing a body of theory about environmental measures. And particular attention will have to be given to developing the logic of, or experimental evidence with which to establish the warrants, because they are the authority for the links between the environmental referent and the human satisfaction referent in any measure.

5.1   Five Realities

As a convenience in evaluating for environmental measures, we divide the world into five realities which can be compared, and operationally describe them as follows:

- Objects such as rooms and buildings and the equipment and items of which they are composed, and the people using them.
- Environments in which objects and people are immersed, including the spatial, luminous, sonic, climatal, stability, time and esthetic environments for individuals; and the size, assortment, location, privacy, flexibility and convertibility of space environments for organizations.
- Standards such as temperature, light levels, etc., and time and use standards which serve over time as guides and goals for the operation of a college or the conduct of people.
- Records of experiences which show the progress being made toward achieving the standards, such as time and use records.
- Opinions of people about the objects and environments, and the standards and records which symbolize them. They are expressed at a single point in time in interviews or on questionnaires.

This gives us fifteen comparisons for field study, each of which may have dozens of comparison possibilities. In the section which follows, we structure only those possibilities which appear to be most promising for the development of environmental measures at this time.

5.2   Evaluation Arguments

Ten comparison statements are proposed. The structure of the argument that might be used to warrant the results is given for the first comparison only. The verb "describes" in each comparison refers to statements shown in Section 3.2 which state cause-effect, necessary but not sufficient, correlative or ranking relationships.

A. Comparing Objects to Similar Objects
1. An evaluator compares the overt behavior of the user(s) of two different objects used for the same activity, and describes differences in physical behavior. e.g. An evaluator compares the physical activities of one lecturer using two different lecterns or a group of students using different chairs, and notes similarities and differences.
Structure of Argument
    Producer-Product Claim: If, after single demonstrations of each, a lecturer is able to select lectern controls correctly more often at one lectern than at another lectern, then the differences in the design are necessary (but not sufficient) to cause the behavioral differences.
    Scales: Physical measures and counts.
    Measurer: Evaluator.
    Warrant: The design of an object is a factor in its use.
    Use of Statement: Prediction.
B. Comparing Environments to Similar Environments
1. An evaluator compares two or more similar kinds of environments used for the same activity, and describes their similarities and differences in performance, comfort, utility, etc.
C. Comparing Opinions to Opinions (Same users)
1. An evaluator compares the opinions of two or more users about the physical characteristics of environments used for the same activity, and describes the similarities or differences of their opinions as to the adequacy of the characteristic for their activities.
2. An evaluator compares the opinions of two or more users about the characteristics of two or more environments used for the same activity, and describes the preferences they have for one or the other for use in their activities.
3. An evaluator compares the opinions of two or more users about the informational content of standard or records for a single environment used for the same activity and describes the similarities and differences of their opinions as to the adequacy of the standard for their activities.
4. An evaluator compares the opinions of two

or more users about the informational content of standards or records for several different environments used for the same activity, and describes preferences they have for one or the other for use in their activities.

5. An evaluator compares the opinions of user(s) about the importance of each environment, goal, or consequences of a room, used for the same activities, and describes how they may be similar to or differ from the rankings of other lecturers.

Warrants for C1 - C5: The user knows best: his opinions affect his activities; the form and content of an environment is a factor in its use; differences of opinions can be studied.

D. Comparing Standards to Standards (For same environments)

1. An evaluator compares two or more standards, for the same environment at a single moment in time, and describes conflict or reinforcement.

2. An evaluator compares standards for using environments at a single moment in time and describes how they conflict or reinforce.

Warrants: If differences can be observed, they can be studied.

E. Comparing Records to Records (For same environments or users)

1. An evaluator compares two or more records for the same environment and describes in what ways the information conflicts or reinforces.

2. An evaluator compares records of users to environments at a single moment in time, and describes in what ways the information conflicts or reinforces.

Warrant: Utilization of an environment is a measure of efficiency: the form and content of environments are determinants for its use.

3. An evaluator compares two or more use records for the same environment before and after, and describes changed conditions.

Warrant: Manipulation of a single variable (the center) while holding all other conditions constant will show the significance of the variable.

4. An evaluator compares two or more achievement records for the same users of an environment before and after, and describes differences.

Non-educational warrants: The room environment has an effect on the amount of learning that takes place in it; manipulation of a single variable (the room) while holding all other conditions constant will show the significance of the variable. There is no way to show cause and effect in comparison tests of this kind, nor can "all other conditions" be held constant. The lecture halls are designed to support the lecturer with A-V media which in turn is assumed to lead to better learning. But ironically, to evaluate this directly is the least promising approach because another variable (the lecturer) is introduced for whom there are no standard scores. However, these kinds of mental achievement tests are firmly established in educational methodology experiments and are useful in evaluating a lecture hall simply to demonstrate through concomitant achievements that as much learning can take place in one environment as in another.

Lesser and Schueler (20), in a recent review of the research literature on the use of new media in teacher education, concluded that this type of testing has "...harvested a rich crop of non-significant findings".

F. Comparing Objects to Environments (Not structured)

G. Comparing Objects to Opinions

1. An evaluator compares an environment to the opinion(s) of the user(s), and describes in what ways the environment is a referent for the opinion.

Warrants: The user knows best: if an observer perceives a difference, it can be studied.

H. Comparing Objects to Standards (Not structured)

I. Comparing Objects to Records (Not structured)

J. Comparing Environments to Opinions

1. An evaluator compares an environment to the opinion(s) of the user(s) and describes in what ways the environment is a referent for the opinion. This would be structured as in "G" above.

K. Comparing Environments to Standards

1. An evaluator compares physical characteristics or operations of environments to environmental measure standards, and describes conformance of the environment to the standard.

Warrant: Experimental evidence.

L. Comparing Environments to Records - this is an internal audit procedure to determine the validity of the records, and is not structured.

M. Comparing Opinions to Standards - structured as in "G" above.

N. Comparing Opinions to Records - structured as in "G" above.

O. Comparing Standards to Records

1. An evaluator compares a standard to a record for environments and describes achievement toward the standard.

Warrant: Manipulation of a single variable (the room) while holding all other conditions constant will show the significance of the variable.

2. An evaluator compares a standard to a record for users, and describes achievement toward the standard.

Non-education warrants: The room environment has an effect on the amount of learning that takes place in it; manipulation of a single variable (the room) while holding all other conditions constant will show the significance of the variable.

Note that there are no standardized tests listed in *Buros Sixth Mental Measurements Yearbook* which contain an environmental-learning factor. The use of any other standardized test, because student matching information is never provided, would only show how the students tested varied from the norm. Thus, the only possibility for the use of this kind of test is to develop one that does have an environment-learning factor. But perhaps none have been developed because the environment is a minor factor compared to others in a learning environment, as we have assumed. Thus, the success of a room for learning purposes at this time can be no more than a conclusion inferred from the results of other evaluation tests.

NOTES

1. Houghten, F.C. and Yaglou, C.D.; ASHVE Report 673; ASHVE Transactions Vol. 29, 1923, page 361; as referenced in ASHVE Guide and Data Book, 1965, page 112.

2. Yaglou, C.D., Riley, E.C. and Coggins, D.I.; ASHVE Report #1031; ASHVE Transactions Vol. 42, 1936, page 133; as referenced in ASHRAE Guide and Data Book, 1965, page 101.

3. Hopkinson, R.G.: The evaluation of the built environment. Inaugral lecture as Haden-Pilkington Professor of Environmental Design and Engineering at University College, London, H.K. Lewis, 1966.

4. Ramsey, C.G. and Sleeper, H.R.: Architectural Graphic Standards: John Wiley and Sons, Inc., New York.

5. Bednar, M.J. and Haviland, D.S. User evaluation of the Spatial Environmental Measure in University Teaching and Research Laboratories: A Methodology Study; Center for Architectural Research, Rensselaer Polytechnic Institute; Nov., 1969; page 2 - 69.

6. Hauf, Kopps, Green, Gassman, Haviland, New Spaces for Learning: Designing College Facilities to Utilize Instructional Arts and Media (Revised Edition), Troy, New York, Rensselaer Polytechnic Institute, 1966.

7. Cantor, David; The Subjective Assessment of the Environment; University of Strathclyde Building Performance Research Unit, 1969.

8. Barowsky, George; Improving Performance of Teacher Education Facilities; BOSTI, State University of New York at Buffalo, 1970.

9. Day, J.P.; Inductive Probability; Humanities Press, Inc; New York, 1961. See p. 279 for the field conditions.

10. Ibid, p. 324.

11. Ackoff, R.L.; Scientific Method; Optimizing Applied Research Decisions, John Wiley & Sons, Inc., New York, 1962, pages 16 - 19.

12. Klapper, J.T.; What we know about the Effects of Mass Communications: The Brink of Hope, in Communication and Culture edited by A.G. Smith; Holt, Rinehart and Winston, New York, p. 538.

13. Wheeler, L.; Behavioral Research for Architectural Planning and Design; Ewing Miller Associates, Terre Haute, Indiana, 1967, page 5.

14. Douglas, Jack; The Social Meanings of Suicide, Princeton University Press, 1968.

15. Cicourel, Aaron V., Method and Measurement in Sociology, The Free Press, New York, 1964, page 25.

16. Lepley, Ray; Value: A Cooperative Inquiry, Columbic Press, New York, 1949; article by Gerger, page 107.

17. Simon, J.L. What Does the Normal Curve Mean? in the Journal of Educational Research, Vol. 61, No. 10, July-August, 1968, page 435.

18. Weaver, L.E.; The Quality Rating of Color Television Pictures, in the Journal of the SMPTE; June, 1968, page 610.

19. Scott, M., New Rules for Suicide; in Psychiatry and Social Science Review, 1968, page 21.

20. Moroney, M.J.; Facts from Figures; Penguin Books, Baltimore, Maryland.

21. Lesser, G.S., and Schueler, H., New Media Research in Education, AV Communications Review, Fall, 1966, page 324.

The Environmental Evaluation of Buildings:
A Worked Example and Technical Specification

by Dean Hawkes

Land Use and Built Form Studies, University of Cambridge
School of Architecture, 16 Brooklands Avenue, Cambridge, England

Abstract

This paper describes work at the centre for Land Use and Built Form Studies (LUBFS) in the University of Cambridge, England, on the construction and application of a computer model to perform room-by-room environmental evaluations of building designs. In this context the definition of the "environment" is limited to the quantifiable components of the visual, thermal and acoustical conditions within buildings.

One of the principle attributes of the model is that its application is not restricted to any particular building type or form. In addition, the data collection and input effort required is not excessive and, within the Cambridge TITAN/ATLAS computer system which it uses, it is possible to make substantial and useful changes to any design by means of the on-line editing facilities.

The process of translating a conventional architectural description of a building into the required data is described and the output produced by the computer is illustrated.

The paper concludes with a brief outline of the logical processes carried out within the model. These are described in full in LUBFS Working Papers Nos. 15 and 29 (1 and 2).

Data collection and input

The input method employed in this model is to present entirely numerical data to the computer by means of punched paper tape or directly through an on-line teletype. Prior to the physical process of input it is therefore necessary to collect the required data. To aid this a series of standard data forms is used upon which the architect is required to describe certain dimensional and physical properties of the proposed design.

Clearly it is important in designing a computer system of this kind to minimize the effort required in data collection. To help

in this respect the concept of Standard Room Types has been devised. This evolved from the realization that, in many modern buildings, large numbers of rooms are similar in many respects. For example, floor and wall finishes are frequently identical and a single type of light fitting might be specified for use throughout the building. To input this repetitive data for each room in a building would be both time consuming and tedious. The Standard Room Type system allows the designer to group together all those rooms which he considers to have sufficient communality of specification and then to input the common data as a single block. For each individual room it is then necessary to collect only that data which is unique. Before the model is run a pre-processing program is used to macro-generate all the data for each room from the raw data. This program also produces a fully annotated output of the data as an aid to data verification.

The process of translating a conventional description of a building into the data required by the model is illustrated in the following example.

Figures 1 and 2 illustrate by means of conventional architectural drawings the simple building which is to be evaluated in this example and show its relationship to adjacent buildings. Table 1 sets out a specification of the properties of surfaces which cannot be communicated directly by drawings and which are required f or the evaluation process.

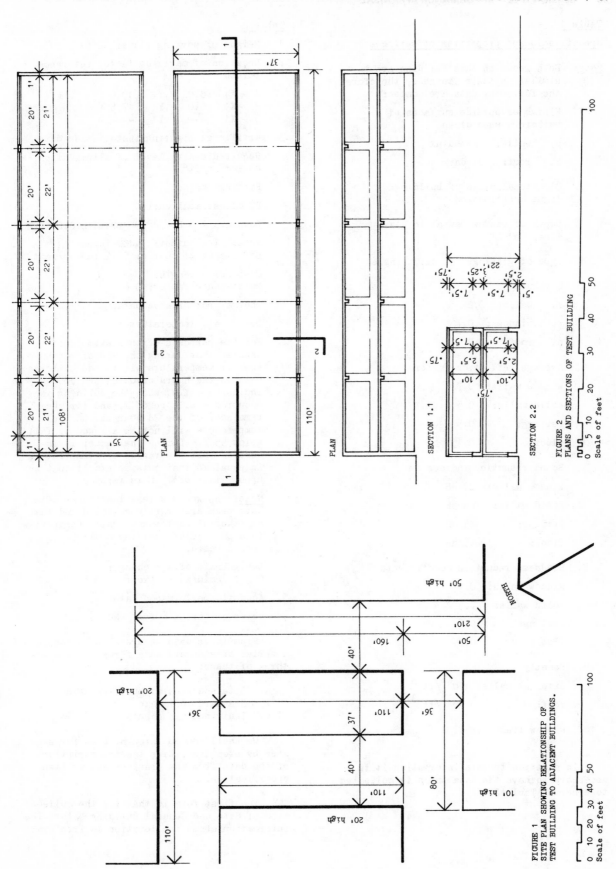

FIGURE 2
PLANS AND SECTIONS OF TEST BUILDING

FIGURE 1
SITE PLAN SHOWING RELATIONSHIP OF
TEST BUILDING TO ADJACENT BUILDINGS.

Table 1

Specification of properties of surfaces

Note: Both rooms in this building are similar in their finishes, therefore the following data are common:

1. Finish of outside surfaces of buildings when clean

    a. walls: medium

    b. roof: dark

2. Structural class of building: light construction

3. Depth of window reveal to glass line: 6"

4. Type of glazing: 32 oz., single

5. U values

    a. walls: 0.2

    b. windows: 0.7

    c. roof: 0.2

6. Average reflection factors

    window walls: 0.7

    solid walls: 0.5

    ceiling: 0.8

    floor: 0.15

7. Sound reduction indices

    window walls: 22 dB

    solid walls: 45 dB

    ceiling: 45 dB

    floor: 45 dB

8. Loudness reduction coefficients

    window walls: 0.1

    solid walls: 0.3

    ceiling: 0.7

    floor: 0.05

9. Density

    external walls: $90^{lb}/ft^3$

    roof: $90^{lb}/ft^3$

10. window frame type: 1

    In addition to this information it is necessary to have the data which is collected together at Table 2.

Table 2

1. Height of working plane: 2'6"

2. Location of daylight factor reference points

    1 X1 0.0 .Y1 10.0
    2 X1 0.0 .Y1 17.5
    3 X1 --- .Y1 ----

3. Artificial lighting installation data

    Required design level of illumination: 40 lumens/ft^2

    Fittings data:

    B2 classification: 6

    Downward L.O.R. 48% Upward L.O.R. 22%

    Total flux output: 4400 lumens.
    Efficiency of source: 52.9 lumens/watt

    Suspension length: 0
    Maintenance factor: 0.8

4. Thermal performance data:

    Design air temperature

    For the purposes of this example it is assumed that during the winter months the air temperature within the building between the hours of 08.00 and 18.00 inclusive - i.e. when the building is occupied - will be 68°F, and for the remainder of the 24 hour period the temperature will not be allowed to fall below 55°F. During the summer it is assumed that the inside air temperature is equal to that outside except that an upper limit of 75°F is imposed

    Note: We would stress that these data have been arbitrarily selected and that any thermal performance data appropriate to a particular building could be incorporated.

    Design rate of air change:
    0 3 ft^3/min/sq ft floor

5. Acoustic performance data

    Noise criterion curve: NC 35

    From these data we are able to complete a series of standard data forms. There are three of these:

    a. Site and general building data
    b. Standard room data
    c. Individual room data

    We shall now go through these forms step by step describing the transcription of the data from the drawings and written specification.

    The first form is that for the collection of Site and General Building Data The information about the location is irrelevant in the present example, but in practice this would be important to enable the appropriate meteorological data to be selected.

Figure 3 shows the site plan from Figure 1 with the basic co-ordinates and the north point superimposed. The co-ordinates are located upon the plan by ensuring that the north point is contained between X and Y. The required orientation data is then simply found by specifying the displacement of north from Y.

Figures 1 and 3 also provide the information which allows us to fill in the location of adjacent buildings data. The procedure here is to specify the locations of the edges of each neighboring building in terms of X, Y and Z.

The determination of the overall dimensions of the building is obvious.

In this case, where we are concerned with a building whose plan is a simple rectangle, there are no subtracted areas to be taken into account

The surface finish of external finishing materials is found from tabulated data where the position of the appropriate material in the table is entered in the data form, a light surface being No. 1, medium No. 2 and dark No. 3. The insertion of the appropriate coefficient is done within the model.

The structural class of the building is again found by reference to tabulated data. Since this is a simple building with only two rooms which belong to the same type we have pnly one standard room to consider.

The first requirement on the standard room data form is to identify the data. In this case the room type is No.1.

The compilation of the next set of information is self-explanatory, the thicknesses of enclosing surfaces being directly derived from the drawings (Figure 4).

"Glazing type" refers to the four glass types defined in tabulated form.

The U-values of the surfaces may be obtained from a number of sources such as the current IHVE Guide (3) and any correction for exposure must be performed prior to the input stage.

The average reflection factors, sound reduction indices and loudness reduction co-efficients are all data which are readily obtainable from manufacturers' technical information sheets and popular textbooks.

The densities of walls and roofs are also easily found.

The best source of design levels of illumination is the IES Code (4). This document specifies levels in the newly adopted metric unit (LUX) and until the model is converted to metric it is necessary to perform the conversion by hand before input.

All the fittings data are readily obtainable from manufacturers' technical literature.

The compilation of the thermal performance data is simply a question of determining the temperature range for the activity to be housed. The rate of air change data relating rates of change to activities is published in the IHVE Guide.

The appropriate Noise Criterion curve may be selected by reference to Beranek's work (5).

The procedure for selecting the window frame type is to calculate the approximate portion of the clear, structural window opening which is obstructed by window frame and then again to refer to tabulated data and quote the glazing bar type whose correction factor most closely corresponds to the proportion calculated. It is difficult to be more explicit than this since the factor is a function of both the geometry and the construction of the window frame.

Policies on the utilization of daylight in a building are clearly a matter which should be discussed between architect and client. It is possible by making use of the model at the design stage to investigate the effects of the alternate policies upon heat loss and gain.

We now turn to the Individual Room Data forms. On these we have to describe those properties of each room which are unique and also those which differ from the properties on the Standard Room Data form.

In the first place it is necessary to specify to which standard type the particular room belongs. Then the floor upon which it is situated and the number given to the room are specified These are required solely to aid identification of output.

The primary location of a room is the point in it where the values of the co-ordinate dimensions X, Y and Z are the lowest possible. Actual room dimensions are easily derived from the drawings.

Moving past the subtracted area data which is not applicable in this example, we define certain surface characteristics. The

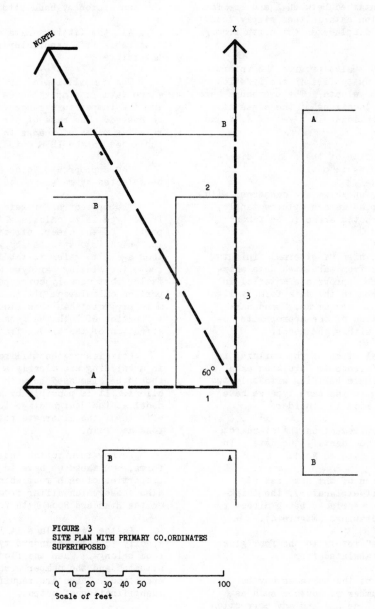

FIGURE 3
SITE PLAN WITH PRIMARY CO-ORDINATES
SUPERIMPOSED

Q 10 20 30 40 50   100
Scale of feet

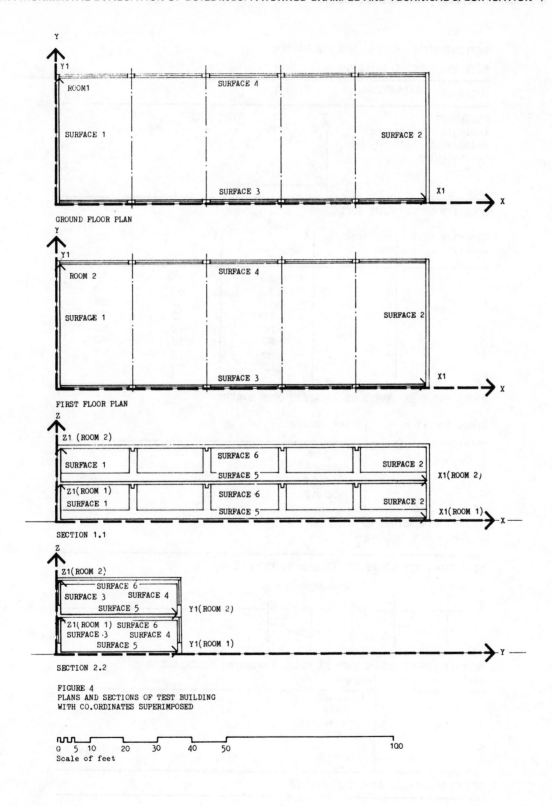

FIGURE 4
PLANS AND SECTIONS OF TEST BUILDING
WITH CO.ORDINATES SUPERIMPOSED

ENVIRONMENTAL PERFORMANCE EVALUATION

SITE AND GENERAL BUILDING DATA

LOCATION CAMBRIDGE

ORIENTATION
Indicate orientation
relative to X/Y
co-ordinates

LOCATION OF ADJACENT BUILDINGS

Opposite wall number	Building edge	X	Y	Z
1	A	−36	0	10
	B	−36	80	10
2	A	146	110	20
	B	146	0	20
3	A	160	−40	50
	B	−50	−40	50
4	A	0	77	10
	B	110	77	10

SOUND PRESSURE LEVELS IN ADJACENT OPEN SPACES

Space location	Noise rating
1	70 dB
2	60 dB
3	80 dB
4	60 dB

OVERALL DIMENSIONS OF BUILDING

X 110   :Y 37   : Z 22

DIMENSIONS AND LOCATIONS OF SUBTRACTED AREAS

Location			Dimension		
X	Y	Z	X	Y	Z

DESCRIPTION OF SURFACE OF EXTERNAL FINISHING MATERIALS

Surface number	Finish
1	Medium
2	ditto
3	ditto
4	ditto
5	—
6	dark

STRUCTURAL CLASS OF BUILDING   2

ENVIRONMENTAL PERFORMANCE EVALUATION

STANDARD ROOM DATA

ROOM TYPE: 1

Thickness of window wall: 1'. 0"
Depth of window reveal to glass line: 6"
Thickness of other external walls: 1'. 0"
Thickness of roof: 9"

GLAZING TYPE: 1

U-VALUES:
Walls: 0.2
Roof: 0.2
Floor: —
Window openings: 0.7

SURFACE PROPERTIES	Average Reflection Factors	Sound Reduction Indices	Loudness Reduction Coefficients
Window walls	0.7	22 dB	0.1
Solid external walls	0.5	45 dB	0.3
Internal walls	—	45 dB	0.7
Ceiling	0.8	45 dB	0.05
Floor	0.15		

DENSITY:
External walls: 90 lb/ft³. Roof: 90 lb/ft³

ARTIFICIAL LIGHTING INSTALLATION DATA:

Required design level of illumination: 40 lumens/ft²

FITTINGS DATA:
BZ classification: 6
Downward L.O.R. 48%   Upward L.O.R. 22%
Total flux output: 4400   Efficiency of source: 52.9 lumens/watt
Suspension length: 0   Maintenance factor: 0.8

THERMAL PERFORMANCE DATA:	Winter Max	Min	Summer Max	Min
Design air temperature	68°F	55°F	75°F	Minimum outside temp.

Design rate of air change/movement   0.5   ft³/min./sq ft floor

---

ACOUSTIC PERFORMANCE DATA:
Noise Criterion curve: 35

Window frame type: 1

Is room to be considered daylit? YES

ENVIRONMENTAL PERFORMANCE DATA

INDIVIDUAL ROOM DATA

ROOM TYPE: 1

Floor: 1 (Ground)   Room number: 1

Primary location: X 1'   Y 1'   Z 0.5'

Room dimensions: X1 108'   Y1 35'   Z1 10'

DIMENSIONS AND LOCATIONS OF SUBTRACTED AREAS

Location			Dimension		
X1	Y1	Z1	X1	Y1	Z1

CHARACTERISTICS OF ROOM SURFACES

	Surface									
	1	2	3	4	5	6	7	8	9	10
Outside surfaces	✓	✓	✓	✓						
Window location			✓	✓						
Sill height			2.5'	2.5'						
Head height			10'.0"	10'.0"						
Location of opening jambs	Y1	Y1	X1 0 x22 28	X1 0 x22 28						
Number of windows in wall			5	5						
Location of closing jambs	Y1	Y1	X1 20 x22 108	X1 20 x22 108						
Blinds, etc.										
Shade factor of blinds										
Transmission factor of blinds										
Glazing type										
Thickness of surface										

ENVIRONMENTAL PERFORMANCE DATA

INDIVIDUAL ROOM DATA CONTINUED

	Surface 1	2	3	4	5	6	7	8	9	10
Depth of reveal to glass line										
U-VALUES										
Walls, etc.										
Window openings										
Average R.F.										
Sound reduction indices										
Loudness reduction coefficients										
Density										
Sound pressure levels in adjacent rooms					44.4					

Height of working plane: $2' \, 6''$

Location of Daylight Factor reference points:
No.1   X1 $0'$;Y1 $10'$:No.2 $0'$ X1 $0'$;Y1 $17.5'$: No.3   X1   ; Y1

Number of refernce points: 2

Window frame type:

Is room to be considered daylit?

ARTIFICIAL LIGHTING INSTALLATION DATA

Required design level of illumination:

FITTINGS DATA:
BZ Classification:
Downward L.O.R.   Upward L.O.R.
Total flux output: Efficiency of source:
Suspension length: Maintenance factor:

THERMAL PERFORMANCE DATA:	Winter Max	Min	Summer Max	Min
Design air temperature:				
Design rate of air change/movement		ft^3/min./sq ft floor		

Number of occupants: 15   Activity group of occupants: 2

indication of the outside surfaces is straight-forward as is the location of walls containing windows.

If the windows in the room are to be fitted with blinds, and their effect upon the thermal transmittance and daylight illumination is to be evaluated, it is necessary to input the data for shade factor and transmission factor. In this example these are ignored and therefore the form is left blank.

All the data in the following sections of the form, up to the sound pressure levels for adjacent rooms, are as the standard room.

The next three items on the data form are concerned with the location and number of the Daylight Factor reference points Firstly, the height of the working plane is established. This is, of course, dependent upon the nature of the activities within the room, but as yet we are only able to handle conventional, horizontal working planes. Selection of the location, in plan, of the reference points requires some care. Beyond this it is simply a matter of describing their position in terms of X1 and Y1 co-ordinates.

It is necessary to specify the number of occupants in each room in order to calculate the heat gain due to their presence. Often it will be possible for the designer to give this information with precision, but in some cases it may be necessary to arrive at a figure via a typical floor space standard for a room of the kind under consideration. In addition to these simple numerical data we have some idea of the kind of activity which the occupants of a room will perform. Figures for these may be found in the IHVE Guide. Finally in this section the time of arrival and departure of the occupants must be specified.

If there are any machines in the room which are likely to prove to be major heat sources their total combined horse-power should be specified. We also include a facility for the inclusion of any other particular heat source which might occur.

Upon completion of this form the next room within the same standard type should be described and so on until that class is completed. Then the next standard type should be selected, if one exists, and so forth until the entire building is described in this form. It should be noted that any single rooms which do not belong to a standard may be input in their entirety on the Individual Room Data forms.

The Output

The model produces a comprehensive analysis of a building on a room-by-room basis. In addition it is possible to request whole building totals, but in general use these have so far been restricted to total heating and cooling loads. The complete list of outputs is given below.

Room Outputs

1. General

    A. Areas of individual enclosing surfaces

    B. Total surface area

    C. Areas of window opening per wall

    D. Total window area

2. Daylight Evaluation

    Calculated values at each reference point of:

    A. Sky component

    B. External reflected component

    C. Internal reflected component

    D. Total daylight factor

    E. Daylight factor corrected for glazing and glazing bar losses

3. Artificial Lighting

    A. Total flux required to provide illumination level specified

    B. Number of specified fittings required

    C. Total wattage of installation

4. Thermal Performance Evaluation

    A. Total heat flows through all external surfaces of space per hour of day selected

    B. Analysis of flows by surface

    C. Analysis of flows through solid and window openings – for window walls only

    D. Hourly total incidental heat gains – occupants, machines, etc.

    E. Hourly gains due to artificial lighting – winter and summer

    F. Losses due to ventilation

    G. Hourly total ventilation requirement

    H. Curves of total heating and cooling load per room

5. Acoustic Evaluation

  A. Maximum acceptable noise level

  B. Actual, calculated noise level

  C. Difference between acceptable
      and actual

Whole Building Outputs

A. Total heating and cooling load for
    whole building

The whole of the output for each room
is extensive. A typical first page, as
produced by the computer for the building
described above, is illustrated below
(Figure 5). The whole of this output has
been published in LUBFS Working Paper 28 (6).

Technical specification of the model

As mentioned above the logical processes
which are performed by the model are described
in detail in LUBFS publications. For present
purposes it is sufficient to state that the
actual design calculations which are performed are all well established and accepted
methods.

The bulk of the daylighting calculations
are based upon the work of Hopkinson and his
colleagues at the Building Research Station (7),
with the principal exception of part of the
rooflight calculation which makes use of the
equation proposed by Arndt (8) for the calculation of the internal reflected component.

The artificial lighting calculations
follow the British Zonal Method (9) and the
thermal stage of the model uses the methods
recommended by the Institution of Heating
and Ventilating Engineers (10). Finally,
the acoustical calculations are based upon
equations published by Parkin and Humphries
(11).

In broad outline the process performed
by the model for each room in a building is
linear. Within individual sub-routines there
are often tests and loops which offer the
ability to handle complex situations, but the
basic process is simple (Figure 6). When each
room has been analysed the model returns to the
beginning and automatically selects the data
for the next room. This process is repeated
until the data is exhausted.

Hardware and Software Background

The system is currently run on the Titan
computer which is situated at The Mathematical
Laboratory, University of Cambridge. Titan is
a prototype Atlas II with 128K of 48 bit core
store and random access backing store provided
by a large fixed disk of capacity 16 million

words. Titan provides a job-shop facility
capable of running 1000 jobs per day and
simultaneously services the Cambridge Multi-
Access system. The system allows up to
20 simultaneous users remote access from
teletypes throughout the University.

The subsystems available under this
system include a complex file-handling system
and advanced editing features. There is also
a wide range of compilers and assemblers. In
particular the standard high level programming
language is USASI Fortran. In fact the Titan
Fortran system has a number of extensions of
USASI Fortran but (it is hoped) no
inconsistencies.

The main virtue of the use of Fortran for
this sort of major package is the ease with
which new subprograms can be independently
tested and then integrated into the system.
The other advantage is that Fortran is the
scientific language to have achieved world
wide use (with Algol a poor second) and so
allows transfer of the package to other
machines.

These advantages seemed to outweigh the
lack of flexibility inherent in Fortran such
as its lack of list processing facilities.

Data Structure

The backbone of a suite of programs of
this type is the data structure used to store
the initial data and to transfer intermediate
results between programs. The main criteria
for a good data structure are ease of creation,
ease of access and efficiency in the use of
storage space and ease of extension for new
programs. Data structures tend to model the
physical or conceptual structure of the object
under study and so one would expect that an
object as complex as a building would lead to
a complex data structure.

The fact that this is not so is due to
several factors; the most important of these
is the absence of inter-room calculations. We
are concerned with the effect of the external
environment of a room, and so ignore inter-
room heat flows. Also the acoustic evaluation
assumes that there are maximum permissible
noise sources in adjacent rooms. All this
means that at any point in the evaluation we
need two separate blocks of data.

Firstly there is a block which is
'common' to all the rooms. This consists of
the site, orientation and adjacent building
data and the various tables including the
meteorological data and so forth. The second
block is that specific to the room. This
includes the various overall and window dimensions and the properties of the surfaces as
well as the lists of the activity and machine

```
ENVIRONMENTAL ANALYSIS
----------------------

FLOOR NUMBER  1, ROOM NUMBER  1.0

  ROOM DIMENSIONS

PLAN                      100.0 X     35.0 FT
HEIGHT                     10.0 FT
WALLS 1 & 2               350.0 SQ FT
WALLS 3 & 4              1000.0 SQ FT
FLOOR & CEILING          3780.0 SQ FT
WALLS 7 & 8                 0. SQ FT
WALLS 9 & 10                0. SQ FT
TOTAL SURFACE AREA OF ROOM 10420.0 SQ FT




WINDOW AREAS OF ROOM
WALL NUMBER
      1                      0. SQ FT
      2                      0. SQ FT
      3                    750.0 SQ FT
      4                    750.0 SQ FT
TOTAL AREA OF ALL GLAZING 1500.0 SQ FT

WINDOW CILL HEIGHT         2.5 FT.
WINDOW HEAD HEIGHT        10.0 FT.

                 DAYLIGHT EVALUATION
REFERENCE POINT SKY COMPONENT INTERNAL   EXTERNAL              CORRECTED
                              REFLECTED   REFLECTED   DAYLIGHT
                              COMPONENT   COMPONENT   FACTORS

      1            0.40%      2.30%       0.30%       3.00%     2.40%
      2            0.85%      2.30%       0.10%       3.29%     2.63%




ARTIFICIAL LIGHTING INSTALLATION
TOTAL FLUX REQUIRED        337607.3 LUMENS
NUMBER OF FITTINGS REQUIRED     77
TOTAL WATTAGE OF INSTALLATION 6381




TOTAL FLOW THROUGH SURFACES OF SPACE,BTU/H

TIME OF DAY WINTER    WINTER    SUMMER    SUMMER
            CLOUDY    CLEAR     CLOUDY    CLEAR
       1   -17458.   -28640.      0.      5191.
       2   -17458.   -29793.      0.      6130.
       3   -17458.   -29822.      0.      6246.
       4   -17458.   -28640.      0.      6904.
       5   -19952.   -28436.      0.      6576.
       6   -19952.   -28436.      0.      5699.
       7   -19952.   -26607.      0.      6599.
       8   -36163.   -42816.      0.     30553.
       9   -38657.   -42699.      0.     36636.
      10   -33669.   -42579.      0.     69289.
      11   -33669.   -38829.      0.    103827.
      12   -31175.   -33699.      0.    122807.
      13   -28681.   -29316.      0.    131783.
      14   -28681.   -25718.      0.    128733.
      15   -28681.   -24699.      0.    108145.
      16   -28681.    -1817.      0.     78472.
      17   -28681.    8517.      0.     55294.
      18   -28681.   -12751.      0.     47058.
      19   -12470.   -24636.      0.     69957.
      20   -12470.   -30421.      0.     95682.
      21   -12470.   -36316.      0.    107056.
      22   -12470.   -28327.      0.     88867.
      23   -14964.   -26468.      0.     16236.
      24   -17458.   -26461.      0.      4880.
```

FIGURE 5
Typical output

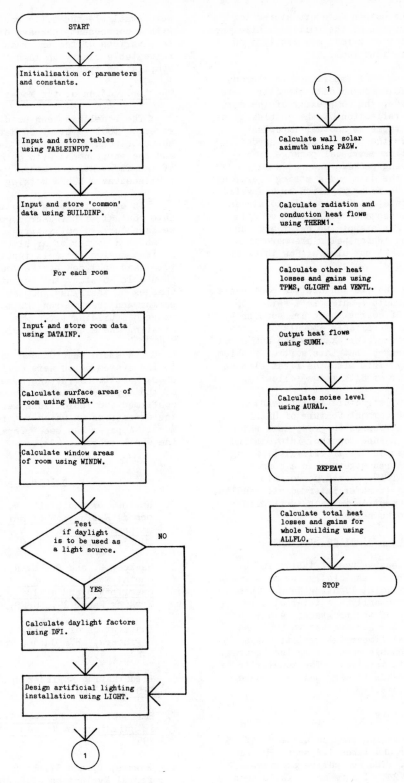

FIGURE 6
Flow chart of
control program

factors. So the common data are stored for the whole evaluation of the building while the specific data for each room are overlaid on those of the previous room.

The next point of importance to discuss is the actual form of the data structure. As pointed out above, the complexity of the data structure is a reflection of the complexity of the object but there is another important factor. This is the type of access needed. For an information retrieval package or a quantity surveying package one needs many cross links in the data and a strong hierarchy. In contrast we do no aggregation or classification of the data apart from simple totals and only need to access a specific list of data in a unique way. For example we never ask the type of question 'Which walls are more than nine inches thick?' but always 'How thick is wall 3 of room 4.2'.

This means that we can use the most basic type of data structure which is a series of simple lists. Of course there are some properties which need variable amounts of space for different rooms, for example the number of windows will change; but this sort of problem is dealt with by lists with the first element giving the number of data items following.

This sort of structure is implemented using the 'named common' feature of USASI Fortran. This allows us to group data which is likely to be needed together into distinct blocks. For example the artificial lighting variables are stored together in a common block named LIGHTFIT. Named common blocks are used also to transfer intermediate results. One has only to mention in each subprogram those common blocks needed.

Techniques in the Evaluation Programs

We make extensive use of tables in the evaluative programs, especially for meteorological and artificial lighting data. This means that we frequently use interpolative routines in many of the programs. A careful study of the tables and evaluative routines convinced us that linear interpolation was quite accurate enough considering the accuracy of the other data involved. The modularity of the evaluation makes it very easy to update or extend the programs.

Run Time Parameters

The preprocessing program needs 8K of store altogether and takes 1.4 secs CPU time to run per room. The evaluative programs if all loaded take 24K of core and take 10 secs CPU time to run for an average room in a building. Unfortunately there is no overlay loader on Titan so we have to load everything we need simultaneously. If an overlay loader

were available the suite would run in 12K but with a consequent increase of CPU time. We keep various of the programs compiled into relocatable binary on magnetic tape to save compilation time.

The Application of the Model

The model has been used extensively as a research tool to study in detail the relationships between the form and detail of buildings and the environment within them. The outcome of the first stage of this work has been published as a LUBFS Working Paper (12).

In order to bring practising architects into contact with research work of this kind we have carried out a series of case studies in which a number of architects saw their current design projects input into the computer and analysed by the model. They were then able to study the output and to make changes to their designs through the on-line editor and then re-run the model. A wide range of building types was studied, demonstrating the model's flexibility.

The exercise produced valuable reactions to the system which were collected through a short questionnaire. As a result the validity of the approach which has been adopted was confirmed and indications were gathered about the directions in which future work should move. A paper has been prepared describing the whole exercise (13).

References

1. Hawkes, D. and Stibbs R. The Environmental Evaluation of Buildings, 1 A mathematical model. Working Paper 15, LUBFS, Cambridge, 1969

2. Hawkes, D. and Stibbs R. The Environmental Evaluation of Buildings, 4 The description and evaluation of rooflights. Working Paper 29, LUBFS, Cambridge, 1970

3. Institution of Heating and Ventilating Engineers, IHVE Guide, The Institution, London, 1965.

4. Illuminating Engineering Society, IES Code, The Society, London, 1968

5. Beranek, L.L. Revised Criteria for Noise in Buildings in Noise Control, January, 1957

6. Hawkes, D. and Stibbs R. The Environmental Evaluation of Buildings, 3 A worked example. Working Paper 28, LUBFS, Cambridge, 1970

7. Hopkinson, R. Petherbridge, P. and Longmore, J. Daylighting, Heinemann, London, 1966

8. Arndt, W. The Calculation of Reflected Daylight in Compte Rendu, Commission Internationale de l'Eclairage, 13th Session, Vol 2, The Commission, Paris, 1955.

9. Illuminating Engineering Society. The Calculation of Coefficients of Utilization. The British Zonal Method. IES Technical Report No. 2, The Society, London, 1961

10. Institution of Heating and Ventilating Engineers, op cit.

11. Parkin, P.H. and Humphries, H.R. Acoustics, Noise and Buildings, Faber, London, 1958

12. Hawkes, D. The Environmental Evaluation of Buildings 5. Explorations. Working Paper 30, LUBFS, Cambridge, 1970

13. Hawkes, D. The Use of an Evaluative Model in Architectural Design. Case Studies. Working Paper 31, LUBFS, Cambridge, 1970

Use of Scale Models as a Stimulus Mode

by Jackie J. H. Lau

Department of Architecture and Building Science,
University of Strathclyde, Scotland
At present with: William Lam Associates, Inc., Cambridge, Massachusetts

Abstract

For reasons of economy and convenience, scale models offer many advantages as a stimulus mode for lighting research. However, little is known of the implications of either reduction in size or the crudity of reproduction on assessment. Theoretical problems of the use of models are discussed together with the findings from a number of experiments on model validity. These experiments indicate general similarity of observer responses to full-size mock-ups and scale models. However, with the tendency towards using more "subtle" measures for environmental evaluation rather than explicit criteria as in psychophysical experiments generally, further work on model validity is advocated.

Introduction

Simulation techniques are often required for purposes of investigating some aspect of the built environment since these techniques tend to be more economical and convenient to manipulate than either using full-size mock-ups or the field mode. In the architectural context, reduced scale physical models have long been used either as a design aid or for the presentation of crystallised ideas to a lay audience. In the lighting field, because of growing concern and interest in the qualitative aspects of lighting, the use of scale models as design and presentation aids is of necessity on the increase. Clearly, however poor a simulation models may be in these fields, experiential evidence suggest that they are preferable and superior to the most commonly used simulation technique - drawings. The use of scale models may be separated into three categories, the use of models as design tools by designers, the use of models as presentation aids and finally the use of models for research purposes. In the first category, models are clearly more advantageous than drawings. As designers are generally trained to visualise, mental adjustments can make the necessary corrections to whatever misrepresentations may occur. In the second

category, should models have some enhancement effect, then perhaps this is probably what the designers want to "sell" the idea to the "client". In the third category, where models are used as the stimulus mode in experimental work, misrepresentation may be of important significance particularly when erroneous data result in totally misconstrued recommendations. This paper discusses the problem of using scale models primarily in the context of lighting research. As demand for design recommendations based on measures of lighting quality is growing, there is likely to be a huge increase in research activity since little work has been carried out to date; and, scale models would be the most likely stimulus mode because of cost and convenience.

Problems of Model Simulation

Careful assessment of the validity of data is carried out in physical experiments using scale models and some knowledge on the effect of size reduction in known (1). However, there is no apparent concern about the validity of model work in qualitative assessment and little information is available. Reduced scale seems to enhance the quality of the object or building interior represented, sometimes to the extend of turning a possibly mundane item into an object of fascination and beauty. Clearly, it would be useful to establish the validity or otherwise of the use of scale models as a stimulus mode and the effect on validity of the degree of crudity or accuracy of simulation. Theoretically, a model can obviously be made to any scale. In practice, however, technical ability of miniaturisation dictate the lower scale limit. Certain ranges of sizes are favoured due to the problem of texture reproduction and the availability of miniature lighting components. From experience of work at the Building Research Station (2), a one-sixth full-size model of a room of approximately 20 sq metres will not present difficulties in manufacture and can be conveniently moved about. However, "perfect" miniaturisation of lighting components are difficult to achieve without great expense. Miniature tungsten filament lamps generally do not have the same performance characteristics, luminous flux output excepted, as their normal size counterparts. Clearly, identical photometric performance may not be important in the case of subjective assessment. But unless we are certain of the physical parameters critical in any assessment, the dissimilar performance characteristics of almost all miniature lamps (compared to normal size) makes the use of scale models open to question.

From physiological considerations, it would seem that a scale of between one-sixth to one-twelfth full-size would be the lower limit for models involving visual judgments. This assumption is based upon known limits of convergence and accomodation of the observer's eyes. The near point of accomodation recedes with age; for the age range of 15 to 25 years, it is 10.25 to 8.50 dioptres (3). However, since observers may be required to look at a model for some length of time, it may be more appropriate to work outside the limit of the nearpoint of comfortable accomodation. Based on clinical experience, it is generally accepted that the near point of comfortable accomodation is one half to two-thirds of the total amplitude of accomodation. For the age group mentioned above, this will be approximately 160 mm. With binocular viewing, however, accomodation is normally accompanied by a convergence of the two eyes. The average near point of convergence is 80 mm from the interocular baseline (4) and this shows no significant variation with age. As the near point of comfortable accomodation is by far the larger of the two dimensions above, this is a highly relevant factor which must be borne in mind when considering the useful limits of viewing conditions in models where no supplementary optical aids are desired. If it proves necessary, the near point of accomodation may be altered by the use of collimating lenses. It has been suggested (2) that the use of collimating lenses of 2 dioptres not only assist accomodation but may even enhance the realism of the model if viewing is monocular, the hypothesis being that "the effect of monocular viewing is to destroy the false stereoscopic effect which arises because the spacing of the two eyes when viewing the model is far greater relative to the size of the objects in the room than it is when viewing a full-size building" and the use of the lens "relax the eye in such a way that it is adjusted for distance as it would be in the full scale building. An explanation would be that cues for size and distance constancies in relation to the scale model are partially obliterated as for instance, when the model is viewed through a modelscope and to a lesser extent when viewing the model from within without the use of optical aids. Thus, the size of the model should be such that any object or surface is at least some 160 mm from the viewing position if no optical aids are to be used; and, depending on the dimensions of the original interior, the lower limit may be one-sixth full-size for the average living room or one-twelfth full-size for a classroom or office interior if the assessment by an observer is to be outwith the model. However, if the assessment is to be from within the model, the scale must be necessarily larger. In this case, not only has the near point of accomodation to be considered but it must also be borne in mind that an object the size of a human head within the model may significantly alter the luminance distribution.

For subjective lighting assessment, in order to minimise any discrepancy, the observer's brightness adaptation level for the model should be the same as for the equivalent full-size room. This can best be approximated by viewing the model from within when the field of view is likely to be similar to the full-size counterpart. If the viewing position is required to be outwith the model, then the observer's adaptation level may either be higher or lower than would be the case compared to the full-size room depending on the luminance distribution of the surrounding field of the model. The possible methods of control of adaptation depend to some extend on the experimental procedure adopted. Experiments on the evaluation of the quality of colour transparencies (5) indicated that the insertion of relatively low-transmittance, uniform, neutral density stimuli between test transparencies appear to minimise distortion in assessment. Thus, the same use of intermediary stimuli could be utilised in the assessment of scale models using the method of category rating scale.

Perhaps the most important aspect of models, and the one about which least is known, is the so-called "scale effect". Generally, a model is made in such a way as to permit the maximum sense of illusion of being in the interior. It is possible that if the scale of the model is too small, there is insufficient detail to provide an illusion of reality and if the scale is too large (say half full-size) the impression of the observer may not be that of a scale model of a large room but rather a small full-size room. The complimentary aspect to the scale of the model is the degree to which details have been reproduced, and this is probably as important, if not more so, in creating the illusion of reality. It is the combined effects of scale and accuracy of reproduction which are pertinent factors of the "scale effect". Whether the illusion of reality can be truly achieved or is even necessary for valid assessment is uncertain.   There is some evidence to suggest that it is not.   A short study (6) on preferences in wall surface lightness used both a semi-abstract model and a realistic model. The realistic model is a furnished living room looking into a patio and the abstract model is a simplified version with no furniture or fitting in it.   Analysis of the data indicates that there is a significant correlation of the rank orders of preferences from the two types of models with Spearman's = 0.91 and P 0.01. Clearly, the degree of representation required would depend on the nature of the assessment and the mechanisms involved in the perceptual process.   At the early stages of an investigation however, the pertinent aspects of the stimuli-response relationship are often unknown.   Since it is feasible to construct a scale model such that all details are present and accurately represented, the more important aspect of model validity may be that of the effect of reduction in size.   It is the question of whether scale models are assessed in the same manner as full-size rooms.

Experimental Evidence

As stated earlier, there is little authoritative information about the use of scale models and its validity.   Of the many lighting criteria currently practised, a number have been the result of experimental work where scale models have been used as the stimuli.   Yet, there has been no serious systematic attempt to validate any of these studies. The only exception has been some field validation work carried out by the Luminance Study Panel of the IES (7) and by Collins (8) on the glare index with the results giving fairly favourable correspondence to the laboratory studies.   The initial work on glare, carried out at the Building Research Station, employed a composite of model and photograph where a black-and-white reflection print was used with cut-outs for light fittings or windows such that the luminance of the glare source (light fittings or windows) can be independently controlled in relation to the surround. Explicit criteria and the method of limits were used, the experiments were thus principally psychophysical in nature.   Though the field studies were useful as a validation of the laboratory work and were intended as such, a little information has been gained on the validity of the simulated stimulus mode used, in this case, a two-dimensional simulation. Also of a psychophysical nature, are the experiments by Holmberg et al (9) and Barthes (10).   Holmberg et al carried out a series of Comparative experiments using different scale models, 1:5 and 1:10 scale, and full-size mock-ups to investigate the relationship of apparent volume of rooms to their depth and width.   Analyses of variance of the data indicated that the different scale models and

the full-size mock-ups gave similar results when the viewing position was standardised though significantly different results occurred when observers were allowed to move around in the full-size rooms.   The study by Barthes, however, on the effect of colour and luminance on attention gave no conclusive evidence on model validity because of the limited parameters investigated.   Of great interest, primarily because the investigation is the only study available which is of a psychological nature , is a series of pilot experiments by Inui (11) on colour harmony using coloured cardboard boxes, colour transparencies and actual interiors.   Factor analysis of semantic differential scores resulted in the same factors, indicating that the assessment of colour harmony is thought of by observers in more or less the same manner regardless of the presentation mode.

Other than the experiments on glare, none of the work described above relate to lighting specifically but rather to the visual environment in general though all have indicated that scale models can usefully serve as the stimulus, even if only in a limited capacity.   In order to investigate the potential of scale models as a stimulus mode in the context of lighting research, the author carried out a series of comparative studies using both one-sixth full-size scale models and full-size mock-ups.   But rather than using explicit and specific criteria as has been common in lighting research in the past (as for example, the experiments on glare), the two criteria used — gloom and pleasantness — are applicable to the visual environment generally as well as to the lighting aspect of the environment specifically.   From pilot studies carried out (12), a gloomy room results not only from a combination of physical entities but also a complex interaction of the individual with the physical environment.   Two experimental techniques were used, the methods of paired comparison and category rating scale.   Observers were asked to assess the relative degree of gloom or pleasantness of a single study-bedroom in the paired comparison experiments.   In the experiments using the method of category rating scale, a 4-category scale with verbal anchors at each end was used, thus

NOT GLOOMY 1 2 3 4 GLOOMY

Since the changes made to the rooms (whether scale model or full-size mock-up) were only to the lighting installation (position of the light, type of fitting and the flux output), the observers were thus implicitly directed to assess their subjective impressions of the different lighting installations.

Analyses of the data from the paired comparison experiments indicated that despite slight differences in photometric terms, viewing position and the presence of individuals in the full-size rooms, responses to the scale models were similar to that of the full-size rooms. Essentially the same rank orders resulted and product moment correlations indicated significant correspondence (P 0.001) between the two sets of Dunn-Rankin scale scores. Analyses of variance (13) indicated that the scale models were similarly assessed as the full-size rooms for both the concepts of gloom and pleasantness in that the effects of the three fundamental lighting variables and their interactions were indicated to be similar. The experiments using the method of category rating scale and the concept of gloom only provided data which confirmed the findings of the experiments using the method of paired comparison. These experiments also indicated that for the particular room layout used, there was no specific advantage in having either different fixed viewing positions or in allowing the observers to move around within the full-size rooms. The status of observer mobility (static position v mobility) did not significantly alter responses though it would appear that there was a higher degree of agreement between observers when assessment was from a fixed position.

Discussion

Within the context of the experiments described above, where assessments of gloom and pleasantness were based on three fundamental lighting variables (albeit implicitly), it would appear that scale models are assessed in the same manner as the full-size mock-ups of the study-bedrooms despite some inaccuracies in representation. However, not unlike the related experiments described earlier, these experiments dealt with a relatively simple stimulus-response relationship. For such experiments, scale models appear to be perfectly adequate provided sufficient safeguards are taken as they should be in planning experiments normally. Perhaps it ought to be stated that the scale models constructed for the author's experiments were as near a perfect replica as possible and as such represent comparatively high cost. Therefore, if it is necessary to have perfect representation it may be more convenient and much more economical to use full-size mock-ups unless the scale models are to be reused. Though research in lighting quality in the past has been relatively simple-minded and are much more of a psychophysical nature there is now an increasing tendency to use psychological measures to ascertain the effects of not one or two variables but the effect of the total environment and the complexity of relationship this implies. In some experiments carried out by the author (12) using the semantic differential and a form of Guttman scale, there is some indication that scale models do differ from their full-size counterparts in that scale models were assessed to be more "beautiful" though equally "friendly". From all these studies, it may be hypothesised that miniaturisation do have an enhancement effect but is not manifested when relatively simple assessments are called for. In such instances, observers appear to be able to "funnel" their critical ability to the task at hand. When the assessment required is of the "affective response" type and the observers' attention are not directed to any specific point , then the validity of the use of scale models is questionable. However, under such circumstances the problem of model validity is equal to that of the validity of artificially created environment in laboratory studies. After all, the full-size rooms referred to in this paper are but full-size MODELS!

Notes & References

1 LANGHAAR, H.L. Dimensional analysis and the theory of models. London, J. Wiley & Sons, Inc. 1951.

2 HOPKINSON, R.G. Architectural physics: lighting. London, Her Majesty's Stationery Office. 1963.

3 DUANE. 1922. Abstracted from Weale, R.A. The eye and its function. London, Hatton Press Limited. 1966. p.73

4 EMSLEY, H.H. Visual optics. London, Hatton Press Limited. 5th edition. Vol. 1. 1955.

5 BARTLESON, C.J. & W.W. WOODBURY. Psychophysical methods for evaluating the quality of color transparencies: II. Control of observer adaptation in categorical judgments. Photographic Science and Engineering. 1962. Vol. 6, No. 1. p.15-18.

6 DEATHRIDGE, J. Research into the determination of desirable inherent light values of wall surfaces in the limited environment. Unpublished Dip.Arch. Thesis. Birmingham School of Architecture. 1963.

7 LUMINANCE STUDY PANEL, IES. The development of the IES Glare Index system. Transactions of the Illuminating Engineering Society, London. 1962. Vol. 27, No. 1. p.9-26.

8 COLLINS, W.M. The determination of the minimum identifiable glare sensation interval using a pair-comparison method. Transactions of the Illuminating Engineering Society, London. 1962. Vol. 27, No. 1. p.27-34.

9 HOLMBERG, L.; S. ALMGREN; A.C. SODERPALM &
   R. KULLER. The perception of volume cont-
   ent of rectangular rooms: comparison be-
   tween model and full-scale experiments.
   Psychological Research Bulletin. 1967.
   Vol. VII, No. 9. Lund University.

10 BARTHES, E. Etude dynamique experimentale
   du champ visuel colore en position de tra-
   vail et de repos en vue de l'establisse-
   ment du projet de conditionnement lumineux.
   Washington, Commision Internationale de
   l'Eclairage Proceedings. Paper P.67.10.
   1967.

11 INUI, M. Practical analysis of interior
   color environment. Tokyo Building Research
   Institute. 1966. Occasional Report 27.

   And in personal communication.

12 LAU, J.J.H. Subjective assessment of artificial lighting quality. Unpublished PhD
   Thesis, University of Strathclyde. 1969.

13 Individual observer rank totals of the
   eight stimuli are used for the analyses
   in the experiments using the method of
   paired comparison. Due to the nature of
   paired comparison data, observers variance
   cannot be revealed as there is an effective
   restriction of numbers to be used by the
   observers such that the sum of rank totals
   of different observers are the same.
   Though the F-ratios may be "inflated" due
   to violation of one of the assumptions in
   the analysis of variance, it is felt that
   the significance levels indicated provide
   an adequate approximation.

Optimisation by Evaluation in the Appraisal of Buildings

by Thomas A. Markus

MA MArch (MIT), ARIBA, Professor of Building Science,
Department of Architecture and Building Science,
University of Strathclyde, Glasgow, C. 1.

Abstract

The paper describes the application of optimisation techniques based on cost benefit analysis. The cost of provision, maintenance and 'failure'-to-provide are used. The use of indifference sets and production functions for design decisions is demonstrated. There is a model of the design process which relates these techniques to those of analysis and design synthesis. The relationship of parts of the system to the whole, and of constraints, is examined in this context.

1   Introduction

This series of articles*has so far explored a number of concepts relating to value, cost, price and a number of techniques by which the designer can attempt to reach the 'best' solution — the one of maximum value. In this paper these ideas are developed in a somewhat different direction. First, a simple model of design decision-making is proposed, in which appraisal is identified as part of the decision process, and evaluation as a part of appraisal. Then there is a brief description of the total system over which the designer has freedom of choice. Next the idea of optimising the state of this complex, interactive system is explored. And finally, some practical and theoretical techniques which could be relevant are described.

2   The Design Decision Process

Most descriptions of design procedure — whether theoretical or based on empirical studies — recognise two basic patterns in the process[1]. (Figure 1). The first is a management process, according to which one phase follows another in time. It divides up the total time available to make the decision into phases which develop from the general and abstract to the detailed and concrete. The RIBA Plan of Work[2], stages A to E, is a well-known example of such a structure. The need to complete by a deadline is emphasised by rules that prevent going back. The attendant failures that would be involved in making this process an iterative one are obvious: continuous re-call of consultants, re-constitution of design teams, inability to key firmly into financial, legal and government action; inability to predict design time and costs; and the arbitrariness of any decision as to how many times to iterate. But the paradoxes of making this a linear process are also obvious: it is a deterministic procedure for an essentially non-deterministic problem. If a design solution can always be novel it is akin to exploration; neither the end of the process nor the resources needed can be predicted. It is rather as if the first trans-Atlantic explorer had been told "We know that there is a Continent to the West, but we do not know how far away it might lie. Here is a ship and 100 men; in 6 months time you much reach it." One could instruct him to reach his goal and offer the necessary and unlimited time to do so; or instruct him to sail for 6 months and report his position. But to attempt to specify both resources and achievements is to programme a paradox — to sail into unknown territory pretending that the journey is on a charted map. This weakness of the "vertical" process (morphology) is to some extent remedied by using an open-ended, iterative decision process at each of its phases — the "horizontal" process.

This decision process appears to have three main parts to it[3].

(i)   Understanding of the problem(Analysis)
This includes the gathering of all relevant information; the establishment of relationships, constraints, objectives,

criteria — indeed the imaginative structuring of the problem. Often, well done, this leads to good and imaginative solutions.

(ii) Producing a design solution (Synthesis)
The problem structure may suggest part or whole solutions. There is a great body of literature and experience suggesting a rich variety of rational, intuitive, ordered and random processes which may be appropriate to different problems and different personalities. The process may result in a single design; or a variety of different designs; or a cluster of similar designs, being variants of a basic type.

(iii) Establishing the performance of the solution (Appraisal)
This is a retrospective act by which the designer establishes the quality of his solution. There are three basic steps in appraisal (Figure 2):

(a) Representation. The solution is modelled in any suitable way. The model might be verbal, mathematical, visual or even 'full-scale' (in this sense a building-in-use is a full and complete 'model' of the design).

(b) Measurement. This is a neutral activity in which the performance of the model is obtained on as wide a variety of counts as necessary. Costs, environmental conditions, flexibility, space utilisation, human response, are amongst those that suggest themselves easily. Such aspects of performance as depend on unpredictable human response — e.g., judgements of the formal qualities of an object, can be obtained by simulation and recording direct responses.

(c) Evaluation. The measured results are now evaluated; cost-benefit analysis; subjective value judgements; comparison with ideal, average or statutory performance standards found in the analysis; conformity to constraints recorded in the analysis — all these and other techniques are appropriate.

In the light of the appraisal the designer may wish to re-design, or even to re-examine and change or develop his analysis. He will iterate these sequences as often as necessary and as time allows and reach a decision.

The entire vertical and horizontal structure, with its iterative feedback loops, is simply illustrated in Figure (1); but the overall sequence followed by a designer may be represented by at least three routes which arise from the paradox of the supposed linearity of the morphology. This creates another, the "double pyramid", paradox. The development of a total design through its sub-systems, components and down to fine details implies, at the analysis stage, a decomposition process; i.e., breaking up the problem into finer and finer detail. At the synthesis stage it implies a clustering or recomposition process; i.e., a building of the total solution from its components. The three possible routes through these two pyramids are indicated by Figure (3).

In the first, the understanding of the problem is carried through all phases, from general to particular, before a design synthesis (with its appraisal) is sought. In this mode the problem of a city is analysed down to its last detail; and the first components to be actually designed would be the most detailed; doorknobs; the last, the complete land use and transport systems.

In the second route each phase of the problem is analysed and solved before proceeding to the next; this mode is the one most often associated with the structure of the design process illustrated in Figure (1).

In the third route, after complete analysis, the synthesis process starts at the general, strategic level and descends to the detailed component.

In each of these an appraisal follows a synthesis, although its nature will vary. Clearly the arrival of industrialised systems of hardware — in which components down to the last detail have already been designed and manufactured — has relevance to the choice of the most appropriate route.

3   The System being Optimised

Organisations which need buildings to house their activities have definable objectives to meet. In order to meet these, they need a certain pattern of activity and behaviour. The setting or environment for this behaviour will influence the degree to which it succeeds in meeting its objectives and will itself be the outcome of decisions about the physical form of the building. Thus the designer is dealing with a complex and interactive system which is simply illustrated in Figure (4)[4].

The objectives of the organisation may be social, economic or cultural (e.g., to do with health, education, commerce or leisure). The activity pattern required to meet these objectives may include activity directly related to production, or communication, control, identification (i.e., establishing the image and self identity of an organisation) and other definable, formal categories. Dependent on the nature of the objectives there will generally also be a host of informal activities which are often vital to the survival of the organisation, its morale and its communication system.

The environmental system consists of two main parts, the spatial environment and the physical environment. The former can be described and measured in terms of the size, number, form, type and linkages between, spaces; and the latter in terms of the visual, thermal, aural and other physical characteristics of the spaces. The building or hardware system can be conveniently described under the constructional system (fabric, structure, components etc.), the services system and the contents system (furniture, furnishings, equipment, fittings etc.).

Whilst the relationship between the four parts are complex they are generally causal in one direction, from left to right on the figure and derivative from right to left, except at the interface between environment and activity where they are mutually interactive and where continuous adaptation takes place in the sense that environments are constantly adapted to activity needs and activity modes are continuously influenced by or adapted to environmental realities.

Also on Figure (4) is included a cost system, for each of the four major parts has a cost, revenue or value attached to it. The hardware costs something to provide; the environment costs something to maintain (energy, cleaning, repair, maintenance); the activities cost something to provide (labour, materials, advertising, waste, etc.); and the objectives have a value in being partially or wholly met. If it were possible to establish all the functional relationships between all the parts of this system and to attach valid cost figures throughout, then the evaluation of any proposed design by cost-benefit analysis, as proposed by Fleming[5], would be feasible and a true optimum could be found. This possibility is discussed further below.

One other interesting propriety of this model and of this way of looking at buildings is that it shows how it is possible to talk about a whole building, or any, even minute, part of it, at any one of the four major levels. For example, it would be possible to describe the hardware of a light fitting giving details of the tubes, diffusers, dimensions and mounting. This would be a type I description. A type II description would specify the environmental output of the light fitting; e.g., its heat output, the emission of total luminous flux or its intensity in a given direction. Clearly this would leave the way open to the selection of alternative fittings with the same environmental characteristics. A type III description would describe the effects of the fitting in terms of human activity or behaviour. It could, for instance, describe a fitting producing illumination in which the maximum error in a standard task would be a specified percentage; or it could describe the score on a standard satisfaction or gloom scale; or the frequency distribution of discomfort glare judgement made by a panel of observers. Since these behavioural responses would also be affected by many other aspects of the environment, clearly the description would now become very open-ended and could lead to a wide variety of combinations of physical hardware sub-systems. At the fourth level one could simply describe, in objective terms, a lighting system; for instance, one that produced a given level of happiness, stability or education. If appropriate language is used at each of these four levels, then the job of writing a specification — that is, producing a prescription — and the job of satisfying that specification by a description — becomes relatively simple. The person or group needing a building starts from level four until they meet and overlap at one of the intermediate levels, the organisation supplying the hardware. To what extent the designer's role lies near one or other end of the spectrum is a question irrelevant to the present paper and obviously highly complex[6].

The last point to note about the description of buildings in these terms is that the statement of constraints, statutory or otherwise, can be made in suitable form at any one of the four levels or at the fifth level in terms of cost limits.

The use of this model, incomplete as it must be, can allow all present and future costs, revenues, resources, effects and values to be placed at the appropriate point in the system.

4   Optimisation

Although the word optimum is often loosely used, it must be clearly understood in the present context to refer to a single best solution. This in turn requires a single criterion for optimisation and in order to fit this article into the remainder in the series, the argument will be based on the use of money as a criterion and on maximising the value or minimising the cost of a solution as an objective. An equally strong argument could be developed in terms of using a physiological or psychological response — say satisfaction — as a single criterion. In raising this issue one should add, perhaps, that although some of the previous authors have treated money as an objective measure of costs or revenues but satisfaction as a subjective or intangible one, this distinction is not entirely valid. Money has simply become a convenient measure by which effort, sacrifice, human values, labour, risk, danger and a whole host of other factors are measured. It is no more objective than desire, satisfaction or sensation. The fact that the price of copper piping for central heating increases overnight and thus alters cost planning for building is merely an outcome of some deep seated problems of human relationship, say in Rhodesia, concerning race segregation, the value of labour and the economic pressures of a country being internationally ostracised. This is no place to develop the history and theory of economic measures or of marginal utility.

It is however very necessary to point out to designers, builders and administrators in the building industry, that there is nothing more objective about money than about a number of other scales of value which could be used. For confirmation of this one has only to look at experiments in which people's evaluation of the worth of money itself is assessed[7] to see that the relationship is not only non-linear but varies from person to person and group to group and that it is not

even static for any individual. Under conditions of risk or danger or poverty, an individual's judgement of the value of a certain increment of money will be quite different from his judgement in the absence of these conditions.

Using the model established in Section 3, it is possible to treat the costs of the first three parts of the system as one side of an equation and the value achieved in the fourth part as the other and to set out to make the value exceed the cost by the maximum possible amount — i.e., a maximum return on investment. Another approach, and that which will be followed here, is to consider the total costs of providing any solution as well as the total cost of not providing it, i.e., "failure" to provide, and by summation to establish the minimum cost, i.e., the optimum solution. A practical example of this technique is the well-known one of the decision as to the optimum thickness t_0 of pipe insulation around a pipe of known diameter carrying a fluid at temperature T1 in an environment at temperature T2, the latter being lower than the former. If the cost of insulation per unit thickness is represented by Figure (5) (this is a non-linear relationship), and if the conductivity of the insulant is known together with the unit cost of heat generation, then Figure (5) will represent the two curves which describe the cost of provision and the cost of failure to provide (heat loss). The saddle shaped summary curve represents the total cost and yields the optimum thickness t_0 at the point where its slope is equal to zero; provision of anything less or greater than this is uneconomic. Mathematical techniques for discovering o-slope points on curves, planes or hyperplanes (either minima or maxima) and for testing whether there are others lower or higher are available for 2, 3 and n-1 dimensional problems; their usefulness is however limited.

This example suffers from three defects in its applicability to most building design problems. The first is that it relies on a few well established functional relationships based on the laws of natural philosophy and economics, second that it deals with only a few variables, and third that it deals with static and not dynamic performance. Most building design problems are both more complex in nature in that they involve many interactive variables and systems, and are also less clear cut in that the functional relationships are not always known. Often, too, the performance of the system changes with time. Nevertheless, the principles of the technique can be applied to many areas of design decision-making and one of its lessons is that it is important to break a complex problem down into as many small "independent" problems as possible. There are few truly independent areas, for even in the case of the pipe the thickness of the insulation would determine the width of duct in which the pipe had to be placed, that in turn might influence the width of corridor in which the duct runs, and that in turn the layout of the rooms, the utilisation of the site and finally the form of the city! However, these links are sufficiently tenuous to allow one to proceed as if the original problem had been independent. Dynamic programming techniques can assist where the system performance varies with time.

In many instances whilst the effects of a decision in activity or organisational terms can easily be predicted, the cost or value of these effects is difficult to establish. This is a central problem, as has already been stated in the previous papers, in any full cost-benefit analysis, and an attempt is made in Section 5 to suggest both research and design techniques which, to some extent, might deal with this difficulty.

There are many cases where functional relationships between variables in the system to be optimised are all linear; all known; where there is a single criterion for optimisation, and where all constraints can be defined. The best known technique for finding the optimum solution in such cases is Linear Programming — a technique for sequential solution of the set of equations describing the criterion function; the functional relationships (expressed as functional constraints — i.e., conditions the solution must obey in order not to break laws of physics, for instance!) and regional constraints (constraints on resources, or freedom of action, arising from the nature of the problem). There is no room to develop this technique here[8]— sufficient to say that it has been successfully used for such problems as minimising the cost of the admixture of different dwellings on a site[9]; minimising circulation distances[10]; and maximising the production of cast concrete panels[11].

5   Evaluation of Effects on Human Responses.

It is often possible to establish a functional relationship between sets of environmental variables and sets of human response variables. These latter may be measured by the use of semantic scales, which attach magnitudes to the way people think and speak about environment or by means of direct observation of non-verbal behaviour. If the response variable is in the form of performance which is relevant to a functional or productive task, it may be a relatively simple matter to attach cost figures to the various levels of performance. For instance, if Figure (6) represents the relationship between illumination and visual performance on a standard task; Figure (7) between the standard task and a known industrial one; and Figure (8) between industrial performance and cost (in terms of time, error, waste etc.) then a similar curve in Figure (9) might reasonably represent the relationship between illumination and cost (of "failure"). Treating the illumination sub-system as independent, the minimum cost (optimum) level of illumination can be found as shown. Such techniques can be of use in considering noise and speech interference; thermal environment and production; corridor width and risk of accident.

In more typical cases the only measure of response that can be reliably obtained is an evaluative one: satisfaction, acceptability, friendliness, gloom, noise measured on ordinal or interval scales. Findings are generally expressed in one of two forms: either a functional relationship between a continuum of an environmental variable and a response variable as in Figure (10); or a frequency distribution of the response at a given point in the response scale. In the latter case it might be, say the mid-point between maximum satisfaction and maximum dissatisfaction on a scale; or it may be the distribution of one response where all are dichotomised into one of two alternatives — say "acceptable" or "not acceptable" as in Figure (11). If either mode is used, how can costs be assigned to various levels of (say) satisfaction or to the frequency distribution?

One way is to establish by reference to simulations or real life, the amount of money required to shift responses by a measurable amount or to turn a "not acceptable" judgement into an "acceptable" one. For instance, if the frequency distribution of "not acceptable" is turned into a cumulative frequency distribution and data on the cost of conversion to "acceptable" is available, then for a homogeneous group of people the sigmoid curve can be read directly as a cost curve. For instance, let us assume that Figure (12) represents the cumulative frequency of "not acceptable" for office workers' judgements of background sound pressure level. Assuming that it is known that an office worker will work in unacceptable noise conditions at a cost of £100 p.a. (say 10% of clerical salary) then the increase in costs with increased noise levels is as in Figure (13) where by the time 75 dBA is reached, all the workers require environmental compensation. Superimposed is the curve representing the cost of preventative measures (duct lining, double glazing etc.). The summation yields the optimum.

One problem which is fundamental to predictive design by cost is to find relationships between measures of hardware systems and their environmental performance, and the costs. For instance, some work has been done on the relationship between the sound attenuation of partitions and their costs. The data was scattered but sufficient for a clear correlation to emerge[12], and took the form shown in Figure (14). One now has a cost(of provision and maintenance) function for sound attenuation. If the behavioural effects of different levels of attenuation can be predicted, and the cost of these effects can be established realistically, then one is in a position to use the optimisation technique suggested by the 3 curves in Figure (14).

It may be objected that the first relationship is tenuous, and so dependent on a host of other factors — current technology, market pressures, materials supply — that it in no sense represents even a weak law. A technological breakthrough may, at any moment, completely nullify even such relationships as are found. This, coupled with the complexity of discovering behavioural effects and costing these, makes the case for predictive optimisation look pretty weak. The only alternative then, however, is to simulate a large number of solutions in every design, obtain accurate and up-to-date costs for each and also the latest data on environmental and

human effects and, if possible, the costs of these latter. This, with the aid of computers and massive data structures would certainly be feasible. However, two reasons still make it seem worthwhile to pursue the more classical, predictive approach. The first, a short-term one, is that computing systems, data structures and personnel for the large and rapid simulation approach will be unavailable or in short supply for some years yet. The second, a long-term one, is that even then, the designer will need a direction in which to progress. He cannot generate solutions randomly, hoping for improved results; he must know why improvement is likely to result and hence have some predictive knowledge. Even more basically than this, unless he carries in his head at least some generally valid relationships of the kind illustrated in Figure (14) then in the multivariate and complex total system he is designing his initial direction will be totally random, and hence have a high probability of cost, performance or human failure which only a near-infinite set of simulations could cure. Relationships are merely formalisations of knowledge available to him and his experience and are discarded at his peril.

Often there is a choice between different combinations of desirable properties — two in the simplest case. Much economic theory and psychological experiment has been carried out into the nature of choices between such combinations. The value or 'utility' of the combination can be plotted in such a way that different combinations of equal utility are represented by an indifference curve. Figure (15A) shows a set of such curves (hypothetical) for different combinations of space heating standards and space in housing. Such a set is an indifference map. With three variables an indifference plane can be drawn; with n variables, represented in a matrix, a hyperplane with n-1 dimensions can be obtained. The curves are generally assumed to be convex in relation to the origin (according to the theory of diminishing marginal utility, now only accepted in the most general case). That is, a small increment of any good is seen as less valuable when added to a large amount than when the same increment is added on to a smaller amount.

If total resources — say for house purchase by an individual, or house construction by a housing authority or the nation — are limited, and can be divided in any way between combinations of two or more desirable properties, then all those combinations costing the same amount can be plotted on curves, planes or hyperplanes of equal cost, sometimes called the production function. Figure (15B) shows a set of equal cost curves (each for a house of different total cost) in which space heating standards and space are considered. These curves are concave in respect to the origin on the basis of the law of diminishing returns (again only true in a general sense) which is held to apply to resource utilisation. That is, if a large amount of something is made, to make an additional incremental amount of it costs less than if a small amount is made.

If these two sets of curves are combined on the same diagram, as on Figure (16), then we get a number of tangent points. Each of these represent an optimal decision; that is, if the satisfaction to be achieved is defined by curve S_2, then the least cost of production which will meet it is represented by point P_x on curve P_2. If the maximum resources available are represented by curve P_1, then the maximum value which can be achieved by them is represented by point P_y tangential to curve S_1. It will be noticed that this technique will not answer the question "what is the optimum amount to invest" — it merely enables the best result from a fixed investment or the least cost investment for a fixed result to be determined. But this is useful, as it represents the degree of freedom in many real situations.

An interesting adaptation of this technique comes from the theory of games. If there are conflicting parties to a decision, each of whom desires the maximisation of a different property, and if an increase in one can only be met by a decrease in the other, then conflict exists. A practical example is the competitive demand on skilled building labour (a fixed pool) for house building and all other types of building. Point P_1, on Figure (17) represents the allocation of labour to the two areas at time t_1. Production function curve F_1 represents the output of houses and other buildings which can be achieved by this pool of labour. As a result of political struggle, the house builders gain extra labour at the expense of the "other" builders, so that at time t_2, P_2 represents the new situation. It will be noticed that this lies on a higher production

function curve, F_2, than P_1, that is some increased efficiency of labour has been achieved. As a result of a second conflict there is a reverse for the house builders, and P_3 is reached. Eventually P_5 is reached, on F_5, where limit of improved efficiency is reached. Both sides have made positive gains, in spite of temporary setbacks, as a result of positively resolved conflicts. But now, any shift must be along the locus F_5 — i.e., the final boundary of labour capacity. Thus P moves up and down this curve, gains for one party being losses for the other and no overall improvement for both taking place with time. Such situations result, usually, in open political conflict or in genuine technological innovation — i.e., the expenditure of energy in pushing the production curve to a new frontier, F_6, which enables conflicts to be resolved within a new area. Many examples of design, production or labour innovation are the result of this type of pressure.

It will have been noticed that of two or more goods or properties being compared to obtain indifference pairs, triplets or sets, one may be money itself. Thus, if pairs can be obtained in sequence (of independent goods and properties) until one can be costed (objectively or subjectively) then all can be costed. Where the goods or properties are interdependent, more complex ordering and ranking techniques are used to give, in the end, similar indifference sets.

Another technique for obtaining the relative values of benefits and disadvantages is to present subjects with simulated solutions in which variables are systematically varied, in combination with each other, and included is either money (e.g., salary) or some easily and objectively costable items. By expressing preferences, in pairs, or judging each solution on a scale, and subsequent variance analysis, the potency of each variable in determining the overall judgement can be obtained. This potency can be taken to be proportional to the percentage of the total variance accounted for by the particular variable; and if one is money, the others may be evaluated in relative terms. One such experiment presented panels of school teachers with verbal descriptions (simulations) of schools having different combinations of headmaster, children, efficiency of buildings, distance from home[13]. Figure (18) shows the pie chart resulting from the variance analysis. Teachers' salaries could easily be included in such an experiment and the cost of all or some variables can be established.

Often evaluations can be obtained from market or field observations. For instance the relative value of different aspects of housing environment may be obtainable from massive samples of sales or rentals, treated factorially and analysed for variance. Sometimes environment is negotiated for money directly — as in certain industrial occupations where the Unions have agreed to standard additional rates for environmental hazards such as heat or dust. On other occasions the sequence of choice — say of houses sold on an estate — will yield rank orders of priorities for various properties.

In business and military situations complex decisions sometimes have to be made in which the optimum involves choices partly determined by predictable outcomes (profit or loss of lives) and partly by subjective value judgements of the relative importance of various objectives and of the amount of risk which is justified in situations only partly predictable. Neumann and Morgenstern[14] formalised the theory of games and recently attempts have been made to apply some of these techniques to planning and design decisions[15]. In these participants may play specific roles, either conflicting or co-operating, and be asked to select from sets of solutions, containing different combinations of variables, the most-preferred. Often this is done sequentially, so that new choices can be made in the light of choices by the other participants, until a stable preference set is reached. Sometimes participants have a fixed resource to allocate between all the solutions (money or votes). If simple preferences and rankings are used, the value (or 'utility') of each solution can be measured by an ordinal utility index. If however it is necessary to compare the differences between various strengths of preferences, it is necessary to have a utility index which has measurable gaps between choices — i.e., a cardinal utility index. Newmann and Morgenstern showed how this could be obtained and the increase in the power of the technique thus resulting. The great difficulty in using such games for building design is the construction of simulations which are rich enough to represent realistically the differences between the

solution sets, and yet quick enough for the game to proceed.

6   Constraints — Financial and Other

Constraints of any kind have two functions: first to limit the designer's area of search; and second to protect society against unscrupulous and ignorant designers. Constraints on resources simply express the limit on what is available. It is clear that often these constraints not only limit freedom of choice but sometimes force designers to adopt solutions which are far from optimal. A practical example will show this.

Let us assume that the design decision to be made concerns the area (A) of window to be used in a school classroom. The cost of provision and maintenance is shown by curve 1 in Figure (19) for a single glazed window of a certain proportion. This includes the variation in the heating plant and heating energy to maintain a fixed design temparature. It is assumed that the effects of noise are represented by the cost of "failure" curve, 2, which also increases monotonically with size. The effects of view, sunlight penetration and general visual character are shown by the monotonically decreasing curve 3. The summary curve 4 shows that the optimum (minimum cost) solution lies at size X_1. However, the 2% minimum daylight factor constraint limits the solution so that $A \geqslant X_2$. The requirement to limit background noise, from a busy street outside, places an upper constraint on $A \leqslant X_3$. Even the area between X_2 and X_3, well away from the optimum, cannot be searched as the cost limit of Y_1 determines $A \leqslant X_4$. Between X_2 and X_4, due to rationalisation of window dimensions, only one size exists — which is the solution! Such examples abound in daily practice; some are even more serious as the constraints are mutually exclusive and prevent a feasible solution from existing.

The need for constraints is obvious; there needs to be, however, careful thought about allowing as much interchangeability between resources as possible so that really economic solutions are not constrained out. Moreover, industrialised building and rationalisation of available components must ensure that the maximum amount of choice exists in the near-optimal areas.

Designers sometimes refer loosely to optimisation by several criteria. This is impossible — one criterion leads to one optimum, another to another. Criteria can be expressed in terms of one another, say by ranking and weighting them and expressing them as a single composite criterion. Alternatively the less important criteria can be turned into constraints around the key one. Since sub-optimisation of sub-systems can lead to a near "pessimum" overall solution unless the sub-system is independent of others, it is not only important to make sure that suboptima are only used in such situations (with their own criteria) but also that, as far as possible, constraints are applied to the least interdependent parts of the system.

The problem of optimising interactive sub-systems has been mentioned, and also that of optimising even a system with independent sub-systems each of which has a different criterion. However another problem which appears much more tractable is common and important. This is that of two or more independent sub-systems, with the same criterion, say cost, where the sum of the sub-optimal (minimum) solution exceeds a constraint on the whole system. (To the extent that an overall system constraint binds all the sub-systems, they are not truly independent.) A simple example will illustrate this.

Consider single storey shed-type factory construction. Three decisions are to be made:

(i) The span between columns
(ii) The amount of roof insulation
(iii) The amount of ceiling sound absorbent

In (i) the cost of the structure increases with bay span; the cost of "failure" in restricting production space decreases as shown in Figure 20; the total cost has a minimum value. The problem in (ii) is similar to the pipe insulation problem already dealt with; Figure 21 shows the cost of provision, the cost of "failure" (heat loss) and the total cost, with a minimum cost, optimum thickness, of insulation. In(iii) it is assumed that the lowering of noise levels resulting from increased absorbent, results in productivity and morale increases which have the costs indicated in the "failure" curve in Figure 22, which also shows the cost of provision of the absorbent and the total cost with its minimum value.

Assume now that if the three optimal values of costs of provision are added together, they exceed the overall cost limit for the factory and the designer is then left with having to choose which of the three decisions, if any, should be optimally decided, with the others shifted to lower, less-than-optimum, cost of provision points; or whether to manipulate all three, and each to what extent. In other words he wants to carry out a sensitivity study to see how he can depart from the three optima with least penalty.

Figure 23 shows a graphical solution based on a technique developed by Maver[16]. On it three curves representing the relationship between the incremental cost of provision and the incremental total cost are plotted with the three optimal solutions represented at the origin; for each of the three decision areas, as well as a fourth for the summated incremental costs of provision and summated total costs. From the origin, on the x axis, representing costs of provision, a sum equal to the difference between the true optimal total cost and the overall cost limit is plotted; this is point x_4. This is projected up onto curve 4 and then across onto curves 3, 2 and 1. From each of these three intersections a line is dropped onto the x axis giving points x_3, x_2 and x_1; these three points represent the amount by which each of the costs of provision of the three sub-systems should be underspent so as to depart least from the true optimum solution.

7   Cost, Responses, Values and Decisions

It may be useful to complete this paper by looking at one or two simple examples where essential information from various sources is brought together in a way for effective decisions.

Example 1. Optimum room size and shape[17].

Rectangular rooms with one window wall and a parallel corridor wall are to be designed, arranged in rows with party walls between them. This is a common built form in hotels, halls of residence, hostels and offices.

On Figure (24) equal area curves A_1-A_4 are drawn. All points of any of these represent x, y coordinate whose product is constant (i.e., they are hyperbolas). On the same Figure equal cost curves C_1-C_4 are drawn. Points along these represent rooms whose constructional, heating, maintenance and other costs are identical. These cross the A curves, on the basis that long narrow rooms with the window-wall on the long side cost more per unit area than those with the party wall on the long side on account of extra external wall costs, longer corridors, more extended service runs, higher heating, cleaning and mainten- ance costs etc. Also plotted on the Figure are curves PA_1-PA_4; these join points which yield room sizes which are perceived, under standard test conditions, to be of equal area. The hypothesis underlying their shape (but unverified) is that a shallow rectangular room, with large window area, appears to be larger than a deep room of the same shape and size with a window at one end. The slope of these curves is shallow, suggesting an effect stronger than that which determines the slope of the cost curves.

This set of data can be used in several ways. If the goal is to provide a specified subjective (perceived) or objective area, then the lowest cost solution can be found. If the cost is given, by a cost limit, then the maximum subjective or objective room area which can be built can be found. If on the graph one plots for each size and shape of room the number of furniture layouts it permits, and then draws curves to connect equal numbers, one can then find, for a given investment, objective size, or perceived size, the room size or shape giving the maximum amount of freedom (or "multi-modality") for the present or the future.

Example 2. Optimum window size[18].
Another example concerns the selection of the optimum size window for an office with four occupants. Figure (25) shows the provision and maintenance cost of a range of window sizes (x axis) with the weighted cumulative frequency responses of "not acceptable" for each size of window (y axis). Window shape is assumed constant and the subjective judgement is a composite of judge- ments relating to view, sunlight penetration and noise.

Any linear function drawn between the two axes represents an indifference line between subjective judgement and money. Thus, if it is assumed that the annual cost of providing "not acceptable" windows for the four office occupants (earning £1,000p.a. each) might be equivalent to the 1% of their combined salaries, then the line x_1 y_1 represents combinations of dissatisfaction and cost where overall cost is constant. Hence any two windows falling on this line have equal total cost. If such an indifference line is tangential to the window curve at any point then, provided the evaluation of "not acceptable" is adhered to, the size of window at the tangent point is the least-cost solution. By altering the slope of x_1 y_1 other evaluations of subjective judgements can be explored, and the sensitivity of the curve to such iterative alterations can be explored.

8   Different Routes to "best" Solution

It will be clear from all that has been said in this and the previous articles that optimising the present and future state of a system as complex as a building, with all its services, environmental conditions and activities is no simple task. Obviously it can be achieved by a host of different techniques and usually has to be achieved by a mixture of them. In Figure (26) the starting point is the designer in search of the "best" solution which lies at the other end of the diagram. It would appear that he can follow one or any combination of 3 basic routes[19].

The first route is the predictive one. Here the designer uses all existing knowledge based on past research and experience, his own personal experience and the results of any specially commissioned research, to enable him to predict what combination of characteristics in his solution will best meet his goals. This kind of route is the appropriate one where the problem has no radically new features and where a lot of experience and research exists.

The second route is the simulation route or, putting it in a more homely manner, the "suck it and see" approach. If the predictive knowledge is inadequate or out of date and there is no time to mount special research, there will be two cogent reasons for making models or simulations of a wide range of solutions and, by iterative adaptations, arriving at a near best solution. The first reason is that some of the physical or cost data is too scattered for any predictable relationships to be feasible. Examples are complex heat flow, intricate lighting solutions or unusual circulation patterns. In all these cases a simulation by an analogue or by detailed computational means may enable the designer to quickly represent a sufficiently wide range of relevant solutions to come out not only with a feasible one but a good one if not the best (since by definition the best in this case is unknown). Many rules of search are available for this kind of exercise.

The second cogent reason for simulation is that in evaluation of the human effects and benefits of solutions there is often no short cut to actually presenting simulated solutions to relevant and representative people and measuring the effects upon them and also obtaining their evaluation of these effects. Measurement may be, for instance, by means of semantic scales on which numerical scores are obtained, and evaluation may be by assigning costs which people are willing to incur to avoid undesirable effects or to obtain desirable ones. Such judgements, whether carried out informally or in the more formal milieu of games, will involve increasing participation in the design process by all those who are likely to be affected by the outcome of decisions.

The third route is the most hazardous and is only taken if the predictive knowledge is unobtainable and if there is an insuperable difficulty about constructing an effective simulation. This route might be called the "multi-modal" route. It involves the attempt to recognise those dimensions of the solution which are likely to be most critical but whose desired properties are most difficult to predict. From this follows the design of a solution which is capable of use in many modes, i.e., it is not a solution at all but potentially a large number of different solutions. An infinitely adaptable solution will cost an infinite amount but is bound to embody within it the best solution. Even a small degree of adaptability, e.g., of spaces and services, may cost a large amount and therefore the decision to build it in is a risky one. Equally

risky, however, is to pretend that one knows the answer from knowledge or simulation when one does not, because the chances of a unique solution, within a set of solutions with random probability of each being appropriate, being the best solution is very small indeed and the cost of failure may be high.

These 3 routes represented in Figure(26) from left to right, are the paths followed, most probably in combination, in almost all design work. Each has a corresponding feedback loop. For the first it is necessary to study the finished object to see whether it does in fact obey the predicted behaviour and if not to alter the body of theory which was used in the light of new experiments and experience. For the second route the feedback loop concerns tests on the validity of the simulations used by observing the behaviour of the real object and comparing it with the behaviour of the simulation. Not least on such validity tests are those designed to answer the question of people's responses to simulations compared to their responses to the real world. The resulting knowledge is added to the pool of simulation theory which will be used in the future. For the third route the feedback loop is that which continuously monitors the behaviour of multi-modal systems (and all real systems are multi-modal to some extent whether designed to be or not) and from this monitoring isolates the dimensions and the degree of adjustment and adaptation which people make to the system over its life. This knowledge is fed back into the pool of knowledge about the behaviour of multi-modal systems and is used in the future. These three feedback loops are properly speaking research activities and make clear that design decision-making and research are complimentary parts of a complete cybernetic cycle and without the support of the corresponding half each is lost. But that is the beginning of another story and serves as a suitable finishing point for this one.

*This article, in slightly amended form, originally formed part of a series in 'Building' and was published August 21st and September 18th, 1970.

References

1 Markus, T.A. 'The role of building performance measurement and appraisal in design method' Architects' Journal, 20.21.67, 1567-73. The paper summarises those models of design method which include the two basic patterns: Levin, Asimow, Pask, Archer, RIBA, Broadbent.

2 Royal Institute of British Architects 'Handbook of architectural practice and management', London, 1967, The Institute.

3 Markus, T.A., op. cit.

4 Based on a model by the Building Performance Research Unit, University of Strathclyde, and first published in Markus, op. cit.

5 Fleming, M.C. 'Building decisions and economic appraisal techniques in practice' Building, 17.4.70, No.16, 73-78.

6 Whitton, D.J.R. 'Performance specifications as contract documents for building work' MSc Thesis submitted to University of Strathclyde, 1970.

7 See for instance Mosteller, F. and Nogee, P. 'An experimental measurement of utility'(1951) and Davidson, D., Suppes, P. and Siegel, S. (1952)'Decision-making; an experimental approach', both in Edwards, E. and Tversky, A. (Ed.) Decision-making selected readings, Penguin Books, Middlesex, 1967.

8 For a general introduction see Churchman, C.W., Ackoff, R.L. and Arnoff, E.L. 'Introduction to operations research' Wiley, New York, 1957, especially Chapters 11, 12 and 13.

9 Krejcirik, M. and Spiler, V. 'Use of computers for determining the optimum development pattern for a residential area' Building Research Station Library Communication No.1235, May 1965, BRS, Watford.

10 Moseley, L. 'A rational design theory for planning buildings based on the analysis and solution of circulation problems' Architects' Journal, 11.9.1963, 525-37.

11 Sebestyen, G. 'Experimental computations connected with the allocation and dimensions of plants producing lightweight concrete medium wall-blocks for dwellings', Institute for Building Economy and Organisation, Budapest, Report No. 116/k-1.

12 Building Performance Research Unit, University of Strathclyde. 'The relationship between one performance criterion and the cost of some boundaries separating school teaching spaces', Report No. GD/27/DW/MM, November 1968.

13 Building Performance Research Unit, University of Strathclyde. Report on Exploratory Studies and Future Plans, Psychological Investigations, January 1968, Report No. GD/11/DC/MW.

14 Neumann, J. and Morgenstern, O. 'Theory of games and economic behaviour' Wiley, New York, 1964.

15 Duke, R.D. 'Gaming simulations in urban research' Michigan State University, 1964. Taylor, J.L. and Carter, K.R. 'Instructional simulation of urban development — a preliminary report' Journal of Town Planning Institute, 53, 10, December 1967.

16 Maver, T.W. 'Systems approach to engineering services' Chapter 4, Draft text for RIBA Textbooks series, 1970.

17 I am indebted to my colleague K. Taylor who first suggested to me the representation of equal room areas by the hyperbolas.

18 Based on Markus, T.A. 'The real cost of a window — an exercise in cost benefit analysis in building design' University of Strathclyde, Report No.62, Feb.,1967.

19 Simplified from model in Markus, T.A. 'Design and Research — Cooperation not Conflict' Conrad, July 1969, 1, 2, 35-38.

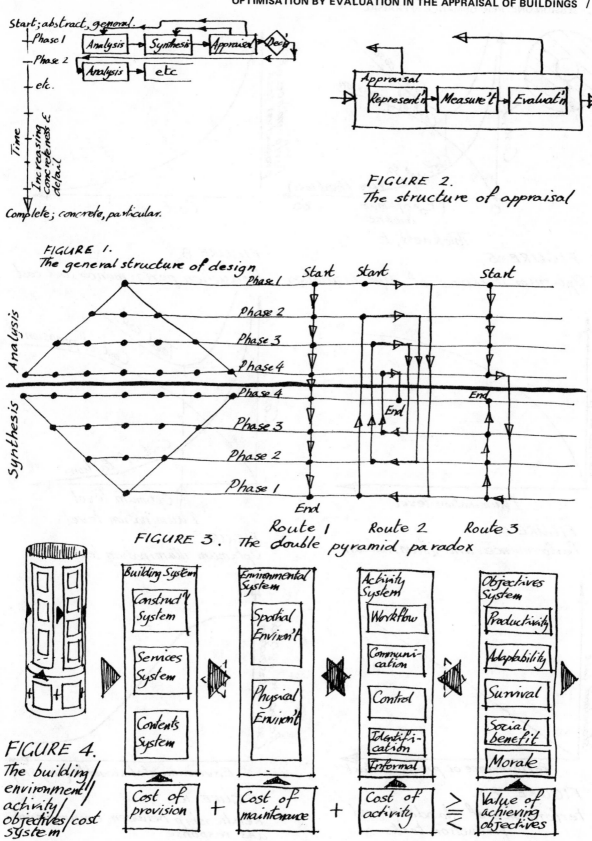

Start; abstract, general.

Phase 1   Analysis → Synthesis → Appraisal → Des'n

Phase 2   Analysis → etc

etc.

Time

Increasing concreteness & detail

Complete; concrete, particular.

FIGURE 1.
The general structure of design

Appraisal
Represent'n → Measure't → Evaluat'n

FIGURE 2.
The structure of appraisal

Analysis

Synthesis

Phase 1
Phase 2
Phase 3
Phase 4

Phase 4
Phase 3
Phase 2
Phase 1

Start   Start   Start

End   End   End

Route 1   Route 2   Route 3

FIGURE 3. The double pyramid paradox

FIGURE 4.
The building/
environment/
activity/
objectives/cost
system

Building System
Construct'l System
Services System
Contents System

Cost of provision

+

Environmental System
Spatial Environ't
Physical Environ't

Cost of maintenance

+

Activity System
Workflow
Communication
Control
Identification
Informal

Cost of activity

≧

Objectives System
Productivity
Adaptability
Survival
Social benefit
Morale

Value of achieving objectives

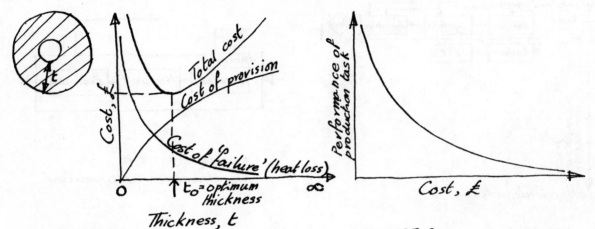

FIGURE 5.
Optimum thickness of pipe insulation

FIGURE 8.
Production performance and cost

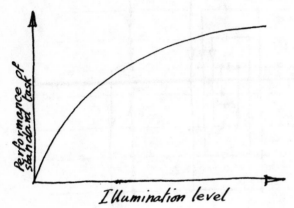

FIGURE 6.
Performance and illumination

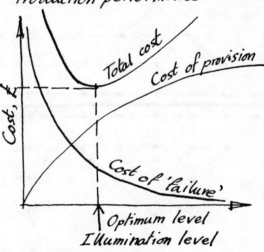

FIGURE 9.
Optimum illumination level

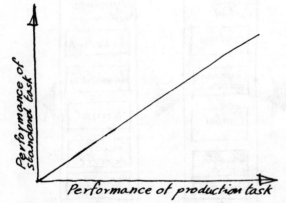

FIGURE 7.
Performance of standard and
production tasks

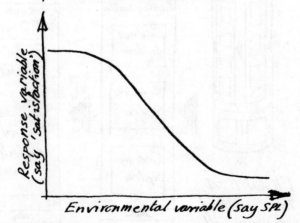

FIGURE 10.
Relationship between environment
and response

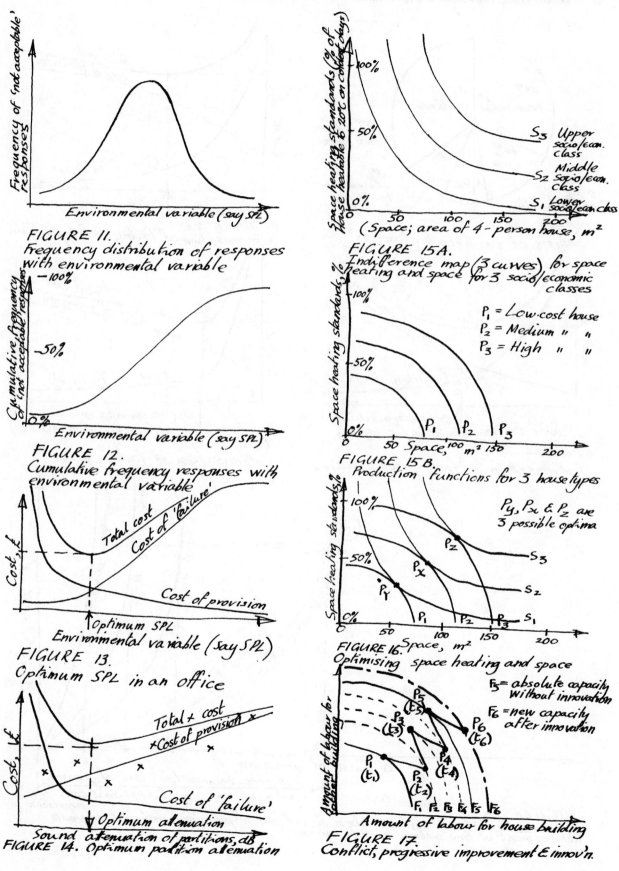

FIGURE 11.
Frequency distribution of responses
with environmental variable

FIGURE 12.
Cumulative frequency responses with
environmental variable

FIGURE 13.
Optimum SPL in an office

FIGURE 14. Optimum partition attenuation

FIGURE 15A.
Indifference map (3 curves) for space
heating and space for 3 socio/economic
classes

P_1 = Low-cost house
P_2 = Medium "   "
P_3 = High   "   "

FIGURE 15B.
Production functions for 3 house types

FIGURE 16.
Optimising space heating and space

P_Y, P_X & P_Z are
3 possible optima

FIGURE 17
Conflict, progressive improvement & innov'n.

F_5 = absolute capacity
without innovation
F_6 = new capacity
after innovation

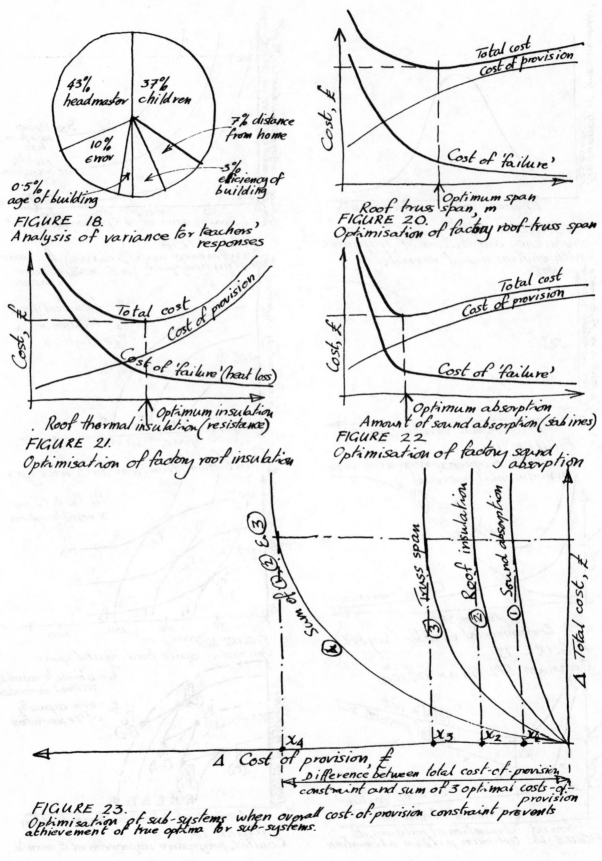

FIGURE 18.
Analysis of variance for teachers' responses

FIGURE 20.
Optimisation of factory roof-truss span

FIGURE 21.
Optimisation of factory roof insulation

FIGURE 22
Optimisation of factory sound absorption

FIGURE 23.
Optimisation of sub-systems when overall cost-of-provision constraint prevents achievement of true optima for sub-systems.

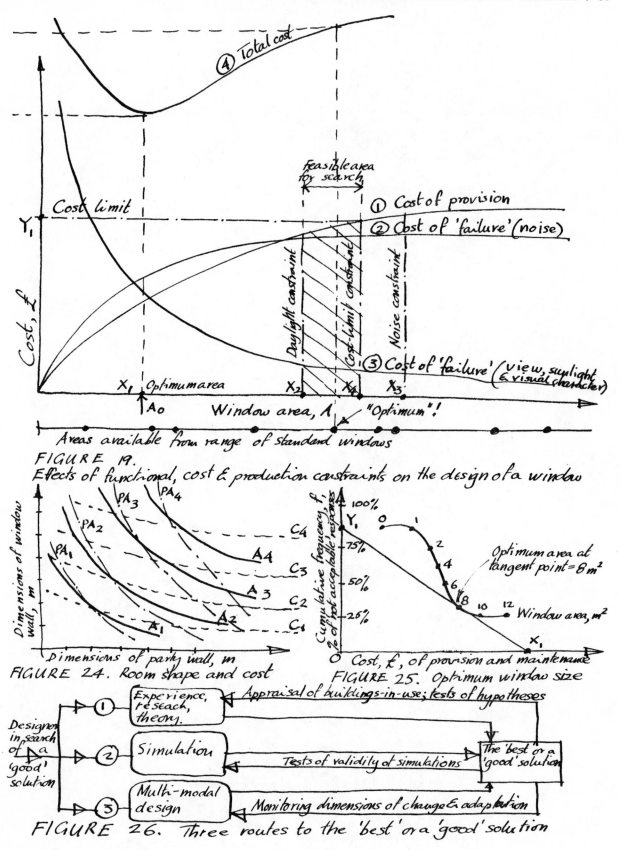

FIGURE 19.
Effects of functional, cost & production constraints on the design of a window

FIGURE 24. Room shape and cost

FIGURE 25. Optimum window size

FIGURE 26. Three routes to the 'best' or a 'good' solution

Environmental Cognition and Behavior

Chairmen: Roger Downs
Department of Geography, Pennsylvania State University

David Stea
Department of Geography, Clark University

David and myself, after editing an issue of Environment and Behavior which dealt with the topic of environmental cognition, felt that there was a great need for a conference session to discuss this exciting but nebulous research area. The central focus of studies of environmental cognition is based on an attempt to explain environmental behavior in terms of cognitive representations of man's spatial environment, these representations being called images.

We suggested to potential contributors that there were five themes delimiting major research questions in the field of environmental cognition, and that these should act as guidelines rather than a definition of legitimacy. These were:

1. elements of an image - what are the main elements (or cognitive categories) of an image? how do these interrelate? is there a common set or do they vary with the particular environment?

2. relations between elements - what are the distance metrics relating elements in cognitive representations? what are the orientation frameworks used to relate elements to each other and to the individual?

3. surfaces - do the interrelationships between the elements lead to a surface: what is the boundary of the surface? is the surface a continuous or discontinuous phenomenon?

4. temporal nature - how stable is the image over time? how far backwards and forwards in time do images extend, i.e., what is the temporal rate of information decay? how do images respond to environmental changes? are there response time lags? what is the nature of spatial learning?

5. covariations with other features - what is the spatial extent of the image, i.e., the spatial decay of information? is there a hierarchy of images, each one associated with a specific spatial behavior? how do all of these factors vary with cultural, socio-economic and personal correlates?

We also requested that contributors should offer critical evaluations of their research methodologies since the development of accumulated knowledge is crucially dependent upon the nature of the hypotheses developed, the operational definitions employed, the samples selected, and the analytic techniques used. Given the adolescent state of the field, this methodological issue is one that we feel should be discussed at the session itself in more detail.

We selected seven papers primarily to offer a broad coverage of the whole field in the hope that they would generate active discussion in the session. Lowrey's contribution deals with the topic of distance metrics in an urban context, stressing both methodological problems of data analysis and collection, and the effect of personality variables on distance judgment functions. Appleyard investigates the process of inference as it effects the cognitive image of cities - in particular, he shows the effect of past experience and learning upon the number of cognitive elements and their interrelationships. The paper by Golledge and Zannaras is strongly linked to that of Appleyard in that it presents a conceptual framework and methodology for understanding how people perceive cities; that is, what type of cognitive models they develop. A final paper dealing with an urban environment, that of Brown, Holmes and Jakubs, discusses activity systems, the behavioral products of cognition, as a manipulable system for environmental design.

The paper by Cox and Zannaras presents a conceptual framework for understanding how people delimit spatial areas which serve as the basis for organising and ordering environmental information. Blaut and Stea provide an overview of the developmental processes and stages of spatial learning, drawing together existing theories from psychology with examples from their extensive experimental and methodological studies. The paper by Kaplan is also theoretical in nature, and develops a model of how environmental information is cognitively organised and stored.

Roger Downs

Notes on Urban Perception and Knowledge

by Donald Appleyard

Professor of Urban Design, Departments of Landscape Architecture and
City and Regional Planning, University of California, Berkeley

Urban perception and knowledge are special instances of general perceptual and cognitive processes, which are not unified in any single theory of perception (Allport, 1955). For the environmental planner this lack of theoretical coherence is a problem. Studies in environmental perception are fragmented, and the environment is viewed with different emphases by the various professions and disciplines concerned with it. (Kates 1966, White 1966). The following notes result mostly from my studies of urban perception in Venezuela and Boston (Appleyard, 1969a, 1969b), together with some reading of the psychological literature. (1) From these studies three characteristic types of urban perception appeared to be dominant: operational, responsive and inferential.

Many elements in the city are perceived because of their operational roles. As a person uses the city, performing various tasks, he selects particular aspects of the environment for the purpose of carrying out these tasks. The details of traffic circles, islands and intersections are often exaggerated far beyond proportion in subjective maps. The noting of quite inconspicuous buildings at primary decision points appears to be part of the same orientational need. Some way of anchoring such points is essential and the most salient element around, however small, is drawn in to perform that role. Isidor Chein has described well how such an operational environment consists of goals, barriers, noxiants and other elements related to purposeful action. (Chein 1954). Goal seeking is certainly a dominant characteristic of automobile travel. (Appleyard et al, 1965). Operational perception is common in other aspects of urban perception. Children know the doorsteps of their houses, where they sit, and recall floor materials, street furniture and pavements on which they play. This kind of perception, directed by activities and operations in the environment, is frequently neglected in environmental planning and design. Yet the environment that interferes with the performance of tasks is probably the most frustrating.

The role of operational perception may be important, too, in the currently fashionable exploration of complexity. Operational complexity, where an environment can be used in many ways, may be much more satisfying than one which creates complex images, just as so many seemingly interesting toys turn out to be extremely dull to play with, while simple looking pieces of equipment provide endless amusement.

In other circumstances perception is much more responsive to the configuration of the physical environment. Bright, isolated, singular, and distinctive elements intrude on the operational search patterns of the traveller, or catch the eye of a gazing passenger. Perception under these circumstances is more passive than active. Signs, billboards, gas stations, water, people occur within the operational view patterns of travellers on the circulation system, or are noticed in peripheral vision while the traveller was engaged in some other search. These are the 'imageable' elements of the environment which Lynch has described in such detail (Lynch, 1960). They are not necessarily visual, they can be distinctive sounds, smells, or tactile experiences. Their imageability depends on the intensity of certain characteristics and their relative singularity or uniqueness in their particular context (Appleyard, 1969c).

Finally, perception is inferential and probabilistic in nature. As we grow up, we develop a generalizable system of environ-categories, concepts, and relationships which form our coding system for the city - our personal urban model. When we encounter a new city, we match each new experience against our general expectations: events are "placed," (2) never-before-seen buildings are identified as belonging to a particular class of building, functional and social patterns are inferred. Apparently significant places are noted, while those that seem trivial are screened out.

Perception in this sense can be seen more as a cognitive decision process, fitting categories, predicting probabilities, forming and testing hypotheses. It is well described in the writings of Jerome Bruner. The wider our urban experience and the more conventional the structure of the city, the quicker and more accurate will be our acquisition of knowledge. Those items of the environment which occur more frequently will be more accessible in our reference system and will stand a good chance of being identified. (3) For opposite reasons, more related to curiosity, the unfamiliar or unusual will also be noticed. This paradoxical attention to both familiar and unfamiliar features in a new environment is difficult to understand unless the multiple motivations of urban inhabitants in any situation are acknowledged.

As yet, we know rather little about these environmental probabilities, either in their objective form or in the common predictions of urban inhabitants. (Brunswick 1943) The conservative nature of this model is probably essential for our mental stability. It has some obvious limitations, however. It makes difficult the absorption of new experiences, and if the environment is ambiguous or incongruous, can very often be a source of error. (4)

The tensions between environmentally dominant responsive perc ption and the mandominant operational and inferential perception appear to be fundamental to our environmental experience. Our discourse with the environment, which is in any case a sporadic one, is continually shifting between subjective and objective, personal and environmental poles, according to our familiarity, experience, mood, the task at hand and the configuration of the environment.

While these perceptual dispositions do shift, from moment to moment, it is also fairly certain that individuals emphasize one or the other as enduring dispositions. Some hold operational values high, others are more concerned with response to the environment, still others search for meaning, objectivity and symbolism. Many of the conflicts in the design professions are rooted in these personality differences (White, 1966).

As a consequence of these varying types of perception, urban knowledge is a complex collection of varyingly perceived items, qualities, and events. Not surprisingly, it is a multi-modal representation of the city. (5) Many aspects of the city are re-

called as actions. Certain trips on featureless roads resemble personal movements more than the roads themselves when recorded on subjective maps (Appleyard, 1970). Descriptions of journeys often concentrate on changes in alignment, stops, congestion and other action events. Such actions and movements, when repeated endlessly, become trans formed into spatial images (Mandler, 1962). The single most common attribute used by our subjects to describe buildings was their 'location'. Even when a person had no visual image of a building he could remember where it was. Many elements are recalled as images. Buildings are described by their physical size, coloring, shape, materials, style, and other imageable qualities. Lastly, elements, particularly larger districts which sometimes have no homogenous image, are labelled by name, number, or some other symbol of their presence. These three modes of perception are successively passed through in our early cognitive development (Bruner, 1966). In adults, while the symbolic mode is dominant, the enactive and iconic modes are still the substance of our environmental experience.

A particular building can thus be recalled by the activity a person engages in when he is there, as an image, or as a name, category, or graphic symbol learned through social communication, from a map or sign. Although society has developed and elaborated symbol systems (verbal, numerical, and graphic) for representing and communicating environmental experience, urban experience is predominantly direct rather than symbolic. Many events are absorbed and represented in the memory as actions or images without transformation as enactive events or iconic images, while others are labelled, categorized, or interpreted for some particular purpose or through habit or experience. Our representation of the urban environment is therefore the product of two information systems, the substance of direct experience and the indirect language of communicating that experience. We receive information directly from the environment and indirectly from several other sources, friends, strangers, the news media, maps, and books. To translate and combine these sources into a coherent network of knowledge, action sequences, associated images, and symbolic structures, many of them fragmented, must be correlated and matched. This is a formidable task, which takes considerable learning ability. For those with less education it is sometimes overwhelming, and the representations of those who travel about cities solely by transit are notoriously fragmented.

Urban perception and knowledge are varyingly schematic in character. In an effort to organize the flux of environmental experience, we frequently, though not always, resort to methods that simplify, structure, and stabilize it. "Thinking," says Bruner, "is an act of categorization." So is perception a great deal of the time. We learn in childhood to develop generalized concepts for classes of events and objects so that new experiences can be fitted into an existing scheme of experience. In processing visual material, people use such devices as identifying regularities, grouping similar or contiguous events, emphasizing separation, continuity, closure, parallelism, and symmetry.(6) In situations of changing stimulus, rhythms and cycles are identified (Johanssen, 1950). There also appear to be limits to our processing capacities which force us into strategies that reduce the number of items we have to recall (Miller, 1956). The effort has been called cognitive economizing (Attneave, 1954). The tendency is not entirely one of skeletonizing. Nonexistent features are sometimes imported to make memory more coherent or meaningful, hence, the process of remembering has been called 'reconstructive' rather than 'reproductive.' (7) In the cognitive representations of large cities, people have to schematize drastically if they are to gain any overall comprehension of urban structure. They extract dominant reference points, a group of districts, or a single line of movement on which to hang their recollections. These simple patterns and networks are the common stereotypes of utopian city design.

Our representations of a city are just as likely to be incremental and disjointed. There exists no pure and complete processing of information; there is no clean entity that words like schema and image sometimes imply. Fragments of direct experience , more often the results of responsive perception, endure unchanged and unassimilated while other events are organized into conceptual systems. Sometimes they possess special survival value and become sharpened in recall (Allport and Postman, 1958) while others are screened out, but many linger on the edge of memory, half recalled, to be only grasped with effort. Sometimes these representations remain in conflict. A building passed on the journey to work is given the wrong name because the name was mentioned in another context. You approach a familiar intersection from a new direction and fail to recognize it. Environmental errors like these are happening all the time.

Partly these errors are due to the difficulty of organizing a vast amount of discontinuous experience but perhaps we also find it unnecessary to organize all experience. This messy characteristic of urban knowledge makes it especially difficult to investigate.

We can at best hope only for glimpses of a person's store of recollections, seeking to detect regularities among them, realizing that every item will not fit perfectly into a schema.

The final quality of environmental knowledge we shall discuss is its relatively inaccurate or non-veridical character (Bruner, 1957). Except for known parts of the city, we depend on very little environmental information to make our inferences. Such errors are often relatively harmless orientational mistakes, but occasionally a misunderstanding can mean the loss of an opportunity, the missing of a job, and a general feeling of inefficiency. It is striking how many people express feelings of guilt when not able to respond to questions about their city. Misinterpretations of the character of other population groups were made in one of our surveys, when garbage was seen on the streets, or when signs were noticed on the walls. It is easy to draw prejudicial conclusions from inadequate information. Much of our environmental knowledge is little more than rumor (Allport and Postman, 1958) - not to be trusted.

The structure of urban knowledge, therefore, is difficult to grasp and full of seemingly contradictory qualities. It can be both concrete yet abstract, schematic yet disjointed, conventional yet imaginative. As a mental counterpart of the environment, it contains elements and attributes which are classed in concepts and categories, and structured in spatial systems and systems of meaning, yet, given the formlessness and complexity of most cities, it is also fragmentary, partial, and inaccurate. It is evolutionary in nature and adaptive to all kinds of demands. As anyone who has given interviews will know, the aspects of knowledge revealed will depend on the question. Indeed, one of the important implications for those who try to probe the nature of urban knowledge, is that interpretations should be made from a variety of responses, graphic, written, and oral to questions which symbolically or in reality place respondents in different kinds of urban situations.

The idiosyncratic and pluralistic nature of urban experience and knowledge have not been discussed here, although they present the greatest conceptual difficulty for the urban designer. But that will have to be another paper.

NOTES

1. Many of these ideas germinated during my stay at M.I.T. in discussions with Kevin Lynch, Stephen Carr, Carl Steinitz and in seminars at the Harvard Center for Cognitive Studies.

2. Tolman identified a "placing need" as a fundamental motivation in perception (Tolman, 1951).

3. Bruner suggests that perception depends "upon the construction of a set of organized categories in terms of which stimulus inputs may be sorted, given identity, and given more elaborated, connotative meaning." The person "builds a model of the likelihood of events, a form of probability learning" (Bruner, 1957).

4. "when....expectations are violated by the environment, the perceiver's behavior can be described as resistance to the recognition of the unexpected or incongruous. ....Among the perceptual processes which implement this resistance are (1) the dominance of one principle of organization which prevents the appearance of incongruity and (2) a form of 'partial assimilation to expectancy' which we have called compromise" (Bruner and Postman, 1949).

5. In his book on cognitive growth, Bruner asserts that children pass successsviely through three modes of representing their environment: the enactive, the iconic, and the symbolic, as part of their cognitive development (Bruner, Olver, and Greenfield, 1966). From our surveys it appears that, once learned, all three modes are employed in representing the environment.

6. The Gestalt psychologists pioneered the investigation of environmental schemata, and although Attneave and Hochberg have convincingly suggested that perceptual organization is more a matter of imformation processing and cognitive economizing than of innate properties of the perceptual machinery, their empirical findings still stand (Wertheimer, 1923; Hochberg, 1953; Attneave, 1954).

7. Bartlett's classic study of memory Remembering, based primarily on the recall of stories, remains one of the most useful and readable analyses of memory processes. (Bartlett, 1932). Paul's statistical analyses of the same stories substantiates many of Bartlett's earlier findings (Paul, 1959).

REFERENCES

1. Allport, F. H. Theories of Perception and the Concept of Structure (John Wiley, New York, 1955).

2. Allport, G. W., and L. J. Postman. "The Basic Psychology of Rumor," Transactions of the New York Academy of Sciences, II, 1945, VIII, pp. 61-81.

3. Appleyard, D., Lynch, K., and Myer, J. R. The View from the Road (M.I.T. Press, Cambridge, 1965).

4. Appleyard, D. "City Designers and the Pluralistic City," Regional Planning for Development, ed. Lloyd Rodwin, et al. (M.I.T. Press, Cambridge, 1969) Chap. 23, pp. 422-452.

5. Appleyard, D. "Signs on Urban Highways; Messages, Audiences, and Media," Dot Zero (1969) pp. 26-31.

6. Appleyard, D., "Why Buildings Are Known," Environment and Behavior, 1969, 1, 131-156.

7. Appleyard, D. "Styles and Methods of Structuring a City," Environment and Behavior, 1970, 2, 100-117.

8. Attneave, F. H. "Some Informative Aspects of Visual Perception, Psychological Review 61, (1954) pp. 183-193.

9. Bartlett, F. C. Remembering (Cambridge University Press, 1932).

10. Bruner, J. S. and Leo Postman. "On the Perception of Incongruity: A Paradigm," Journal of Personality, 1949, 18, 206-223.

11. Bruner, J.S. "On Perceptual Readiness," Psychological Review 64, (1957) pp. 123-152.

12. Bruner, J. S., Goodnow, J, and Austin, G. " Study of Thinking," Science Editions paper (1962).

13. Bruner, J. S., Olver, R. R., and Greenfield, P. M. Studies in Cognitive Growth (Wiley, New York, 1966).

14. Brunswick, Egon. "Organismic Achievement and Environmental Probability," Psychologi-Review, 1943. 50 No. 3, 255-272.

15. Carmichael, L., Hogan, H. P. and Walter A. A. "An Experimental Study of the Effect of Language on the Reproduction of Visually Perceived Forms" Journal of Experimental Psychology, 1932. 15, 73-86.

16. Chein, I. "The Environment as a Determinant of Behavior," _Journal of Social Psychology_ 39, (1954) pp. 115-127.

17. Hochberg, J. E. and McAlister, E. "A Quantitative Approach to Figural 'Goodness'". Jour. Exp. Psychology 46, 361-364 (1953).

18. Johanssen, G. _Configurations in Event Perception_ (Almquist and Wiksell, Uppsala, 1950).

19. Kates, Robert W. "The View From the Bridge," _Jour. of Social Issues_, 1966, 22, 1-140.

20. Lynch, K. _The Image of the City_, Cambridge, Mass.: MIT Press 1960.

21. Mandler, George. "From Association to Structure" _Psychological Review_, 1962, 69, 415-426. 1.

22. Miller, G. A. _Psychology: The Science of Mental Life_, (Harper and Row, New York, 1962).

23. Paul, I. H. _Studies in Remembering_ (International University Press, New York, 1959).

24. Tolman, E. C. "A Psychological Model," eds. Parsons and Shils, _Towards a General Theory of Action_ (Harvard University Press, Cambridge, 1951), pp. 279-361.

25. Wertheimer, M. "Principles of Perceptual Organization," translation of Untersuchugen zur Lehre von der Gestalt, II, _Psych. Forsche._, 1923, 4, 301-350, eds. D. C. Beerdslee and M. Wertheimer, _Readings in Perception_ (Van Nostrand, New York, 1958) pp. 115-135.

26. White, Gilbert F. "Formation and Role of Public Attitudes" in H. Jarrett (ed.), _Environmental Quality in a Growing Economy: Essays from the Sixth R.F.F. Forum._ Baltimore: Johns Hopkins University Press, 1966, 105-127.

Urban Activity Systems in a Planning Context

by Lawrence A. Brown, John Holmes and John F. Jakubs

Department of Geography, The Ohio State University

Abstract. This paper considers urban activity systems with the purpose of identifying elements of the system which are capable of being employed as planning levers for environmental design. The transportation system and set of interaction opportunities are noted as being important, and particular attention is given to the latter. Drawing upon previous work it is concluded that the opportunity set may be so used in a city-wide context, but preliminary empirical analysis leads us to doubt its utility in a more highly localized context.

Introduction

The study of urban activity systems focuses upon interaction between sets of elements within the urban environment. On one level the urban area itself may be seen as a single activity system which contains a number of inter related sub-systems (1). More often, however, researchers examine a single one of those sub-systems as an activity system. Examples include the study of office linkages in the central business district (CBD) (2), the study of inter-industry linkages within a metropolitan area (3), and for the household, the study of social interaction (4), the journey to work (5), and shopping trip behavior (6).

This paper is concerned exclusively with spatial aspects of household activity systems. It has been suggested that urban activity systems are an important consideration in urban planning (7). If this is so, certain aspects of urban activity systems must be capable of manipulation by the planner so as to affect the urban environment. Identifying and discussing the nature of these levers constitutes the major focus of this paper. In this sense, environmental design consists of identifying aspects of the environment that can be manipulated to bring about the desired living conditions.

To a large extent urban spatial structure and the spatial behavior of urban residents form a circle of causality. Spatial behavior is constrained and shaped by the location of existing opportunities for interaction such as work places, retail stores, theatres, and schools. At the same time, the spatial behavior of the urban resident in part determines the arrangement of opportunities, in particular the location of new opportunities and of defunct ones.

Ideally we would like to know how people use their urban areas and how their spatial behavior might respond to changes both in urban structure and in their own circumstances. We would then be in a better position to evaluate the impact of planning on the urban resident and the impact of the response of the urban resident upon the planned and unplanned aspects of the urban environment.

One approach towards this end is to construct a simulation model which would allow experimentation with different activity systems, different activity system characteristics, and different environmental characteristics. In order to accomplish this, three aspects of activity systems must be accounted for: the time spent in performing each activity, the sequencing of activities, and the spatial manifestations of each activity (8). Previous work in the area has tended to focus on just one or two of these three aspects, and much more preliminary work must be carried out before such a task can be accomplished. Indeed, Chapin and Logan (9) note

It may seem that the possibility of developing a model system for simulating activity routines is still far in the future, and this may well prove to be the case.

Thus, we know of no attempt to build

and test an overall model of household activity systems. As a step in this direction, however, we here lay some groundwork and explore some implications of this approach.

Background
Time Budget Studies

Much work in this aspect of activity systems has been done by sociologists. This follows classic work by Sorokin and Berger (10) which analyzed the duration and sequence of activities for various population groupings, the typical number of people participating in each activity, and the motives behind participation in certain activities. Daily time budget studies have been used in the Soviet Union and Eastern Europe countries for economic planning purposes, whereas in the United States they have been used mainly in studies of leisure and market research for the mass media (11). A number of transportation-land use surveys of metropolitan areas have collected data relating to the amount of time spent in out-of-home activities and in travel to such activities, but these seldom have been used.

This trend appears to be changing. In a recent paper, Chapin and his colleagues consider the use of time budget aspects of human activity systems for rational policy making decisions in metropolitan areas (12). As an example, Chapin and Brail first examine a range of background variables to determine which are significantly associated with classes of frequently occurring activity. Second, they group respondents by socio-economic status and, by controlling such variables as sex, stage in life cycle, and employment characteristics, test for variation between groups for selected categories of discretionary activities. This work, then, is a start towards predicting time aspects of activity structure given a set of personal characteristics.

Sequencing of Activities.

Studies of activity sequencing have focused upon activities for which travel from the home to some other location is required. Typical studies are those of Hemmens, Marble, and Nysteun (13). These structure the analysis in a Markov chain format with activity classes representing states and the probability of going from one activity to another being represented as a transition probability. Activity classes include home, work, shopping, school, social-recreational, and personal business. Transition probabilities for permutations of these activity states have been estimated from survey data for Buffalo, Pittsburgh, Chicago, and Cedar Rapids. Surprisingly, they find few trip patterns that involve more than one activity, indicating little association or linkage between activities. However, when activities are defined more specifically to distinguish between different land uses of the same general type (such as department store, foods-drugs-liquor, and eating and drinking), significant linkages are found. The role of socio-economic characteristics has also been considered.

This work, then, provides a start towards predicting the sequencing of activities given a trip purpose and personal characteristics of the household. It does not assist us, however, for activities that do not involve travel.

Spatial Form of Activity Systems.

The most commonly considered aspect of household activity spaces is their distance decay property (14). The approach taken is to tabulate frequency of interaction by distance from the source of interaction (such as the household's residential location) and to fit a mathematical function that views interaction between two locations as a function of the distance separating them. The activity space in such a formulation is conical in shape and centered upon the original residence site.

A second relevant model has been developed by Moore (15). This postulates that urban activity spaces are a function of both the travel preferences of households (which for simplicity may be seen as a distance decay function centered on the residence site), and the location of opportunities for interaction for each activity (termed the opportunity set). For the case where the opportunity set is most dense at the CBD and decreases as a function of distance from the CBD, the resulting activity space is sectoral with a center of gravity between the CBD and the household. Although not explicitly stated in these terms, a similar approach is used in gravity formulations of aspects of planning models, such as that by Lowry (16). There, the interaction between two places is seen as a direct function of the opportunities for interaction in each place and an inverse function of the distance separating them.

The premise that sub-populations differentiated on the basis of socio-economic attributes will have spatially dissimilar activity patterns also has been examined (17). In general, such differences do appear to exist. Suburban higher income groups tend to have activity systems which are more spatially extensive than those of inner city lower income groups. However,this may well be a function of their relative proximity to opportunity sets, as well as the variance in cognitions of the city according to socio-economic characteristics. Thus, since major shopping opportunities lie in the CBD, the activity patterns of lower income groups that tend to be located more towards the inner city would naturally exhibit less spatial extent.

This work, then, provides a start towards predicting the spatial pattern of activities given the location of the household, its socio-economic characteristics, and the spatial distribution of the relevant opportunity set. Interestingly, of the three approaches reveiwed (time budget,sequencing of activities, and spatial form of activities), the third is the most operational, providing us not only with an indication of interaction regularities, but also with a methodology for predicting them.

Implications for Environmental Design.

It was argued earlier that modeling urban activity systems might put one in a position to assess the impact of alternative planning policies. The object of such an exercise, of course, is to identify elements of the activity system the manipulation of which will have effect upon the urban environment. Consideration of the cursory review just completed renders a distinct impression that research has identified few activity system levers for use by the planner. There are, however, two exceptions: the urban transportation system and the opportunity set for a given activity.

To illustrate this clearly, consider the studies of intra-urban migration by Adams and Brown and Holmes (18). The former, in examining Minneapolis, identified migration patterns that exhibited sectoral bias along the axis passing through the original residence site and the CBD and directional bias away from the CBD and towards the urban periphery. The latter in examining Cedar Rapids, Iowa, a medium-sized town, found little sectoral bias and a directional bias

slightly towards rather than away from the CBD. In reviewing these differences, Brown and Holmes stated:

Consider first that each household has a preference structure for spatial interaction which essentially reflects a least effort principle. Thus, given that transportation costs per distance are the same in every direction, the interaction preference surface will be symmetrical about the household's location and exhibit distance bias properties. The existence of a major transportation artery near the household will distort the interaction preference surface, making it elongated along the artery. The preference surface for spatial interaction will influence the activity pattern of the household, which is a basic element in the formation of its cognitive map of the urban area, and its spatial search behavior in seeking a new residence site.

The preference structure alone, however, is not sufficient to define a household's pattern of spatial interaction. The locations of activities which are the concern of that interaction, collectively termed the opportunity set, also must be considered. For shopping trip behavior, for example, the opportunity set would consist of store locations, while for migration the opportunity set would consist of locations of suitable vacancies.

An observed pattern of spatial interaction results from the amalgamation of the space preference and opportunity set structures. It has been shown that the outcome of this amalgamation may be an interaction pattern that is quite dissimilar from the spatial form of either the household's interaction preferences or opportunity set. For example, given a space preference structure that is symmetrical about the household with distance bias properties and an opportunity set that is bivariate normal and centered on the CBD, the resulting activity surface will be peaked between the household and the CBD, and spatially ellipsoid in form.

Similarly, the outcome of Adams' model in terms of expected migration patterns can be seen to result from assumptions not only about the spatial form of the city, but also from resulting assumptions about the spatial form of the opportunity set for household activities, the spatial form of interaction preferences, and the spatial form of the opportunity sets for residential vacancies (the vacancy market). Alteration of any one of these four sets of assumptions would lead to a different expected migration pattern. Particularly critical in reconciling Adams' findings with ours is the spatial form of the opportunity set for residential vacancies and the spatial form of interaction preferences. An important factor in the formation of these is intra-urban population densities and their distribution, which vary according to urban characteristics, an especially important one of which is overall population size. Thus, for smaller towns, as compared to large ones, we would expect that opportunity sets for vacancies be more uniformly distributed and that interaction preference surfaces be less distorted by major urban arteries. These expectations are consistent with the empirical findings reported.

Accepting the argument of Brown and Holmes, the importance of the urban transport system and the opportunity set for a given activity as planning levers is evident. While the former has received much attention (19) the latter has received almost none. This is surprising since the opportunity set is easily manipulated through planning legislation such as zoning.

At this juncture we know little about opportunity sets and their explicit role in the dynamics of activity systems. As a step away from this situation, the following section presents preliminary empirical analyses that consider the role of opportunity set characteristics in shopping trip behavior.

Empirical Analysis.

In order to gain preliminary insight into the role of opportunity set characteristics in influencing household choice behavior, analysis was undertaken to answer the following questions. (1) Does the distance of a given element of the opportunity set from a given household influence the likelihood that it will be chosen as a destination by that household? (2) If distance does play a role in determining which elements of the opportunity set are chosen for contact, does that role vary according to the characteristics of the household? (3) Does consideration of perceived distance rather than actual distance improve the researcher's ability to account for the

choice behavior of households?

As a part of a project on consumer behavior directed by R.G.Golledge of the Department of Geography, The Ohio State University, there were obtained 293 personal interviews with households sampled from an area covering most of the north half of Columbus, Ohio. For the present study, we employed the following information from that survey: the household's location, the stores where it usually shopped for food supplies, the frequency of visits per week to each of these stores, the three shopping areas thought of by the respondent as being closest to his residential location, and the length of time the household had been located at its present address.

Clearly, the actual distances of one household in the sample to its set of shopping opportunities may be quite different from those of another household, owing to their relative locations. Thus, actual distance is not a suitable metric for comparing the choice behavior of two households. Rather, distance was defined as an ordinal metric. All stores within the area were first divided into "large" shops or supermarkets, and "small" shops such as corner stores and small groceries. For each sampled household in turn, the stores in each subset were ranked in terms of their distance from the home location. In the ordering process, city block distance was used. That is, the distance between location at $(x_1 y_1)$ and $(x_2 y_2)$ was defined to be $D(1,2) = |x_1 - x_2| + |y_1 - y_2|$. Due to the lack of diagonal streets in the study area, this distance measure approximates true conditions as well as any other simple function. The set of large stores was 30 in number, while there were 39 small shops. Sample size was restricted to 280 due to incomplete data.

Relative frequencies of choice were calculated for each of the 30 rank ordered distance classes in the large store set and for each of the 39 rank ordered distance classes in the small store set. Thus, from column A of Table 1, 41.7% of all trips to large stores or supermarkets were to the closest one while 47.3% of all trips to small stores were to the closest small store (column B). Similar analyses were carried out for sub-sets of the household sample, such as those who shopped at only one supermarket (column E) versus those who went to more than one supermarket (column F), those households that had resided in the area not more than one year (columns H and J) versus those who had resided in the area more than one year (columns G and I). Analysis of the influence of perceptual distance was also undertaken. In the latter, the set of opportunities was restricted to be those supermarkets in one of sixteen pre-defined shopping areas. Relative frequencies for shopping areas ordered both on the basis of actual distance and perceptual distance are given in columns C and D, respectively.

Plots of columns A and B in Table 1 indicated that the relationship between order distance to a given shopping opportunity and frequency of choosing that opportunity might be approximated by a discrete form of the negative exponential function, $Y=ae^{-bx}$. In this function, which monotonically decreases with increasing values of x and is concave upward, Y denotes frequency of selection, x indicates ordered distance to the opportunity, and a and b are parameters. Logarithmic transformation of this equation yields a linear model that can be fit by regression procedures. This model was applied to the supermarket opportunity set and to the small store set both for the entire sample. It was found to be a good predictor. For the supermarket case an r^2 value of .984 was obtained, while for the small shops r^2 was .743, both significant at the .01 level of confidence. Although alternative descriptive models may provide better fits, this analysis does demonstrate that there exists a significant relationship between order distance to an opportunity and frequency of choice. The possible use of such a relationship in models of choice behavior, and the association with earlier work on distance decay functions using actual, rather than ordered distance, is apparent (20).

Examining Table 1, it is clear that although distance does play a role in determining choice behavior for grocery trips, it is by no means the only determinant. It had been expected, in fact, that the influence of distance would be greater than was actually obtained. For the total sample, for instance, approximately 35% of the choices were to supermarkets other than the three closest ones (column A). Such a result may be due to differences between perceived distance and distance as we defined it. However, examination of columns C and D fails to support such a hypothesis. These provide information similar to that in column A except that here only supermarkets in the sixteen major shopping areas are considered. Further, and more importantly, in column C these opportunities are ordered by actual distance while in column D they are ordered according to cognitive distance measures of the subjects. These statistics show that for actual distance the three closest shops are chosen 81.5% of the time, while cognitive distance alters this likelihood but slightly, to 84%.

While this limited analysis cannot be used to state that perceptual aberrations play no role in spatial choice making, it does indicate that at least for grocery shopping this may be the case. Clearly, then, if we are to understand the relationship between opportunity set characteristics and the spatial form of activity spaces, properties of the system other than distance must be considered. In particular these properties may be of two types: one relates to remanent behavior, especially by households relatively new to the area; a second type acts as stimuli in guiding the choice of the urban household.

At the present time, Table 1 is in the process of being analyzed to identify the existence of significant differences in spatial choice behavior among the subgroups. Although these findings are not presently available, some general impressions can be gleaned from a casual inspection. A striking similarity exists among the columns of Table 1. Whether classified on the basis of length of residence, number of opportunities habitually utilized, or type of opportunity, the behavioral patterns are much the same. However, distinctions do exist. Table 2, indicating the largest differences between the columns expressed in cumulative forms, shows that columns C and H were involved each time a sizable difference prevailed. The opportunity set associated with column C consisted only of supermarkets located in shopping areas. Since other retail establishments are located in close proximity to each of these supermarkets, we assume that the distinctiveness of column C reflects the fact that multiple purpose trips alter the characteristics of household choice behavior.

The distinctiveness of column H is because the choice pattern of newcomer households with regard to supermarkets is more dispersed than other groupings. This provides support for the notion that newcomer households search out an area for suitable opportunities before settling into a patterned behavior that focuses in upon one or a few stores (21). The implication is that newcomers first engage in what Gould has called space covering search, followed by space organizing

TABLE 1. RELATIVE FREQUENCIES OF GROCERY
SHOPPING TRIPS BY DISTANCE ORDER
CLASS

ORDER	A	B	C	D	E	F	G	H	I	J
1	.417	.473	.467		.454	.378	.429	.350	.486	.416
2	.105	.125	.219	.840	.108	.101	.112	.062	.122	.136
3	.143	.133	.126		.123	.164	.151	.094	.132	.136
4	.052	.030	.077		.069	.034	.056	.026	.037	.000
5	.034	.038	.050		.031	.037	.030	.057	.037	.045
6	.031	.030	.024		.023	.039	.020	.092	.022	.061
7	.027	.035	.004		.015	.039	.025	.037	.027	.068
8	.034	.006	.005		.023	.045	.038	.012	.000	.030
9	.025	.000	.009		.031	.018	.024	.026	.000	.000
10	.018	.011	.016	.160	.023	.012	.010	.062	.014	.000
11	.015	.009	.003		.015	.015	.026	.009	.011	.000
12	.009	.000	.000		.008	.010	.008	.013	.000	.000
13	.020	.011	.000		.023	.016	.023	.000	.014	.000
14	.015	.000	.000		.015	.014	.005	.071	.000	.000
15	.016	.027	.000		.015	.018	.019	.000	.033	.000
16	.002	.022	.000		.000	.004	.000	.009	.027	.000
> 16	.040	.052	.000		.023	.057	.034	.078	.038	.106
Total No. of Stores	30	39	16		30	30	30	30	39	39

Column A: All Subjects, Supermarkets (n=280)
Column B: All Subjects, Small Stores (n=280)
Column C: All Subjects, Supermarkets in Shopping Areas, Actual Order Distance (n=280)
Column D: All Subjects, Supermarkets in Shopping Areas, Perceived Distance (n=280)
Column E: Subjects Who Shop at One Store, Supermarkets (n=130)
Column F: Subjects Who Shop at More Than One Store, Supermarkets (n=124)
Column G: Nonmovers in the Last Year, Large Shops (n=236)
Column H: Movers During the Last Year, Large Shops (n=44)
Column I: Nonmovers in the Last Year, Small Shops (n=236)
Column J: Movers During the Last Year, Small Shops (n=44)

TABLE 2. MAXIMUM DIFFERENCES BETWEEN COLUMNS
OF TABLE 1. EXPRESSED IN CUMULATIVE
FORM

	A	B	C	E	F	G	H	I	J
A	-	.076	.188	.040	.043	.031	.185	.086	.071
B	-	-	.140	.060	.119	.057	.225	.016	.073
C	-	-	-	.155	.223	.165	.357	.127	.206
E	-	-	-	-	.083	.025	.222	.059	.084
F	-	-	-	-	-	.071	.125	.129	.145
G	-	-	-	-	-	-	.216	.067	.074
H	-	-	-	-	-	-	-	.245	.182
I	-	-	-	-	-	-	-	-	.089
J	-	-	-	-	-	-	-	-	-

search which is spatially more intensive, followed eventually by patterned behavior (22). Similar evidence to support this spatially sequential nature of search was found by Brown and Holmes in examining search in intra-urban migration (23). They found that spatial patterns of search in terms of the migrant's original residence were quite extensive, skewed in one direction, and appeared to be space covering as the migrant sought out generally acceptable areas as destinations for migration. Search patterns in terms of the chosen new residence, however, were spatially constrained, circular in form, and appeared to be space organizing as the migrant pinpoints a new residence.

Concluding Remarks.

This paper has focused upon spatial aspects of household activity systems. Its purpose has been to identify elements of the system which are capable of manipulation by the planner so as to have an effect on the urban environment. Environmental design in this sense consists of identifying aspects of the environment that can be manipulated to bring about desired living conditions.

Surprisingly, the literature on activity systems provides little insight into potential levers for environmental design by planners. However, two critical elements were identified: the transportation system and the set of interaction opportunities. Primary attention was given to the latter since it has seldom been considered in such a framework.

On a macro-level of spatial aggregation, that is, in a city-wide context, there is ample indirect evidence of the relevance of the opportunity set to household activity patterns and its capability of being employed to channel those patterns in desired directions. Examples of such evidence are to be found in the work by Brown and Holmes on intra-urban migrant lifelines and the search behavior of intra-urban migrants (24). Nevertheless, we know of no study that explicitly examines the role of the opportunity set at the macro-level. Until such a study is undertaken, judgment must be reserved.

In this paper we presented preliminary analyses of the opportunity set for one type of activity and the ways in which households respond to its locational characteristics. Although this is admittedly a highly limited analysis, it provides very little, if any, support for the use of the op-

portunity set as a planning lever on the micro-scale. Distance (or ordered distance) alone apparently is not the quality to which households respond in choosing a destination for grocery shopping. Before the potential use of the opportunity set on the micro-scale is dismissed, however, an attempt must be made to identify those qualities to which consumers do respond, how they operate in conjunction with one another and the nature of consumer response to different opportunity set situations. If this is to be done successfully, a study must be undertaken that considers qualities other than the spatial, and opportunity sets other than groceries. Needed, then, is a study that encompasses more of the system than does the preliminary work presented here.

This system is very complex, and in our present state of ignorance it is difficult to know which of its aspects is sufficiently important to warrant extended empirical study. Given an empirical finding, it is also difficult to know how it relates to the activity and urban system as a whole, since we have no satisfactory model of those systems. However, our bits of knowledge and related theory are extensive enough that construction of such a model may be possible, either in a verbal or computer simulation format. This would permit experimentation with different assumptions about the activity system and urban form. It should lead to a better understanding of the system and a better idea of what research is relevant both in terms of the model and an environmental design context. Our experience in other areas of urban research, notably migration, leads us to be optimistic about such a possibility.

Notes

(1) Goddard, J. "Multivariate Analysis of Office Location Patterns in the City Centre: A London Example," Regional Studies , 2(1969), 69-85.

(2) Goddard, J.,op.cit., footnote 1. Rannells, J. The Core of the City (New York: Columbia University Press, 1956).

(3) Artle, R. The Structure of the Stockholm Economy (Ithaca: Cornell University Press, 1965).

(4) Cox, K.R. "The Genesis of Acquaintance Field Spatial Structures: A Conceptual Model and Empirical Tests" in K.R.Cox and R.G.Golledge, eds.

Behavioral Problems in Geography: A Symposium (Evanston: Northwestern University Studies in Geography Number 17, 1969). Chapin, F.S. and H.C. Hightower Household Activity Systems: A Pilot Investigation (Chapel Hill: Institute for Research in Social Science, 1966).

(5) Taaffe, E.J., B.J. Garner, and M.H. Yeates, The Peripheral Journey to Work: A Geographic Consideration (Evanston: Northwestern University Transportation Center, 1963).

(6) Bucklin, L.P., Shopping Patterns in an Urban Area (Berkley: University of California Press: 1967).

(7) Chapin, F.S.,"Activity Systems and Urban Structure: A Working Schema," Journal of the American Institute of Planners, 34 (1968), 11-18.

(8) Chapin, F.S. and H.C. Hightower, op.cit., footnote 4. Chapin, F.S. and T.H. Logan,"Patterns of Time and Space Use," in H.S. Perloff, ed. Quality of the Urban Environment (Baltimore: Johns Hopkins University Press, 1969). Hemmens, G.C. "Analysis and Simulation of Urban Activity Patterns," Socio-Economic Planning Sciences , 4 (1970), 53-66.

(9) Chapin, F.S.and T.H.Logan, op.cit. footnote 8, page 312.

(10) Sorokin, P.A. and C.Q. Berger, Time Budgets of Human Behavior (Cambridge: Harvard University Press, 1939).

(11) British Broadcasting Corporation, The Peoples Activities (London: His Majesty's Stationery Office, 1965). de Grazia, S. Of Time, Work, and Leisure (New York: Twentieth Century Fund, 1962). Szalai, "The Multinational Time Budget Research Project," American Behavioral Scientists, 10 (1966).

(12) Chapin, F.S. and P.K. Brail, "Human Activity Systems in the Metropolitan United States," Environment and Behavior, 1 (1969), 107-130. Chapin, F.S. and T.H. Logan, op.cit., footnote 8. Chapin, F.S. and H.C. Hightower, op.cit., footnote 4. Chapin, F.S., op.cit., footnote 7.

(13) Hemmens, G.C., The Structure of Urban Activity Linkages (Chapel Hill: Institute for Research in Social Science, 1966). Marble, D.F, A Simple

Markovian Model of Trip Structures in Metropolitan Regions," Papers of the Regional Science Association, Western Section , 1 (1964), 150-156. Nysteun, J.D. "A Theory and Simulation of Urban Travel," in W.L.Garrison and D.F.Marble eds. Quantitative Geography, Part I: Economic and Cultural Topics (Evanston: Northwestern University Studies in Geography Number 13, 1967).

(14) Marble, D.F. and J.D.Nysteun, "An Approach to the Direct Measurement of Community Mean Information Fields," Papers of the Regional Science Association, 11 (1963), 99-109.

(15) Moore, E.G. "Some Spatial Properties of Urban Contact Fields," Geographical Analysis,2 (1970). Moore, E.G. and L.A. Brown, "Spatial Properties of Urban Contact Fields: An Empirical Analysis," Research Report Number 52, Northwestern University Department of Geography, 1969.

(16) Lowry, I.S., A Model of Metropolis (Santa Monica: Rand Report RM-4035-RC, 1964).

(17) Kansky, K.J. "Travel Patterns of Urban Residents," Transportation Science , 1 (1967), 261-286. Horton, F.F. and J.F. Hultquist, "Urban Travel Patterns as a Function of Household Attributes," Xerox, University of Iowa Institute of Urban and Regional Research, 1969. Hanson, S. and D.F.Marble "A Study of Urban Travel Linkages," Xerox, Northwestern University Department of Geography, 1969.

(18) Adams, J.S. "Directional Bias in Intra-Urban Migration," Economic Geography , 45 (1969), 302-323. Brown, L.A. and J. Holmes, "Intra-Urban Migrant Lifelines: A Spatial View," Xerox, Ohio State University Department of Geography, 1970.

(19) Meyer, J.R., J.F. Kain, M. Wohl, The Urban Transportation Problem (Cambridge: Harvard University Press, 1965).

(20) Marble, D.F. and J.D.Nysteun, op.cit., footnote 14.

(21) Golledge, R.G. and L.A.Brown, "Search, Learning, and the Market Decision Process," Geografista Annaler, Series B, 49 (1967), 116-124.

(22) Gould,P.,"Space Searching Procedures in Geography and the Social

Sciences," Working Paper Series Number
1, University of Hawaii Social Science
Research Institute, 1966.

(23) Brown, L.A. and J. Holmes,"Search
Behavior in an Intra-Urban Migration
Context: A Spatial Perspective,"Xerox,
Ohio State University, Department of
Geography, 1970.

(24) Brown, L.A. and J. Holmes, op.cit.
footnote 18. Brown, L.A. and J. Holmes,
op.cit. , footnote 23.

The Perception of Urban Structure:
An Experimental Approach

by Reginald G. Golledge and Georgia Zannaras

The Ohio State University

Abstract. While many geographers have investigated the physcial structure of urban areas, few have attempted to examine the perceptual structure of these areas. While we have descriptive models which tell us that cities are concentrically zoned, or appear in wedge and sector form, as multiple nuclei, or some combination of each of these physical structures, we have at present no idea as to whether individuals perceive city structures in the same form as our descriptive models. This paper outlines a method for determining how a sample of individuals perceive the structure of urban places. The total experiment includes a combination of laboratory and field methods. Only the conceptual basis and the laboratory section of the analysis is reported in this paper. The major ideas in the paper had their origins in the detailed experiments of psychologists studying cognitive and purposeful behavior. The basic hypotheses presented in the paper are that the way cities are perceived will influence the behavior of individuals in urban areas; particularly with respect to the selection of direct and least effort routes. The experiment is designed to be tested in small to medium-sized cities which have one major focal business area (that is, a central business district). The paper as currently constituted reports mainly on the theoretical basis of the study and the experimental section ; however, procedures are outlined to show how the field analysis will verify the laboratory results.

Introduction

In many sciences such as physics, chemistry, economics, and psychology hypotheses are tested in rather strictly controlled cirsumstances. For example, if a chemist wants to examine the action and reaction of two substances on each other, he first isolates the substances and then conducts an experiment in such a way that exogeneous variables are eliminated or strictly controlled. Economists and psychologists have followed the lead of many of the pure sciences in terms of exerting controls on their experiments. For example, the economist frequently works in a spaceless society with a group of rational beings; this eliminates much of the variability in consequent behavior due to the variability in the environment and differences among individuals. Psychologists also conduct experiments such that the number of external stimuli that have to be considered as influencing the outcome of the experiment are controlled. Geographers, particularly those concerned with human behavior, have rarely tried to achieve the same source of control over their experiments.

Since one of the major arguments of geographers interested in the use of behavioral appraoches to solve geographic problems is that the traditional models of geography should incorporate more valid assumptions concerning human behavior and the actions of individuals, it seems relevant at this stage to suggest some methods for isolating variables that should be incorporated into standard, explanatory models. The aim of this paper, therefore, is to indicate how relevant behavioral concepts can be isolated and examined under laboratory conditions prior to their wholesale testing in the field. The specific purposes of the paper are first to show how the selection of environmental cues helps structure mental images of urban areas, and second to show how these images affect urban travel behavior.

The selection of environmental

cues can be likened to the process of concept identification - a specific form of learning. In a typical concept identification experiment, individual subjects are presented with a variety of stimuli over a range of time periods and are requested to make some specified judgement about the stimuli. The judgement may be a pairing of stimuli or the selection of specific stimuli based on preselected cues. One may be interested in the number of trials, the time elapsed, or the number of errors made by the subject prior to the identification of a particular cue and the successful completion of an experiment. Once a particular cue is identified, then repititions of the experiment should result in reduced time, fewer trials, and fewer errors prior to successful completion of the task. Concept identification provides the individual with sets of expectations about what he will see when presented anew with the cue selection problem.

The relationship between cue selection and the perceptual process is suggested by Carr and Schissler. Each individual possesses a set of expectations as to what he will see when driving on an urban road. These expectations are the result of previous similar experiences and the individual's general learned model of the form of the city. The individual is ready to perceive those elements that have a high probability of occurrence in the immediate environment in which he finds himself. His behavior is related to the elements he perceives (1). In the experiment undertaken in this particular paper, an attempt is made to infer what a subject perceives from his consequent behavior.

City Structure and Cognitive Processes
In a recent AAG resources paper, Gould has argued the following: "Whenever we enter a new area of learning, we must acquire a body of simple but fundamental concepts and terms from which we can build more complicated structures and carry on more difficult discussions." (2) Geographers in the past have succeeded in building up a number of simple and fundamental concepts concerning the structure of cities and the interrelationships of segments of cities. Currently, there is increasing interest in both the behavior of individuals within these structures and the way that the structures are perceived by individuals. Investigation of problems of perception

at an individual level have been undertaken with the hope that commonly held perceptions across groups of people will be found (3). Ideally, it is hoped that the perceptions of city structure that are found in this way will conform to the physical models that have been derived from objectively analyzing the locations of parts of the city in space. Up to the present, most of the work concerned with the perceptual structure of cities has focused on a few subsets of the urban structure. These include such things as the view from the road (4) or perceptions of small parts of the city that are regularly viewed on journeys to work. Other attempts (5) have concentrated on examining the precision with which individuals can locate individual features within an urban area. The next step, admittedly a major step, is to try to find if individuals have a perception of an entire urban area and if that perception is stylized in some way that it conforms to one or another of the major theories of physical structure that currently exist. In other words, we have had in the past suggestions that cities are structured concentrically by zones, or by wedges and sectors, or in terms of multiple nuclei, or in some combination of each of these. It is our purpose to try to determine if one or another of these particular forms dominates the way that we construct our mental images of urban areas.

We are also interested in seeing if we actually perceive different urban structures differently. That is, we wish to examine the problem of whether or not an individual will impose, say, a concentric zonal type structure on all urban places whether they are concentrically zoned or whether they take one or another of the forms previously mentioned. This, in essence, closely follows Gould's statement that we must acquire a body of simple and fundamental concepts and terms so that we can examine more complicated structures. We are beginning to talk freely of individual's perceptions of the city without as yet understanding if they perceive the city as a whole, or alternatively if they perceive cities in a certain structure form. It is our suggestion that if individuals do impose a formal structure on their city images, then the types of structure they impose will influence all their actions in the city. In particular, it will influence the direct nature of these trips, and may influence the selection of different subparts of the urban area which are patronized by such individuals.

Several researchers have recognized an existing relationship between city structure and the cognitive processes in the spatial behavior of individuals (6). Although these relationships have been postulated, there has been no complete investigation of how a learned model of a city is developed nor how the perceptual and physcial structures of a city influence behavior in its environs. The research proposed here examines the role the spatial structure of the city plays in the development of spatial images of the city as evidenced by a particular spatial behavior, that is, movement to the city center. The objectives of the research are as follows:

1) To identify the relevant environmental cues utilized by the individual in the development of his mental image of the city.
2) To determine the degree to which the cues selected are the same regardless of city structure.
3) To ascertain whether one particular city structure facilitates the development of mental images of the city.
4) To see if the nature of the structures perceived influences travel behavior.

A Conceptual Framework for the Investigation of Spatial Images and Behavior in Varying City Structures

Tolman's theory of behavior as a purposive and cognitive process provides a framework for relating images which are private and actual observable behavior (7). He argues that an act of behavior involves recognition of a goal, a means of getting to or from the goal, and facts exhibited relative to the selective identification and subsequent use of the shortest route, the most direct route, and so on. The purposes of behavior are exhibited as persistences through trial and error to get to or from a given goal. The cognitive nature of behavior is reflected in the organism's cognizance of the nature of the environment for mediating such gettings to and from This aspect is of prime interest in studies of spatial behavior since it allows the organism to build a "tentative cognitive map indicating routes and paths and environmental relationships which finally determines what response, if any, the organism will make" (8).

Geography has always expressed interest in the structure of the environment and in man's movement or spatial behavior within that environment. It is easy to conceive of the environment as consisting of stimuli such as buildings, and supports such as paths. The stimuli and supports are associated in both a sequential and hierarchical fashion. The observer builds his cognitive map from the existing environmental features by selecting and organizing those which are meaningful to him. In moving through space toward a specific location (goal), the individual uses this "mental map" as a guide and consults a "conventional map" only when the "mental map" lacks coherence. A conceptual framework such as the one above should enable the researcher to examine the role that spatial structure plays in the development of spatial images of the city as evidenced in a particular type of spatial behavior, that is, movement to the city center.

Research Concern

Two of the four previously stated objectives of this research were concerned with the identification and selection of environmental cues. Environmental cues consist of buildings, signs, traffic lights, parks, and so on. These items exist in all urban places. Their order and sequence in the environment, however, differs with the overall design of cities. At any one time there will be a great number of cues present in the environment. The individual, however, will select, organize, and endow with meaning only those cues which are relevant for him at that moment or which are a regular part of his "experience" of the city. Although each individual's selection and therefore image is unique, there is substantial agreement between individuals with similar experiences and characteristics. Thus, it is valid to speak of common images (9). The research focuses on these common images

Using the conceptual framework from above, the following hypotheses are examined: (10)

Hypothesis 1. a) It is hypothesized that the relevant cues selected by subjects will be the same in all structures of similar size.
b) Since the order relationships of the

Figure 1: The Environmental Cue Scale

Circle the number that tells how often you notice the following
features as you travel to the city center.

1. Never 2. Rarely 3. Occasionally 4. Fairly often 5. Frequently

_____

1	2	3	4	5	1.	shopping centers
1	2	3	4	5	2.	railroad tracks
1	2	3	4	5	3.	direction signs
1	2	3	4	5	4.	school buildings
1	2	3	4	5	5.	banks
1	2	3	4	5	6.	churches
1	2	3	4	5	7.	movie theatres
1	2	3	4	5	8.	restaurants
1	2	3	4	5	9.	open space areas such as parks or green squares
1	2	3	4	5	10.	speed limit signs
1	2	3	4	5	11.	the city skyline
1	2	3	4	5	12.	traffic congestion
1	2	3	4	5	13.	traffic lights
1	2	3	4	5	14.	street width changes
1	2	3	4	5	15.	billboards
1	2	3	4	5	16.	bridges
1	2	3	4	5	17.	neon lights in business areas
1	2	3	4	5	18.	rivers
1	2	3	4	5	19.	hills
1	2	3	4	5	20.	freeway system
1	2	3	4	5	21.	number and spacing of freeway exits
1	2	3	4	5	22.	industrial buildings (factories)
1	2	3	4	5	23.	public buildings
1	2	3	4	5	24.	residential quality changes
1	2	3	4	5	25.	residential density changes (spacing of houses)
1	2	3	4	5	26.	smog
1	2	3	4	5	27.	buildings become more numerous and closer together
1	2	3	4	5	28.	major department stores
1	2	3	4	5	29.	slums
1	2	3	4	5	30.	construction work

cues will vary in different structures, man's spatial behavior will vary in different urban structures.

Hypothesis 2. It is hypothesized that given several paths to the city center, man will select the path having the shortest perceived distance between himself and the city center.

Hypothesis 3. It is hypothesized that given the opportunity to select among equal distance routes, man will more often select the one that first turns in the direction of the goal (the city center).

Research Design

The first phase of the research consisted of a preliminary study involving the identification of relevant environmental cues. Environmental cues were solicited from twenty respondents located in the city of Columbus, Ohio. The technique used was informal discussion related to the features respondents noticed as they traveled in the city. Two uses were made of the data collected in this way. First, a scale of environmental cues including such features as stores, buildings, signs, etc. was developed by conducting a content analysis of the free flowing responses of sample members, then including all items that were mentioned by three or more members. (11) (See Figure 1: The Environmental Cue Scale (12)) Once this scale was developed, it was then administered to a new sample of one-hundred fifty subjects chosen from Ohio State University and its branch campuses at Marion and Newark. The purposes of this experiment were threefold:

a) to test Hypothesis 1 concerning the communality of cues across structures

b) to provide an idea of each subject's awareness of the environment for testing later hypotheses

c) to provide information for structuring laboratory experiments (i.e. constructing maps

and models).

The second phase of the study involved examining the respondent's behavior in structured environments through the use of a number of laboratory experiments. Initially, each respondent was presented with several maps of hypothetical cities. (See Figure 2, 3, 4 (13).) Figure 2 was a concentrically zoned strucutre; Figure 3 was sectorally structured; and Figure 4 was a combination of the two patterns. As can be seen from the figures, maps contained marked cues such as traffic lights, buildings, and so on. All maps were given the same cues, but the positional relationships among the cues differed with each city pattern. When presented with a map each respondent was instructed to outline an effective pattern of travel for the purpose of obtaining a high order good, that is, a good that is found only in the city center. Records were made of the cues occurring on the trip selected and those that were not used. During the selection process, the respondents were asked to identify which cues they used in selecting the route. The purpose of this experiment was to test Hypotheses 1b, 2, and 3. To obtain the data necessary to test all the above mentioned hypotheses, the experiment was performed nine times; three trials were allocated to each type of city structure. The instructions given on each trial were:

First trial: Mark a travel route you might take to purchase a good or service found in the city center.

Second trial: From the several alternative routes leading to the center, mark the route that you would take if you desired to minimize the actual distance you traveled.

Third trial: All the routes are of equal length, mark the one you would take to the city center.

A comparison of the performance of the respondents with respect to the structures indicated the degree to which the structure facilitates image formation and thus, behavior.

A second method of examining the research problem involved the use of table models rather than maps. This method provided a correction factor for map-reading deficiencies. The table models were simply constructed

with movable parts so that the number
and pattern of environmental stimuli
could be manipulated. (See Figure 5)
The procedure for collecting data from
this experiment was the same as that
used in the map section.

A third and final laboratory
method involved the use of slides.
This method was closer to reality, but
it still allowed the researcher some
control over the experimental situation. Slides were presented in a
random order. Respondents were asked
to look at each slide and identify the
locale of the slide. Locale names such
as fringe, center, etc. were provided
for each subject on a test form. When
a locale was selected, subjects were
asked to give a reason for their identification. The reason involved the
identification of some environmental
cues shown in the slide.

The final phase of the research
involved an actual field study. While
laboratory studies allowed the researcher to control the number of cues
and paths presented, this final phase
permitted a discussion of the correlation between the behavior in the
laboratory and "reality" situations.
The cities of Marion, Newark, and
Columbus, Ohio, were used for the field
study. Each city represented one of
the three patterns commonly associated
with city structure.

Conclusion

This paper has outlined a procedure for examining perceptual structures of cities. It has been largely
concerned with the way city images are
built up. Because of the complexity
of real world experiments, the problem
suggested laboratory experiments as
prerequisites to analysis in the field.
As such it indicated a desire to understand the theories, concepts, and
methods pertinent to the study before
applying them in the field. While
only the basic concepts and research
design are presented at this time, it
is anticipated that preliminary results
will be available by October.

Notes

1. S. Carr and D. Schissler, "The
City as a Trip," Environment and Behavior, Volume 1 (June 1969), 33.

2. Peter Gould, Spatial Diffusion
Resources Paper Number 4 (1969), 3.

3. Kevin Lynch, The Image of the
City (Cambridge: Massachusetts Insti-
tue of Technology Press, 1960); K.
Boulding, The Image (Ann Arbor:
University of Michigan Press, 1956).

4. Kevin Lynch, op. cit., (1960);
S. Carr and D. Schissler, op. cit.,
(1969).

5. R. G. Golledge, R. Briggs,
and D. Demko, "The Configurations of
Distances in Intra-Urban Space,"
Proceedings of the American Association
of Geographers, Volume 1 (1969), 60-
65.

6. Kevin Lynch, op. cit., (1960);
S. Carr and D. Schissler, op. cit.,
(1969); T.R. Lee, "The Psychology of
Living Space," Transactions of the
Bartletts Society (1963-64), 11-36.

7. E.C. Tolman, Purposive
Behavior in Animals and Man (New York,
Appleton-Century-Crofts, 1932).

8. E.C. Tolman, "Cognitive Maps
in Rats and Men," Psychological
Review, Volume 55 (1948), 192.

9. K. Lynch, op. cit., (1960),
7.

10. The basic ideas inherent in
these hypotheses had their origins in
the studies by psychologists of rat
behavior in mazes. See, for example,
J.F. Dashell, Direction Orientation in
Maze Running by the White Rat,
Comparative Psychology Monographs,
12 (Baltimore: Hopkins Press, 1930);
E.C. Tolman and C.H. Honzik, "Degrees
of Hunger, Reward, and Non-reward and
Maze Learning in Rats," University of
California Publication in Psychology,
Volume 4 (1930), Publication in
Psychology, Volume 4 (1930), 241-257;
C.H. Honzik, The Sensory Base of Maze
Learning in Rats, Comparative Psychol-
ogy Monographs, 13 (Baltimore: Hopkins
Press, 1936); E.C. Tolman, "Determiners
of Behavior at a Choice Point,"
Psychological Review, Volume 45 (1938),
1-41.

11. The rationale for this lower
limit is found in Bayesian Analysis;
see L.J. King and R.G. Golledge,
"Bayesian Analysis and Models in Geographic Research," Discussion Papers
Series, Number 12, Department of Geography, University of Iowa, Iowa City,
Iowa.

12.   The scale in Figure 1 represented the initial attempt to formulate
a scale of environmental cues for the
research reported. The final scale is
still being processed and will be
reported on at the meeting.

13.   The figures referred to in
the text were not available for the
present publication date.

Designative Perceptions of Macro-Spaces:
Concepts, a Methodology and Applications

by Kevin R. Cox and Georgia Zannaras

Department of Geography, Ohio State University

Abstract. The conceptual focus of the
paper is provided by the spatial schema;
this may be defined as the set of locational classes along with the locational and non-locational attributes of
those classes which are used to organize and order incoming information
about the environment. Such schemata
are developed for a variety of spatial
contexts and are of great utility in
communication and search behavior.
Given this conceptual framework, a
methodology is provided for identifying
the classes employed in developing
schemata; this methodology is then
applied to two specific geographical
contexts: the states of the U.S.A. and
the cities of North America.

Introduction

A brief perusal of some recent
psychological literature suggests that
psychologists are increasingly interested in the influence which perceptions of ambience have upon man's behavior. Geographers have recently
evinced a similar interest but largely
because such perceptions of space are
ultimately reflected in human behavior
which has locational implications.
This paper is written with the latter
viewpoint in mind but it draws on a
concept developed largely in psychology -- the concept of the spatial
schema (1). This concept has also gone
under the names of mental map or cognitive map.

Specifically we have three purposes in writing this paper. Firstly,
to specify in more concrete terms the
notion of spatial schema; second, to
present a methodology capable of capturing at least some of the attributes
of the schemata which people have; and
thirdly, to apply this methodology to
two specific content areas: the spatial schemata which people develop from
the states of the United States; and

the spatial schemata which they use
when thinking of the larger cities of
North America. These applications are
presented less for their own substantive interest and more for exemplifi-
cation purposes and for identifying
some critical research questions.
Each of these tasks is taken in turn.

The Concept of the Spatial Schema

In our sensory and verbal contact
with the surrounding environment we
receive a great variety of perceptions
of places: some of these concern non-
locational aspects of places such as
their business concerns or their racial composition; others of these
perceptions concern the relative locations of places: how close they are
to other places, etc. In order to use
that information in navigating,
searching, and generally manipulating
our environment we clearly need some
way of ordering it, eliminating the
redundancies in it and occasionally
extracting via a more-or-less reliable
inference procedure more knowledge from
it than might at first seem possible.
The problem of ordering is considerably
aided by our learning of the similarities and differences which exist between places. Such similarities form
the basis of a classification of locations in terms of both locational and
non-locational criteria: a set of
locational pigeon holes, therefore, in
which we can place incoming information. A simple example is provided by
the inner city-suburban dichotomy
which most of us use in, say, searching for a residential site in a new
city.

Elsewhere Terence Lee has defined
the concept in similar terms as:
"...an inner representation of space
that is originally built from the
disposition of desired objects, but
which later becomes an abstraction, a

series of metaconcepts which organize the objects, facilitate navigation and allow us to coordinate our behavior with that of others. They have been described as spatial schemata. They are obviously constructed from past sensations, myriads of "wherenesses" which have become organized into a structure in the form of an image, that is, something that is available for examination when required. New perceptions from the external environment are given meaning by their connection to it" (2).

All movements in space call for some type of schema. We have schemata for our home, our neighborhood, the town in which we live, and the nation of which we are citizens. It is possible to conceive of a range of schemata therefore from those applicable to micro-spaces at one end of the scale to the macro-spaces represented by nations.

While the resultant classification or spatial schema is based on actual sensory and verbal contact with the environment, however, it clearly has an eventual existence of its own with a power to affect the information which will be selected for ordering; information which cannot be fitted into the schema tends to be discarded until, presumably, the utility of the schema appears to be prejudiced by its inaccuracy or lack of comprehensiveness. The organized structure of this spatial schema, therefore, has a tendency for self perpetuation: earlier perceptions are considerably more important than later perceptions since they provide the basis for a core of meaning in the schema to which later perceptions must be assimilated.

In discussing the characteristics of spatial schemata, it is useful to discuss at the outset certain basic dimensions along which they can be classified. In particular we would like to distinguish two classificatory dimensions in our typology of schemata. Firstly, we can classify in terms of the type of perception which forms the basis for the schema: there are, on the one hand, schemata based on purely designative perceptions of places; perceptions of location, social composition, climate, topography etc., which are devoid of all evaluative content. It is schemata such as these with which we will be primarily concerned in this paper. There are on the other hand, however, schemata based on appraisive perceptions. Such schemata contain a very strong evaluative component and have been already quite extensively tackled in the geographical literature (3). Operationally this literature has focused upon mental maps of residential desirability which provide some insight into the values which people put on the places in their different locational pigeon holes for this residential activity. The schemata revealed in this way are presumably based on appraisive perceptions of the environment around us.

The second dimension along which we can arrange schemata refers to the locational specificity to which they pertain. On the one hand, for example, we develop schemata applicable to highly specific content areas: we have schemata of the United States, for instance, or the city in which we happen to live and, indeed, of the world as a whole. On the other hand, we also develop more general schemata applicable to a wide variety of specific content areas. Perhaps one of the best examples which we have of this is the general schema which most of us have of the city and which we apply in moving around in a city which is strange and unknown to us. We tend in fact to have a schema which classifies locations within the city into concentric zones: higher order retail functions in the downtown area, the Negro ghetto not too far out from there, followed by a zone of older housing structures inhabited largely by working class whites proceeding out eventually to the ring of white, middle class, and generally low density, suburbs. The reality of this general schema is illuminated very readily by our use of it when searching for a new residence in a new town. In like manner we have a general schema which classifies urban places: we tend to expect larger places to be further apart and to have a greater variety of retailing, service and entertainment functions. Again anyone who doubts the validity of this should consider his own behavior when planning overnight stops for an automobile trip across the United States.

All schemata, however, whether general or specific, and whether based on appraisive or designative perceptions, tend to have certain characeristics in common. Firstly, for example, they tend, like all classifications, to have a marked hierarchical structure. Thus while we may think of the United States as divisible into a certain number of regions we also tend to think of each region as divisible into states; and our schemata may also envisage the further subdivision of at least some of those states into smaller regions: Upstate New York versus Downstate New York, for instance. An interesting example of such hierarchical structure concerns the degree to which the fineness of the hierarchization for a specific schema is dependent upon the location of the observer: it seems highly likely, for example, that we tend to subdivide areas closer to us in space in much greater detail than areas further away. Not only that but we tend to project this aspect of schemata on to other people when communicating with them. This is apparent in cocktail party conversation which revolves around the issue of "Where are you from?". If the anchor location is Columbus, Ohio responses to this question will range from Springfield, Ohio through Southern Ohio, Kentucky, Pennsylvania etc. to England. The Englishman is most unlikely to respond with the answer "The Midlands of England" since it is unlikely to be meaningful in terms of the schemata probably prevalent at the cocktail party. Still less is he likely to respond with the answer "Leamington Spa". In brief the fineness of the hierarchization of schemata deteriorates with distance from the observer and this is intuitive in our handling of communication with others.

Within this hierarchical structure of the schema each class can be seen to have certain properties based on perceptions of the constituent places. Given that each class consists of places -- towns, states, areas, counties etc. -- each class has certain internal locational characteristics relating the constituent places of that class one to another: it may be, for example, that the member places in a class are all perceived as geographically close to each other. Or on the other hand the class may be seen as locationally discontinuous, as for example, with a schema which groups towns by size. The internal arrangement of places within a class may also produce certain characteristic shapes as with the donut image which most of us have of that class of places which we call "the suburbs."

We also tend to think of the classes in our schemata as having certain external locational characteristics relative to each other. If the states of the U.S. form the classes of our schema for instance we may perceive Missouri as being contiguous with

Mississippi. Thus, in the New Yorker's Map of the United States (4) there were a variety of locational errors of this type which exemplify the perceptions of relative location which we apply to the classes of our schemata.

Finally we may tend to perceive the places in our classes as having certain non-locational attributes in common which serve to tie them together in bonds of similarity. Hominy grits, poverty, and a highly stratified social system may serve to link places in the Southern states into a class or region in our schema. We also use a distinct set of social, economic, and housing density criteria to differentiate suburbs from inner cities.

Clearly these characteristics of the classes in our schemata need not be accurate spatial images of the real world. We have already referred to the distortions of the relative locations of states inherent in such cognitive maps as the "New Yorker's Map of the United States." Identifying the constituent places in the class, however, allows us to relate the spatial image to the real world. Such deviations of course are of considerable value in understanding behavior which departs from that predicted on certain assumptions about behavior within a real world context as opposed to behavior within a perceived context.

In summary, the schemata which we have contain classes of places organized in some hierarchical manner; the classes in our spatial image, moreover, have certain internal locational characteristics, external locational characteristics and some non-locational attributes. These characteristics of the spatial image derived from certain perceptions of places may be more or less accurate in terms of the real world characteristics of the places constituting the class.

While these schemata are probably unique for individuals, however, it seems likely that there is also considerably similarity across individuals within identifiable groups sharing certain sensory and/or verbal experience of the environment. Groups based on life cycle, social class and ethnic status seem particularly relevant in this respect. Orleans, for example, has drawn attention to the contrasting schemata which blacks and whites have of the Los Angeles area (5). The schema of the less travelled black is spatially much more constrained and incomplete then that of the white.

It also seems highly likely that

the criteria employed in developing schemata change with alterations in travel behavior and in vicarious verbal experiences of places. An interesting contrast, for example, concerns the contemporary tendency for people in the more developed societies to view their nation as divisible into regions which have a locational status with reference to the nation as a whole: the Midwest, the West, the South, the Midlands, the Northwest etc. Such classes contrast markedly with those characteristic of an era of more limited locomotion and spatial experience: New England, Genesee, the Home Counties, Provence, etc. As criteria change so we would expect schemata to change.

The final comment concerns some possibly speculative relationships between the essentially discontinuous image of space implied by the schemata and perceptions of a more continuous space. It seems likely, for instance that the fragmentation of spaces into classes strongly defined by proximity may exercise an effect on our perceptions of the distances to various locations: if two places are in the same class of our schema then they may be perceived as geographically closer together than two places which are in different classes respectively. Thus, if one perceives Ohio and Indiana as being part of the Midwest and Pennsylvania as part of the East one might underestimate the distance from (e.g.) Columbus, Ohio to Indianapolis relative to one's estimation of the distance from Columbus to Pittsburgh. Likewise the average Britisher may perceive a Welsh county such as Flint to be closer to another Welsh such as Cardigan than to any English county which is objectively closer to Flint than Cardigan.

Again the locational and hierarchical characteristics of schemata may afford some insight into the usual tendency for people to overestimate shorter distances relative to longer distances. Given the hierarchical structure of schemata and a tendency for the hierarchy to be more finely developed in the immediate vicinity of the observer it seems plausible that the psychological principle of closure would tend to bring more distant places perceptually closer to the observer; this would be a result of the perceptual contraction and resultant distance distortion as apparent in the "New Yorkers Map of the United States."

Given this conceptual overview the remainder of this paper adopts a more

restricted focus: briefly that of a methodology for identifying the schemata which people have of specific macro-spaces. We shall also confine ourselves to those schemata which are based on designative rather than appraisive perceptions since that latter problem has already received considerable methodological attention. We now proceed to a consideration of methodology and then to some applications.

A Methodology for Identifying Specific Schemata for Designative Perceptions

The methodology developed here is derived from the work of a group of political scientists at the University of Michigan who have been carrying out extensive questionnaire surveys into the structure of international attitudes in the public at large (6). One aspect of the investigation has been the identification of perceptions of cross-national similarities: "Questions about the perceived similarity of countries were asked concerning 17 countries, chosen so as to represent all major regions of the world. Each country in turn served as the anchor country and the respondent was asked to indicate which three of the remaining 16 countries were most similar to the anchor...it was hypothesized that this rather unstructured task would give us meaningful insights into the perceptual and cognitive maps of interrelationships among countries typical of people with various educational and social backgrounds. Further, we felt that multidimensional analysis of this data would indicate meaningful attitude structures, subject to dimensional interpretation"(7). The consequent analysis did indeed reveal the existence of dimensions of perceived variation -- in particular a Developed-Underdeveloped dimension and a Communist-non-Communist dimension.

Given this basis for a methodology, therefore, assume that a study group is given the names of subareas of some larger area such as a nation -- the departments of France, for example. They are asked to take each subarea in turn as an "anchor subarea" and identify the three other subareas which they regard as most similar to the "anchor subarea." The resultant choices of the study group can then be placed in a matrix in which C_{ij} gives the number of times that subarea j has been chosen as similar to anchor subarea i. Division of each cell entry by 3M, where M is the size of the study group, yields Pij, the probability that subarea j has been chosen as similar to anchor subarea i.

Manipulation of the data tableau in some of the ways suggested by Hefner et. al., might plausibly provide evidence of the classes used in the schemata or cognitive maps of which, presumably, the choices are a function. Factor analysis of the Pij matrix, for instance, might permit the identification of <u>dimensions of choice</u> such that subareas loading high and in the same direction on a particular factor would frequently be chosen together as the most similar subareas to particular anchor subareas. In this way it would be possible to identify sets or classes of subareas which are regarded as similar to one another either by a simple mapping of the loadings for each factor or by a multivariate grouping applied to the leadings for a set of factors.

Clearly the methodology has limitations from the viewpoint of providing a comprehensive view of the properties of schemata characteristic of groups of respondents. Most importantly, it only assists in establishing the classes which are employed in schemata. The results of such an analysis would tell us nothing conclusive about the locational characteristics of schemata or about the attributes employed in deriving these schemata; only inference with a shaky logical foundation could provide us with some idea of the criteria used by examining the real world characteristics of the places constituting the classes.

Nevertheless we believe that the identification of such classes is important in the overall process of identifying the properties of schemata. They afford a reasonably objective means of defining the classes which people use and they also afford a control in further investigation over variance in the classes characteristic across a set of individuals. The significance of this can be readily grasped by considering the problems of asking a group to draw cartographically their spatial images of the United States; almost certainly there would be some differences in the sets of classes identified. The investigator could of course specify beforehand the classes to be used but without the procedure which we have outlined above such classes might bear precious little relationship to those which constitute the spatial image of the average respondent.

What we envisage in investigations of spatial schemata therefore is a two stage research process. The initial stage would establish classes in the manner which we have outlined above. The second stage would ask for cartographic depictions and/or verbal descriptions of these classes from the respondents involved. It is with the first stage that the remainder of this paper is concerned.

Application of the Methodology

Partly by way of example and partly by way of pointing out problems and possibilities in the application of the research methodology we have applied it to two specific content areas for which people develop schemata: 1) the states of the United States; 2) the cities of North America. The limited question which we have asked is, what are the classes which constitute the schemata which students have of these specific geographical aggregations. Perceptions of similarity allow us to establish such classes.

The States of the U.S.A.

The methodology briefly outlined above has therefore been applied to the perceptions of state similarity across the states of the U.S.A. of a study group of 40 undergraduates at The Ohio State University with little or no geographical backgorund. To each of the 40 students a list of states was administered and each student was instructed to: "Take each state in turn and select the three states most similar to it. Similarities should be evaluated in as many ways as you think states differ." Students were given 20 minutes to perform this task.

The resultant choices were then taken off the schedules and inserted in a Cij matrix. The cell entries were converted into percentages of row totals. The high proportion of zero entries in this matrix suggested that for most anchor states there is a considerable degree of study group consensus as to the most similar states.

In order to identify the classes of the cognitive maps held by the students, the Pij matrix was factor analyzed. Prior to this, however, the diagonal cells of the matrix were inserted with values equivalent to .33: technically this was done in order to maximize the correlations between the variables representing choices for different states; conceptually the approach can be defended on the grounds that the state <u>most</u> similar to a state is the state itself.

The variables factor analyzed, therefore, are state similarity choices with <u>one variable for each of the 48 states</u>. The <u>observations</u> are the <u>48 anchor states</u>. Loadings are on state choices while scores are computable for anchor states. The loadings are presented in Table 1. In interpreting the factor loadings, states which have similar loadings on the same factor can be regarded as being perceived as similar and belonging to the same set; states which have very different loadings on the same factor, on the other hand, can be interpreted as being perceived as correspondingly dissimilar and in different sets of the schemata involved. In this treatment only loadings in excess of $\pm.4$ have been employed in identifying classes of states: these classes have all been mapped on to Figure 1 in order to conserve space.

The first factor appears to be bipolar in form differentiating areas on an East-West basis. In one sense the Mississippi River proves an almost perfect boundary line with almost entirely negative loadings to the west and almost entirely positive loadings to the east. Closer inspection of the loadings, however, reveals that the map has two epicenters: a cluster of relatively high positive loadings in what is commonly regarded as the East, stretching from Maryland in the south to Vermont and New Hampshire in the north; and a cluster of relatively high negative loadings in the Mountain States and adjacent Plains States to the east. In the light of the roles which the so called East and so called West play in popular symbology the importance of this basic dimension in the conceptual spaces of the students is perhaps not surprising. On Figure 1 the locational identities of these classes are referred to as the "<u>Northeast</u>" and the "<u>Mountain</u>" or "<u>West</u>" respectively.

The second factor describes a second dimension of the cognitive maps superimposed upon the East-West factor and differentiates between two of the classic regions of the U.S. -- the <u>South</u> and <u>New England</u>. (See Fig. 1) The regional images, moreover, reveal considerable subtleties of judgement which accord well with more objective criteria of regional definition. There seems, for example, to be a clear perception of a Southern Borderland with such states as Kentucky, Virginia,

Arkansas and North Carolina receiving rather more modest loadings than the Deep South of Georgia, Alabama, Louisiana and Mississippi. Interestingly enough the atypicality of Florida, Texas and Oklahoma was also recognized though the Deep Southern characteristics of South Carolina appear to have been less clear to the students

The third factor in contrast with the first two factors, is not bipolar. Loadings on a few contiguous states in the Great Lakes area are very high and negative but are not counterbalanced by high, positive leadings elsewhere in the U.S. What is being depicted by this factor, therefore, is a perceived area of homogeneity which we might call the <u>Midwest</u>. As with the South this has a core area consisting of states with loadings in excess of $-.5$ (Wisconsin, Minnesota, Illinois, Indiana, Michigan and Ohio). This core area is surrounded by another tier of states all with negative though low loadings; the residue of the nation is characterized by relatively low loadings.

Of particular interest in this factor, however, is the high degree of clarity with which the regional core is perceived. This is indicated not only by the large differences in loadings between the core area and the surrounding tier of states but also by the magnitudes of the loadings for the core states. Ohio, Michigan, Indiana and Illinois all record loadings of at least $-.70$. On no other factor do loadings exceed $-.70$. Such clarity may be related to the fact that the perceptions are those of Ohio students and we may therefore be dealing with a phenomenon akin to the spatial discrimination effect in the "Mental Maps of Residential Desirability" literature (8). Just as the greater degree of discrimination accorded to states surrounding the home state is a function of familiarity, so the high loadings on factor 3 may suggest a high degree of consensus which likewise originates in a familiarity factor.

The three remaining factors may be disposed of more briefly. Factor 4 appears to be extracting a rather more surprising dimension of the conceptual spaces. It would appear that a considerable degree of homogeneity was accorded by the students to a polyglot group of states in the Midcontinent including on the one hand some states which we would regard as Great Plains states -- Nebraska and Kansas particu-

FACTORS

Location	I	II	III	IV	V	VI
Alabama		-.66			-.40	
Arizona	-.45					+.40
Arkansas		-.48		-.40		
California						
Colorado	-.61					
Connecticut	+.55	+.52				
Delaware	+.50					
Florida				-.42		
Georgia		-.70				
Idaho	-.53					-.53
Illinois			-.82			
Indiana			-.70			
Iowa	-.40			-.53		
Kansas	-.47			-.65		
Kentucky		-.48			+.54	
Louisiana		-.60			-.44	
Maine		+.47				
Maryland	+.48					
Massachusetts	+.50					
Michigan			-.81			
Minnesota			-.57			
Mississippi		-.63				
Missouri				-.51		
Montana	-.59					-.49
Nebraska	-.47			-.60		
Nevada	-.60			+.40		
New Hampshire	+.47	+.52				
New Jersey	+.48					
New Mexico	-.42					+.49
New York	+.44					
North Carolina		-.52				
North Dakota						
Ohio			-.74	+.41		
Oklahoma				-.41		+.43
Oregon						-.64
Pennsylvania						
Rhode Island	+.54	+.50				
South Carolina		-.51				
South Dakota	-.42					
Tennessee		-.57			+.49	
Texas						+.44
Utah	-.60					
Vermont	+.44	+.50				
Virginia		-.40		+.40	+.60	
Washington						-.66
West Virginia				+.41	+.54	
Wisconsin			-.61			
Wyoming	-.61					

Table 1: Factor Loadings on the U.S. states: for purposes of clairty, only loadings greater than +0.4 or less than -0.4 are shown.

larly -- and some states which are on the periphery of the Midwest as in the case of Iowa and Missouri. We have called this class the "Midcontinent."

Factor 5 appears to be largely an Appalachian factor with high loadings for West Virginia, Kentucky, Tennessee and Virginia. This is also of interest

in that it suggests that there is a perception of similarity accorded to an area of the nation not usually regarded in geography textbooks as a region in the classic sense. Factor 6 is possibly also surprising in that it draws a contrast between two regions which one would not have expected to have pre-

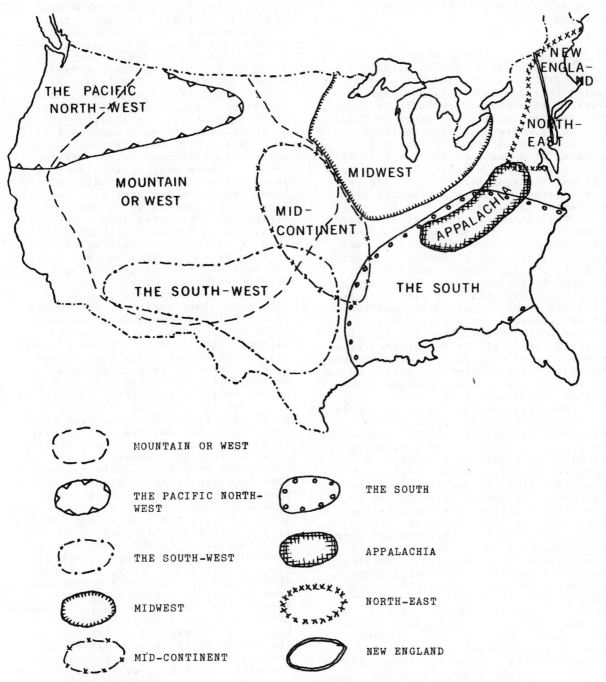

Figure 1: Locational Classes of Student Schemata of the U.S.A.

sented such clear images -- the Pacific Northwest and the Southwest.

These notes suggest that it is possible to conceive of a system of classes or regions corresponding to the schemata of the students by placing the areas of homogeneity revealed by the

factors into some sort of simple hierarchical classification: on the one hand we have the West which can be broken down into the Pacific Northwest, the Mountains, the Southwest and the Midcontinent; on the other hand we have the East comprising the South,

Appalachia, the Midwest and New England.

The Cities of North America

The procedure used in examing state similarity choices was also applied to a sample of sixty cities of varying size located in North America; the selected cities are shown in Table 2. In this instance, the variables. factor analyzed are city similarity choices with one variable for each of the sixty cities and the observations are the sixty anchor cities. The factor loadings on the city choices are presented in Table 2.

The factors on the city data were more difficult to interpret than those obtained from the state choices. Each factor represented a greater complexity than is usually encountered and this complexity raised doubts regarding any simple classification of city choices. Students seemed to use a combination of attributes in selecting similar cities and consequently, only the first four factors could be interpreted with any degree of confidence. As with the American states material reported on above only the loadings greater than +.4 or less than -.4 were used.

The first factor can be described as a Cosmopolitanism-Provincialism dimension of differentiation. As can be seen from Table 2, the factor is bi-polar in form. It summarizes a complex cluster of characteristics. Geographically the negative loadings outline a peripheral distribution of the largest cities in the sample (see Figure 2); an examination of these cities suggests that they are the more cosmopolitan of North American urban centers and that they perform service functions for wide surrounding areas. On the other hand, the positive loadings relate cities which are small interior regional centers. These cities (Fort Wayne, Lexington, Little Rock, Macon, Memphis, Mobile, South Bend, Wheeling) have a considerably more provincial image than the cities picked up by the cosmopolitan end of the dimension. In contrast the cosmopolitanism of the larger cities is illuminated and emphasized by the way in which they ignore the international boundary. Clearly however, the cities at the two opposite poles of the dimension can be differentiated in more ways than in terms of their relative degrees of cosmopolitanism and provincialism.

The second factor is also bi-polar in form and can be interpreted as a

factor which differentiates between two urban systems: the Great Lakes Urban System and the Southwest Urban System (see Figure 3). This factor is also complex in its nature. The first distinguishing characteristic is locational the positive loadings clustering in the Southwest and the negative loadings clustering in the Great Lakes area. Distinctive sets of communication linkages underline this proximity criterion, the Great Lakes cities in particular being tied together commercially by a network of water transportation. Studies of airline transportation have also underlined the degree to which southwestern cities are integrated into a network focussing on Dallas-Forth Worth (9).

A further interesting feature of this factor appears in its possible contrast of the environmental quality of the two areas. The cities in the Southwest are more open in physical structure, less polluted, and less industrialized than those around the Great Lakes. The factor seems to differentiate in fact between a set of cities characterized by nineteenth century forms of industrialism and a set of cities which are more contemporary in their industrial composition.

The third factor is also a bipolar factor, but it is perhaps the simplest of the factors. It is certainly a factor of location: the negative loadings summarize cities in the traditional South while the positive loadings relate cities in the Midwest. In examining the positive loadings, however an interesting aspect appears. Only the smaller more provincial Midwestern cities appear to have larger loadings on this factor: the larger cities of the region such as Minneapolis, Kansas City, Milwaukee, Chicago and St. Louis are absent and seem to have been abstracted from the surrounding region. It is as if people perceive larger cities as having an existence independent of the surrounding region while smaller cities are associated more with their regional context. Consistent with this idea is the fact that on the first factor, the more cosmopolitan cities were derived from a variety of regional contexts, spreading in particular over the international boundary.

The fourth and final factor which could be interpreted is a Canadian factor. It is more uni-polar thus the other factors. There is only one positive loading greater than .4, (Dallas), although a number of other cities in

FACTORS

Location	I	II	III	IV
1. Albany				
2. Albuquerque		+.55		
3. Atlanta			-.44	
4. Baltimore				
5. Binghamton				
6. Boston		-.41		
7. Buffalo		-.47		
8. Cedar Rapids				
9. Charlotte				
10. Chicago	-.50	-.45		
11. Cleveland		-.57		
12. Dallas		+.50		+.40
13. Denver		+.59		
14. Detroit		-.56		
15. Des Moines			+.48	
16. Duluth			+.41	
17. El Paso		+.59		
18. Erie				
19. Evansville			+.46	
20. Fort Wayne	+.43		+.50	
21. Grand Rapids				
22. Harrisburg				
23. Houston		+.55		
24. Huntington				
25. Indianapolis				
26. Kansas City				
27. Lexington	+.50			
28. Little Rock	+.45		-.41	
29. Louisville	+.50		-.40	
30. Los Angeles	-.54			
31. Macon	+.51		-.44	
32. Manchester				
33. Memphis	+.56		-.58	
34. Minneapolis				
35. Milwaukee				
36. Mobile	+.47		-.56	
37. Montreal	-.41			-.65
38. New York	-.58			
39. Omaha			+.43	
40. Ottawa				-.73
41. Philadelphia	-.43			
42. Pittsburgh		-.55		
43. Providence				
44. Salt Lake City		+.43		
45. San Diego				
46. San Francisco	-.53			
47. Seattle				
48. Shreveport				
49. South Bend	+.41		+.48	
50. Spokane				
51. St. Louis				
52. Tampa				
53. Terre Haute			+.44	
54. Toledo		-.41		
55. Toronto	-.43			-.78
56. Tucson		+.57		
57. Vancouver				-.72
58. Wheeling	+.47			
59. Wichita				
60. Winnipeg				-.78

Table 2: Factor Loadings on North American Cities: for purposes of clarity, only loadings greater than +0.4 or less than -0.4 are shown.

the Southwest have loadings in this direction. Four of the five Canadian cities in the study have high negative loadings though Montreal is noticeably absent from the list. The factor testifies to the strength of political units as the bases of spatial schemata and this recalls the significance which the English-Scottish boundary has in the mental maps of residential desirability of British school leavers (10).

Concluding Comments

In this paper we have pro gressively narrowed down our focus from a broad conceptual treatment of spatial schemata to a methodology designed to capture a limited but important aspect of those schemata: the classifications of locations upon which they are based. Specific applications of this methodology do allow us, moreover, to extract certain dimensions of variation along which students appear to differentiate places. While it might be difficult to define the boundaries of locational classes with exactitude, we are probably given a good idea of their conceptual relationships one to another: we know, for example, that Iowa is much more likely to be grouped with Missouri than with Ohio.

The methodology, however, raises certain questions and two in particular concern us here; first, to what extent do such measures constitute a valid measure of the dimensions of differentiation employed by students? Secondly, what are some of the important avenues of research which need to be developed in the future?

With respect to the first question, it is clearly important that there be a close relationship between the geographical units which form the building blocks of spatial schemata and the geographical units employed in the method-

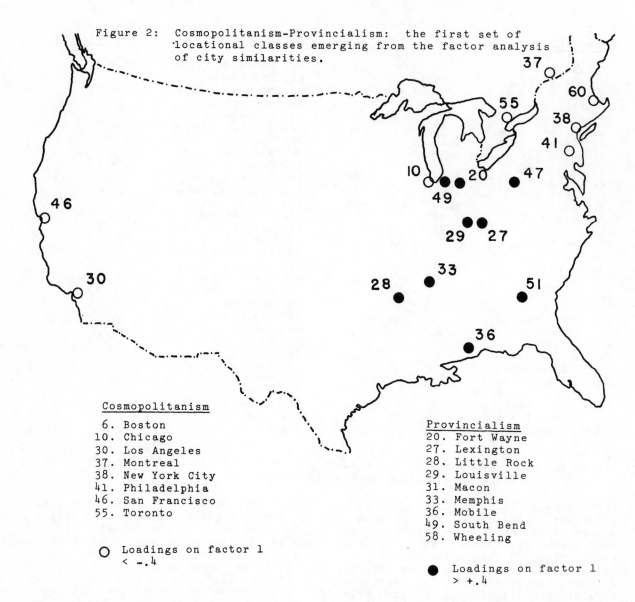

Figure 2: Cosmopolitanism-Provincialism: the first set of locational classes emerging from the factor analysis of city similarities.

Cosmopolitanism

  6. Boston
 10. Chicago
 30. Los Angeles
 37. Montreal
 38. New York City
 41. Philadelphia
 46. San Francisco
 55. Toronto

○ Loadings on factor 1
   < -.4

Provincialism

 20. Fort Wayne
 27. Lexington
 28. Little Rock
 29. Louisville
 31. Macon
 33. Memphis
 36. Mobile
 49. South Bend
 58. Wheeling

● Loadings on factor 1
   > +.4

ology. In the case of the students we assumed (e.g.) that the states of the U.S.A. provided meaningful units. Certainly counties would not have and the use of states in mass communication and informal interaction in the U.S.A. suggests that these do provide the individual observations upon which the classes of schemata are based. Clearly, however, this is an important consideration in any research probing the nature of schemata.

Also, with respect to the problem of validity, there is the question of _forcing_ classification where it doesn't exist in the schemata. It is possible, for instance, that such forcing was present in the methodology as we applied

it. We did call for specifically 3 similar units whereas in fact, three may not have existed in the individual schema or in fact there may have been more than 3. We also employed a sample in the case of the North American cities so that the student could have faced the situation where the cities he thought most similar to a specific anchor city did not appear on the list at all. In retrospect it is probably advisable to employ universes rather than samples and also to adopt a looser arrangement as to the number of places to be selected as similar.

Major research questions for the future include the problem of the

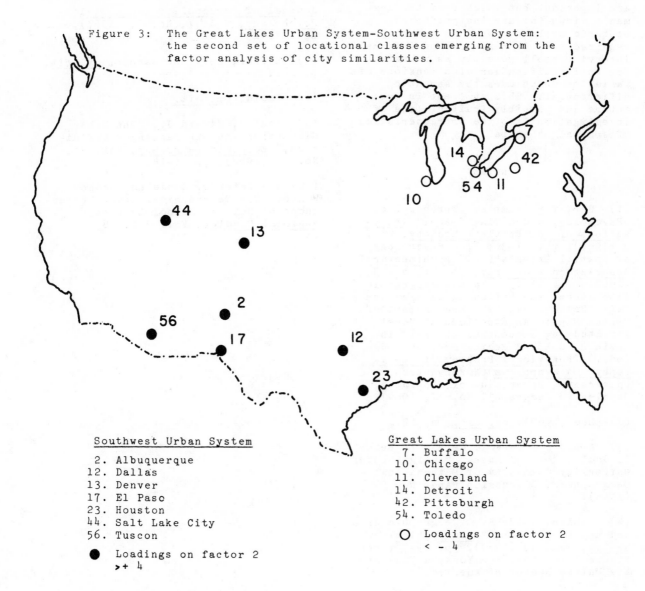

Figure 3:   The Great Lakes Urban System-Southwest Urban System:
the second set of locational classes emerging from the
factor analysis of city similarities.

Southwest Urban System

   2. Albuquerque
  12. Dallas
  13. Denver
  17. El Paso
  23. Houston
  44. Salt Lake City
  56. Tuscon

  ● Loadings on factor 2
    > + 4

Great Lakes Urban System
   7. Buffalo
  10. Chicago
  11. Cleveland
  14. Detroit
  42. Pittsburgh
  54. Toledo

  ○ Loadings on factor 2
    < - 4

criteria which people use in classifying places. The two applications presented in this paper suggest that relative location is very important but why
should this be? Is it that location
itself provides a cue to the individual,
for example; or is it a perception of
spatial autocorrelation in the attri-
bues used as criteria. Thus, the Great
Lakes cities could have been grouped
together in one class because they are
located near to each other; alternatively the raison d'etre of the class
might reside in similarities of industrial structure and urban environment
across those cities. Alternatively, of
course, it might be a mixture of the

two mechanisms, the perception of locational proximity providing a cue for
assumptions of spatial autocorrelation.
   Whatever the criteria employed we
clearly have a set of puzzling problems
related not only to the classifications
which do emerge -- why the Midcontinent,
for example -- but also to those which
don't. We fully expected urban size to
be a major criterion in the North
American cities case, for instance, but
apparently it wasn't. In investigating
this problem, moreover, we are in a
sense professionally handicapped in
that as geographers, we are likely to
project on to the students' perceptions,
geographical differences which we think

are important but which from the lay-
man's viewpoint are insignificant,
esoteric or both. What is probably
required here is some sort of informal
interview tool, possibly as a basis
for an identification of dimensions of
variation which uses the semantic
differential. This at least is one
future and possibly fruitful line of
investigation into the characteristics
of spatial schemata.

NOTES

(1) See, for example: Terence Lee,
"Psychology and Living Space," Transactions of the Bartlett Society, Vol.
3 (1966), pp. 11-36; "The Psychology
of Spatial Orientation," Architectural
Association Quarterly, Vol. 1, No. 3,
(1969), pp. 11-15. In the geographic
literature, the following is also useful: David Stea, "The Measurement of
Mental Maps: An Experimental Model
for Studying Conceptual Spaces," in
Kevin R. Cox and Reginald G. Golledge
(eds.), Behavioral Problems in Geography: A Symposium (Northwestern
University, Department of Geography,
Studies in Geography, No. 17, 1969).

(2) Lee (1969), op. cit., p. 12.

(3) A basic reference here is: Peter
R. Gould, "Mental Maps," Michigan Inter
University Community of Mathematical
Geographers, Discussion Paper No. 9
(1966).

(4) Tobler, Waldo R., "Geographic Area
and Map Projections," Geographical
Review, Vol. 53 (1963), pp. 59-78; see
Figure 1 for the "New Yorkers Idea of
the United States of America."

(5) Orleans, Peter, "Urban Experimentation and Urban Sociology," in
Science Engineering and the City
(Washington, D.C.: National Academy
of Sciences, Publication 1498, 1967).

(6) See for example: Robert Hefner,
Sheldon G. Levy, and H. Lester Warner,
"A Survey of Internationally Relevant
Attitudes and Behavior," Peace Research
Society (International), Papers, Vol. 7
(1967), pp. 139-150; John P. Robinson
and Robert Hefner, "Perceptual Maps of
the World," Public Opinion Quarterly,
Vol. 32 (Summer, 1968), pp. 273-280;
and John P. Robinson and Robert Hefner,
"Multidimensional Difference in Public
and Academic Perceptions of Nations,"
Journal of Personality and Social
Psychology, Vol. 7, No. 3, (1967),
pp. 251-259.

(7) Hefner, Levy and Warner, op. cit.
p. 141.

(8) Gould, op. cit.

(9) Taaffe, Edward J., "The Urban
Hierarchy: An Air Passenger Defini-
tion," Economic Geography, Vol. 38,
No. 1, (1962), pp. 1-14.

(10) See Peter R. Gould and Rodney
White,""The Geographical Space Prefer-
ences of British School Leavers,"
Regional Studies, Vol. 2 (1968).

The Role of Location Processing in the Perception of the Environment

by Stephen Kaplan

Department of Psychology, University of Michigan

Abstract

Evolutionary considerations, anomalies in visual perception, and physiological and anatomical data provide support for the two-visual system hypothesis. In addition to the well-documented contour-processing system, there is also a largely independent location processing system that codes size, motion, number, and texture, as well as locus. This system appears to be flexible, parallel, high in capacity and unobtrusive in its operation. It is essentially analog, reflecting its suitability for the guidance of locomotion over a continuously varying terrain. A caution is raised concerning the excessive reliance on slides, on verbal report, and on concepts based solely on alphanumeric data.

The purpose of this paper is to provide some cautions and some guidelines for students of visual perception working at the psychology/environment interface. More specifically, this paper deals with recent developments that have led to a broadened conception of the processing of visual information, a critical link in how man perceives and thinks about his environment.

A pivotal concept in the modern psychology of perception is that of contour. Sharp edges, borders, and lines are prominent features of the visual world. Further, there is considerable evidence that single cells in the visual cortex respond to different kinds of contour information (Hubel & Wiesel, 1962). For example, some cells may be most sensitive to horizontal lines, some to lines at a 45° angle, and so on. Based on the pervasiveness of contour and the evidence for a physiological mechanism that codes contour into the activity of conveniently discrete elements, it is hardly surprising that some psychologists have concluded that the perception of contour is visual perception (e.g., cf. Thompson, 1969).

There are, however, a number of grounds for doubting this identity. First, there is the perspective provided by evolutionary considerations. Many of the aspects of the visual world that appear most essential to survival in a difficult and dangerous world seem quite far removed from contour. Secondly, there are a

number of phenomena of visual perception that appear to be analog in nature, and are difficult to interpret along the essentially digital lines of the contour processing system.

The evolutionary perspective, although not widely held among psychologists, is not unfamiliar to students of psychology and environment (e.g., Shepard, 1966; Sommer, 1969; Hall, 1966; Carroll, 1970; Griffin, 1969). In considering the sorts of visual stimuli important to survival, it is useful to remember that at one point in man's prehistory his line was probably represented by a small, ground-dwelling undifferentiated mammal (Diamond & Hall, 1969). For such an animal, locus would seem to be of the greatest importance.

Motion, that is, a change in locus, appears to be another essential kind of stimulus information. Stimuli that move demand immediate attention. Besides motion in a plane, motion toward, called looming by Gibson (1969), and motion away appear critical. What one does with respect to a moving stimulus is, in turn, largely a function of size. Additional information a small animal might find helpful includes some rough indication of form and a notion of how many objects are present. Finally, texture, as the most general and pervasive guide to depth (Gibson, 1946), would be a useful addition to any animal concerned with making his way over uneven terrain.

As with the evolutionary considerations, several perceptual phenomena are also difficult to handle on the basis of contour alone. Figural aftereffects provide a striking example of a distortion of locus without a corresponding distortion of the figures in question. For example, after prolonged inspection of a pattern made of two adjacent squares and two distant squares, a pattern of four evenly spaced squares appears askew. The squares on the same side as the close together inspection squares appear far apart; likewise the squares on the side of the far apart inspection squares appear close together (Kohler & Wallach, 1944). The squares in this example tend to retain their crisp contours; the primary distortion is one of locus.

The strange behavior of solid figures in the fixed retinal image paradigm is another case in point. While portions of outline figures disappear in a discrete, all-or-none fashion, a solid figure appears to crumble (Heckenmueller, 1965). This clearly suggests that surface is coded differently from contour. (Surface here is assumed to be a location-like concept related to both size and texture.) Blurred images, that is, images with impoverished contours, likewise behave in an anomalous fashion (Fry & Robertson, 1935).

It thus appears that both adaptively crucial kinds of information and rather out-of-the-way perceptual anomalies point to the indispensability of the concept of location. Location is characterized by continuity; it is essentially an analog concept. Contour, by contrast, is largely digital; a given element may code the presence of a horizontal line while its neighbor may be concerned with some quite different feature.

These sorts of data suggest a fairly simple mechanism. Consider a two-dimensional array of elements in the brain corresponding point by point with the retina (the familiar topological representation of the gestalt visual brain). In such a system, locus might be coded by the peak of activity in the matrix of elements. (The point of maximal excitation concept is a familiar one in discussions of figural aftereffects and apparent movement, cf. Osgood, 1953.) Size would then be coded by the spread of activity about this point. Motion, of course, would be represented by a change in locus. Motion toward would be progressive increment in size, and motion away, a progressive diminution in size. Rough form and a crude notion of the number of objects present both appear to depend on the distribution of activity in the matrix. Unconnected loci could code number up to some limit (in humans the numbers of objects directly perceived, i.e., without counting, is approximately five -- providing no particular strain on the matrix interpretation). Rough form would arise from the configuration of connected loci, and from their sizes.

This proposed mechanism may at first glance appear simply to push the problem one step back, and in a sense this is true. The translation of the various patterns of excitation of matrix elements into reliable codes may in large part depend on learning. The hypothesized mechanisms for this learning are very general (that is, they are equally pertinent to the broad problems of pattern recognition) but their complexity puts them beyond the scope of this paper. In brief, a distance-biased random net composed of a large number of elements provides a structure in which any class of excitation patterns will tend to result in peak activity in a restricted set of elements "deeper" in the system (i.e., farther

from the sensory interface). This convergence on a few elements that come to represent the class of events in question is discussed in greater detail in Kaplan (1970). Quite independent of the particular learning patterns involved, it appears that the location system might be considerably more flexible than the largely prewired contour system.

The conception of location processing discussed here was developed (some two years ago) solely on the basis of psychological data, and in fact flew in the face of most physiological data known to the author. There was, however, supportive physiological data in the literature at that time and more has been forthcoming (e.g., Schneider, 1969). This physiological research has centered around a primitive visual center, the superior colliculus. This tegmental visual system is the major processing region for vision in some animals and still functions in primates, including humans (Trevarthen, 1968, 1969). It is known to be related to the control of head and eye movements. It has rather undiscriminating receptive fields. That is, any element in this system is excited by a stimulus in the appropriate retinal region, quite independent of details of its form. [It should be pointed out that the elements in the tegmental system in cats are highly motion sensitive; the majority of them not only code motion but motion in a particular direction (Sterling & Wickelgren, 1969). Primate data, while similar in most respects, does not show this dependence on motion (Wurtz, 1970).] Thus, the available evidence is consistent with the simple matrix view of location processing.

Additional physiological evidence supports the further hypothesis that this system codes texture as well. For example, in cats the receptive fields vary in visual angle from 5° to 50° (Sprague et al., 1968). This means that different elements would be firing in the presence of fine as opposed to coarse texture.

Thus a convergence of evidence from a variety of sources supports the hypothesis of an at least partially independent location processing system. While there is a great deal yet to be learned about this system, a certain basic set of properties is beginning to emerge. This system appears to be uniquely important to those interested in how man experiences and builds maps of his visual world. It also appears to operate by rules quite different from those characteristic of the extensively studied contour-processing system.

The location processing system appears to be important in the directing of attention. Not only does it play a central role in the orientation of head and eyes, it also appears to have all the properties required for Neisser's (1967) pre-attentive process, that is, for the initial aspect of visual perception that precedes the construction or hypothesis-testing stage. Neisser argues for a system that is rather crude, and highly parallel; the location system appears ideally suited to this role.

In addition to its attentive (or "pre-attentive") function, this system is intimately concerned with locomotion in space (Held, 1970). Trevarthen (1968) refers to this component of visual information processing as "ambient vision." Certainly the wide visual angle characteristic of the system, its sensitivity to texture, and its capacity to process a continuous surface make it ideal for this function.

Since the system described here is necessarily a very primitive one, existing in comparatively simple animals, one is tempted to conjecture that it might operate largely outside the realm of consciousness, even in more complex organisms that have presumably developed some degree of consciousness. Indeed, as Trevarthen (1968) pointed out, traversing an uneven terrain appears in humans to be a reasonably efficient yet largely unconscious process. Thus it is possible that humans may have feelings about stimuli and may even be able to act on the basis of such stimulus information without being aware of taking in the information in question. In fact, the relative neglect of location processing by psychologists may be in part due to this very unobtrusiveness.

Another special feature of this system is its flexibility. The proposed matrix model depends heavily on learning for the establishment of coding patterns, and the available data are in line with this hypothesis. Held (1970) points out that studies of relearning with distorting lenses strongly support the distinction between the two systems. Subjects learn to localize effectively under such conditions while still experiencing contour distortion, suggesting the superior flexibility of the location system as well as the validity of the distinction.

Further information about the unique properties of the location system comes from research with dot patterns. As Held points out, dot patterns, in failing to define a contour, must be handled in terms of location. He finds illusions are perceived differently when defined by dots instead of contours, and further, that the act of pointing on the part of the subject yields data like that produced by dot stimuli (whether the stimuli are in fact contours or dots). A study requiring the location of dots in a visual array was carried out by Hill (1969). Since the traditional 7±2 channel capacity limitation found with alphanumeric visual stimuli has not been found with tactile patterns, Hill used dots to translate the tactile pattern into the visual mode. This visual task, like the tactile one, failed to show the channel capacity ceiling. Pachella (1970) indicates that in addition to

confirming this result, he has found that the usual steady increase in performance as a function of increasing duration fails to hold for dot patterns.

The evidence, fragmentary as it is, seems to point clearly to a high capacity, highly parallel, highly flexible, and highly unobtrusive system. It appears also to be concerned, quite literally, with getting along in the world.

The existence of such a system has numerous implications, both theoretical and practical. We have become deeply concerned with how man experiences his environment; with his reactions to buildings and cities, to parks and to wilderness. In this research we cannot with confidence substitute slides for space. The architect's model serves as a paradigm of the substitution of contour information for location information. Several studies have suggested that the planner's view of a city is markedly different from the experience of those who live there. Man may have strong preferences for certain spatial configurations. We must not assume that the individual's failure to mention some feature indicates that it plays no role. In matters of space intuitive and nonverbal inference patterns cannot be ignored.

There is a growing interest in the way man builds maps of the world in his head. In understanding this process we should consider cautiously information processing rules based on studies of alphanumeric visual material. It appears that not only the experience of space but also the process of locomotion itself are dependent upon a system which has received little study and which appears to operate by its own rules.

References

Carroll, J. W. Man and animal: Changing concepts. Fish and Wildlife Service, US Dept. of Interior. 1970.

Diamond, I. T. & Hall, W. C. Evolution of neocortex. Science, 1969, 164, 251-262.

Fry, G. A. & Robertson, V. M. The physiological basis of the periodic merging of area into background. American Journal of Psychology, 1935, 47, 644-655.

Gibson, E. J. Principles of perceptual learning. N.Y.: Appleton-Century-Crofts, 1969.

Gibson, J. J. Perception of distance and space in the open air. AAF program report #7, 1946. Reprinted in D. C. Beardslee & M. Wertheimer (Eds.) Readings in perception Princeton, N.J.: Van Nostrand, 1958.

Griffin, R. M. Jr. Ethological concepts for planning. Journal of the American Institute of Planners, 1969, 35, 54-60.

Hall, E. T. The hidden dimension. Garden City; N.Y.: Doubleday, 1966.

Heckenmueller, E. G. Stabilization of the retinal image: A review of method, effects, and theory. Psychological Bulletin, 1965,

63, 157-169.

Held, R. Two modes of processing spatially distributed visual stimulation. In F. O. Schmitt (Ed.) The neurosciences: Second study program. N.Y.: Rockefeller University Press. In press.

Hill, J. W. Preliminary experiments for comparing the perception of simultaneous and sequentially presented tactile and visual point stimuli. Unpublished manuscript, Stanford Research Institute, 1969.

Hubel, D. H. & Wiesel, T. N. Receptive fields, binocular interaction and functional architecture in the cat's visual cortex. Journal Physiology, London, 1962, 160, 106-154.

Kaplan, S. Perception and thought: Getting along in a difficult and complex world. Unpublished manuscript, University of Michigan. 1970.

Kohler, W. & Wallach, H. Figural aftereffects. Proceedings of the American Philosophical Society, 1944, 88, 269-357.

Neisser, U. Cognitive psychology. N.Y.: Appleton-Century-Crofts, 1967.

Osgood, C. E. Method and theory in experimental psychology. N.Y.: Oxford, 1953.

Pachella, R. G. Personal communication. 1970.

Schneider, G. E. Two visual systems. Science, 1969, 163, 895-902.

Shepard, P. Man in the landscape. N.Y.: Knopf. 1966.

Sommer, R. Personal space: The behavioral basis of design. Englewood Cliffs, N.J.: Prentice-Hall. 1969.

Sprague, J. M., Marchiafava, P. L., & Rizzolatti, G. Unit responses to visual stimuli in the superior colliculus of the unanesthetized, midpontine cat. Archives Italiennes de Biologie, 1968, 106, 169-193.

Sterling, P. & Wickelgren, B. G. Visual receptive fields in the superior colliculus of the cat. Journal of Neurophysiology, 1969, 32, 1-15.

Thompson, R. F. Neurophysiology and thought: The neural substrates of thinking. In J. F. Voss (Ed.) Approaches to thought. Columbus, O.: Merrill. 1969.

Trevarthen, C. B. Two mechanisms of vision in primates. Psychologische Forschung, 1968, 31, 299-337.

Trevarthen, C. B. Experimental evidence for a brain-stem contribution to visual perception in man. Presented at Conference on subcortical visual systems. MIT, June, 1969.

Wurtz, R. H. Personal communication. 1970.

[1]A far-ranging discussion of this topic with Dr. Richard Held and the helpful comments on an earlier draft by Dr. Gerald E. Schneider are greatly appreciated.

Distance Concepts of Urban Residents

by Robert Allen Lowery

CONSAD Research Corporation, Pittsburgh, Pennsylvania

Abstract

An interview procedure was devised to enable the scaling of distances to facilities as judged by urban residents. Scaling parameters were then analyzed in regard to socio-economic characteristics of the residents. The facilities chosen were examples of each of ten types, including parks, bus stops, schools, etc. Each of 138 subjects chose an example familiar to him of each type. Items were presented in a paired comparison format and subjects recorded their judgments on simple-line diagrams. Results suggested that residents may have different distance judgment functions for different types of facilities, but this evidence was not convincing. Driver status and sex were identified as factors influencing judgment behavior.

Introduction

The purpose of this paper is to present an analysis of some socio-economic characteristics of urban residents as related to their spatial behavior. In the present paper, the activity called spatial behavior includes both judgments of distances, as well as actual trips. In other words, it includes any behavior, subjective or overt, which is pertinent to, or influenced by, physical distances and relative physical distances among locations. The objective of the study reported here was to record subjective spatial behavior as judgments of physical distances in the urban environment.

More specifically, the report deals with people's responses to ten types of public service facilities: shopping centers; bus stops; libraries; terminals for trains, airplanes or buses; schools; parks; public parking lots or garages; expressway interchanges; post offices; and hospitals. These ten types were selected because of the variety of uses they represent and because of their public service nature. Spatial behavior related to distances to these types of facilities was hypothesized to vary in relation to people's socio-economic characteristics. Several methodological maneuvers were necessary to test this hypothesis. In particular, attention was directed toward the problem of defining subjective distance scales, and toward the problem of separating the effects of the facilities themselves on judgments from the effects of socio-economic characteristics.

Procedure

In order to measure physical distances in the present study, facilities and residences were located, using a latitude-longitude scale, and kilometer distances between residences and facilities were calculated. These physical distances were converted to natural logarithms to make them compatible with data obtained from the spatial behavior-measuring procedure. The 138 subjects in the study were selected by resurveying one part of an urbanized area which had been partitioned and sampled for a previous study. The data were obtained in a house-to-house interview procedure. The neighborhoods in which the subjects lived were widely dispersed, but all were within the city limits of Baltimore, Maryland. The median annual household income of the sample was about $6,300.

Each subject named an example of each of ten types of facilities. Together they named 500 different facilities and defined their locations for later measurement by the latitude-longitude scale.

The smallest physical distance obtained, 0.01 kilometers, was between a subject's home and a bus stop, but various other facilities named, including post offices and an expressway interchange, were found less than 0.2 kilometers from subjects' homes. The largest distance was a hospital 23.94 kilometers from the home of the subject who named it. Thus, the logarithmic scale for kilometer distances ranged from -4.60517 to 3.13549. In the present study, values on this transformed scale are referred to as log kilometers.

Before further analyzing these log distance measures, it is useful to consider the comparable measuring procedure for distance judgments, i.e., the measuring procedure for spatial behavior. In the present study, an interview procedure was designed for obtaining the behavioral measures; the physical distances were measured later. The interviewer asked the subject to name, for each type of facility, an example which he had recently visited or with which he was familiar. He then asked the subject to define the facility locations by street or block.

After the interviewer obtained the name and location for an example of each of the ten facility types, the subject was presented with a series of distance judgments diagrams on which he marked lines to indicate distances. Horizontal lines were presented in pairs, one as a standard line and the other as an unknown distance. Each line was labeled with a type of facility, each type being paired with each other type once. Since the subjects made judgments of the ratio of two lines, the responses were analyzed as ratios of the length of the line the subject marked, divided by the length of the standard line. The facilities were paired in a conventional paired comparisons format for one presentation of each pair. This type of format produced a symmetric matrix of ratio judgments in which half the cells were filled with inverses of the values in the diagonally opposite cells. Values in the main diagonal were set at 1.00. (1)

Although the responses were in the form of ratios, the range and distribution of the ratios made it reasonable to transform them to natural logarithms and to use their log's as the basis for analysis. For a set of nine

values plus the arbitrary 1.00, all having one facility in common, a least squares estimate of the log of the judged distance is the mean of the logs of the ten values. These means were calculated, resulting in one such value for each facility for each person. These ten values for each subject are called subjective scale values. (2)

For all ten facility types, the judgment ratios most commonly occurring were between 0.01 and 3.05, giving logarithms of about -4.1 to +1.1. A few subjects tended to make extreme judgments, and a few ratios were as high as 14.8 ($\log_e 14.8 = 2.70136$). For both log kilometer and subjective scales, the extremely high values were rare. In summary, the important principles of the physical distance and behavioral measuring procedures were:

1. The interview judgments consisted of a set of judgment ratios which yielded a subjective scale of ten values for each subject.

2. The physical distance measurements yielded a $\log_e$ kilometer scale with range similar to that of the behavioral measurements.

As a second part of the interview in which the facility locations and the distance judgments were recorded, the respondent was asked several questions about his household conditions. The hypothesis which suggested these questions was, as mentioned earlier, that spatial behavior varied according to the experience and household conditions of the subject. This rather general hypothesis suggests several directions for the data analysis to proceed, only two of which will be discussed in this paper.

Analysis

The first step of analysis to be discussed dealt with the characteristics of the subjects' judgments in relation to the physical distances. This analysis includes the results of the scaling procedure applied to the data for the various types of facilities. The second type of analysis deals with the relation between psychophysical data and household characteristics.

Judgments and Trips

Some analysis of the physical distance data itself is useful in order to understand the trip behavior related to the judgments the subjects made. The trips reported were to facilities with which the subjects were familiar or which they had recently visited. Except for this restriction, subjects were allowed extensive freedom in specifying an example for each type of facility. The 138 subjects named 82 schools and 86 parking lots and garages. There were 39 parks and 40 expressway interchanges named, and 30 libraries and 31 post offices. In other words, some similarities appeared in the numbers of different examples of facilities that were named.

These similarities raised two questions. First, were there similarities in the distances that people traveled for the facilities that were named with equal frequency? Second, were there similarities in the way the distances to these facilities were judged?

In order to answer the first question, average distances traveled to each facility type were compared with frequencies. In the case of two of the pairs of facility types which were named with about the same frequency, the average distance traveled to each was substantially different. Subjects traveled about 1.7 kilometers further for expressway interchanges and garages than they did for parks and schools. In the case of the third pair, libraries and post offices, the distances traveled were about the same. (See Table 1.)

In order to answer the second question, the scale values for judgments, as well as physical distances, were used. Each subject interviewed had been measured on each of ten facilities and each facility was connected to a physical distance from the subject's home to it. Thus, there were physical distance and behavior scales consisting of ten values each for each subject. Means of these values were used to evaluate both a psychophysical function and error scores for all subjects. Using logarithms in a regression formula produces a function of the form,

$$\log Y = a \log X + b,$$

where a represents the regression coefficient or slope and b represents the scale constant

or Y-axis intercept.

Table 1
Number of Facilities of Each Type
Named By All Subjects and Geometric
Mean of Distances from Homes

Type	Number	Kilometers*
Shopping center	64	1.64
Bus stop	109	0.57
Library	30	1.15
Terminal	9	5.28
School	82	0.96
Park	39	1.79
Parking garage	86	2.72
Expressway int.	40	3.49
Post office	31	1.17
Hospital	21	2.54
Total	511	21.31

*This is the geometric mean of the distances to facilities named from the homes of 138 subjects. In other words, the distances from each subject's home to the specific facility named were measured and the sum of their logarithms was divided by 138.

The linear function reflects an exponential curve relationship of the form,

$$Y = bX^a + e$$

in the original data, where e represents a residual. (3)

The apparent linearity of the graph of this function (See Figure 1) suggested that subjects had judged the facilities in a similar manner, presumably according to a common subjective rule. Nevertheless, the range of the exponents (regression coefficients) was rather broad. A few subjects showed exponents that were bizarre, presumably because of misunderstanding or disregarding the interview instructions (See Table 2).

Table 2
Exponent Values

	a < 0.0	0.0 < a < 1.0	1.0 < a
Number of subjects	4	129	5

Figure 1
Means of Scale Values for Ten Facilities
(each point represents 138 subjects)

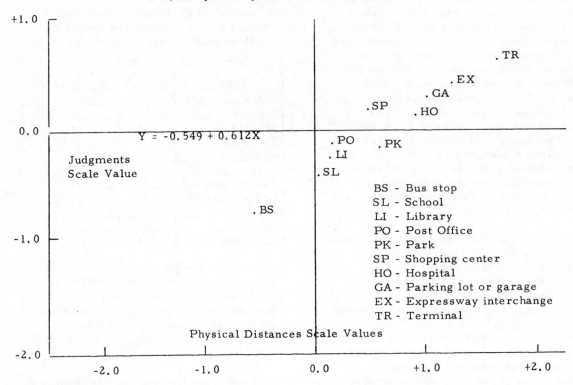

More information on differences among facility types was obtained by calculating separate regression functions for each facility. In other words, each subject's physical distance and judgment scales were divided into ten pairs of values, and a regression equation was calculated for each facility type using the scale values for that type.

In looking at the regression analysis for each facility type, a useful idea is that a single "average" person produced all the scales, judging all the facilities from all of his multiple residences. Thus, it is reasonable to look at how his judgments changed for different facility types. His exponents (or regression coefficients) varied somewhat, between 0.26 and 0.39 for seven facilities, and decreased toward zero for bus stops, libraries, and post offices; all three of these also were associated with small physical distances. Schools, however, while associated with the second smallest mean log physical distance, had a relatively high exponent of 0.3413.

One way to look at these relationships

is to define groups of facility types having similar values, as shown in Table 3.

Bus stops and libraries are characterized by short physical distances and low regression coefficients. Of these two, bus stops showed a high standard error of regression while libraries showed a low value for this parameter. In other words, short physical distances were judged in a slightly different way than were long ones, but even for some long distances, especially those associated with expressway interchanges, there were large errors from the regression line.

In addition to libraries, post offices and hospitals showed low regression errors. These three types are dissimilar in physical distances, but they do happen to be the lowest three in variability of judgment scale points, i.e., the distribution of subjective scale values about the mean for each facility was narrow. Perhaps the narrow distribution shows a cultural stereotype: no matter where these facilities are, everyone judges them at about the same distance.

Table 3
Facility Groups

Regression Coefficient (exponent)		
0.06 - 0.25 bus stop library post office	0.25 - 0.35 terminal school expressway interchange	0.35 - 0.40 shopping center park parking garage
Standard Error		
0.30 - 0.40 library post office hospital	0.40 - 0.45 shopping center terminal parking garage park	0.45 - 0.55 school expressway interchange bus stop
Log_e Kilometer Distance		
-0.05 - 0.15 bus stop school library	0.15 - 1.0 post office shopping center park hospital	1.0 - 1.7 parking garage expressway interchange terminal

Schools, expressway interchanges, and bus stops have the three highest Y-error values. Again, these three are not similar in their physical distance values. Thus, looking at the extreme values for the facility regression errors suggests that the factors involved in distance judgment behavior, including physical distance itself, have different effects on judgments within different ranges of distances and for different types of facilities.

Socio-Economic Variables

Data were obtained in the interviews not only for distance judgments but also for a series of socio-economic or household condition variables. Two of these were dichotomous: driving status and sex, and were analyzed by t tests. Nine others were treated as continuous variables using product moment correlation formulas.

The two dichotomous household variables showed strong relations to several psychophysical variables. In addition, some of the variables which did not show significant t values have significant interpretations.

Specifically, no differences appeared in real distances traveled or standard deviations of real distances traveled. Drivers, non-drivers, men, and women all traveled about the same mean number of kilometers to facilities, and they all showed about the same variability in the distances they traveled.

For drivers and non-drivers, the regression coefficient ($p < 0.005$) and the regression line errors ($p < 0.025$) were both significantly different, rather strong evidence of a completely different way of thinking about distances (See Table 4). For drivers, the mean regression coefficient and the mean regression line errors were both larger than they were for non-drivers. There is no simple way to translate these results into statements about behavior, but there are some tentative interpretations. Drivers have a significantly different exponent for their distance judgment function, and they make sloppy or careless mistakes. Or, drivers log kilometer distances resemble more closely a linear function of log kilometer distances, but there is also more error in their judgments. Non-drivers have a lower exponent for their distance function, but their judgments conform more closely to the derived function or judgment rule. How far away a person thinks a place is may or may not be related to where it really is, but non-drivers are less variable about where they think it is than drivers are.

Men and women are alike on their psychophysical functions but differ on regression line errors ($p < 0.005$). Both sexes have similar ideas of the ordering or interrelation of distances but men are always more confused than women. When the subjects are divided into drivers and non-drivers and sex differences are tested in each sub-group, these differences tend to fade away. The driver/non-driver distinction is undoubtedly the more important of the two two-valued variables. In looking at the actual values, female non-drivers had the lowest regression line errors of all four groups, while male non-drivers had the highest. Male drivers had the highest regression coefficient and male non-drivers the lowest.

Since the driving status variable shows the major strong effect on distance judgments, a possible conclusion is that whether a person is a driver determines the distances he travels to facilities. It should be noted, however, that the mean for 138 subjects of all log kilometer distances scale is 0.4982, which represents the mean of 1,380 values. The standard deviation of the scale means is 0.9729, suggesting wide variability among individuals, all of which cannot be attributed to a single binary variable.

Each of nine other household variables for each subject was paired with physical distance and regression parameters. The nine household variables measured age, education, and family composition. Of about 90 correlation coefficients calculated, none exceeded 0.30. For the small number of variables available, multiple regression procedures were not considered appropriate.

sented later for separate facility types raise some doubts. These analyses showed a wide range of exponents for different types of facilities. No concept or theory was found to account for the way in which the exponents varied.

Investigations of exponents for various sensory modalities have noted the dispersion of these exponents, and have suggested that a given exponent is characteristic of, and reasonably constant for, a given modality such as taste, touch, or hearing. (4) The work on specifying the modality exponents has taken place in a larger context of investigation of, and controversy about, the psychophysical law. This larger context will be ignored here, but it is important to consider the implications of the notion of modality constants.

Table 4
Results of T Tests

	Male	Female	Drivers	Non-Drivers
Number of Subjects	45	93	63	75
Regression coefficient T, p	0.4780 -0.3239	0.49551 .40	0.5568 -3.1925	0.3834 .005
Y - intercept T, p	-0.1718 -0.9799	-0.2510 .20	-0.3034 2.4431	-0.1632 .01
Y - axis errors (residuals) T, p	0.4251 -2.7316	0.3111 .005	0.3845 -1.9814	0.3178 .025
	(All values are means of logarithms)	(All values are means of logarithms)	(All values are means of logarithms)	(All values are means of logarithms)

Discussion

There are two points of discussion which arise in light of the above mixed results. They are the psychophysical problem of motivational bias, and the geographic problem of neighborhood locations.

Constant Exponents and Motivational Bias

Although the roughly linear plot of logarithms in Figure 1 is interpreted to mean a single psychophysical function exists for urban distance concepts, the analyses pre-

The range of these constants is from less than 0.1 for smell up to 3.5 for electric shock. Variability of the constant for any given modality has been noted, but no theory has sought to incorporate such variability, which is sometimes attributed to experimental conditions. Similarly, individual subject departures from the function determined for a group have been attributed to temporary conditions. These temporary conditions are sometimes called motivational bias, but are rarely considered as constant factors in perception, since constant factors are presumably all reflected in the exponent.

Experiments on emotional involvement and distance to cities by Bratfisch(5) have suggested that some variability in exponents characterizes the relation between subjective and objective distances. Using distances among European and Asian cities, he found exponents ranging from 0.58 to 1.07. Without stating any specific hypotheses, he suggests that further investigation deal with concepts such as emotional involvement, estimated importance, and interest. These concepts are seen as influencing a person's concepts of subjective distance, but their relation to objective or physical distance remains obscure.

Thus, these studies of subjective distance conclude that a link between subjective or judged distance and other subjective conditions exists, but that there is no such link between subjective distance and physical distance. It may be that if distances within one city had been used as stimuli, an association among all three types of concepts would have been found. In any event, variability in the exponent of the psychophysical functions suggests that substantial differences in subjective judgment rules exist, whether because of past experience and other motivational factors or because of some discontinuous feature in the stimuli.

Two points are important for further work on this tangle of problems. One point is that the total variability in exponents, while substantial enough to need explanation, is not substantial enough to submit conveniently to experimental investigation. In other words, there really is a lot of variability due to experimental effects. A diverse set of variables for investigation of the associations among the three phenomena is needed.

Second, it is eminently desirable that connections between distance judgments and socio-economic characteristics be established, without intervening variables, such as interest or emotional involvement, intriguing as these may be. For those who are faced with development and investment decisions, connecting distances likely to be traveled with available socio-economic features is much more useful than knowing that emotional involvement is an important but unknown factor.

Neighborhood Choices

The second discussion point deals with the relation between distance concepts and the geographic concept of neighborhoods. One of the most persistent concepts in analyses of urban space has been the notion that neighborhoods exist. Although census tracts and transportation districts have been invented, the neighborhood as a unit of urban space continues to be popular, perhaps because the term continues to show up in interviews and popular writing about cities. (6)

One of the more disturbing aspects of the concept is that it seems to have very concrete meanings to people who use it as an everyday, household term. Commonly heard phrases such as: "You can play outside, but don't go out of the neighborhood," "Well, there goes the neighborhood," "Those vandals were from outside our neighborhood," and others, have continued to frustrate social scientists who wish to understand people's concepts of distances, boundaries, and space. Analyses of neighborhood changes accompanying renewal or transportation projects have provided some insight into the meaning of neighborhood, but only in relation to these disruptive events.

Lynch(7) originated a direct approach to measurement of the concept by testing graphs or pictorial interview techniques which partly identified important features or "cues" associated with neighborhood labels, such as "Back Bay" and "Scolley Square." Studies of the type conducted by Lynch have suffered from the lack of measurement techniques to apply to spatial behavior. Although the present study contributes little to neighborhood theory, it does provide some suggestions as to how further neighborhood content or area research might be directed.

In the plot of log kilometer versus judgment scale values (Figure 1), five facility types fall into a lower group, below the X-axis in this figure, and these five are types which could commonly be considered desirable neighborhood facilities: bus stops, schools, libraries, post offices, and parks. All have been judged closer to subjects' homes than they really are, and parks in particular have been wildly exaggerated in a closer direction. Perhaps the X-axis on this graph represents a neighborhood boundary for facility types. The facilities within the neighborhood (below the X-axis) are judged in such a way that their plot suggests a downward convex curve. The facilities above the X-axis plot on any of two or three possible curves.

Another feature of the five closest-judged facility types is their common structural nature. Three are commonly monolithic structures of striking architectural design and four are frequently equipped with flagpoles. In agreement with the importance of cues or special features noted by Lynch, perhaps these types of facilities contribute to a commonly held concept of neighborhood.

There is, however, little consistency in the judgment errors associated with these five types. Bus stops and schools are among the most confusedly judged, while libraries and post offices are judged precisely. In other words, there is reasonable accuracy in the ordering and in the relative distances of the five types, but much variation in the consistency or dispersion of the judgments for each type. These differences are difficult to translate into conventional concepts, but they suggest a certain complexity of connections between people's distance judgments and the places they go.

Notes

(1) Further description of the paired comparisons technique can be found in Henry David, The Method of Paired Comparisons, New York, Hafner Publishing Company, 1963; and Lennart Sjoberg, "A Study of Four Methods of Scaling Paired Comparisons Data," Scandinavian Journal of Psychology, 6, 1965, pp. 173-185.

(2) For a more detailed description of this scaling procedure and a proof of the least squares estimate, see Warren Torgerson, Theory and Methods of Scaling, New York, John Wiley, 1958, pp. 108-111.

(3) The use of psychophysical functions and their exponents is described in various reference works, including Duncan Luce, Robert Bush, and Eugene Galanter, editors, Handbook of Mathematical Psychology, New York, John Wiley, 1963,

pp. 273-293.

(4) Two reviews of psychophysical functions for various modalities are: S. S. Stevens and Eugene Galanter, "Ratio Scales and Category Scales for a Dozen Perceptual Continua," Journal of Experimental Psychology, 1957, 54, pp. 377-411; and Duncan Luce, Robert Bush, and Eugene Galanter, editors, Handbook of Mathematical Psychology, New York, John Wiley, 1963, p. 277.

(5) Oswald Bratfisch, "A Further Study of the Relation Between Subjective Distance and Emotional Involvement," Reports from the Psychological Laboratories, The University of Stockholm, Stockholm, Number 208, 1966.

(6) A thorough attempt to sort out the neighborhood phenomenon was made by Suzanne Keller, Neighbors, Neighboring and Neighborhoods in Sociological Perspective, Athens, Athens Technological Institute, 1965. Other discussions include Bernard Frieden, The Future of Old Neighborhoods, Cambridge, Massachusetts, Massachusetts Institute of Technology Press, 1964; and Harold Bracey, Neighbours: Subdivision Life in England and the United States, Baton Rouge, Louisiana State University Press, 1964.

(7) Kevin Lynch, The Image of the City, Cambridge, Massachusetts, The Massachusetts Institute of Technology Press, 1960.

Session Three:
Design Education
Chairman: Peter Manning
School of Architecture, Nova Scotia Technical College

It is to be hoped that the major question, "What is Environmental Design?", might be attempted and answered by the EDRA Conference as a whole. In the design education session, more specific questions will be raised:

(1) What should be taught in an education for Environmental Design?
(2) What emphases and orientations are most important?
(3) In this education, what is the place of science and research?
(4) What organizations and methods of teaching might be considered?
(5) What aptitudes and attainments are required of Environmental Design students?
(6) On what bases might students be selected for inclusion in such a program?

The five papers selected for discussion bear upon these questions. One by one, they will be summarized by their authors and discussed by the session, each separate discussion being then extended to the questions raised above. Finally, an attempt will be to establishment overall agreements and disagreements.

Peter Manning

Systems and Environmental Design

by Geoffrey Broadbent

BA (hons) (Arch) (Manc) ARIBA, Head of the Portsmouth School
of Architecture, Portsmouth Polytechnic

Abstract

The paper opens with a discussion of
design processes for general application and
questions their viability with reference to
differences in the range and complexity of
information required for designing in different fields. It refers to the author's
Environmental Design Process as an attempt
to control the flow of information into
architectural design and suggests that this
is a special case of a more general structure within which all the factors relevant
to the design of buildings can be plotted
systemically. The nature, difficulties and
advantages of systems thinking in general are
discussed and the paper concludes with
reference to systems applications in the
architectural education programme at
Portsmouth.

Introduction

The first ten years or so of design
method studies have been concerned largely
with the identification and description of
generalised procedures which could be used by
designers in different fields. That was a
worthwhile aim, but for many reasons - some
of which have been discussed at previous
EDRA meetings - it seems unlikely now to be
realised. Designers in different fields
certainly will share common techniques -
derived from operational research, systems
analysis, cybernetics, information theory,
creativity studies and so on, but the ways
these are put together into coherent design
processes probably will vary from field to
field.

Information for the Designer

The nature, quantity and quality of the
information required in design varies greatly
from one field to another. Architecture and
chemical engineering for instance, have much
in common (see Gregory 1969). Both are
concerned with more or less closed vessels
within which environmental conditions have
to be controlled and with means of trans-
porting people and chemicals between these
vessels. But whereas the same chemicals, in
similar quantities, will behave consistently
in the same environment, the architect knows
that individuals will show quite different
responses to the environment he designs.
They will differ in physiological responses,
not to mention the aesthetic and symbolic
values which, whether he likes it or not,
they bring to the perception of architecture.

Differences, arise then because range
and complexity of the factors which have to
be taken into account vary greatly from one
field to the other. It is virtually
impossible in any design field, but
especially where "human" values have to be
taken into account, to ensure that all the
relevant factors have been considered, interrelated with others in the decision making
process, and allowed to play their appropriate
part in determining the final design.

So most design processes, as distinct
from design techniques resolve themselves
into attempts to control this flow of
information, on the twin assumptions that
if the designer has too little information,
then his decisions will be inadequate,
whilst if he has too much, then he may have
the greatest difficulty in actually reaching
a decision. Some design theorists (e.g.
Alexander 1969) assume that given the same
problem, all designers, eventually, will
collect the same information, knowing .
intuitively when to stop. Others, such as
Drucker (1955), in the field of management,
suggest that no decision-maker ever can
have all the information which theoretically
he needs, that his skill, in fact, lies
essentially in making viable decisions on
the basis of incomplete information. Others
again, such as Jones (1969) have written of
the "information explosion" which afflicts
the designer whose enthusiasm for "briefing"
leads him to pursue every piece of data to

145

its logical conclusion, whilst government agencies, research institutions and the technical press in many countries, provide the raw material for such an explosion by their unremitting production of reports, analyses, working papers, statutory constraints, design check lists, and so on. Best (1969) has analysed three contrasting design processes in terms of information flow - Alexander's, Aalto's and a student's of design method, concluding that in each case, and in different ways, the designer had to effect a homomorphic reduction of the information available before he could cope with it in his designing. Needless to say, the chosen process of reduction itself affected considerably the nature of the final design.

Clearly it will help the designer if some means can be found of helping him decide what information is essential to his task, thus helping him collect precisely what he needs, but at the same time protecting him from the information explosion. A simple check list will not be enough. He needs a rather more comprehensive structure which also tells him what to do with the information he has collected. The Environmental Design Process, which I described to the Portsmouth Symposium of 1967, was intended to be just that, and whilst it has been described in detail elsewhere (Broadbent 1969); the premisses on which it was based are relevant here.

Environmental Design Process

It is based, as one might expect, on a series of assumptions, deriving in this case from the historic origins of architecture as described by Clarke (1952), Mongait (1961) and others in the mammoth hunters' tent and other primitive forms of dwelling. Invariably when man started to build, he put the available materials together to form a shelter, in such a way that the indigenous climate at a particular (and inhospitable) place was modified, thus providing internally conditions within which human activities could be carried out conveniently and in comfort. I assume that architecture still possesses this primary function, although the concept of climate may be extended to include social, political, economic, cultural and aesthetic climates, in addition to the phsyical one, whilst the notion of comfort may be broadened to include other forms of sensory stimulus; certain activities will need a "stimulating" environment. In order to design a building, therefore, one needs three kinds of information; concerning the pattern of activities which it is to house, the available site, and its indigenous climates, and the technology of building available for reconciling the two.

The process goes on to describe how this information can be used in the design of buildings and with certain modifications that has been used quite extensively in architectural education. It allows inexperienced students to design buildings well, because among other things, it forces them to consider interaction between the various kinds of information available to the building designer. But that also suggests a possible limitation; it is directed specifically towards the design of buildings, on particular sites, according to particular sets of functional requirements, so that it may result in a fit between building and activities which is so close that changes in use become difficult. It is intended to lead also towards physical solutions, in terms of built form - and is unlikely therefore, to result in a new pattern of organisation, a vehicle of some kind, a life-support package or some other non-building solution.

These limitations led to the search for a more generalised approach - keeping strictly within the field of environmental design. Markus (1969) suggested the basis for such an approach in the structure for building appraisals which he described to the Portsmouth Symposium, against which certain aspects of the building fabric, and of human demands on that fabric, are plotted in terms of four "systems"; the building system, the environment system, the activity/behaviour system and organisation objectives. This classification is extremely useful, within its defined limits, because it deals in the interactions between different classes of factors, but it leaves out any references to the site, adjacent buildings, climate, and so on, into which the building may be placed, on the grounds that by definition any "system" operates within an "environment" and that the latter therefore needs no further description. There are certain advantages, however, in describing this physical environment so that the pressures it imposes on the building's design can be taken into account. They can be subsumed overall within an environmental system Interactions between people - the client's requirements, the users' needs (physical, social and psychological), can be taken to form a human system. The architect's task, then hinges on the design of a building system which will reconcile and interrelate the two. The overall pattern of interrelations between th ese three systems then can be plotted on a chart (Chart 1).

This chart could be expanded in many ways. Certainly we should analyse each system as Markus does, in cost/benefit terms, and one could elaborate each of the systems further, not to mention the subsystems within them. But before we do this we should test each addition against a simple question: "Does this

CHART I – INTERRELATIONS IN BUILDING DESIGN

ENVIRONMENT SYSTEM		BUILDING SYSTEM		HUMAN SYSTEM	
CULTURAL CONTEXT	PHYSICAL CONTEXT	BUILDING TECHNOLOGY	INTERNAL AMBIENCE	USER REQUIREMENTS	CLIENT OBJECTIVES
	The site as given in terms of:	Modifications of external environment to provide suitable ambience for specified activities by means of:	Provision of physical conditions for performance of activities in terms of:	Provide for specified activities in terms of the following needs:	Return for investment in terms of:
Social	Physical characteristics:	Available resources in terms of:-		Organic:	Prestige
Political	climatic	cash		hunger & thirst	Utility
Economic	geological	materials		respiration	Provision for change
Scientific	topographical	labour/equip.		elimination	Housing of particular
Technological				activity	activities so as to
Historical	Other constraints:	Structural systems	Structural mass	rest	encourage user motiv-
Aesthetic	land use	mass	visible surfaces		ation.
Religious	existing built	planar	space enclosed	Spatial:	Security
	forms	frame		functional	
	traffic patterns			(inc.fittings)	
	legal	Space separating		territorial	
		system:			
		mass		Locational:	
		planar		static	
		frame		dynamic	
		Services system:	Sensory environment	Sensory:	
		environmental	lighting	sight	
		information	sound control	hearing	
		transportation	heating/vent	heat & cold	
				smell	
		Fittings system:		kinaesthetic	
		furnishing		equilibrium	
		equipment			
				Social:	
				privacy	
				contact	

(G H Broadbent, adapted from T L Markus: Building-Environment-Activity-Objectives model)

new factor affect, in any way, the shape of a
room, the size of a window, or any other
aspect of the physical form of the building?"
It is tempting, for instance, to add to the
section on human needs further appetites,
instincts, interests and ideals. But no human
instinct, as far as I know, ever affected,
say the shape of a window; such proliferations
merely confuse the issue rather than clarify-
ing it.

The chart will encourage us to do several
things. It suggests, for instance, that the
Environmental Design Process is only one way
out of the many which are possible, of treating in sequence the various factors which must
be considered in the design of a building.
But provided that one covers all the factors
eventually, and considers the interactions
between them, the order in which one takes
them is immaterial. It seems quite legitimate,
for instance, to <u>start</u> with the building
fabric system, moving later to the human and
environmental systems; this has been the
approach of much of so-called systems building.

Systems Approach

This concern for interactions between a
multiplicity of factors has come to be known
as a system approach, which tends to be con-
fusing, because over the past ten years or so,
the word "systems" has acquired quite different connotations for designers in different
fields. In the United States it is associated
largely with urban systems; problems of land
use, locational analysis, transportation and
so on are generalised in terms of mathematical
models, so that individual cases can be
subject to analysis by computer. We are
familiar with this usage in the UK but we
still use the word more often in the context
of systems building. Another popular usage
is concerned with information systems;
generalised structures against which information can be classified - often for computer
storage and retrieval - whilst there is a
growing, if less specific interest, in the
application of systems thinking to psychological and/or social issues.

Anyone who uses the word "systems",
therefore, is liable to be misunderstood.
Certainly it is a very flexible word; for
which my Oxford dictionary suggests three
major uses. In the first place, it refers
to a complex whole consisting of interconnected things or parts, such as a
planetary system; secondly it may be applied
to a body of organised knowledge, such as the
Hegelian, or some other system in philosophy,
and thirdly, it may indicate a scheme of
classification such as the UDC system, CI/SfB,
a system of notation and so on. So, clearly
the data structures use is legitimate - it
matches the third definition, but one wonders

to some extent about the urban systems and
systems building approaches. It is a matter
of what one means by wholes, parts and inter-
connections. Alexander discusses this usage
in a very sensitive essay (1968) describing
also the concept of "generating systems" -
kits of parts, with the rules for using those
parts, such as language, building systems, or
even the genetic code.

A notable attempt to clarify, once and
for all, the general concept of systems, is
described in General Systems Theory (GST)
by von Bertalanffy, who claims to have
invented it, c. 1935 - 37.

> " Whilst in the past, science tried to
> explain observable phenomena by reducing
> them to an interplay of elementary units
> investigable independently of each other,
> conceptions appear in contemporary science
> that are concerned with what is somewhat
> vaguely termed "wholeness", i.e. problems
> of organisation phenomena not resolvable
> into local events, dynamic interactions
> manifest in the difference of behaviour
> of parts when isolated or in a higher
> configuration, etc., in short, "systems"
> of various orders not understandable by
> investigation of their respective parts
> in isolation. " (von Bertalanffy 1955)

At this level of definition, GST may seem
vague, inconsequential and tentative compared,
say with cybernetics, which has a hard core
of technological achievement to its credit.
Both are concerned with the drawing of
analogies between living organisms and
machines - in both directions - but whereas
cybernetics - according to Weiner (1947), is
concerned specifically with the science of
control and communication, GST takes a much
broader view.

Von Bertalanffy claims that the feedback
systems of cybernetics are merely a special
case, however important, within the overall
range of self-regulating systems which GST
studies. Von Bertalanffy himself was concerned
with the mechanisms by which a given embryo
will develop into a particular kind of
organism, with ways in which the organism
grows to a particular size, maintains itself
as a whole within a constantly changing
environment, seeks out particularly goals
in a purposeful way and so on. This involves
a study of the ways in which information
necessary for the organism's development is
passed into it genetically and used to control
that development.

Distinctions are drawn in general systems
theory, between closed systems and open
systems. The former might consist, say, of
sealed vessels containing certain chemical
processes. In time, such processes will

reach a state of maximum entropy, a state of equilibrium in which no further reactions can take place. No energy is needed to maintain this state, nor will energy be released by it.

An open system, by contrast, will be open to its environment. Material will pass into, through and out of it and energy will be exchanged. But whilst this flow of material and/or energy will vary, according to the state of the environment (an animal may find itself without food for several days) the system as a whole will maintain itself in a state of near-equilibrium. GST has its own version of feed back, known as homeostasis. This concept was first described by Cannon (1939) who was concerned with the ways in which living organisms maintain themselves with reasonable constancy even though they interchange material and energy with the environment - they are "open" to it, whilst their bodily structures are inherently unstable, subject to constant growth, damage and repair. Homeostasis applies particularly to those mechanisms by which material and energy within the organism are maintained within rather fine limits affecting, say internal temperature, osmotic pressure, salt and other chemical concentrations in the blood, posture and so on. None of these remains entirely constant in the living organism which is why Cannon used the word homeostasis instead of equilibrium.

But we are still lacking in a rigorous definition of system; Angyal (1941) takes us some way towards this in considering the differences between a system and a relationship. A relationship, according to Angyal, needs only two members, between which relations can be established in terms of position, size, colour, shape or other observable factors. Compound relationships may also be formed in which A is related to B, B to C and so on. But they still do not form a system unless, overriding all these relationships there is a "whole" of some kind, within which the various elements are distributed and to which each participates by virtue of its position in the whole. For Angyal, a system is a distribution of members within a dimensional domain. The members are not significantly connected except with reference to the whole.

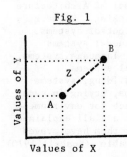

Fig. 1

Values of Y

B

Z

A

Values of X

The crucial differences between a relationship and a system are indicated in Fig.1. in which the linear relationship Z, between A and B, tells us nothing about their position in the system, whereas co-ordinates about X and Y enable us to locate them precisely within the whole.

It is clear then, that most uses of systems are concerned with wholes and with the ways in which a whole is greater than the sum of its parts. Such thinking was called "holistic" by J C Smuts (1961), biologist and one time premier of South Africa, who used this term because he believed that in living organisms at least, it stemmed from some kind of life-force. We may prefer "wholistic" as having fewer connotations of piety, but whatever we choose to call it, holism has its difficulties. Others, long before Smuts, had been concerned with wholes, Aristotle and Hegel, each had tried to establish a philosophy in which the whole of human knowledge would be inter-related in one vast system. Popper (1957) and others have criticised these aims on the grounds such wholes can never be the subject of scientific enquiry. He questions the possibility of considering even a limited concept like "society" in holistic terms. For if each part is related to every other, and some parts will be related to things outside that particular society, then before very long one will be concerned with the whole of human knowledge, which as one tries to encompass any part of it, is constantly changing in other directions. Clearly this is a serious hazard when systems thinking is applied in design; it is liable to trigger a further information explosion.

One further difficulty with systems is that they tend to be hierarchical. Weiss (1969) comments on the reasons for this. The brain, for instance, contains a vast number of cells, estimated at some 10^{15}; many of them die during the course of a lifetime, yet the nervous system continues to function systemically. That suggests an overriding pattern of organisation which, to survive change and decay must be hierarchical. The whole is more than the sum of its parts because of this organisation - if the pattern is disrupted, then the system ceases to work effectively.

This hierarchical view of systems - in which each component has its rightful place and must keep to that place - permeates all systems thinking. It is noticeable for instance, with increasing political concern for problems of conservation, pollution and so on, that the ecologists who have the public ear, want very much to confine man within the ecological niche they have determined for him. Nor is this sinister aspect of systems thinking particularly new. Oponents of the Nazis in Germany used to speak of Der System, a political structure in which everyone knew his place, and kept to that place if he wanted to stay out of trouble.

Reasons for Taking a Systemic View

If the concept of system is fraught with such dangers, why should we want to pursue it? The answer, for environmental design, is that most of design failures arise from our refusal to take a systemic view. Such failures do not worry the designer - he has an easier time of it when he takes a fragmented view of his task - but they do worry the user, who may suffer abominably when parts of the environment which the designer considered separately, begin to interact when the system is brought into use.

A simple example which Musgrove (1966), and I (1971) have discussed, concerns the laboratory experiments which were used to set up daylighting standards in British Schools (Weston 1962). Children were asked to read algebra texts, under laboratory conditions, where it was easy to set up a configuration in which subject and light source were arranged in specific physical relationships. Emission from the light source could be adjusted within very fine limits and the level of illumination at the working plane, or even on the book, could be measured very precisely. The subjects' performance, in terms of reading speed and accuracy could be measured at different levels of illumination, and furthermore, objective measurement could be supported by verbal statements. As a result of all this - and other experiments to establish standards to sky luminance - a daylight factor was devised which ensured that even in the worst case, each pupil could see 2% of the sky from his desk.

Yet to provide the daylight factor thus established, the whole of one wall in each classroom has to be glazed substantially to a height of ten feet. And because one environmental factor - daylighting - was considered in isolation, other problems arise. Heat loss, solar heat gain, glare, distraction, noise penetration and so on are all affected by window size, and this has lead to serious criticisms, by the users, of post-war British schools (Manning 1967).

Analogous problems seem to arise wherever the classical method of physics - the isolation and manipulation of a single variable - is applied to the investigation of man's relationship with his environment. Such experiments essentially are non-systemic.

Other problems arise whenever, say, decisions on a building's structure are made in isolation - without reference to the environmental control properties which different building materials may or may not possess. This accounts for the inherent deficiencies, in terms, of environmental quality of most light-and-dry building systems.

Even greater problems may arise when single aspects of the urban system are isolated and treated analytically. This is particularly true where transportation networks are designed without reference to the social and psychological problems which traffic noise, and other forms of environmental pollution will cause (Pahl 1968).

If we are to avoid this kind or problem, then we shall have to take a systemic view of design. The difficulty, as we have just seen, is that many studies which have the word systems in their title - such as urban systems and systems building, are essentially non-systemic. One truly systemic approach might be to think in cybernetic terms, observing in use the things we have designed, monitoring where they are going wrong and using the information thus obtained as feedback into a new design process. The RIBA Plan of Work (1965) envisages feedback of this kind (Markus calls it feed-forward) as the final stage of the design process. It is fairly common also to describe the whole design process in cybernetic terms, so that every decision is monitored, its effects observed and fed forward to form part of the information on which further decisions are based. Matchett uses such a feedback process in his course on Fundamental Design Method (1969) whilst Beer (1966) has outlined a cybernetic process for the design of a factory.

The intention is admirable, as far as it goes, but such processes, essentially, are concerned with the design of closed systems in the form of finite objects. GST suggests that an open system approach might be even more rewarding. One could then design for changes in use or, better still, design objects which monitor what the user is trying to do, and modify themselves accordingly. One envisages, say, a building consisting of open spaces, lightly enclosed. People arrive and start to do things; the building observes them, decides what they are trying to do and adjusts itself to fit their needs in terms of spatial enclosure, environmental conditions, equipment and so on. Much of this is feasible already from a technological point of view, and possibilities of this kind have prompted a wide-ranging interest in the School of Architecture at Portsmouth in systems thinking. We have looked at computer systems, control systems, cybernetics, eco-systems, general systems theory, information systems, language systems, psychological systems, social systems, systems analysis, systems building, systems engineering and urban systems, trying in each case to assess their relevance for environmental design education. These are all explained in the glossary, and some of them have proved already to be immensely valuable (Russell 1970).

The difficulty is that they tend to group themselves into "hard" applications and "soft" applications, which on the face of it, have very little in common. The former include computer systems, control systems, systems analysis, systems engineering and urban systems -all of which are thoroughly relevant to our courses in architectural technology. They tend to be concerned as one might expect, with the quantifiable aspects of design.

But some of our studies also tend to the "soft" end of the spectrum; this is true of ecology, perhaps the oldest systemic discipline of all, which used to be exclusively a matter of verbal description. Even now the relationships with which ecology is concerned tend to be so complex that mathematical models simply cannot be built for them.

It is not surprising therefore, that whilst the "hardliners" tend to dismiss such descriptive approaches as non-scientific, and essentially trivial the "softliners" reply quite rightly that, much "hardline" thinking as we have seen is essentially non-systemic. Yet both factions are concerned with describing reality in terms of analogies: one uses words, the other uses numbers. Echenique (1970) proposes a 3-dimensional system against which different kinds of model can be classified, and I have suggested elsewhere (Broadbent forthcoming) that all types of model - numerical, verbal, spatial representation and analogue - should be treated with equal respect. Each has its uses, and by demonstrating this within a structure such as Echenique's, it may be possible to effect a reconciliation between the "hardliners" and the "softliners". Certainly we find the full range is essential to a comprehensive design education.

Applications

Students in their undergraduate years at Portsmouth are introduced to a good many systems concepts, the fundamentals of information systems, energy transfer and movement systems, systems building, computing and quantitative methods, ecology, systematic design methods and urban systems. Much of what they are taught results from our exploration at post-graduate and research level and again, a good deal of this originates in a system point of view. We offer a series of options to post-graduate students, one of which, Integrated Building Services, applies certain aspects of systems engineering to the integration of services within the building as a whole.

We refuse to separate out computing, or even systems analysis, as separate disciplines on the grounds that these present a number of quantitative techniques which may, or may not, be useful in design. Our observation

elsewhere suggests that where these are developed outside the context of designing, they tend to "take over" so that there is a progressive failure to solve real design problems. One sets up artificial problems instead because they are amenable to computer analysis, irrespective of whether anyone actually wants to solve such problems. Nevertheless, we have developed - within the context of designing - a number of programmes concerned with pattern generation, the evaluation of building designs using a simple building system, the location of activities within a two dimensional grid (in terms of "distance" and "interrelationship" measures) and various cluster routines. A space-co-ordinate program enables us to apply semantic differential techniques a) in the evaluation of buildings from an aesthetic point of view and b) in the generation of building form, by using semantic space as an analogy for physical space. Current developments are concerned with movement systems, urban systems, economic models, 3-dimensional planning models analogue computer simulation of environmental control systems, and so on. (O'Keefe 1970).

A good deal of our work on information systems has been facilitated by the installation of a microfilm retrieval system, consisting of a 3M processor camera and reader-printer, a card-to-card copies and an Ozalid production printer. These, with ancillary equipment, enable any document up to 1010mm x 760mm to be copied on to 35mm microfilm, mounted in an 80 column punched card and delivered within 40 seconds. This can then be printed out: same size, enlarged or reduced, so that whole areas of teaching and research have changed in character. It solves the inherent dilemma in professional education of whether to teach practical detail, which means that the student has little understanding of the principles on which new developments can be based - or to teach principles, which means that he has no store of practical details when he goes into practice. The microfilming system enables us to store details which the student can retrieve by applying the principles he has learned, and the critical faculty he has built up, to their selection.

The most rewarding aspect of these systems in the School of Architecture is that they begin to show links again between various aspects of environmental design which, for historical reasons, had tended to fragment. This is nowhere clearer than in the application of language systems to the study of architectural symbolism. Language in this sense, is defined as a set of symbols and a system of rules for using them (but see Glossary). Rules thus detected in the study of language can be applied in other fields as they have been in anthropology

(Levi-Strauss 1968), food and costume
(Barthes 1967) not to mention architecture
(Jencks and Baird 1969, Bonta 1970). In one
simple study, the students considered a
series of committee rooms, observing the form
of each chair, and its spatial relationship
with other chairs, tables and with the room
as a whole! The chairman's chair, for
instance might differ from the others in
having arms, a higher back, deeper upholstery,
and so on. These particular attributes -
and the chair's location in relation to other
chairs, signify the status of its user. One
could also distinguish the chairs which were
to be used by committee members, secretaries
and observers. This kind of analysis can be
applied to many aspects of architecture, and
clearly it can be used in design. It is
obviously relevant in the planning of a
courtroom, or a suite of offices, but it is
surprisingly effective in the planning of
other building types. The beauty of such
language systems is that they allow symbolic
values and other "intangibles" to be treated
by methods which are applicable also to structures, environmental standards and other
quantifiable aspects of design.

It seems, therefore, that a systems
approach, in its many ramifications, really
can be used to help the designer take an
overall view of his task. It may help us
even to avoid the incipient danger that,
because certain factors in design are easily
quantifiable, they are given greater weighting
in design than those which are not. In other
words it gives us a way of structuring the
intake of information into design in which
all the relevant factors are allowed to play
their appropriate part in determining the
final design.

GLOSSARY OF SYSTEMS CONCEPTS[*]

1.0 Computer System: seems to have three
    distinct uses.

1.1. Integrated unit of personnel, computer
     hardware and sortware which are available
     for data processing.

1.2 Interrelated set of hardware consisting,
    for example, of a central processor with
    peripheral input, output and storage devices.
    Ambiguity can be avoided by describing a
    set of such physical units as a configura-
    tion.

1.3 Method of analysing a particular class of
    problem using a given set of mathematical
    models often sold as a package or suite of
    programmes.

[*] (The word Glossary is interpreted strictly:
    the entries represent my own gloss on the
    various concepts)

2.0 Control Systems

2.1 Application of cybernetic principles to the con-
    trol of machines; described as "Automation" by
    D S Harder who devised a system of inter-
    linked, self-regulated machines for the
    manufacture of automobile engineers(Ford
    Motor Company 1946).

2.2 An advanced system might consist of computer
    controlled machines, interlinked by a
    hierarchy of computers collating orders,
    controlling stock, programming work to
    different machines in man-computer dialogue
    with management. It may be, under these
    circumstances, that the uniformity of
    product which has been traditional in mass
    production leads to over-use of some
    machines and under-use of others, so that
    for the efficient deployment of machines,
    automation requires diversity of product
    rather than uniformity.

3.0 Cybernetics: see text

4.0 Eco-System

    A term describing all the living and non-
    living components of the environment,
    together with the interactions between
    them. Ecology was probably the first
    discipline to take a systemic view in its
    concern for relationships between living
    organisms and their environment. It is
    usual to locate the components within a
    structure consisting of four trophic levels:

4.1 Raw materials - such as minerals in the soil,
    water, carbon dioxide and so on.

4.2 Producer organisms - such as plants, which
    utilise the sun's energy in photosynthesis
    to combine the raw materials, thus forming
    carbohydrates, fats, proteins, vitamins
    and so on.

4.3 Consumers - including herbivores, which
    utilise the producers as sources of their
    energy, carnivores, which feed on the
    herbivores (or other carnivores) and
    omnivores, which feed on both.

4.4 Reducers - such as bacteria and fungi which
    feed on dead organic matter, thus convert-
    ing it back into raw materials.

    In a well adjusted eco-system, these will be
    a homeostatic relationship between these
    four levels and increasing concern is being
    expressed, politically, at the ways in which
    man's activities, especially those connected
    with the growth of large cities, are upsett-
    ing the whole earth eco-system.

5.0 General System Theory : see text

6.0 <u>Information Systems</u>: Refers to three quite different concepts

6.1 The structure against which an entire field of knowledge may be classified; e.g De wey, UDC, Cl/SfB and so on. Consistent with the third Oxford Dictionary definition of system, but technically a holotheme.

6.2 Analogous with computer system: the entire system of personnel, hardware and software available for the collection, representation, classification, storage retrieval and transmission of information. May be manual, mechanical or computer aided; where computers are involved, it is usual to describe any input to the system as data and any output as information.

6.3 Technical term used to describe an intermediate level or organisation in the holotheme; consisting of units, assemblies, systems and combines.

7.0 <u>Language Systems</u> : two major uses

7.1 In the definition of language itself as a set of signs and a system of rules for using them.

7.2 In a technical sense the word systems refer to the way in which one word relates to others by virtue of shared meanings, derivations, position in a paradigm (table of declension or conjugation), rhyme and so on. Systems, in this sense, are distinguished in linguistics, which refer to the ways in which words afford structural support to each other within a sentence. Two further concepts from linguistics may help to show why language is more than a simple kit of parts with a set of rules for using them.

7.3 A linguistic sign, according to Saussure (c.1905-11) consists of two components a <u>signifier</u> - the word, pattern of speech sounds, marks on paper and so on by which one tries to communicate an idea, and a <u>signified</u> - the thought or concept which one is trying to convey. Ogden and Richards (1923) add a third component to these first two, the <u>referent</u>, which is the person, place or thing one is communicating about.

7.4 Our personal selection of signs from the available list was called <u>speech</u> by Saussure, to distinguish it from <u>language</u>, which is a shared, public thing - a system of values agreed by social contract. This social contract is necessary because the relationship between signifier and signified is essentially arbitrary. The letters h-u-t denote a small building; so do the sounds we utter when we read them. Initially, any other signifier would have done just as well, but the meaning of hut is now agreed so none of us can change it if we hope to be understood. Yet in systems analysis and computing generally some 3000 such relationships between

signifier and signified have been fractured (Chandor 1970) i.e. new words have been coined or old ones given new uses.

7.5 There have been several attempts recently to use the methods of structural linguistics in the analysis of architecture (Jencks and Baird 1969), which suggest that eventually, aesthetic and other "intangible" aspects of environmental design may be brought within an analytical structure compatible with those appropriate for the physiological, social structural and other quantifiable aspects.

8.0 <u>Psychological Systems</u>:

8.1 Gestalt theory that wholeness and organisation are basic features of all mental processes and behaviour, so that any situation can be understood only when its constituent parts have been organised into a systemic whole.

8.2 Application of cybernetics and general system theory to the analysis of psychological processes, e.g. Gibson's description of the external senses as interrelated, perceptual systems.

9.0 <u>Social Systems</u>: uses in ascending order of <u>precision</u>

9.1 Set of social units; individuals, groups, institutions and the conventions by which they are interrelated.

9.2 Use of generalised analogies from other fields, e.g. Comte's and Marx's use of evolution, Spencer's of the living organisms, and Homan's of the concept from physical sciences, to describe patterns of social organisations.

9.3 Application of cybernetics and general system theory to the analysis of social phenomena; e.g. Buckley's Sociology and modern systems theory.

10.0 <u>Systems Analysis</u>: development of operations research which, instead of distinguishing between individual techniques such as decision theory, theory of games, linear programming, queuing theory, network analysis, and other simulation methods deals in mathematical models which may be used for various purposes.

10.1 Generally a middle to lower management function in which these models are used in the implementation of policy decisions taken at executive level. The aim, usually is to analyse the organisation itself, or various processes so that the most effective use can be made of available man-computer systems.

10.2 The system analyst will have at his fingertips a repertoire of methods which may be used in accounting, stock control, plant allocation and so on. Given any class of problem - in management, economic or physical planning he can suggest which techniques would be most appropriate.

10.3 A typical systems analysis procedure (Chandor, Graham and Williamson, 1969) might form an effective process for re-design, rather than for de novo design; in the following stages: (1) definition of the problem (2) monitoring of the existing system in action (3) analysis of data thus collected with a view to determining requirements for the new system (4) design of the new system so as to make the best use of available resources (5) documentation of the new system and communication to those who will be affected by it (6) implementation of the new system and long-term maintenance of it.

11.0 Systems Building: Method of building by analogy with certain aspects of systems engineering, in which standardised components (doors, windows, wall panels, structural frame and so on) are designed and prefabricated in the factory in such a way that they can be delivered to site and assembled there rapidly. Given a massive programme for a single building type - schools, houses and so on, systems building allows for extensive pre-planning and bulk ordering of components in advance, with attendant production and cost advantages. May also speed up processes by which Building Regulation and other statutory approvals are obtained, on grounds that the method of construction is standardised and known. May be superceded by automated systems (see control systems) in which, uniformity of components is undesirable.

12.0 Systems Engineering: originally synonymous with engineering design (e.g in Goode and Machol 1957) systems engineering also has much in common with Operational Research (e.g in Churchman, Ackoff and Arnoff 1957). Hall (1962) distinguishes between them by suggesting that Operational Research is concerned with the application of scientific methods, process and techniques into the management functions of existing organisations, military, commercial, industrial and so on, whereas systems engineering includes the design of new enterprises, their long range planning and overall development. Design therefore, is only a part of systems engineering which will include the definition of a need, the selection of objectives, the synthesising of systems, analysis of these systems, selection of the best alternative and planning for action.

12.1 Systems engineering takes from General Systems Theory some basic definitions.

"A system is a set of objects with relationships between the objects and between their attributes." (Hall 1962) and the idea that such a system will operate within an environment: "For a given system, the environment is the set of all objects outside the system: (1) a change in whose attributes will affect the system and (2) whose attributes are changed by the system".

12.3 Systems engineering, fundamentally, is a highly sophisticated development of design for mass production (based on methods devised initially by Brunel (c.1805) for making rigging blocks at Portsmouth Dockyard, extended to produce building components (Crystal Palace 1851), automobile components (Henry Ford 1911) and so on, reaching its apotheosis in the electronics industries (e.g. RCA Victor c. 1935) in which individual components - transformers, resistors, capacitors and so on, are available from stock and can be plugged into circuits laid out according to known principles. As individual components are redesigned and plugged into the circuit, so the circuit performance as a whole will improve, even though overall, its layout remains the same. The circuit will have an input, such as a radio signal, throughout it the form of electric currents and an output in the form of a current powerful enough to drive a loudspeaker. The throughput will be modified or transformed as it passes into, through and out of each component; analogies can be drawn from this into any system into which matter (goods, traffic, people), energy (electricity, heat) or information (spoken, written, punched on tape) can be made to flow, and will be transformed in the process. This is clearly true of people moving into, through and out of buildings.

13.0 Urban Systems: Abstraction from the total urban system of those aspects, e.g. land-use, location, economic growth, population growth, transportation and so on, which are susceptible to analysis by the use of mathematical models.

13.1 A typical location model showing the ways in which industry, housing and services are distributed geographically, may be used to predict the effects of future developments on the interrelationships of these three functions.

13.2 Demand for future highways may be predicted by plotting the origin and destination of communications in various modes, e.g. telephone messages, flow of people and goods, extrapolating future trends, location of new activities and predicting demands on the transport system at some specific time in the future.

13.3 Few urban systems models are sophisticated enough to take into account the psychological and social implications of land use, location, transportation and so on.

REFERENCES:

Alexander, C. A. : Notes on the Synthesis of Form, Cambridge Mass., Harvard U.P. 1964
- Systems Generating Systems, in Architectural Design, 12/68
Angyal, A. : A Logic of Systems, reprinted in Emery, F. E. Systems Thinking, Harmondsworth Penguin 1969
Barthes, R. : Elements of Semiology, London, Cape, 1967
Beer, S. : Cybernetics and Management, London, EUP, 1959
- The World, the Flesh and the Metal; the Prerogative of Systems, in Nature, 16/1/65
Bertalanffy, L. von : General System Theory, reprinted in General System Theory, New York Braziller 1969
Best, G. : Method and Intention in Architectural Design, in Broadbent and Ward 1969 (see below)
Bonta, J. P. : (in preparation) A Semiological Design Method, Buenos Aires and Portsmouth Schools of Architecture (Mimeo)
Broadbent, G. : Notes on Design Method, in Broadbent and Ward 1969 (see below)
- (forthcoming) Design in Architecture, Chichester and New York, Wiley
Broadbent, G. and Ward, A. : (eds) Design Methods in Architecture, London, Lund Humphries, 1969
Buckley, W. : Sociology and General Systems Theory, New York, Prentice Hall, 1966
Cannon, W. B. : The Wisdom of the Body, New York, Norton, 1939
Chandor, A. : A Dictionary of Computing, Harmondsworth, Penguin, 1970
Chandor, Graham and Williamson : Practical Systems Analysis, London, Rupert Hart-Davis 1969
Churchman, Ackoff and Arnoff : Introduction to Operational Research, New York, Wiley, 1957
Clark, J. D. G. : Prehistoric Europe, London, Methuen, 1952
Drucker, P. F. : The Practice of Management, London, Heinemann, 1955
Echenique, M. : Models, a Discussion in Architectural Research and Teaching, RIBA, May 1970
Emery, F. E. : Systems Thinking, Harmondsworth, Penguin, 1969
Gibson, J. J. : The Senses Considered as Perceptual Systems, London, Allen and Unwin 1968
Goode and Machol : Systems Engineering - an Introduction to the Design of Large-Scale Systems, New York, McGraw Hill, 1957

Gregory, S. A. : Morphological Analysis, some simple Explorations, in Broadbent and Ward 1969, (see above)
Grinker, R. R. : (ed) Towards a Unified Theory of Human Behaviour, New York, Basic Books 1965
Hall, A.D. : A Methodology for Systems Engineering, New York, van Nostrand 1962
Jencks, C. and Baird, G. : Meaning in Architecture, London, Barrie and Rockliff 1969
Jones, J. C. : The State-of-the-Art in Design Methods, in Broadbent and Ward 1969 (see above)
Levi-Strauss : Structural Anthropology, London Allen Lane, 1968
McLoughlin, J. B. : Urban and Regional Planning; a Systems Approach, London, Faber, 1969
Manning, P. : (ed) The Primary School, and Environment for Education, Liverpool, Pilkington Research Unit, 1967
Markus, T. A. : The role of Building Performance Measurement and Appraisal in Design Method, in Broadbent and Ward 1969 (see above)
Matchett, E. : Fundamental Design Method Training, (seminar papers) Bristol, Engineering Employers, West of England Association 1969
Mongait, A. L. : Archaeology in the USSR, Harmondsworth, Penguin, 1961
Musgrove, J. : The Dangers of Scientism, Architectural Review, July 1966
Ogden, C. K. and Richards, I. A. : The meaning of meaning, London, Routledge, 1923
O'Keefe, J. : A Brief Report on the use of Mathematics with Design Studies, Portsmouth School of Architecture, 1970 (mimeo)
Pahl, R. E. : Spatial Structure and Social Structure, London, Centre for Environmental Studies, Working Paper 10, 1968
Popper, K. : The Poverty of Historicism, London, Routledge, 1957
R.I.B.A. : Plan of Work for Design Team Operation in Handbook of Architectural Practice and Management, London, RIBA 1965
Russell, B. : Design and Systems Theory, Portsmouth School of Architecture, 1970 (mimeo)
de Saussure, F. : Course in General Linguistics, London, Peter Owen, 1960
Smuts, J. C. : Holism and Evolution, New York, Viking, 1961
Spearman, C. and Wynn Jones, L. : Human Ability London Macmillan, 1950
Weiner, N. : Cybernetics, New York, Wiley, 1948
Weiss, P. A. : The Living System, Determinism Shunned, in Koestler, A. and Smythies, J. R. Beyond Reductionism, London Hutchinson, 1968
Weston, H. C. : Sight, Light and Work, London, Lewis, 1962

Student Selection and Concept Attainment in Architectural Education

by Adrian R. Hill

BSc, PhD, FBOA, Experimental Cartography Unit,
Royal College of Art, London England

Abstract

A comparison is made between the accuracy performance scores obtained on the A-C Test for concept attainment by student-entrants on an Architecture course, and the sessional results in three examinable subjects for the same students at the end of their 1st, 2nd and 3rd academic years. It is concluded that the A-C Test is unsatisfactory as a means of student selection on the basis of architectural ability.

Architectural Education and Academic Achievement

In a recent enquiry into student progress, the University Grants Committee(1) showed that architecture courses throughout Great Britain have an abnormally high proportion of undergraduates who withdrew through academic failure. This was 20%, whereas the national average academic failure rate was only 9.5%. The significance of this figure is made the more dramatic when it is realised that no more than 2 or 3% variation existed between fields of study in the withdrawal rate for reasons other than academic failure. Furthermore, architecture was shown to have the highest overall percentage of undergraduates leaving without a first degree and it also topped the list of subjects for the proportion of students completing the course but failing to obtain a degree. These figures are discouraging, and demand that studies be made not only to ascertain the major factors responsible for academic failure but also to provide the means for improving the academic success rate.

Causes of Academic Failure

Of the many factors in higher education which govern a student's academic progress, at least three are outside his control. These are the techniques employed for student selection, teaching and assessment of performance, and by their mere subjectivity different standards are known to exist between the universities. In this paper we are only concerned with the aspect of student selection but it can clearly be seen that the above three factors are inter-dependent. Failure to recognise the importance of any one such factor detracts from the value of efforts expended in the other two.

In selecting students as to their appropriateness to a particular degree course, the selector is frequently faced with a dearth of empirical evidence upon which to base his judgments. Dependence upon the examination results in the General Certificate of Education is not altogether very reliable, (2). The personal interview can also be misleading because of the possibility of numerous situational effects influencing the behaviour of both the interviewee and interviewer, (3). Some attempts aimed at overcoming such deficiencies have involved the use either of aptitude tests (4) or of specially designed projective tests. In the field of architectural student selection, Freeman et al (5) have reported successful results with two tests. One was the Wechsler Adult Intelligence Scale and the other was a practical aptitude test (A-C Performance Test 1) which they had developed and described a few years earlier (6). This latter test is a concept attainment test which has been designed specifically with the aim of incorporating those concepts such as size and shape which are frequently encountered in architecture. It is the results of a recent application of this test which has provided the basis of this paper, but before discussing the data of the present study let us briefly examine the role of concept attainment in architecture.

Assessing Architectural Concepts

An important part of a successful architect is his ability to think creatively. It would be extremely valuable, therefore, if we could base the selection of students for the course in architecture on a measure of some aspect of their creative ability. This belief is strongly supported by the studies of Getzels and Jackson (7) who have shown that intelligence (I.Q.) and performance on various creativity tests are equally and independently successful indicants of scholastic achievement. Hence, since many selection methods in education are related to measures of I.Q. this suggests that potentially high achievers are being rejected.

In a study of higher thought processess, especially creative thinking, Guilford (8) has identified that there are essentially three kinds of intellectual factors, namely cognition, production and evaluation factors. The production factors may further be subdivided into convergent and divergent thinking abilities. Convergent (ie. reductive) thinking implies the narrowing down of possibilities in the production of the one possible answer to a problem, whereas divergent thinking requires the production of as many answers as possible. In architectural design, convergent thinking can have an inhibiting effect because it implies that alternative solutions are not considered. On the other hand, divergent thinking will involve originality, fluency and flexibility in design in addition to aspects of elaboration and evaluation. This sense of intellectual resourcefulness can range from fluency in handling rather basic architectural concepts such as shape, space and colour, to providing flexibility in complex total design concepts. For assessment purposes it is more convenient to concentrate on the basic and simple concepts, and it is upon these that the A-C (Performance) Test is based.

In applying the principle of concept attainment as a means of assessing academic achievement, M'Comisky and Freeman (9) proved that their test possessed specifically architectural concepts when they demonstrated that 2nd year students of architecture performed better on the test than did economics students of comparable age and intelligence. A subsequent investigation, (again on 2nd year students) provided

evidence that the test was likely to prove a useful tool in student selection by measuring the capacity for the development of architectural ability, (10). The present study was aimed at attempting to replicate this latter investigation.

Description and Use of the A-C Test

The A-C Test is a Vigotsky-type blocks test with the addition that it enables differentiation between divergent and convergent tendencies in thinking. It involves the grouping and category naming of sixteen small wooden blocks each of which differs in terms of colour, shape, size, height, weight or hollowness. Some of these characteristics are related, eg. size and height; others are unrelated, eg. colour and weight. Performance on the test may be scored for accuracy in sorting the blocks and time taken in carrying out the sortings made. Only the accuracy scores are reported in the present study, thus providing scores for both the 'divergent','convergent' and 'total' (ie.'divergent' plus 'convergent') parts of the test. (The administration of the test is described in M'Comisky (11).)

Subjects

The subjects were 54 students of architecture, (from 17 to 24 years of age), who were tested on the A-C Test within their first two weeks of commencing the course. At this stage they were unlikely to be influenced by the major principles involved in the discipline of architecture. Examination marks in three examinable subjects were obtained for the same students at the end of their 1st academic year as well as in comparable subjects at the end of their 2nd and 3rd years. However, due to academic failure there were only 43 students in the 2nd year and 42 in the 3rd year.

Results

As would be expected, intercorrelations between the 'divergent', 'convergent' and 'total' accuracy scores on the A-C Test showed that the 'divergent' and 'convergent' measures were entirely independent ($r=0.229$, not sig.), whereas the 'divergent' with 'total' and 'convergent' with 'total' were both highly correlated, ($r=0.716$ and $r=0.825$ respectively, $p < 0.01$). (12)

The mean accuracy scores in the present investigation are in very

close agreement with the comparable
scores for pre-entry students reported by Freeman et al (13), thus suggesting a degree of invariance in the
test for two separate sample populations. Also, both these sets of mean
scores for the pre-entry students on
the 'divergent' and 'convergent' parts
of the test were lower than those obtained by Buttle et al (14) on 2nd year
students. This would tend to support
the assertion that pre-entry students
had a general lack of understanding of
architectural concepts.

Comparisons were then made between
the accuracy scores of the pre-entry
students and their sessional examination marks in three course subjects
obtained at the end of their 1st, 2nd
and 3rd years. The three examinable
subjects were selected on the basis of
incorporating a fairly extensive use
of some of the concepts involved in
the A-C Test. They were as follows:
1. Architectural design, (practical
   design work)
2. Building construction
3. Geometry (1st year) and
   Structures (3rd year)
(There was no comparable Geometry or
Structures subject offered in the 2nd
year of the course.) The first two
mentioned of these three examinable
subjects are identical with two of the
subjects selected by Freeman et al (15)
thus facilitating a comparison between
the two investigations.

In the Freeman study all the analyses were made using the Fisher exact
probability test which is a nonparamet-
ric statistic for determining whether
the scores from two independent random
samples all fall into one or the other
of two mutually exclusive classes.
When arranging the 2nd year examination
marks according to the ten best and ten
poorest students and comparing them
with the A-C Test 'divergent' scores,
Freeman et al showed that the difference
in 'divergence' scores in favour of the
best ten students in each of the architecture subjects was statistically
significant at the 0.05 level. In the
present study, however, none of the
results in either of the examinable
subjects for the 1st, 2nd or 3rd years
showed a significant agreement with the
'divergence' scores, (Fisher exact
probability test).

Rank order correlations were performed between the 'divergent', 'convergent' and 'total' accuracy scores
obtained for the pre-entry students
with the marks for the same students in

each of the above three examinable
subjects at the end of each of the
three academic years. All the correlations were extremely low, ranging
from -0.189 through +0.279, and only
two were just significant at p=0.05.
These were, 1st year Building construction with 'total' score (r=+0.279)
and 3rd year Architectural design
with 'divergent' score (r=+0.263).
However, in view of the large number
of correlations made (ie. 24), one of
these correlations is likely to occur
as significant at the 0.05 level merely by chance, so caution must be
observed when considering the relevance of the above two 'significant'
results.

During the course of administer-
ing the test a record was kept of the
order in which concepts were used in
the section on divergent thinking.
This was undertaken because one of the
main requirements of a concept attainment test is that the array of possible concepts must be encountered in
an order over which the subject (ie.
student) has no control. A Kendall's
coefficient of concordance on the
pooled 'divergence' scores of all students showed the order of concept
usage (over four concepts) to be significant at p<0.001, (W=0.475). The
importance of this order is further
emphasised by the identical order of
frequency totals from which it appears
that the 'shape' concept is approximately twice as frequently (and perhaps
twice as easily) attained than the
'height' concept.

What is of interest from this aspect of the results is that the order
in which concepts were used bears a
close similarity to the order in which
concepts are attained and understood
by children (16). There is here,
perhaps, material for further research
into discovering to what extent the
order of concept usage in an adult is
influenced by the ontogenetic development in childhood.

But to limit the discussion to
the immediate implications of the
results, further experimentation on
the order and frequency of concept
usage is undoubtedly desirable in order
to establish weighting factors for the
various concepts for the purpose of
avoiding marked non-liniarity in the
'divergence' score on the A-C Test.
Such a procedure would help to eliminate the bunching together of the higher accuracy scores without substantially increasing the length of the test.

Conclusions

The failure to replicate the previous successful application of the A-C Test as a student selection technique in architecture would indicate that, in its present form, the test is inappropriate for general usage. However, the theoretical implications of the test in measuring some aspect of creativity offers promising potential in the field of student selection and reasons for this lack of success should be examined further. Two possible sources for this lack of success may be sought either in differences in the teaching or assessment techniques between the two schools of architecture concerned in the two studies. Certainly, on the aspect of teaching, there is slight evidence to suggest that the academic achievement of students at the school used for the present study was, on average, above that present in the Freeman sample, (17).

On the relationship between concepts and teaching, Goodnow (18) has found that children with a low socio-economic status and semi-schooling performed better on judgments of space, weight and volume than did those children who had more schooling. It would seem that this difference may be due to a greater fluidity in learning in the former situation, thus allowing a greater opportunity for the development of certain concepts. Such an arguement would be supported by the experiments of Canter et al (19) who showed that an architecture student's ability to discriminate in the use of certain concepts for describing plans and elevations of houses is highly dependent upon the teaching philosophy behind an architectural course. Further support for this effect of teaching on concept attainment may also be found in the work of Abercrombie (20) who has shown that experience and familiarity with past events significantly affects the way in which we perceive and think about the world around ourselves.

Future studies on student selection therefore, will need jointly to consider both the aspects of teaching and assessment if the generality of a technique is to be developed. But, whatever developments are made in the way of student selection for architecture, there is an urgent need for a collective effort amongst the schools in Great Britain to determine why its academic failure rate is more than twice that of the national average.

Notes

1. University Grants Committee, Enquiry into student progress. H.M.S.O., London (1968)
2. BARNETT,V.D. & LEWIS,T. A study of the relation between G.C.E. and degree results. Journal of the Royal Statistical Society, pp.187-226 (1963)
3. ARGYLE,M. The psychology of interpersonal behaviour. Penguin Books (1967)
4. OLIVER,R.A.C. A test of scholastic aptitude. University Quarterly, June (1962)
5. FREEMAN,J., M'COMISKY,J.G. & BUTTLE D. Student selection: a comparative study of student entrants to architecture and ecomomics. International Journal of Educational Science. 3,(3), pp.189-197 (1969)
6. BUTTLE,D., FREEMAN,J. & M'COMISKY, J.G. The measurement of ability in architecture. The Builder, 10th September, pp.537-539 (1965)
7. GETZELS,J.W. & JACKSON,P.W. Creativity and intelligence. Wiley, New York, (1962)
8. GUILFORD,J.P. The structure of intellect. Psychological Bulletin 53,(4), pp.267-293 (1956)
9. M'COMISKY,J.G. & FREEMAN,J. Concept attainment and type of education. International Journal of Educational Science, 2, pp.47-50 (1967)
10. FREEMAN et al. Op. cit.
11. M'COMISKY,J.G. The A-C (Performance) Test 1. Psychology Department, University of Hull, England, Mimeograph (1961)
12. All correlations quoted in this paper are Spearman rank order correlations unless otherwise stated.
13. FREEMAN et al. Op. cit.
14. BUTTLE et al. Op. cit.
15. FREEMAN et al. Op. cit.
16. PIAGET,J. The child's conception of space. Routledge and Kegan Paul, London (1956)
17. University Grants Committee, Op. cit.
18. GOODNOW,J. A test of milieu effects with some of Piaget's tasks. Psychological Monograph 76, pp.1-22 (1962)
19. CANTER,D., JOHNSON,J., & M'COMISKY J.G. Familiarity with architectural

concepts and academic achievement
of architecture students.
Perceptual and Motor Skills, 27
pp.871-874 (1968)
20. ABERCROMBIE,M.L.J. The anatomy of
judgement. Penguin Books (1960)

Research Oriented Architectural Education

by Gunter Schmitz

Associate Professor, Director - Project Development, Research Center,

College of Architecture and Environmental Design,

Texas A & M University, College Station, Texas 77843

Abstract

Two practical experiments of architectural education and research are described. One of these experiments is the way the former School of Design in Ulm, Germany saw the role of the architect in the building process more than a decade ago and educated in its research oriented program architecture students consequently to become contributive in the building team. Methods used in problem solving and results from various levels of study are presented. The second case history concerns the architectural Research Center at Texas A&M University which combines a program for graduate education with applied research and development research in environmental design problem areas of public concern. The Institute tries to contribute to progress in architecture and the environmental design disciplines through careful selection of problems, through programming, rational methodology, interdisciplinary approach, consequent system orientation, and the dissemination of results for their effective utilization. Nature and results of some recent projects are explained.

Some conclusions are tentatively drawn from the experiences gained at both institutions: A profound orientation towards research should happen early in a students career. The structuring of a comprehensive research oriented curriculum and its continuous annual improvement seems to be easier accomplishable in new schools. Such a school should be university affiliated. Practical architectural research programs can be established at virtually any school and graduate students can benefit greatly from participating in contract research. However, such programs should feed back into the school's academic program to improve the general educational curriculum which should assist interested students to prepare themselves theoretically for a research career.

Introduction

Applied research and development research in architecture is necessitated by many determining trends of our time. The most important of these are: the in-terdisciplinary complexity of architectural design problems; the increasing economical and social importance of building tasks; the rational cooperation of building teams; the mechanization and industrialization of the construction process; the mass demand of building products; the application of new materials and production methods; the formulation of standards and building codes; the increasing consciousness of the anonymous user for environmental quality, functional design, and precision of details and finishes; the continuous process of change regarding user requirements within constructed facilities; etc. To meet successfully the challenge of these (commonly known) trends, scientific investigations, systematic experiments, developmental research, exemplary pilot projects, and refined methodical design process have to be utilized.

The architect's job is more complex and characterized by public concern today than ever before and predictably even more so in the future. But as man always resists change, schools of architecture are no exceptions. They even tend to be particularly slow in adjusting their programs to the exigencies of our world in change. The purpose of this paper is not to analyze why they are so slow in acknowledging the dynamic changes of recent years, nor is it to demonstrate a hypothetical model of new more relevant schools of architecture, although this might make much sense. I intend rather to describe in brief two practical experiments related to research oriented architectural education. Both examples can be criticized readily because of their many imperfections. But in both cases two educational institutions made practical contributions (with varying degrees of comprehensiveness and risk) to the adequate education of the new generation of architects.

One of these experiments is the way the School of Design in Ulm, Germany, saw the role of the architect in the building industry and consequently educated its architecture students to contribute to the tedious industrialization process of building. The second case study deals with the College of Architecture and Environmental Design at Texas A&M

University which has been successfully conducting architectural research and systems development tied into its educational program for several years. Both case studies are presented independently, stating first some background data pertinent to each institution and presenting subsequently some typical work examples.

Ulm School of Design (1955-1968)

Concepts and Organization

The School of Design in Ulm, Germany is historical now after it was closed by the Government in December 1968. It used to be a private institution with an unconventional progressive and well organized four years curriculum for the education of systems architects, product designers and graphic designers. Its admission levels were high, the tuition fees minimal, and its capacity always limited to a maximum of 160 students with a faculty to student ratio of 1:8. In addition to an interdisciplinary and international permanent faculty of 20, the school relied in its program on 35 visiting professors from various related disciplines and with a variety of nationalities. Since its origination in the mid-50's the school always attracted students internationally, the percentage of foreign students oscillating between 45 and 55 percent. The programs offered education in three departments: The Department of Building educated architects capable of solving building problems posed by mass demand through the utilization of industrial organization and production processes. The Department of Product Design was concerned with the education of industrial designers competent in product design areas of every day use, public use, and work environment. The Department of Visual Communication was oriented towards design problems in modern mass communication media (press, commercial design, television, etc.) and in technical communication. As can be suspected, a multitude of interactions occured between these three departments of the school by overlappings of professors, design problems, seminars, etc.

Annexed to the academic departments were Research and Development Institutes working on practical problems within each design discipline. This work usually was contracted by industry and private or public organizations.

Department of Building

The studies in the Department of Building were directed more to prepare architects for the assumption of increased responsibility delegated to them by the progressing industrialization process of building, than merely to train specialists in various technologies. The education program, by its exclusive objectives unique in the world, presupposed an excellent professional background from the student: studies in the field of architecture or civil engineering at a University (intermediate degree) or technical level (full degree) or alternatively three years of professional training in architecture or engineering plus professional practical experience (site supervision, industrial production, etc). Candidates were selected for admission to the department by their transcripts, their previous works and the maturity of professional attitude. All admissions were on a probationary basis. Attendance at the lectures, seminars, and practical design work was decided by the professor. Some professors required oral or written examinations at regular intervals, whereas some others preferred a global statement of the student's progress. At the end of the probation term in the first year, and at the end of each year the students were reviewed by a board of the departmental professors. This review very rarely involved grading, as it took the form of a written judgement.

The programs of the first and second year took into account the excellency of the student's basic professional knowledge. This knowledge was systematically supplemented by systems oriented studies, qualifying him for research and development work in the field of industrialized building and its architecture in the third and fourth year. There was no degree offered after the second year, but the upper two years clearly were devoted to advanced work on a graduate level. The final degree was granted only after the successful completion of the full course of four years of study including thesis work and a colloquium in the last year.

The school intended to prepare its architectural students to solve complex design problems responsibly on a rational basis. It communicated the necessary technological and scientific knowledge. And as the architect should be very conscious of the implications of his activities to humanity, the professional training at the same time was an education towards social, political, and cultural responsibility. The Department of Building assisted to transform the architectural practice from the common state of an empirical, intuitive, and individualistic activity within the arts and crafts tradition into a state more in equilibrium with the physical and intellectual demands of our industrialized civilizations.

One main rationale behind the department's teaching philosophy implied the utilization of building systems rather than individual static architectural creations to solve today's building needs. In a time characterized by rapid changes, only systems of coordinated components will guarantee the necessary flexibility of architectural solutions, which could be best described as open-ended solutions, able to adapt.

The department's educational program was structured very methodical. The exercises were given to the student in deliberate abstract formulation in order to stimulate his imagination. The complexity of the problems grew gradually and the student learned to control the various design factors step by step. Twelve short term problems in the first year were followed by three projects in the second. All problems required from the student a continuous effort to rationalize the design process and often included the necessity to utilize own experiments.

The problems trained the student to collect information, to utilize and interpret exact data, to define assumptions, to formulate hypotheses, to establish syntheses, to generate innovative solutions, and to select optimal ones. No matter what the complexity of the studied object was - a building component, a building type, or a building system - the student was supposed to conceive of it as a result of industrial production and organization. The decision making process was performed under a continuous dynamic movement of the student's creative mind. Some projects of the second year could be distinguished by their typical accents on particular determinants of the given problem. If, for instance, the development of an optimal organization of a functional set of rooms was of primary interest, the structural problems remained secondary, and the following project inverted the order of priority. This method offered to the student an opportunity to deal more profoundly with certain subproblems, to detect special possibilities which never would have come to his mind if he had been forced to concentrate on all design factors, and to see contradicting situations which would result in the elaboration of necessary compromise solutions. The objectives of other projects had been more comprehensive studies, comprising all the necessary functional, structural, technical, economic, and aesthetic aspects. The purpose of these exercises was as follows: teaching of fundamental principles for the design of architectural components systems and its buildings; training in rational decision making and specific design methodologies including experiments; training in both responsible individual work and collective teamwork; training precise presentation and communication techniques; stimulation of "systems thinking" to achieve flexible end results.

The introduction of system concepts in architectural design has become an urgent worldwide problem. In dealing practically with these basic exercises the student got acquainted with the most important design principles of industrialized building and its architecture.

A considerable part of the lectures in the first two years was attended jointly by students of different departments. The lectures in Mathematical Techniques for Design were an introduction into the fields of combinatorics, topology, and logistics.

This course set down an important basis for activities like positioning, joining, connecting, distributing and standardazing of elements. Courses in applied Sociology, Psychology, Economics, etc. communicated fundamental insights into scientific disciplines vitally important to contemporary architects. Our profession has to become more and more perceptive and responsive to human needs caused by, and satisfied by, characteristics of the built environment. If the architect wants to explore and demonstrate possibilities for physical betterment, it is his fate to be in constant interaction with society, a fact which requires from him an excellent knowledge of Sociology. The course in Cultural History of the 20th Century helped the students to clarify their position in the historical process, whereas History of Modern Architecture dealt with special facts. An oeuvre, an architect, a school, a tendency, or a doctrine became the object of a profound analysis. The supplementary course in Socio-Dynamics of Culture analyzed trends in our rapidly changing contemporary socio-cultural environment. And for their ultimate role as coordinators, the future architects and designers were prepared by lectures on Cybernetics and Theory of Systems. Specific theory courses for the Department of Building included the important Technology course comprising materials, construction, and production processes, oriented towards technical problems of industrialized building. From the course in Structures the students got insights into alternative structural systems. The lectures and exercises of Constructive Geometry were intended to bring the students to a high level of consciousness regarding the geometry of polyhedrons, curves, and surfaces. A course on Modular Coordination clarified the theoretical basis of the necessary dimensional normalization, typification, and standardization in the building industry. In the lectures on Environmental Phsyics the students learned to correlate the influences of temperature, humidity, sound and solar exposure to the design concept of a building product. The courses in Mechanical Equipment covered heating, conditioning, mechanical supplies, lighting, electricity, etc. Seminars in Advanced Structures dealt with particular methods of prefabrication and with complex lightweight structural systems.

From the third year on the design problems became architectural research projects. In conducting the projects, efforts were made to simulate actual conditions. The students were consulted by experts—engineers, sociologists, building contractors, industrialists, economists, etc. These consultants were selected according to actual conditions in the particular project. They advised at appropriate intervals and participated in many intermediate decisions of the design phase. Furthermore, all visiting professors in the theory courses, which had by their specific field of knowledge a certain relationship to a current project, were pledged to consult in their speciality. All projects of the third year were elaborated in team work. Their duration (3 to 9 months) was determined according to the complexity of the problems and the size of the particular team. The seminars on Technology and the lectures on Political Economy were continued. In the seminar on Economy of Building the students were trained to evaluate the economic consequences of their design decisions. Questions like optimal story height, width of a building, number of floors, space utilization, or repetition problems were investigated with special regard to the costs of construction. Further seminars covered the areas of Management, Organization of Building Processes, Elements of Urbanism, History of Industrialized Building, and Programming Techniques.

The students of the fourth year were almost released from theory courses. During the first two trimesters they worked on projects. Later on they devoted their time entirely to their diploma thesis, which comprised a theoretical and a practical part. The final degree candidate selected his thesis themes in conjunction with a professor of his department who later acted as principal advisor of the thesis. The student further proposed for each part of the thesis two co-advisors, who could be taken from outside (industry, profession, science, government, etc) if he so preferred. As a principle the diploma candidate started with the thesis in April and submitted it at the end of September. After these six months the candidate finally proved his knowledge and professional maturity in all fields of his education in a formal coolquium with a board of professors.

Some work examples of the Ulm School of Design might help to illustrate the research orientation of its thinking and didactic efforts. (Slides on: Grid Transitions; Circulation Graphs; Box Unit Building System; Joining and Connecting Problems; Volume Configuration System; Catalog of Room Sizes; Apartment Planning Grids; Prefabricated Sanitary and Kitchen Components; Prefabricated Homes in Panel Construction; Integrated Building Structure; Low Income Apartment Studies)

Institute for Industrialized Building

As mentioned earlier there were developmental research projects pursued within the Ulm School of Design, most of them in separate "Institutes" as contracted research. One of them was the Institute for Industrialized Building, working like the (academic) Department of Building in problem areas of modern industrial technology impinging on architecture. The students benefited indirectly from its real research and development projects, as the staff of the research institute as a rule simultaneously was involved in their teaching too. Considerable information resources of the research institute were also available to the interested student. Some typical work examples of the Institute will serve to indicate its field of action. (Slides on: Box Unit Building System in Concrete; Ring Unit Building System in Concrete; Polyfold Facing Panel System; Formwall Partitioning System; Twin Membrane Structural Panel)

The Successor

The Ulm School of Design is no longer existing. The reputation it enjoyed after only 13 years of existence was due mainly to the proven results of its curriculum, its teaching methodology, and its system oriented research and design processes. Its former teachers and students are working now singly or in small groups all over the world. The School's facilities, reopened in late 1969 as a state institution, are known as the Institute of Environmental Planning of the University of Stuttgart. It will serve as a place for advanced graduate studies in the environmental planning sciences of building, industrial design, and visual communication. The school is no longer departmentalized but problem-oriented. The new beginning is humble. Six new professors with thirty of the former students in their final year and twenty new (mainly monodisciplinary) students programming their interdisciplinary problems and curriculum. Although the new team seems also to concentrate part-time at least in trying to manipulate the past, one should wish success to the new institution. Only the future will show if the new start will lead again to a dynamic, progressive and exemplary school, comparable with the ancestors it is most obliged to, the former Ulm School of Design and the famous Bauhaus.

Architectural Research Center, Texas A&M University

Goals, Structure, and Program

The circumstances leading to the establishment of the present architectural research program at Texas A&M University in 1963 can be stated quite simply: a new chairman in newly built facilities in an existing School of Architecture, decided to set up a University Center in the field of architectural research. Impressed by the earlier experience and concept of building research within the Ulm School of Design, the chairman made an extensive and thorough analysis of the previous fourteen years of architectural research and testing at Texas A&M University. The establishment of an Research and Graduate Center was the outcome.

The primary goal of this Center was stated to be the application of University research resources to actual, practical problems of social and economic significance within building science and the environmental design fields. The Center was to contribute to the advancement of architecture and building through meaningful research and development projects and through the dissemination of results for their effective utilization. This program was – and still is – based upon applied rather than basic research, and great emphasis has been placed upon coordinating this research with development projects, that is to say, controlling its results through exposure to production and use.

Recently the prime aims of the Research Group have been articulated more precisely as focusing on the development of adaptable systems (systems of order, component systems, product systems, circulation systems, signage systems, etc.),to improve the efficiency of environmental facilities and their building processes in the various phases of planning, design, construction, cost control, functional performance and change. The improvement of architectural technology and the human physical environment is studied in close relation to selected building types (i.e. hospitals, mental institutions, children day care centers, low income housing, port facilities, etc.). The development of open-ended, flexible system solutions for these particular areas (sometimes demonstrated in pilot projects) is the immediate objective. However, it is hoped, that by systematic research and development related to specific building types, some theories, principles, and concepts might ultimately evolve which are of general practical use for non-intuitive, critical and rational approaches to building tasks in the future.

The second goal of architectural research at Texas A&M University is education at the graduate level in research and development. This is accomplished by three complementary programs: (1) the research assistantship program, allowing graduate students to participate actively in actual research and development work at a national and international level, under the direction of professional research architects and with a wide range of consultants; (2) a curriculum of graduate courses, specifically organized to involve the student in a broad core of research methodology, systems orientation, and in more specialized courses relating to his field of interest; (3) a professional development program exposing the graduate student externally to real situations in related problem areas of professional research and development.

The administrative structure of the Research Center within the University (the Land Grant College of the State of Texas founded in 1876) is complicated. Embedded in the College of Architecture and Environmental Design, the Institute is its official research branch and is also part of its graduate program in Architecture. The Institute is also responsible to the University's Research Foundation and the Texas Engineering Experiment Station (established in 1914) operating under the administration of the College of Engineering. This four-fold responsibility requires the unrestricted attention of a full-time administra-

tive Director in charge of budgets, administrative management, project promotion, formal research applications, and general representation of the Center. He is assisted by a full-time Director for Project Development in charge of coordinating and guiding the various research project teams by continuous advice in conceptual, procedural, and quality aspects. Each project is directed by a Principal Investigator, responsible for the coordination of his particular project team. These teams consist of two to six people, mostly graduate students (some of them non-architects), or selected under-graduate architectural students, and sometimes include research associates from project related scientific disciplines. The management of the projects by the Project Directors entails scheduling, allocation of funds and manpower, and continuous coordination of team work during the entire developmental process.

The graduate students come from different disciplines (e.g. architecture, management, industrial design, systems building, construction, sociology, psychology, medical care, hospital administration, etc.) to be part of multi-disciplinary problem solving teams. The opportunities offered to the graduate student in research are unusual and broad. He is encouraged to develop and apply rational problem solving techniques. He participates in interprofessional teams working with various organizations and agencies. He can travel, meet experts in various fields and may attend conventions and lectures which occur in connection with the varied ongoing research projects. The present graduate program in Architectural Systems Development foresees 16 to 24 months for a master's degree. Candidates for a newly introduced Doctor in Environmental Design also have the opportunity to conduct architectural r&d work in the Research Center.

From a staff consisting of a newly appointed head and a part-time secretary in fall 1963, the research group has grown to the present 6 full-time and 1 part-time professional staff, 10 research assistants and 3 full time secretaries of the Institute. The fortunate fact that the Research Institute with its shop and photo lab is housed independantly in its own building permits informal contacts and the exchange of ideas and information at any time between staff members. The arrangement of the administrative area as well as the two open studio/conference areas which are subdivided flexibly according to the requirements of the project teams, encourages staff and students to stay in continuous interaction and to keep informed of each other's work.

Projects
The operation of the architectural Research Center   is financed by University seed money

(state funds), and its own sponsored or funded research projects. Seed money originally permitted the School of Architecture to hire the first qualified and imaginative research staff and is still appropriated to the Center for the initiation of new projects. Research projects sponsored from the outside are contracted and centrally administered through the University's Research Foundation. Overhead costs for these services of the University run up to 43% of wages and salaries. Part of the money retained, however, serves for balancing salaries, for a limited time, if research programming efforts should happen to fail in raising outside funds.

Sixteen r&d projects have been conducted since 1963. Seven were sponsored and nine were exploratory. The project areas include problems in inner-city transportation and circulation, health facilities, housing, mental health facilities, day care, education, recreation, and port facilities. Interestingly enough, all sponsored projects – with one exception – fall into the category of health or mental health. All projects sponsored over more than one year – with one exception – required intensive solicitory research and development efforts from 2 to 4 months long. Starting from the fall of 1968, some of the exploratory efforts could not be followed up because of heavy involvement in current funded research projects. (Slides on 5 typical projects)

Methodology

Although the student might be assigned to one single long range research project only during his entire time as a master's student, he greatly benefits from this experience. He participates in various phases of architectural research, from programming to the documentation of results. He is a substantial part of a project team involved in r&d work with realistic goals, objectives, and solutions. The results are publicized widely and sometimes have national or international significance – a complete novum to the student who used to think and work within the limitations of academic exercises. But most important, he learns general methods and techniques of architecture oriented research which are not necessarily only problem confined. Throughout the entire research and development process, great emphasis is placed on a methodical, rational elaboration of system solutions.

After a tentative formulation of the problem and objectives, a comprehensive examination of the literature and an analysis of the problem are made. This leads to a clarification and possibly limitation of the original tentative statement of the problem and objectives. A pilot study then proves the feasibility of a variety of tentative solutions. After these exploratory projects with their feasible tentative solutions have been initiated, and only at this stage, formal proposals are submitted to potential sources of funding (government, agencies, industry, foundations, etc.). These proposals emphasize very specific objectives and give a detailed description of the methodology.

Upon funding, a thorough analysis, review, and extension of the preliminary problem analysis begins, taking advantage of experience gained in developing the first range of tentative solutions. Specific sub-procedures are worked out as well as sub-objectives together with development criteria and rating systems. During the development phase, the utilization of modern technology, methodology, and management is emphasized. All projects are characterized by being applied and developmental rather than basic research, and most will result in the development of system solutions with carefully coordinated sub-components allowing adaptation processes to be part of the solutions, thus opening them up to changing user requirements.

Demonstration units must be built in many cases to test the research results under actual use conditions. In any case, projects have to be evaluated after completion by multi-professional teams, to determine if original objectives have been met.

In problem solving, both logic and imagination are utilized in a step by step sequence with many necessary feedbacks. The use of operational sciences as well as decision theory helps to optimize the solutions. Group discussions are emphasized as well as control of the development work by model building and testing (shapes, forms, fabrication, materials, structures, connections, prototype parts, or entire components). In complex problems, the use of dynamic simulation models with variable inputs will be utilized to determine circulations, interdependencies, network behavior, etc. The various steps in decision making during the entire development process are documented in a comprehensive work report for future reference.

Observations

The differences between both institutions – the Ulm School's Department of Building and the architectural Research Center at Texas A&M University – are obvious. Positive aspects in the Ulm experiment were the private status of the school, the progressive integration of several scientific disciplines into a four years architectural curriculum, the close interaction between three related design disciplines with advanced teaching philosophies, and the high professional level of both faculty and admitted students. Its negative aspects are obvious too. The Ulm School of Design was not university affiliated, very limited in size, did not offer an undergraduate degree after the first two years, had an isolated location, was not sufficiently funded by governmental or private sources, and en-

countered continuously the public resistance of the do-
minating conservative part of its country. It also
clearly separated contracted r&d work from education.

The advantages of the Research Center are distinct:
it is university integrated, it offers graduate programs
with degree plans, students participate in actual contracted r&d projects . Disadvantages of the Research
Center are : its limited capa-
city restricted by its present size, its complicated
organizational structure within a conservative state
university administration resulting in a considerable
bulk of necessary basic paper work, the limited time
that graduate students can participate in the r&d process - often necessitating the phasing-in of several
student generations into the same long-range project
with obvious losses in work efficiency, and its non-
urban location. The currently non-research oriented
architectural programs in this country furthermore effect that admitted graduate architectural students
rarely show sufficient knowledge in either basic research techniques or important neighboring disciplines.

Both places which I tried to describe, have distinct differences, but also certain features in common: both are concerned with the education of
young professionals; both presuppose from their students the mastering of basic professional skills and
the basic knowledge of the status quo of their art or
science as admission standards; both institutions are
research oriented utilizing rational decision making
and scientifically controlled design processes; both
are (in varied degrees) multidisciplinary oriented
and try to educate professionals which will be able to
work in teams and to direct interdisciplinary teams
themselves; both places are not concerned to educate
architects for traditional private practice; in the selection of their problems, they are society oriented
rather than middle-income-private-client conscious—
their humanistic concern places more emphasis on
fulfilling the physical needs of society than merely
embellishing its products or buildings; both hold human worth above material value and insist on control
and redirection of the flow of technology so as to
benefit the whole of society; both think in terms of
adaptable systems and dynamic processes, permitting
flexible open-ended solutions of the built environments; both institutions try to contribute to the education of the next generation architects who will be
concerned to initiate, promote, or direct the development of systems where necessary, and who will be
capable of implementing these component systems in
a continuous adaptation process into unique solutions
for unique human needs in unique situations.

My experiences with research oriented architectural education so far are related to these two institutions, but I hope they can be of use for necessary

re-evaluation processes to update inadequate current architectural curricula. There is a small van-
guard in the profession now promoting research,
systems, and process thinking in schools of architecture. But many more architectural research institutes in university environments are needed.
They will have different origins, facilities, and resources and necessarily will vary in concept, direction, and capacity. But they should supplement
each other in their activities. Some kind of coordination on a regional, national, and even international level will become inevitable if duplication
of energy, time, and effort is to be avoided, together with a waste of valuable funds.

The benefits of architectural research and development integrated into the universities will be substantial: Students will be profoundly influenced
towards solving the problems of the built environment more scientifically than in the past; if the
necessary theory programs are available, the student
might even be encouraged to prepare himself thoroughly for a future research career. The profession can improve its designs by the application of
system solutions, and it will be able to attach systematically rational data to its design processes; in
its frequent role of coordinating building teams it
can act increasingly from a basis of communicable
knowledge rather than purely personal preferences
or assumptions. Architectural schools, once they
have included research oriented programs into their
own research and development institutes, will regain
recognition as the thinking centers of the profession
and the building industry; it is hoped that more and
more schools will be able to redirect their resources
to the practical solution of pressing problems of social, economic and technical significance. The
building industry will certainly be influenced by
exemplary research and development results, by new
insights into the building process, by progressive system concepts and by contributions to technical knowledge in building science. Lastly, society will benefit through the improved physical environments
produced by more rational decisions; environments
which hopefully are responsive to continuously
changing physical and intellectual needs; for all
architectural research and development efforts have
to be ultimately directed towards that human purpose.

The next generation architects will indeed face
quantitative and qualitative problems of unprece-
dented magnitude. It is on us educators now to
equip them with the necessary knowledge, insights,
capabilities, and team spirit which will enable
them to contribute to the advancing humanization
process of this our earth. It is not too late.

Bibliographic References

"Architectural Education in the Hochschule fur Gestaltung at Ulm, Germany". 20 page prospectus of the Department of Building, HfG Ulm, 1966.

"Hochschule fur Gestaltung Ulm, Lehrprogramm". HfG Ulm, 1966/67 and 1967/68.

Ulm, journal of the Ulm School of Design, numbers 1-21, 1958-1968.

Gunter Schmitz, "Environmental Design Education, Hochschule fur Gestaltung Ulm", Connection, the magazine of visual arts at Harvard, vol. 5, no. 2/3, pp. 25-32, 1968.

Gunter Schmitz, "Education, Research and Development in Industrialized Building at the School of Design Ulm, Germany", paper presented at the annual AIA/ACSA Teachers' Seminar, Montreal, 1968.

G. Mann, J. Patterson, G. Schmitz, "The Graduate Program in Health Facilities Research at Texas A&M University", World Hospitals, Journal of the International Hospital Federation, vol. 4, October 1968, pp. 179-188.

Gunter Schmitz, "Architectural Education – Systems Oriented", paper presented at the Joint Conference ACSA/ASC-AIA (East Central Region/Great Lakes Region), Ball State University, Muncie, Indiana, 1969.

Gunter Schmitz, "University Integrated Architectural Research – A Case Study from Texas A&M University", Industrialization Forum, vol. 1, no. 2, Jan. 1970, pp. 13-22.

Session Four:

Urban Systems and Planning Theory

Chairman: Alfred Blumstein

Urban Systems Institute, School of Urban and Public Affairs, Carnegie-Mellon University

Correlates of Mobility among Retired Persons

by Frances M. Carp

Ph.D., University of California Medical Center, San Francisco, California

Abstract

Generally, retired people go about very little in their communities. This immobility seems inimical to development of creative and satisfying life-styles in this new phase of the personal history, and retired people express displeasure with their inability to get about. There are, of course, wide individual differences in mobility and satisfaction. This variance is used in the present study to investigate factors which may influence mobility behaviors and attitudes: characteristics of older persons, circumstances of life in retirement, and the kind of transportation which is available.

Leisure is thought to be favorable to personal fulfillment and cultural advance (1, 2,3). On the other hand, free time has long been recognized as a psychological problem (4). Martin (5) points out that in the decades after Ferenczi wrote, free time increased in Western society and there was commensurate rise in mal-adaptations, "giving us today a socio-psychological problem of the first magnitude" (p.148)

As more and more people live into later maturity (6) and retirement age creeps downward (7), society is creating a new leisure period in the normal life-history (8). This emerging period of retirement leisure occurs at a time in life when people tend to be at their most mature and experienced (9), and relatively well educated and in good health (10). Given a supportive and stimulating milieu, this "new social class" (11) may lead rich and satisfying lives, and contribute to the well-being of society.

For the majority of persons, retirement will be spent in cities and their suburbs (12). The environment is of crucial importance in determining the adaptation of older persons (13). The urban environment can isolate and stultify the person who has left the work force, and present him a serious problem in regard to free time, or it can stimulate and support his fulfillment as an individual and facilitate his contribution to the general welfare.

The degree to which the environment meets a person's needs and improves the quality of

his life depends not only upon what exists in the community but also upon his access to these resources. The physical presence of other persons and services is not enough. People may be lonely in a crowded city (14,15,16). They may not use services designed for them. The elderly ill tend not to make use of medical facilities which, in the judgment of physicians, they badly need (17). Small proportions of retired persons take part in senior center activities, though these centers are designed to help such persons fill their time with meaningful activity (18,19,20). Those who attend senior centers may be least in need of their services (21). This may be true also for public housing (22).

No doubt the gap between existence and utilization of community resources for retired people has many determinants (23). Information is one factor (24). Transportation may be another. When old people were asked what services they needed, a large proportion named transportation (25). In addition, many who said their primary needs were medical, recreational, or religious explained that the reason was not absence of the service but lack of a way to get to it.

The Study

Retired people go about in the community very little (26). On his first visit to this country, Bracey (27) commented on how few old people he saw about the streets. Generally, retired people are not well pleased with this inability to get about; and they think they would go more places, and more often, if suitable transportation was available (26). To what extent are the low mobility and the dissatisfaction due to transportation, and to what extent to characteristics of persons and other circumstances of their lives in retirement? One way to gain information on these issues is to look at the personal, situational and transportational differences which are associated with individual differences.

This is a study of some correlates of mobility behaviors and attitudes among retired persons in an urban area. It investigates factors that influence the extent to which a retired person gets about outside his home to engage with the society in which he lives: to shop, visit family and friends, use various services, and enjoy entertainment; and factors which may determine the means of transportation he usually uses. It explores factors related to his satisfaction with his arrangements for getting places. This paper presents results from the first phase, which was conducted in San Antonio. A cross-validation phase is being carried out in San Francisco.

For convenience, the sources of variance in mobility, transportation and satisfaction were divided into five categories: characteristics of the individual, the location of his residence within the urban-suburban complex, the neighborhood in which he lives, the household composition and family situation within which he leads his life, and the transportation facilities he uses.

Characteristics of Persons

Chronological Age. The possibility must be considered that age accounts for much of the variance in the mobility of retired persons. Transportation systems are increasingly complex, they emphasize speed, and they involve change. For all these reasons, chronological age might be an important factor. Mobility may be related to age because of sensory motor decrements, because of the rigidity of older organisms, or because of over-learning of outmoded mobility behaviors.

The "ridigity" of the older personality remains in doubt. Some studies seem to document it (28,29,30,31,32,33), others to disprove it (34,35,36,37,38). The tyranny of habit is less in doubt. Clearly, "overlearning" increases resistance to forgetting (39,40,41, 42,43). Long practice of motor skills can ingrain them so that they become automatic and highly resistant to extinction (44,45,46,47, 48).

Over a lifetime, a person builds up a repertory of cognitive and motor skills which enable him to navigate his world. However, as transportation systems are altered or if he must change from one mode of transportation to another (for example, when he can no longer drive an automobile) his deeply ingrained habits become inappropriate. They may interfere with acquisition of new skills (49). "Spontaneous recovery" (50) of old habits may present hazards. A driver may revert and respond to the traffic light high and ahead, rather than to the newer arrow low on the left, and turn left into oncoming traffic (51).

Not only in learning new transportation skills but even in continuing to perform old ones, the older person may be at a disadvantage. With age, sensory acuity diminishes, strength and agility decline, and responses slow (52). Perpetual-motor changes decrease the ability to respond correctly to complex stimuli (53). This decrement is emphasized when there is pressure for speed (54). Body balance becomes less secure, both when walking and when standing in place (55,56). There is an increasing tendency to lose equilibrium and fall (57,58). The consequent loss of confidence must be a further handicap. Generally, laboratory studies suggest that vehicular and pedestrian accommodations are increasingly problematic and hazardous, and therefore deterrent to mobility, as people age. Therefore age was included in this study of mobility behaviors and attitudes.

Health. On the other hand, time elapsed since birth may not be a critical variable in accounting for individual differences in mobility. Among "the old," chronological age may be a poor index of ability to get about; both biological and behavioral scientists have pointed to the need for more accurate indexes of "agedness" (59,60). The model of sickness and health may be more useful. Disease and disability rates increase in later life but, on an individual basis, there is no necessary concurrence between age and health (61). Definition of health is a problem (10). On the theory that S's rating is most relevant to his tendency to get about and do things, it was the measure used in this study.

Socioeconomic Status. The mobility problems of older persons are magnified by low income. A third of persons aged 65 and over live below the poverty line (62,63). Nearly all experience a sharp reduction in income at the time of retirement, and this "relative deprivation" may be important. Transportation options are limited for those with little money, and they are at least narrowed for nearly all retired persons. To provide an index of earlier socioeconomic status for this study, the work previously performed by male Ss (or that of female Ss' husbands) was categorized into job levels (64). Current income and quality of housing were indexes of present status.

Sex. Sex differences must always be considered (65). They seem especially likely in regard to mobility behavior in old age because of sex differences in gait and stance, and in the tendency to fall. Also, sex interacts with other variables relevant to mobility, such as longevity, income, marital status, and likelihood of living with children. The majority of older persons are women (66). Most older women are widowed (6). Generally they are the most impoverished (67). Old women are more likely than old men to live with their children (68), which may give them better access to automobiles as passengers. Women's transportation histories may be different from those of their male peers. Some women past 60 or 65 today never drove (69), just as they never voted (25). For some members of this generation, suffrage and automobiles are men's affairs.

Location of Residence

Situational as well as personal factors

may be related to mobility. Where a person lives may have an important bearing. Trips out of the home probably vary with distance of residence from the center of town. Many factors interact with location in influencing mobility of behaviors. For example, distance from the city center is related to the extent of public transportation services and to the likelihood of car ownership, as well as to socioeconomic status. No doubt such factors also help to determine why people live in the parts of town they do.

Distance from the city center was included as a variable in the study, in order to assess its importance in accounting for mobility and clarify its relationships with other variables. A basic premise was that peripherality-centrality of residence is an important correlate of mobility behaviors and attitudes, without making any assumption about cause and effect. San Antonio, the city in which these data were collected, is outlined by an almost circular highway. The central downtown intersection lies almost exactly at the geographic center. Using this intersection as the focus, concentric circles were drawn to define five zones. Radiuses were adjusted in relation to the older population of the city, in order to represent in the sample their number in each zone: central city; downtown but outside the center; urban-suburban interface; old, inner suburbs; and new, outer suburbs.

Characteristics of the Neighborhood

Regardless of where a person lives in the city, characteristics of his immediate neighborhood probably are important to his mobility habits.

Age Composition. Rosow (20) found that old persons in neighborhoods with high proportions of older residents enjoyed more neighborhood sociability and received more help from neighbors. Other investigators (27,16) are less sanguine about the superiority of age-similar neighborhoods, and some (70) deplore the "geriatric ghetto." The issue needs clarification. If age-segregated neighborhoods are better contexts for life during retirement, their residents should show differences from residents of "normal" neighborhoods in the important area of mobility. To the extent that the immediate neighborhood does not meet needs, ways of getting out of it are imperative. To the extent that sociability and assistance are provided by neighbors, visits with them should be more frequent, visits outside the neighborhood less important, and therefore frustration with transportation problems less acute.

According to Rosow: "Half measures are relatively ineffective...and strong concentrations of old people are a necessary condition" (20, p. 298). In the present study, age-homogeneous neighborhoods were hotels and apartment houses restricted to the retired or elderly, and residential blocks in which all households included a retired person.

This study tested the effects of neighborhood age-composition throughout the city. Rosow's Ss were drawn from apartment buildings in the Cleveland metropolitan area. In the present study, within each of the zones based on distance from the city center, equal members of Ss were selected from age-homogeneous and age-heterogeneous neighborhoods. A list of age-homogeneous residences within each of the five zones was compiled, and a "roster" of residents (without names) was prepared for each zone. From this roster, subjects were drawn at random.

To select residents of age-heterogeneous neighborhoods, the residential blocks within each zone were numbered. Blocks were selected at random. The interviewer drove to one corner of the block so selected; he then alternated starting at the northwest, northeast, southwest, and southeast corner. To avoid the bias of disporportionate amounts of data from houses on corner lots, the interviewer rolled dice to determine the dwelling to approach first. If there was no retired person in that house, he proceeded around the block in the direction in which he started. If there was no retired persons in that block, he went to the next block selected by the table of random numbers.

Ethnic Composition. Mobility behavior and satisfaction may vary according to the ethnic composition of a neighborhood. Public transportation tends to be less adequate in minority areas (71). Generally, economic conditions are more depressed there also (63), so that car ownership must be more difficult. Health is generally worse among the minority-group old (17), which would further inhibit mobility. Also, extent of "neignboring" and of confinement to the neighborhood are related to ethnic background (72,24).

The ethnic composition of the neighborhood rather than the background of the individual was used in this study. Generally they are the same. However, in regard to transportation facilities and schedules, as well as habits and attitudes, the neighborhood composition seemed more relevant. Difference between minority-group members who live in an ethnic ghetto and members of the same minority who live in other parts of town are being explored in the second phase of the study. The issue in the present report is whether transportation is a more severe problem for people who retire in ethnic-minority neighborhoods. Though there is some mixing, most residential neighborhoods in San Antonio were easily identified as Mexican-American, Afro-American or Anglo-American. Mexican-American neighborhoods comprise a sufficient proportion of San Antonio that any reasonable sampling plan would provide adequate representation of them, for statistical purposes. However, to insure that there were sufficient numbers of Ss from Afro-American neighborhoods, it was necessary to oversample them.

Neighborhood ethnicity was predetermined throughout the city by two observers, and color-coded on the map. Arbitrary quotas were set for selection of Ss according to the predominant ethnicity of the neighborhoods in which they lived: 15%-20% Afro-American, 25%-30% Mexican-American, and 55%-60% Anglo-American. A simple minority-majority division was made for this analysis of mobility determinants: Afro-Americans and Mexicans vs Anglo-Americans.

Personal and Family Characteristics

Mobility probably is influenced by the person's immediate milieu, his household and local family. The person who lives with others should be less frustrated by mobility problems than the one who lives alone (27,16). The presence or absence of a spouse may be particularly important. Transportation may be less of a problem for those who have children or relatives nearby (73). Length of residence at the present address may be an influence. The newcomer must acquire entire sets of transportation and mobility information and habits. To clarify the roles of these variables and of such characteristics as age, sex, income and health, subjects were selected at random within the locational zones and the neighborhood quotas.

Transportation Facilities

Habits of going about and satisfaction with ability to get places must be strongly dependent also upon facilities for transportation. "In America, the ability to go places depends so very much on the ability to drive an automobile without which you may be literally marooned in your own house" (27,p. 185). The ex-driver may have special difficulty because, late in life, he must learn completely different sets of information and skills in order to get around. Access to rides in cars driven by others may well influence the ability to get places, as may the accessibility of public transit.

Mobility Behavior and Attitudes

The 18 variables discussed above were viewed individually and in interaction as they related to each of 34 items of mobility behavior and satisfaction. Some items have to do with frequency of going to certain destinations: to see children, other relatives, friends, and the doctor; to stores, meetings, religious services, the library, the theater, a senior center, a sports event, or on a trip. Others relate to satisfaction with transportation to these places. Still other items have to do with frequency of using various means of transportation: automobile, bus, taxi, feet, train and plane; and satisfaction with them.

Data Collection and Subjects

Data were collected in individual interviews which typically lasted two and a half hours. Interviewers in Mexican-American neighborhoods were bilingual members of the Mexican-American community. The 709 subjects were a 1.3% sample of the city's retired population. Mean age was 67.5; 82% were 65 or over. Four per cent were under 50 and 4.5%, 85 or older. The group was comprised of 40% men and 60% women, while national figures for people aged 65 and older are 43% and 57% (74). The median yearly income of $1797 was close to the national median for persons 65 and over (74). During working years, most men (and women's husbands) had held jobs in the middle levels (64). Only 9% had been at professional or top managerial levels, and 8%, unskilled laborers.

Order of Importance of Person-Situation Variables

A stepwise multiple-regression analysis was run between the set of 18 person-situation variables and each mobility variable. For each analysis, the initial step involved identification of the person-situation variable which had the highest zero-order correlation with the mobility variable. The second step identified a second person-situation variable: the one which, together with the first had the highest multiple-correlation with the mobility variable. In each subsequent step one more person-situation variable was added into the system until none which remained in the pool would significantly increase the coefficient. Tables 1 and 2 summarize the selection of person-situation variables in the 34 multiple-regression analyses: Table 1, in regard to frequency of going places, and Table 2, for satisfaction with transportation to these destinations.

Table 1: Correlates of Frequency

Rank	Variable	Among 1st 4	1st Variable
1	Health	12	3
2	Location	9	3
3	Ethnicity	8	0
4	Income	6	3
5	Has car	6	2
6	Age	6	0
7	Housing	5	2
8	Household	5	0
9	Job level	4	1
10	Other kin	3	2
11	Time at address	3	1
12	Sex	3	1
13	Children	3	1
14	Exdriver	2	0
15	Other driver	2	0
16	Distance to bus	1	0
17	Age of neighbors	1	0
18	Marital status	0	0

Health. Assessment of one's own health was the most important variable in regard to frequency of going places and satisfaction with arrangements for getting there. People who expressed favorable views of their health tended to go out more often and to be better satisfied with their transportation. This is consistent with responses when they were asked what was the most important problem for them in relation to mobility. Over half (52%) put health in first place.

Table 2: Correlates of Satisfaction

Rank	Variable	Among 1st 4	1st Variable
1	Health	12	5
2	Has car	9	2
3	Location	8	3
4	Job level	5	0
5	Sex	4	1
6	Income	4	0
7	Ethnicity	4	0
8	Household	3	0
9	Other driver	4	0
10	Housing	3	2
11	Children	3	1
12	Other kin	2	1
13	Time at address	2	1
14	Age	2	0
15	Marital status	1	0
16	Exdriver	1	0
17	Age of neighbors	1	0
18	Distance to bus	0	0

Location. Distance of the person's residence from the center of the city ranked second in accounting for frequency of going out, and third in regard to satisfaction with transportation. In general, centrality of residence was associated with high frequency of going out and satisfaction in regard to transportation, while peripherality was associated with infrequency of going out and dissatisfaction with transportation.

Car Ownership. Having or not having an automobile ranked within the first four "determinants" of outing frequency and transportation satisfaction. It was second only to health in regard to satisfaction. Generally, people who had cars tended to go more and to be better satisfied about their transportation. Car ownership interacts in an interesting fashion with location of residence. The proportion of people who had cars was very small in the inner city and increased from zone to zone toward the outer suburbs. Despite this distribution of car ownership and the association of car ownership with frequent outing and transportation satisfaction, residents of the inner city tended to go more and to be better satisfied about their mobility than were people who lived farther out. Being without a car was common but not much of a handicap in the downtown area; the really housebound and dissatisfied people were those in the suburbs who did not have automobiles.

Socioeconomic Level. An index of past or present socioeconomic status ranks fourth in importance in regard to both frequency and satisfaction. Present income is the fourth most important correlate of frequency of going places, and level of previous job is fourth in importance in regard to satisfaction with

transportation. Quality of housing, another index of socioeconomic status, was seventh in importance in regard to frequency of going out and tenth in regard to satisfaction with transportation. Generally, people in higher socioeconomic brackets tended to go more and to be better satisfied with their transportation to the places they went.

The importance of finances was indicated also by responses to the direct question regarding the most important problem in regard to mobility. Money was second only to health. It was the critical issue for a third of these people. Ss were also asked to what extent they thought money would solve their transportation problems. Answers were recorded on a seven-point scale running from "completely" to "not at all." A multiple regression analysis was made of the determinants of this score, using the same pool of 18 person-situation variables. Predictably, socioeconomic indexes accounted for most of the variance in the importance of money. The most important correlate was current income. Those in upper brackets were likely to say that more money would not help, and those in lower brackets to say that money would solve their problems. Those with good incomes either had no mobility problems or their problems were not amenable to solution in terms of dollars, while the very poor thought they could get about much better if they had additional funds. Tying for second importance were qualtiy of present housing and previous job-level. Persons in poor housing and those who had worked in unskilled and semi-skilled jobs tended to say money would solve all their problems, while persons in good housing and those who had been in professional or managerial positions were less sanguine about the extent to which additional money would help. Ownership of an automobile was relevant also: persons who had cars tended to downgrade the importance of additional money, and those without cars to emphasize it. Age and health were additional factors: older members of the group and those in poor health were less optimistic than the younger and healthier in regard to the capacity of money to solve their transportation difficulties.

Neighborhood Ethnicity. Third in importance in regard to frequency of going places, and seventh in regard to satisfaction with transportation was ethnicity of neighborhood. Generally, residents in minority neighborhoods tended to be less mobile and to express less satisfaction with their transportation.

Other Determinants. Men tended to go less and to complain more about their transportation than did women. There was a tendency to greater mobility and higher satisfaction with transportation among people who had someone to drive them places and those who had children and other relatives in the area; on the part of the less old, and those who had lived relatively long at the present address. Exdrivers tended to be especially limited in going places and disgruntled about transportation. Age composition of neighborhood, marital status, and distance to the nearest bus stop did not account for much of the variance in any index of mobility or satisfaction. (In the second phase, a different measure of access to bus service is being used. Often the nearest stop is not the one to which a person must go to catch a bus to a desired destination. Also, the schedule may be frequent of infrequent.)

Determinants of Getting to Various Destinations

The relative importance of the person-situation variables is different from one type of trip to another, as is efficiency in accounting for the variance in mobility behavior and transportation satisfaction. Table 3 summarizes the results of 26 of the regression analyses in terms of the final multiple-correlation coefficients and the number of person-situation variables which entered into each of them.

Table 3: Variance in Mobility

Mobility Variable	N of Variables	R
Visit Children (f)	3	.84
Satisfaction	4	.82
Visit Other Relatives (f)	4	.80
Satisfaction	5	.78
Visiting Friends (f)	6	.57
Satisfaction	6	.60
Going to Doctor (f)	6	.58
Satisfaction	3	.50
Grocery Shopping (f)	4	.59
Satisfaction	4	.63
Other Shopping (f)	6	.65
Satisfaction	5	.65
Attend Meetings (f)	6	.57
Satisfaction	5	.59
Attend Church (f)	5	.60
Satisfaction	6	.57
Going to Library (f)	4	.66
Satisfaction	5	.66
Theater-Going (f)	8	.62
Satisfaction	7	.63
Senior Center (f)	6	.57
Satisfaction	5	.57
Sports Events (f)	4	.53
Satisfaction	5	.55
Travel (f)	5	.61
Satisfaction	5	.60

Children. By far the most important determinant of frequency of going to visit children and of satisfaction with transportation for these visits was whether children lived in the city. Obviously, people whose children lived far away went to see them less often, and gave lower marks to the transportation. Within the city, frequency of going to children was negatively related to the centrality of the retired person's home. Suburbanites tended to pay most visits to children, and city-center residents, least. This may be related to the fact that more suburbanites owned cars, and

that few people had children within walking distance. People in minority neighborhoods reported more visits to children. Retired persons most satisfied about visiting their children were those who, in addition to having children close by, had good health, someone to drive them to see the children, and relatively good incomes.

Other Relatives. As with children, proximity of the persons was the most important determinant of frequency of visits and satisfaction with transportation. Having a car to drive or a ride with someone else was also influential. However, people in ethnic minority neighborhoods, who were unlikely to own automobiles, paid frequent visits to family members. Retired people who had no children in the area tended to see other relatives more frequently than did those with children nearby. In regard to satisfaction with transportation for family visits, income was second in importance after proximity of relatives. Retired persons with low incomes, without automobiles, in poor health, and whose homes were distant from bus stops tended to be most dissatisfied with their means of transportation.

Friends. Health rating was the strongest correlate of how often visits were made to friends and of how well satisfied the person was with the trips. People who lived alone, and those who could drive themselves or had someone to take them in an automobile went most often. People who had no children in the area visited friends more often than persons who did. Important determinants of satisfaction with transportation, in addition to health, were having a car or a ride in another's automobile. People who lived near the city center tended to be better satisfied than people who lived in outlying areas. People who lived alone, and those who had no children in the area tended to be better satisfied with arrangements for seeing friends than were persons who lived in larger households and those who had children in the city.

Doctor. Understandably, health was the variable most strongly associated with frequency of visits to a doctor. People who rated their health favorably tended to go seldom. Infrequent visits were characteristic also of those in poor quality housing and with low income, those who lived alone, those who had lived only a short time at the present address, and those who lived far from a bus stop. Satisfaction with transportation was determined primarily by whether the person drove. If he drove, he probably was well satisfied; if he did not drive, he probably assessed his transportation negatively. Other correlates of satisfaction were quality of housing and distance from the city center. Residents of poor housing were more likely than those in good housing to express dissatisfaction. Residents of the inner city tended to be better satisfied than those who lived farther out.

Grocery Shopping. Not having a car was the most important concomitant of frequent grocery shopping trips. Persons who had given up driving tended to shop most often. Persons who lived alone and those in poor housing also tended to make frequent shopping trips. On the other hand, those who considered their health poor went infrequently. Poor health was the factor most closely associated with dissatisfaction in regard to transportation. Nearly as important was lack of an automobile. Ex-drivers were especially disgruntled. Those who lived alone or with only the spouse tended to be better satisfied than those in larger households. Men tended to be less well satisfied than women.

Other Shopping. In regard to shopping for items other than food, health was the leading correlate of both frequency and satisfaction. People who lived near the city center, and those who lived farther out and had cars, tended to shop frequently. Non-drivers who lived outside the heart of town, people in poor housing, men, and the very old seldom or never shopped except for food. People in good health, drivers, and those who lived near the city center tended to be satisfied with their transportation. Those who lived alone or with a spouse tended to be better satisfied than those in larger households. Generally men were less satisfied than women.

Meetings. People in poor housing and those with poor health were least likely to attend meetings. People most likely to go were those who had someone to drive them or who could drive themselves. Frequent attenders tended to be long-time residents at the present address, and persons living alone. Determinants of satisfaction were similar to those of attendance. Persons in poor housing, those who had moved within the year, those who had no one drive them, and those in poor health tended to be dissatisfied.

Interestingly, people more likely to be dissatisfied with their transportation to meetings were those who had children living in the area. As mentioned above, people with children nearby made fewer trips to see other relatives and friends, and were likely to express dissatisfaction about their transportation for these visits. Proximity of children was favorable only to frequency of trips to children and satisfaction with these trips. The findings suggest that, while children pick up parents for visits to their own homes, they may not be so obliging about taking parents to see friends or other family members or to meetings. Reduced desire for other associations when a child is available may be a factor in the low frequencies. However, the consistent dissatisfaction argues against this as a complete explanation.

Religious Services. People who had children or other relatives in the area attended church less frequently. This suggests that the family does not provide a significant amount of transportation to church for retired persons, and that participation in a religious congregation may be more important to the older person who does not have immediate participation in a family group. Other factors associated with infrequent church attendance were poor health, substandard housing, and short residence at the present address. Men attended less frequently than women. Health was the variable most strongly associated with satisfaction with transportation: those in poor health were less satisfied. Next in importance was sex: men tended to be dissatisfied with their means of getting to church. In some instances this sounded like a rationalization for infrequent attendance. People in substandard housing were more likely to be dissatisfied with the way they go to church, as were those who had no car and no one to drive them. Again, people who had children or other relatives in the area expressed more dissatisfaction with their transportation to church.

Entertainment. Location of residence was the most important correlate of frequency of going out for entertainment. Those who lived in the city center tended to go most often, and those in the outer suburbs, least. Theater-goers also tended to be wealthier, healthier, younger car owners who were living with spouse, and who had held jobs at higher levels. Those least likely to go out for entertainment were exdrivers and those with low incomes. The people relatively well satisfied with transportation were those who lived near the center of town, who had good health and were relatively young, and those who had held jobs at high levels. Other factors making for satisfaction were having a car or a ride with someone, or being close to a bus stop.

Library. Few of these people ever went to a library. Those most likely to use one had lived a short time at their present address, lived near the center of the city, had held high-level jobs, and did not have children in the area. Those dissatisfied with transportation tended to be non-drivers, long-time residents of the same address, in substandard housing, out from the center of the city.

Senior Center. Senior Center attendance was uncommon, and findings in relation to it are influenced by a sampling bias: persons in good housing were more likely to attend senior center activities, as were persons in age-segregated neighborhoods. These findings are artifacts of the inclusion of senior centers in retirement residences. Their residents comprise a small fraction of the total group, but a majority of senior center participants. These findings probably mean only that people who live under the same roof with a senior center are more likely to use it. Coincidentally, the housing was good and was restricted to the elderly. People with housing was good and was restricted to the elderly. People with low incomes and those who lived alone were more likely to go to senior centers than were those who had more money and lived in households with other people. Those who had worked in high-level jobs, and those who had someone available to drive them places tended not to go to senior centers.

Sports Events. Sex was the basic determinant of attendance at sports events: men went much more frequently. Militating again attendance were low income, very old age, and poor health. Availability of relatives in the area was negatively correlated with satisfaction regarding transportation. Again there is the pattern of dissatisfaction with transportation on the part of those who had family nearby.

Travel. Income was the strongest correlate of trip taking. Travel was also facilitated by healthy, relative youth, living in the suburbs, and driving or having someone to drive. Dissatisfaction was strongest among those in poor health, the poor, and persons who could not drive and had no one to drive them.

Determinants of Means of Transportation

The regression analysis also looked into the means people used to get from one place to another. (See Table 4)

Table 4: Variance in Transportation Mode

Mode	N of Variables	R
Drives car (f)	1	.94
Satisfaction	2	.92
Driven by others (f)	4	.64
Satisfaction	5	.59
Bus (f)	5	.72
Taxi (f)	5	.62
Walking (F)	4	.76
Satisfaction	6	.74
Train (f)	4 .	.53

Driving. Frequency of driving an automobile could be well estimated from one item of information: whether the person had a car. Most people who had a car drove it every day. Ownership of a car is strongly correlated with high income, good housing, high job level, and residence in the suburbs. People who had automobiles and sufficient incomes to finance their upkeep tended to be well satisfied.

Driven by Others. People most likely to be driven by others tended to have no cars, to be in poor health, to live in substandard housing, and to have worked at menial jobs. Dissatisfaction was expressed primarily by the people who had rides. This was explained by the appearance in the regression analysis of one more item: availability of a driver. The primary source of dissatisfaction was the amount of chauffeuring. They needed more.

Bus. The best predictor of how often a person took a bus was whether he had a car. If he had no car, he was likely to take a bus;

if he had a car, he was not. Nearly as important was residence toward the center of the city. The very old, those in poor health, and those who lived far from a stop, seldom took a bus. Satisfaction with the bus was inversely related to use of it. People who had cars and drove them "everywhere" considered the bus good, while those who were dependent upon the bus gave it low marks.

Taxi. People who lived alone and near the center of the city, those who did not have cars, and especially the exdrivers, were most likely to take a taxi. The very poor and people who had children in the area were not likely to take one.

Walking. Location was the most important correlate of walking as transportation. People who lived near the center of town walked most, those in the outer suburbs, least. People who had cars and those in poor health walked little. Men were more likely than women to use walking as transportation.

As with the bus, people who walked were less favorable about it than were people who used other means of transportation. People in the center city, where most of the utilitarian walking went on, were dissatisfied with walking as a form of transportation, as were the people, throughout the city, who had no cars. Suburbanites who went everywhere by car, were very favorable in their evaluation of walking. Men and the relatively young, among both of whom walking was relatively common, were negative toward it; and people who were far from a bus stop were negative in their assessment of walking.

Train. As would be expected from the data on taking trips, traveling by train was associated with high income. It was also more common among people who lived alone, and those who had no relatives in the area, and ex-drivers.

Plane. Unexpectedly, current income was not the primary correlate of plane travel, but third in order of importance. Those who traveled by plane tended to have retired from high-level jobs and to live in the suburbs, with spouse. Those who did not fly tended to live in substandard housing toward the center of the city, and to have low incomes.

Summary and Implications

These findings accent the importance of health and socioeconomic factors in relation to the mobility of retired persons. The unwell and the poor were least mobile and least satisfied. Car ownership was important in determing how much a person went about, and even more critical in relation to satisfaction with transportation. Generally, people who did not drive found it difficult to go to most places. Location of residence was important also, and its effects interact with those of socioeconomic status and car ownership. City-center residents tended to go out more often and to be relatively well satisfied, despite the fact that few had cars. Residents in ethnic-minority neighborhoods tended to be less pleased with their arrangements to go places. Having children in the area was favorable in regard to family visits but was related to dissatisfaction with transportation to other destinations. Age, marital status, age of neighbors, and distance to bus stop were relatively unimportant.

The specifics of these various relationships and their implications will be reported elsewhere. The present very summary over-view of the results indicates that the retired people who are relatively well able to make use of their community resources for creative and enjoyable leisure are those in good health, who either have automobiles or live in the heart of the city, and in ethnic-majority neighborhoods. They have relatively good retirement incomes and housing, and they retired from high-level jobs. On the other hand, community resources tend to be inaccessible, and therefore retirement may constitute a special problem in regard to free time, for people with health problems, those who do not own cars (particularly if they live in the suburbs), those who live in minority neighborhoods, and in substandard housing, and who retired from menial jobs with low retirement incomes.

References

1. Pieper, J. Leisure, the Basis of Culture. New York: Pantheon Books, 1952.
2. Soule, G.H. Time for Living. New York: Viking Press, 1955.
3. Soule, G.H. Free-time - man's new resource. In W. Donahue, W.W. Hunter, D. Doons, H. Maurice (Eds.), Free Time - Challenge to Later Maturity. Ann Arbor, Michigan: University of Michigan Press, 1958. Pp. 61-76.
4. Ferenczi, S. Further Contributions to the Theory and Practice of Psychoanalysis. London: Hogarth Press, 1926. Pp. 174-177.
5. Martin, A.R. Idle hands and guilty minds. American Journal of Psychoanalysis, 1969, 29, 147-156.
6. Metropolitan Life Insurance Company. Expectations of Life in the United States at Age 50. Statistical Bulletin, 1965.
7. Kreps, J.M. & Spengler, J.J. The leisure component of economic growth. The Employment Impact of Technological Change. Appendix, Vol. 2, National Commission on Technology, Automation & Economic Progress. Washington, D.C.: Government Printing Office, 1966. Pp. 353-397.
8. Donahue, W., Orbach, H.L. & Pollak, O. Retirement: the emerging social pattern. In C. Tibbitts (Ed.), Handbook of Social Gerontology. Chicago: University of Chicago Press, 1960. Pp. 330-397.
9. Kleemeier, R.W. Time, activity, and leisure. In R.W. Kleemeier (Ed.), Aging and Leisure. New York: Oxford University Press, 1961.
10. Shanas, E. The Health of Older People.

Cambridge: Harvard University Press, 1962.
11. Tibbits, C. Introduction. Social gerontology: origin, scope and trends. International Social Science Journal, 1963, 15, 339-354.
12. Wirth, L. Urbanism as a way of life. In P.K. Hatt & A.J. Reis, Jr. (Eds.), Cities and Society: The Revised Reader in Urban Sociology. New York: Free Press of Glencoe, 1957. Pp. 593-594.
13. Anderson, J. Environment and meaningful activity. In R. Williams, C. Tibbitts, & W. Donahue (Eds.), Process of Aging. New York: Atherton Press, 1963. Pp. 223-224.
14. Reisman, D. The Lonely Crowd. New York: Doubleday Anchor Books, 1955.
15. Townsend, P. Isolation, desolation, and loneliness. In H. Friis, P. Milhoj, E. Shanas, J. Stehouwer, D. Wedderburn, P. Townsend (Eds.), Old People in Three Industrial Societies. New York: Atherton Press, 1968. Pp. 258-285.
16. Turnstall, J. Old & Alone. London: Routledge and Kegan Paul, 1966.
17. Ostfeld, A.M. Frequency and nature of health problems of retired persons. In F.M. Carp (Ed.), The Retirement Process. Washington, D.C.: Government Printing Office, 1968.
18. Kutner, B., Fanshel, D., Togo, A.M. & Langner, T.S. Five Hundred Over Sixty. New York: Russell Sage Foundation, 1956.
19. Downing, J. Factors affecting the selective use of a social club for the aged. Journal of Gerontology, 1957, 12, 81-84.
20. Rosow, I. Social Integration of the Aged. New York: The Free Press, 1967.
21. Blenkner, M. Comments. In R.W. Kleemier (Ed.), Aging and Leisure. New York: Oxford University Press, 1961. Pp. 418-421.
22. Carp, F.M. Housing and minority-group elderly. The Gerontologist, 1969, 9, 20-24.
23. Carp, F.M. Use of community resources and social adjustment of the elderly. Proceedings of Seminars, 1965-1969. Durham, North Carolina: Duke University Council on Aging and Human Development, November, 1969, 169-176.
24. Carp, F.M. Communicating with elderly Mexican-Americans. The Gerongologist, 1970, No. 2, 10, 126-134.
25. Carp, F.M. A Future for the Aged: The Residents of Victoria Plaza. Austin: University of Texas Press, 1966.
26. Carp, F.M. Mobility and retired people. In E. Cantilli & J. Shmelzer (Eds.), Transportation and Aging, in press.
27. Bracey, H.E. In Retirement. Baton Rouge, Louisiana: Louisana State University Press, 1966.
28. Stone, C.P. The age factor in animal learning: I. Rats in the problem box

and the maze. Genetic Psychological
Monographs, 1929, 5, 1-130.

29. Stone, C.P. The age factor in animal
learning: II. Rats on a multiple light
discrimination box and a difficult maze.
Genetic Psychological Monographs, 1929,
6, 125-202.

30. Kay, H. Learning of a serial task by
different age groups. Journal of Experimental Psychology, 1951, 3, 75-80.

31. Schaie, K.W. Rigidity-flexibility and
intelligence: a cross-sectional study
of the adult life span from 20 to 70
years. Genetic Psychological Monographs,
1958, 72, 1-25.

32. Chown, S.M. Age and the rigidities.
Journal of Gerontology, Vol. 16, 1961,
353-362.

33. Botwinick, J., Brinley, J.F. & Robbin, J.S.
Learning a position discrimination and
position reversals by Sprague-Dawley rats
of different ages. Journal of Gerontology, 1962, 17, 315-319.

34. Bernstein, I.S. Response variability and
rigidity in the adult chimpanzee. Journal of Gerontology, 1961, 16, 381-386.

35. Birren, J.E. Age differences in learning
a two-choice water maze by rats. Journal of Gerontology, 1962, 17, 207-213.

36. Kay, H. & Sime, M. Discrimination with
old and young rats. Journal of Gerontology, 1962, 17, 75-80.

37. Sime, M. & Kay, H. Inter-problem interference and age. Journal of Gerontology,
1962, 17, 81-87.

38. Botwinick, J., Brinley, J.F. & Robbin, J.S.
Learning and reversing a four-choice
multiple Y-maze by rats of three ages.
Journal of Gerontology, 1963, 18, 279-
298.

39. Ebbinghaus, H. Memory. New York: Teachers College, Columbia University, 1913.

40. Krueger, W.C.F. The effect of over-learning on retention. Journal of Experimental Psychology, 1929, 12, 71-78.

41. Krueger, W.C.F. Further studies in over-
learning. Journal of Experimental Psychology, 1930, 13, 152-163.

42. Bartlett, F.C. Remembering: An Experimental and Social Study. London:
Cambridge University Press, 1932.

43. Hebb, D.O. The Organization of Behavior.
New York: Wiley, 1949.

44. Carmichael, L. Manual of Child Psychology.
New York: John Wiley & Sons, 1946.

45. Munn, N.L. Handbook of Psychological
Research on the Rat. Boston: Houghton
Mifflin, 1950.

46. Gagné, R.M. & Fleishman, E.A. Psychology
and Human Performance. New York: Henry
Holt and Company, 1959.

47. Bilodeau, E.A. & Bilodeau, I. McD. Motor-
skills learning. Annual Reviews of
Psychology. Palo Alto, California:
George Banta, 1961. Pp. 243-280.

48. Fitts, P.M. Perceptual-motor skill learning. In A.W. Melton (Ed.), Categories
of Human Learning. New York: Academic
Press, 1964.

49. Guthrie, E.R. The Psychology of Human
Conflict. New York: Harper, 1938.

50. Pavlov, I.P. Conditioned Reflexes. London: Oxford University Press, 1927.

51. Lawton, A.H. Accidental injuries to the
aged and their psychologic impact. Mayo
Clinic Proceedings, 1967, 42, 685-697.

52. Birren, J.E. The Psychology of Aging.
Englewood Cliffs, New Jersey: Prentice-
Hall, 1964.

53. Braun, H.W. Perceptual processes. In
J.E. Birren (Ed.), Handbook of Aging and
the Individual. Chicago: University
of Chicago Press, 1960.

54. Welford, A.T. Psychomotor performance.
In J.E. Birren (Ed.), Handbook of Aging
and the Individual. Chicago: University
of Chicago Press, 1960.

55. Lawton, A.H. & Azar, G.J. Consequences of
physical and physiological change with
age in the patterns of living and housing
for the middle-aged and aged. In F.M.
Carp (Ed.), Patterns of Living and Housing of Middle-Aged and Older People.
Washington, D.C.: Government Printing
Office, 1966.

56. Lawton, A.H. & Azar, G.J. Sensory and
perceptual changes that may influence the
housing needs of the aging. In F.M. Carp
(Ed.), Patterns of Living and Housing of
Middle-Aged and Older People. Washington
D.C.: Government Printing Office, 1966.

57. Droller, H. Falls among elderly people
living at home. Geriatrics, 1955, 10,
239-244.

58. Azar, G.J. & Lawton, A.H. Gait and step-
ping as factors in the frequent falls of
elderly women. Gerontologist, 1964, 4,
83-84.

59. Butler, R.N. The facade of chronological
age: an interpretative summary. In B.L.
Neugarten (Ed.), Middle Age and Aging.
Chicago: University of Chicago Press,
1968. Pp. 235-242.

60. Strehler, B.L. Cellular aging. Annals
New York Academy of Science, 1967, 138,
661-679.

61. Jones, H.B. The relation of human health
to age, place and time. In J.E. Birren
(Ed.), Handbook of Aging and the Individual. Chicago: University of Chicago
Press, 1959. Pp. 336-363.

62. Epstein, L. Income of the aged in 1962:
first findings of the 1963 survery of the
aged. Social Security Bulletin, March,
1964, 27, 3-24.

63. Orshansky, M. Counting the poor: another
look at the poverty profile. Social Security Bulletin, January, 1965.

64. McGuire, C. Index of status characteris-
tics. In C. McGuire (Ed.), Social Status
Peer Status, and Social Mobility. Chicago
University of Chicago Press, 1949.

65. Carp, F.M. Comments on: age and sex differences in stress reactivity in genetically hypertensive and normal control rats. In S.S. Chown & K.F. Riegel (Eds.) Interdisciplinary Topics in Gerontology. Vol. 1. Psychological functioning in the normal aging and senile aged. New York: S. Karger, 1968. Pp. 109-111.

66. National Center for Health Statistics. Vital Statistics of the United States. Vol. 2, Sec. 5, 1963.

67. Epstein, L.A. & Murray, J.H. The Aged Populations of the United States. Washington, D.C.: Government Printing Office, 1967.

68. Stehouwer, J. The household and family relations of old people. In H. Friis, P. Miljoh, E. Shanas, J. Stehouwer, P. Townsend, D. Wedderburn (Eds.), Old People in Three Industrial Societies. New York: Atherton Press, 1968. Pp. 177-227.

69. Carp, F.M. Driving an automobile in retirement, in press.

70. Clark, M. & Anderson, B. Culture and Aging: An Anthropological Study of the Older American. Springfield: Charles C. Thomas, 1967.

71. Stringfellow, W. The representation of the poor in American society. Law and Contemporary Problems, 1966, 31, 142-151.

72. Clark, M. Health in the Mexican-American Culture. Berkeley, California: University of California Press, 1959.

73. Shanas, E. & Streib, G.F. (Eds.) Social Structure and the Family: Generational Relations. Englewood Cliffs, New Jersey: Prentice-Hall, 1965.

74. Brotman, H.B. Who are the aged: a demographic view. Occasional Papers in Gerontology. Ann Arbor, Michigan: Institute of Gerontology, University of Michigan, Wayne State University, November, 1968.

Urban Transit Vehicle Design and Rider Satisfaction

by Robert L. Lepper

Carnegie-Mellon University, Pittsburgh, Pennsylvania

and Robert K. Moorhead

Rensselaer Research Corporation, Troy, New York

Abstract

This paper describes an investigation into the microenvironment of the urban transit vehicle, and offers a general framework for structuring observed human activity in a manner useful to the designer. Sources of psychological stress, entry-exit flow problems, riding problems, and interior design parameters, are identified. A full scale interior mock-up was constructed as a basis for investigating changes in current vehicular interior design. Photography was used as a primary means of collecting data.

The basic assumption of this study is that the designer must observe the social environment of a transit vehicle before he can rationally design alternative interior configurations. Some principles for solving interior design problems are offered.

Introduction

Rider satisfaction is the ultimate measure of transit utility. The individual rider, the ultimate particle of an urban transit system, confronts the reality of the system through its ultimate hard component, the vehicle.

Reality -- real physical contact with the vehicle and one's neighbors, events taking place in real time -- will be repeated ten times a week for a job tripper, 500 times per year.

The study examines the qualities of the experience to real persons in a real world as distinct from the abstractions and quantitative values of trip time, "ride quality", system efficiency and economics. The real rider may be utterly miserable on his first (or one hundredth) trip in a superably air-conditioned and vibration-free vehicle of a splendidly planned new system which operates an ideal schedule at half the fare of the old system. The real rider will be miserable in this abstract and quantitative paradise if he is exposed to, or confronted with, invasion of his person or indignity by neighbors.

The reality of an urban transit vehicle has three aspects. Functionally the vehicle is a collector and distributor of self-programmed or 'volatile' particles.

Sociologically it is an unfocused behavioral setting, the convergence and dispursion of a group governed by pure chance. Psychologically the plan of the setting may distribute the members of the group with greater or less satisfaction to the individual members.

The functions of collection and distribution will progress in random patterns of entry, periodic rest and exit. The design of the processing vessel, the vehicle, may ease or inhibit flow of the 'particles', in this case the riders.

The 'unfocused behavioral setting' is that of a heterogenious group, each member of which has his own destination, sharing a common space for a short period of time -- with the combination of the mix changing at every stop. It lacks the focus of a church service wherein the members of the congregation, however diverse their class origins may be, merge in a common objective. They enter at the same time, stay 'the length of the trip', and disburse at the end of the event.

The rider in an urban transit vehicle is exposed to the behavior of other passengers. The behavior of one person acting on the environment may infringe upon the person of another in violation of the latter's code of propriety. A qualitative vehicle plan will recognize this potential for infringement and seek to control it.

Conventional approaches to 'passenger comfort' conceive the problem in quantitative terms of square feet per person, of dimensional ranges in seats, of noise and vibration tolerance, illumination levels and the comfort index of temperature/humidity ratios, (1). These abstract values become real experience to a passenger who knows that he is squeezed into a hot (or cold), noisy environment, cursed with unpleasant vibration and a low light level. Technology can (and does) alleviate the discomforts of this physiological world. In the psychological world all men are not brothers.

In a psycho-social world - which is the world of an urban transit vehicle - people will vary in physical agility, in psychological toughness, in degree of pasivity or agressiveness of temperament and in behavioral codes.

A group of passengers who are sharing an ideal physiological environment of sight, sound, temperature, and vibration can be seething in psychological distress stemming from bodily contact with each other.

It is the purpose of this study to examine this psycho-social reality. Hopefully, modification of vehicular design can minimize or eliminate some sources of distress. Alleviation, a rise in standards, would be immeasurable boon to the captive rider. The rider with modal choice who may be attracted to the system by promise of increased convenience at reduced cost, would not be lost through alienation.

Urban rapid transit is social recognition of the right of mobility. In pursuit of fulfillment of this right, urban rapid transit can be seen as minimum accommodation for those who have no modal choice. It can be seen also as an alternative mode for those who do; that is, for those who choose to leave their private vehicles at home rather than to compete for their space on the freeway or for parking space in the CBD.

Minimum accommodation invites the rejection by one social class of the code of behavior of another. The rejection can lead to a de facto one-class system, patronized only by those who have no alternative. Minimum accommodation is inherently hostile to the physically disabled. The latter is a class which is, in fact, deprived of the right of mobility.

An unwholesome inference of upgrading a system is that of attracting a wider patronage from the well-off. A more wholesome view would see that an upgraded vehicle would benefit all men alike. A neighbor's wet umbrella against the leg of rich or poor is just as wet. The goal of 'equal protection' applies equally to those who share and those who differ in social codes. A de facto one-class system need not settle for minimum physiological standards only.

Indignity to person, or its threat, can occur within as well as across class lines. Nonetheless, it is predictable that potential indignity to person and heterogeneity of patronage are in inverse ratio. As threat goes down the variety of social mix goes up and vice versa.

The comparative studies of vehicle plans analyze conditions of psycho/social stress which are directly traceable to the plans themselves. An alternative plan is proposed for reduction of the stress potentials.

Development of Vehicular Plans

The contemporary urban transit vehicle is an obsolete hybrid of the pre-urban society. The first public carrier, the omnibus, began operation in New York in 1830, two years after the founding of the Baltimore and Ohio Railroad, (2). The omnibus or "carryall", by definition, carried anyone with the price of the fare. Prior to the omnibus, wheeled mobility was restricted to the gentry, and to owners or hirers of a private carriage. The gentry had no psycho-social problems with fellow travelers.

The urban transit vehicle is short-haul with the 'stages' measured in city blocks rather than in miles. Its precedent in public carriers, the post or stage coach, was long haul with the spacing of the posts or stages set by the endurance of the propulsion units, the horses. With steam propulsion able to pull larger loads at higher speeds it was logical that the first railroad passenger vehicles were stage coaches carried piggy-back on flat cars. The subsequent rail coach was a logical extension of its horse-drawn predecessor. Increase the number of benches; face all the benches in the direction of travel. The resultant plan resembles a mobile meeting hall.

The major characteristic of a meeting hall is its cycle of use. In general the participants in a meeting flow in a linear pattern. They gather, move easily into their seats, stay 'the length of the trip', exit together at its end. As any air traveler or church goer will know there is turbulence at exit. The participants will maneuver for advantage but, however competitive they may be the flow is one-directional. The commuter train is a variable of this linear flow. It will collect its inputs at stages down the line for a mass output at the terminal. The process will be reversed in the evening.

An urban transit vehicle is short-haul. The short-haul vehicle with short intervals of start and stop is a collector and distributor of random boardings and destinations. Each stop is both a destination and an origin. Rider flow is two-directional.

This cycle of use differs sharply from the meeting hall precedent yet the latter persists as prototype for all transit vehicles.

In the muscle society of the early 19th century, just fifty years after James Watt, any widespread access to wheeled mobility was a major advance in satisfaction of a social need. The vehicle plan having 'solved the problem' of mass transit, the energies of the entrepreneurs could flow into expansion of track mileage, to safety and to physiological 'comfort'. Congestion with its inevitable face-to-face interaction would be taken as a matter of course. A system of class or premium fares would minimize congestion for the well-to-do in the long haul train or plane or the short haul Paris subway.

The meeting hall plan of folk ingenuity remains the model-substantially unmodified. The model of a century ago is the major source of contemporary dissatisfaction with urban transit.

Environment of the Vehicle:
Isolation of Relevant Variables

The meeting hall plan has defects of its own for the long trip. These defects are compounded in the short trip vehicle. These defects, of two types, are identifiable in two cycles in time--the physical turbulence of entry-exit at the stop (the vehicle is at rest but the riders are in motion) and the psycho/social interactions of riding companions (the vehicle is in motion while the riders are at rest). The former are productive of confusion, shortlived irritation and time delay. The latter have high potential for stress producing situations persisting in time with profound dissatisfaction to riders. The design of the vehicle can unwittingly intensify rather than alleviate these problem areas. The meeting hall plan tends to intensify them.

Entry/Exit flow problems: sources of dynamic stress indentified

In the meeting hall plan of the long haul vehicle or the conventional aircraft, the loading flow--one directional--moves smoothly as entering passengers move into the seats. They are out of the flow. Air travelers will know that exit will be less smooth. Riders, for and aft, pressing to exit will clog the aisle.

It is apparent that bench seats at right angles to the axis of the vehicle are analogous to the bulkheads of a ship or the baffles of a chemical vessel. They impede the flow. In the long haul vehicle the relation of stop-start to rest time is a period of momentary inconvenience leading to long rest. In the short haul start-stop vehicle with the components of the load redistributed at every stop, the bench seats add impedence to the near constant state of aisle turbulence. The flow pattern is one of agitated mix of exited riders maneuvering for the door, weaving to pass obstructions such as standees, packages and canes while the vehicle is still in motion. Stop-Exit! The turbulence is repeated by the entering riders who, their competitive instincts aroused, move aggressively in hope of a seat. The vehicle will start up with the redistribution process still underway.

A current double seat described as generous (40" in width) may make extended baffles of the passengers shoulders. The range of shoulder dimensions is given as 14.6" - 22.8". Two upper-percentile seat mates will find the one on the aisle over-hanging the latter by as much as four or five inches. The man on the aisle is doomed to the role of human baffle with a buffeting of his shoulder from any shift in aisle movement. This condition is illustrated in Figure 1.

The man on the aisle will seek to minimize his role. He will compress his seatmate. Forced seatmates of varying mix--two large, one large/one medium, one large/one small, male/female, etc.-- have high potential for generating psychological stress in each other.

Easing of the rigid baffles of the meeting hall vehicle may be accomplished by swinging the benches against the wall. The extended knees and feet of the seated riders are more flexible than the fixed seats. The longitudinal plan guarantees that all passengers, seated and standing, entering and leaving, will participate in aisle turbulence. The traditional meeting hall and longitudinal plan impose an acquiescence, sullen or good humored, in the inevitability of indignity to person at any stop.

Riding Problems

While time delay as a product of aisle turburence is distributed equally among all riders, turbulence, or obdily contact will generate unequal tolerances among the individuals who compose the mix. While the tough may be indifferent, not all riders are tough.

In American Society it appears that the individual is expected to exert a kind of discipline or tension in regard to his body, showing that he has his faculties in readiness for any face-to-face interaction that might come his way in the situation. . .that failure to exhibit 'presence' is a normal, understandable expression of alienation, (3).

The luck in face-to-face interaction that might come a passenger's way in the drawing of a seatmate (or mates, one on either side, in longitudinal seating) can place great strain on the maintenance of presence. (i.e. the concealment of one's annoyance in the face of unpleasant encounter.)

Sources of Stress Identified

The luck of the draw in a seatmate in any pattern of side-by-side seating or face-to-face standee invites any of the following states, conditions, or actions, separately or in combinations, originating with a seatmate:

> Elbows
> Shopping bag/Brief case
> Nasal Allergies
> Newspaper
> Wet rainwear or gear
> Soiled clothing
> Body odor
>
> Sprawler
> Sleeper
> Drunkard
> Ogler
> Baby

These are supplemented by irrational prejudice towards passive persons of different skin pigmentation, age, eccentricities of dress or personal adornment such as beards, beads and length of hair of which he disapproves. Any seasoned rider can expand the list.

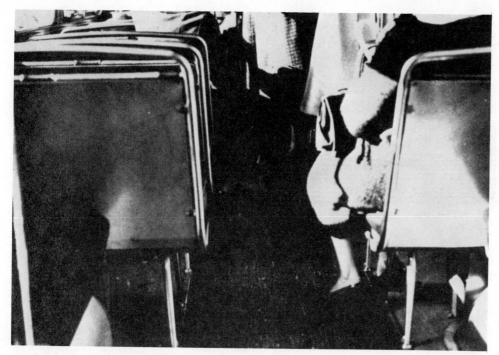

Figure 1 - Human Baffle: Transverse Seating Arrangement

These states generated in passivity may be painful enough. Compounded by malice or hostility the stress may be extreme. The delemma of the seated victim is a double bind. A seat is a property. It will be relinquished only under extreme provocation. To relinquish is to lose 'face' or 'presence', to yield under duress. Yet immobility produces vulnerability to external threat. The standee, mobile, is free to take evasive action without loss of face. However, a standee without access to a stabilizing hand grip is not to be envied. His agonizing imbalance is also a menace to his neighbors.

Design Variables: Vehicle Interior

The physical variable which affect the psycho/social aspects of rider-satisfaction are briefly, as follows:
- seating configuration
- individual seat design
- aisle width
- stanchion design and placement
- door width, placement, number
- entry-exit flow patterns

Other design variables such as lighting, heating, ventilation, etc. are related to problems of physiological comfort and are adequately covered in the literature.

Development of Appropriate Models

The development of appropriate models is a necessary prerequisite to offering any design alternatives which can hope to achieve the goal of increasing rider-satisfaction. The following conceptual models attempt to (1) identify problem areas in an overall context, (2) offer a sociological model which "explains" how stress is generated and (3) relate stress-producing variables to particular design variables.

General Analytic Framework

For the purposes of analysis the diagram illustrated in Figure 2 provides a framework for viewing two general problem areas. Problems related to entry-exit can be considered 'dynamic' with the emphasis on momentary bodily contact, while problems associated with actual riding can be considered 'static' with the emphasis on behavioral stress producing situations.

A vehicle is a clear cut enclosed behavioral setting separated from the rest of the world. While the setting is a two phase cycle of rest and motion the difference in ratios between the two phases in short and long haul vehicles is of fundamental importance to rider satisfaction.

At stop the entrant, a goal oriented actor seeks a place of security-hopefully a seat, at worst, some sort of solid handgrip for the duration of his ride.

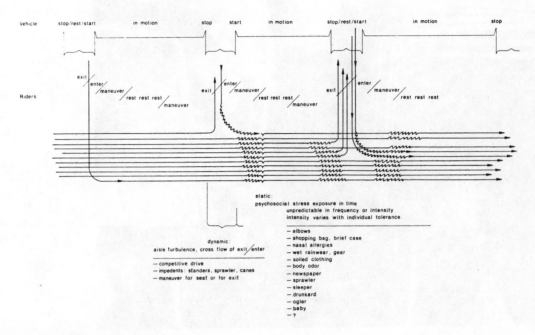

Figure 2—General Analytic Framework

(There will be others who have boarded at prior stops; there will be others boarding with him.) The actor will exercise a strategy of choice. He will be influenced not only by the distribution of seats or supports available. He will calculate a strategic location for ease of exit modified by an intuitive (or experienced) estimate of desirable seatmates.

The long haul vehicle will have, by definition, a short loading phase relative to its time in motion. The strategy of choice described will, in train and aircraft, take place in neat separation from the phase of the vehicle in motion. In the short haul vehicle the loading-and exit-phase bears no relation to the distribution of the entrants and exitings. The phases of the cycle overlap. The vehicle, manned or automatic, is presumed safe for motion the instant the doors are closed. Well into the motion phase of the vehicle the entrants will be distributing themselves. Meanwhile, those exiting at the next stop are in counterflow, making for the door, lest they will be carried beyond their stop. In automatic vehicles as elevators, passengers well know maneuvering is mandatory. In a short haul transit vehicle, the aisle turbulence is escalated by the baffle system of the rigid seats and those riders in a state of 'rest'.

The entrant will surmount this aisle turbulence in having made a choice of rest position in the vehicle. He will have moved from physical, dynamic, to a passive or 'static' state. He will also have become a member of a sub-set of two, three or four seatmates and standees in close face-to-face encounter. His

"fit" or degree of compatibility with his sub-group will be a matter of physical size complicated by sex. The five variables of large/medium/small and male/female produce a large number of potential combinations of mix.

A indeterminate number of these combinations are obviously conducive to psychological stress of indeterminate intensity to one or all of the members of the sub-set. Assuming a set of physical compatability the setting is ripe for the potential disruptions inherent in the actions, states, conditions and prejudices previously outlined.

The rider in either a short or long haul vehicle may be exposed to identical conditions of aisle turbulence and of stresses generated within his sub-set. His ride and his response to it, will be affected in an indeterminate way by differences in the rest-motion cycle of the vehicles. These differences are frequency and duration. In short haul vehicles the aisle trubulence at peak hours may well occur at every stop together with a change of mix in the sub-set.

Vehicle as a Behavior Setting

Reference has been made earlier in this report to the term "behavior setting".

"Some social occasions, (a funeral, for example), have a fairly sharp beginning and end. . .Other occasions, like Tuesday afternoon downtown, are very diffuse indeed. . .In those cases the very useful

Figure 3—The Aircraft Drama

term employed by Barber and his associates, behavior setting, might be sufficient.
(4) The behavior setting is then the scene
where in general patterns of social codes
will operate. The specifics of the list
of states and actions originating with
individual riders will fall outside these
general patterns.
The behavior setting of a transit vehicle can be seen
as a system of rewards and punishments (or a "use-
pleasure-avoidance-pain profile") weighted on the
side of potential for punishment. The designer of
the setting (the vehicle) might well approach his
task by seeking minimization of potential for
punishment.

Each of the items in the preceding list can be
seen as a threat to dignity of person, an invasion of
privacy and a threat to security and to property in
a setting which is superficially 'orderly'.

These actions and states of passengers are of
a class separate from the inevitable give-and-take
of bodily contact in the street or in the entry-exit
flow of a crowded aisle. The chance buffet of the
street is quickly over. The stress producers of a
vehicle differ in kind from street contact. Once
encountered, they are either continuous or carry the
threat of recurrence. The rider under such stress
in time could not care less that he is enjoying a
bargain in physiological comfort.

Behavioral Codes

The lapse of the sleeper offending against a
neighbor may or may not suggest variables of code
between participants. The offender may awaken to
be shocked at or indifferent to his lapse. His
neighbor may have understanding of a state of fatigue
yet be outraged at being its random victim. The
event may be judged regrettable by either or both of
the participants. The emotion generated may be
intensified by differences in behavior codes.

The 'baby-gambit' is well known to air travelers.
A couple with a baby are participants in the linear
boarding pattern which finds only single aisle seats
available. The family will be reunited with incred-
ible speed. The traveler who is chosen as seatmate
will yield his seat, instantly. His code may call for
the gallantry of reuniting a separated family at some
sacrifice to himself. He also extricates himself from
an unnerving encounter with a potentially formidable
seatmate.

> "One finds a very pervasive difference
> between middle and lower class males in
> American Society. Those who work without
> a tie, in clothes they do not have to
> worry about keeping clean, and persons
> who can afford to touch and to be touched
> . . .need not maintain a tight orientation
> in public social situation.(5)"

The tensions generated between or within participants by the states and actions listed may then be aggravated by differences in class codes of behavior. (This is not to imply that members of a homogeneous class are incapable of offending each other). The ideal transit vehicle would accommodate a mix of sex, age and class with a minimum of friction in face-to-face interaction. Conversely, a vast investment in system development can deteriorate into a mobile ghetto through failure to accommodate such a mix.

A Case in Point

The scene, illustrated in Figure 3, a photograph from an advertisement in the New Yorker for a manufacturer of permanent press fibres, discloses two and one-third seats of a three-across aircraft array. Two males the focus of the scene, sprawl comfortably in their resplendently crease proof jackets, the man in the middle spreading his elbow generously over the airspace of his two seatmates. On his right, a male companion apparently finds no threat to his dignity, no offense to his person, no stress on his sense of presence. Compared similarly, the two males are friends. The elbow of a friend is a tolerable intrusion.

The cropped photo revealing only the arm of the rider on his left, a woman, gives no hint of her feelings. One may assume that she feels threat to dignity, offense to person and stress on presense. The elbow of a stranger who has a social obligation to control it but who does not is a painful intrusion. There is strong irony in this scene. This wrinkle conscious middle class American male in clothes he does not have to worry about (wrinkling) . . . need not maintain a tight orientation in (this) public social situation. "It frees him to spill over into a neighbor's territory. The inference: designers have an obligation to be aware of the predator and to seek means to inhibit his field of influence.

Alienation is a state which may work up, down or across social strata. The aircraft drama is working across. The three persons of the setting are apparently, of the same socioeconomic status. The 'pervasive difference between middle and lower class' males in American Society suggests alienation upward. Those persons who are indifferent to touching and to being touched by the environment are likely to affront those who are not--and quite without intent. A person whose care in dress and manner of behavior radiates distaste for bodily contact will alienate downward.

A vehicle plan which minimized bodily contact in time would minimize opportunity for generating these infinite shades of alienation by any definitions of up, down or across. One may control the behavior of the sleeper by inhibiting his need to sleep. One may provide the potential victim with

some defense from the sleeper. In the latter alternative each may go about his 'voluntary' behavior unconditioned by his neighbor. No-one's 'presence' is challanged. To sleep is not a lapse of behavior. Ideally such a plan, recognizing the unquantifiable value of human dignity would seek 'equal protection' consistent with freedom of action. In the aircraft drama a realignment of the seating may permit the relaxed sprawl as acceptable behavior to a neighbor. Realignment frees the sleeper to sleep while it frees his neighbor from intrusion. The physical setting may strongly modify the behavioral setting.

The Standee

The standee on a transit vehicle has one specific advantage. Not bound by fixed position he may take evasive action in the face of threat (except, of course, in the case of maximum congestion in the vehicle.)

It may be axiomatic that, given a choice, most riders would prefer sitting to standing. Apparently the Long Island C. C. with no standees, adopts this axiom as self-evident. There are risks inherent in this assumption. Either the planning assumes stabilization of the population with demand and supply in equilibrium or that the standee will do his standing on the station platform rather than in motion. The latter situation, waiting time, is less than ideal. It is predictable that standees will infiltrate the vehicles in peak hours. The internal maneuvers between those with handgrip and those seeking to enter or leave the vehicle will generate painful dissatisfaction.

If there are standees, then there must be provision for stability--a hand grip. The short-haul vehcile, with its random flow of entries, rest and exits requires provision for aisle flow in order to function at all. The lack of provision for stability for standees who are 50 percent of vehicle capacity seems a perpetration of a major source of rider dissatisfaction.

Standees, of course, stand in the aisle. The conventional in service vehicle has two rows of standees, back to back, with some form of hand grip available to each. There is an unspecifiable passage space between them, hopefully, for flow of entry and exit. In peak hours this space, too, is clogged with standees. The standees in this middle row find themselves bolcked from access to a handgrip by the shoulder-to-shoulder pack of the outer rows. The standee in the middle row finds himself both agonizingly insecure and a floating menace to his neighbors.

The Method of Study

Photographic records of rider behavior on in-service

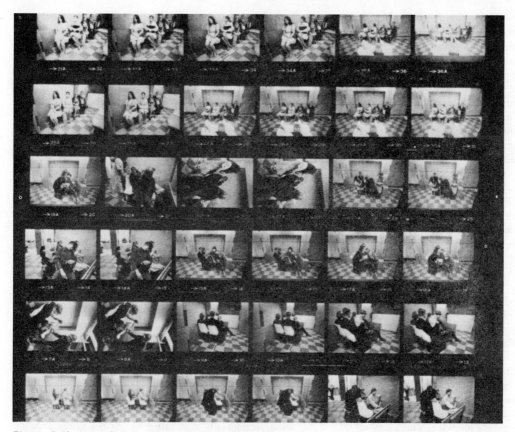

Figure 4-Photographic Data From Vehicle Mock-Up

vehicles was used as basis for a flexible wall, full-scale mock-up of a simulated vehicle, as illustrated in Figure 4. The width of the floor area was arbitrarily set at 8' - a common vehicle dimension.. The floor pattern is one of one-foot modules to provide reference for rough territorial definition (and disintegration). The one-foot module is continued on the transparent wall. Apart from the convenience of the latter to the photographer, the walls gave the sense of vehicle scale to subjects and observers alike as well as positive resistance to physical movement of seated subjects.

The bucket seats - not proposed as designs for vehicle seats - nevertheless have specific advantages for the study. Their tapering backs while providing body support, reveal clearly the spill-over of seated pairs on each other and on the aisle. With positive confinement of the buttocks (at 19" one inch over the maximum percentile), they demonstrate the accommodating processes of the subjects in hunching their shoulders. The seats provide a uniform element for the comparison of the three arrays of seats.

Some Principles for Solution

The analysis and findings of this study point toward the need to either redesign the current 40-150

passenger vehicular interiors in such a manner that they minimize psychological stress and problems of entry and exit or to abandon them in favor of a "mini-vehicle". While this study has its origin in the problem of altering current urban transit vehicles, it acknowledges the necessity for further research into mini-car systems as a viable alternative to vehicles which may have outlived their utility.

Within the framework of current vehicular design two solutions suggest themselves. Eliminate the wide range of possible passenger subsets by removing the seats. Give everyone the mobility of the standee. This solution, apart from its indifference to fatigue and disability, suggests the brutal congestion of the cattle train.

The second solution - a subsetting of one for seated passengers - would reduce the variables of face-to-face interaction to two - that of setter to standee.

A shift of axis of the seat to an angle other than the transverse or longitudinal axis of the vehicle will produce a subset of two.

The psycho/social gain of the shift is economically feasible. Its feasibility derives from two sources: the relevant dimensional relationships of the human body to the seat and to the characteristics of pack.

The dimensions of conventional seating bear no obvious relation to the 'particles' the seating is intended to accommodate. The 'generous' 40" double seat bears no relation to the 22.8"(x2=45.6') upper percentile shoulders or to the 18" (x2=36") upper percentile buttocks. Since all people sit on their buttocks, an 18" seat will accommodate all comers. However, the 4.8" excess of shoulders over buttocks remains to be accounted for.

A look at a group of persons in close contact, either standing or seated, will show a congestion plane at shoulder level. Figure A5, a conventional vehicle pack, shows this shoulder-to-shoulder pack. Situation A is described as "covering 79 percent of a surface with 21 percent exposed while a 'triangular array' (B) covers as much as 91 percent of the surface with only nine percent exposed."(6)

Lest it be argued that people are not beer cans for which situation B is applicable it may be stated that situation A is a beer can or shoulder-to shoulder pack. Situation B with no shoulder contact will have no congestion plane for seated passengers. That is, the single seat in series at angular axis is clearly defined private territory or a pack related to people rather than to beer cans.

The private territory allows for orientation by twist of the neck or of the torso, freedom of elbow movement without intruding upon others or being inturded upon. The sleeper, drunkard, baby, seeker after handkerchief, sprawler, etc., project or fall into space behind the neighbor, at worst, into the airspace over his knees. The parcel or briefcase can lie parallel to the seat axis out of the aisle. (The aisle wideth gains 2" to 2.5" per side with the shift in axis). Women have responded that the angular axis forestalls direct stare of an ogler across the aisle. The threat inherent in continuous contact with an irritant (soiled or wet clothing), or of one with the possibility of recurrence (a sneeze), is virtually eliminated.

The major need of the standee is his physical stability. Physical stability may be assured by a hand grip. Lack of access to a handgrip is a real and painful threat. A double stanchion, by separation of shoulder to shoulder pack, increases availability of handgrip in peak load congestion.

A vehicular plan of such promise might well increase in range of acceptability among riders with varying codes of behavior.

Summary and Conclusions

The major concerns of this study have been to give focus to the realities of independence from others through identification of principles underlying rider irritations and to propose principles for an increasing measure of independence.

Traditionally, congestion in urban transit, the desire of masses of people to enter and leave an area at the same time, assumes that independence and congestion are mutually exculsive. The study reveals that traditional seating plans limit independence in two ways. One, as baffle systems they impede floor within the vehicle. Two, the longitudinal and transverse plans impose upon riders sub-sets of prolonged face-to-face relationships which carry a variety of threats to independence. The threats, physical and psychological, derive from both real bodily contact and from differences in codes of behavior among riders of varying socio/economic and occupational groups. If a threatening event takes place it is intensified by either duration (as soiled clothing) or possibility of recurrence (a sneeze).

Threat is a more serious matter to both rider and the system that the chance recurrence of an unpleasant event on one ride in ten (or one in a hundred). Underlying the fact that any preventable event which happens is one too many is the side effect that some victims will shun future use of the system. A system satisfied with travel time as definitive measure is unwittingly designed for a physically agile and the psychologically tough. A victim of threat is more likely to seek alternatives to use of the system than he is to figure the odds on frequency of recurrence of threat. A rider without alternatives is condemned to face whatever threats come up.

Within current vehicular capacities (40-150 passengers) innovations in interior arrangements appear limited from the viewpoint of eliminating sources of stress. A seating plan with a diagonal axis indicates a relief from the baffle in flow of aisle movement and a position of relative independence to the heretofore vulnerable seated passenger. A double stanchion, by separation of shoulder to shoulder pack, increases availability of handgrip in peak load congestion.

A logical next move would be the testing of these principles in an experimental in-service vehicle along with further investigation of the implications this study may have for the development and testing of mini-car systems in urban areas.

URBAN TRANSIT VEHICLE DESIGN AND RIDER SATISFACTION / 191

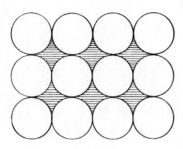

Figure A5

Figure B5

Notes

1. For a discussion of the physiological aspects of vehicle design see Chapter 3, p. 25-36 of Qualitative Aspects of Urban Personal Travel Demand, Abt Associates, Inc., August 1968, prepared for the U.S. Department of Housing and Urban Development.

2. For a short discussion of the history of urban transit vehicles see Chapter 1, p. 1-6 of Principles of Urban Transportation, Frank H. Mossman, ed., The Press of Western Reserve University, 1951.

3. Goffman, Irving. Behavior in Public Places, The Free Press of Glencoe, New York, New York, 1963.

4. Design and Performance Criteria for Improved Nonrail Urban Mass Transit Vehicles and Related Urban Transportation Systems, Washington, D.C., National Academy of Engineering, 1968.

5. op. cit., Goffman, p. 203

6. Loeb, Arthur A., "The Architecture of Crystals", Module, Proportion, Symmetry, Rhythm, G. Kepes, ed., 1966.

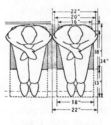
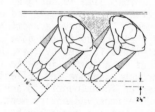

Situation A   Situation B

Downtown: An Economic-Environmental Simulation Game

by Wesley H. Long

The Pennsylvania State University

Abstract

This game is designed to bring out inter-actions among economic and environmental deci-sions. Teams have economic interests focused by their roles in the game and environmental interests focused by their habitation loca-tions in a town. They vie individually through exchange and collectively through an elected Town Council to achieve economic gain and an improved environment. Conflicts encoun-tered between teams and between teams and Town Council when they attempt to realize both the goals simultaneously replicate in miniature and in a collapsed time frame the strains and tensions experienced by a real community.

Introduction (1)

The instructional purpose of this game is to bring out some of the conflict between the economic development of a community and its environmental quality. Teams of players repre-senting interest groups in a town make explic-it economic decisions which have explicit and implicit environmental content. The economic and environmental decisions made by one team have an impact on all teams. Results of deci-sions are made explicit at the end of each round of play as teams receive income and en-vironmental information with respect to their own team and to the community as a whole.

A unique feature of this game is the use of two types of currency: money and environ-mental quality units (EQU's). The latter are used to measure the environmental quality of the town and the share each team has in the town total. As explicit and implicit environ-mental decisions are made the total EQU's for the town and each team's share will change. The impossibility of maximizing two quantities with different measures (dollars and EQU's) simultaneously exposes the players to the real-ization that there are no clear cut solutions to community planning. However, by providing a unit of measure for environmental quality, implicit trade-offs can be discovered and the conception of making choices among ambiguous alternatives is brought out.

The game takes place in a town represen-ted by a map which is 5 by 10 city blocks (see Figure 1a). (2) Land use in the city blocks is homogeneous and already established so that no blocks are vacant. Each block has a block factor assigned to it which indicates the rela-tive desirability of the block as a commercial location. These block factors are to be view-ed as economic laws based on the location of a block relative to the center of the business district and are not subject to arbitrary change by town legislation. However, the pro-posed town plan (Figure 1b), which is the is-sue that the Town Council must decide on imme-diately after election, has economic effects which do alter some of the block factors. Gross receipts for commercial land use are higher for higher block factors. Conversely, the desirability for habitation is inversely related to the block factors. A team's share in the environmental quality units generated by the community is smaller if the blocks where they live have higher block factors.

Teams are designated by interest groups in the town such as retail store owners, apart-ment house owners, business employees, univer-sity employees, etc. The teams designated are not the only ones possible or desirable, but a limited number of teams is necessary to allow for reasonable time for play. Each team spec-ializes in its economic activity and owns some property which represents its places of habi-tation. The business teams also own their commercial locations.

The steps of play are as in Table 1. These will be described below in the section on experience with the game.

Table 1
Steps of Play

0. Receive Income and Environmental Qual-ity Units from Game Control for year 0 (example year).

   End of year 0

1. Hold Boro Council election.

2a. Legislative Period: Boro Council makes decisions on proposed town plan, zoning, public land use, taxes, etc.

2b. Business Period: teams make property transactions and have buildings constructed.

3. Tax rates posted by Boro Council clerk.

Table 1 (continued)

4. Control posts public information.

5. Income and Environmental Quality calculations made by teams.

6. Receive Income and Environmental Quality Units from Control.

End of year 1

Repeat steps 2 through 5 with Election at beginning of every odd year.

The following sections of the paper give detailed descriptions and mathematical analyses of parts of the game in order to expose its inner workings and interactions.

Economic Part

Each team receives gross income and incurs expenses and taxes, thus arriving at its net income. However, the initiators of business activity are the Retail and Apartments teams. They can build additional units of their businesses and presumably would do so based on their expectations of the profitability of these actions. The Bank and Contractor teams are more or less passive aids in business expansion providing loans and construction services respectively, but they cannot add any new units of their business. However, since the income of these two teams depends to a great extent on such expansion they should be sympathetic to it. The Bank has limited loan capacity and Contractor has limited construction capacity so the competition between Retail, Apartments, and Council (and other teams to some extent) can result. Thus, the game assumes that players will adopt the role of their team and strive to increase team income by expanding the economic activity of the town.

The gross income of Retail and Apartments depends positively on Town population, the location of the business units (block factors), and negatively on the degree of traffic congestion. Bank gross income depends on the amounts of local loans outstanding. Contractor gross income depends on the amount of construction and maintenance undertaken by all the teams and Council. The net income of each of these teams is arrived at by subtracting wages, taxes, interest, and maintenance from gross income. Retail and Apartments can convert some of their domicile properties to commercial use (but not all since they must live in the community) and they can buy blocks from other teams.

The equations governing the Retail team will be used to illustrate the determination of business income.

(1) $GRIN = POP*RIF*(1.0-TCF)$

Gross retail income (GRIN) is equal to Town population (POP) times a retail income factor (RIF) times 1.0 minus the traffic congestion factor (TCF). The equations for POP and TCF which are the result of decisions by all teams are given below.

(2) $RIF = REF+RMBF$

RIF is designed to increase as the number of retail blocks expands (retail expansion factor: REF) and to depend on the economic desirability of the retail block locations, the retail mean block factor (RMBF).

(3) $REF = NRB*RERT$

Thus, REF increases at a given rate (RERT, retail expansion rate) as the number of retail blocks (NRB) increases. This provides an incentive to expand the number of retail blocks in search of greater retail sales.

(4) $RMBF = (SUM(RBF(I),I=1,NRB))/NRB$

The incentive to locate near the center of business activity is provided by using RMBF, the mean of the retail block factors (RBF). If locations away from the business center are selected as retail locations this mean declines and retail sales are lower than if locations near the center are chosen.

This forced centralization of business activity is perhaps more characteristic of the past history of cities than of the present day, but tension in game design between playability and reality dictates simplifications. Another example of such a simplification is the lack of the possibility of vertical expansion, say by building apartments over commercial locations. The author feels that the pedagogical objectives of exhibiting conflict and trade-offs would not be enhanced by adding these aspects of reality.

(5) $NRIN = GRIN-RWAG-RTAX-RINT-RVMA$

Net retail income (NRIN) is determined by subtracting retail wages (RWAG), retail taxes (RTAX), retail interest (RINT), and retail voluntary maintenance (RVMA) from gross retail income.

(6) $RWAG = RWRT*NRB$

RWAG is the product of a retail wage rate (RWRT) per retail block and the number of retail blocks (NRB).

(7) $RTAX = TRAT*RAV$

RTAX depends on the property tax rate (TRAT) set by the Town Council and the assessed value of the property owned by the Retail team (RAV). Thus, Retail will try to influence Council decisions on taxes and assessments.

(8) $RINT = LRAT*RLON$

RINT is the product of the loan interest rate (LRAT) on whatever loans the Retail team has outstanding (RLON). RVMA depends on what the team wishes to spend on maintenance. Complete maintenance can be obtained by spending 5 per cent of the original construction cost per year.

Gross and net Apartments income is computed in almost exactly the same manner so that both these teams are subject to the same kind of economic costs and incentives. Bank and Contractor gross incomes are determined in a different manner, but their net incomes are computed in much the same way as for the Retail and Apartment teams.

Business Employees receive income in proportion to the number of commercial blocks at the end of the year. University Employees and

a) Existing Land Use

	30	32	34	36	38	40	42	44	46	48
2	1	2	3 APT	4 RET	4 RET	4 BAN	4 RET	3 RET	2 APT	1
4	1	2	3 CON	3 TOW	3 RET	3 RET	3 APT	3	2	1
6	1	2	2	2	2	2 LOT	2	2	2	1
8	1	1	1	1 SCH	1	1	1	1 PAR	1	1
10	1	1	1	1	1	1	1	1	1	1

b) Proposed Town Plan:
New Downtown and
One-Way System

	30	32	34	36	38	40	42	44	46	48
2	4	4	5	5	MALL	5+5	MALL	5	5	4	4

One-way Street

	30	32	34	36	38	40	42	44	46	48
4	4	4	4	4	4	4	4	4	4	4
6	3	3	3	3	3	3	3	3	3	3
8	2	2	2	2	2	2	2	2	2	2
10	1	1	1	1	1	1	1	1	1	1

The existing land use is designated as follows:

APT	Apartment block	LOT	Parking Lot
RET	Retail block	SCH	School
BAN	Bank	PAR	Town Park
CON	Contractor	blank	Family block
TOW	Town Hall		

Zoning boundaries: inner zone is commercial; middle zone is
apartments; and outer zone is residential.

Figure 1. Land Use, Zoning, Block Factors, and Proposed Town Plan

Students receive a fixed amount per year. From these figures are subtracted necessary expenses (a high percentage, say 80, of gross receipts), taxes, and maintenance to arrive at savings rather than net income. These teams all own residential property, part of which can be sold, and rent apartments from the Apartments team. The savings computation will be illustrated for Business Employees.

(9) BEIN = BWRT*NBB

Business Employees income (BEIN) is the product of the business wage rate (BWRT) and the number of bu ness blocks (NBB).

(10) BESV = BEIN-NERT*BEIN-BETX-BEVM

Business Employee saving is the result of subtracting necessary expenditures, taxes (BETX), and maintenance (BEVM) from income. Taxes and maintenance are computed in the same manner as for business teams. Necessary expenditures are the product of the necessary expenditure rate (NERT) and income.

The total net income of the town is one of the measures of performance of the town that is posted for all teams to see at the end of each round. This is the sum of the net incomes of all business teams and the savings of nonbusiness teams.

Business activity affects a number of variables concerning the town as a whole and in turn is affected by these variables.

(11) POP = APRT*NAB+FPRT*NFB

Population (POP) depends on the number of apartment (NAB) and family dwelling (NFB) blocks and the population rate per block for each use (APRT, FPRT). Thus, the construction of apartment blocks and the conversion of family blocks to other uses are decisions which determine the total population.

(12) TLEV = POP*NBB

Since the interaction of population with businesses gives rise to traffic movement, the traffic level (TLEV) in the town is the product of population and the number of business blocks.

(13) TCF = TLEV/SCAP

Finally, the ratio of traffic level to street capacity (SCAP, determined by Council) is the traffic congestion factor (TCF). As traffic rises, relative to street capacity, congestion rises, lowering Retail and Apartment income. Private decisions on business expansion affect traffic in the town and traffic affects Business income, thus pressures for public action arise to alleviate traffic problems.

To illustrate the interactions among decisions by Business teams the effect on retail gross income (GRIN) of the addition of one apartment block, other things being equal, is presented below. Repeating equation (1), GRIN = POP*RIF*(1.0-TCF).

From equation (11) population depends on the number of apartment and family blocks so apartment construction influences GRIN positively from this source. From equations (12) and (13) apartment construction and the consequent increase in population increases traffic

congestion so there is a negative influence on GRIN from this source.

$$(14) \quad \frac{d(GRIN)}{d(NAB)} = MRBF(APRT\text{-}FPRT\text{-}\frac{1}{SCAP}$$
$$(APRT^2*NAB(2NRB+3NAB)\text{-}2APRT*FPRT$$
$$*NRB\text{-}FPRT^2*2NFB(NRB+NAB)))$$

The net influence shown in equation (14) depends on all the population rates and the number of apartment (NAB), family (NFB), and retail (NRB) blocks existing at the particular time when the extra apartment building is built.

Environmental Part

Each team owns some residential property all of which cannot be sold so that they are forced to maintain a stake in the community by living there. The location of residential property is used to distribute the community environmental quality units among teams. Thus, environmental repercussions of economic decisions are felt by all teams, not only those making the decisions.

The environment is quantified in an arbitrary way with various aspects of it being assigned values in terms of environmental quality units. These units are a type of currency which teams possess by virtue of their share of the community's environmental factors. The environmental factors apply only to residential and apartment blocks and are arrived at by subtracting the block factor for the given block from 6. Each team computes its share of the town's total environmental quality by multiplying the percentage of the town's total environmental factors it holds by the town's total environmental quality units.

The game is limited in its treatment of environmental questions as can be seen from Table 2 in which a few environmental aspects are listed for each type of land use and the environmental quality units (EQU's) assigned to each are entered. Trees is chosen as an environmental aspect because many active protests against construction focus on the issue of tree removal. Open space is chosen because it is a common phrase in planning rhetoric and convenience is chosen to illustrate the nonvisual aspects of the environment. The common questions of air and water pollution are not treated and, although reality may indicate explicit inclusion, the implications involved may not provide any gain in terms of showing the impact of community development on the environment.

Table 2 shows some of the trade-offs of environmental quality arising in the course of community development. The construction of a retail block to replace a residential block is a net gain to the community in terms of the block totals, but since an increase in business outlets increases the traffic level the net gain may be lost as population increases. This is more likely to happen due to the fact that traffic level is the product of population and

Table 2
Environmental Quality

Environmental Quality Units for any block:

Land Use	Environmental Aspect			Block Total
	Trees*	Open Space	Convenience	
Retail	0	0	100	100
Shopping Mall	5	1	30	36
Bank	0	0	0	0
Contractor	0	0	0	0
Boro Hall	0	0	0	0
Parking Lot	0	1	0	1
Apartment	5	5	0	10
School	5	5	**	10±
Residence	10	10	0	20
Park	50	20	100	170
Streets				
4-lane	20	0	0	20
6-lane	0	0	0	0

* Maximum trees permitted. Some die each year.

** $-10\left[\dfrac{\text{Town population}}{\text{No. of schools}} - 70\right]$

Environmental Quality Units for town as a whole:

Add $\frac{1}{5}$ (Parking Capacity - Traffic Level)

Subtract Total deterioration = 5% original construction
cost of property
- maintenance expenditures

business outlets. Attempts to compensate for traffic level by increasing parking capacity lead either to building more parking lots which mean a loss in environmental quality relative to other land uses or to street widening which destroys trees and again degrades the environment. Avenues for escape are available through the building of parks and schools. A similar but more direct chain of reaction eminates from apartment construction on residential land. There are net losses in substituting for residential land use, increasing traffic level, and increasing population per school.

Equation (15) shows the determination of the total environmental quality units (TEQU).

(15) $\text{TEQU} = \text{SUM}(\text{EQRT}(I), I=1, \text{NTB}) + \text{N4LB} * \text{STRT} + \text{ARAT} * (\text{PCAP} - \text{TLEV}) - \text{SCRT} * ((\text{POP}/\text{NSCH}) - \text{SCOP}) - \text{TDET}$

The environmental quality rate (EQRT) for each block depends on the land use of the block. These are summed over the number of town blocks (NTB). To this is added the product of the number of blocks with 4-lane streets (N4LB) and the number of trees planted along such a block (STRT); if a block has six lanes there are no trees along the street. Increased parking capacity (PCAP) is desirable

to shoppers, but increased traffic level (TLEV) is not so the first has a positive sign and the second is negative; both are multiplied by an automobile rate (ARAT). The population per school (POP divided by the number of schools (NSCH)) is compared to an optimum ratio (SCOP) and the difference multiplied by a school rate (SCRT). Thus, if population per school rises environmental quality declines. Finally, total property deterioration (TDET), the amount of total maintenance required for property upkeep which is not undertaken, has a negative sign.

The change in TEQU realized from building a park where a family block had been located would involve the difference between the EQRT for parks and that for family blocks. Furthermore, since population changes, the population per school and the traffic level are changed. The total change is presented in equation (16).

(16) $\dfrac{d(\text{TEQU})}{d(\text{NPRK})} = \text{EQRT}(\text{PRK}) - \text{EQRT}(\text{FB}) + \text{SCRT} * \text{FPRT}/\text{NSCH} + \text{ARAT} * \text{FPRT} * \text{NBB}$

Governmental Part

An election of the Town Council is held immediately after the explanation of the game is accomplished by examining the results of the dummy year (year zero) for which all calculations have been done prior to play. The issue of the adoption of the plan or keeping the existing situation is given to the players in order to focus the players' attention on the development of the town.

Each team nominates one or more candidates for the 3-man Town Council and an election is held in which the person with the highest vote total holds office for 4 years and the others for 2 years. Thus, a majority on the Council can be changed quickly if the original Council obtains the displeasure of the teams.

The vote distribution (indicated in Table 3) is designed to provide tension between the business teams and the employee teams. Neither has enough power to elect a clear majority, so some accommodation must be made in the process of which the questions of community development and environmental quality will be discussed and compromises made. As the game proceeds and the results of decisions are seen, renegotiation of old agreements and new electoral coalitions may arise thus bringing home to the players some of the strains in community relations resulting from economic and esthetic concerns.

Town Council operates by majority vote. Its powers (listed in Table 4) include the usual ones as well as those of acting as zoning board of appeals and school board. Also, it must determine compensation in condemnation decisions. One of the key decisions of Council is determining street capacity (SCAP); it affects business profit and the environmental quality of the town.

Table 3
Vote Distribution

Students - 1 vote
Bank, Contractor, Retail, Apartment - 2 votes each team
University Employees, Business Employees - 4 votes each team

Table 4
Town Council Powers

A. Traffic (to start, all streets 4-lane, two-way with on-street parking)
1. Determine street width (4- or 6-lane) around any block.
2. Make streets one- or two-way around any block.
3. Allow or prohibit on-street parking around any block.

B. Public land use
1. Buy from Contractor construction of:

parking lots	parks
tree planting	Town Hall
malls	demolition
schools	maintenance

C. Private land use
1. Determine zoning
2. Condemn property for public use

D. Determine tax rate

E. Borrow from Bank at 10% interest

(17) $SCAP = (LCAP+PCAP)/(LCAP/PCAP)$

The capacity of the street system to carry traffic depends on how many lane widths streets are, how many lanes are devoted to traffic movement and to parking (and how many parking lots there are) and whether the lanes are one-way or not. The capacity of each block to carry traffic and contain parking is determined from Table 5. These capacities are summed over all blocks to obtain the traffic lane capacity (LCAP) and parking capacity (PCAP) of the whole town. These two quantities are combined in the preceding formula to obtain the street capacity of the town (SCAP). This formula is designed to make the street capacity respond positively to both lane capacity and parking capacity (the numerator) but to enforce a balance between lane capacity and parking capacity (the denominator). Thus, the Town Council cannot merely abolish on-street parking to increase land capacity because the decrease in parking involved makes the actual capacity fall.

Interaction Among Parts

Economic-Environmental. Economic development is motivated in the game by the positive relation between sales of the Retail and Apartment teams and population, and the simultaneous relation that apartment construction increases population. Since Contractor and Bank income both are heavily dependent on expansion of such commercial activity, a natural commonality of interest arises to undertake development. This development has direct environmental effects in that traffic levels are increased, open space and trees decline, and schools become crowded.

The game is thus designed to bring out conflicts between economic development and environmental quality. These conflicts are not irresolvable, but care and planning are necessary for their resolution; thus, environmental and developmental enthusiasts must work together in the interests of the whole community.

Economic-Governmental. The natural coalition for economic development mentioned above will be a strong voice in Town Council for ordinances to increase parking spaces and traffic flow, and to expand commercial zoning boundaries. Because Business Employee income is also influenced by economic expansion they may have a development interest, but because their stake in the environment is larger this may influence their political choices also. University Employee and Student incomes are determined outside the community so their interests should be environmental.

Table 5
Street Capacity

LCAP = Traffic Lane Capacity per block
PCAP = Parking Capacity per block

Street Width

Traffic Flow	4 lanes		6 lanes	
	Parking on street	No parking on street	Parking on street	No parking on street
Two-way	LCAP= 80 PCAP= 40	LCAP= 120 PCAP= 0	LCAP= 160 PCAP= 40	LCAP= 200 PCAP= 0
One-way	LCAP= 120 PCAP= 40	LCAP= 160 PCAP= 0	LCAP= 200 PCAP= 40	LCAP= 240 PCAP= 0

Shopping Mall reduces LCAP and PCAP by 25%
Parking lots hold 50 cars, i.e., PCAP= 50

$$\text{Street Capacity (SCAP)} = \frac{LCAP + PCAP}{\frac{LCAP}{PCAP}}$$

As the Council attempts to provide public services, it must obtain land if it is to construct schools, parking lots, and parks. Since no land is vacant condemnation inevitably has economic consequences. First, taxable land is removed from assessment roles and tax rates are increased on other land. Second, condemnation of commercial land will reduce sales. Conflicts may arise between the role Council plays as an agent of economic development and its role as provider of public services. Thus, the tensions between community economic development and the provision of supporting public services that are necessitated by this development are brought out during the play. Again conflicts are not irresolvable but also not simply solved, so that players gain an appreciation for these problems.

Environmental-Governmental. The Council's impact on the environment is widespread. Parking decisions affect parking capacity; changing street widths change the number of trees; building street malls, schools, and parks changes the EQRT on such blocks; and zoning decisions by affecting allowable land use change the scope of private land use changes.

Since most of these actions have economic consequences also, the Council becomes the arena for debate on the trade-offs between economic development and environmental quality. Furthermore, since economic and environmental decisions by individual teams have environmental effects on all teams and government is able to limit individual action, recourse will be made to Council to mitigate these side effects.

Experience with the Game
This game was developed in connection with the Earth Week program at The Pennsylvania State University by a volunteer group of faculty and students. Including the process of testing and revising the game and its use one afternoon during the Earth Week program the game was played four times. This experience will be exposited by explaining the steps of play and describing how players reacted at each stage.

Step 0 is a dummy round using precalculated transactions to illustrate the role of each team and the flow of play in the game. To become familiar with records and calculations teams receive income and EQU's based on pre-assigned decisions.

Initially one round of actual play, that is involving team decisions, was programmed to take place before the Council elections, but teams were so reluctant to make economic decisions before the election and the subsequent decision on the proposed town plan, that the election was made the first step.

Pre-election bargaining involved trading team votes for promises of Council votes on the proposed town plan. The expected coalitions developed: Business vs. University Employees and Students with Business Employees being the swing group. Their candidate usually received the most votes in the election. Initially three plans were provided for, the other two being the new downtown and the one-way system separately, but the combination of the two always was adopted.

After the Council election the legislative and business periods run simultaneously. Council deliberates on the proposed plan and other town ordinances and businesses buy or sell land and construct new retail and apartment units. This period was characterized by land speculation based on knowledge that Council would vote for the plan and increase the commercial value of some lots and by attempts at closed Council sessions and demonstrations against them. In general there was a good deal of involvement in acting out the votes of private interests using inside information and citizens attempting to make information available to all.

Council also was quite active. Usually zoning boundaries were changed or land was condemned for public use. One Council zoned almost all the town commercial and saw the town EQU's decline as commercial development lowered the environmental quality of many blocks. Another Council condemned land for parks at a great rate and suffered a skyrocketing tax rate because of the loss of land from the assessment roles. The trend seemed to be towards an enthusiastic monism. With longer periods of play the results of these extremes could have been absorbed to lead to some balanced policy, but desk calculators (the game has not been computerized) made the play so slow that there was no time for this kind of learning in a single session.

The legislative period ends with public announcement of Council decisions. The teams are then given time to make any further business decisions based on Council's announcements. Maintenance expenditures tended to be neglected. They are voluntary and the only penalty for neglect is lower town total EQU's. Apparently the diffuse repercussions and press of large decisions was responsible. During the Earth Week session the two employee teams used some of their land to build parks: privately financed parks for public use, but this was an uncharacteristic action.

At the end of the business period the assessed value of the town is added up (it depends on business and Council decisions as to land use) and divided into Council's net expenditures (expenditures minus borrowings) to determine the tax rate per dollar of assessed value for the year. These rates tended to change radically between rounds due to the sporadic nature of business and Council decisions so that some teams lost money at times.

With the posting of tax rates business and employee teams can calculate profits and saving. Game Control collects this information and posts the Town net income. It also computes and posts Town total EQU's and teams calculate their share in the total. With this posted information the course of income and EQU's from period to period is available for all to see. Decreases in either of these totals quickly became political issues in the next Council election.

Summary

Decisions concerning economic development and environmental change made by individuals have repercussions on the environment and the economic life not only of those individuals, but all others in the community as well. The game described in this paper is designed to bring out these interactions in the course of play. Teams have economic interests focused by their designated roles in the game and environmental interest focused by the designated habitation locations in the game. They vie individually through exchange and collectively through an elected Town Council to achieve economic gain and an improved environment. The conflicts encountered within a team, between teams, and between teams and Town Council when they attempt to realize both the goals simultaneously replicate in miniature and in a collapsed time frame the strains and tensions experienced by a real community.

Notes

(1) The author wishes to acknowledge suggestions made and assistance rendered in the development of this game by Imre Kohn, Leonard Olson, John Archea, and other members of The Urban Scene committee of the Earth Week program at The Pennsylvania State University.

Also, the author's having played City I at the Washington Metropolitan Center has influenced the design of this game.

(2) This figure and all tables are examples actually used during the Earth Week program at The Pennsylvania State University, Spring 1970.

Mathematical Models to Facilitate Design and Management of an Environmental System

by Manohar D. Nasta and John Keith Beddow

College of Engineering, Department of Industrial and
Management Engineering, Iowa City, Iowa 52240

Abstract

In order to resolve the crisis of our
environment, we must manage it in exactly the
same way and using similar management techniques as with any other system. This paper presents an account of a mathematical modelling
technique which it is believed will be a very
powerful tool for use by environment managers
in their policy and decision making processes.
The technique presented here is called "Input-
Output Analysis". In broad terms it can be
used to describe the interrelationships between all of the activities which are occurring
within a given system.

The technique is simple to use and understand. It can be programmed on a computer and
therefore it can be applied to all or to portions of the system by clerical staff available. The technique enables administrators to
plan on a day to day, month to month or year
to year basis or any other time period, in
response to the changing demand upon the
system.

In this paper both deterministic and
probabilistic input-output models of an environmental management system are developed and
illustrated with the help of hypothetical
examples. Finally, the limitations of the
models are discussed and recommendations for
future work are suggested.

Introduction

To resolve the crisis of our complex
environment, in effect we must manage it in
exactly the same way as with any other system.
Mathematical modelling is a useful tool in the
design and management of systems. This paper
presents an account of a mathematical modelling
technique which it is believed will be a very
powerful tool for use by environment managers
in their policy and decision making processes.
The technique presented here is called "Input-
Output Analysis". In broad terms it can be
used to describe the interrelationships between
all of the activities which are occurring within a given system.

Input-output analysis has been used in
large scale economic problems, in connection
with resource allocation and planning in
educational systems and also in the design and
management of hospital-health services sytems
(1-10). However, the state of art in all of
these previous applications has been confined
to deterministic input-output analysis. In
this presentation, a probabilistic input-output
technique is developed via a more conventional
(although modified) deterministic model. It is
believed that the application of deterministic
input-output analysis presented here is unique
and also that the probabilistic model, developed from it, is a new technique which will
permit one to solve more realistic problems
than the conventional input-output analysis is
capable of dealing with alone.

The main difference between the deterministic and probabilistic techniques is that
in the deterministic technique we deal with
the means of the variables, whereas in the
probabilistic technique we deal with the
stochastic nature of the variables concerned.

The technique of input-output analysis has
some special features which make it of the
utmost utility in its application to an environmental management system. These features
include:

1. The input-output technique describes in a
   quantitative manner the flows of work
   within a system.
2. The technique also describes the interrelationships between all of the work flows
   which are considered in the system.
3. The technique is simple to use and understand. It can be programmed on a computer
   and therefore it can be applied to all or
   to portions of the system by clerical
   staff available.
4. The technique enables administrators to
   plan on a day to day, month to month or
   year to year basis or any other time
   period, in response to the changing demand
   upon the system.
5. If a new facility, operation or procedure
   is in planning stage, the input-output

technique can be used to give quantitative answers to what will be the effects of the new facility throughout the total system.

6. This technique will yield quantitative measures of the sensitivity of the system to technological innovations introduced into the system.

In this paper both deterministic and probabilistic input-output models of an environmental management system are developed and illustrated with the help of hypothetical examples which, for the sake of brevity, are restricted to environmental pollution problems. Finally, the limitations of the models are discussed and recommendations for future work are suggested. The organization of this paper is as follows:

Part A   The Deterministic Model
    I.   Assumptions and Nomenclature
    II.   Construction and Use of General Hypothetical Model
    III. Numerical Example to Illustrate Model
    IV.   Conclusions and Recommendations

Part B   The Probabilistic Model
    I.   Advantages of the Probabilistic Input-Output as Compared with Deterministic Input-Output Analysis
    II.   Assumptions and Nomenclature
    III. Construction and Use of the Probabilistic Hypothetical Model
    IV.   Numerical Example to Illustrate the Model
    V.   Conclusions and Recommendations

Part A The Deterministic Model

I. Assumptions and Nomenclature

The basic assumptions of the model are:

1. The elements of the flow matrix are known and constant. That is they do not vary over the period of the analysis.
2. The unit of measurement of the inputs can be different. The symbols used are defined as follows:

N = The Number of sectors into which the environmental management system is divided.

X = The ($N \times 1$) vector which represents the outputs of the sectors of the system.

Y = ($N \times 1$) vector which represents the outputs delivered outside the system in order that the environmental management system can satisfy the demand by the community which it serves. The final demand constitutes the quality of the environment required by the people. It may be measured most conveniently in terms of reduction of levels of various

pollutants by   certain predetermined amounts.

X_j = Total output of sector j.

Y_j = Output delivered outside the system by the jth sector.

x_{ij} = Amount of output of sector i absorbed by sector j.

b_{hj} = Amount of basic input of the h type to the jth sector.

B_h = Total amount of basic input of type h.

II. Construction and Use of the General Hypothetical Model

The derivation of the general deterministic model consists of the following steps:

1. Choosing a measure of effectiveness.
2. Construct the equations for the flows of activities in the different sections and present in the form of an input-output table.
3. Construct the equations involving the interdependence coefficients.
4. Express the total output vector in terms of the final demand vector.
5. The use of the model.

Two of these steps are discussed below:

1. Choosing a measure of effectiveness for the model to be constructed consists essentially of choosing the units of measurement for the inputs and the outputs of the different sectors of the environmental management system.
2. An input-output flow table (shown in Table 1) summarizes the observed relationships between the inputs and outputs associated with the set of activities comprising the hypothetical environmental management system. These activities are divided into two classes. One class consists of intermediate activities which are produced and used within the system but are not directly demanded by the community; rather they are used as inputs by other intermediate activities and by final activities. The other class consists of final activities or services which are those directly demanded and used by the community. These are the standards of the environmental quality set by the community.

The sections of the system are itemized in two ways in the table; in a row of sectors (numbered 1 to 17) which produce services and in a column and row are divided into intermediate and final activities. The upper portion of the table describes the basic inputs (the endowment) of labor, equipment and facilities. The extreme right hand side of the table shows in one column the set of final services demanded and used by the community and in the last column the total output of the sections of the system. This total output consists of all the services used within the system (the intermediate services) plus all of the services used by the community (the services used by the community (the final demand).

By referring to the input-output flow table it will be observed that the flow equation corresponding to the first producing sector is:

$$x_{11} + x_{12} + x_{13} + \cdots x_{1N} + Y_1 = X_1$$

where x_{11}, x_{12}, ... x_{1N}, Y_1 and X_1 have meanings previously specified.

Similarly the flow equations for the 2nd, ... ith and Nth sectors are:

$$x_{21} + x_{22} + \cdots + x_{2N} + Y_2 = \ddot{X}_2$$

$$x_{i1} + x_{i2} + \cdots + x_{iN} + Y_i = X_i$$

$$x_{N1} + x_{N2} + \cdots + x_{NN} + Y_N = X_N$$

Similarly the flow equation for the basic input of the first type shown in Table 1 is:

$$b_{11} + b_{12} + \cdots + b_{1N} = B_1$$

and the flow equation for the basic input of the h type is:

$$b_{h1} + b_{h2} + \cdots + b_{hN} = B_h$$

The above equations can be written in the matrix notation as follows:

$$A\ X = Y \tag{1}$$

where,

$$A = \begin{bmatrix} -(\dfrac{x_{11}}{X_1} - 1), & \dfrac{x_{12}}{X_2}, & \cdots\cdots\cdots, & -\dfrac{x_{1N}}{X_N} \\ -\dfrac{x_{21}}{X_1}, & \dfrac{x_{22}}{X_2} - 1), & \cdots\cdots\cdots, & -\dfrac{x_{2N}}{X_N} \\ \cdot & \cdot & & \cdot \\ \cdot & \cdot & & \cdot \\ \cdot & \cdot & & \cdot \\ -\dfrac{x_{N1}}{X_1}, & -\dfrac{x_{N2}}{X_2}, & \cdots\cdots\cdots & -(\dfrac{x_{NN}}{X_N} - 1) \end{bmatrix} \tag{2}$$

if we represent the element in the ith row and jth column of the above matrix by a_{ij} then matrix A can be rewritten as follows:

$$A = \begin{bmatrix} a_{11}, & a_{12}, & \cdots, & a_{1N} \\ a_{21}, & a_{22}, & \cdots, & a_{2N} \\ \cdot & \cdot & & \cdot \\ \cdot & \cdot & & \cdot \\ \cdot & \cdot & & \cdot \\ a_{N1}, & a_{N2}, & \cdots, & a_{NN} \end{bmatrix}$$

$$X = \begin{bmatrix} X_1 \\ X_2 \\ \cdot \\ \cdot \\ \cdot \\ X_N \end{bmatrix} \tag{4}$$

$$Y = \begin{bmatrix} Y_1 \\ Y_2 \\ \cdot \\ \cdot \\ \cdot \\ Y_N \end{bmatrix} \tag{5}$$

Finally, to express X in terms of Y we premultiply both sides to (1) by the inverse of the matrix A, which is A^{-1}. This gives:

$$A^{-1}AX = A^{-1}Y, \text{ which gives:}$$

$$X = A^{-1}Y \tag{6}$$

Similarly the interdependence coefficient matrix for the basic input of the first type is derived as follows:

$$\frac{b_{11}}{X_1} X_1 + \frac{b_{12}}{X_2} X_2 + \cdots + \frac{b_{1N}}{X_N} X_N = B_1$$

and in general for the basic input of the h type is

$$\frac{b_{h1}}{X_1} X_1 + \frac{b_{h2}}{X_2} X_2 + \cdots + \frac{b_{hN}}{X_N} X_N = B_h$$

In the matrix notation the above equation can be written as follows:

$$C\ X = B \tag{7}$$

where

$$C = \begin{bmatrix} c_{11} & c_{12} & \cdots & c_{1N} \\ \cdot & \cdot & & \cdot \\ \cdot & \cdot & & \cdot \\ \cdot & \cdot & & \cdot \\ c_{h1} & c_{h2} & \cdots & c_{hN} \end{bmatrix} \qquad (8)$$

$$c_{\ell m} = \frac{b_{\ell m}}{X_m} \quad \ell = 1 \ldots\ldots\ldots h, \qquad (9)$$
$$m = 1 \ldots\ldots N$$

and the matrix

$$B = \begin{bmatrix} B_1 \\ B_2 \\ \cdot \\ \cdot \\ \cdot \\ B_h \end{bmatrix}$$

5. In this section the use of this hypothetical input-output model (equation 6) will be illustrated as shown below:

   a. Question: What are the most obvious advantages to an environmental management system in making use of this model?
   Answer: The first advantage is that the administration is required to identify and quantify all the work flows occurring in their system. This procedure evaluates all of the elements of the (N x N) "A" matrix in the model (equation 2).

   b. Question: How does this model permit an administration to respond to a changing demand for the services of the system?
   Answer: The model relates the final demands on the sections (Y) to the total outputs of those sections (X) via the the "A" matrix. Therefore if Y changes from Y to Y' then the new outputs X', which the administration would have to provide is given by:

   $$X' = A^{-1}Y' \qquad (10)$$

   This assumes that the elements of A are constant over the period of analysis and planning. This means that when the level of activity varies within a certain range during the period of anal-

ysis, the output of the ith sector utilized by the jth sector (X_{ij}) per total output of the jth sector (X_j) is always constant over the time period of the analysis. That is to say:

$$\frac{x_{ij}}{X_j} = \text{constant} = a_{ij} \qquad (11)$$

Therefore the new inter-sectional flows can be computed from the relationship

$$x_{ij}' = a_{ij}X_j'$$

where x_{ij}' is obtained from equation (11).
In exactly similar manner, using equations (7, 8, and 9) we can write the new flows from the basic inputs to the various sections:

$$b_{\ell m}' = C_{1m}X_m' \qquad (12)$$

Also the new total basic input of the hth type is given by

$$B_h' = CX' \qquad (13)$$

c. Question: What will be the effect of increasing the output of the ith sector (X_i) either by increasing the endowment or by technological innovation?
Answer: By increasing the basic inputs to the ith section, X_i is increased. Consequently, elements of the "A" matrix alter and A becomes A'. Therefore using these two new matrices in the model, the new total output of the system to the community (Y') is found:

$$Y' = A' X' \qquad (14)$$

d. Question: In what section of the system should the administration invest for effectiveness? That is, how sensitive individually are all the sections of the system to fresh endowment?
Answer: Once the model is established for a specific system, it is an easy matter to change one or more of the elements of the "A" matrix and compute the effect upon the total outputs. Using the model repeatedly in this way, one can identify the element which when changed will produce the maximum effect on a specific output. This procedure will deliniate the most sensitive parts

of the system and therefore will
facilitate policy making, including
investment policy.

III. Numerical Example to Illustrate the
Model

1. Purpose of this example is to illustrate
the use of the model to answer question
5b in section AII of this paper.

2. The Hypothetical System Used. A hypothetical but typical environmental management
system might contain some or all (or more)
of the following sections:

1. Research Type 1 Hardware
2. Research Type 2 Software
3. Research Type 3 Systems
4. Industry
5. Agriculture
6. Fishing
7. Legislation
8. Waste Disposal
9. Water Plant
10. General Administration
11. Routine Testing
12. Human Quality
13. Air Quality
14. Water Quality
15. Soil Quality
16. Animal Quality
17. Plant Quality

Keeping in mind that sections 1 through 11
are activities which are either directly or
indirectly producing or reducing pollutants in
the systems, we shall designate these as intermediate activities. Sectors 12 through 17
constitute the maximum levels of pollutants
permitted by the community. They are demands
made directly by the community and they are
therefore defined as final demands or required
quantities.

The whole system, consisting of 17 sectors,
uses the basic inputs which can include the
following:

Utilities
Manpower
Equipment
Space

In this example we shall consider a small sample
only of these basic inputs, comprising

Labor Type 1
Labor Type 2 (Professional Services)
Space

These basic inputs are used by the intermediate and final activities in the manner
shown in Table 1. The figures in this table
have been devised to illustrate the application
of the model. They represent the interactions
between the various sectors of the system. The
Table should be interpreted in the following
way: Consider for example the section entitled
Research Type 2. This has a total output of

12 cost units during the period of analysis.
This means that the funds expended upon the
activities of this section amount to 12 cost
units. The services of this sector are not
directly used by the community. Therefore the
final demand for this sector is zero cost
units. However, many sectors of the environmental management system require the services
of Research Type 2. For example, as shown in
Table 1, industrial waste consumes 3 cost
units of this service; municipal waste consumes
2.5 cost units and water quality takes 0.5 cost
units, all over the time period of analysis.
These services plus all of those being used by
the other sectors add up to 12 cost units,
which figure constitutes the total output of
the section entitled "Research Type 2".
Similarly, examination of Table 1 shows the
total outputs, final demands and intersectional
flows of all the other sections of the environmental management system.

3. Method of Solving the Problem. Because
the problem is to respond to the increased
(or changed) final demand of the community
for the services of the environmental
management system, it is necessary to estimate quantitatively these new final demands
and in turn, the input-output model developed earlier, to compute the new intersectional flows, the new basic inputs and
the new total outputs.

A set of new estimated final demands for
all of the sections of our hypothetical
environmental management system is shown
in Table 2. The numbers in this table
have been previously chosen so that the
final demand on some sections are decreased,
on others increased and on others remaining
the same, compared with the starting situation, as illustrated in Table 2.

The interdependence coefficients (that is
the elements of the "A" matrix) have been
calculated by using equation 2. With these
coefficients and the new final demands, by
using equation 7 we can calculate the new
total outputs of each section (X'). Finally
with the help of equations (8) and (9) and
the new total output matrix we can compute
the new intersectional flow matrix given in
Table 2. And also the new basic input
flow into the various sections. This basic
input flow matrix is given in the top
portion of Table 2.

IV. Conclusions and Recommendations

1. Input-output analysis applied to a environmental management system helps management
to formulate policies, which involve problems of resource allocation, in a quantitative manner.

2. Because input-output analysis replaces
qualitative planning and decision making
with quantitative planning and decision

making, cost effectiveness is increased
throughout the whole system. This factor
also applies when management is considering new innovations in the system.

3. The input-output technique can be usefully
applied to subsectors, sectors, whole
ecosystems or even to groupings of such
systems with corresponding benefits.

4. Because much of the raw data required for
input-output analysis is usually already
available within current accounting procedures, the extra cost of introducing and
operating an input-output program should
be well within the budget of the system
being considered.

5. In this paper, one very specific and
important use of the input-output technique
has been illustrated in the example. It
has been shown that the model can be used
directly to compute the new basic inputs,
the new intersectional flows and the new
total outputs of the sections in response
to a new demand by the community for the
services of the environmental management
system. In Section II-5, the uses of the
model to solve other important problems in
environmental management systems, have been
discussed. The reader is referred to that
section for further details.

6. The deterministic input-output technique is
not a panacea. For example, many if not
all real systems are probabilistic rather
than deterministic in nature. In addition;
inherent in the deterministic model is the
assumption that the system is linear, and
there is no guarantee that this will be the
case in a real situation. These topics are
discussed more fully in Part B of this
paper.

Part B The Probabilistic Model

I. Advantages of the Probabilistic Model
Compared with the Deterministic Model

The advantages in using the probabilistic
model when compared with the deterministic
type are:

1. The deterministic model can only be used
to compute average responses to changes
whereas the probabilistic model gives more
realistic answers. For example, the final
demands constitute a matrix of random
variables, each element of which follows a
probability distribution. The use of the
model allows one to evaluate the probability distributions which the responses will
follow as a consequence of change in the
distributions of the final demands.

2. The probabilistic model facilitates con-
tingency analysis for the system.

3. To the administrator the probabilistic
model incorporates what is perhaps analogous to what the safety factor is to the
engineer. For example, it will allow

administrators to design their systems
such that for a given endowment, they can
fulfill the demands made upon the system
with a predetermined assurance.

4. Because of the probabilistic nature of
the model, it will allow an administration
to quantify the degrees of flexibility in
the changes which it must make in order
to cope with the altered demands for the
services from the system.

5. The probabilistic model will allow quantitative policy formulation on matters
of resource allocation where hitherto a
subject set of rules may have been used.

II. Assumptions and Nomenclature

The nomenclature and assumptions of the
probabilistic model are the same as those for
the deterministic model except for their stochastic nature. Thus each variable in the
probabilistic model is a random variable
following a specific distribution.

III. Construction and Use of the
Probabilistic Model

For the deterministic model presented in
Part A, it was assumed that the intersectional
flows (x_{ij}'s), the final demands (Y_i's) and
hence the total outputs (X_i's) of all sections
remain constant over the period of analysis.
As most real systems are probabilistic in
nature, in this section we will extend the
above model to encompass the advantages listed
in Section I of Part B and then illustrate its
use with the help of a series of questions and
answers.

In the probabilistic model x_{ij}'s and Y_i's
are considered to be random variables having
known probability distributions. Also the
total output of ith section is given by

$$X_i = \sum_{j=1}^{n} x_{ij} + Y_i$$

Therefore the total output X_i is a function of the random variables x_{ij}'s and Y_i.

Using the equation (1) we get the relationship between the final demands (Y_i's) and
the total outputs (X_i's) as

$$Y = A X \tag{16}$$

With the help of equations (15) and (16)
we can simulate the probabilistic nature of
the real system by following a series of steps
outlined below:

Step 1.   Generate x_{ij}'s following a distribution D_{ij} having a mean $\bar{x}_{ij}$ and variance σ^2_{ij}.

Step 2.   Generate Y_i's following a distribution D_i having a mean Y_i and variance σ^2_i.

Step 3.   Compute X_i's by using equation 15.

Step 4.   Determine matrix A by computing its elements using equation 2.

Step 5.   Calculate A^{-1}.

Step 6.   Generate new values Y_i''s following a distribution D_i' having a mean Y_i' and variance σ_i'.

Step 7.   Compute the $\bar{X}'$ matrix by using the model.

Step 8.   Compute the new x_{ij}'s as follows
$$x_{ij}' = a^{old}_{ij} X_i' \quad \text{(equation 8)}.$$

Step 9.   Repeat steps 1 thru 8 about 1000 times. (This number was found by trial and error to give a satisfactory frequency plot.)

Step 10. Print out the new distributions of x_{ij}'s, X_i's, Y_i's.

Step 11. Print the distributions of old x_{ij}'s, X_i's, Y_i's.

Step 12. Compare means and variances of the old and new distributions of all the random variables in the model.

The use of the probabilistic input-output model is illustrated as shown below:

a. Question: What is the most obvious advantage to an environmental management system in making use of this model?
Answer: The first advantage is that administration is required to identify and quantify all the work flows occurring in the system. This consists of collection of the data to evaluate the probability distributions of the elements of the (N x N) "A" matrix in the model (equations 15 and 16).

b. Question: In what way does this model differ from the deterministic model?
Answer: Refer to advantages 1 to 4 given in Section I of Part B of this paper.

c. Question: What additional information does this model provide to the administrators to answer question 5b, given in Part A.
Answer: The use of the probabilistic model gives the administrator the probability distributions which the responses will follow as a consequence of change in the distributions of the

final demands. This enables him to design the system such that for a given endowment, he can fulfill the demands made upon the system with a predetermined assurance. It also allows the administrator to quantify the degree of flexibility in the changes which he must make in order to cope with the altered demands for the services from the system.

d. Question: How will the probabilistic model help the administration to decide in what section of the system he should invest for maximum effectiveness? That is, how sensitive individually are all the sections of the system to fresh endowment?
Answer: Once the model is established for a specific system, it is an easy matter to change the parameters of one or more of the probability density functions of the elements of the new "A" matrix and compute the new probability distributions of the new final demands and new total outputs of the system. Using the model in this way it will allow quantitative policy formulation on matters of resource allocation where hitherto a subjective set of rules may have been used.

IV. Numerical Example

1. The purpose of this example is to illustrate the use of the probabilistic model to answer question 5c in Section III of Part B of this paper.

2. The hypothetical system used is the same as the one described in Part A   Section IV. For the probabilistic model Table 1 gives the mean total outputs, mean final demands and mean intersectional flows of all the sectors of the environmental system. Table 2 shows the variances of the distributions of the intersectional flows and final demands. Table 3 shows the means of the distributions that the new final demands follow. These figures are also hypothetical and serve to illustrate the hypothetical example of the model. The numbers in this table have been purposely chosen so that the final demands on some sections are decreased, on other increased and on other remaining the same, compared with the starting situation, as illustrated in Table 1.

3. Methods of solving the problem. Because the problem is to respond to the changed final demand of the community for the services of environmental system, it is necessary to estimate quantitatively the new distribution of final demands and in turn by stimulating the input-output model developed earlier, to determine the

a. New distribution of the sectional flows (x_{ij}').

b. New distribution of the basic inputs ($b_{\ell m}'$).

c. New distributions of the total outputs (X_i').

A computer program has been developed to simulate the model which has been derived in this paper. Up until the time of writing, this program has been used to answer questions (a) above. The answer consists of 289 graphical representations of the frequency plots of x_{ij}'s. From which means and variances of interest can be computed.

4. Interpretation of Results. Consider element x_{ij}; of the flow matrix:

This represents the amount of output of section i used by section j. Therefore the distribution of x_{ij}; will represent the distribution of the flow from section i to j. The graphs of the distributions of x_{ij}'s for sectors and are given in Figures 1 through 4 respectively. Features which are of importance in the design and management of each case and the items of information which are of importance in designing and managing of real systems include the following:

a. x_{ij}' maximum and x_{ij}' minimum.

This information provides the administrator with the upper and lower limits of the amount of work flow (x_{ij}') from section i to section j. This provides him with a very realistic and quantitative basis for designing capacity and resources of the particular section under consideration. For example by referring to frequency plot x_{13} we know that for the period of analysis the flow in cost units from the Research I to the Research III section should lie in the range (.15 to 7.8). This range (.15 $\leq x_{ij}' \leq$ 7.8) defines the flexibility of the Research I in relationship to the Research III section. This frequency plot gives the corresponding probability that x_{ij} will lie in this range. Hence one can determine the probability that the section will be able to meet the demands of another section lying in a certain range (say 1,6).

b. Although means and variances of x_{ij}''s are not printed out directly at this

stage of the development of the program, it is apparent that this information along with the model can be utilized to advantage in the manner outlined in sections A1 to A5 of the introduction of this paper.

Conclusions and Recommendations

1. A probabilistic model of an environmental management system has been developed using input-output analysis. It is believed that this is a unique contribution to the technique of input-output analysis.

2. Probabilistic input-output analysis is a more realistic method of solving problems than is the deterministic approach and certain aspects of this superiority have been discussed in this paper.

3. In Part B of this paper the specific and important use of the probabilistic model has been illustrated by a numerical example. Using the model to calculate the new distributions of the intersectional flows (x_{ij}''s) in response to a changed final demand. These results provide the environmental managers with a more realistic basis for designing the capacities of the various sections of the system under consideration as compared to the deterministic model. This additional information consists of the following points:

a. Frequency plot of the x_{ij}''s.

b. The maximum value of x_{ij}.

c. The minimum value of x_{ij}.

4. Additional to the extra information about the x_{ij}' elements which the probabilistic model makes available is the important feature that it can be used to design each individual section of the system that it will operate within stated limits with a preselected degree of assurance.

Notes

1. Bowles, Samuel. "The Efficient Allocation of Resources in Education." Quarterly Journal of Economics, 81 (May, 1967), 189-219.

2. Dantzig, George B. Linear Programming and Extensions. Princeton, N.J.: Princeton University Press, 1963.

3. Fetter, Robert B., and Thompson, John D. "Computer Models for the Design and Utilization of Hospital Facilities." Paper presented at the 22nd National Meeting of the Operations Research Society of America, Philadelphia, Pa., November 7-9, 1962.

4. Fisher, W.D. "Criteria for Aggregation in Input-Output Analysis." Review of Economics and Statistics, 40, No. 3 (August, 1958), 250-60.

5. Hurwicz, Leonid. "Input-Output Analysis and Economic Structure." The American Economic Review, 44 (December, 1955), 626-36.

6. Koza, Russell C. "The Use of Micro-Structural Input-Output Systems Analysis in Educational Resource Allocation Decision Making." Paper presented at the Joint TIMS/ORSA Meeting, San Francisco, May, 1968.

7. Levine, Jack B., and Richard, W. Judy. "The Integration of Simulation Models and Program Budgeting in University Planning and Administration." Paper presented at the Joint TIMS/ORSA Meeting, San Francisco, May, 1968.

8. Miernyk, William H. The Elements of Input-Output Analysis. New York: Random House, 1965.

9. Nasta, M. D.; Beddow, J. K.; and Shapiro R. A. "A Deterministic Model for a Hospital Health Services System". (To be published.)

10. Nordell, Lawrence P. A Dynamic Input-Output Model of the California Educational System. Technical Report No. 25, Center for Research in Management Science, University of California, Berkeley, California, August, 1967.

Table 2. Criteria for the Determination of the Standard Deviation

Mean of the Random Variable (R.V.)	Variance of the Random Variable ($\sigma_{R.V.}$)
$0 < R.V. \leq 3$	0.2
$3 < R.V. \leq 10$	1.0
$10 < R.V. \leq 20$	2.0
$20 < R.V. \leq 50$	3.0
$50 < R.V. \leq 100$	4.0
$R.V. \geq 100$	5.0

Table 1

		1	2	3	4	5	6	7	8	9	10	11	12	13	14	15	16	17	
Number	Labor 1	25	20	10	250	50	5	15	100	10	50	20	40	20	30	10	20	15	680
Number	Labor 2	30	25	15	100	50	2	25	20	15	50	10	25	15	20	10	15	10	437
$(M)	Equipment	1	1	1	15	3	1	0	3	5	0	1	5	3	1	1	2	1	44
Sq Ftx10³	Space	50	60	10	20	10	1	5	13	5	10	5	6	10	15	4	3	10	237

Absorbing Sectors (1–17): Research 1, Research 2, Research 3, Industrial Waste, Municipal Waste, Ag. Fish Water, Legislation, Waste Disposal, Water Plant, General Administration, Routine Test, Human Quality, Animal Quality, Plant Quality, Soil Quality, Water Quality, Air Quality

	Producing Sectors	1	2	3	4	5	6	7	8	9	10	11	12	13	14	15	16	17	Final Demand	Total Output
1 $(M)	Research 1	0	5	0.5	6.5	2.5	0	0.5	2	1	0.5	1	0.5	0.5	0.5	0.5	0.5	0.5	0	23
2 $(M)	Research 2	0	0	0.5	3	2.5	1	0.5	0.5	0	0.5	1	0.5	0.5	0.5	0.5	0.5	0.5	0	12
3 $(M)	Research 3	0.5	0.5	0	1	1	1	0	1	0.5	0.5	1	0.5	0.5	0.5	0.5	0.5	0.5	0	10
4 Ton (M)	Ind. Waste	0	0	0	0	0	0	0	30	20	0	0	0.1	0.2	0.1	50	60	70	0	230.4
5 Ton (M)	Municipal Waste	0	0	0	0	0	0	0	20	15	0	0	0.1	0.1	0.1	40	50	40	0	165.3
6 Lbs(th)	Ag. Fish Water	0	0	0	0	0	0	0	0	0	0	0	0.2	0.2	0.2	40	10	0	0	50.6
7 Time	Legislation	40	50	60	150	200	50	0	200	100	100	0	20	60	50	40	30	60	0	1260
8 $(M)	Waste Disposal	2	0.5	1	85	50	20	0	0	5	1	1	0	0	0	0	0	0	0	200
9 Gallon	Water Plant	1	0.5	1	10	15	0	0	5	0	1	1	0	0	0	0	0	0	0	345
10 $(th)	General Adm.	0.5	0.5	0.5	0.5	0.5	0.5	0.5	0.5	0.5	0.5	0.5	0.5	0.5	0.5	0.5	0.5	0.5	0	85
11 $(th)	Routine Test	0	0	0	0	0	0	0	0	0	0	0	1	1	1	1	1	1	0	6
12 ngm/per	Human Quality	0	0	0	0	0	0	0	0	0	0	0	0	0	0	0	0	0	10	10
13 ngm/ani	Animal Quality	0	0	0	0	0	0	0	0	0	0	0	0	0	0	0	0	0	10	10
14 ngm/pla	Plant Quality	0	0	0	0	0	0	0	0	0	0	0	0	0	0	0	0	0	5	5
15 ngm/amb	Soil Quality	0	0	0	0	0	0	0	0	0	0	0	0	0	0	0	0	0	3	3
16 ngm/gal	Water Quality	0	0	0	0	0	0	0	0	0	0	0	0	0	0	0	0	0	10	10
17 ngm/amb	Air Quality	0	0	0	0	0	0	0	0	0	0	0	0	0	0	0	0	0	10	10

Table 3

No. Units

		1	2	3	4	5	6	7	8	9	10	11	12	13	14	15	16	17	
1 Number	Labor 1	38.8	31.1	15.6	387.1	77.6	8.2	23.3	156.0	15.5	77.7	30.8	60.0	30.0	48.0	16.7	30.0	22.5	1069.5
2 Number	Labor 2	46.6	38.9	23.4	154.9	77.6	3.3	38.9	31.2	23.3	77.7	15.5	37.5	22.5	32.0	16.7	22.5	15.0	667.5
3 $(M)	Equipment	1.6	1.6	1.6	23.2	4.7	1.6	0.0	4.7	7.8	0.0	1.5	7.5	4.5	1.6	1.7	3.0	1.5	68.1
4 SqFTx10³	Space	77.6	93.4	31.2	31.0	15.5	1.6	7.8	20.3	7.8	15.5	1.7	9.0	15.0	24.0	6.7	4.5	15.0	383/6

	Producing Sectors	1	2	3	4	5	6	7	8	9	10	11	12	13	14	15	16	17	New Final Demand	New Total Output
1 $(M)	Research 1	0.0	7.8	0.8	10.1	3.9	0.0	0.8	3.1	1.6	0.8	1.5	0.7	0.7	0.8	0.8	0.7	0.7	0	34.9
2 $(M)	Research 2	0.0	0.0	0.8	4.5	3.9	1.6	0.8	0.8	0.0	0.8	1.5	0.7	0.7	0.8	0.8	0.7	0.7	0	19.5
3 $(M)	Research 3	0.8	0.8	0.0	1.5	1.6	1.6	0.0	1.6	0.8	0.8	1.5	0.7	0.7	0.8	0.8	0.7	0.7	0	15.6
4 Ton (M)	Industrial Waste	0.0	0.0	0.0	0.0	0.0	0.0	0.0	46.8	31.0	0.0	0.0	0.1	0.3	0.3	83.3	90.0	105.0	0	356.6
5 Ton (M)	Municipal Waste	0.0	0.0	0.0	0.0	0.0	0.0	0.0	31.2	23.3	0.0	0.0	0.1	0.1	0.2	66.7	75.0	60.0	0	256.6
6 lbs(th)	Ag. Fish Water	0.0	0.0	0.0	0.0	0.0	0.0	0.0	0.0	0.0	0.0	0.0	0.3	0.3	0.3	66.7	15.0	0.0	0	82.6
7 Time	Legislation	62.1	77.8	93.5	232.3	310.5	81.6	0.0	312.0	155.2	155.5	0.0	30.0	90.0	80.0	66.7	45.0	90.0	0	1882.2
8 $(M)	Waste Disposal	3.1	0.8	1.6	131.6	77.6	32.6	0.0	0.0	7.8	1.6	1.5	0.0	0.0	0.0	0.0	0.0	0.0	0	258.2
9 Gallon	Water Plant	1.6	0.8	1.6	15.5	23.3	0.0	0.0	7.8	0.0	1.6	1.5	0.0	0.0	0.0	0.0	0.0	0.0	0	53.6
10 $(th)	General Adm.	0.8	0.8	0.8	0.8	0.8	0.8	0.8	0.8	0.8	0.8	0.8	0.7	0.7	0.8	0.8	0.7	0.7	0	13.2
11 $(th)	Routine Test	0.0	0.0	0.8	0.0	0.0	0.0	0.0	0.0	0.0	0.0	0.0	1.5	1.5	1.6	1.7	1.5	1.5	0	10.0
12 mgm/person	Human Quality	0.0	0.0	0.0	0.0	0.0	0.0	0.0	0.0	0.0	0.0	0.0	0.0	0.0	0.0	0.0	0.0	0.0	15	15.0
13 mgm/animal	Animal Quality	0.0	0.0	0.0	0.0	0.0	0.0	0.0	0.0	0.0	0.0	0.0	0.0	0.0	0.0	0.0	0.0	0.0	15	15.0
14 mgm/plant	Plant Quality	0.0	0.0	0.0	0.0	0.0	0.0	0.0	0.0	0.0	0.0	0.0	0.0	0.0	0.0	0.0	0.0	0.0	15	15.0
15 mgm/amb	Soil Quality	0.0	0.0	0.0	0.0	0.0	0.0	0.0	0.0	0.0	0.0	0.0	0.0	0.0	0.0	0.0	0.0	0.0	8	8.0
16 mgm/gal	Water Quality	0.0	0.0	0.0	0.0	0.0	0.0	0.0	0.0	0.0	0.0	0.0	0.0	0.0	0.0	0.0	0.0	0.0	5	5.0
17 mg/oc	Air Quality	0.0	0.0	0.0	0.0	0.0	0.0	0.0	0.0	0.0	0.0	0.0	0.0	00.0	0.0	0.0	0.0	0.0	15	15.0

Changing Racial Residential Patterns

by Henry Sanoff
Associate Professor of Architecture

Man M. Sawhney
Associate Professor of Sociology

Henry K. Burgwyn
Research Assistant

and George Ellinwood
Research Assistant

North Carolina State University, Raleigh

Abstract
        This investigation deals with
the "flight of whites" in terms of
their varying behavior as functions
of their social and economic background and their attitudes towards
and perceptions of the changes in
their neighborhood that a non-white
entry would bring about. It is also
concerned with the influence of a new
non-white neighborhood on the property values of the adjacent all-white
neighborhood through the analysis of
price behavior of a control and test
neighborhood.

        The findings suggest that the
rate of racial change is influenced
by the level of white demand, the
level of Negro demand, the number
and race of families that wish to sell
their houses and the interactions of
these three variables.

        (This project was financed by a
title 1 grant from the Higher Education Act of 1965 and coordinated with
the Urban Affairs and Community Service Center, North Carolina State U-
niversity.)

Introduction
        Residential segregation occupies
a critical position in the changing
patterns of race relations. It not
only inhibits the development of informal neighborly relations between
white and Negroes but ensures the segregation of a variety of public and
private services and facilities.

        It is clear that race has been a
more important factor in the residential structure of southern cities
than in other regions of the country.
The pattern of residential differentiation included an adaptation to the
presence of a large Negro population,
but in areas usually set aside for
them. However, racial patterns of
neighborhoods are beginning to change.

        The following study is a syste-
matic investigation of one of such
changes. It dealt with the impact of
a predominantly Negro neighborhood
built in the vicinity of an all-white
neighborhood. The object of the study
was twofold. First, it was concerned
with "the flight of whites" in terms
of their varying behavior as functions
of their social and economic backgrounds, their attitudes and perceptions of the neighborhood changes resulting from the close proximity to
this Negro neighborhood. Second, the
study deals with the effect of the
Negro neighborhood on the property
values of the adjacent white neighborhood. The reason for this phase
is succinctly described in the following statement:

> "The rate of racial change in a
> neighborhood varies widely and
> is not as commonly thought, sim-
> ply a measure of differences in
> the intensity and extent of pre-
> judice and discrimination. Ra-
> ther, differences in rates are
> due to variations in all the fac-
> tors which affect the level of
> white demand, the level of Negro
> demand, the number and race of
> families who wish to sell their
> homes, and the interaction of
> these three variables" (1).

Historical Development of the Turnkey
III Project

        In June 1968 the Raleigh Housing
Authority solicited proposals for the
construction of 216 units of public
housing under the Turnkey III Program.

        When Apollo Heights was selected
as the site for the 216 units of

Turnkey Housing, the Local Housing Authority had on file nine hundred applications for public housing occupancy. However, since the family income limits for Turnkey III are slightly higher than conventional low rent public housing, additional applications were solicited by the LHA.

Applications received above the income limitations of Turnkey III were turned over to real estate brokers who could arrange FHA 235 below interest loans and interest supplements to low income families. The maximum annual income limits of this program ranged from $5-6000, while those for Apollo were $4500-5000. Under the FHA 235 Program the home buyer is required to provide 20% of his income to repay the mortgage loan at 8% interest (2). While the mortgages can be repaid in periods ranging from ten to forty years most low income families utilize the long term mortgages. The FHA 235 mortgage insurance is for 100% of the mortgage, hence requiring no down payment by the home buyer (3).

A certain portion of the funds allocated by Congress for the FHA 235 Program were earmarked for financing the sale of existing housing to low income families at prices below $15,500 (4). Hence, the realtors who had been supplied lists of families whose incomes qualified for FHA 235 mortgages needed access to existing housing that would be purchased under the $15,500 ceiling. Since the large, predominantly Negro, Apollo Heights Project was being constructed adjoining white Stratford Park, the realtors could reasonably expect a substantial number of white families to place their homes on the market (5). To ensure that Stratford Park whites did sell, realtors circulated printed information describing the Apollo Heights project and the anticipated racial composition (6). Some realtors assured white families that housing would be provided for them in all white neighborhoods if they would sell or trade their present homes (7). Subsequently, realtors acquired many of the homes in Stratford Park during the construction of the initial increment of Apollo Heights housing which was the first visible indication of change. The realtors, however, could not sell any of the white homes in Stratford Park to Negro families. The National Association of Real

Estate Boards maintains a code of ethics which states that "a realtor should never be instrumental in introducing into a neighborhood a character of property or use which will clearly be detrimental to property values in that neighborhood" (8). Consequently, until Apollo was occupied by Negroes, realtors could sell housing in Stratford to white families only for fear that black entry would cause property values to decrease sharply. However, once construction of Apollo Heights began in March 1969, the realtors could proceed to sell homes in Stratford Park to Negro families.

It is important to note that action taken by the Federal government in the field of housing policy from 1935 to 1950 made discrimination against Negroes a condition of Federal assistance (9). In the underwriting manual of 1938 it stated that "if a neighborhood is to retain stability it is necessary that properties shall continue to be occupied by the same social and racial classes" (10). Consistent with this theory, the FHA because of its conviction that declining property values would result from a mixed neighborhood, thus endangering the long range financing involved, formerly insisted that residential projects desiring FHA-insured financing draw up restrictive covenants against non-whites. In recent years FHA has adopted the opposite position, refusing to insure projects where a written racially restrictive covenant exists. Concerning property values and race, the Underwriting Manual now states, "the tendency of user groups to seek compatible conditions can sustain and enhance, diminish or destroy neighborhood desirability..." If a mixture of user groups is found to exist, it must be determined whether the mixture will render the neighborhood less desirable to the present and prospective occupants (11).

When the first increment of the construction of Apollo was completed, twenty eight families moved in, of which twenty four were Negro. Construction continued in increments of forty houses and by February 1970, 116 families had moved into Apollo Heights (107 of which were Negro). When the project was completed in the summer of 1970, 90% of the 216 homes were occupied by Negro families (12).

PINECREST

STRATFORD PARK

The research findings are being presented in two sections: A. A Property Values Study and B. An Attitudinal Study.

Property Values Study

The influence of Apollo Heights on property values in Stratford Park was investigated by comparing the price behavior in Stratford Park, the target area, with another similar neighborhood, Pinecrest (control neighborhood).

To compare price behavior of each neighborhood over time, multiple listing records were used to provide a representative sample of sales over a two-year period. An index of sales was computed to control for the diversity of type and size of house sold and yet yield the overall market price trends. This index was computed by dividing the selling price by the original price paid when built.

In order to determine the financial gain from home sales under various loan arrangements, an index of return on equity was computed by subtracting the selling fees and unpaid mortgage principal from the selling price. The remainder or residual was then contrasted with the equity (selling price minus unpaid mortgage principal). This percentage (residual/equity) provides an indication of loss of sales under various loan arrangements.

The value of property changes over time can only be realistically known after a sale. To assess the value of a property, one must analyze the individual's role as a buyer and seller of his home, hence the value index gives an indication of the changing worth of property. While the

original cost of the home when built is publicly recorded, the purchase price of subsequent sales is not. It is for this reason that the sales index and return index (rather than the value index) have been utilized in this report. The relationship of the sales and return index provides an operational definition of the term property value: the greater the sales index and the greater the return index, the greater the value of the property and vice versa.

Level of Sales

The level of sales in Pinecrest has been relatively stable in the last decade. The number of sales in any six-month period has never risen above fifteen or fallen below seven as shown in Figure 1. Until 1969 the sales level in Stratford was similarly stable with a half year range of eight to eighteen sales.

It was during 1969 that Apollo Heights was constructed and when the level of sales in Stratford increased sharply to twenty-four in the first half of the year. When the sales level was plotted for 1968-69 as shown in Figure 2, it is clear that the sales increase in Stratford begins in the summer of 1969 with an increase of four to five sales a month. The sales continued to increase to a peak of eighteen in December.

Since a two to three month period is usually required to sell a home, it can be assumed that the homes sold in the summer of 1969 in Stratford were placed on the market that spring during the construction of Apollo Heights. During the first five months of 1969 fifteen homes in Stratford Park were sold to white families. It is interesting to note that of the

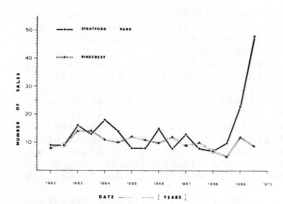

Figure 1:
HOUSING SALES: 1962 to 1970

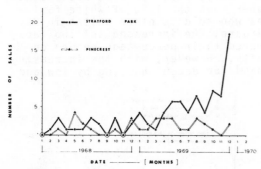

Figure 2:
HOUSING SALES: 1968 and 1969

initial six non-white sales in June,
three involved the Local Housing
Authority. The LHA purchased parcels
of vacant land in January 1969.
Three homes purchased by Negro fami-
lied were adjacent to lots on which
the LHA was constructing the Turnkey
Housing. These sales occurred before
the initial occupancy of new homes in
Apollo Heights in July. The first
increment of new homes in Apollo
Heights was occupied in July and subsequently, more non-white families
began purchasing homes in Stratford
Park. From August to November twen-
ty-one Negro families moved into the
neighborhood.

As the extent of Negro entry increased in October and November, so
did the non-white demand, as indicated by the thirteen sales to Negro families in December. The sales summary for 1969 indicates that 59% of
the sales in Stratford Park were to
non-white families. By the end of
February 1970, Negro families occupied

48% of the homes in the Stratford
Park neighborhood. While the Negro
homes are located in close proximity
to Apollo Heights, the spread is increasing towards the white areas.

The sales index for Pinecrest increased from about 1.3 in early 1969
to around 1.5 by the end of the same
year. This increasing level over time
is a result of rising selling prices
due to inflation. This line of inflation (13) shown in Figure 3 indicates
a general increase in the value of
property. The return index for Pinecrest (Figure 4) indicates that selling
fees during 1968-69 had remained relatively stable allowing an average
return on equity of 72%. Hence, the
line of inflation for Pinecrest should
give an accurate picture of property
values in both the test and control
neighborhoods since they were originally similar. In Figure 3 the line
of inflation for Pinecrest should
give an accurate picture of property
values in both the test and control
neighborhoods since they were originally similar. In Figure 5 the line of
inflation for Pinecrest has been superimposed on the sales index graph for
Stratford Park. The Stratford sales
index closely follows the line of inflation until the summer of 1969 when
it decreases from 1.30 to 1.15.

The low sales index of 1.25 in
Stratford during April, May and June
resulted from white families selling
to other white families. These white
families who sold had financed their
homes in the early 1960's with FHA or
VA (14) loans at 4 to 6% interest.
The present rate for such loans being
8%, thus increased substantially the
finance payments that families have
to pay to acquire new housing comparable to that in Stratford Park. In addition to the low sales index during
this three-month period, the return
on equity index for FHA-VA sales also
decreased slightly due to the lower
selling prices (See Figure 6). Both
these decreases indicate an initial
decline in property values in Stratford
Park.

Effect of Non-White Entry
When the construction of Apollo
began in March, a new market was comprised of moderate income Negro families who could arrange FHA or VA financing (15). The initial Negro families purchased homes during the latter part of the "panic" sales period.

Consequently, the sales index of white families who sold to Negroes in June and July decreased from 1.25 to 1.15. However, as a result of increased Negro demand, the sales index in August and September increased over the line of inflation. The white families who sold to the initial Negro buyers benefited from both high sales index and percentage of return on equity (See Figures 5 and 6). Consequently, the initial decrease in property values caused by "panic" sales was reversed by this new upswing. However, the combination of high mortgage interest rates and the limited number of Negro families who could qualify for FHA or VA financing served to curtail the new market by the end of September.

In the fall of 1969 a second new market was opened for the homes in Stratford Park. Realtors facing a "tight" money period began to utilize the FHA 235 Program to finance the sale of homes in Stratford to low and moderate income Negro families. The limited selling price required by the 235 Program ($15,500) decreased the sales index from 1.45 in late September and October to 1.25 in November as shown in Figure 5. This decrease in the sales index (and the selling price) in November was followed by a substantial increase in the number of sales in December (13 as compared with 6 in November) as indicated in Figure 1. This increase in sales can be attributed to the increased demand of low and moderate income Negro families for decent housing in Raleigh.

The white families in Stratford who sold under the FHA 235 Program in the fall of 1969 received a lower percentage of return on their equity (56%) as shown in Figure 7. While their sales index of 1.30 was slightly higher than the 1.25 of white families who sold to other whites in May and June, the increased selling fees lowered their percentage return on equity. However, with the increasing demand for decent housing by low and

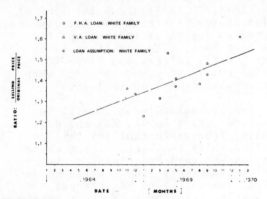

Figure 3:
PINECREST SALES INDEX

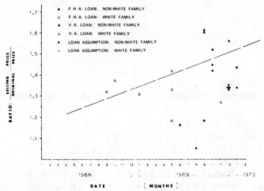

Figure 5:
STRATFORD PARK SALES INDEX

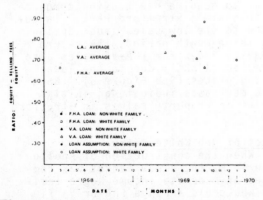

Figure 4:
PINECREST RETURN INDEX

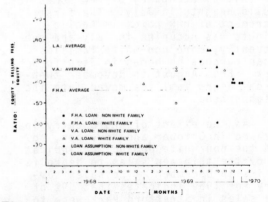

Figure 6:
STRATFORD PARK RETURN INDEX

moderate income Negro families and the increase in the selling price ceiling on FHA 235 morgaged homes to $18,500 (effective January 1970) the sales index for Stratford should increase to at least the line of inflation. This increase will cause a stabilization in the value of property.

Finally, it is clear that property values arise from a number of economic variables - original cost of the home, selling price of the home, selling fees, and loan arrangements. The term sales index and return on equity give the above variables an operational meaning. When compared they can give a picture not only of the total market (sales index) but also the individual profits (return on equity).

Factors Influencing Change
The process of racial transition has been stimulated by a rapid increase in the numbers and income of the Negro population as well as the absence of a sufficient quantity of newly constructed houses elsewhere in the city. Most evidence suggests that the logical area to undergo racial change is on the periphery of established non-white sections. The new Apollo Heights neighborhood, however, suggests the characteristics of a stable non-white neighborhood. Hence, the movement into Stratford Park is the natural extension of the Negro neighborhood. While the initial sales resulting from the implications of Apollo were to white buyers, it rapidly became evident that they were not willing to pay a satisfactory price.

Rapid transition in the Stratford Park area was the product of numerous influences: liberal mortgage terms, sustained Negro demand, a substantial supply of houses of moderate value, rising prices and considerable availability of high quality housing for whites in other sections of the city.

The evidence from this study though not conclusive, does suggest that unless the Negro population in Raleigh has access to other residential areas, Stratford Park will not become interracially stable. Rapkin (16) suggests that if the non-white population of a neighborhood is above 40% then the demand of white families will

be zero, thus causing the neighborhood to turn completely non-white in about five years. Since there has been 45% non-white entry in Stratford it seems very likely that the neighborhood will eventually become non-white.

Other findings suggest that many whites living in predominately white sections of mixed areas had no objections to or even awareness of the small percentage of Negroes nearby (17). When this percentage was exceeded and the proportion of Negroes continued to increase, many white residents chose to move to other areas. It is suggested that the threshold of acceptance is rather low perhaps much lower than the proportion of Negroes in the population of the city.

If the pattern of Stratford Park becomes a typical case, it implies that a pattern of predominately Negro communities will emerge, irrespective of a few hard core whites who will remain and a few more who may move to the area for a variety of reasons.

It seems clear from this study that even in the South the fear whites have of property values declining with Negro entry to their neighborhoods is unfounded. It is only when the scale of non-white entry is sufficiently great to cause "panic selling" that property values will temporarily decline. Even when a neighborhood panics and a very large number of whites put their houses or the market simultaneously, the excess supply will certainly be absorbed quickly by a new market. This situation is particularly pertinent when there is an inadequate availability of decent housing in the city.

It may be useful to go beyond the findings of this study and examine other relevant factors. The housing alternative available within the city must be related to the size of Negro demand. Although Negroes comprise approximately one quarter of the total population in Raleigh, they constitute 40% of the families earning less than $5000 (18).

Demands from this group will need to be met by moderately priced units in the existing stock. In order to diminish the number of all-white neighborhoods available to lower middle income white groups, who (like in Stratford Park) will prefer to move, a policy which produces dispersed, integrated neighborhoods must be followed. It is also clear that if owners of existing housing and real estate brokers pursued a policy of non-discrimination, alternative opportunities for all white neighborhoods would disappear.

Attitudinal Study

Survey research technique was used in Stratford Park, where mass relocation of white families occurred when it was realized that 216 Turnkey III housing units built adjacent to the white area were going to be predominately Negro. A questionnaire was administered to 50% of the white residents of Stratford Park in an attempt to understand and explain the causes of the apparent white exodus.

The results of this inquiry are consistent with the prevalent view that residential integration, even today, poses a serious threat to those living in all-white neighborhoods. In this predominately lower middle class residential area, a large number of white families had already relocated prior to this investigation. However, the mass relocation had not ceased. The data indicated that a great majority of those interviewed had either already decided to move or considered that the decision to relocate in the near future was a possibility.

The mass relocation was not simply an expression of white families desire not to have Negro neighbors. Rather, the white families that had decided to relocate realized that from racial segregation in residential areas arises de facto groups, children's peer groups and in many other activities in which the area itself is a focal point. The reasons for relocation given by the respondent were deterioration of schools, contact with Negro children, etc. Also, since these activities involve a number of families that know each other, the decision by one family to relocate was affected by similar decisions of other families. A large proportion of respondents planning to relocate indicated that they did know some other families that had left Stratford Park or were planning to leave. Also, a comparatively greater proportion of

the families who were more social (high casual neighboring index) had decided to relocate. Many of these people seemed to leave the area because of apprehensions and fears about the quality of life in the neighborhood after their friends moved away and Negroes moved into their neighborhood and into Apollo Heights. It is also significant that in comparison to the families that were not planning to move, those that were relocating had a more pessimistic outlook for the future of their neighborhood. It is unfortunate that many people (79.3%) expressed a wish that the mass relocation had not started. Half of the white respondents also expressed the opinion that property values would have remained the same, ins pite of Apollo Heights, if all the white families had decided to remain in the neighborhood. This is the advice they would offer to other white families confronting similar situations. Most of these families had already made plans to relocate.

Also, the fear of decline in property values due to the proximity to Apollo Heights did not have as much influence on decisions to relocate as was expected. This was evident from the fact that home owners were not the only ones leaving. Home and apartment renters were also moving from the Stratford Park area. This is not to deny that a decline in property values was a fear. In fact, home owners did express this fear as a reason to leave. It is also evident from the study that many families did take an economic loss when they sold their homes. This probably explains the fact that very few (10%) of those families who had been living in Stratford Park area for nine or more years were planning to relocate. These families apparently had large equities in their properties. It is especially ironic that the loss could have been prevented if the white families had decided to stay in the Stratford Park area.

Other data that explain mass relocation relate to the fact that a majority of the respondents thought that Apollo Heights would make their neighborhood a less desirable place for white families to live (45.6%), would result in deterioration of local schools (62.0%) (Table 1) and would lower the neighborhood as a place of white children to grow up (41.8%) (Table 2). These facts probably explain why families with more children or younger children were leaving more frequently (Table 3). Comparatively fewer families with junior or senior high school age children were planning to relocate. These parents were probably less worried about the changes in the de facto segregation in schools, recreation and other neighborhood-centered activities.

It is interesting that some of the commonly used demographic factors did not seem to be related to the respondents' decision to relocate. For example, the respondents who had had Negroes as co-workers or whose children were going to schools with Negro children were as likely to relocate as those who did not have Negro co-workers or whose children did not have Negro schoolmates. Similarly, annual family income did not show any relationship to the decision to relocate or stay. Nor did the accuracy of respondents' information on Turnkey III housing seem to be related to their decision on relocation. Those who had accurate information about the amount of down payment required for ownership title or the income range that qualified a family for occupancy in Apollo Heights were as likely to relocate as those who over -- or under -- estimated the two amounts.

One factor which seems to have had an important bearing on decisions to relocate was the individual's own description (political) of himself. Those who described themselves as liberals or moderates were less likely to leave than those who described themselves as conservative or reactionaries.

Rapid transition in the study area was the product of numerous other influences: federal assistance programs, sustained Negro demand, a substantial supply of quality houses of moderate value, rising prices, considerable activity by professional real estate operators and ready availability of higher quality housing for whites in other sections of the city.

The extensive turnover was also in considerable measure the result of a lack of community effort to prevent panic selling. In neighborhoods that have remained stable over a period of years, organized community efforts have played a significant role. They can be summarized as follows:
   A. Neighbor organization to prevent panic selling.
   B. Attract white families to the areas.
   C. Discourage questionable practices among real estate brokers.
   D. Stop telephone and mail solicitation of a panic generating character.

There is an additional factor which appears to be vital in determining the rate of transition in an area. This refers to the predictions of white families concerning the eventual racial mix of their neighborhood and their apprehensions regarding the possibility of inundation by Negro families of lower socio-economic class.

Table 1: RESPONDENTS CLASSIFIED BY THEIR PERCEPTION OF HOW APOLLO HEIGHTS WOULD EFFECT THEIR SCHOOLS IN THEIR NEIGHBORHOODS

Response	Number	%
No Effect	19	24.1
Improve	3	3.8
Deteriorate	49	62.0
No Response	8	10.1
Total	79	100.0

Table 2: RESPONDENTS CLASSIFIED BY THEIR PERCEPTION OF HOW APOLLO HEIGHTS WOULD EFFECT THE LIVES OF WHITE CHILDREN IN THEIR NEIGHBORHOOD

Response	Number	%
No Effect	26	32.9
Improve	13	16.4
Deteriorate	33	41.8
No Response	7	8.9
Total	79	100.0

Table 3: RESPONDENTS CLASSIFIED BY THEIR DECISION ON RELOCATION AND BY NUMBER OF CHILDREN

| Decision on Relocation | Number of Children | | | | |
| | 2 or Less | | 3 or More | | |
	No	%	No	%	Total
Planning to Relocate	23	44.2	6	23.1	29
Not Planning to Relocate	29	55.8	20	76.9	49
Total	52	100.0%	26	100.0%	78

Table 4: RESPONDENTS CLASSIFIED BY THEIR DECISION ON RELOCATION AND BY THEIR PERSONAL ACQUAINTANCE WITH FAMILIES PLANNING TO RELOCATE

| Decision on Relocation | Acquaintance with Families | | | |
| | Yes | | No | |
	No	%	No	%
Planning to Relocate	25	53.2	4	12.9
Not Planning to Relocate	22	46.8	27	87.1
Total	47	100.0%	31	100.0%

Conclusions and Implications

With the proposed national goal of 26 million new housing units in the next decade, the major issues to be confronted refer to the strategies and policies necessary to prevent residential disruption, maintain residential stability, yet house the many non-whites without contributing to panic fears.

Essentially two sets of factors seem to bring about mass relocation. First is the fear of economic loss which is used as a rationalization for many actions by home owners and many practices of real estate brokers and financial institutions. Secondly there is the fear that racial mixing would decline the social status of the neighborhood and disrupt established association patterns and life styles.

When many white owners have these two apprehensions, they may panic and instead of organizing to remain, frantically list their homes for sale and compete with each other for buyers.

Such a sudden rise in the supply of homes in a small market area may well mean that not enough buyers can be found, whether white or non-white. Homes may not sell for weeks, even months; and when they do, it may be at prices that had to be discounted so sharply to attract buyers from a wide radius. The result is that prices may fall, just as the homeowners had feared, strengthening their belief in the notion that "Negroes hurt value".

Also, mortgage lenders may feel that the entry of non-white families into a first class residential area may cause values to drop. Consequently, lending policies for that area may be modified. The percentage of loan to appraisal will be reduced. The appraisals themselves may gradually move downward because of subjective value judgments influencing the appraiser's objective approach. As a result, the effective demand for homes in that area will be lower than it would be under ordinary circumstances, because potential buyers cannot get as large loans as before. (19) In this way Robert Merton's self-fulfilling prophecy produces real results. He states that "a false definition of the situation evolving a new behavior which makes the originally false conception come true".(20) It is likely that neither the home owners nor the lender are aware that their own beliefs had influenced their actions that brought about results they have feared.

Concern with maintaining property values is the major reason put forth in defense of barring Negroes from middle class "white" suburbs. However, on the basis of the most comprehensive study yet made of actual price trends on house sales in middle class home owning neighborhood undergoing non-white entry, as compared with price trends in comparable control neighborhoods without non-white entry, Laurenti reached two broad conclusions:

"First, price changes which can be connected with the fact of non-white entry are not uniform, as often alleged, but diverse. Depending on the circumstances racial change in a neighborhood may be depressing or it may be stimulating to real estate prices and in varying degrees. Second, considering all of the evidence, the odds are about four to one that house prices in a neighborhood entered by non-whites will keep up with or exceed prices in a comparable all white area. These conclusions are chiefly based on observations of real estate markets in a period of generally rising prices. This period, however, was characterized by unusually strong demand for housing, particularly by non-whites who had been making relatively large gains in personal income. These conditions seem likely to continue into the foreseeable future, and, therefore, the main findings of the present study may be valid for many neighborhoods certain to experience the entry of non-whites." (21)

The findings of Laurenti's report place in doubt existing beliefs concerning the harmful effects of nonwhite occupancy on property values. Studies of the price behavior in San Francisco, Oakland and Philadelphia suggest that if such beliefs were rooted in fact the statistical evidence of this investigation would have shown downward shifts of neighborhoods price levels following changes in the racial pattern. In fact, few such shifts took place in the areas studied, and where they did occur they were moderate.

The price effects of racial changes on a neighborhood seem to depend largely on the rate and urgency with which whites add homes to the housing supply in relation to the strength of non-white housing demand. There is evidence that resistance of white people to buying or renting in racially mixed neighborhood is greatly reduced when the non-white group is not perceived as becoming the numerically dominant element. From the point of view of maintaining the stability of racially mixed areas, white demand, therefore, becomes the single most important factor. Unless there are white buyers, no areas entered by Negroes can preserve its interracial

character; rather, it would become all Negro. A panic "flight" by white owners may hasten the process. Every home occupied by a white family will be put up for sale unless white buyers can be found. The transition process may be extremely rapid or slow but it will eventually occur without white buyers.

Alternately, they could stabilize the neighborhood by accepting Negro entrants as they would any new neighbors. If this is the case, the number of neighborhoods containing small numbers of non-white will increase. Opportunities to escape living near non-whites by choosing exclusive neighborhoods will become fewer and as this process continues, race should gradually lose its importance as a consideration in the real estate market.

"It has been argued that racial prejudice originated as a means of justifying and buttressing social practices which had, for socially influential groups, the economic function of exploitation of Negro labor. With time some of the original economic value of the exploitation of Negro labor has diminished; yet prejudice and the social practices on which it is based still flourish despite the loss of much of their original function. Various social practices of discrimination, exclusion and segregation tend to create the conditions for the continuation of prejudices and as a result, social practices and social attitudes mutually support and reinforce each other." (22)

While the modification of race relation relies upon (a) a change in the political-economic relations, (b) a change in the socio-economic status of Negroes, (c) elimination of social practices of discrimination and (d) destruction of prejudicial attitudes, it is clear that attempts to change significant social attitudes must be directed not only toward the individual, but also toward the social institutions and social norms which determine the individual's values. The social influences of friends, family, authority, etc. help to shape an individual's behavior and the stability of a new belief structure rests primarily in the culture of the group.

In the final analysis it is attitudes that will determine the ultimate racial composition of an urban area. With increased occupational and social and economic equality, perhaps one day neighbors will be chosen on a basis other than the color of their skin.

Notes

1. Chester Rapkin and William Grigsby. "The Prospect for Stable Interracial Neighborhoods" in B.J. Frieden and Robert Morris (ed.) Urban Planning and Social Policy. Basic Books, Inc., New York, 1968. Palmore, Erdman and Howe, John, "Residential Integration and Property Values", Social Problems, Summer 1952, Vol. 10, No. 1.

2. The Secretary of the Department of Housing and Urban Development determines the interest to be paid on FHA-insured mortgages. In December 1969 Secretary Romney set the rate at 7-1/2% plus 1/2% mortgage insurance premium paid to FHA.

3. A two hundred dollar investment is required by the FHA and may be used to cover closing costs and items of prepaid expense, such as utility connections.

4. The Housing Act of 1968 set the maximum selling price for FHA Section 235 but it has since been revised to $18,500.

5. Seymour Sudman, Norman Bradburn, and Galen Gockel, "The Extent and Characteristics of Racially Integrated Housing in the U.S.", Journal of Business, Graduate School of Business of the University of Chicago, Vol. 42, No. 1, January 1966. "Less than 10% of the neighborhoods in the South are to any degree integrated.

6. Seemingly this practice deviates from the Federal Fair Housing Law, Title VIII of the Open Housing Law of 1968, which states: "it shall be unlawful for profit to induce any person to sell or rent any dwelling by representations regarding the entry or prospective entry into the neighborhood of a person or person's of a particular race, color, religion or national origin."

7. Certain realtors related that they will accept a family existing home as partial payment for a more expensive new home.

8. National Association of Real Estate Boards, Code of Ethics, adopted in 1950. The old 1924 version read: "A realtor should never be instrumental in introducing a neighborhood a character of property or occupancy, member of any race or nationality or any individual whose presence will clearly be detrimental to property values in the neighborhood." This clearly segregationist ethic has set the tone in residential housing, particularly in the South.

9. Charles Abrams, "The Housing Problem and the Negro" in Parsons and Clark (ed.) Who Has the Revolution or Thoughts on the Second Reconstruction.

10. Federal Housing Administration, Underwriting Manual, 1938, Sec. 937.

11. Ibid., Rev. 1952, Sec. 1320.

12. This information was obtained from the Raleigh Housing Authority.

13. The line of inflation was determined by the "leat squares" method.

14. The average during 1968-69 for fees are comprised of 6% realtor commission, 6% for discount points, and 3% closing costs as related by local realtors.

15. Both the Federal Housing Administration and the Veteran's Administration maintain a ceiling on the interests charged by lending institutions handling mortgages they insure or guarantee.

16. Chester Rapkin, The Demand for Housing in Racially Mixed Areas, University of California Press, 1960, p. 68.

17. Seymour Sudman, op.cit. Also found this.

18. Bureau of Census, Census of 1960, North Carolina.

19. Lugi Laurenti, Property Values and Race, University of California Press, Berkeley and Los Angeles, 1961.

20. Robert K. Merton, "The Self-Fulfilling Prophecy", The Antioch Review, VIII #2, Summer 1946, p. 208.

21. Lugi Laurenti, Property Values and Race: Studies in Seven Cities, University of California Press, Berkeley, Los Angeles, 1960, pp. 52-3.

22. Morton Deutsch and Mary E. Collins, Interracial Housing: A Psychological Evaluation of a Social Experiment, University of Minnesota Press, 1951.

Session Five:

Micro-Ecological Behavior Systems

Chairman: Irvin Altman

Department of Psychology, The University of Utah

This session focuses on micro-ecological aspects of man-environment relationships, with a particular emphasis on interpersonal relationships. The papers are a blend of theoretical and empirical analyses of different facets of interaction in relatively molecular settings, with several themes running through individual papers and the collection of papers as a whole. A major theme is that an understanding of micro-ecological aspects of interaction requires a systems orientation. That is, behavior occurs at many levels of functioning - verbal, nonverbal, use of the environment - involves subjective cognitive-perceptual processes. Also, such behaviors occur in complementary, substitutable, coherent sets. Furthermore, understanding such systems involves drawing on several disciplines and approaches, and the use of a variety of research methods. Finally, micro-ecological systems are but subsystems in larger man-environment systems, and it is likely that similar and overlapping principles apply at several levels of functioning.

Within this general framework, the paper by Nancy Marshall will focus on subjective, internal aspects of privacy, as well as linking such states to overt use of the environment. Her paper, therefore, emphasizes that part of the

system concerned with internal states of individuals.

The papers by Starkey Duncan and Fred Steele spell out different levels of man-environment "systems", with Duncan concerned with dyadic interpersonal relationships in a particular setting. His strategy is to weave together verbal, nonverbal, and other facets of behavior to yield a complex picture of interpersonal exchange. Steele presents a systems approach to larger scale man-environment settings, with emphasis on dimensions of effective organizational functioning.

The papers by Allan Wicker and Edwin Willems fall within a Barker strategy of research to man-environment relationships, with Wicker presenting a general approach to behavior setting congruence, and Willems presenting data involving a specific application of this research strategy.

Taken together the papers in the session fit into a framework of man-environment relations which recognizes the importance of considering several facets of behavior simultaneously and of viewing such phenomena in systems terms. Furthermore, the papers demonstrate a spectrum of research methods appropriate to studying various facets of man-environment relationships.

Irvin Altman

223

Session Five.

Micro-Ecological Behavior Systems

Chairman: Irwin Altman

Department of Psychology, The University of Utah

Towards a Grammar for Floor Apportionment:
A System Approach to Face-to-Face Interaction

by Starkey Duncan, Jr.

University of Chicago

Abstract

Face-to-face interaction involves
a number of diverse communication channels, including language, paralanguage,
body motion, proxemics, and the use of
artifacts, among others. A program of
research is described which treats the
phenomena of face-to-face interaction
as having the characteristics of a system: that is, as having a set of standard units, the use of which is governed
by rules. One aspect of face-to-face
interaction is floor apportionment, a
mechanism by which interactants manage
the smooth exchange of speaker and auditor roles in a conversation. Results
of a study of floor apportionment as a
communication system are reported.

Face-to-face interaction has been
defined by Goffman as having to do with
"a person's handling of himself and others during, and by virtue of, his immediate physical presence among them...."(2)
This paper will be concerned with the
study of face-to-face interaction as a
communication system.

Face-to-face interaction is accomplished through a number of communication
channels. The first channel to be mentioned would be language. This is the
channel about which we know the most.
Language has been the object of scholarly
inquiry for centuries. Enormous quantities of raw data have been amassed on
languages around the world, and complex
grammars have been written for the phonological and syntactic components of
these languages.

But language is only one channel
for face-to-face interaction. There is
an entire realm of communication behaviors which have not traditionally been
included in the study of language. These
behaviors, often referred to as "nonverbal" (3), occur in a number of channels:

Body motion, or kinesics (4), or
visible behavior (5) includes such behaviors as gestures of the hands, feet,
shoulders, and head. Also included are
facial expressions, eye movements, and
posture.

Paralanguage (6) includes voice
qualities, speech pauses and nonfluencies, and such nonlanguage sounds as
laughing, yawning, and grunting.

The general area of the use of "social and personal space and man's perception of it" (7) has been christened
"proxemics" by Hall. Proxemics may be
considered to include both the social
use of space in such contexts as conversational distance and the phenomena related to territoriality, a concept which
has been discussed in detail by Altman.(8)

There are signalling phenomena related to olfaction.

There are patterns of tactile interaction, based on the skin's sensitivity
to pressure and temperature. Austin (9)
has suggested the term "haptics" for this
channel.

The use of artifacts is an integral
part of face-to-face interaction. This
channel would include dress, cosmetics,
the handling of personal objects, such
as clipboards, handkerchiefs, eyeglasses,
and ballpoint pens, and the use of what
Altman (10) has called "environmental
props."

The striking thing about this richly
varied area of face-to-face interaction
is that, in relation to language, the
entire area has been virtually untouched

by systematic research until very recently. Why was all this not included from the beginning of scholarly inquiry into language? Regardless of the reasons for this surprising neglect, the present upsurge of interest, both popular and scholarly, in nonverbal aspects of communication may eventually remedy our present severe shortage of both raw data and hard research evidence in this area.

While for purposes of discussion I have distinguished the linguistic from the nonlinguistic aspects of face-to-face interaction, I doubt that this type of traditional dichotomous thinking is maximally productive for research. I assume that there is considerable integration among all aspects of face-to-face interaction, and that departure from this integration is itself a significant communication event.

Like many predecessors and colleagues, I approach research on face-to-face interaction with the presuppositions that this form of communication is (a) composed of standard units, which (b) are used according to specific rules. (c) These units and rules are hierarchically organized, such that units on a lower level combine in a lawful manner to form units on the next higher level. Finally, (d) face-to-face communication is context specific. (11) That is, there are appropriate communication forms for given interpersonal situations and given physical settings.

The presupposed characteristics of face-to-face interaction mentioned above, most importantly the first three, suggest that face-to-face interaction has the properties of a system. While there are a great number of different types of systems, the essential elements of a system are (a) a set of units, and (b) a set of rules which define the interactions among these units. (12, 13, 14)

The specific system model which we have adopted for research on face-to-face interaction is that of linguistics. While linguists do not use terms such as "system," modern grammars are complex systems in precisely the sense discussed above. A grammar specifies the standard units of a language, both phonological and syntactic, and describes the rules which govern the uses and interrelationships of these units. Within this context, the

research reported here represents the first step in a program of research designed to develop a grammar for face-to-face interaction.

Our use of the grammar model has been facilitated by our finding that, for the phenomena analyzed to date, the units in the nonverbal aspect of face-to-face communication are, like those in language, discrete. That is, they are perceived by the participants as cues which are either displayed or not displayed. While I would expect that continued investigation will indicate that many other aspects of face-to-face communication have a similarly discrete character, there seems to be no reason to expect a priori that all of this sort of communication is discrete.

To anticipate the discussion below, we have chosen the communication mechanism of floor apportionment (15) as a starting place for our attempt to construct a grammar for face-to-face interaction. The function of the floor-apportionment mechanism is to regulate the smooth exchange of speaker and auditor roles. Through floor apportionment these roles can be exchanged in an orderly manner, with a minimum of simultaneous talking by the two participants. The floor-apportionment mechanism is considered to be one of a number of communication mechanisms, such as those discussed by Scheflen. (16) These mechanisms serve the function of integrating the performances of the participants in a number of ways, for example, regulating the pace at which the communication proceeds, and monitoring deviations for appropriate behavior.

Before describing the proposed system for floor apportionment, the transcribing and sampling procedures should be briefly described.

Transcription

The first step in a general research program on the structure of face-to-face interaction was the development of a careful, explicit transcription of interaction behaviors. This transcription included linguistic, paralinguistic, and body motion behaviors of participants in a dyad, as follows:

Language

A careful phonological transcription

was made of the segmental phonemes, following the system developed by Trager and Smith. (17) Close attention was paid to verbal slips, mispronounced words, speech nonfluencies such as stutters, and unexpected forms, such as failure to add "s" for plurals, "ed" for past tenses, and the like. The suprasegmental phonemes, commonly referred to as intonation, were likewise transcribed according to the Trager-Smith system, with minor modifications. Intonation includes the phenomena of stress, pitch, and terminal junctures. These junctures are composed of contours of pitch, intensity, and duration occurring on the final syllable of phonemic clauses.

Paralanguage

This term, proposed by Trager (18), refers to the wide variety of vocal behaviors which occur in speech but are not a part of the formal linguistic system. A number of paralinguistic behaviors were transcribed, the most important of which were (a) intensity, (b) pitch height, (c) extent (drawl/clipping), (d) tempo, (e) various types of pauses, and (f) vocal lip control (rasp/openness).

Body Motion

In contrast to paralanguage, there was for body motion no available transcription system which could be readily applied to interview behaviors. Our approach to transcribing body motion stemmed from the observation that, within a given interaction situation, an individual uses a remarkably small number of different body movements. The total number of different movements for any one body part is quite limited, even when the conversation is relatively animated. In this circumstance it is possible to inventory the movements used in the interview under consideration, assign either arbitrary or descriptive labels to the different movements, and then to transcribe body motion for that individual in that situation. As other interaction situations, involving either the same or different participants, are subsequently transcribed, new behaviors will be observed, thereby necessitating additions to the original transcription system. The result is a system, not theoretically comprehensive, but firmly grounded on actual observation and readily expandable

to cover newly observed behaviors.

Included in the transcription were: (a) head gestures and movements (nodding, turning, pointing, shaking, etc.), and direction of head orientation; (b) shoulder movements (e.g., shrugs); (c) facial expressions, such as could be clearly seen--since our videotapes did not include close-ups of the participants' faces, fine detail could not be observed; (d) hand gestures and movements of all sorts (each hand recorded independently); (e) foot movements (each foot recorded independently); (f) leg movements; (g) postures and posture shifts; and (h) use of artifacts, such as pipe, kleenex, papers, and clip board.

Coordination of Body Motion and Speech Transcriptions

In the transcription, speech syllables were used to locate all transcribed events. Thus, the movements of both participants were located with respect to the syllables emitted by the speaker, or to the pause between two syllables.

Sample

The system described below was based, not on a representative sampling of interview behaviors, but on an intensive analysis of behaviors within a single interview. The rationale for this research strategy rests upon assumptions concerning the nature of communication, as discussed above. Crucial to the strategy are the assumptions that (a) communication is a highly structured, standardized activity, and (b) this structure is shared by members of a culture. While within a culture there will be at least some variation among individuals in their repertoires of nonverbal behaviors as there is in their vocabularies and dialects, considerable generality may be expected in the rules for constructing messages, for coordinating communication channels, and for integrating a dyadic interaction, just as there is generality in linguistic rules. As has often been pointed out, this generality of basic structure is, in fact, necessary for communication to exist.

The interview upon which the transcription and analysis were based, was a preliminary interview held at the Counseling and Psychotherapy Research Center at the University of Chicago. This preliminary interview is part of the routine intake procedure at the Counseling and Psychotherapy Center, and the client was a regular applicant for therapy. The two participants had had no contact with each other prior to this interview.

There are several advantages to using preliminary interviews for this type of study. Within a rather compressed period of time a wide variety of types of interaction may be encountered, from simple information giving, such as address, etc., to more emotionally-laden discussion of reasons for applying to therapy. At the same time, there is a strong intrinsic motivation for the interview, namely an application for therapy, thereby avoiding the more artificial research situation in which unacquainted subjects are simply brought together and asked to discuss anything which might be of mutual interest.

In terms of size, the nineteen minutes of transcribed interaction is simultaneously very small and very large, depending upon one's perspective. From the point of view of the wealth of communication engaged in each day by an individual, the transcription is quite brief. On the other hand, this transcription is believed to be unique in its breadth and duration. The time involved in making such a transcription was great, involving the better part of an academic year. (Subsequent transcribing has proved to proceed more rapidly, once solutions are found to initial transcribing problems. Nevertheless, the process is a best laborious.)

As an indication of the amount of material available in this 19-minute stretch of interaction, a few descriptive statistics may be cited. The interviewer spoke 1089 words which were organized into 375 phonemic clauses, while the client spoke 1695 words, with 668 phonemic clauses.

A transcription of a second dyadic interaction has just been completed and is being added to our data pool. Further transcriptions are being planned.

Floor Apportionment

Once the transcription was completed, inquiry was begun into the manner of segmentation of utterances by speakers. The question asked of the data was whether or not cues could be found which serve to break the stream of speech into a series of shorter units. An analogy, but not a model, for this would be the use of punctuation marks and capitalization to break a series of written words into groups.

Beginning with a scrutiny of various types of intonation patterns, initial analysis suggested that certain intonation patterns and various nonverbal behaviors operated almost interchangeably to break utterances into units composed of one or more phonemic clauses. It was then noticed that these behaviors, while usually occurring singly or in pairs, sometimes occurred in larger clusters, typically at the end of a speaker's utterance. This observation led to the further inquiry into the basic topic of this paper: floor apportionment.

The proposed system for floor apportionment in a dyad will be presented in terms of (a) basic variables in the system, and (b) rules of interaction, defining the relationships among the variables. Finally, (c) rules of correspondence will specify the relationships between the system variables and empirical behaviors.

There will be two major classes of variables: speaker variables and auditor variables. Within each of these main classes there will be several subclasses. Rules of interaction will define the relationships among these subclasses, as well as between the two main classes.

As discussed above, the variables in the system are discrete. That is, they represent signals which are either displayed or not displayed. This being the case, we shall, in line with a widely-used linguistic convention, denote the display of specific variables with a "+" and those not displayed with a "-."

Because the purpose of the floor-apportionment mechanism is to minimize simultaneous talking by the participants, the phenomena which the system attempts to predict are (a) the presence or absence of silence, and (b) the presence or absence of simultaneous talking. These phenomena will be designated in the system as ± silence, and ± simultaneous, respectively. Of the four possible combinations of these variables, the following two will be predicted by the system:

$$\begin{bmatrix} - \text{ silence} \\ - \text{ simultaneous} \end{bmatrix} \text{ and } \begin{bmatrix} - \text{ silence} \\ + \text{ simultaneous} \end{bmatrix}.$$

$\begin{bmatrix} + \text{ silence} \\ - \text{ simultaneous} \end{bmatrix}$ did not occur in the interview analyzed, because the participants did not allow appreciable periods of silence to occur. The fourth logical possibility is not physically possible: $\begin{bmatrix} + \text{ silence} \\ + \text{ simultaneous} \end{bmatrix}$.

Auditor Variables

There are four subclasses of auditor behaviors: (a) accompaniment behaviors (designated as ± accompaniment); (b) floor requesting (± requesting); (c) floor taking (± taking); and (d) silence (± silence). The specific behaviors which comprise each of these subclasses will be discussed below in the section on rules of correspondence. Floor-requesting behaviors, while widely supposed to exist, have not yet been identified in the interview and will not be included in the grammar.

A simple rule relates each of these subclasses to each of the others: they are mutually exclusive. Any subclass

designated by a "+" to indicate that it is present for the auditor requires that all other subclasses be designated with a "-."

Speaker Variables

There are three subclasses of speaker behaviors in the system: (a) floor retaining (designated as ± retaining); (b) regular floor yielding (± regular); and (c) superordinate floor yielding (± superordinate). Of the subclasses of speaker behaviors, superordinate floor yielding and floor retaining are mutually exclusive. The possible combinations of speaker behaviors are as follows:

	Regular	Superordinate	Retaining
1.	+	-	-
2.	-	+	-
3.	-	-	+
4.	+	+	-
5.	+	-	+
6.	-	-	-

Between-Class Rules

The rules relating the respective speaker and auditor behaviors to the predicted results are presented below. "S" preceding a set of brackets refers to the speaker; "A" refers to the auditor.

1. $S\begin{bmatrix} \text{any} \end{bmatrix} + A\begin{bmatrix} \text{silence} \end{bmatrix} \rightarrow \begin{bmatrix} - \text{ silence} \\ - \text{ simultaneous} \end{bmatrix}$

An auditor response of silence to any speaker behavior results in the speaker's continuing without simultaneous talking. The obvious alternative--that the speaker also falls silent--was not observed in the transcribed interview and thus was not included in the system.

2. $S\begin{bmatrix} \text{any} \end{bmatrix} + A\begin{bmatrix} + \text{ accompaniment} \end{bmatrix} \rightarrow \begin{bmatrix} - \text{ silence} \\ \pm \text{ simultaneous} \end{bmatrix}$

Accompaniment behaviors of the auditor to any speaker behavior may lead either to simultaneous talking or to the speaker's continuing without simultaneous talking. The data clearly show that the auditor may make accompaniment behaviors, whether or not simultaneous with the speaker's talk, without disrupting the interaction. Disruption would most likely result from a conspicuous lack of accompaniment behaviors by the auditor. An important point for floor apportionment is that accompaniment behaviors do not result in the auditor's taking the floor. There may well be rules for the placement of accompaniment behaviors with regards to the speaker's speech, but these rules have not yet been determined.

The following rules all concern the predicted results of the auditor's attempting to take the floor.

3. $S\begin{bmatrix} + \text{ regular} \\ - \text{ superordinate} \\ - \text{ retaining} \end{bmatrix} + A\begin{bmatrix} + \text{ taking} \end{bmatrix} \rightarrow \begin{bmatrix} - \text{ silence} \\ - \text{ simultaneous} \end{bmatrix}$

The auditor's taking the floor in response to the display of regular floor-yielding behaviors results in a smooth exchange of speaker--auditor roles in the conversation.

$$4. \quad S \begin{bmatrix} - \text{ regular} \\ + \text{ superordinate} \\ - \text{ retaining} \end{bmatrix} + A \begin{bmatrix} + \text{ taking} \end{bmatrix} \rightarrow \begin{bmatrix} - \text{ silence} \\ - \text{ simultaneous} \end{bmatrix}$$

$$5. \quad S \begin{bmatrix} + \text{ regular} \\ + \text{ superordinate} \\ - \text{ retaining} \end{bmatrix} + A \begin{bmatrix} + \text{ taking} \end{bmatrix} \rightarrow \begin{bmatrix} - \text{ silence} \\ - \text{ simultaneous} \end{bmatrix}$$

The meaning of a superordinate floor-yielding signal is that the auditor invariably responds by taking the floor, and that this response never results in simultaneous talking. Superordinate signals may or may not occur with regular floor-yielding signals. The presence or absence of regular signals with superordinate signals is irrelevant.

$$6. \quad S \begin{bmatrix} - \text{ regular} \\ - \text{ superordinate} \\ - \text{ retaining} \end{bmatrix} + A \begin{bmatrix} + \text{ taking} \end{bmatrix} \rightarrow \begin{bmatrix} - \text{ silence} \\ + \text{ simultaneous} \end{bmatrix}$$

The auditor's taking the floor in the absence of signals from the speaker relevant to floor apportionment results in simultaneous talking. This situation represents a breakdown of the floor-apportionment mechanism.

$$7. \quad S \begin{bmatrix} - \text{ regular} \\ - \text{ superordinate} \\ + \text{ retaining} \end{bmatrix} + A \begin{bmatrix} + \text{ taking} \end{bmatrix} \rightarrow \begin{bmatrix} - \text{ silence} \\ + \text{ simultaneous} \end{bmatrix}$$

$$8. \quad S \begin{bmatrix} + \text{ regular} \\ - \text{ superordinate} \\ + \text{ retaining} \end{bmatrix} + A \begin{bmatrix} + \text{ taking} \end{bmatrix} \rightarrow \begin{bmatrix} - \text{ silence} \\ + \text{ simultaneous} \end{bmatrix}$$

The auditor's taking the floor in the presence of the speaker's display of floor-retaining signals invariably results in simultaneous talking. This situation results in a breakdown of the floor-apportionment mechanism. Floor-retaining signals may be displayed in the presence or absence of regular floor-yielding signals. When displayed in the presence of regular floor-yielding signals, floor-retaining signals may indicate that the speaker is almost, but not quite, ready to yield the floor.

Rules of Correspondence

Regular Floor-Yielding Cues

Before proceeding with a detailed description of regular floor-yielding cues, the general structure of this variable may be described as follows: (a) The speaker indicates his yielding of the floor by conjointly displaying a minimum number of discrete cues. These cues will be displayed simultaneously and/or in tight sequences. (b) Regular floor-yielding cues are found in a wide variety of communication modalities: content, syntax, intonation, paralanguage, and numerous aspects of body motion. (c) When the proper number of regular floor-yielding cues is properly displayed by the speaker, the auditor is more likely to attempt to take the floor; and when he so attempts, he is likely to be successful, with no simultaneous talking. (d) The functioning of regular floor-yielding cues in floor apportionment appears to be a direct extension of a general system for segmenting the speaker's communication, as briefly mentioned above.

The number of regular floor-yielding cues required to constitute a floor-yielding signal by the speaker is a number N, determined empirically, which can vary, probably within very small limits, among dyads. When $N-2$ cues are displayed, it is believed that the speaker is indicating a segmenting of his communication on a level lower than that of floor yielding. An auditor's attempt to take the floor in response to $N-2$ cues or less will result in simultaneous talking. The display of $N-1$ cues is a transition phenomenon, not fully understood. When $N-1$ cues are displayed, the evidence for both participants in our dyad indicates that the auditor attempts to take the floor a moderate number of times, and that these attempts result in simultaneous talking a moderate number of times.

With respect to specific behaviors,

seven regular floor-yielding cues were discovered for the therapist:
1. <u>Syntax</u>. The use of a grammatical question form, defined as the placement of the verbal auxiliary before the subject, as in "Are you leaving now?"
2. <u>Syntax</u>. The completion of a grammatical clause, involving a subject-predicate combination.
3. <u>Intonation</u>. The use of any pitch level--terminal juncture combination other than 2 2| at the end of a phonemic clause. Following the Trager and Smith (1957) notation system, the 2 refers to an intermediate pitch level, neither high--3--nor low--1. The single bar juncture "|" at the end of the clause refers to a sustention of the pitch at the level previously indicated. Thus, 2 2| refers to a phonemic clause ending on an intermediate pitch level, which is sustained, neither rising nor falling, at the juncture between clauses.
4. <u>Paralanguage</u>. A drop in paralinguistic pitch and/or loudness, and/or the appearance of rasp, in conjunction with a terminal clause, either across the entire clause or across its final syllable or syllables.
5. <u>Paralanguage</u>. Drawl on final syllable or on the stressed syllable of a terminal clause.
6. <u>Body Motion</u>. The termination of any hand motion or gesture while speaking, or the relaxation of a tensed hand position (e.g., a fist) while speaking. Following Kendon (1967), hand motions used while speaking will be termed "gesticulations."
7. <u>Body Motion</u>. Turning of the head toward the auditor. This observation is in line with the speaker's part of the gaze-direction pattern discovered by Kendon (1967).

There were also seven regular floor-yielding cues discovered for the client.
1. <u>Content</u>. The appearance of one of several stereotyped expressions, typically following a substantive statement. Examples are "you know" (most often heard); "you know but uh"; "you know, so I don't know"; "or something, you know what I mean"; and the like.
2. <u>Intonation</u>. The use of any pitch level--terminal juncture combination other than 2| at the end of a phonemic clause. Exactly as for the therapist.
3. <u>Paralanguage</u>. A drop in paralinguistic pitch and/or loudness, in conjunction

with a terminal clause, either across the entire clause or across its final syllable or syllables. Exactly as for the therapist, except that rasp is not considered.
4. <u>Paralanguage</u>. A drop in paralinguistic pitch and/or loudness, in conjunction with one of the stereotyped expressions described above under "Content." These expressions typically followed a terminal clause but did not often share the same paralanguage.
5. <u>Body Motion</u>. Turning of the head toward the auditor. Exactly as for the therapist.
6. <u>Body Motion</u>. The termination of any hand motion or gesture while speaking, or the relaxation of any tensed hand position while speaking. Exactly as for the therapist.
7. <u>Body Motion</u>. A relaxation of the foot from a marked dorsal flexion. (Throughout the interview the client's legs were stretched out in front of her and were crossed at the ankle.) From time to time one or both feet would be flexed dorsally, such that they assumed a nearly perpendicular angle to the floor. Their falling, as a result of relaxing the flexion, was the cue.

Accompaniment Behaviors

Accompaniment behaviors (19) include head nods and such readily-identifiable articulations as "m-hm," "yeah," "I see," and "right." The head nods and articulations may occur either together or separately. Other types of accompaniment behaviors have been tentatively identified, but are not necessary to account for the behavior of this dyad.

Superordinate Floor-Yielding Cues

The analysis revealed a special subset of floor-yielding cues which were designated superordinate cues. These cues had three distinctive characteristics: (a) the auditor responded each and every time one of these cues was displayed, (b) regardless of the presence or absence of other floor-yielding cues, and (c) response to a superordinate cue never resulted in simultaneous talking.

When the client was speaking, there were two superordinate cues: (a) bringing a kleenex to the face (which occurred here only during crying), and (b) asking a question of the therapist. It should be noted that crying occurred without bringing a kleenex to the face and was not superordinate.

When the therapist was speaking, there was one superordinate cue: putting his pipe in his mouth.

Superordinate cues were relatively infrequent. For the client, the kleenex-to-face cue occurred seven times; the question cue occurred three times. For the therapist, the pipe cue occurred three times.

Until further data are gathered on superordinate cues, it may be best to regard them as a rather special case. The generalizability of the cues is somewhat questionable. It seems possible that a cue becomes superordinate, not so much as a result of the floor-yielding system of a speaker, as of the response proclivities of the auditor.

Floor-Retaining Cues

There appear to be certain cues which signal that the speaker is not yet ready to yield the floor, regardless of floor-yielding cues being displayed. The floor-retaining cues we observed seemed to accompany situations in which the speaker is almost, but not quite, ready to yield the floor. Auditor response while floor-retaining cues are being displayed invariably resulted in simultaneous talking.

A single floor-retaining cue was identified in the dyad under study: the therapist's hands being in motion. Even when the therapist had begun a sequence of floor-yielding cues, such as turning his head toward the client, he did not yield the floor until his hands had come to rest from whatever gesticulations they had been engaged in.

The client's responding before the therapist's hands had come to rest position accounted for almost 50 per cent of the simultaneous talking when the therapist was speaking.

No such floor-retaining cues were identified for the client, possibly because the therapist succeeded in avoiding responding whenever these cues were displayed by the client. Because of their nature, floor-retaining cues can only be positively verified when they are violated by the auditor.

Results

It was stressed above that floor apportionment involves a communication system, requiring coordinated behavior by both speaker and auditor. For this system to function properly, there must be appropriate display of floor-yielding cues by the speaker, and then appropriate behavior by both auditor and speaker following the cue display. One conclusion following logically from these considerations is that, while a single dyad is being studied, there are data available for two behaviorally distinct and conceptually independent floor-apportionment systems: (a) one in which the client is the speaker and the therapist is the auditor; and (b) one in which the therapist is the speaker and the client is the auditor. Evidence will be presented below for each of these two systems.

Tables 1 and 2 present the findings for regular floor-yielding cues in relation to the predicted results of the system. The percentage is given of simultaneous talking resulting from the auditor's floor-taking response to a given number of regular floor-yielding cues by the speaker. In addition, it might be expected that the auditor would be more likely to respond by taking the floor when the speaker displays higher numbers of regular floor-yielding cues. While this result was not predicted by the system, these floor-taking percentages are also given in the tables.

Table 1
Therapist Response
to Client's Regular Floor-Yielding Cues
and Resulting Simultaneous Talking

Client Cues Displayed	Therapist Response			Simultaneous Talking		
	N	N	P	SD	N	P	SD
1	41	2	.05	.03	2	1.00	.00
2	29	2	.07	.05	2	1.00	.00
3	26	6	.23	.08	3	.50	.20
4	25	14	.56	.10	2	.14	.09
5	13	8	.62	.13	1	.13	.12
6	6	4	.67	.19	1	.25	.22
7	6	3	.50	.20	0	.00	.00
Σ	146	39			11		

Table 2
Client Response to
Therapist's Regular Floor-Yielding Cues
and Resulting Simultaneous Talking

Therapist Cues Displayed	Client Response				Simultaneous Talking		
	N	N	P	SD	N	P	SD
0	17	2	.12	.08	2	1.00	.00
1	33	4	.12	.06	3	.75	.22
2	44	9	.20	.06	3	.33	.16
3	24	17	.71	.09	3	.20	.10
4	12	7	.58	.14	0	.00	.00
5	4	1	.25	.22	0	.00	.00
6	1	1	1.00	.00	0	.00	.00
Σ	135	41			11		

In general, the tables show that simultaneous talking was at a maximum (100%) when very few numbers of regular floor-yielding cues were displayed. There was then a transition point of two therapist cues and three client cues at which a moderate amount of simultaneous talking resulted from auditor response. Finally, the critical number of regular floor-yielding cues appeared to be four for the client and three for the therapist. When the critical number of cues was displayed by the respective speakers, simultaneous talking dropped to a minimum, and auditor responsiveness reached a maximum.

No tables are presented for superordinate floor-yielding cues. Predictions for these cues were perfect: the auditor always responded by taking the floor, and simultaneous talking never resulted.

Similarly, when the auditor responded by taking the floor when floor-retaining cues were displayed by the speaker, simultaneous talking always resulted.

Discussion

The data and the system which have been presented for floor apportionment are the first step of a projected program of research designed to develop a grammar for face-to-face interaction.

It should be pointed out that, with regard to developing grammars for interaction, there are two separate but closely interrelated approaches which a structural analysis may take. We may study the behaviors of individuals; or, as in this paper, we may consider a dyad as a communication system and attempt to describe the rules for interaction in that

dyad. Both approaches are aimed at understanding the rules for communication shared by members of a communication community.

In the first case--that of individuals--the approach is similar to that for language, except that the inquiry is expanded to include both language and non-language behaviors. The researcher would be seeking to define classes of communication behaviors on the bases of their form and distribution in the stream of communication. For example, are there rules for the use of gestures, definable in terms of the gestures' consistent distribution with respect to other body movements, paralinguistic features, content themes or words, intonation patterns, or grammatical structures?

In contrast to studying individual communications, this research took the approach of studying the dyad as a communication system. For dyads, the purpose of structural study is to formulate behavioral rules for the development and smooth functioning of interactions.

These two perspectives on communication organization--focusing on individual messages, and focusing on the dyad as a communication system--are seen as highly interrelated. Consideration of either aspect leads rapidly to consideration of the other. For example, if a study of individual communication structures uncovered definite behavioral regularities (communication units) involving consistent, repeated clusters of behaviors occurring in specifiable contexts for individual communicators, then we would immediately be interested in observing the effects of these units on the interaction.

With respect to the floor-apportionment system discussed in this paper, several general observations may be made. First, all communication channels examined contained floor-apportionment cues: content, syntax, intonation, paralanguage, and various aspects of body motion.

Second, the cues do not seem to be specific or idiosyncratic to an individual but rather appear to have a general character. For floor apportionment signals, it is not the specific behavior which is important, but rather a general property of that behavior. This generality should greatly facilitate the effectiveness of the communication mechanism. For example, in body motion, the gesture, regardless of what it is, must cease or noticeably relax. Similarly, for paralanguage there must be a drop in pitch and/or loudness, regardless of the vocal pattern from which the drop occurs. For intonation, there must be a deviation from the 2 2| pattern. Among speakers of American English, this pattern is undoubtedly universally held and almost certainly the most common single intonation pattern. On the basis of these generalized deviations or relaxations, an auditor can correctly perceive the floor-yielding aspect of gestures and vocal patterns which are entirely new to him. The syntactic cues are likewise general: the use of a question form or the completion of a clause. The role of head orientation in floor apportionment has been previously documented by Kendon. (20) This is a specific behavior but most likely is universally held in the Anglo-American language community.

In regard to the two speaker--auditor systems in a dyad, it may be well to point out that the number of such systems increases with the number of participants in the interaction. Specifically, there are $n(n-1)$ different speaker--auditor systems possible in a group, when n equals the number of participants in that group. This circumstance greatly complicates the communication picture, at least for purposes of analysis. For example, a triad has six possible speaker--auditor systems, whereas a dyad has only two. One conclusion might be that it would be well to concentrate on dyads, at least in the early stages of structural research. Of course, the extent to which all of the logically distinct speaker--auditor systems in an interaction are actually different in a behavioral sense is an empirical question.

Several lines of inquiry suggested by our findings to date on floor apportionment have been initiated in our laboratory. An intensive analysis of accompaniment behaviors by the auditor is underway: what behaviors are included in this class; where are they located in the stream of speech; and what effects do they have on the interaction? Some floor-retaining and floor-requesting signals have been tentatively identified and are being pursued. An interesting class of displacement behaviors, in the ethological sense, has been observed and is under

study. These behaviors by the auditor appear to follow frustrated attempts to take the floor. Meanwhile, other aspects of dyadic structure are being explored; and our present findings are being checked on our second transcribed dyad.

It appears from our experience that, once this sort of inquiry is begun, a rapidly-expanding network of related phenomena is established.

The primary obstacle to research in this area is the lack of raw data: the difficulty of developing an adequate transcription, coupled with the dearth of transcriptions already made by other investigators. It is hoped that some similar transcriptions will be made in other laboratories, and that some pooling of raw data can be arranged.

Transcribing is made difficult by both the behavioral detail and breadth required. While it is unquestionably more convenient for certain types of communication studies to focus on selected behaviors, such as smiling, gaze direction, or a particular set of gestures, it appears that for studies of communication structure, the broadest possible behavioral inclusiveness is the strategy of choice. This inclusiveness is desirable because of (a) the probable complexity of communication structures, (b) the probably high interrelatedness of behaviors in different channels, e.g., gestures and intonation, and (c) our present lack of empirically-based knowledge concerning just which behaviors are important for communication.

In particular, the inclusion of language with nonlanguage behaviors is believed to be of crucial importance to the coherence of the results reported here. Our experience with these data suggests that a thoroughgoing understanding of the systematic aspect of face-to-face interaction is unlikely without careful consideration of both language and nonlanguage components.

Notes

1. This study was supported in part by grants MH-16,210 and MH-17,756 from the National Institute of Mental Health, and grant GS-3033 from the Division of Social Sciences of the National Science Foundation. I wish to express my appreciation

to Ray O'Cain for his contributions to the phonological transcription, and to Diane Martin for her contributions to the body motion transcription and to the data analysis. I am indebted to Dick Jenney, who served as therapist for this study.

2. Goffman, E. Behavior in public places. New York: Free Press, 1968, p. 8.

3. Duncan S. D., Jr. Nonverbal communication. Psychological Bulletin, 1969, 72, 118-137.

4. Birdwhistell, R. L. Introduction to kinesics. Louisville: University of Louisville Press, 1952.

5. Kendon, A. The role of visible behavior in the organization of social interaction. In M. von Cranach, & I. Vine (Eds.), Symposium on human communication. London: Academic, in press.

6. Trager, G. L. Paralanguage: A first approximation. Studies in Linguistics, 1958, 13, 1-12.

7. Hall, E. T. The hidden dimension. Garden City, N.Y.: Doubleday, 1966, p. 1.

8. Altman, I. Territorial behavior in humans: An analysis of the concept. In L. Pastalan and D. H. Carson (Eds.), Spatial behavior of older people. Ann Arbor: University of Michigan-Wayne State University Press, 1970.

9. Austin, W. M. Personal communication.

10. Altman, I. An ecological approach to the functioning of social groups. Paper presented at the NATO Symposium on Man in Isolation, Roman, October 1969.

11. Schefler, A. E. Human communication: Behavioral programs and their integration in interaction. Behavioral Science, 1968, 13, 42-55.

12. Bertalanffy, L. V. General Systems Theory, New York: Braziller, 1968.

13. Miller, J. G. Living systems: Basic concepts, Behavioral Science, 1965, 10, 193-237.

14. Meeham, E. J. Explanations in social science: A system paradigm, Homewood, Illinois: Dorsey, 1968.

15. Kendon, A. Some functions of gaze direction in social interaction. Acta Psychologica 1967, 26, 22-63.

16. Schefler, A. E. Human communication.

17. Trager, G. L. and Smith, H. L., Jr. An outline of English structure. Washington, D.C.:

18. Trager, Para-Language.

19. Kendon, A. Some functions of gaze direction in social interaction. Acta Psychologica 1967, 26, 22-63.

Ecological Analysis of a Hospital: Location Dependencies in the Behavior of Staff and Patients[1]

by William F. LeCompte and Edwin P. Willems

University of Houston, Baylor College of Medicine

Abstract

This is a report of an ongoing analysis and evaluation of the Texas Institute for Rehabilitation and Research in Houston, Texas, which provides comprehensive rehabilitation to persons with spinal cord injuries. The major investigative purpose has been to use methods that would yield quantitative documentation of (a) the nature of the hospital as an environmental system, and (b) the nature of the interface of the hospital's delivery system with patient behavior and experience. The first is provided by a behavior setting survey of the hospital (as developed by Roger G. Barker) and the second by firsthand observations of patients. Against the framework of the behavior setting analysis, the observational data provide a fine-grained, quantitative picture of patient behavior, hospital delivery, and the locational dependencies in behavior and delivery. This research can be seen as a prototype or model for other investigations of environmental dependencies in human behavior.

Introduction

Our talk today will describe what we have discovered about the treatment environment of patients with injuries to the spinal cord, through the convergent application of two methods. The methods to be described are different in level of analysis and in their data base, but the two can be used to focus on a critical aspect of any environment designed for people; namely, the actions of individuals within a defined location. The relevance of this work for environmental design seems clear; the field, at present, consists of a host of untested behavioral assumptions embedded in a structural context. The present methodology is proposed as one way to articulate and generate data on these assumptions.

Method 1: The Behavior Setting Survey (William F. LeCompte)

As defined by Roger Barker (2), and as used in previous research, the behavior setting unit represents a stable combination of one or more extra-individual patterns of behavior surrounded by a non-psychological milieu. Slide 1 presents three defining characteristics of any behavior setting. The following slides illustrate these points visually in a number of locations around the hospital.

Slide 2: Here is one of the most typical hospital settings; namely, a one-man office.

Slide 3: This area, called the prevocational skills area, is interesting because it provides an illustration of the need for one of the defining characteristics; to the left of the picture is a fragile white screen that marks the boundary of this setting. Its function is to inform one that he is entering a different place. As a boundary, its function is more symbolic than real. That is, it does not filter out auditory stimuli, and it is too low to effectively stop all visual cues. But the inhabitants of the prevocational skills area need it to define their territory.

Slide 4: This setting has been labeled as "trafficways" in view of its dominant action pattern of locomotion. It is included to illustrate the variety one finds in situations.

Slide 5: Here is a typical laboratory at the hospital. Note the high degree of individual attention to projects and the lack of social interaction. The two people at the far end of the lab are conversing in low tones about a project, but there is little disruption of the others.

Slide 6: This is a typical ward of the hospital; one sees occasional signs of boundary maintenance as in this slide, but generally wards function as a rich, open behavior setting.

Slide 7: Let's turn to the "classic" areas of the treatment environment in a rehabilitation facility. Here is the general physical therapy area.

Note the vast amount of specialized equipment in this room. The area in the center has been affectionately designated as the "fishbowl" and is specialized for the administrative and clerical tasks that physical therapists do. However, the boundaries here are transparent to allow the staff to observe their patients.

Slide 8: In this close-up of the "fishbowl" area, we can see some of the ways in which the exclusiveness of this area is maintained, despite the visual access to outsiders. Note the narrow entrances and the impossibility of defining the area as a traffic-way. Intruders sense that they must not enter and wait, passively, to be noticed.

Slide 9: This slide depicts quite a different organization. It is the occupational therapy (OT) department taken with a wide-angle lens. To your right is the recreational therapy and to your left is the general OT area. The doors lead to other OT settings such as a kitchen, a woodshop, and a driver simulation room. Contrary to physical therapists, the occupational therapists apparently prefer closed-in areas for specialized activities. In general, there are more than twice as many settings in OT than in PT.

Slide 10: Finally, here is a view of a weekly meeting of the rehabilitation team. Note that patients are not present here.

The Behavior Setting Survey:

With this much as introduction, then, let me describe the behavior setting survey of the treatment environment. To begin with, the slides illustrate one facet of this approach that is basic to an understanding of the method: the units of analysis here are not created by an investigator, but rather are discovered by him in his survey.

In other words, they exist within the defined phenomena, in the same way as do cells for a biologist or planets for an astronomer. The task of the scientific investigator is to achieve a more precise and quantitative description of these naturally occurring phenomena.

In the behavior setting survey of the treatment environment, 122 of these units were reliably discriminated at a level of interdependence corresponding to the everyday experience of their inhabitants. Hence, the total treatment environment within the hospital consists of 122 equivalent units which can be systematically described in countless ways, depending on the interest of an investigator. For our purposes, let me mention some general findings regarding

different parts of the treatment environment.

Perhaps the most general question to be considered is: To what extent is the treatment environment devoted to direct patient-care activities? The next slide has been prepared to provide a visual answer to that question—it is based on the Occupancy time index, defined as the product of the total number of people in the setting times their average duration or stay within the setting. The cumulative result is then multiplied by the number of times the setting happens within the survey year.

Slide 11: The occupancy time for each setting has been represented in this figure as a circle, the area of which increases proportionately to the total person-hours-per-year occupancy of that setting.

The total treatment environment of the hospital is represented here. The 76 settings above the horizontal line are the patient sector of the treatment environment while the 46 settings below the line constitute that part of the treatment environment in which patients are not found. The latter constitute the "backstage" in Goffman's (3) sense, where important decisions are made by professional staff regarding the fate of the patients. Some representative backstage settings include: Weekly chart rounds where a doctor reviews his case load; departmental staff meetings; offices of heads of departments. To the left of the vertical line bisecting the patient sector of the treatment environment are the "classic" treatment areas. They constitute somewhat more than 25 per cent of all settings. The remaining settings in the patient sector, to the right of the vertical line, include a cafeteria, walking rounds, and all other nontreatment settings in which patients are found.

In general, the total occupancy time of the patient sector is nearly five times as large as the non-patient sector of the treatment environment. Hence, one would expect to find approximately a five-to-one difference in occupancy time of professional personnel on the average.

Table 1 presents the actual percentage of occupancy times in back- and frontstage settings. The first column, territorial range, contains the percentage of the 122 settings in which each type of personnel is found.

Physicians have the highest territorial range, entering over half of the settings in the treatment environment, while vocational counselors have the narrowest range, entering less than one-quarter of the 122 settings. Despite this evidence of an extremely broad territorial range, Table 1 shows that far from maintaining a five-to-one ratio of occupancy time

Table 1

Overall Territorial Range and Percentage of
Occupancy Times for Hospital Personnel
in Frontstage and Backstage Settings

Occupational Group	Overall Territorial Range	Contribution to Occupancy Times (% of Total)	
		Patient Sector (N=76)	Nonpatient Sector (N=46)
Physicians	55%	4.9%	17.5%
Aides and Orderlies	32	34.4	7.3
Nurses	43	20.2	6.2
Administrative Personnel	49	13.2	47.6
Physical Therapists	29	2.8	3.7
Occupational Therapists	25	4.9	4.2
Social Workers	39	6.0	3.1
Vocational Counselors	24	2.5	3.3
Other Occupations	--	11.1	7.0
Totals	--	100.0	100.0

between patient and nonpatient sectors of the treatment environment, physicians actually reverse the expected proportions. That is, they occupy nonpatient settings nearly four times more than patient settings. Only administrative personnel are as remote from patients. Aides, orderlies, and nurses constitute frontline groups, while other professions seem to distribute their time more evenly.

Turning now to a consideration of the treatment environment as a whole, the behavior setting data are capable of generating quantitative, precise inter- as well as intra-environmental comparisons. Many writers have described aspects of institutions which care for a target population 24 hours a day (e.g., Goffman, 4). Such descriptions are typically rich in qualitative detail and correspondingly poor in quantitative analysis. Before presenting some comparative data, let me digress for a moment to describe another useful unit.

One of the most important classifications of the inhabitants of behavior settings relates the amount of control a person has over the activity in the setting. Leaders and active functionaries within settings are called "performers," while customers, audience, and onlookers are referred to as "members." We have found that a classification of settings on the basis of their performers is an important taxonomic step in studying the treatment environment. Such a classification has been labeled a "genotype."

Genotypes:

In brief, two settings are judged to be in the same genotype if at least 75 per cent of the time spent by performers in them is spent by people with equivalent backgrounds (Barker, 2, Pp. 80-89). For example, 12 of the 122 behavior settings were found to have physicians in single leadership positions. These constitute a single genotype, and it can be compared with another genotype in which physicians and nurses share leadership positions. In general, the 122 settings form a total of 52 genotypes, each controlled by a different combination of performers. If the number of settings in an environment provides a measure of the size or "extent" of the place, then the number of genotypes can be considered a measure of the "variety" one finds in that place. It answers the question, "How many different kinds of things are there here?"

Consider the following analogy. A farmer may tell you that he has 100 acres under cultivation, with four different kinds of crops. Number of settings can be considered equivalent to acres in the analogy, and number of genotypes to the four types of crops. Just as the 25-to-one ratio of acreage to crops is meaningful, the setting-to-genotype ratio can tell us the relation of extent to variety within the treatment environment.

Hospital-Town Comparisons:

Barker (2) has provided a number of structural indices from a small midwest town, surveyed during 1963 and 1964. Table 2 summarizes the data from both hospital and town environments on both extent and variety measures. These data bear on the question of the similarity between community types.

Table 2

Ecological Comparisons between
TIRR and Midwest, Kansas

Item	TIRR	Midwest	TIRR/MW X 100
No. of Behavior Settings	122	884	14%
No. of Genotypes	52	198	26%
Genotype/Setting Ratio	.430	.225	191%
Total Occupancy Time	1,316,185 hrs.	1,822,004 hrs.	65%
Time/Setting Ratio	10,800	2,129	197%

The data in Table 2 tell an interesting story; the hospital is far less extensive than the community, and it provides only about one-quarter of the variety one encounters in the small town. However, one finds nearly twice the amount of variety per unit setting in TIRR than in Midwest. The hospital records only about two-thirds the occupancy time of the town, yet here again one finds almost twice as much occupancy per unit setting in the hospital than in the town.

The town data in Table 2 include only community behavior settings; obviously, the addition of family settings would give rise to much greater figures. However, the hospital data obviously do not include the homes of the working personnel. In that respect, then, it seems quite legitimate to compare the two environments.

Let me summarize this part of my talk to provide a contextual framework for Dr. Willems' description of the patient observation methodology. After his presentation, I shall return to discuss some more specific findings regarding the settings actually inhabited by the patients in his observation sample. We have found the treatment environment to be structured into a backstage and a frontstage with the various types of hospital personnel positioned accordingly. The physician seems to operate as a kind of "backstage" controller, receiving inputs about patients indirectly and sending decisions back through the network to frontline personnel. Further, the entire treatment environment seems, in comparison to the small community, to be a more specialized but more densely populated place, with greater diversity per unit setting.

Method 2: Direct Observation
(Edwin P. Willems)

Against the framework of the overall environmental survey of the hospital presented by Dr. LeCompte, we were in the position to study the interface between the treatment environment and the behavior and experience of its primary target population: the patients.

What do patients do? What does their behavior look like in terms of events, structure, pace, and dynamics? In what ways, predicted or not, do the behavioral repertoires and activities of patients change as they progress through the hospital's program of treatment? From the standpoint of patient behavior, what happens in the various subparts--the behavior settings--of the hospital; how can the various behavior settings be characterized in behavioral terms? How does the behavior and experience of patients change, and how does the impact of the hospital change as patients move from one subpart of the hospital to

another? These questions and others like them point to several notable issues. (a) They point to the crux, the payoff point, of hospital functioning--they point to the direct interface between the hospital system and the behavior and experience of patients. (b) Furthermore, such questions point to the kinds of data for which students of design and behavior have been pleading. As is true in so many other areas of human behavior, these questions are usually answered through a combination of crude, hit-or-miss observation, retrospective summaries, interviews, anecdotes, and a host of beliefs, assumptions, and pet ideas. In order to generate a more systematic, quantitative pool of data to answer such questions--and taking out procedural cues primarily from the work of Herbert F. Wright and Roger G. Barker (5)--we began a program of direct observation of patients; patients actually in the hospital at the time of the behavior setting survey that Dr. LeCompte has described.

Twelve adult patients with high spinal cord injuries and involved in comprehensive rehabilitation programs at the Texas Institute for Rehabilitation and Research made up the observational target group, including eight males, four females, a mixture of races and ages, and patients who varied from early in treatment to predischarge. For each patient, a continuous descriptive protocol was generated, based upon continuous firsthand observation of his behavior and situation for one day, beginning at 5:00 a.m. and ending at 11:00 p.m. To obtain the protocols, a team of three observers was assigned to each of the patients. On a patient's appointed day, the team assigned to him rotated in two-hour observation shifts. A minimum of strictures was placed on the observational process--observations were recorded in the everyday language of the observers. All observations were dictated into small, battery-operated tape recorders and in general, each passing minute of clock time was noted. A series of systematic editorial and clerical steps then yielded what we were after: twelve 18-hour protocols, totaling 216 hours of patient time, representing on-the-spot descriptions of what the patients did and including enough of the context of their behavior to make it intelligible.

Our first analysis, keyed to answering some of the questions mentioned earlier, has been based upon a distinction between molar and molecular events in the behavior streams of the patients, or between what we call chunks and bits. The analysis assumes that a protocol captures and describes the ongoing experience-behavior stream of a patient and that the events in the behavior stream include things the patient does, things that are done to him or with him, and segments in which the patient is idle or passive. For our purposes, our major coding unit, a chunk, is a molar event in the behavior stream of a patient which (a) can be readily characterized by a single principal activity, (b) begins at a clearly described starting point, (c) occurs over time in a characteristic, regular manner, with all its essential accompaniments, and (d) ends at a clearly described stopping point. One necessary condition for marking a chunk is that the patient himself be directly involved in it. Thus, if the patient is clearly described as having been involved in two distinct, molar, principal activities at the same time, two chunks are demarcated as occurring simultaneously. Chunks are marked off with major brackets. To each chunk marked on the protocol, the following items of information are attached: (a) a descriptive label for the chunk; (b) how long the chunk lasted; (c) who, out of 31 categories of other persons, was directly involved in the principal activity of the chunk, and how many such persons were involved; (d) who instigated the chunk; (e) the degree of involvement by the target patient in the principal activity, on a scale from active participation through passive participation, to resistive participation; (f) the number of other persons in the immediate situation, but not directly involved in the principal activity of the chunk; (g) the beginning clock time of the chunk; and (h) the specific behavior setting in which the chunk occurred.

The protocols describe more than the molar behavior events, or chunks. We have focused on two kinds of short, fleeting social encounters ("bits")-- fleeting intrusions by others in the patients' behavior streams. The bits of the first type are directed toward the patient's care, safety, comfort, or treatment. The second type includes greetings, fleeting small talk, and other short, but purely sociable, encounters. Each is accompanied by a code for who was involved in it. Finally, transfers (from bed to wheelchair, etc.) and transports to formally scheduled events are coded as chunks. Other changes of location or position are indicated by a separate code.

For our analysis, one person coded an entire protocol, after which a second person coded a portion of it independently. Across seven independent checks, involving a total of 730 minutes of protocol time and four independent coders, pairs of coders agreed on 84 per cent of their accounting for protocol time in terms of chunks (6). A second coder then studied each protocol in its entirety and he and the original coder resolved any questions and disagreements that arose (7).

In order simply to illustrate some general characteristics of the data we are retrieving from these observations, I shall summarize several aspects of the behavior and experience of four of the twelve patients. All four were males, but, by date of admission and progress through the hospital's program of comprehensive rehabilitation, two were early in treatment and

two were advanced, or predischarge, at the time the observations were made.

The first two examples illustrate descriptions of topographical or structural aspects of behavior. Table 3 shows the total number of separate major behavior stream events, or chunks, that occurred in the days of the early and advanced patients, as well as the number of different kinds of chunks that occurred.

Table 3

Summary of Numbers of Chunks

	Total number of chunks	No. of different kinds of chunks (out of 41 kinds)
Early patients	139.5[a]	21.0
Advanced patients	193.5	27.5
Advanced/Early	1.39	1.31

[a]Entries are averages for two patients.

Here is a behavioral documentation of what we commonly assume, or at least hope: as the patient progresses in treatment, his behavioral day becomes fuller, more eventful, and more differentiated. The first two lines show this progress in terms of absolute numbers and the last line shows it in terms of ratios of advanced patients over early patients.

Table 4 shows structural aspects in terms of behavioral overlapping. The first column summarizes the average total number of observational minutes

Table 4

Summary of Overlapping, by Instances and Time

	Observational Minutes	Instances of Overlap	Overlapping Minutes	% of Total (Col. 1)
Early patients	1020.0	23.5	77.75	7.6%
Advanced patients	1080.0	51.5	180.00	16.7%
Advanced/ Early	----	2.19	2.32	2.20

available as a baseline; the second column records the number of times that behavioral chunks occurred simultaneously, or in overlapping fashion, for each set of patients; and the third column shows the average number of observational minutes that involved overlap. The last column summarizes the proportion of overlapping minutes to total observational minutes. The table summarizes the extent to which the behavior streams of the patients proceeded in multiple file as against simple, single file. The ratios in the last line indicate that the behavior streams of the advanced patients marched along in complex, multiple patterns more than twice as often, more than twice as long, and in more than twice as high a proportion of total time as the behavior streams of the early patients. In summary, the data in Tables 3 and 4, which exploit only the number of chunks, the chunk labels, and the length code, illustrate that the behavior of early and advanced patients differs in overall richness, differentiation, and complexity.

There are many dimensions on which the overall diversity and variation in the experience of patients can be documented from these observational data. The data in Table 5 exploit the chunk codes for transfer and transport and the other change-of-location codes to provide one picture of environmental diversity and change to which the patients were exposed. From left to right, the columns summarize (a) location changes within one room, (b) movements across the boundary of one room, (c) movements across the boundaries of more than one room, (d) totals of these three kinds of changes of location, (e) the number of separate behavior settings entered, and (f) the number of times they entered behavior settings. First,

whereas advanced patients also ranged in and out of immediate rooms (second column), probably reflecting the fact that they were in wheelchairs and could move themselves.

I have focused on the distinctions between two early and two advanced patients and the "normalizing" of behavior streams with progress in rehabilitation to provide a relatively straightforward illustration of the validity and usability of the kinds of data we have obtained with the procedures we have described.

We are finding such data indispensable in the documentation of many aspects of the system for delivering care, treatment, and service to patients. Dr. LeCompte will now present some general characteristics of the 19 behavior settings that were actually entered by the 12 patients we observed, after which we shall demonstrate some of the ways we are using the observational data to study environmental dependencies in patient behavior.

Home Range Characteristics of the 12 Patients (William F. LeCompte)

David Stea's (8) term, "Home Range," is an ecological concept that can be useful to key in to the results of the present study. We have defined the home range of this sample of patients as the total number of behavior settings penetrated by them during the day in which they were observed. Table 6 contains a list of the 19 settings in the home range of these patients.

Perhaps the first item to be considered regarding these data relates to their validity; to what extent

Table 5

Changes of Location and Behavior Setting Entries

| | Movements | | | | No. of Different Behavior Settings Entered | No. of Behavior Setting Entries |
	Within Room Only	Across One Room Boundary Only	Past More Than One Room	Total		
Early Patients	13.0	0.0	7.5	20.5	5.5	16.5
Advanced Patients	35.0	7.0	29.5	71.5	11.5	56.0
Advanced/Early	2.69	---	3.93	3.49	2.09	3.39

as the entries in the last line indicate, the advanced patients were involved in much higher numbers of location changes of all types than were early patients. Second, early patients were either involved in movements within rooms (transfers, etc., first column) or major transports about the hospital (third column),

does the sample of 12 observation days reflect the general occupancy time of patients at TIRR? In order to generate data on this question, estimates of patient occupancy time were calculated separately from the protocol records and from the behavior setting survey for each setting. The last two columns in Table 6

Table 6

Home Range of the 12 Patients in the Observation Sample

Behavior Setting		Total Occupancy Time	Patient Occupancy Time Estimates	
			(From Behavior	(From
No.	Name	(Person-Hours/Year)	Setting Survey)	Sample)
1.	Nursing Wards	317,828 hrs.	21.00 hrs.	12.22 hrs.
2.	Self-care Ward	117,192 hrs.	19.00 hrs.	13.30 hrs.
7.	Dental Clinic	4,860 hrs.	1.00 hrs.	.59 hrs.
10.	Physical Therapy Area	26,475 hrs.	.68 hrs.	2.97 hrs.
12.	Electrical Stimulation	261 hrs.	.52 hrs.	.14 hrs.
13.	Occupational Therapy Area	22,430 hrs.	.08 hrs.	1.14 hrs.
16.	Recreational Therapy Area	5,935 hrs.	1.00 hrs.	1.37 hrs.
20.	Job Clinic	360 hrs.	1.50 hrs.	.11 hrs.
22.	Men's Lounge	1,150 hrs.	-0- hrs.	.10 hrs.
24.	Hallways	207,750 hrs.	.01 hrs.	.12 hrs.
26.	Korner Store	2,667 hrs.	.01 hrs.	.03 hrs.
27.	Food Machines	73,444 hrs.	.25 hrs.	.63 hrs.
28.	Waiting Area	30,021 hrs.	.25 hrs.	.33 hrs.
29.	Cafeteria	24,732 hrs.	1.00 hrs.	1.62 hrs.
35.	X-Ray Laboratory	2,781 hrs.	.25 hrs.	.41 hrs.
40.	Photography Studio	4,453 hrs.	.12 hrs.	.02 hrs.
49.	Doctor's Office	4,740 hrs.	-0- hrs.	.15 hrs.
111.	Schoolroom	4,720 hrs.	1.50 hrs.	.79 hrs.
112.	Evening Recreation	3,750 hrs.	1.50 hrs.	1.13 hrs.
	Total	855,549 hrs.	49.67 hrs.	37.17 hrs.

provide estimates from the behavior setting survey and from the protocol records, respectively. In both cases, the figures represent average occupancy times for a single patient during one occurrence of the setting.

The patient occupancy estimates from these two sources are remarkably close, as is apparent in Table 6. The total times are within 12.5 hours of each other. More impressively, the product-moment correlation between the two estimates across the 19 settings is +.98. It seems clear that the set of 12 observation days furnishes an extremely accurate sample of patient occupancy within the home range.

Turning to the home range itself, perhaps the first item of interest is its smallness. This list of 19 behavior settings constitutes only 15 per cent of the total number of settings in the treatment environment, and with regard to genotypes, only 37 per cent are included. Thus, the patients' days occur within quite narrowly defined boundaries, even within the rather narrow confines of the treatment environment.

Although the home range is, thus, restricted in number of settings and in genotypes, it is interesting that the total occupancy time in the patient home range accounts for more than 75 per cent of the total

time in the patient sector. In other words, these 12 patients are located where the action is in the treatment environment.

Physical Structure of the Patient Habitat:

As might be expected from the enormous occupancy time of the patient home range, the physical size of these settings tends on the average to be quite large. We have measured this with an index called the "longest look." It is simply the number of feet in the diagonal from one corner of the setting to the opposite corner, representing the longest possible view within the setting. Longest look data for the patient home range provide a mean value of nearly 55 feet, compared to 35 feet for all settings entered by patients, and 27 feet for backstage settings.

Interpersonal Structure of the Patient Habitat:

The variety of members of the rehabilitation team in the patient home range is also impressively large. Taking the eight occupational groups displayed in Table 1 and adding another seven groups that were not displayed, we constructed a "people variety" index by tallying the number of times in each setting that at least one member of a group appeared as a regular inhabitant. The mean people variety for the patient home range was 6.58, significantly larger than the mean of 4.45 for all settings entered by patients or the mean of 4.09 for backstage settings.

Despite this evidence of greater variety in personnel, however, the behavior setting survey data show that patients had an unequal probability of encountering various types of personnel. Ranking the 15 groups in the rehabilitation team on the basis of their contribution to yearly occupancy time in the home range provides an index of differential exposure to patients. Far in excess of any other group are aides and orderlies with a figure above 150,000 hours. Next in frequency are nurses, with nearly 80,000 hours of exposure. Secretaries, custodians, and occupational therapists appear next most frequently with approximately 20,000 hours of exposure each. Volunteers occur in the next category with about 16,500 hours. Three members of the rehabilitation team appear next, with about 11,500 hours, namely, physical therapists, physicians, and social workers. Only dietitians, vocational counselors, and bracemakers have fewer hours of exposure in the patient home range than physicians. One very clear implication of these data on performances is that the "frontline" groups tend to involve poorly trained, low power occupations, while the appearance of physicians is proportionately few and far between.

Finally, I would like to characterize some aspects of the "social weather" of the patient home range. To what extent are the people in these behavior settings involved in certain characteristic activities? The data show that the most prevalent action patterns are those involving social interaction, clerical activities, and nutrition, while treatment and recreation occur in about 50 per cent of the settings. Somewhat less present are actions such as physical evaluation, maintenance, and activities devoted to improving personal appearance. Nearly completely absent are research and religious activities.

In closing, let me try to summarize some of the main features of these contextual data on the structure of the patients' habitats. We have found the patient home range to be larger both in physical size and in population than typical behavior settings in the treatment environment, to possess, on the average, a greater variety of occupational types, and to include a vastly greater exposure time of low level performers than skilled rehabilitation personnel. Noticeable by their lack of exposure in the patient home range are such groups as physicians, social workers, and physical therapists. Almost completely absent from patient home range are dietitians, vocational counselors and bracemakers. Characteristic activities in the patient

home range include social interaction, nutrition, clerical jobs, with some recreation and treatment, while physical evaluation, personal appearance, religion, and research seem to be underrepresented.

With this much of a chart to help us survey the ecological terrain over the patients' habitat, let us turn to Dr. Willems' observational data to discover how individual behavioral indices fit into this picture.

Behavioral Landscapes: Location Dependencies in the Home Range of Twelve Patients
(Edwin P. Willems)

Dr. LeCompte has presented the actual home range of the 12 patients who were observed so intensively, and he has described that home range. In the parlance of the ecologist, he has, first of all, presented the overall ecological survey of a particular habitat--the hospital. Then, using the actual occupancy and behavior of a subpopulation--the patients-- as the criterion, he has demarcated a special subpart of the habitat as the home range of the patients, and he has described that home range by some of its general social, environmental, and behavioral characteristics. We come now to the final questions of this presentation: Considering the day-long observations of the 12 patients, how did their behavior distribute itself over the behavior settings that constituted their home range? And, what were some of the critical dependencies on location that occurred in their behavior?

Across the 12 patient protocols, our coding system yielded a total of 1815 chunks and the addition of lengths of these chunks yielded a total of 14227 chunk minutes. Table 7 displays the way in which these behaviors were distributed across several behavior settings, in terms of per cents of chunk

Table 7

Distribution of Chunk Minutes by Behavior Setting in Which They Occurred

	No. of Minutes	% of Total
1 Stations 1-3	5082	35.7
2 Station 4	4709	33.1
10 General PT Area	1704	12.0
13 General OT Area	749	5.3
16 Recreational Therapy	403	2.8
24 Hallways	395	2.8
29 Cafeteria	348	2.4
Other	837	5.9
Total	14227	100.0

minutes that occurred in each. Several things stand out: (a) Ninety-four per cent of the patients' chunk minutes occurred in the 7 settings displayed. (b) That means that 94 per cent of the patients' behavior time was captured by fewer than six per cent of the hospital's 122 behavior settings. (c) In fact, about 69 per cent of the patients' behavior time was spent in only two settings--the two wards or primary living areas.

Table 8 characterizes three of these settings in more detail, in terms of the distributions of patient behaviors that occurred within each. These data indicate that in addition to capturing a high proportion

Table 8

Characterizations of Three Settings By Patient Behaviors Occurring in Them

(2) Station 4 (4709 Chunk Minutes)

	N	%
Idle	1149	24.4
Nursing Care & Hygiene	1045	22.2
Conversing	828	17.6
Sleeping	666	14.1
Eating Scheduled Meal	217	4.6
Passive Recreational	151	3.2
Transferring	129	2.7
Telephoning	126	2.7
Exercise & Performance Training	123	2.6
Other	275	5.8

(10) General PT Area (1704 Chunk Minutes)

	N	%
Exercise & Performance Training	1025	60.2
Conversing	317	18.6
Idle	161	9.4
Transferring	110	6.5
Other	91	5.3

(29) Cafeteria (348 Chunk Minutes)

	N	%
Eating Scheduled Meal	213	61.2
Conversing	131	37.6
Other	4	1.1

of patient behavior, the wards were also quite diverse and complex in terms of patient behavior. The cafeteria, on the other hand, was a much more specialized setting for patients, being devoted to eating and conversing.

We turn now to a more dynamic, inferential, and program-oriented aspect of patient behavior. From our codes, it is possible to retrieve (a) the total number of waking and non-idle chunk minutes for the patients, (b) the number of chunk minutes in which

the patients acted alone, and (c) the number of chunk minutes instigated by the patients themselves--all differentiated by behavior settings. With total waking and non-idle minutes as the baseline, averaging the two per cents for acting alone and patient instigation gives us an index of the extent to which the behavior streams of the patients were under their own control, or, if you will, an index of patient independence. Table 9 displays indices of independence for the seven behavior settings that contained the largest amounts of patient behavior. The highest rates of behavioral independence by patients were associated with the cafeteria and hallways, two settings which

Table 9

Indices of Patient Independence for Seven Behavior Settings

	Total Chunk Minutes[a]	Index of Independence
(29) Cafeteria	346	64.3
(24) Hallways	387	48.1
(1) Stations 1-3	3003	29.7
(2) Station 4	2894	23.9
(13) General OT Area	697	15.1
(10) General PT Area	1543	7.5
(16) Recreational Therapy	388	.2

[a]Excludes Idle and Sleeping time.

are only tangential to the formal program of rehabilitation. By contrast, three settings that lie at the heart of the formally defined program of rehabilitation--physical therapy, occupational therapy, and recreational therapy--produced the lowest rates. Another way to summarize these data is to say that when the patients moved from cafeteria and hallways --two settings that are complex and demanding, but peripheral to the formal rehabilitative process--to the more formal treatment settings, the message somehow got through that they were to be much more dependent and docile.

It is possible that these differences in rates of independence were produced by different patients who entered the settings at varying rates. To test this alternative hypothesis, we calculated combined indices of independence for (a) cafeteria, hallways, and wards; (b) occupational therapy, physical therapy, and recreational therapy; and (c) each of the 12 patients. In the case of each patient, the results corroborated the pattern found above; for all 12 patients, the index of independence dropped dramatically as they moved from cafeteria-hallways-wards to occupational therapy–physical therapy–recreational therapy.

Data such as these not only point to powerful location dependencies in the dynamics of behavior, but they should be useful to those who wish to evaluate how their programs are being carried out. The use of patient instigation and acting alone to measure variations in independence among settings is only one example of what the observational data enable us to do. We have analyzed associations between independence and types of behavior and differences among patients. We have studied differences among patients, settings, types of behavior, and involvements by various persons with the patients for their effects upon behavioral zest, as measured by patient initiative and degree of involvement. We are planning analyses which exploit--singly and in various combinations--dimensions of behavior such as numbers of chunks per hour, rate of overlapping, and degree of involvement to make inferences about behavioral pace.

* * * * *

We have presented only a few sparse illustrations of our approach to the study of human environments: overall environmental analysis with convergence down to the way in which the moment-by-moment behavior of inhabitants distributes itself within that environment. The general investigation of environment and behavior can benefit from the application of strategies similar to these because de facto environmental dependencies should be our point of departure. If this be so, then there is no substitute for being present to observe and measure behavior when and where it occurs.

Notes and References

1. The research reported here and the preparation of this paper were supported by Research and Training Center No. 4 (RT-4), Baylor College of Medicine, funded by Social and Rehabilitation Services, USDHEW.

2. Barker, R. G. Ecological psychology. Stanford, California: Stanford University Press, 1968.

3. Goffman, E. The presentation of self in everyday life. Garden City, New York: Anchor Books, 1959.

4. Goffman, E. Asylums. New York: Doubleday, 1961.

5. Wright, H. F. Recording and analyzing child behavior. New York: Harper & Row, 1967.

6. In order to check agreement on the ratings attached to the chunks, we selected 43 chunks on whose demarcation two coders had agreed exactly. Out of these 43 chunks, pairs of raters agreed on the following number and per cents: T code--39 (90.7%); O code--41 (95.3%); I code--40 (93.0%); DI code--38 (88.4%); RP code--33 (76.7%).

7. Details of the entire observational and coding process are presented in: Willems, E. P., & Vineberg, S. E. Procedural supports for the direct observation of behavior in natural settings. Houston, Texas: Texas Institute for Rehabilitation and Research, 1970.

8. The writers are indebted to David Stea for a copy of an unpublished manuscript which contains the text of his paper presented at a symposium at the University of Michigan in 1968.

Environmental Components of Orientations Toward Privacy

by Nancy J. Marshall

James Madison College and

Multidisciplinary Social Science Program, Michigan State University

Abstract. Orientations toward privacy were identified and individual differences in orientation assessed by means of the Privacy Preference Scale. Six subscales were constructed from principal components analysis of the scale, centering around preferences for non-involvement with neighbors, seclusion of home, solitude, privacy with intimates, anonymity, and reserve. In an adult sample, orientations were related by means of multivariate analysis of variance and canonical correlation to (a) density of the past and present environments, (b) features of the physical environment affecting potential privacy, and (c) privacy-oriented behavior and social norms regarding privacy.

Privacy and Environmental Design. Privacy can be viewed as a dimension for describing behavior that deals with control over interaction with others, the domain of privacy including (a) behavior that is oriented away from others and (b) the presentation of barriers to the behavior of others oriented toward the self. Understanding privacy-oriented behavior involves understanding the circumstances under which persons desire to withdraw from others, the preferred means of withdrawal, and the features of the physical environment which can aid or hinder control over interaction, as well as individual differences in dispositions to seek privacy.

The concept of privacy is of interest to the social psychologist, the environmental psychologist, and the designer, and as such can serve as a focus for interdisciplinary research. In terms of the preceding definition of privacy, the social psychologist is largely concerned with studying the process of withdrawal from interaction or of control of interaction and involvement with others in contrast to his more usual study of interaction processes. The environmental psychologist is interested in the relationship between privacy-oriented behavior and the physical environment, for privacy can be controlled by manipulating either the environment or one's position in the environment.

To the designer, questions of privacy are involved in decisions about visual and auditory separation within the home and between dwelling units, and about levels of density within the neighborhood, city, or region. Defining privacy as the ability to control the amount and kind of interaction one has with other persons, the dilemma for designers becomes that of providing flexibility for choosing either privacy or interaction with others when desired [1]. The data needed as input to the design process include how people define privacy and how they prefer to obtain it (are both auditory and visual privacy necessary in all situations?), and the range of individual differences in privacy preference (assuming that a succession of persons with different desires may need to be accommodated). The implications of the complexity and cultural relativism of the concept of privacy for designers has been discussed by Rapoport [2].

In another context, concern about population growth and its ecological implications has led to interest in identifying an optimal level of density. Among the arguments made for low density is that of a human "need" for privacy that is thwarted by high density living. There is clearly a need for information about individual differences in privacy preferences, the amount of adaptation to crowding that takes place, and about alternative means of gaining privacy when the solitude of low density living is unavailable.

The Concept of Privacy. The core of the concept of privacy lies in the ability to control the degree to which others have access to the self. One can conceive of a continuum of 'facts' about the self ranging from the most to the least personal, similar to what William James [3] called the empirical self or Lewin [4] the centrality of inner personal regions. Privacy involves control over disclosure of those facts to others of varying intimacy.

The concept of privacy can be differentiated into its component parts by identifying ways of controlling both input and output. A major means of controlling how much others know about one involves limiting verbal disclosure of facts about oneself, of thoughts, of beliefs, and of opinions. Achieving this kind of privacy is a function of both self-control and the demands made by others for information.

Closely related to self-disclosure is the idea of social distancing and related norms as means of providing privacy. Levy (5) suggested that when physical distancing becomes impossible, as in prisons, army barracks, or slum apartments, "it would appear that people make use of psychological distancing mechanisms. Enforced physical contact often leads to the maintenance of 'emotional distance'." In addition, norms dealing with privacy or informal systems for communicating desire for privacy may be developed within families, friendship circles, or societies.

Privacy may also be controlled through the use or erection of physical rather than psychological barriers, including visual barriers, auditory barriers, and increased distance between self and others.

Anonymity is a means of gaining privacy by being "lost in a crowd," coming into contact with a great many people who do not know one as an individual. This is the privacy afforded by the city rather than the small town which has been so strongly defended by Jane Jacobs (6).

Plan of the Study. Three purposes of the study of privacy to be presented here were:

1) to explore in more depth the concept of privacy by means of a questionnaire assessing preferences for different kinds and degrees of privacy in a variety of situations. How closely related are preferences for one kind of privacy to preferences for the others? Is privacy a unitary concept, an internal goal or end, and the components merely interchangeable behaviors toward this end which are adapted to the particular environmental conditions presented (7)?

2) to relate attitudes toward privacy to the physical and social environment of an individual, partly to reveal how he attempts to achieve levels of privacy appropriate to his preferences. Behaviors surveyed focused on entertainment preferences, preferred and achieved modes of interaction with neighbors and friends, and amount of time spent alone. Environmental variables related to available privacy included physical arrangements within the home and within the neighborhood, number of persons lived with, and amount of noise.

3) to relate density levels in an individual's past and present environment (home, neighborhood, work) to his preferred level of privacy, using adaptation level theory as developed by Helson (8) as a source of hypotheses. The discussions of privacy appearing in popular literature are generally based on the assumption that privacy is a basic need; it would follow from drive reduction theory that depriving one of privacy would increase attempts to gain privacy, and should be reflected in higher scores on a measure of privacy preference. In contrast, adaptation level theory postulates an adaptation to past and current levels of input; thus a decrease in available privacy should over time lead to a decrease in preferred levels of privacy.

Method. An 86-item scale called the Privacy Preference Scale (PPS) was constructed containing statements about preferences for privacy in a variety of situations. This scale was an expansion of an earlier scale which focused on the college enviornment, and contained items representing the factors labeled solitude, anonymity, and control over self-disclosure appearing in the factor analysis of the earlier scale. In addition, items dealing with privacy for units larger than one, noise as an intrusion, and the inviolacy of personal possessions were included. Cutting across these content areas were items dealing with control over input and output involving several sensory modalities and kinds of barriers. The items were presented as a summative scale with five response alternatives: strongly agree, agree, undecided, disagree, and strongly disagree.

An environmental questionnaire was constructed to assess the amount of privacy, both potential and realized, in the individual's present and childhood physical and social environments, and the number of others interacted with on the job and off. To facilitate adequate coverage of the entire domain of inquiry, the items sampled from a variety of situations (home, work, recreation) and relationships (with family, neighbors). Assessment of privacy within the home included measures of perceived privacy and crowding, time spent alone, presence of physical barriers between areas, and norms concerning their use. Assessment of privacy from neighbors included perceived privacy, visual and auditory barriers, and entertaining preferences. Another group of questions inquired about the number of people with whom one preferred to relax on evenings and weekends and the quality of the interaction involved in the preferred activities, whether solitary, coacting (acting in the presence of others but not interacting, such as watching movies), and interacting. Information about the following variables in the childhood environment was obtained: amount of open space, crowding, and closeness of relationship with siblings.

Subjects. The samples selected for study consisted of second-semester sophomore students (n = 149) from a commuter junior college in the outer suburbs of the San Francisco Bay area, and a sample of their parents (n = 101). The junior college chosen for study draws students from largely upper-middle class suburbs, but also from lower-middle class suburbs closely connected with local industries. The Privacy Preference Scale was given to both the student and adult samples, and the Environmental Questionnaire only to the adult sample.

Results. Factor analysis of the Privacy Preference Scale was employed as a means of identifying orientations toward privacy. Principal components analysis of the combined samples produced seven major rotated factors, six of which appeared in separate analyses of both the adult and student samples. Subscales were constructed based on the latter six factors to yield measures of orientations toward privacy more differentiated than that offered by the over-all Privacy Preferency score. The six factors included the following orientations:

1) Intimacy. This factor was largely concerned with the size of the unit involved in situations requiring privacy; e.g., several items dealt with being able to get away from others with an intimate or with one's family. The adult and student samples, as reflected in the differences in the factor analyses of their respective data, differed in the nature of the desired intimate relationship; while the student would tend to disclose a great deal about himself in order to gain intimacy, the adult was concerned with retaining a degree of privacy even within the intimate relationship.

2) Not neighboring. These items dealt with disliking the tendency of friends or neighbors to drop in without warning, and with a preference for non-involvement with neighbors. The factor reflected two not necessarily related means of gaining privacy: through expressed or implied norms about when others might visit and through choice of persons other than neighbors as close friends, distance presumably allowing more control over the relationship.

3) Seclusion. Items loading on this factor dealt with visual and auditory seclusion of the home, placing it out of sight and sound of neighbors and traffic. Seclusion entailed a tolerance for being alone, and a willingness or preference to be unacquainted with neighbors.

4) Solitude. This factor reflected a desire to be alone at times, without differentiating between being alone but with others nearby (as in one's room) and being far from others. The possibility of being alone "mentally," with others present but not intruding on one's thoughts, was included.

5) Anonymity. The central theme of this factor was the anonymity of urban living; items dealt with being able to attain privacy in a large city because "everyone wouldn't know everything about you" as opposed to the interest in and involvement with others in a small town. The student factor, unlike the adult, also reflected a liking for the noise and traffic of the city; noise did not seem to be

a drawback to city life for the students.

6) Reserve. This factor dealt with a preference not to disclose much about oneself to others, particularly if the others were not known very well. Several types of items involving self-disclosure were written, covering the depth of disclosure (how much one was willing to disclose to even the closest friends) as well as the breadth of disclosure (how much one preferred to disclose to acquaintances or strangers). Many of the items in the latter category, expressing liking to be "open and honest with others" or to have few really intimate friends, did not load highly on this factor. The differences in emphasis of the adult and student factors were similar to the age group differences on the intimacy factor. The adults emphasized not revealing much about themselves to friends until they had known them a long time, while students emphasized not revealing themselves to "persons I don't know very well."

Comparison of the orientations revealed in the factor analysis to those discussed in the introduction shows two that are identical (Reserve, and Anonymity), and two that could be construed as the use of physical barriers of one kind or another (Solitude and Seclusion). Not Neighboring seems to involve a control over the self-disclosure that might be forced by physical proximity. No factor was specifically concerned with emotional distancing, although items representing this possibility were included.

The correlations of the subscales with overall privacy preference (PPS) and the intercorrelations of the subscale scores are presented in Table 1. All of the subscales were significantly related to PPS ($p < .01$), with the Neighboring and Solitude scales correlating the highest. Intercorrelations of the six subscales showed two major groupings. The first centered on strong relationships among Anonymity and Neighboring, predictable from the item overlap (two items appeared on both subscales), and Reserve. The second showed a strong relationship between the Solitude subscale and both Seclusion and Intimacy. The latter would seem to indicate that preference for solitude in this sample did not indicate complete withdrawal from others or reclusiveness. Rather, the same persons who preferred times of solitude had strong preferences regarding being with intimates at other times.

The substantial relationships between Reserve and the Neighboring and Anonymity subscales may indicate a functional relationship between the subscales, in that controlling involvement with neighbors is one means of controlling self-disclosure. Several case studies of suburban communities, such as that of Kuper (9), show non-involvement with neighbors as one means of avoiding a relationship in which it could easily become difficult to control the amount of time spent with another

Table   1

Correlations of Privacy Subscales with PPS Total Score; Subscale Intercorrelations for Adult and Student Samples

Scale	Anonymity	Not Neighboring	Reserve	Solitude	Seclusion	Intimacy
Privacy Preference (Adult & Student)	.51**	.65**	.52**	.63**	.56**	.47**
Not Neighboring						
Adult	.61**					
Student	.54**					
Reserve						
Adult	.35**	.27**				
Student	.29**	.24**				
Solitude						
Adult	.17	.34**	.11			
Student	.04	.17*	.26*			
Seclusion						
Adult	.10	.36**	.08	49**		
Student	.05	.18*	.20*	.45**		
Intimacy						
Adult	.14	.18	.28**	.40**	.35**	
Student	.12	.06	.23**	.39**	.24**	

*p < .05
**p < .01

and the amount of disclosure. Fava (10) found that the urban setting, which tends to offer more opportunity for anonymity, had lower levels of neighboring than the suburban setting, even with social correlates of neighboring such as marital status, home ownership, residential stability, and age controlled. The relationship between Neighboring and Seclusion is logical in that a person wanting involvement with his neighbors would find it more difficult if secluded.

The subscale intercorrelations revealed that, while there may be different orientations toward privacy or different means of attaining privacy that are conceptually separable, there existed strong relationships between many of them as measured by personal preferences.

Environmental Density and Privacy Preference. Predictions about privacy preferences were made from three sets of variables, dealing with density of the living situation in childhood, density of the present living situation (including density within the home and within the neighborhood), and job density (number of persons interacted with on the job). It was hypothesized, based on adaptation level theory, that high levels of density in the past environment would be related to preferences for low levels of privacy.

Of the significant relationships found between past environmental density and privacy preferences, none involved the subscales of most relevance to adaptation level theory, Seclusion and Solitude. There seemed to be, on the whole, a minimal relationship between past environment and present privacy preferences, and the existing relationships were not particularly relevant to adaptation level theory. The most interesting were positive correlations of both over-all privacy preference (PPS) and preference for anonymity with average size of town lived in. In addition, high perceived crowding of the childhood environment was positively related to preference for low self-disclosure.

Correlation of job density with the number of persons subjects preferred to interact with in other situations (when entertaining, when relaxing) revealed only one significant correlation. Although the relationship was in the direction predicted by adaptation level theory, in that persons who interacted with a relatively large number of others on the job preferred to entertain larger groups, the lack of correlation with the other measures served to lower confidence in the hypothesis.

The hypothesis of a relationship between density or crowding in the present environment and preference for privacy paralleled that for past environment, predicting that high levels of density would be related to low preference for privacy, particularly as measured by the Solitude subscale. Three of the measures of density within the home (number of persons in the home, visual openness of rooms, and judged privacy in the home) were significantly related to total score on PPS in the direction predicted by adaptation level theory. The hypothesized relationships with the Solitude subscale, however, did not appear. None of the correlates of density in the neighborhood seemed particularly interpretable using the concept of adaptation level.

The over-all force of the data presented here is toward a general lack of relationship between preferred levels of privacy and actual privacy (past and present), with the relationships that did appear tending to support adaptation level theory more than drive theory. These findings also suggest that there was not a very good fit between privacy preferences and the opportunities available in the environment for attaining privacy. Supporting this conclusion was the finding that the responses of persons with high preferred privacy fell between "about right" and "not quite enough" on a question asking them about the level of privacy in their present home environment; the responses of persons with low preferred privacy centered on "about right." The fit between preference and environment, then, was better for the group showing low preference for privacy, even though persons with high preference for privacy tended to have more actual privacy (lived with fewer people and had fewer rooms that were visually open to each other).

Environmental and Behavioral Correlates of Privacy Preferences. Two sets of variables were constructed from the items on the Environmental Questionnaire, combining items into more manageable composites. One, the Privacy-oriented Behavior Composites, assessed behavior that would influence the amount of available privacy. The Environmental Privacy Composites assessed variables in the physical environment of the home or neighborhood that would influence available privacy. These two sets of variables or composites were related to three levels of PPS by means of multivariate analysis of variance (overall multivariate F not significant in either case) and to the privacy subscales by means of cononical correlation (significant canonical r's ($p < .01$) of .61 and .50 with Environmental Composites, .56 with Behavioral Composites). As a means of integrating the information about the relationships between expressed privacy preferences and both the behavioral and environmental variables revealed in these analyses, sketches will be drawn of the "average" individual belonging to each of the privacy orientations. Since the behavioral and environmental information was obtained only from the adult sample, the sketches will apply only to them.

1) Privacy Preference Scale. First is the "privacy-prone" individual, who shows an inclination toward privacy in a wide variety of situations (high scorers on PPS). The high value he places on privacy is reflected in the choices choices he would make in buying a home: he would give up adequate lighting from outdoors if it meant having enough privacy, and would choose separate bedrooms for his children in place of a family room. Although he lives with few other people and has few rooms that are visually open to each other, he tends to state that he does not have enough privacy. He does not enjoy dropping in on others, nor having others drop in without warning. His past environment is notable for the large proportion of time spent in large towns.

2) The orientation toward privacy in the neighboring relationship emphasizes a dislike of casual visiting by friends and neighbors, and a dislike of high involvement with neighbors. The person oriented toward "not neighboring" lives with fewer other persons than does the neighboring person, and would be more likely to favor privacy over light, and separate bedrooms over a family room if a choice were necessary. His non-neighboring orientation is reflected in not liking, and not liking others, to drop in without warning, and his avoidance of neighbors as close friends. When entertaining, he prefers to invite a small number of persons. He would be more likely to choose to attend a ball game on weekends, where he would be coacting with a large groups of people, than to interact with a small group of others.

3) The orientation toward privacy exemplified by the "seclusive" person is characterized by preference for a house that is visually and auditorily secluded from other houses and by an associated tolerance for being alone and being unacquainted with one's neighbors. Neighbors do not usually drop in to visit the seclusive individual without being invited, nor does he drop in on them. More than the non-seclusive, he tends to prefer solitary weekend activities. The seclusive does not differ, however, in the actual seclusion of home, as measured by such variables as number of houses visible, lot size, distance to nearest neighbors, and auditory privacy.

4) The orientation toward solitude reflects a desire to be alone at times, to have some time away from even family and close friends. Although his physical environment does not tend to differ from that of an individual who is not solitude prone, the "solitude-prone" person is more likely to feel he does not have enough privacy. His orientation is strongly reflected in his activity preferences: he prefers solitary activities or those with low levels of interaction, particularly shunning activities involving interacting rather than coacting with a small group of others; he

prefers to entertain few people, and does not enjoy dropping in on others.

5) The anonymity of city living is the major emphasis of the orientation toward anonymity, with minor emphasis on non-involvement with neighbors. The "anonymity-prone" individual is likely to have lived much of his life in a large town, and is particularly likely to have spent more time in a metropolitan area and less time in a rural area than the anonymity-avoiding individual. He felt that his childhood home was crowded, and tends to have low privacy in his present home (he has no place to be alone and inadequate auditory separation of areas within the home). Although he tends to dislike casual visiting (dropping in without warning) and does not choose neighbors as friends, he dislikes solitary evening activities.

6) The orientation toward reserve focuses on being unwilling to reveal very much about oneself to casual acquaintances, and on liking visual privacy from neighbors. In addition to perceiving his childhood home as crowded, he feels his present home is crowded and lacks sufficient privacy, although he lives with fewer people than the high discloser. He tends to choose weekend activities involving interaction with large groups of people and to avoid those that involve coacting with less than six persons.

7) The orientation toward intimacy involves the desire for privacy for a unit larger than one, especially for privacy with a close friend or with the family. This person is likely to have lived in a metropolitan region, in a single family dwelling as a child, and to live near where he grew up. His present environment is characterized by high privacy within the home, since he lives with few others and has high visual privacy from neighbors. He generally prefers to interact with few others in the evening, but tends to interact with many others on the job. His behavior and that of his associates reflect respect for privacy norms: people tend to call before dropping in, ask permission before entering a private room, and keep private doors closed.

These characterizations seem distinctive enough to justify identifying six separate orientations toward privacy. Undoubtedly, more could be identified, but these promise to be fruitful in exploring further the individual differences in preferred modes of exerting control over interaction with others.

Notes

1. Chermayeff, Serge, & Alexander, Christopher. Community and privacy. New York: Doubleday, 1963.

2. Rapoport, Amos. Observations regarding man-environment studies. Man-environment Systems, January, 1970.

3. James, William. The principles of psychology. New York: Holt, 1890.

4. Lewin, Kurt. Principles of topological psychology. New York: McGraw-Hill, 1936.

5. Levy, Leo. The quality of urban life. In Urban America: goals and problems. Washington, D. C.: U. S. Government Printing Office, 1967. Pp. 100-112.

6. Jacobs, Jane. The death and life of great American cities. New York: Random House, 1961.

7. Based on Simon's model of environment-behavior relationships, in Herbert Simon, The sciences of the artificial. Cambridge, Mass.: M. I. T. Press, 1969.

8. Helson, Harry, Adaptation-level theory. New York: Harper & Row, 1964.

9. Kuper, Leo. Blueprint for living together. In L. Kuper (Ed.), Living in towns. London: Cresset, 1953.

10. Fava, Sylvia. Contrasts in neighboring: New York City and a suburban community. In W. Dobriner (Ed.), The suburban community. New York: Putnam, 1958. Pp. 122-131.

Architecture and Organizational Health

by Fred I. Steele

Private Consultant, 71 Hancock Street, Boston, Massachusetts

Abstract

This paper discusses some dimensions for looking at the impact of physical settings on organizational health. The dynamic processes described come out of the author's observations while working as an organizational consultant. The criteria of organizational health used are those proposed by Bennis: adaptability and problem solving; reality-testing; and sense of identity. A number of important physical setting properties are identified as influencing these three criteria, and examples are given. The properties include: physical distance; functional distance; interference; visibility; mood; power cues; and boundaries.

Introduction

There is an old vaudeville joke which has a husband returning home unexpectedly in the afternoon and surprising his wife and her lover, who hides in the bedroom closet. The husband throws open the door and bellows, "What the hell are you doing in my bedroom closet?" The lover, standing shivering in his underwear, shrugs and says, "Everybody's got to be someplace ...."

That is true not only for individuals, but for organizations as well. Every system of people who have joined together for some kind of joint effort has some kind of physical setting in which they operate. It may be one building, or a series of buildings, or offices scattered around the country, or a combination, but each of those is "someplace" and provides the setting for the organization's activities. Yet we know relatively little about the impact that different kinds of settings have on the functioning of organizations. Although there has been a real explosion of interest and work on tying together design and its impact on behavior, most of the attention to date has been at the individual and small group level, with much less attention on the organization.

In this paper I would like to focus on the complex area of the impact of physical settings on human organizations. I will discuss three criteria of organizational health, the impact that space can have on these dimensions and the decision processes that influence these spatial arrangements, and provide examples of dynamic processes between space and the system.

The Concept of Organizational Health

For me, the most useful means of conceiving "health" of an organization comes from those writers who have looked at systems of different complexity (a one-celled animal, a woods animal, a man, a group, etc.) as having similar fundamental functions which they must perform over time in order to be "healthy" -- that is, to survive and fulfill their existence without destroying themselves in the process. These functions are seen as basic to an organism dealing with the world in a competent fashion.

Following this line, Warren Bennis developed what he called the "criteria of organizational health", ((1) ch.3) to try to get away from single, static measures of organizational performance which may describe a point in time but tell you little about the state of the system and its potential future performance or survival. He then proposed three criteria of organizational health which are more process-oriented and which come from the studies of mental health of individuals and from general systems theory. Briefly, these three criteria are:

1. Adaptability and problem solving This is essential for doing the tasks of the system, and for reacting flexibly to changing external or internal conditions. The higher the rate of change in an organization's environment (market, source of supply of people, clients, or users, etc.), the more critical this flexibility becomes.

2. A sense of identity.This is concerned with the extent to which the organization's members know what it is trying to do (its goals) and share perceptions of what the organization looks like -- what its structure is, who are its members, what their roles are, and so on. Bennis suggests that this sense of identity is sharpest when four entities are congruent (matched) with one another: (a) the manifest organization (publicly described on the charts); (b) the assumed organization (the one members would draw to show how things actually happen); (c) the extant organization (the true system as it exists and could be discovered through study); and (d) the requisite organization (what it should be like for what it is trying to do in its environment). When these four are basically the same, then the system has a clear sense of identity.

3. Reality-Testing. This involves having processes for accurately perceiving the properties of the field in which the organization exists (including both the internal organization itself and what goes on outside it). The emphasis here is on two aspects: getting enough information to know when things have changed or are changing, and getting undistorted information, so that accurate descriptions of the

world (as much as can be known)are used as inputs to problem solving and to maintaining the sense of identity.

Having given the flavor of these process criteria for health of a system, I will now take each in turn and present some examples of the ways in which an organization's setting can affect the health of the system. Since one of the main reasons for writing this paper is to stimulate more explicit research on this area, it is not surprising that there are few systematic studies to report at this point. The comments that follow are for the most part based on my own work in consultation to various kinds of organizations, where I have been recording examples of the impact of spatial arrangements on the system.

Adaptability and Problem Solving
Perhaps the most ubiquitous spatial factor in organizational problem-solving is that of relative placement of people: how far or how near people are to one another in terms of energy required (or perceived) to have contact. We could call this "functional distance." The impact of this is often seen in relational problems between central offices and field offices. Lack of contact makes it difficult to work through problems, since separation keeps pieces of the problem unshared. By the time they get warmed up when they are together the time may be used up, and they separate again and the crust starts reforming.

The most striking example of this I have seen lately was a company that was organized functionally and had two main locations, (45 min. drive) apart. This was a transition period in shifting the total system from one location to the other, and during it there was a great deal of difficulty in operating efficiently, especially in reacting quickly to problems. They had been used to calling spontaneous short meetings to check information, but this became almost impossible when 1½ hours travel time was thrown in for each meeting.

In other instances, the actual physical separation may be nowhere near this great-- it may only be a few hundred feet in the same building--but the <u>functional</u> <u>distance</u> may be large. For instance, one person described how he had to reach a collaborator in another department: "Go from my office to the other end of the building, take the elevator to 14, get off, take another elevator to 21, walk to the other end of the building (above my own office)...." The result: "I go there much less frequently than I really need to."

The impact of these separations on the system's ability to solve problems would depend of course on the degree to which people need to share ideas, information, reactions, etc., for particular tasks. What makes functional distance a critical variable is that a system will often set up places for people and groups based (loosely) on some criteria of interaction and maintain that distribution even when the needs change radically. I have found a number of instances of project task forces being formed and members keeping their old offices in their functional areas; this makes it difficult for the new group to form.

Besides distance and/or floor differences the arrangement of facilities (walls, pathways, lounge areas, noise-producing activities) can also inhibit contacts. People who are in diferent corridors or sectors of a building may have a low probability of having second order interactions--that is, those contacts which are not vital to doing their job (they go out of their way to have those), but which are useful and stimulating if they occur.

Another facility which influences adaptability is the presence or absence of different-sized meeting spaces. I have known numerous instances when it would have helped a client system if we could have gathered together groups of 50 or more, yet there was no place to do that. If these (and other) areas are not available, then groupings in the system tend to occur based on available spaces--which may or may not fit task needs. An even simpler example is the tendency of groups to stop listing ideas when they use up their immediate blackboard or newsprint space. One member once said "I just realized that all our problems are two blackboards long."

The actual correlation between complexity of the problem and what they put on the two boards could be fairly low.

Inflexibility of space in terms of change (high spatial viscosity-- see(2)) will also hinder adaptability. For example, a professor friend of mine searched in vain for an available classroom that did not have all the seats bolted down facing the front (from which all wisdom was expected to flow). He wanted to innovate in his teaching style, but he finally gave up since there was no setting which would promote or even allow the kind of interaction he wanted to promote among the students.

The physical setting may also be a better or worse medium for practicing problem-solving and developing skills in this process. It is a good medium for this because the variables and results are usually concrete, visible, and understandable. An organization can have processes of spatial decision making that either add to the competence of its members or do not. Most organizations fall into the latter category.

As my final instance of the influence of space on adaptability, I want to touch on a process that is not very well understood at this point. This is the impact of a place on individual or group <u>mood</u>: its existential messages and the way these vary for different people. We all know that places feel different in terms of such dimensions as warm-cold, formal-informal, frantic-peaceful, and so on. Although there is little systematic data on this, observations indicate that places have mood-setting capabilities: a group meeting in the library of an old mansion will feel different than a group meeting in a store-front in the central city, or than a class meeting in an austere classroom. The messages of these places are different about values, goals, relationships, and the like; and these tend to trigger off fantasies and memories in the people using them (of this and similar places). These associations in turn help determine the kinds of associations and ideas generated by the group, and can therefore influence both the definition of problems and the solutions that are generated. A system's setting can also generate a false view of the conditions around it (such as the slick building in a depressed area). Finally, the mood of a place can affect peoples' desire to be there or not. A place that people like will have more members there on the average; this can mean both more energy available and greater inter action when problems arise.

Sense of Identity

A clear sense of identity for the system and its subparts means that it knows where it is going and what it looks like. Organizational identity can be described on many dimensions: values, goals, power and status structures, interests, strengths and weaknesses, potentials, styles of life, reporting relationships, other communication networks, and rules and regulations. A clear sense of identity for a system would mean that these are mutually perceived by different members of the system, and that they are what is required for that system to be effective.

An organization's physical structure is one of the most visible ways of getting a feel for what it "is". One major way in which space influences identity is through the symbolic language of space that develops about status in the organization. In many systems an insider can tell exactly where someone is in the hierarchy simply by looking at his place. This language can be a help to a clear identity, or it can confuse it; formal position and actual power in getting things done are not necessarily the same. If the physical language reflects rigidly just the formal categories, it may inhibit executives who would like to reward real contributions. If this kind of split exists, members may also discount the meaning of the spatial language, as in the case of the retired vice president who has a plush office to which he comes to read the paper.

A second factor is one also mentioned under adaptability: the physical closeness or separation of members of the system. Locations of people can facilitate or inhibit their sense of who they are in the organization and what it looks like. The history of

home-office/field relations is filled with complaints from the field that they have no sense of how things happen in the whole system. This can be true at the same location, too: people in "backwater" offices in a far corner can forever feel out of what is happening and fuzzy about themselves in it.

Sometimes, however, this phenomenon can promote a sense of identity for the sub-unit, such as when a university department is in an old building together and develops a strong cohesion. This can be costly to the system as a whole, however, if cooperation is actually needed across boundaries. A company often buys more trouble than gain when it begins to spill out into overflow rented space all over town. In the reverse direction, a group of lawyers in a large organization resisted a move to the company's central location, since their separation had allowed them to set their own pace and life style. Yet it made more sense for the total system that they be near the people who were their daily clients.

The structure of boundary zones can also serve as a block to a perception of shared identity between groups. These zones are the areas that may say "keep out" to non-members, through closed doors, walls, unclear entrances, gauntlets to run (such as the secretary who screens people), or actual rules about who can enter. The more there are "backstage areas" (in Goffman's terms), the lower the likelihood of people in the system being able to accurately perceive that subgroup and how it fits into the whole.

By contrast, an area that is open to entrance but also quite clearly a personal area (with personal items, art works, new arrangements of furniture, etc.) can help others understand what that group is about and who is in it.

A related factor that impinges on interpersonal as well as intergroup relations is that of visibility of people to one another. One feature of the open office landscape design is that it allows people to see one another and get a picture of the "comings and goings" of the system. In a study of short-term community development (3), I found that a group which had a setting which allowed members to see one another as they moved about or gathered for meetings seemed to facilitate development of a cohesive community, and a setting that blocked this visibility helped to inhibit community development. If an organization can structure its spaces can have both privacy when they choose and observability of major movements and interactions, this should facilitate both individual and group sense of identity.

Another spatial factor in system identity is the cues that the organization's facilities provide to itself and the outside world about its values and preferences. The public image of a company is often formed this way, even if it does not always occur as planned. A firm may build a new building to say that they are "progressive,modern, and efficient," and be read as "cold, technological, inhuman, and insensitive," (especially if they destroyed a landmark in order to build their new box).

Another problem with spatial identity and choices is that often there is not agreement about central qualities. Its facilities can reflect this, as in the case of the graduate business school that bought an historic building and built a new concrete and glass wing out the back. This beautifully captured their felt demands to be both change-agents pushing business to new frontiers and the guardians of traditional values.They at least represented this clearly and nicely in their building--many organizations show this through totally bland choices which illustrate their lack of clarity about identity.

Reality Testing
    The final criterion of organizational health was a system's ability to obtain necessary information in an undistorted form about both its internal state and the world around it. At the most general level we can say that settings that block free information flow or encourage distortions will inhibit reality testing more than those that do not.

We have already considered the rigid separation of territories between groups in a system. This can be costly if it leads to restrictions in the sharing of information necessary to either

group. Sheer physical distance can also have this effect, as when the corporate officers at headquarters get out of touch with what is going on at field locations.Lack of contact not only reduces information, it makes the field groups feel that they are outsiders.When they do actually go to other locations, the time required allows ample warning and a "grand tour" is set up for a controlled route,allowing them to see a carefully managed "reality" (reminiscent of the rennovation of building fronts by the Soviets for the Tashkent conference several years ago).The separation and feelings of threat from the top lead the visitors to be treated like outsiders, not members of the same joint effort.

Therefore, facilities that are close together can promote a clear picture of what goes on.At the same time, they also allow the possibility of distortion. For example,an executive who wants to raise an important(for him)issue with another whose office is visible nearby can wait until he sees the other come out and the "accidentally" bump into him and mention the issue in casual conversation. If proximity were not in his favor he probably would have to initiate the contact more directly,which would give a more accurate picture of his concern.

Distortions or reduced information flow also occur in settings that reinforce social distance.Great differences in luxury between a boss' and subordinate's offices can promote a systematic "good news" bias in the subordinate's reports in that office. Social workers have reported similar difficulty in getting valid information from clients if interviews are held in a caseworker's office that is well-appointed compared with the client's spaces.Similarly,the boss on the top floor of his organization's offices is less likely to sense the mood or climate of the system than is one who is located in the middle.In fact, I have seen cases where day-to-day screening of the "executive suite" from real life was so complete that they must have wanted it that way.

In a similar process, whole organizations can help or hinder their sense of reality by where they locate.If an organization such as a community action group wants to get accurate feedback about its effects on the client community, it must not locate itself somewhere else or build barriers to entry.

One final effect of space on reality testing is the phenomenon of privacy. It is well known that people are open to different degrees when they are in private and public (as felt by them) settings. The open office layouts may have the mixed effect of promoting more general interaction and visibility and at the same time reducing the depth of sharing about difficult issues. Of course this results from a joint working of the physical and social space: a person is not as open when he feels he will be overheard (spatial) and he feels that it would be a bad thing to be overheard (social). If the norms promote trust and sharing, then public spaces can enhance the depth of sharing. A president-vice-president team decided to have their desks in the same area on the assumption that whatever one was dealing with was fair game (and in fact important) for the other to at least be aware of. The result, as they report it, is a greater sense of teamwork than thought possible before.

Properties in the Setting

Rather than give more examples, I would like to provide a brief list of some of the dominant qualities of the setting that have recurred in my observations. These represent in essence some dimensions that could be used by designers in conjunction with data about a social system to create spaces that will promote rather than deteriorate the health of that system.

* Physical Distances- the location of people and groups near or far from one another.
* Functional Distances- arrangements of facilities and their impact on the energy required for face-to-face contact in the same general location.
* Interference- traffic patterns, noise etc. that block concentration.
* Visibility- the extent to which arrangements allow people to see each other and to see movement.
* Themes/Mood- cues of the arrangements, decorations, or past history of a place that increase the prob-

ability of certain thoughts, associations, or feelings.
* Power Cues- the degree to which the setting has reminders about who has more and less power.
* Power cues/Historical-reminders in the setting about how it got that way--who made the decisions.
* Boundaries- the degree of clarity and permeability of divisions between different groups, and between the system and its environment.

There is one final process issue which is likely to affect system choices about their spaces. The main theme here has been that the quality of an organization's settings influences its health as a system. Unfortunately the converse also tends to be true: a healthy organization will be more likely than an unhealthy one to make good choices about its spaces. It will get more accurate information, process it better, understand more about the need for flexibility, and have a better sense of what it is and where it is going. This suggest what many designers already know in practice: it is difficult to engage in a healthy design process with an unhealthy system. This also suggests that a design project would be more effective if linked to a social system diagnosis and, if appropriate, with developmental activities to increase the system's competence in making spatial (and other) decisions.

References

(1) Bennis, Warren, Changing Organizations, New York: McGraw-Hill, 1966.

(2) Steele, Fred, "Physical Organizational Development," in H. Hornstein et al (eds), Strategies of Social Change Glencoe: The Free Press, 1970 in press.

(3) Steele, Fred, "The Impact of the Physical Setting on the Social Climate at Two Comparable Laboratory Sessions," Human Relations Training News, Vol. 12, No. 4, 1968.

Processes Which Mediate Behavior-Environment Congruence: Some Suggestions for Research[1]

by Allan W. Wicker

Department of Psychology, University of Illinois

Abstract

It is suggested that Barker's behavior setting is a useful environmental unit, but that research on this unit should go beyond static description to consider the following question: What events or processes mediate the influence of environments (behavior settings) on behavior? In this context, several psychological theories are discussed: operant learning, observational learning, behavior setting theory, a model of adaptation to environments, and social exchange theory. Several suggestions for research are offered.

The Importance of the Immediate Socio-Physical Environment

When social scientists take the trouble to observe the same person or group in a number of different naturally-occurring settings, they invariably conclude that the immediate socio-physical environment is an important determinant of behavior (cf. Barker, 1965, 1968; Bijou, Peterson, & Ault, 1968; Ellsworth, Foster, Childers, Arthur, & Kroeker, 1968; Gump, Schoggen, & Redl, 1957, 1963; Raush, Dittman, & Taylor, 1959; Raush, Farbman, & Llewellyn, 1960; Willems, 1969). For example, Harold Raush and his colleagues reported that the interactions among eight-to-ten-year-old boys were generally friendly in settings where food was available (breakfast, lunch, dinner, snacks) but that in structured competitive games, interactions not required by the games were often hostile.

The importance of the immediate situation has also been shown by research involving self-reports of subjective states rather than observation of overt behavior (Endler & Hunt, 1966, 1969; Moos, 1968). To illustrate, Rudolph Moos reported that staff members of a psychiatric hospital rated their feelings as being considerably more sociable and friendly at lunch than in community meetings of patient groups.

In short, the available evidence suggests that both overt behaviors and psychological states are affected as socio-physical environments change. A corollary to this conclusion is that most of the time, most people behave in ways that are compatible with or adaptive to their immediate social-physical environments. This is not to suggest, of course, that everyone in the same situation behaves in the same way, but rather that most of the various behaviors which occur are at least compatible with, if not facilitative of, the setting. The behaviors being referred to here are relatively molar, goal-directed acts, such as talking, drinking, sitting, marching, etc. The fit between the immediate socio-physical environment and the behaviors within it is hereafter referred to as behavior-environment congruence.

Reactions to Incongruence between Behaviors and Environments

Laymen generally take the phenomenon of behavior-environment congruence for granted. When people see someone behaving inappropriately in a setting, they often made broad inferences about the traits the deviant individual possesses, inferences which would not be made about non-deviants. The person may be labeled as hostile, crude, sick, ignorant, or careless, depending upon the nature of his deviant behavior, his apparent knowledge of what is appropriate, and his apparent freedom to behave in other ways (cf. Heider, 1958; Jones & Davis, 1965; Steiner, in press). And depending upon how he is labeled, he may be expelled, ignored, physically restrained, laughed at, or instructed by those observing his actions.

Some reactions to incongruence between behaviors and environments are illustrated in the following excerpt from John Steinback's The Grapes of Wrath. In the excerpt, two rural Oklahoma children are exploring a camp which their family entered late the preceding night. Their first experiences with a modern toilet are described:

> Ruthie...led the way into the building. The toilets lined one side of the large room, and each toilet had its compartment with a door in front of it. The porcelain was gleaming white. Hand basins lined another wall, while on the third wall were four shower compartments.
>
> "There," said Ruthie. "Them's the toilets. I seen 'em in the catalogue."

The children drew near to one of the toilets. Ruthie in a burst of bravado, boosted her skirt and set down. "I tol' you I been here," she said. And to prove it, there was a tinkle of water in the bowl.

Winfield was embarrassed. His hand twisted the flushing lever. There was a roar of water. Ruthie leaped into the air and jumped away. She and Winfield stood in the middle of the room and looked at the toilet. The hiss of water continued in it.

"You done it," Ruthie said. "You went an' broke it. I seen you."

"I never. Honest I never."

"I seen you," Ruthie said. "You jus' ain't to be trusted with no nice stuff."

/Later, Ruthie tells her mother that Winfield has broken a toilet./

Ma was apprehensive. "Now what did you do? You show me." She forced them to the door and inside. "Now what'd you do?"

Ruthie pointed. "It was a-hissin' and a-swishin'. Stopped now."

"Show me what you done," Ma demanded.

Winfield went reluctantly to the toilet. "I didn' push it hard," he said. "I jus' had aholt of this here, an--" The swish of water came again. He leaped away.

Ma threw back her head and laughed, while Ruthie and Winfield regarded her resentfully. "Tha's the way she works," Ma said. "I seen them before. When you finish, you push that."

/The children leave and Ma remains to wash up. She hears a step behind her and turns around./

An elderly man stood looking at her with an expression of righteous shock.

He said harshly, "How you come in here?"

Ma gulped, and she felt the water dripping from her chin and soaking through her dress. "I didn' know," she said apologetically. "I thought this here was for folks to use."

The elderly man frowned on her. "For men folks," he said sternly. He walked to the door and pointed to a sign on it: MEN. "There," he said. "That proves it. Didn' you see that?"

"No," Ma said in shame, "I never seen it. Ain't they a place where I can go?"

The man's anger departed. "You jus' come?" he asked more kindly. "...if you want a ladies' toilet, you jus' go on the other side of the building. That side's yourn." (Steinback, 1939, pp. 409-412.)

In the example, inappropriate behaviors in the unfamiliar restroom led observers to respond with laughter and harsh questioning, which in turn led the newcomers to feel embarrassed and to change their behaviors. The present paper is concerned with events, such as those described, which occur to shape behavior to be compatible with the immediate situation. Before discussing the processes which mediate behavior-environment congruence, however, the question of how the environment can most profitably be conceived will be considered.

The Behavior Setting: A Useful Environmental Unit

It should be kept in mind that any conception of the environment which dichotomizes components into environmental and non-environmental features undoubtedly oversimplifies complex interrelationships (Proshansky, Ittelson, & Rivlin, 1970). However, such breakdowns may be necessary for research purposes.

One way of conceiving of the environment is to include only inanimate physical features, such as furniture, walls, and spatial arrangements of objects, and to exclude the behaviors of people. This approach has the advantage of conceptual clarity, since stimuli can be readily classified as physical or behavioral, but it does not adequately represent the range of stimuli to which a person is exposed, since social inputs are ignored (Gump, 1967).

A second alternative is to view the environment as a network of social roles and norms, of expectations and rules of proper behavior. Advantages of this approach include the possibility of representing several simultaneous sources of influence on the individual (as in role conflict) and the possibility of representing hierarchical and/or horizontal components of environments (as in an organization chart). But actual environmental events in terms of overt behaviors may not coincide with the expected or prescribed patterns, and physical aspects of the environment are given secondary status or may not be represented at all.

A third conception of the environment is reflected in the behavior setting unit, which includes both physical components and overt behaviors (rather than expectations). A behavior setting has the following characteristics: (a) one or more regularly occurring or standing patterns of behavior (for example, lecturing, listening in an academic class), (b) behavior patterns which are compatible with and closely related to the physical characteristics of the place in which the behaviors occur (for example, chairs in a classroom all face the front, the blackboard used by the lecturer is in a location readily visible from the chairs), and (c) temporal and physical boundaries (for example, class begins at 8:00 and ends at 8:50; it occurs within an area bounded by four walls; the behaviors in the class are different from those in the hall, just outside the boundaries). (See Barker, 1968, pp. 18-91 for precise rules regarding the identification of behavior settings.) The following are examples of kinds of public (non-family) behavior settings: church worship services, softball games, banks, sheriffs' offices, grocery stores, taverns.

Research by Barker and his colleagues has examined the behavior of the same individuals across different behavior settings, as well as the behavior of different individuals in the same settings. The research has shown behavior settings and characteristics of behavior settings to be important determinants of the overt behavior of children, adolescents, and adults (cf. Barker, 1965, 1968; Barker & Barker, 1961; Barker & Gump, 1964; Willems, 1967; Wicker, 1968, 1969b, 1969c; Wicker & Mehler, in press). This conclusion might appear to be an artifact, in that one of the criteria for identifying behavior settings is the existence of regularly-occurring patterns of behavior. However, in most of the investigations suggesting setting influences on behavior, observers have not merely noted whether or not people show the standing patterns of behavior. Rather, components of settings, such as population density, have been related to finer variables, such as degree of participation in the behavior patterns. Moreover, the problem is avoided if one observes the behavior patterns of a setting and then later observes the behaviors of people entering the setting for the first time. In this case the newcomers' behaviors do not serve as a basis for identifying the setting; if they come to engage in the standing patterns of behavior, it is not due to the procedures employed in selecting environments.

In the remainder of the present paper, the environment will be conceived of in terms of behavior settings, and unless otherwise stated, the terms, behavior settings, setting and environment will be used interchangeably.

The process of identifying and describing behavior settings requires non-interfering, unobtrusive observers, who note the physical and temporal aspects of the settings, as well as the patterns of behavior which occur. Kenneth Craik (1970) has suggested that such an "ecological analysis" of designed environments can be useful to environmental psychologists and designers in that it provides information on what actually occurs within settings, and also permits the study of spatial aspects of behavior.

Craik's suggested ecological analysis and much of the research on behavior settings focus on more or less static descriptions of settings and the events which occur within them. The questions asked are "what takes place, where it takes place, and when it takes place (Craik, 1970, p. 24)." Such data can be extremely informative and useful. See, for example, studies of hospital environments by Gump and Jones (1970) and Proshansky, Ittleson, & Rivlin (1970).

An Additional Question: "Why?"

There is, however, a complementary question which is of fundamental scientific importance and which has practical implications for the environmental disciplines. Stated most simply, the question is why do predictable, regular patterns of behavior occur within the boundaries of settings? What experiences do people have which lead them to change their behaviors as they go from one setting to another? And how is it possible for people to behave appropriately when they enter an unfamiliar setting? What mechanisms exist in settings to keep the behaviors of the occupants within the range acceptable to other people and congruent with the physical features of the setting?

Obviously, the question of why people show behavior-environment congruence is not easily answered, and relevant evidence will more difficult to obtain than descriptions of settings. In order to study the dynamics of the man-environment relationship, investigators must carefully select naturally-occurring settings so as to maximize the probability of obtaining relevant data. Suppose one is interested how children come to show the required behavior in a school classroom, for example, proper use of desks, blackboards, when to speak, when to listen, and so on. He would probably find much relevant data at the first few sessions of a kindergarten class attended by children who had not previously been to nursery school. Specific kinds of acts (for example, the teacher's instructions regarding how to behave) must be given special attention, and sequences of events (for example, children's reactions to instructions, and the teacher's responses to the children's acts) carefully noted. Extended observations over time (for example, from the first kindergarten session until the setting stabilizes) would be necessary (cf. Altman & Lett, 1970). In order to study certain specific questions, natural settings might be systematically modified (cf. Weick, 1968) or special environments created (cf. Altman & Haythorn, 1967).

Some Possible (and Partial) Answers to the Question, "Why?": Suggestions from Selected Psychological Theories

In the remainder of the present paper, several psychological theories of behavior are examined in an attempt to understand some of the processes which mediate behavior-environment congruence. These include operant and observational learning theories, behavior setting theory, a model of adaptation to the environment, and reward-cost analysis. Suggestions for future research, and possible implications for environmental planners will be discussed.

Operant Learning

Theory

One rather obvious answer to the question of why people behave in ways congruent with their immediate environments is that they have learned to do so by trial and error. Inappropriate behaviors may have been followed by negative reinforcers, i.e., stimuli which reduce the probability of the behavior, and appropriate behaviors followed by positive reinforcers, i.e., stimuli which increase the probability of the behavior (cf. Bijou & Baer, 1961, 1965; Millenson, 1967; Skinner, 1953). The source of reinforcement may be the social environment, as when a parent praises a child for using an eating utensil properly (positive reinforcement), or scolds him for standing on a rocking chair (negative reinforcement). Physical laws also operate to provide consistent reinforcement contingencies for some acts involving the physical environment. For example a child may experience the negative consequence of not getting any food when he tries to eat soup with his fork. And standing on a rocking chair is likely to result in a fall and consequent pain.

There are relatively few behaviors, if any, which are consistently followed by positive or negative reinforcers, regardless of the situation. Rather, the same behaviors which are positively reinforced in one situation may be negatively reinforced in another situation. People are able to obtain positive reinforcements and to avoid negative reinforcements by attending to certain environmental cues, or discriminative stimuli, which signal what consequences will follow from a given act. Any aspect of the environment which a person is capable of perceiving may become a discriminative stimulus if in its presence certain responses lead to different consequences than the same responses to in its absence. For example, the behavior of continuing through an intersection without stopping is sometimes positively reinforced by moving quickly and smoothly with the traffic and at other times is negatively reinforced by being ticketed by a policeman. By attending to the traffic signal, which serves as a discriminative stimulus, a driver obtains information about what will be the consequence of proceeding through the intersection. Here is another example: to renters of slum tenements, the presence of a front stoop on a building has come to serve as a signal (a discriminative stimulus) that teenage gangs are likely to congregate, and to rent an apartment in such a building is likely to lead to trouble (Sampson, 1970).

Behavior settings serve as discriminative stimuli to their occupants. Loud, boisterous behavior may be positively reinforced in some settings, such as neighborhood taverns, parties, and football games, but negatively reinforced in other settings, such as physicians' offices, funeral chapels, and golf tournaments. It should be noted, of course, that behavior settings are extremely complex patterns of stimuli, involving physical objects, people, and patterns of behavior within a bounded area, and that any one component or combination of components can serve as a discriminative stimulus. For example, a combination of stimuli may make up the discriminative stimulus signaling to a student that talking aloud is negatively reinforced: the physical setting of a school classroom, the presence of the teacher, the presence of quiet classmates, the ringing of the school bell at the beginning of the class.

As they create and modify environments, designers also create and alter discriminative stimuli and consequently, the behaviors which occur within the environments. A good example of this comes from the study of a psychiatric ward by Ittelson and his colleagues (Ittelson, Proshansky, & Rivlin, 1970). These investigators noted that an overheated, poorly furnished solarium was rarely used by patients. When drapes were installed to keep out the hot sun and more comfortable furniture was added, the patients began to occupy the room more frequently and to show increased social behavior. For the patients, the refurnished aspects of the room came to signal that entering the room would lead to different consequences than it formerly had--they would be more comfortable and there would be people with whom they could talk.

Suggestions for Research

Unfortunately, there appears to be little research on the question of which specific stimuli or classes of stimuli (for example, physical objects, presence or absence of other people, behaviors of other people, spatial arrangements of objects and people) serve as the discriminative stimuli for behaviors in naturally occurring settings. Perhaps the best approach is systematically to alter stimuli in a setting and to observe directly the responses of the occupants. For example, one might ask subjects to prepare several meals in one or the other of two kitchens of different design, and then observe their behaviors as they worked. Similar procedures could be employed for virtually any design feature whose effects one wished to investigate. Such experiments, although costly, seem to be very much worthwhile, especially when the information obtained is used in making decisions which will affect large numbers of users.

Owing to the cost of this procedure, however, it seems necessary to consider alternative strategies which more or less approximate the ideal suggested. One possibility would be to follow the logic employed in Harry Triandis' (1964) exploratory study involving what he calls the behavior differential, a questionnaire composed of scales on which respondents indicate the likelihood that they would show each of a number of behaviors toward a given stimulus person. Adapting this procedure to the study of environments might involve preparation of a set of photographs or drawings of rooms (or buildings, parks, etc.) which are identical except for one or several features: wall color, styles of furniture, presence of windows, a fireplace, etc. A list of behaviors which conceivably might occur in the rooms would be prepared. Subjects would be asked to indicate the likelihood that they would engage in each of the behaviors in each room pictured. This information could be used in numerous ways. For example, designers thus might be able to determine if their conceptions of how a room will be used coincide with the judgments of potential users.

It should be noted that in the above suggestion, subjects are not asked to rate their liking for or perceptions of a setting or components of settings. Recent research has suggested that subjects' judgments about how they would respond in hypothetical situations are consistently better predictors of actual behaviors than are traditional measures of attitude (Wicker, 1970). In fact, a recent review of the social science literature on the relationship between verbal expressions of attitudes and overt behaviors toward the attitude objects, led to the following conclusion:

> The studies cited...have covered a wide range of subject populations, verbal attitude measures, overt behavioral measures, and attitude objects. Taken as a whole, these studies suggest that it is considerably more likely that attitudes will be unrelated or only slightly related to overt behaviors than that attitudes will be closely related to actions. . . . Only rarely can as much as 10% of the variance in overt behavioral measures be accounted for by attitudinal data (Wicker, 1969a, pp. 65-66).

Although none of the studies in the review used designed environments as attitude objects, it is difficult to think of any reason why the attitude-behavior relationship should be any stronger in that area than in any other. And in fact, the report by Proshansky et.al.(1970) that features of the physical environment rarely enter into users' awareness suggests that this lack of saliency may make the attitude-behavior relationship even weaker when designed environments are studied.

Strictly speaking, a given feature of the environment serves as a discriminative stimulus for a person because of his prior experience, and thus one can speak of a discriminative stimulus in a general sense, that is, as applying to many people, only when he has reason to believe that many people have had similar experiences with the stimulus in question. While some stimuli probably do serve as discriminative stimuli for large segments of a culture (for example, traffic signs) others may serve as discriminative stimuli for smaller subgroups (for example, front stoops on apartment buildings) or for single individuals. Thus in conducting research of the kind suggested above, an investigator should be careful to include

in his sample, representatives of all groups to which he wishes to generalize the results. Also, if one examined responses from a broadly selected sample, he should compare the responses of any subgroups, such as social classes, sexes, age groups, races, for which he might expect different training experiences.

Another approach to understanding the learning aspects of behavior-environment congruence would be to observe parents or other adults as they train children to behave in new environments, noting the techniques of training, and the cues pointed out to children (for example, "don't run in the living room," cf. Schoggen, 1963; Dyck, 1963). One could study naturally occurring settings such as the kindergarten class referred to earlier, or specially created novel settings which are of theoretical or practical importance.

Observational and Instructional Learning

Theory

In the operant learning paradigm, in order for learning to occur a person must emit a given behavior, which is followed by a positive or negative reinforcer. The learning process to be considered now is observational learning, in which a person's behavior is affected merely by his observations of the actions of other people and the consequences of their acts. In many instances, observational learning is a more efficient and less dangerous way of acquiring behaviors than by trial and error (Bandura, 1965; 1969). For example, a newcomer to an apartment house who observes that his neighbors keep everything under lock and key may imitate their behavior without himself ever being a theft victim.

Observational learning appears to play an important role in the acquisition of behaviors in unfamiliar behavior settings. It is much more efficient for new occupants to attend to the behaviors of others in a setting, and then to imitate them, than to act on impulse and see what consequences follow. This suggests that for the newcomer, the physical aspects of settings may be less important than social aspects. Physical aspects may have an indirect influence, however: the first occupants of a setting may have responded to and been conditioned by the physical environment, with later occupants merely using the learned behaviors of others as cues.

In some instances, the use of written or spoken instructions or rules may be an even more efficient way of acquiring situationally-appropriate behavior than by watching others or by trial and error. (Of course, acquisition of word meaning is based on observational and operant learning, so these processes are not really bypassed.) For example, signs such as "NO RUNNING" and "SHALLOW WATER: DO NOT DIVE" appearing at a swimming pool warn newcomers of potentially dangerous situations. They need not dive themselves nor see someone else dive to learn the consequences of diving near the sign. Signs and instructions contribute to behavior-environment congruence in another way, namely, by directing people into the settings appropriate for the behaviors they wish to enact. Signs such as "MEN" and "FIRST NATIONAL BANK" help assure that people entering these labeled settings will not expect to engage in a behavior pattern which is not available there.

Suggestions for Research

Relating observational learning and instructional learning to behavior-environment congruence suggests several questions for research. One question is how the newcomer selects a behavior pattern to enact from among the various behaviors he sees in a novel setting. A newcomer to a Protestant worship service would observe different behaviors by the pastor, the choir, the ushers, and members of the congregation. Presumably he would follow the behaviors of the congregation, but the basis for his selection of those behaviors is not clear. It could be related to the fact that the members of the congregation are more numerous, that they appear to be more like him, that they are least active, or because of other factors. One way to study this problem would be to place research subjects in settings where the characteristics of the other occupants (e.g., their similarity to the subjects) or their behaviors (e.g., activity level) were systematically varied, and then to observe how these characteristics affect subjects' choices of behavior.

Also, researchers might shift their attention from the behaviors of individuals to characteristics of settings by noting the number and kinds of cues which settings provide to newcomers, and whether the cues are compatible. In some settings, the only cue for proper behavior may be the actions of other occupants, while in other settings cues may be multiple and redundant (cf. Altman & Lett, 1970; Bugental, Kaswan, Love & Fox, 1970). For example, a newcomer to a church worship service might observe several cues that he should stand before singing a hymn with the congregation: besides the congregation's rising to their feet, the organist may strike a sustained chord, the minister may rise and gesture for the congregation to rise, and the program may state that all hymns are to be sung standing. Cues can also be multiple and dissonant, for example, persons might be observed smoking in a room where "NO SMOKING" signs are posted. It might be expected that there would be more cues to proper behavior, and more redundancy of cues, in public settings where newcomers are often found, such as church worship services and tourist attractions, and in settings where inappropriate behavior could result in serious harm to setting occupants, such as zoos, race tracks, and swimming pools.

Preliminary research on these questions

might involve asking subjects to visit behavior settings which are as different as possible from any they have attended before, and which permit them to become actively involved in the ongoing activities. They could then report the behavior patterns occurring in the setting, which of the behavior patterns they engaged in, and the influences on their choice of a behavior pattern, such as the behavior of other people, the physical characteristics of the setting, and spoken or written instructions.

The question of how people adapt to unfamiliar settings or unfamiliar objects in settings should be of interest to planners and architects. In fact, one way of evaluating designed environments might be to observe the ease with which newcomers adapt to the environments when there are no experienced users present. That is, do designers see to it that the occupants of newly created or modified environments are not left to inefficient trial and error learning procedures? Do they provide filmed models or detailed instructions to facilitate usage? And do they assume the responsibility of providing information about the use of environmental features to all subsequent users? For example, how often are house plans permanently installed in new houses so that subsequent occupants can locate wires, water pipes, and so on?

Behavior Setting Theory: A Feedback Model

The conditions which must be met to keep any behavior setting functioning are numerous and complex. Not only must the behavior of the human components be kept within a tolerable range, but the physical components must also function within limits: most settings have implicit requirements regarding noise levels, temperatures, and condition of equipment. Barker (1968) has recently proposed an information-processing, feedback model which attempts to represent the mechanisms which occur to keep setting events within the bounds acceptable to setting occupants.

Theory

Barker's basic assumption is that people obtain satisfactions from the settings they occupy, and thus they actively seek to maintain the settings. Setting occupants act as they have a sensory mechanism which receives and transmits information about the setting to an executive mechanism, which tests the information against the occupants' criteria of adequacy for the setting. If the perceived events, whether social or physical in origin, are judged adequate (not disruptive or dangerous to the setting), occupants employ operating mechanisms, that is, they continue to show the standing patterns of behavior in the setting and continue to receive satisfactions. However, if the events are judged to be disruptive or potentially dangerous to the setting, occupants will employ maintenance mechanisms to bring about changes to restore the setting to a condition which permits their goals to be pursued. Two forms of maintenance are proposed: deviation-countering mechanisms, by which the occupant takes steps to counteract or alter the interfering conditions, and veto mechanisms, by which the person eliminates the interfering conditions. The effectiveness of the maintenance mechanism is then evaluated via the sensory and executive mechanisms: If the maintenance mechanism proves successful, occupants switch to operating mechanisms ("business as usual"). If the maintenance mechanism proves unsuccessful, they continue to employ maintenance mechanisms until the potential threat is corrected.

The operation of maintenance circuits is of particular relevance to behavior-environment congruence. These circuits may involve one person's actions toward a single other setting component, as when a teacher ejects an unruly child from a classroom, or they may involve induction of maintenance forces to other inhabitants. Barker gives the following example of the latter process:

The director of a play notes (sensory mechanism) that the behavior setting Play Practice is not going well, that it is inadequate for the program of the setting and for his goals within it (executive mechanism): the sets are not ready, the lines are not learned. One deviation-countering course he could take (executive mechanism) would be to construct the sets and drill the cast himself (maintenance mechanism). Another would be to bring the state of the setting as he sees it to the attention of some deviant members of the cast, e.g., provide input about the state of the setting to member A and member B. If A and B were to agree with the director's observations (sensory mechanism) and with his evaluation (executive mechanism), actions (maintenance mechanism) along maintenance circuits would increase, and three members would exhibit increased activity via maintenance mechanisms, rather than one (Barker, 1968, p. 175).

It should be kept in mind that not all maintenance circuits in settings occur via human channels, nor do they necessarily act upon human components of settings. For example, thermostatically-controlled heating and cooling systems keep temperatures in settings from becoming too cold or too hot (deviation-countering mechanism).

Suggestions for Research

Most of the research relevant to Barker's model has dealt with the ways setting occupants cope with problems of undermanning, i.e., the lack of sufficient personnel to carry out setting functions (e.g., Barker & Gump, 1964; Wicker, 1968, 1969b, 1969c; Wicker & Mehler, in press; Willems, 1967). A number of important research questions in this area remain to be studied. However, for the present purposes it seems more appropriate to suggest research questions which are more closely related to physical aspects of the environment.

One such question is how people respond to and evaluate the designed environments, such as apartments and offices, which they occupy. Suppose, for example, one wanted to learn about reactions to the married student apartments provided by a university. For each of the mechanisms proposed by Barker, relevant information could be sought. Sensory mechanism: To what features of the apartments are residents most sensitive? Relevant information might be obtained by keeping records of requests for maintenance and complaints to apartment managers, and by asking residents to name what are for them the most salient aspects of the apartment they occupy. It would also be of interest to learn if certain occupants are more sensitive to certain features than are others. For example, couples with children might be more concerned about the availability of play areas and the volume of traffic nearby than childless couples, who might be more concerned with noise from playgrounds and lack of privacy due to the play territories of children. Husbands might be concerned about the absence of space for storing tools; wives might be more concerned with a refrigerator which is too small. Executive mechanism: What are the plans or programs which residents hope to accomplish in the apartment, that is, what are the criteria against which the apartment features are compared? Some couples may be more interested in using their apartments for social events, while others may intend to use them primarily for study. Operating mechanism: What behaviors are carried actually out in the apartment? Maintenance mechanism: How do occupants respond to annoying design features? Deviation-countering mechanism: Do they attempt to alter some features, by, for example, installing additional refrigerators, shower hoses in bathrooms, electric space heaters, etc.? Vetoing mechanism: Do they refuse to use certain areas or furnishings for their designed purposes and merely ignore them? What factors influence whether users will attempt to modify an undesirable design feature, or to refuse to use it? Answers to questions such as these might provide a basis for evaluating designed environments.

Model of Adaptation to Environments

Another process which mediates behavior-environment congruence is the selection of settings by the individual on the basis of his ability and desire to perform the standing patterns of behavior (Barker, 1968, p. 31). Braginsky, Braginsky, and Ring (1969) have explored this problem by examining the "style of adaptation" employed by persons who enter a new community offering a variety of behavior settings. Their model assumes that "(1) the needs, attitudes, goals and interests that a person has at the time of entry into a new environment, as well as his previously learned techniques for adaptation, determine (2) where and how he will spend time in the new environment...which, in turn, influences among other things, (3) what he learns about his new milieu, how long he will remain a resident there, and how visible he is to other members (Braginsky, Braginsky, and Ring, 1969, pp. 78-79)."

Their investigations in a mental hospital are consistent with these assumptions: Some patients entered settings which were highly visible to the hospital staff (for example, group psychotherapy), and showed appropriate behavior in these settings in order to bring about their discharge. Other patients, for whom the hospital served as something like a retreat or resort, avoided the settings most visible to the staff and instead frequented pleasure-oriented settings (for example, the gym and the canteen). The latter group, usually long-term patients, sometimes varied the degree of "normality" of their behaviors depending upon whether they believed the information was to be used to decide about placing them on a locked ward or to decide about their discharge (Braginsky, Braginsky, & Ring, 1969, Chap. 2).

Social Exchange Theory

Theory
The model of adaptation to environments proposed by Braginsky and his colleagues is compatible with a more general formulation of the social psychology of groups proposed by Thibaut and Kelley (1959). Thibaut and Kelley's discussion focuses on the dyad, a two-person relationship, and "begins with an analysis of interaction and of its consequences for the two individuals concerned (p. 10)." Their approach involves examing a "matrix formed by taking account of all the behaviors the two individuals might enact together. Each cell in this matrix represents one of the possible parts of the interaction between the two and summarizes the consequences for each person of that possible event (p. 10)." For each possible action by individuals A and B, there are associated costs and rewards. Rewards are gratifications resulting from the fulfillment of a need or drive, and costs are factors which may inhibit or deter the enactment of a given behavior. It is assumed that net outcomes for A and B resulting from A's given act and B's given act can be specified by subtracting the costs from the rewards.

This reward-cost analysis can most easily be related to behavior-environment congruence and to the model proposed by Braginsky, et.al. by modifying the dyad so that A represents an individual who is considering entering a setting or who has already entered it, and B refers to the behavior setting, rather than a second person. The interaction matrix would then consist of all the possible behaviors A

might enact in the setting, and all of the possible setting events (primarily behaviors by setting occupants) which might affect A. Thus for every possible combination of behaviors of A and B, outcomes for A and B would be specified in the matrix.

To consider a simplified example involving a 2 x 2 matrix, a mental patient might show "normal" or "sick" behaviors in the canteen, and the canteen employees and other occupants might eject the patient or permit him to remain. For each possible behavior of the patient and the other setting occupants, there would be specifiable outcomes. Conceivably, the only cell in the matrix which would have positive outcomes for both the patient and the setting would be the cell representing "normal" behavior by the patient and allowing the patient to remain.

Thibaut and Kelley describe two kinds of standards for evaluating outcomes of interaction: (a) the comparison level, which is "the standard by which the person evaluates the rewards and costs of a given relationship in terms of what he feels he 'deserves'," based on "all of the outcomes known to the member, either by direct experience or symbolically (p. 21)," and (b) the comparison level for alternatives, which is "the standard the member uses in deciding whether to remain in or to leave the relationship," that is, "the lowest level of outcomes a member will accept in the light of available alternative opportunities (p. 21)." Two distinct standards are proposed, since a person may remain in a relationship he regards as unsatisfactory merely because the other available alternatives are still worse. In order for a dyadic relationship to form and continue, both members must experience outcomes which are above their comparison levels for alternatives. Thibaut and Kelley also point out that one alternative which members usually have is being alone, that is, severing the relationship without forming another.

In person-setting dyads, then, the person must be able to obtain outcomes which are more satisfying than those in other settings available to him; otherwise, he will abandon the setting for another more desirable one. (It is hard to conceive of a choice to participate in no setting, with the possible exception of suicide.) The setting, also, must receive outcomes from the person's behaviors which are more satisfactory than those obtainable from other persons who are available to enter and participate in the setting; otherwise, the setting will reject the person and select another, more promising one. Or if the person's behavior provides poorer outcomes than his absence, the setting may reject him without a replacement. It should be kept in mind, however, that there may be heavy costs to a setting for ejecting a person: he may cause a disturbance, initiate legal action, etc.

To continue the example cited earlier,

the patient in the canteen may grow tired of sitting around. He could get up and run around the canteen, but the costs for such behavior would probably be so great that the outcome would be below his comparison level for alternatives. He thus might choose to go to the gymnasium where the outcomes for running are much higher. If he should run in the canteen, however, the outcome for the setting if he were left alone would probably be below its comparison level for alternatives, and its occupants might therefore seek to cease the relationship by ejecting the patient.

The relevance of the concepts of outcomes and comparison levels to problems faced by urban planners can be illustrated with an example from a Chicago newspaper. The article describes the case of a woman who chose to live in an apartment house in a slum area rather than accept an offer of an apartment in Chicago's Cabrini-Green housing project:

> "This place isn't anything to write home about, but I've lived in worse."
>
> She peers thru her window at the street outside. There is no front stoop on her building, a favorable feature from a tenant's viewpoint, because it means teen gang members can't congregate.
>
> The street is dotted with grocery stores, bars, even a laundromat just around the corner. So people are moving around most hours of the day. You have the feeling that if you called for help, someone might come.
>
> But friends of Mary Lou's who live in Cabrini must walk blocks thru deserted streets to buy a loaf of bread or stop in for a beer. Lots of open space is nice--but not at night (Sampson, 1970, p. 18).

Although Mary Lou may consider her apartment somewhat unsatisfactory, she clearly regards it as better than the housing project. Stated in terms of the theory, her outcomes from living in the apartment are below her comparison level, but above her comparison level for alternatives.

Suggestions for Research

One rather obvious implication for research from Thibaut and Kelley's theory which is illustrated in the above example is this: if one is interested in finding out what people want in housing or other designed environments, he should seek to learn whether they prefer one feature over another, and not whether they happen to "like" or "dislike" each feature. He should also be aware of the social consequences of planning decisions. People may like freshly-painted rooms and modern plumbing features, but might not choose apartments having them if doing so means living in fear of personal attack.

As can be seen from the discussion in the preceding section, Thibaut and Kelley's reward-

cost analysis has the advantage of being able to deal with both the selection of settings by persons and the selection of persons by settings. These issues are also interesting problems for research. Let us consider a relatively simple case. Suppose we wish to predict which of two available settings a person will choose to enter. The person could be asked to rate on a continuum of liking each of a number behaviors which might be enacted in one or both of the settings. He could also be asked to rate each of these behaviors a second time, indicating his perception of the degree to which the behaviors are approved or disapproved in each of the settings. One would then predict entrance into the setting for which there was the closer fit between the person's liking for the behaviors and perceived setting approval of the behaviors.

If one wished to predict whether the person would remain in the setting entered, it would be desirable to obtain degree of approval ratings of the behaviors from the regular setting occupants. The closer the correspondence between the individual's liking for the behaviors and the average approval of the behaviors by setting occupants, the more likely it is he would remain in the setting. (This assumes that the person has previously engaged in the behaviors rated; to the extent this is not true, predictions of whether he will remain in the setting would probably be less accurate.)

Conclusion

It has been argued that a fundamental problem in the study of the man-environment relationship is the question of why naturally-occurring socio-physical environments, such as behavior settings, come to be important determinants of human behavior. The major theme of the present paper is that current psychological theory can contribute to an understanding of this problem. Each of the theories discussed is in some ways unique, but there are also numerous points of convergence, suggesting that an attempt to integrate them into a general model may be worthwhile.

One implication of the present attempt to apply the theories to the phenomenon of behavior-environment congruence is the following: Research must reflect the interdependencies of the man-environment relationship. Studies must not treat persons or settings merely as objects to be measured, but rather as interacting components of a system. Complexities must be grappled with, even at the expense of the niceties of research design. Quick and easy research studies must be replaced by careful, thoughtful attempts to understand the dynamics of settings. Research problems must dictate research methods and the choice of measuring instruments, and not the reverse.

Another broad implication for research suggested by the present paper is that the study of adaptations to new or modified environments may prove to be more valuable than investigations which begin after adaptations have taken place. Longitudinal studies which trace the sequence of events leading to stable man-environment relationships are costly but necessary.

References

Altman, I., & Haythorn, W.W. The ecology of isolated groups. Behavioral Science, 1967, 12, 169-182.

Altman, I., & Lett, E.E. The ecology of interpersonal relationship: A classification system and conceptual model. In J.E. McGrath (Ed.), Social and psychological factors in stress. New York: Holt, Rinehart & Winston, 1970.

Bandura, A. Vicarious processes: A case of no-trial learning. In L.Berkowitz (Ed.), Advances in experimental social psychology. Vol. 2. New York: Academic Press, 1965.

Bandura, A. Principles of behavior modification. New York: Holt, Rinehart & Winston, 1969.

Barker, R.G. Explorations in ecological psychology. American Psychologist, 1965, 20, 1-14.

Barker, R.G. Ecological psychology: Concepts and methods for studying the environment of human behavior. Stanford, Calif.: Stanford University Press, 1968.

Barker, R.G. & Barker, L.S. Behavior units for the comparative study of cultures. In B. Kaplan (Ed.), Studying personality cross-culturally. New York: Harper & Row, 1961.

Barker, R.G. & Gump, P.V. Big school, small school. Stanford. Calif.: Stanford University Press, 1964.

Bijou, S. & Baer, D. Child development. Vol. 1 New York: Appleton-Century-Crofts, 1961.

Bijou S. & Baer, D. Child development. Vol. 2 New York: Appleton-Century-Crofts, 1965.

Bijou, S.W., Peterson, R.F., & Ault, M.H. A method to integrate descriptive and experimental field studies at the level of data and empirical concepts. Journal of Applied Behavior Analysis, 1968, 1, 175-191.

Braginsky, B., Braginsky, D., & Ring, K. Methods of madness: The mental hospital as a last resort. New York: Holt, Rinehart, & Winston, 1969.

Bugental, D.E., Kaswan, J.W., Love, L.R., & Fox, M.N. Child versus adult perception of evaluative messages in verbal, vocal and visual channels. Developmental Psychology, 1970, 2, 367-375.

Craik, K. H. Environmental psychology. In New direction in psychology. Vol. 4. New York: Holt, Rinehart, & Winston, 1970.

Dyck, A.J. The social contacts of some Midwest children with their parents and teachers. In R.G. Barker (Ed.), The Stream of Behavior, Appleton-Century-Crofts, 1963.

Ellsworth, R.B., Foster, L., Childers, B., Arthur, G., & Kroeker, D. Hospital and community adjustment as perceived by psychiatric patients, their families and staff. Journal of Consulting and Clinical Psychology, 1968, 32, (5, Part 2).

Endler, N.S., & Hunt, J. McV. Sources of behavioral variance as measured by the S-R Inventory of Anxiousness. Psychological Bulletin, 1966, 65, 336-346.

Gump, P.V., & James, E.V. Patient behavior in wards of traditional and modern design. Report prepared for The Environmental Research Foundation, 2700 W. Sixth St., Topeka, Kansas, 1970.

Gump, P.V., Schoggen, P., & Redl, F. The camp milieu and its immediate effects. Journal of Social Issues, 1957, 13, 40-46.

Gump, P.V., Schoggen, P., & Redl, F. The behavior of the same child in different milieus. In R.G. Barker (Ed.), The Stream of Behavior. New York: Appleton-Century-Crofts, 1963.

Ittelson, W.H., Proshansky, H.M., & Rivlin, L.G. The environmental psychology of the psychiatric ward. In H.M. Proshansky, W.H. Ittelson, & L.G. Rivlin (Eds.), Environmental psychology. New York: Holt, Rinehart, & Winston, 1970.

Jones, E.E., & Davis, K.E. From acts to dispositions: The attribution process in person perception. In L. Berkowitz (Ed.), Advances in experimental social psychology. Vol. 2. New York: Academic Press, 1965.

Millenson, J. R. Principles of behavioral analysis. New York: Macmillan, 1967.

Moos, R. H. Situational analysis of a therapeutic community milieu. Journal of Abnormal Psychology, 1968, 73, 49-61.

Proshansky, H.M., Ittelson, W.H., & Rivlin, L.G. The influence of the physical environment on behavior: Some basic assumptions. In H.M. Proshansky, W.H. Ittelson, & L.G. Rivlin (Eds.), Environmental psychology. New York: Holt, Rinehart, & Winston, 1970.

Raush, H. L., Dittman, A. T., & Taylor, T. J. Person, setting, and change in social interaction. Human Relations, 1959, 12, 361-378.

Raush, H. L., Farbman, I., & Llewellyn, L. G. Person, setting and change in social interaction. II. A normal-control study. Human Relations, 1960, 13, 305-332.

Schoggen, P. Environmental forces in the everyday lives of children. In R. G. Barker (Ed.), The stream of behavior. Appleton-Century-Crofts, 1963.

Simpson, G. Tenement more "human" than hirise. Chicago Today, August 16, 1970, p. 18.

Skinner, B.F. Science and human behavior. New York: Macmillan, 1953.

Steinbeck, J. The grapes of wrath. New York: Viking, 1939.

Steiner, I. Perceived freedom. In L. Berkowitz (Ed.), Advances in experimental social psychology. Vol. 5. New York: Academic Press, in press.

Triandis, H. Exploratory factor analyses of the behavioral component of social attitudes. Journal of Abnormal and Social Psychology, 1964, 68, 420-430.

Thibaut, J.W., & Kelley, H. H. The social psychology of groups. New York: Wiley, 1959.

Weick, K. Systematic observational methods. In G. Lindzey & E. Aronson (Eds.), The handbook of social psychology. Vol. 2. Research methods. (2nd Ed.) Reading, Mass: Addison-Wesley, 1968.

Wicker, A. W. Undermanning, performances, and students' subjective experiences in behavior settings of large and small high schools. Journal of Personality and Social Psychology, 1968, 10, 255-261.

Wicker, A. W. Attitudes versus actions: The relationship of verbal and overt behavioral responses to attitude objects. Journal of Social Issues, 1969, 25 (4), 41-78. (a)

Wicker, A. W. Cognitive complexity, school size, and participation in school behavior settings. Journal of Educational Psychology, 1969, 60, 200-203. (b)

Wicker, A. W. Size of church membership and members' support of church behavior settings. Journal of Personality and Social Psychology, 1969, 13, 278-288. (c)

Wicker, A. W. An examination of the "other variables" explanation of attitude-behavior inconsistency. Unpublished manuscript, Department of Psychology, University of Illinois, 1970.

Wicker, A. W. & Mehler, A. Assimilation of new members in a large and a small church. Journal of Applied Psychology, in press.

Willems, E. P. Sense of obligation to high school activities as related to school size and marginality of student. Child Development, 1967, 38, 1247-1260.

Willems, E. P. Direct observation of patients: The interface of environment and behavior. Paper read at American Psychological Association Convention, Washington, D. C., 1969.

Footnote

[1]Preparation of this paper was facilitated by a grant from the National Institute of Mental Health, United States Public Health Service (Grant No. 1 R03 MH18598-01). The author is indebted to Irwin Altman and J. Richard Hackman for valuable comments on an earlier draft of this paper.

Session Six:

Design Information Systems

Chairman: Charles Burnette
Institute of Environmental Studies, University of Pennsylvania

The Design of Comprehensive Information Systems for Design

by Charles Hamilton Burnette

Ph.D., A.I.A., Institute for Fundamental Studies,
University of Pennsylvania, Philadelphia 19104

Abstract

If general information systems to facilitate environmental design are to supercede the growing collection of specialized programs and services, a better appreciation of the problems and possibilities of such systems is needed. A lack of theory to guide the design of comprehensive systems, the proliferation of more or less specialized and arbitrary high level languages, unintegrated data, inadequate capacity for describing relationships, the complexities of large scale operating systems, and the magnitude of the information problems posed by environmental design have conspired to discourage, confound and diffuse effort. Yet despite these difficulties, progress is being made. Modular, machine independent, user oriented fourth generation software has emerged. Its contribution is discussed. The on-line control of such software by the problem solver by means of a meta-linguistic organization of role oriented subsystems is suggested and outlined. A broad involvement with the problems of comprehensive design-oriented systems is encouraged.

Introduction

Generally speaking most applications of the computer to architectural problems have been limited by their goals, their conceptual approach, and by the programming language or operating system used. They have not been designed to facilitate the direct entry, manipulation and communication of large quantities of information by persons working steadily at computer terminals. Yet, architects and others involved in the design of the environment need to facilitate the entire range of their problem solving activities. If they are to practice a discipline of organization and synthesis they need an integrated system for information handling, documentation and communication that fits in with their natural habits of thought and expression

The task of formulating and implementing an information system of such scope is not well understood. This paper briefly outlines some of the issues, present capabilities and future possibilities for the design of such systems. The intent is to encourage thought and effort toward their realization.

Background

A cursory review of several of the issues to be met by a comprehensive design oriented system is offered as background. Information Retrieval: In practice today information retrieval means the accession of gross units of information through the use of labels, descriptors and, occasionally, graphic symbols. It normally does not mean the retrieval of phrases or other fragments of substantive information embedded in text or pictures. Those systems which retrieve data such as unit costs or quantities for processing are usually very limited by format, content and program structure and are better thought of as data processing systems. Information retrieval implies a more open ended approach and one characterized by a lack of information regarding the exact content of a system. Thus, a problem of identification must be solved in order to obtain information in such a system.

Three approaches to this problem presently dominate the design of IR systems. Coordinate indexing is an approach which applies several indexing terms to each unit record, each term effectively narrows the search space to the limited set of records having all the terms cited. Precise retrieval of a unit record depends on citing all terms or those which are unique to the record. Normally, more records are retrieved than are desired. In coordinate indexing there is no syntax among terms to aid in recognizing their relative importance regarding the document they index. While coordinate indexing systems tend toward a stable vocabulary with time, this vocabulary is usually controlled by professional indexers working through a thesaurus containing synonyms and other lexical controls. Such control is costly and imposes delays in the handling of information that would be intolerable in a design-oriented system. The tendency today is to encourage users to provide key words, and to automate the vocabulary control function of the thesaurus. Coordinate indexing has been appropriately applied to the abstract retrieval system of the Industrialization Forum magazine.[1] The paper by Professor Colin Davidson discusses this application.

The Key Word In Context Scheme presents the key descriptors of a unit record in the context of the title or descriptive phrase in which they occur. The natural syntax of this expression establishes the relative import of each term and assists interpretation. Periodically produced (batch processed) indexes permute the terms to display them each in alphabetical order accompanied by the other terms of the phrase and the accession number of the document. Such indexes are easy to scan and are particularly appropriate for periodical publications and occasional information. They have been employed by the Index Medicus of the Medlars System of the National Institutes of Health.[2]

Classification schemes such as in the Uniform System for Construction Specifications, Data Filing and Cost Accounting[3] have been the traditional means of structuring information for retrieval. These schemes are usually very limited in the subject vocabulary (class labels) which they employ. As a consequence their vocabularies tend to become obsolete even as they become familiar. "Faceted classification" as distinct from subject classification is a relatively new and less familiar approach to classification. It involves a normative partition of the entire domain of a system according to some relatively independent, exhaustive and useful set of viewpoints or facets regarding the problem field served by the system. In practice, in the Coordinated Building Communications System facet classification has been used to unite subject classification with coordinate indexing.[4] This author has proposed a less rigid use of facet classification as a linguistic device along the lines of the form-class conception of language. This application is based on a partition of all information according to its role in a message situation, unit record or statement.[5]

In general, despite the fact that the need for precise identification and retrieval is both critical and immediate in a design-oriented system, there is presently no operating, computer-aided system by which users may identify, structure and retrieve information according to their immediate needs. Most retrieval schemes in the building industry rely on conventional published indexes and microfilm or microfiche records.[6,7]

Interpretation and Compilation: The human interpretation of information in computers today depends largely on the user's knowledge of the conventionalized meanings of the higher level languages which he must use to express his problems (aided occasionally by verbal "comment" that is not processed). These languages are often the ad hoc result of design by committee. They are usually designed to deal with some particular class of problems or to capitalize on some recognized potential. The conventions which result are usually rather arbitrary, unnatural and awkward to use for someone whose primary concern is with the problem he wishes to solve. In large and complex systems, and particularly among time sharing systems, the language which the user employs to communicate with the system tends to be more important or complicated than that which he uses to solve his problems.[8] The design of interpreters or compilers to produce the object code from the input of the higher level languages is also typically ad hoc and machine dependent. Only in a few languages such as L6[9] or IPL-V[10] does the expression in the higher level language correspond closely to assembly language, thereby reducing the task of compilation and the levels of translation required.

Descriptive Specification: The information contained in computerized data banks is almost invariably highly fragmented from a substantive point of view as a result of the specialized goals and declarative conventions of higher level languages. File organization and data structures, even in list processing languages, are also closely tied to the conventions of the language. As a result the user's ability to directly understand and manipulate description in a file as well as the efficient maintenance of the files themselves is usually compromised by the language form by which information is established. This issue of file structure for descriptive specification is addressed in the papers by Charles Davis and Ted Myer in these proceedings. From the substantive point of view computer aids to the preparation of construction specifications and the master specifications with which they deal are often thought of as the foundation of future data banks. However, specification systems today are designed primarily to manipulate text, rearranging it to accord with selected formats. They have very little flexibility with respect to the substantive aspects of the information they manipulate and, being verbally oriented, do not offer facilities for the coordination and maintenance of both graphic and verbal data. A design oriented information system should seek ways to organize verbal and visual description from a common data base leaving the form of output to the user.

Presentation of Information: As just suggested, the form in which information should be displayed or published depends primarily on the needs of the user. Traditionally, verbal and visual description have been handled differently as drawings and written specifications. In addition, paper media tended to force the author of information to either try to anticipate the user's need or to ignore it. The computer, however, offers the possibility of widely different forms for input and output and provides the capability to immediately publish only that information needed for a given task or felt need. Yet today most printout is tied to the particular program being processed rather than being at the discretion of the user. The processing of graphic display is still in its development phase.

Operational Specification: Most programs available to the architect or environmental designer are sequences of logical or numerical operations arranged in a relatively inflexible structure in order to efficiently achieve narrow goals. For example, take A, add to B, put into C, if C greater than X, do D. Similarly, most programs for the design of heating systems, elevators, cut and fill and the like are based on mathematical models which describe the phenomenon with which they deal. These programs typically depend on a complete theory or descriptive specification of the phenomenon. Decision making is aided through the manipulation of a few well defined variables.

On the other hand, programs for network scheduling of construction or resource allocation are less restricted with regard to substantive elements of description but have been limited in the kinds of decisions which they facilitate (i.e., time relationships, costs, etc.). In summary, the writing of design-oriented programs regardless of their application is presently at the cottage industry level, and is producing incompatible products that are not easily modified or integrated into the design process. Programming is not yet a highly organized process for the assembly of modular components into systems open to change.

Evaluation: While useful documentation of architectural programs is only now beginning to emerge[11] there is almost no dynamic evaluation and analysis of the performance of programs, of the way users employ them, or of their effective value. While errors in language use are flagged by the compiler, more general analysis is left to the individual program. Information of the operation of the system itself is directed almost exclusively to those who staff and run it rather than to the problem oriented user who would ultimately like to discover efficiencies in his media as he uses it more and more.

Significant Developments: ICES and AED

The incompatibilities of existing programs and the lack of a framework for their integration and evaluation present problems to the pooling of present capabilities. Two technical developments which may alleviate these problems somewhat are: 1) the emergence of virtual machine control programs such as CP67[12] which allow several users to specify desired machine configurations in a large computer to process programs written for another system; 2) microprocessing in which whole (LSI) memory segments may be individually programmed to allow faster processing on newer equipment of programs written for slower equipment. The approach to coordinated design-oriented systems is more clearly suggested by the concepts of modular software engineering, embodied in the ICES System (Integrated Civil Engineering System) and the AED (Automated Engineering Design) System.

ICES contains four major features: 1) a set of engineering subsystems, each designed to facilitate the work of a particular area of civil engineering; 2) a set of command structured problem-oriented languages used to operate these systems; 3) a command definition language (CDL) and an extension and expansion of Fortran (ICETran) to permit new languages to be designed and embedded in the system or to modify those which exist; 4) an executive system for the above. The philosophy of ICES is user oriented. It has been designed to allow a systems programmer to engineer a dedicated system, and to allow the user to program such a system to solve particular problems. The user may also employ programs developed by others. The command definition and structuring approach favors the user's natural vocabulary somewhat while the free formatting of command identified processes or parts of processes permits him to follow the sequence of solution which he prefers. Both features aid the research and evolution of increasingly efficient and effective design procedures.[13] However, user programs in ICES are

essentially conceived for sequential (command by command) processing. Due to the command structure they are weak in their ability to define and operate on the relational data which is often the most critical information in the design process. It has been noted that many pages of ICES-Build commands are needed for even a greatly simplified description of a simple building.[14] The reduction of this large amount of input probably depends on the ability to integrate the data base (on a larger and more organized basis than the present "common" provides), and to flexibly define relations in substantive description in addition to the present capabilities for defining dynamic arrays for data management.

The AED System sprang from the same background as ICES and offers many similar software engineering features in a significantly different approach. This approach rests on: 1) a general purpose language AED-0, an extended version of ALGOL 60; 2) a library of off-the-shelf components software packages often interlocked closely with the compiled features of the language itself. (For example, the Input-Output Buffer Control Package (IOBCP) provides a common operating system interface to all hardware devices for sequential character and word files. It includes control of logical and physical records, buffering and timing.) The physical form of all such AED software components "is an integrated package of routines - atomic functions which provide input arguments to others so that molecular functions can be built, sub-atomic functions which control detailed mechanisms and prepackaged molecular functions (for redundant needs). These functions are integrated because they share an interlocked set of common variables and data structures.[14] Thirdly, AED provides tools for generating new systems when it is no longer feasible to adapt off-the-shelf components. For example, a subsystem which builds lexical items provides inputs to another system which constructs tables for structuring statements which in turn may help generate either an interpretive or compiling translator. Such features as plex programming (a generalization of list processing) and phrase substitution (permitting embedded assignment and the replacement of a single identifier by an entire program) provide the kind of relational facilities which seem appropriate for design-oriented systems. Perhaps the most important aspect of AED is that it stems from a carefully worked out and rationalized modularity which allows both data and processes to be modeled at various levels of generality in an integrated way that is machine independent. AED is apparently thought of primarily as a means toward the engineering of software systems dedicated to particular problems rather than as a general system for on-line problem definition and solution. Nevertheless its principles of organization suggest the general character of such a system.

A Proposed Approach

Given this background the remainder of the paper will attempt to roughly characterize a system for the design discipline that builds on the AED and ICES experience but which would be intended for general on-line problem solving. The amount of data with which the architect deals, the complexity of his descriptive task and the variety of the considerations which he must make relative to his information leaves no doubt that a design-oriented system must ideally be a large scale interactive system working on integrated data bases. "It becomes worthwhile to enter and update large amounts of data because a single item of information can be entered or revised by one member of a design team and be accessible to all other team members."[15]

If the computer is to become the principal medium for information handling, documentation and communication and thus the principal instrument of the building industry some more natural links to the common understanding of a large body of users than presently exists is needed. The design of such a system is a meta-linguistic problem and involves a completely different approach than the design of a language or program dedicated to a particular class of problems or a specialized need. The goal should be a language-like organization through which the structure and use of the system becomes clearly comprehensible to its users rather than a collection of language conventions keyed to particular expressions. While the AED System is linguistically conceived it is not manifested to the user as a normative guide for his expression. What is needed is a linguistic format like a sentence through which the user works to construct his meaning and its processing counterpart. An English sentence provides a model of such an organization in that it is partitioned into nominals, verbals, adjectivals, etc., that is, into words or phrases which play a recognizable role in the expression as a whole. This model may be generalized to roles in problem solving, categories in operational definitions, information types and other useful paradigms.[16] It can offer a naturally comprehensible organization guide to the construction and use of different software components of the AED variety. A brief review of how such a system might be constituted follows and is represented by Figure 1. For the figure each block represents a role oriented subsystem and the links between blocks indicate the general dependency or syntax between them. The user establishes the role, structure and processing of information by the way in which he establishes and links it within the limitations of the role oriented subsystems and the systematic relationships which hold between them.

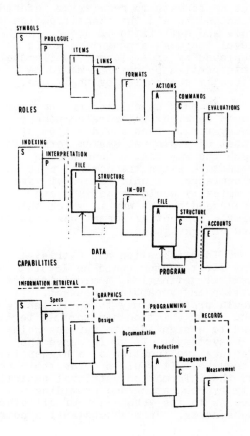

CONTENT OF SUBSYSTEMS

While each subsystem might be used to contribute to or mediate a particular unit record they would also facilitate a summary categorization by role or type of the information in all unit records. This recognition of the type or role of data might be extended to the very complex descriptions or processes through a kind of phrase substitution which would range from the overall content of a system to the content of the assembly statements themselves. Said otherwise, one might in effect categorize the content of a system according to the conventionalized roles and recognize the same roles in a message unit or an expression at the level of a programming language. If these recognitions are similarly flagged and freely substituted one could descend into the machine (as it were) through a kind of phrase substitution modularity. The level of generality of the substituted phrases would be recognized through the structure of use. Thus direct programming by a user would make use of the same cognitive distinctions through which he comprehends the content and use of the system as a whole. This could effectively reduce the interface between user and machine to a discrete set of formats to regularize information and to aid the identification of role and definition of scope. Higher level language expressions would be replaced by those formats while their interpretive processing would be directly controlled by their use.

In this speculated system there would be eight software component subsystems. Each would implement one facet of a general system format in much the way that a noun phrase structure plays the nominal role in a sentence. A unit record of varying complexity would be defined and processed by the way in which this single sentential format was elaborated or aggregated.

Identification and Retrieval: The first system would be devoted to lexical definition, nominal identification and vocabulary control. It would provide a way to establish terms and their relationship to other terms and to assign them to various roles (subsystems). It would serve the declarative function of a higher level language. It would provide the core of the information retrieval capability by regulating and providing access to the vocabulary of all other subsystems. From a substantive point

of view it would permit any author or subsequent user of information to establish any indexing terms which seem appropriate or useful. This additive vocabulary lends itself to coordinate indexing as a means of narrowing the search field. A further narrowing of the field would result by categorizing terms according to the subsystem to which they refer or are assigned. A facility for both the system and the user to discover and declare synonyms based on such role oriented categorization would also effectively reduce the vocabulary and the search space. This facility for recognizing and relating terms would also provide a basis for the study of word use and communication. From such analysis profiles of the word use of individuals could be developed and used to automatically cue him when material related to his interests is added to the system. The automatic translation between technical vocabularies could be similarly facilitated.

Interpretation and Assembly: Because the interpretation of information by man or machine depends on conventions of use there should be a distinct subsystem which established these appreciations of particular messages both for the user (an "introduction" to the content and purpose of a unit record) and the machine (directives to the compiler regarding the unit record). If this executive subsystem worked at the level of a substantive record which might itself be constituted from subordinate records through phrase substitution what one has is a model of the "comment" statements in a given message, a library representation of the structure of the unit record, as distinct from a directory of its contents, a record of its primary antecedents and related unit records,[17] and directives which inform the compiler regarding the assembly and interpretation of the information referenced by the unit record. Packaged together all interpretive and assembly problems relative to a logical record could be localized. From a substantive point of view this system could be of particular value to the job captain or architectural programmer in setting up directives to staff and monitoring their implementation. It could also help in recognizing and using those modular units appropriate to a given purpose which have already been built and established in the system,(i.e., AED)-like components).

Substantive Information-Data Banks: There would also be a distinct subsystem through which to inventory the object data in a unit record and in the system as a whole. This subsystem would be restricted to non-operational substantive information in order to optimize its function as an object file. It would be designed to facilitate the natural accumulation, flexible assembly and selective use of data through a listing of items in a unit record that was itself defined in terms of a list of the attributes and values of the item. The attribute list for each item (or the item list for a unit record) would be open ended to enable new information to be added as required, to build an exhaustive description of each item or to build the scope of a record. This exhaustive description would be edited by the preceding two subsystems according to immediate need. While broadly used to establish any element of a descriptive problem or statement this subsystem would be of particular utility to material suppliers, manufacturers and others who must supply resource information and to specifiers or accountants who must work most directly with the unit type of data involved.

Relational Information and Data Structures: The fourth subsystem would be devoted entirely to the organization and storage of relational information pertaining to the elemental information inventoried in the preceding system. By modeling relational information through representations in the form of trees, strings, networks, etc., in a completely distinct subsystem the correlation, coordination and comparison of like or unlike items or organizations would be facilitated. Only descriptive relationships possible to the items in the elemental subsystem would be modeled - operational relationships describing processes or behaviors being reserved for another subsystem. The relational subsystem for object description would be used for working out assembly, organization and fit, for setting up spatial coordinates and relative locations and for the coordination of structural, plumbing, heating, electrical and other functional lay-outs. Such a system would be of particular use to planners, designers and others involved in the acts of judgment, organization and synthesis.

Because it is a subsystem for structuring substantive data elements only (as distinct from unit records or the various data management link ups) it would provide a focus for optimizing the construction, storage and handling of complex descriptions.

Representational Information - Input Output: There would be a distinct subsystem for all input-output functions serving all peripheral equipment (similar to the IOBCP component of AED). But this would contain both character and word capabilities and graphic display control. It would govern the formatting of all information at the interface between man and machine. It would include a means for giving boundaries to visual forms specified dimensionally and locationally in the data bank and data structure subsystems. At the level of programming language and below it would regulate punctuation and other delimitors. This would facilitate error checking and user notification as an integral part of the input-output component. Graphic programs such as perspective generation and map plotting would perhaps also be integral to the display processor of this component yet work on data collected and initially organized by the central system. Text manipulation programs would belong to this component rather than the central program inventory. The user would work directly with this subsystem through a general format reflecting the eight-part organization of the system as a whole. This general format would organize the access to the specialized formats of the role-oriented subsystems and would be the main instrument for understanding and structuring input and output. Thus, it would be the main linguistic convention that the user would have to learn.

Operational Information - Program Bank: This system would be for operational elements what the data bank of the third system is for object information. It would inventory operations, parts of processes and processes available to the programming user. It would also inventory the substantive information describing elemental activities, events or behaviors in the real world. It may be thought of as a listing of available computational operations (or routines) or real world behaviors from which particular processes or functional models could be assembled. At the level of a unit record it may be thought of as the collection of operational events pertaining to the data specification. The manner in which this inventory is referenced as well as its context in a unit record would signal the difference between machine and substantive information. By this joint inventory the matching of routines with the behavior they describe would be facilitated, gaps in procedural knowledge could be handled judgmentally and simulation would be facilitated.

Control Information - Program Structure: To facilitate direct on-line program building and execution there would be a command system interlocked with the operations, partial processes and programs of the preceding subsystem. This system would be used to structure a program by reference to the program store which would in turn reference data in the data bank or the data structure bank and ultimately drive a compiler or interpreter to generate or execute the object code for a unit record. There would be differences in the mode of commands to signal structuring for the compiler or the interpreter and to permit storage of the command structures in the program store.

Evaluative Information - System Analysis and Feedback: A final system to maintain records and help in the analysis of the operation of the system and the flow of information rounds out the overall system. This subsystem would facilitate analysis and quantification by functioning as a work pad for deriving answers during problem solving and as a recording device and data bank for those substantive and procedural quantifications which are to be retained or continuously monitored. This subsystem would be of particular value to a researcher as well as the operating personnel of the system. It should operate over all of the previous subsystems and provide an evaluative portion for each unit record. The system should be designed to allow several console commanders to constantly monitor the use of a multiprogramming setup.

The implementation of such a system as is suggested would seem beyond the realm of possibility had not ICES and AED already been developed. The rationalization linking language form and role oriented cognitive distinctions, which is at the heart of the proposal for an on line programmable information handling and communication systems, springs from the author's efforts to develop a meta-linguistic approach to computer representation, one more related to human behavior than present day programming languages.[18] The important point to make, however, is that it is reasonable and potentially worthwhile to continue on the path toward an integrated design-oriented information, documentation and communication system for the building industry rather than to surrender completely to the expedient solution and the partial answer.

Notes

1. Wert, Leonard. "Information Retrieval and Industrialization Forum," Industrialization Forum, School of Architecture, Box 1079, Washington University, St. Louis, Missouri 63130. Volume 1, Number 1, October 1969, page 11.

2. Luhn, H. P. Key Word in Context Index for Technical Literature, IBM, August 1959.

3. The American Institute of Architects, et al. The Uniform System for Construction Specifications, Data Filing and Cost Accounting, Title One, Buildings. The American Institute of Architects, 1735 New York Avenue, Washington, D. C., 1966.

4. Bendslev, Bjorn; Burgess, David. "Coordinated Building Communication," The Architects Journal, Architectural Press Ltd., 9-13 Queen Ann's Gate, London, SWI, England, 25 March and sequel.

5. Burnette, Charles. "A Linguistic Structure for Architectonic Communication," Response to Environment, The Student Publication of the School of Design, North Carolina State University, Raleigh, North Carolina. Volume 18, page 101.

6. IDAC System, 425 East 53rd Street,
    New York, New York 10022.

7. Showcase Corporation, Showcase
    Building, 6230 John R. Street,
    Detroit, Michigan 43202.

8. Sammett, J. E. Programming
    Languages. Prentice Hall, Inc.,
    Englewood Cliffs, New Jersey,
    1967, page 87.

9. Knowlton, K. C. $_6$A Programmer's
    Description of L^6, Bell Telephone
    Laboratories Low Level Linked
    List Language. Bell Telephone
    Laboratories, Murray Hill, New
    Jersey, February 1966.

10. Sammett, Op. cit., page 388.

11. Stewart, C.; Teicholz, E.; Lee,
     K. Computer/Architecture
     Programs 1, 2, 3. Center for
     Environmental Research, 955
     Park Square Building, Boston,
     Massachusetts 02116.

12. Bairstow, J. "Many From One:
     The Virtual Machine Arrives,"
     Computer Decisions. 850 3rd
     Avenue, New York, New York 10022.
     January 1970, page 28.

13. Teague, L. "Research in Computer
     Applications to Architecture,"
     Harper, N., editor. Architecture
     and Engineering, McGraw-Hill,
     New York, New York 1968, page
     197.

14. Ibid., page 210.

15. Ross, D. "Fourth Generation
     Software: A Building Block
     Science Replaces Hand-Crafted
     Art," in Computer Decisions,
     850 3rd Avenue, New York, New
     York 10022, April 1970, page 38.

16. Teague, Op. cit., page 211.

17. Burnette, Op. cit.

18. Bolt, Beranek and Nerman.
     Development of Notation and Data
     Structure for Computer Applica-
     tions to Building Problems,
     PB 174 795, Clearinghouse,
     Springfield, Virginia 22151,
     March 1969.

An Operating System of Building Information

A Case History of Applied Research, conducted jointly by teams at
Washington University, St. Louis, the Universite de Montreal and
the University of California at Los Angeles

**Research Team: Professor Colin H. Davidson, Mr. Michel Jullien,
Mr. John Roberts, Mr. Helmut Schulitz and Mr. Leonard Wert.
Notes prepared by Professor Colin H. Davidson
and Mr. John Roberts.**

Abstract

The project is described as applied research; it has grown up, in response to the information system needs of "Industrialisation Forum" - a quarterly publication at Washington University and the Université de Montréal. Experience shows the advantages of co-ordinate indexing for information storage and retrieval, compared to subject classification; procedures are described and the importance of a controlled vocabulary common to the indexer and searcher is discussed. Generation of the Thesaurus of Common Noun Key Words needs careful study; new logical rules have been devised for establishing hierarchies of terms - these introduce the new relationship: Part Term/ Whole Term to the current Narrower Term/Broader Term. In addition, the concept of Proper Noun Keywords is introduced and their rôle in information storage and retrieval discussed.

Introduction: Reasons for the Project

Today, research workers and practitioners in almost every field are faced with the increasingly time-consuming problems of information retrieval. The building industry is no exception; indeed, the fragmented structure of the industry contributes to the problems of information retrieval and information flow. Members of the team are active in the field of applied building research and as a result of suggestions made at the 1968 ACSA (1) seminar, it was decided to confront this set of urgent requirements and respond to them. Our immediate response was to launch "Industrialisation Forum". (2) Since that time, our research work in information science, necessary for the production of "I.F.", has assumed an importance in its own right. However, our research findings can (and, through publication dead-lines, have to) be applied and tested in practice; risks of yielding to expediency, and taking short cuts, can be minimised by conscious planning. We feel that this relationship between our research and its application most useful.

In the early stages of planning "I.F.", two important decisions were made: firstly, that the publication would not only contain information, but should constitute, by its nature, an information system so that readers could re-trieve the information as their need arose; secondly, that the publication should be aimed toward anyone interested in the current changes in building (which are commonly called "industrialization") and should not reflect the information habits of any single group. The result of these decisions (made in the early summer of 1969) are embodied in "I.F.", the first issue of which (October 1969) included a description of the system prepared by Leonard Wert. (3)

Since the publication of "I.F." vol. 1, no. 1, the project team has necessarily been applying its original decisions to subsequent editions of the periodical. However, our interest in, and emerging skills in, information have been leading into other task areas. These are described in greater detail later in these notes.

The Principles of Information Handling: Post-Co-ordination

Several of the members of the project team had suffered from the current building information classification systems - U.D.C., SfB and so on. All of these systems fail to operate as effective guides for information storage and retrieval for several reasons: firstly, no document treats one subject only; secondly, each reader approaches each document with a specific slant corresponding to his interests at a particular moment in time; thirdly, subjects and areas of interest change, going beyond the original scope of the classification system.

Consequently, it was decided to extend the method of post-co-ordination - developed in other fields - into our own subject area, which was beginning to be described as "building science and technology".

Post-coordination (which could also be called "post classification") allows decisions about the relevance of the information in any document to be determined by the person who retrieves the document and not by the person who puts it into storage, as is the case with subject classification. The routines employed are probably familiar to many people by now, and comprise the following steps (presented here in outline):-

A. Information Storage

1. A document (book, report, letter, etc.) is received into the library; it is given an accession number;

2. It is read, and the concepts it contains are described by the selection of up to ten to fifteen keywords chosen from the controlled vocabulary (see next section); these words are displayed somewhere on the document where (a) they serve a control function and (b) they constitute a list of the concepts in the document (quite often an abstract is prepared at this time, it will carry the same accession number and the same keywords);

3. Special cards are prepared, one for each new keyword, and the accession number of the document is entered on it (this may be written or may be punched out - as in the case of perforated cards of some sort). In the case of keywords that have been found in some document earlier, and for which keyword cards have already been made, the existing card is brought out, and the accession number of the new document is added to it.

4. The keyword cards are filed alphabetically, and the document is put away in a location which is uniquely described by the accession number given to it (the accession number is a "zip-code" for the "address" of the shelf or file where the document is located and nothing more).

B. Information Retrieval

1. A person requiring a document about some subject (and he may or may not know that such a document exists), describes the concepts that constitute his area of interest, and about which he seeks information, using keywords selected from the controlled vocabulary; we explain the significance of the keywords later on in these notes. Experience shows that the searcher may use from five to ten words;

2. He picks out the keyword cards corresponding to his selection. Any accession number common to all of the cards he has chosen will indicate the address of documents about his subject. Note that accession numbers common to most of the cards will indicate documents about a large part of his area of interest;

3. He goes to the shelves and retrieves the document(s).

In this sequence: (a) the person who enters the keywords does not classify the document, he merely describes it using the controlled vocabulary and this stage should be as objective as possible; (b) the person who retrieves the document "classifies" his interest by his choice of keywords from the controlled vocabulary. There is no a priori res-

triction on his interest; rather his unique interest is expressed in terms of combinations of keywords whose meanings are carefully controlled.

Search Patterns

Our experience through observation of other information systems under operating conditions e.g. KWIC, SfB, UDC, etc. has led us to believe that there are two distinctly different types of information search: firstly, there is the general search where the researcher is not sufficiently well acquainted with the search area he is defining to give any clues other than the general concepts of his requirements; he does not know if any information exists in the area he is attempting to describe nor is he aware of the existence of other researchers active in the area; at best he can describe his problem in terms of a set of Common Noun Keywords such as exist in published thesauri. Secondly, a search may be undertaken by the researcher who either has definite knowledge that a document exists or can suggest the names of organisations or people responsible for the document, its physical form or its approximate date of publication. For example, it is common to be asked a question of the form: "Do you have that paper published by the National Research Council on Modular Coordination?"

Proper Noun Keywords

Through our observation of information searches in practice, we realized that the "additional" clues provided by the researcher who was already familiar with his subject were extremely important. Since the aim is rapid and effective retrieval of information, these clues must be taken advantage of. Consequently our retrieval system makes considerable use of these clues, which we call "Proper Noun Keywords" (to distinguish them from the Common Noun Keywords described earlier in these notes).

Proper Noun Keywords can be coordinated in the same way as Common Noun Keywords, either together or in combination with Common Noun Keywords. Furthermore a PNK search can always be followed by a Common Noun Keyword search in answer to a subsequent (explicit or implicit) request "What else do you have in this area?"

One of the advantages of the use of Proper Noun Keywords is that they do not require defining and so the equivalence of words selected by librarian and researcher is automatic. Some cross-referencing may be necessary, however, where the order of words in a Proper Noun Keyword is not certain or where abbreviations are employed.

Having described the two different types of searches which were observed, it was realized that the first type (the general search) could be translated into the second type (the restricted search) with the help of the information system operator, for this person can fulfill the rôle of the experienced researcher and start the search by coordinating the Proper

Noun Keywords of sources familiar to him. In this way, the system operator acts in a manner which resembles the experienced librarian. It is important, however, that he should follow up his PNK search with a CNK search, in order to be sure that the information store has been thoroughly combed. The intervention of such a "specialist" may greatly increase the effectiveness of the system in the general search.

The use of PNK's, as opposed to CNK's, assumes particular importance in, for example, an office information system, where the names of clients, members of the staff, projects,etc.. can all become PNK's (though obviously some care is required in deciding which ones to use).

Controlled Vocabulary: Thesaurus of Common Noun Keywords

Two reasons are usually given to explain the need for controlled vocabularies: to restrict the number of terms allowed and to make clear the relationships between them. The degree of control required depends directly upon the information to be stored in the information system. For example, in the legal profession, where documents not only constitute the working material of the lawyer but also contain words and phrases the interpretation of which is the process of law, current research projects in legal information systems (4) have found it impossible to either restrict the number of keywords or to define relationships between them. In the building industry, this is not the case. Documents are only a medium for the transfer of information and it is possible to define terms ahead of time; indeed, this is desirable because practitioners in the building industry come from a wide range of backgrounds whereas those in the legal profession have all the same fundamental education.

The success of the storage and retrieval of information by this method depends very considerably on the equivalence between the choice of keywords by the librarian when describing each concept in any document and the choice of keywords by the searcher when describing each aspect of his subject. To ensure this equivalence in choice of words (or at least to minimize the risk of divergent choices) a common, or controlled vocabulary of Common Noun Keywords is indispensible.

A number of controlled vocabularies exist such as the E.J.C. thesaurus (5). Quite apart from the fact that these thesauri are not oriented towards the area of "building science and technology",they also present some serious weaknesses due to their having (i) too many terms and (ii) too loose a structure. In this situation, the risk that any one concept can be described by different terms (terms of differing generality or slightly different meaning) is very real.

On the first point, namely to avoid the generation of an excessive number of terms, present thesauri attempt to avoid synonyms through the USE instruction ("use for" (UF) being the

reciprocal); thus a single word may serve for several where there is not a significant difference of meaning. We return to this point further in these notes.

On the second point, namely the loose structure, the usual thesauri have terms listed alphabetically, most of which are accompanied by their "broader terms (BT)", "narrower terms (NT)", and "related terms (RT)". For any term X, the narrower term describes "a type of X" (the broader term is the reciprocal). Any term in the same area (or areas) of interest is listed as an RT (with reciprocal entries); the RT form is used rather loosely and often includes near synonyms (the Case-Western Thesaurus of Educational Terms (6) tries to establish rules to cover the related term form).

Taking into account the peculiarities of the building industry (the fragmented nature of information flow) and having reviewed the work already accomplished in other fields, it was decided that the sort of thesaurus of Common Noun Keywords required was one with the following characteristics:-
(i) A minimum set of operational terms, the terms themselves to remain as closely as possible in user language; this can be achieved by a more frequent use of the USE/UF qualification.
(ii) An organised hierarchical structure to improve consistency in indexing, storage and retrieval of information.

In studying these aspects of establishing a controlled vocabulary, one further relationship (the whole term/part term, WT/PT relationship) was found to exist between terms; it is useful to make this clear in the thesaurus, to avoid (a)"straining" the Broader Term/Narrower Term relationship to include relationships which are not properly so described, or (b) "falling back" on the Related Term category, which can be better used. This WT/PT relationship has been introduced between words and a logical series of questions or rules to introduce words into the vocabulary has been established. These are described in the next section.

The purpose of the introduction of the WT/PT relationship is to enable rules for the selection of Common Noun Keywords (CNKs) to be set up more easily and in this sense there are two inter-related advantages. Firstly, an indexer should not be confronted with a large number of "narrower terms" to any one given keyword particularly if the relationships between these "narrower terms" and the main keyword are inconsistent as has been indicated. For example, in traditional thesauri, DOOR HANDLES and WOODEN DOORS are both "narrower terms" of DOORS, yet each bears a different relationship with DOORS. In more complex cases, an indexer may select a word which does not bear the same relationship to the "broader keyword" as the original document suggested and hence control is lost. Secondly, different indexing rules apply to WT/PT relationships than to BT/NT relationships and the application of these rules minimises the frequency of "nil returns" or "noise". In all cases, we believe, keywords should be as specific as possible while adequately covering the concept. However, when the term chosen is part of a BT/NT relationship, an indexer should - after selecting the original term - progress upwards in the hierarchy; how far up will depend on (a) the word composition of the specific term chosen, and/or (b) whether other specific terms in the same area are chosen. For example, the relationship between FRAMES and CONCRETE FRAMES is BT/NT; if a document is indexed by the keyword CONCRETE FRAMES only, a searcher interested by frames would not retrieve the document unless the original document had also been key-worded with the Broader Term, FRAMES.

This situation does not exist with the WT/PT relationship. An article on DOOR KNOBS is not of interest to the researcher requiring information on DOORS. If a searcher is interested in other parts of doors, then he will select each of them independantly and organize his search accordingly.

To avoid the inclusion of an excessive number of keywords, it was decided to extend the USE/UF form to include words which may be different in meaning but which can be brought together for the purposes of information storage and retrieval. A specialist using this thesaurus could always over-ride the USE/UF form suggested for his own areas of specialisation if greater depth of concept definition is required (this can be called the construction of a "micro thesaurus"). This is done by taking some or all words out of the USE/UF category for a specific subject area, i.e. a set of keywords, and structuring them in the usual way (see next section) so that they bear a relationship with the word which previously was used in their stead. Such structuring can only be successful if the specialist is able to define the words accurately in his own terms. For example, while one recognizes that TOLERANCES and GAPS are different, for the purposes of the general purpose thesaurus, one can describe GAPS as USE:TOLERANCES because it is doubtful that any article including the concept GAPS would not also mention TOLERANCES nor that anyone searching for GAPS would mind being directed through the thesaurus to conduct a search through TOLERANCES. The specialist can, as we have pointed out, reverse this decision and maintain GAPS, and at the same time further introduce such narrower terms as MINIMUM GAPS. The aim is to minimize the risk of doubt when selecting keywords.

Procedures for Constructing a Common Noun Thesaurus

The subject area which was of concern to us, and therefore which was to be served by the thesaurus was defined as "building science and technology". In fact the area was defined by a set of general keywords, selected on the basis of usage and structured according to logical questions (see fig 1a & b). Having established these preliminary general keywords, it became possible to determine the extent of the work (an important question in terms of programming) and to decide upon a plan of action for completing the work in an organised and logical way such that the degree of completion would always be known.

Within this framework, the procedures which have been developed for the generation of a controlled vocabulary can be described as follows:-

(i)   A general keyword within the larger framework is selected e.g. ACOUSTICS, MODULAR COORDINATION, SYSTEM BUILDING etc.

(ii) Words are collected from earlier thesauri, glossaries, research reports, books, articles etc.

(iii) These words are divided into groups by, for example, their semantic nature. This is merely to reduce the random list of words into manageable sets.

(iv) Definitions are agreed (specialists are consulted where the research team does not have the appropriate knowledge); note that often, negotiation is necessary on some specific meaning which is declared through the annotations contained in a "Scope Note (SN)".

(v)   Words which can adequately be covered by other terms through the USE/UF form are "eliminated" from the processing (note that these words are not "lost" since they will appear in the thesaurus not as keywords but accompanied by the appropriate annotation and its reciprocal.

(vi) Words are picked out in pairs (using "common sense" for guidance) and a logical sequence of questions is run through. This shows whether the terms under consideration have a BT/NT relationship or a WT/PT relationship, whether they are related terms (RT) within the same hierarchy or whether they are not related at all (see fig 1a & b).

(vii) A relationship chart is prepared showing the initial hierarchy (see fig 2a & b).

(viii)Groups of words bearing any of these relationships to each other are re-assembled by means of a computer programme (the purpose of which is simply to display all the words in the area having relationships between them all in clusters); a question is then asked of each of these sets of keywords as follows: "which single keyword describes the ideas contained within this set of keywords?" If the resulting keyword already exists within the hierarchy being compiled, then the hierarchy is as complete as the original set of words allowed. If on the other hand, some of the resulting keywords are not in this hierarchy, a search is made to see if they exist in other hierarchies. If this is so, then relationships between hierarchies are established. Note that if these keywords do not exist in other hierarchies, it may be because the hierarchies have not been fully developed. Alternatively, the concepts generated by these keywords may fall outside the area of interest as defined.

(ix) If new keywords are produced as a result of re-assembling the original keywords, then steps (iv) - (viii) are repeated until such time as no new relationships appear. The process is thus iterative and the relationships become better defined with each cycle and more comprehensive with the increasing completion of the entire subject area.

(x) Individual cards are prepared for each keyword showing its immediate surroundings in the hierarchy and a revised hierarchical display is drawn (as completely as the advance of the work will allow see fig 3).

(xi) The alphabetical list of keywords is updated to include those just generated.

At the time of writing, the final format for the display of hierarchical relationships has not been designed.

Generation of Proper Noun Keywords

Words which describe other than the factual content of a piece of information may be described as Proper Noun Keywords. The following are categories of Proper Noun Keywords:-

(i) The names of authors responsible for the literature.

(ii) The names of organisations (e.g. universities, publishers, etc.) responsible for the publication of the information.

(iii) The date of publication.

(iv) A geographical reference to the information (usually by country).

(v) A set of Proper Noun Keywords describing the physical nature of the information as follows:

       ABSTRACTS
       ARTICLES
       BIBLIOGRAPHIES
       BOOKS
       DOCUMENTS
       FILMS(MOTION PICTURES)
       ORGANISATIONS
       PERIODICALS
       PUBLICATIONS LISTS
       SOUND RECORDINGS
       STATISTICS

Whereas Common Noun Keywords have to be selected ahead of time by experts in the field and structured accordingly, Proper Noun Keywords are generated automatically avoiding the problems of selection, definition and structuring. Some cross-referencing is necessary e.g. when abbreviations are used, but cross references can be built into the Proper Noun Keywords either by cross reference cards or search instructions for computer operation. The use of PNKs has already been described, in the context of rapid searches by experts.

Proper Noun Keywords describing the physical nature of the information have already been generated for the abstracts published in IF and it should be noted from the list in (v) above, that it is sufficient to select only one Proper Noun Keyword to describe the physical nature of the information. Often this class of PNKs helps with the actual physical retrieval of the document, since quite probably they correspond to types of storage facilities; indeed it is possible to regard these PNKs as an adjunct to the accession number "addresses" of the documents.

Use of the Thesaurus: Relationship to Other Work

The immediate relevance of this work is to develop a workable Common Noun Thesaurus (i.e. controlled vocabulary of keywords) in our subject area. The hierarchy is not a classification of words (pre-classification anyhow is to be avoided at all costs); it allows the librarian and the searcher to recognise at a glance how general or how specific within and between hierarchies any word must be, and thus guide them in the choice of word that corresponds most exactly to the generality or specificity of the concept under consideration. At the present time, more comprehensive rules for indexing are being prepared.

The thesaurus is needed above all for IF; it would be risky to continue to generate words in isolation. Also it is, in our opinion, a necessary (and unavoidable) first step in the setting up of any wider information services or data banks, which is something else that we are beginning to undertake (see next section of these notes).

It is essential that there should be as few thesauri as possible in use at any one time. Our group has been in contact with other people working on thesaurus generation on the North American Continent and elsewhere, though little work is being done on building industry thesauri. In fact it seems that although building information systems have been the subject of considerable theoretical study, few people have been fighting with the practicalities of operating an ongoing system for the building industry.

One major exception is the Thesaurus being developed for the Canadian Department of Industry, Trade and Commerce - a first edition of which is due for publication at the end of the summer of 1970. Having been in contact with the team working for the Canadian government, we believe and hope that there will be compatibility between our thesauri - at least as far as the allowable word lists are concerned.

Use of the Thesaurus: Information Systems

Our group is constantly aware of the problems of finding information - both in teaching and consultancy work - yet although a considerable amount of research and development results are presently available, few people are in a position to collect them and compile them into a common post-coordination type system based on a commonly accepted thesaurus.

At the time of writing, our team is involved in three levels of initiative in the area of information systems. Firstly, the ground rules have been established for a formal information link between groups at Washington University, St. Louis, the Université de Montréal and the University of California at Los Angeles; this will involve sharing the work of information collection and the preparation of abstracts and exchanging abstracts with agreed keywords. Secondly, it is proposed to agree keywords with several institutions, particularly Laval Université, Québec who are setting up a housing information system (this will allow people to use a common routine for information searches at any of the universities in question). Thirdly, it is proposed to extend our work to include setting up and operating building science informations systems to government agencies through contracts.

As work on developing the thesaurus proceeds, many other advantages of the logical structuring of words are being discovered. Since the words correspond to concepts in the field of building science, the structuring of words implies a structuring of the concepts on the same logical basis. This would appear to offer all sorts of interesting indications in other areas, e.g. when setting up a curriculum or planning a research project or establishing checklists for various stages of design and planning.

Conclusions

These notes have described experiences in the practicalities of information handling - from the early design-publication stage with Industrialisation Forum to the current forays into building science information systems. The critical decision is to use post-coordination instead of any of the creaking classification systems with which the building industry is bedevilled. The critical research phase is then the development of rules for word generation and word selection.

The advantages of using a common thesaurus are many, though in certain circumstances it may be necessary for different users to develop certain areas to greater depth; even so, it is possible to agree "translation" rules to pass from one thesaurus to another, i.e. from one information stores.

Notes

(1) "The Impact of Industrialisation on the Design of the Built Environment", AIA/ACSA Teachers' Seminar 1968, Montréal.

(2) "Industrialisation Forum; Building: Systems Construction Analysis Research", published quarterly jointly at Washington University, St. Louis and the Université de Montréal.First issue October 1969.

(3) Wert, L.,"Information Retrieval and 'Industrialisation Forum'", "Industrialisation Forum" volume 1, number 1, pp. 11 - 17. (Includes a short bibliography).

(4) "DATUM", a system of information storage and retrieval developed by the School of Law, Université de Montréal.

(5) "Thesaurus of Engineering and Scientific Terms", Engineers' Joint Council, New York, 1967, 690 pp.

(6) Barhydt, Gordon C. and Charles T. Schmidt et al., "Information Retrieval Thesaurus of Educational Terms", The Press of Case Western Reserve University, Cleveland, 1968, 133 pp.

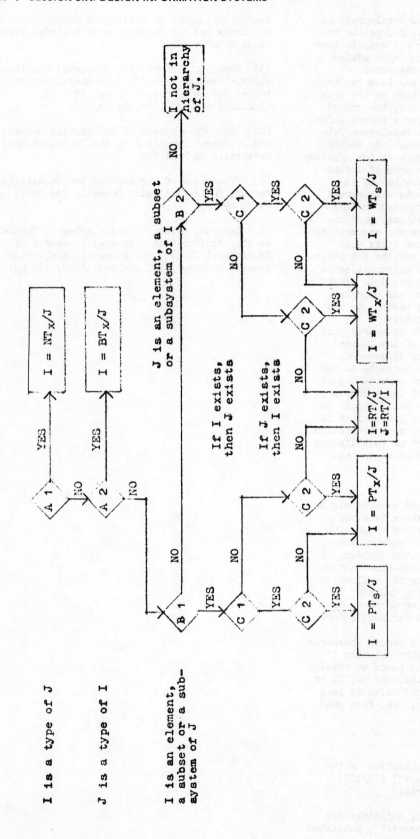

I is a type of J

J is a type of I

I is an element,
a subset or a sub-
system of J

Fig. 1a. Question-sequence used to determine what is the relationship between two terms ("I" & "J").

Notation: NT = narrow term, BT = Broad term, PT = part term, WT = whole term, RT = related term.

suffix 's' denotes specific PT or WT (next level in hierarchy), 'x' denotes general NT, BT, PT or WT at an unknown level above or below the term (to be determined by other word pairing).

Fig. 1b Examples of the Question—Sequence.

Example 1.

I = "Modular Dimensions"
J = "Tolerances"
A_1: Are "Modular Dimensions" types of "Tolerances"? No
A_2: Are "Tolerances" types of "Modular Dimensions"? No

B_1: Are "Modular Dimensions" elements, subsets or subsystems of "Tolerances"? No
B_2: Are "Tolerances" elements, subsets or subsystems of "Modular Dimensions"? Yes

C_1: If "Modular Dimensions" exist, do "Tolerances" exist? Yes
C_2: If "Tolerances" exist, do "Modular Dimensions" exist? No

Therefore: "Modular Dimensions" is a whole term (WT_X) of "Tolerances"

Example 2.

I = "Tolerances"
J = "Manufacturing Tolerances"
A_1: Are "Tolerances" types of "Manufacturing Tolerances"? No
A_2: Are "Manufacturing Tolerances" types of "Tolerances"? Yes

Therefore: "Tolerances" is a Broader Term (BT) of "Manufacturing Tolerances"

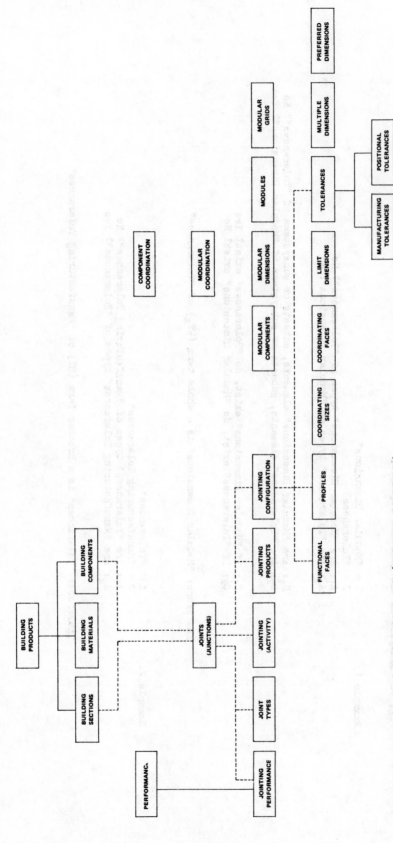

Fig. 2a. Part of a hierarchical display of key-words (in-house working format).

———— NT/BT relationship

- - - - - PT/WT relationship

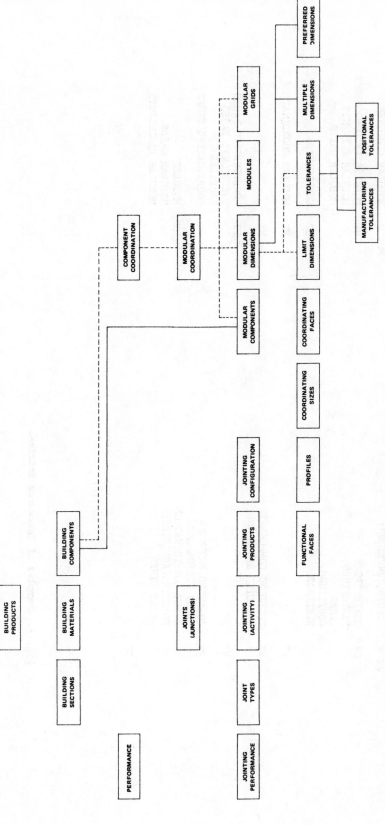

Fig. 2b. Part of a hierarchical display of key-words (in-house working format).

———— NT/BT relationship

- - - - - PT/WT relationship

JT 2   JOINTS(JUNCTIONS)

UF   CONNECTIONS
     FASTENINGS
     LINKS
     COUPLINGS
     BINDINGS

BT

WT   BUILDING COMPONENTS
     BUILDING SECTIONS

NT

PT   JOINTING PRODUCTS
     JOINT PERFORMANCE
     JOINT CONFIGURATION
     JOINTING(ACTIVITY)
     JOINT TYPES

RT

MOD 2   MODULAR COMPONENTS

UF   MODULES IF COMPONENTS
     MODULAR ELEMENTS
     MODULAR UNITS

BT   COMPONENTS

WT   MODULAR COORDINATION

NT

PT   COORDINATING FACES
     FUNCTIONAL FACES
     PROFILES
     COORDINATING SIZES

RT   MODULES
     MODULAR GRIDS
     MODULAR DIMENSIONS

Fig. 3. Examples of Thesaurus Entries.

An Architectural Data Management System

by Charles F. Davis, III

Davis, Speake and Associates — Architecture, Planning, Engineering;

Davis, Kennedy Consultants

Abstract

A data management system for architectural information is introduced. (1) Goals
for system development have been primarily to
increase the amount of information which may
be brought to bear effectively on the design
process; to reduce the time required for
searching and organizing of information which
occurs in practice; provide the potential for
storage and use of feedback information from
construction and use of the designed environment.

The system is based on a simple paradigm: an assembly may be described as a linear combination of components; components are
either elements or assemblies. The present
state of development is described together
with projected applications of the system.
Some of these are cost analysis, component
selection, specification preparation, storage
and retrieval of programmatic information,
cross referencing to standard details.

Apologia and Introduction

ADMS is an Architectural Data Management
System. The primary commitments to it are as
a stopgap measure and as an initial step in an
evolutionary process. The capability to automatically store, manipulate and retrieve information has existed for years. Yet little
use has been made of this capability within
the building industry. ADMS, admittedly, may
not be able to handle the whole gamut of information relative to buildings. However, the
greatest problem and expense in establishing a
data management system is the collection and
organization of the data base. ADMS is immediately applicable for this task, is simple to
use, flexible, and has substantial early payoffs. When it is superceded by more sophisticated and complete systems, the data base
should be easily converted by the computer to
a new format and organization.

The Motivations for ADMS

There were several aspects of the environment which motivated the development of
ADMS. First, a constantly enlarging amount of
information is being created. It is being
produced with such rapidity that the information is often unrelated, or at best, poorly
organized. Handling, retrieving, organizing,
and using the information is consequently expensive. For example if a comparison of interior wall systems is to be made on the basis of performance, it is necessary to go to
various references to search for the relevant
information. There is one set of references
for masonry walls, another for drywall assemblies and so on. There is one source of information for cost, another for sound transmission, another for sound absorption, another for fire rating, etc. Making an enlight-
ened decision under the conditions will result in a financial loss for the design firm.
The cost will be greater than the fee for
making the decision.

The second motivational aspect of the environment is the increasing complexity of the
problems which face architects. They are becoming larger in scale, and involve more complex activities. Furthermore, information is
being developed about aspects of design which
were never given consideration before. Few
had thought that systematic consideration
might be given to how the form of a window can
respond to what is involved in looking out of
it until Christopher Alexander began talking
about a pattern language.(2).(3)

Thirdly, the power of the computer is not
being utilized by the professions. It appears
that this is due to the nature of design. In
design we are seeking after elegant, simple
solutions to complex problems. There are many
considerations, factors, and limitations which
determine form, but form is a single response.
The complexity of the problems requires that
programs be extensive in scope, or if limited,
then very closely interrelated. It also requires large amounts of input. Use of the
computer requires the coding of extensive information into machine readable form. It also
involves the assimilation of it which may involve time and costs that make the output too
expensive whether or not the computer is used.
As a result, the analysis is performed only
when the problem is extremely critical. At
other times no analysis or consideration may
be given to certain aspects of the problem.

Goals

Based on these observations a set of goals for the development of ADMS were formulated. The most general goal is to improve the quality of the designed environment through improving the design process. It was felt that in light of the observations several sub-goals would make significant contributions toward meeting this general goal. First the amount of information which may be effectively brought to bear on the design process should be increased. This goal is modified by the limitation that the information should be organized so that its usefulness throughout the design process is maximized. Secondly, the number of aspects of designing the environment which may be given consideration should be increased, and they should be integrated into the design process. Thirdly, the time allotted to design should be increased. Stated another way, the level of the designer's concern should be raised. Rather than spending time finding information, he should be asking more significant and penetrating questions. I remember hearing a structural engineer placating those who argued that the computer could replace the engineer.(4) He said that experience showed that once the designer was no longer bound to performing calculations he was free to ask better questions. The problem has been how the computer could free architects to ask such questions. There is actually little calculating done in architectural design. Of course, there are the time consuming tasks of drafting or the recording of decisions. The computerization of these tasks would be inefficient because preparation of the input would take as much time as doing it all by hand. Now it is obvious that an architect basically transforms information. It is in this conceptual framework that the computer can be a powerful tool in the hands of an architect.

The second general goal is to improve the quality and accuracy of the information which an architect uses. This may be done by improving feedback from the construction and use of the designed environment. Once there is a mechanism for receiving and using feedback information other than the ears and mind of one individual the impact of such information will be significantly increased. It will no longer be like the high pitched scream of acoustical feedback in a sound system. It will become so important that architects will seek it out. It may become possible that the record of a firm's or the profession's experience can be a significant contribution to the education of a new generation of architects.

The quality of information may also be improved by increasing the crossfeed of information between the academic-research communities and the practicing architects. It will become possible for researchers to enter their conclusions and findings into the system and provide up-to-date information and facts for use by the practicing architects. Such a systematic updating might even replace many of the refresher courses which have become necessary for professionals after they have been in practice for a few years.

Operations of ADMS

These goals lead to an operational description of ADMS. ADMS should allow the user to efficiently define and describe building components for storage in a master file. Components can be of several types existing in parallel: construction, activity, program or spatial. ADMS should allow the use of these predefined components to describe and define higher level components. It should allow the creation of a job file for use in modeling a specific project. The job file should exist throughout the life of the project, from an initial meeting of the architect and client to the completion of construction. It should store information as it is transformed from preliminary programmatic considerations to the finalized description of the building and its construction. ADMS should allow cross referencing of information both inside and outside of the system to components within it. It should allow the use of a library of service routines to process the information in the master file or the job file. Some of the potential uses will be discussed below.

Paradigm

ADMS is based on a simple paradigm which allows these operations. It consists of three definitions.

1. A constructed object is an assembly.
2. An assembly is a linear combination of components.
3. A component is an element or an assembly.

Consider two examples of construction components: a drywall assembly and a door assembly. Remember that there are other kinds of components. These are selected because they are easy to illustrate. Programmatic, spatial and activity components are analogous to these. One can combine specified quantities of gypsum board, metal studs, screws, taping and finishing in a specified manner and define a drywall assembly.(Fig.1) Assemblies (e.g. the metal stud assembly) and elements (e.g. gypsum board) are being combined to form a higher level assembly.

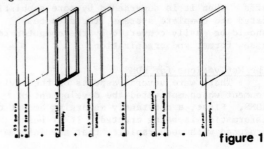

figure 1

Likewise, combine metal door frame, door, hinges, lockset to define a door assembly. (Fig.2)

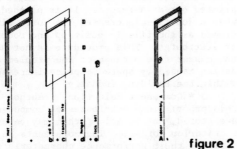

figure 2

At a higher level these components (the drywall and door assembly) may be used to define another component, a specific. (Fig.3) Here previously defined assemblies are being combined to form a higher level assembly.

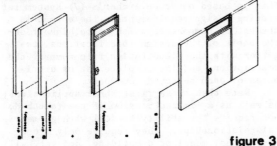

figure 3

At an even higher level a set of walls could be created out of distinct walls.(Fig.4)

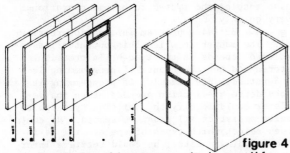

figure 4

Continuing this process, it is possible to describe an entire building as an assembly of construction components. See note 5 for a description of the method used for storing geometrical relationships.

Associated Information

Certain information is attached to or associated with each component. There are nine types of such information.

1. Name. Component description and related information is accessed externally by using the component name.

2. Type. This data item indicates the class to which the component belongs. For example, interior walls, exterior walls, ceilings, teaching spaces, learning activities, classrooms, etc. All components within one class have the same set of attributes. As many types as described may be created. In the system they are treated as components which are classified as a type. That is, the type of "WALL-AB" may be "INTERIOR-WALL" and the type of "INTERIOR-WALL" is "TYPE".

3. Units. These are the units in which the component is measured. For example, square feet, square yard, a square, cubic feet, hours, dollars, pounds, tons.

4. Illustration. This is the file number of a graphic description of the component. At present this points to a location outside of the computer system. If it is desired or necessary to store graphical information within the system, this data item could very well point to a location within a computer file. An illustration might be a standard detail, a diagram, an element in a pattern language, a photograph, etc.

5. The entry date and utilization information. These two data items are stored within one word. Both are created and kept up-to-date automatically by the system. The entry date is the date on which the information was entered or last updated. Utilization refers to the number of times a component is a member of higher level assemblies. A component may be deleted only when this count is zero. Otherwise information would be lost or errors would occur.

6. References. These are pointers to information outside the system. This information can be specification paragraphs in a master specification file, catalog data, research reports, etc.

7. Attributes. These are quantifiable characteristics of a component, either desired or actual. A construction component would have actual performances, e.g. weight, height, sound transmission class, fire rating, location. A programmatic one would have desired attributes, e.g. light level, desired temperature.

8. Description. This is any data which is meaningful to the user but not necessarily to the computer. For example, comments could be associated with a component. Generally it is used to store a precise description to aid in recognizing or remembering the component. Eventually it may be used for key word indexing to simplify the interface of the master file and the various users.

9. Composition or cost. This data is a set of pointers to the storage locations of the components of an assembly together and the amount of each component in the assembly. In construction components, the composition is actual. In programmatic ones the composition is assumed. Cost is considered the composition of a construction element.

Data Structure

Figure 5 is a diagram of the data structure. The name, type, units, illustration, entry date, and the set of four pointers are stored in a random access file composed of records which are two words long. The composition pointer of an assembly points to a header in this file. The first word in the header points back to the assembly (required for garbage collection) and the second contains the number of components. Following the header is a list of the storage locations of the components and the quantity of each. The other data files are random access files composed of one word records. The respective pointers of a component point to a header which is two records long. The first record is the point back and the second is the number of words of data which follow. If five specification paragraphs are to be associated with a component which is stored in the 4095th location in the master file, the first record would contain "4095", the second would contain "5", and the next five records would contain coded references to the appropriate master specification paragraphs.

Present Capabilities

At present, only the programs which maintain the master file are operationally part of the system. (6) A GE Mark II time share system is being used to run the programs and store the data. All programming is in Fortran IV though conversion is now under way to PL-1 for use on a IBM 360-65. The following operations may now be performed:

1. Adding and deleting components.
2. Attaching and detaching references, attributes, descriptions and composition.
3. Updating information.
4. Retrieving information.
5. Automatic garbage collection (compressing of the file by removal of obsolete information when the files are full.)

Potential Applications

With this simple data structure a wide range of applications are possible. Some of the potential applications are described below. At this time a number of application programs are operational but have not yet been tied into the data base. They have been written so that they will easily interface with ADMS. These are marked by an asterisk and the authors are noted in parentheses. All others are projected and will be available in the not too distant future.

1.* Preparation of specifications. (Michael D. Kennedy, University of Kentucky) The actual text of the specifications is outside the system. Since specification paragraphs are keyed into the construction components as references, it is possible to trace the structure of the assembly (e.g., the building) and compose a list of the relevant specification paragraphs. This list may then be processed by a specification assembling program. The "sub-master" specification thus created may be reviewed and marked up for input to a specification editing program.

2.* Cost Analysis (Author of this paper) A trace may be made of the composition of any assembly down to its basic elements. At this point costs are stored. Then by retracing the steps of the decomposition the costs and quantities at each level may be summed and printed out as a report. It is planned that when a job file is created the costs will be summed as the file is built up and recorded as attributes. This procedure is not used in the master file because of the problem of updating caused by sporadic price increases within the building industry.

3.* Component Selection. (Author of this paper) Since attributes of components are stored, any or all of them may be used as a criterion for selecting components on the basis of their performance characteristics. The program which will be modified to serve this data base allows the designer to specify performances which are important to the selection, their relative importance, and the relative values of various levels of performance. This is based on Bruce Archer's (7) system for stating design requirements. The output is the set of components which score highest on the basis of the design specifications, together with the illustration file number, the description, and the complete set of attributes of each selected component.

Note that these first three applications, as well as a limited version of the fourth do not require the ability to deal with geometrical relationships. They require only a one dimensional model of a building, and yet, will yield significant payoffs to subsidize future development. This initial simplification has also enabled the system to become operational very quickly.

4. Building program information retrieval. The manner in which this potential is developed depends on the type of information stored and how the nature of programming is understood. For example, if programming is considered a selection process, then the designer could specify the building type and receive a list of all possible spaces. He could then select which types of spaces will be in the building. Later, he could retrieve information on each space. If programming is considered a design process then the designer might begin with a similar consideration of activities. In either case the final results would be something like a list of spaces and relationships with certain desired attributes and assumed composition, and the interrelationships of the spaces. This will eventually be the initial step in creating a job file. From this point the designer becomes more specific, adds information to the model or changes information from the assumed to the confirmed status. (8)

5.* Heat gain-heat loss calculations (Miller and Weaver, Consulting Engineers of Birmingham, Ala.) This is normally the province of the mechanical engineers and will continue to be so. The consulting engineers with whom the firm of Davis, Speake and Associates works have computerized major portions of the

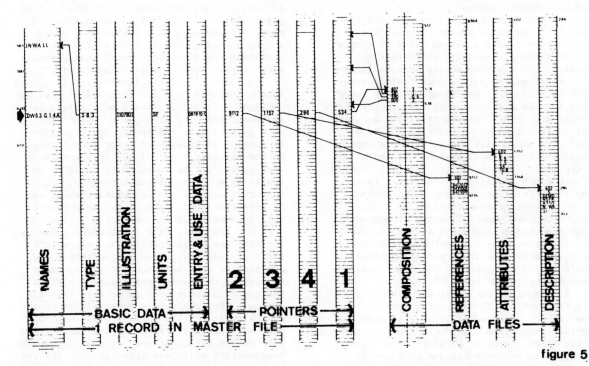

figure 5

required calculations for the design of an HVAC system. The equivalent temperature differential and solar radiation tables are stored in random access files. The attribute data in ADMS on exterior walls includes u-factor and density. Eventually the load program will refer to a job file for the building description and use this exterior wall information to determine which sections of the tables should be extracted. Also the desired attributes of temperature, humidity, air changes per hour etc., could be used by the HVAC design system to set design requirements. In the long run it will become possible for the consultants to modify the job file with the output of their system. This is one example of the way in which the various people concerned with a building project may communicate via the computer. These may include the client, consultants, architect, contractors, supervisors, etc.

6. Schedule preparation. In the future, door, window, hardware, and finish schedules may no longer be required or considered the best way of communicating such information. The necessary information will be stored within the computer system. It then may be converted to schedules, or order forms for subcontractors, or dimensions for masons and carpenters.

7. Plans (Michael D. Kennedy) and perspectives (Author of this paper) It will be possible to have graphic output which will record the present state of a design. Plan graphics are presently limited to location of components and titles of spaces. The rather complicated aspect of notes and dimensions has

not yet been undertaken by any of those involved in the development of ADMS. The perspective program was test model of this system and allows manipulation of geometrical components in three dimensional space.

These are some of the more obvious uses of ADMS and as such represent the applications which will be among the first to be implemented. These application programs will be relatively easy to implement. The next major task will be the development of routines to create and maintain the job files.

Evaluation
The overall performance of a system may be understood as the results from a series of tradeoffs. For example, the design of an automobile engine may involve tradeoffs between power and pollution control, fuel consumption and power, pollution control and maintenance, cost or profit to the manufacturer and any of the other performances. The variations in performance among a set of engines may be determined analytically. However, which engine is selected as the best will depend on the relative values attributed to the various performances. Innovative design seeks to establish a new set of tradeoffs which will bring the ranges of performance into a closer relationship with existing values. Competing systems can be evaluated on the basis of a comparison of the tradeoffs which limit their potential. The more important characteristics of ADMS are listed below, and the tradeoffs to which they give rise are discussed. (9) It is left to the reader to compare and evaluate the various architectural

data management systems.

1. There is conceptually only one dimension of variation at each level. This characteristic of the system makes it simple to understand and use, and simplifies programming. It can also create serious limitations which may require a good deal of ingenuity to overcome. For example, it is impossible to make a stair a component in the masterfile and then to use it to create another stair. If the floor to floor height is altered, the slope will change or the number of treads and risers will change. If the width of the stair is altered, the landings change in both width and length. One stair is not simply a multiple of another. The problem can be somewhat circumvented by creating a "step" component and a "landing" component. These may then be sized and assembled into many different stairs. Another way to avoid the problem is to write a special program to handle stairs and use only the lower level components from the master file.

2. The information of the system is not at a fine grain. In describing drywall components, for example, it is wise to generalize the information. Rather than keep track of the exact length of metal studs or floor track, it is better to assume an average amount per square foot of wall. Otherwise, the information would be so voluminous that it would be impractical to store it all. It is probable that any system that proposed to store such fine grained information would be impractical.

3. The simplicity of the paradigm gives the system an innate flexibility. The University of Alabama Medical Center in Birmingham is planning to use this system as a space and facilities management system (SFMS). The data will be slightly different from the data stored in ADMS, and the modular service programs will be completely different. However, the basic data structure will be practically identical. In SFMS a component will belong to several classes instead of belonging, as in ADMS, to only one. The similar structure will enable direct transfer of information from ADMS to the space and facilities management system. The tradeoff for a simple data structure is a more complex program structure for the various applications. The system becomes differentiated only as application programs are developed. What makes ADMS basically different from SFMS are the application routines. The option for a simple data structure has been chosen to expedite initial development, as well as to enable the interface of ADMS with related data structures.

4. The easiest applications to implement are specification preparation, cost analysis, component selection, and drawing retrieval. These applications will not require the use of a job file or the capability for handling geometrical relationships. They are expected to produce major

savings. Thus, the system will yield a high payoff for the initial implementation with payoffs increasing at a lesser rate during subsequent development. The initial implementation can subsidize future development and create a natural motivation for it.

5. Not all of the information is sorted in the computer system. This has several advantages. It reduces costs of storage, development and data conversion. Since the data may still be referenced by the system it remains an integrated information system. On the negative side, if the information were stored in the computer it could be potentially more useful and effective. It is felt that most of the information which can be effectively manipulated by the computer will be stored within the system.

6. The basic file maintenance routines for ADMS are operational. This allows the tasks of data collection, organization and encoding to proceed immediately. Programs to service the system and insure a profitable operation have only to be tied into the system. They can easily be available on a month's notice. This rapid initial development will probably result in a slower growth rate in the future because of the programming complexities which are inherent with the simple data structure.

7. Extensions of the system capabilities may be made incrementally by adding program modules which service the data base. This allows relatively small investments to produce recognizable benefits in a short time.

NOTES

1. Concept development was undertaken at the University of Kentucky, School of Architecture. Program development has been primarily done at Davis, Speake and Associates-Architecture, Planning and Engineering of Birmingham, Alabama. Professor Michael Kennedy has made valuable contributions to concept development and is converting the system to PL-1 at present. The comments and reactions of numerous other people have been helpful in the evaluation of the system. Among these are Lavette Teague of Skidmore, Owings and Merrill; Charles Burnette of the Institute of Environmental Studies, University of Pennsylvania; and Ted Myer of Bolt, Baranek and Newman, Boston.

2. Alexander, Christopher and Ishikawa, M. Silverstein, A Pattern Language Which Generates Multi-Service Centers, Center For Environmental Structure, Berkeley.

3. Montgomery, Roger, "Pattern Language," Architectural Forum, Volume 132. No. 1, January-February, 1970, pp. 53-59.

4. LeMessurier in discussion at Boston Architectural Center's Computer Conference in 1964.

5. In the master file, construction com-

ponents, destined for use in a job file, are described in appropriate basic units (i.e., a square foot, each, a linear foot). For example, a square foot of drywall will be described rather than some particular sized panel or wall. The information, such as cost, attached to it will be general rather than specific. When a wall is created in a job file, its general attributes will be taken as those of the generalized wall in the master file. The size and location attributes, which make the wall unique in the job file, will be assigned by the computer as the job file is created. The geometry of the arrangements of components is to be handled in two ways depending upon the use to which the component is to be put. At present, geometrical relationships of the components of the basic assemblies (those in the master file which are used to create specific components of a specific installation) are only recorded in standard details filed outside of the system but referenced by it. The geometrical relationships of specific components in the job file are to be considered a subset of the general attributes of the components. Prior to assigning construction components to the job file, it is assumed that there will exist a set of spaces which have been located and sized, and an adjacency matrix. Walls will then be attached to the sides of these spaces, ceilings to the tops; and floors to the bottoms. Automatically these components can be sized and their location recorded as attributes. On the basis of the adjacency matrix common walls will be automatically attached to the adjacent spaces. Openings may be likewise inserted in the walls for doors and windows. Continuation of this process will lead eventually to a geometrical description of a large part of a building. There may be parallel descriptions of the structural and mechanical systems of the building.

At this time it is still possible that components in a job file may have a distinct set of data attached which would consist only of the dimensional and locational attributes. This arrangement will reduce retrieval time but will add programming complications. Further evaluation will be required before a decision is made.

6. These operations are controlled by a set of simple commands. Command words are in all caps. Data items are enclosed in parentheses. Options are enclosed in brackets and separated by semicolons.

a. NEW (component name) (type) (illustration) (units). This command enters into the master file a new component together with the standard descriptive information.

b. OLD (component name). This command sets the system pointer to a component which has previously been entered into the master file, and retrieves from the master file the information relative to it.

c. DELETE. This command deletes the component presently located by the system pointer, if the deletion is permitted.

d. ATTACH-
[REFERENCES-(number), (code to references);
ATTRIBUTES-(values);
DESCRIPTION-(any symbols);
COMPOSITION-(number), (name, amount) . . . (name, amount)]
This command attaches to the component presently located by the system pointer the specified information.

e. DETACH-
[REFERENCES;
ATTRIBUTES;
DESCRIPTION;
COMPOSITION]
This command removes the connection between the specified information and the component presently located by the system pointer by setting the respective data pointer to zero.

f. UPDATE-
[TYPE (new type);
ILLUSTRATION (new illustration);
UNITS (new units)]
This command updates the information specified by substituting the new data for what was presently entered.

g. MODIFY-
[REFERENCES (number) (list of codes to references);
ATTRIBUTES (number) (name, value) . . . (name, value);
DESCRIPTION ("any symbol");
COMPOSITION (number) (name, amount) . . . (name, amount)]
This command updates the information specified for the component presently located by the system pointer. Any data that is duplicated is subsequently omitted. Any new data is added to the list.

h. LIST-
[REFERENCES;
ATTRIBUTES;
DESCRIPTION;
COMPOSITION]
This command lists the specified information on the component presently located by the system pointer.

i. DESCRIBE
This command lists all the information on the component presently located by the system pointer.

7. Explicated at the First International Conference of The Design Methods Group in Cambridge, 1967. The presentation should be contained in the following reference when it is published.

Moore, Gary T. (ed), Emerging Methods in Environmental Design, MIT Press, 1970. (?)

8. I am indebted to Lavette Teague of Skidmore, Owings and Merrill for this notion of assumed and confirmed data.

9. See also the evaluation of the planned method of handling geometrical data in note 5 above.

An Information System for Component Building

by Theodore H. Myer

Bolt, Beranek & Newman, Inc.

Abstract

An information system for building design is explored as a case history, with emphasis on the characteristics most important to the user. Experience with the system suggested that key criteria are the effectiveness with which designs are represented in the computer, and the ease with which users can work with the stored material. The design of a simple information system that appears to meet these criteria is described.

I. Introduction

This paper describes research carried out in collaboration with Carl Koch and Associates, Architects, under the sponsorship of the Urban Development Corporation of New York State. The project grew from a desire to apply computer technology to the information problems of component building design.

Our working context was Carl Koch's Techcrete building system. Techcrete is based on precast floor planks and bearing wall panels; post tensioning techniques enable construction of high- as well as low-rise buildings. Our partcular focus in this project was the use of Techcrete in the design of a mixed public and private housing complex of about 1000 units for a site near New York City (1).

Within this context we wanted to investigate a computer system capable of managing design information and supplying a number of separate retrieval, analytic, and reporting functions. We approached this by developing a limited initial system, putting it into practical use, and

letting our experience in using the system guide its further development. By this means we gained not only a practical working tool, but also some insight into the nature and applicability of information systems in architecture.

In the work, our greatest concern was to find an effective way to represent building designs in the computer. The representation would have to carry information satisfying the various functions to be included in the system. More importantly, we felt, it would have to be convenient to work with. This suggested ease of assembly and editing as key criteria, and most importantly "naturalness" in the sense of reflecting the designer's own ways of thinking about and organizing architectural material.

What resulted was an initial system with incremental cost estimation as its main function. Once in use, the system became more general. At this writing it includes or will shortly include reporting functions for net and gross areas, heat and cooling loads, and various schedules. Also, during use the system's data base evolved into a cataloguing and control tool for Techcrete, and a pool of design information upon which to draw in establishing new designs. At present we are adding a graphic capability and plan to extend the system to aid in manufacturing and construction.

II. The Initial System

We selected construction cost estimation as a first goal, since we felt it would require an initial system with most of the important components needed in a subsequent, more elaborate system. Within the general framework of cost estimation, we were particularly concerned with incremental estimation (2,3). That is, we wanted the designer to be able to test design changes for their effect on construction cost, in a continuous manner throughout the design process. That goal was met by building an initial system with four main components:

1) A representation for building designs.

2) A library of building components containing cost and other information about each component. The component library provides a base for building the design representation, and a source of cost data for estimation.

3) A series of commands for assembling and modifying the design representation.

4) Computer programs that perform quantity surveys, compute costs, and issue cost reports.

Figure 1 shows the functional relationship of these four components. Physically, the system resides in a DEC PDP-10 time-shared computer, under control of the TENEX time-sharing system under development at BBN. Communication and data input take place through remote Teletype terminals. Reports can be output via Teletype or line printer.

INITIAL SYSTEM

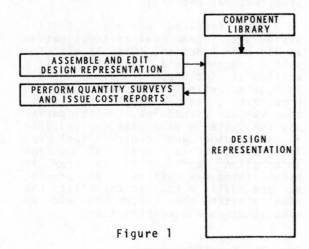

Figure 1

To represent buildings in the computer, we selected a tree structure (4). Similar techniques for organizing design information have been used by a number of other workers (5,6,7,8). Carr (5), in particular, gives a lucid

explanation. We chose a tree structure as likely to meet our demands for ease of manipulation and "naturalness". In addition, the tree quite easily supports cost computation.

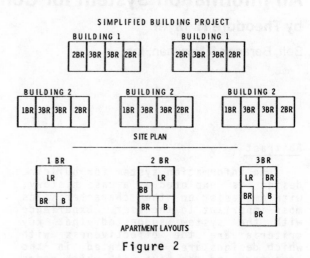

Figure 2

To illustrate how a building project can be mapped into a tree representation in the computer, Figure 2 shows a grossly simplified building Project and Figure 3 shows its representation in computer memory. As indicated in Figure 3, the tree is made up of nodes and branches, with nodes standing for groups of things and branches pointing to other nodes to indicate what and how much of it belongs in each group. For example, the top node, named "PROJECT-1", stands for the entire project and is made up of five buildings - two of type 1 and three of type 2. Each building in turn is a group of apartments. Each apartment comprises lower-level groupings accounting for its interior components and structural envelope.

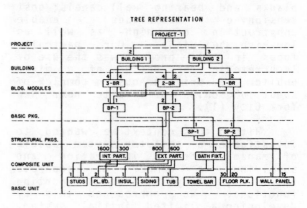

Figure 3

This aggregation into groups continues down through the structure, until at the bottom one reaches the elementary components from which the project is built.

In computer memory, nodes comprise data blocks. Within a node, branches are represented by pointers to other nodes. Each branch has an associated number indicating how much of the second node is contained in the first. The tree structure permits rather efficient use of computer memory because, as with multi-level "instances" in computer graphics, or nested subroutine calls in ordinary programming, each component or assembly is defined just once and then referred to or "called" when needed.

As well as being compact, the tree structure allows considerable flexibility. Though Figure 3 suggests seven levels and specific uses, the designer can employ as many levels as wanted for whatever purposes he has in mind.

Although most branches in Figure 1 descend one level, there is nothing to prevent branches that descend multiple levels or none at all. This permits low-level components or groups to be "tacked on" to groups much higher in the structure. For example, exterior light fixtures (at the bottom level) might be added to the project (at the top) in this way. This also makes it easy to create slightly modified versions of standard groupings. For example, a modified three-bedroom apartment might reference the standard version and be augmented by a few extra square feet of interior partition.

Closely related to this augmentation capability is the possibility of subtracting from a standard by using negative branch quantities. This proved useful in the actual project in permitting modified versions containing fewer of one component or another than the original.

Finally, although the tree in Figure 3 ascends to a single node at the top, there is nothing against multiple top nodes, and this is sometimes useful. With the actual project, this permitted useful subgroupings of the buildings. For example, one collection of "top" nodes called out groups of buildings segregated by height, while another pair of nodes separated the project

into public and private sectors. These partitionings of the data were useful in serving design and legal needs of cost estimation.

Thus the central component in the information system is a flexible and rather loosely organized tree structure, to be approached very directly by the designer in formulating design representations.

As suggested by Figure 3, elements of the system's second major ingredient, the building component library, form the bottom of the tree. Actually, this data is kept in a separate part of computer memory and referred to by branch pointers in the nodes that lie above it. In the initial system the library contained an identifying code for each component, a text description, the CSI and FHA categories to which the component belongs, and certain temporary storage registers to hold component quantities during estimation.

The component library forms the most permanent part of the data base, changing only as the building system itself is changed. In contrast, the tree structure that represents a given building project will grow and change as the design is built up and successively modified. Furthermore, at any given time, the component library may support any number of separate tree structures, each describing a different project.

INITIAL SYSTEM COMMANDS

DATA ENTRY AND EDITING

DEFINE NODE___LEVEL___
    BRANCH QUANTITY

KILL NODE___
PUT BRANCH___ON NODE___QUANTITY___
TAKE BRANCH___FROM NODE___
REPLACE BRANCH___OF NODE___WITH BRANCH___
QUANTIFY BRANCH___OF NODE___QUANTITY___

ESTIMATION AND LISTING

ESTIMATE STARTING AT___REG/INV___FORMAT___SORT___
REPORT COSTS FORMAT___SORT___
LIST FROM LEVEL___TO LEVEL___
LIST NODE___

Figure 4

To assemble and manipulate design representations, the system includes simple commands (Figure 4) that refer directly to tree elements. These commands govern the creation and destruction of nodes and the modification of node contents. To create a node (Define) one specifies its level, names it, and then lists the branches and their quantities that form its contents. To remove a node (Kill) one need only give its name. To change node contents, one can add (Put) or remove (Take) branches. Although these four commands suffice for all functions, two more were included for convenience. Replace is equivalent to Take followed by Put; Quantity allows one to change quantity without otherwise affecting node contents. As an added convenience, Take, Replace, and Quantity can modify all nodes, if desired, rather than a single named node. This allows one to do such things as replace all occurrences of one building component with another.

Internally, the assembly and editing commands are backed up by appropriate indexing, retrieval, and storage management programs. As editing occurs these programs access and modify the tree structure.

The remaining commands in Figure 4 govern the estimating and reporting functions that form the fourth component of the initial system. To perform conventional cost estimates, a simple "tree-walking" program performs the equivalent of a quantity survey on the tree structure. It does this by tracing down all possible branches, collecting branch quantities as it goes, and accumulating them in temporary registers at the bottom of the tree. A reporting program then computes and tabulates component and total costs.

The tree-walking program can be started off at any point in the tree. If started at the top, it will yield an estimate for the whole project. If started somewhere else, it will yield a quantity survey and cost estimate for the node selected. Figure 5 shows two reports for the tree shown in Figure 3, one covering the whole project and one covering just the one bedroom apartment. These were produced by starting the program at nodes Project-1 and 1-BR respectively. This ability to begin the takeoff process anywhere permitted separate estimates of individual apartments, buildings, and other design subgroupings of the project.

Figure 5 shows just one of several possible report formats. Component tabulations can be sorted, if desired,

by CSI or FHA categories. As well as detailed tabulations, summary reports can be produced giving category totals or just the final total.

NAME	DESCRIPTION	QUANTITY	MATERIAL COST		LABOR COST	
			UNIT	TOTAL	UNIT	TOTAL
STUD	2+1/2" MET STD (S. F)	171600	.32	54912	0.00	0
PLBD	1/2" GYP BD	288000	.08	22400	.13	36400
INSL	2" BATT INSULATION	63200	.05	3160	.05	3160
SIDG	METAL SIDING	63200	.27	17064	.20	12640
TUB	BATHTUB	60	35.00	2100	20.00	1200
TBAR	TOWEL BAR	120	1.00	120	.50	60
WALL	PRECAST WALL PANEL	50	864.00	43200	432.00	21600
FPLK	PRESTRESSED FLR PLK	1000	90.00	90000	47.00	47000
TOTAL BASIC COSTS				232956		122060
	INSURANCE & TAXES ON LABOR @ 30%			36618		
	TOTAL LABOR			122060		
	SUBTOTAL			391634		
	GENERAL CONDITIONS @ 5%			19582		
	SUBTOTAL			411216		
	OVERHEAD & PROFIT @ 10%			41122		
	SUBTOTAL			452337		
	BOND @ 1%			4523		
GRAND TOTAL COST UNIT PRJ1				456861		

COST REPORT -- UNIT PRJ1   PAGE 1

NAME	DESCRIPTION	QUANTITY	MATERIAL COST		LABOR COST	
			UNIT	TOTAL	UNIT	TOTAL
STUD	2+1/2" MET STD (S. F)	1500	.32	480	0.00	0
PLBD	1/2" GYP BD	2400	.08	192	.13	312
INSL	2" BATT INSULATION	600	.05	30	.05	30
SIDG	METAL SIDING	600	.27	162	.20	120
TUB	BATHTUB	1	35.00	35	20.00	20
TBAR	TOWEL BAR	2	1.00	2	.50	1
WALL	PRECAST WALL PANEL	2	864.00	1296	432.00	648
FPLK	PRESTRESSED FLR PLK	20	90.00	1800	47.00	940
TOTAL BASIC COSTS				3997		2071
	INSURANCE & TAXES ON LABOR @ 30%			621		
	TOTAL LABOR			2071		
	SUBTOTAL			6689		
	GENERAL CONDITIONS @ 5%			334		
	SUBTOTAL			7024		
	OVERHEAD & PROFIT @ 10%			702		
	SUBTOTAL			7726		
	BOND @ 1%			77		
GRAND TOTAL COST UNIT 1-BR				7803		

COST REPORT -- UNIT 1-BR   PAGE 1

Figure 5

The downward direction of the quantity survey program suggested reversing the procedure, starting with unit costs at the bottom, and extending costs and quantities up through the structure above. In contrast to the ordinary estimate, which analyzes a single node in detail, this procedure computes the total cost of each node in the tree. We called the resulting output an "inverted" cost report because the processing involved is, loosely speaking, the inverse of the ordinary case. In practice, inverted reports provide a convenient tool for analyzing the relative cost contributions of different parts of a project. For example, one such report shows, for every node, the cost contributed by each of its branches.

The Estimate command starts either of the two estimating processes and allows one to select an initial report format. Report Costs permits additional reports on the data generated in a prior estimate. The

List commands provide for tabulations of tree and component library contents.

III.   Practical Experience and Extensions

Once complete, we put the system to work, and tested it during several stages in the design development of the housing project. Figure 6 shows a model photograph of the project; its 1000-odd units were grouped into three-, six-, ten-, and eighteen-story buildings. Inside the computer, the project required a tree of 10 levels and about 200 nodes.

As expected, the system's chief value was its ability to do incremental and comparative estimation. It was possible to test such things as differing apartment layouts and alternative groupings of apartments into buildings, for their effect on total project cost. It was also useful to compute unit apartment and building costs, and to compare costs for public and private sectors. After each series of definitive design changes, we ran a complete series of cost reports, which formed one basis for subsequent design work.

Figure 6

During this testing phase we began to add new functions. We have completed report functions that tabulate floor areas and compute total areas for each type of precast panel used in a design. These functions use tree-processing techniques similar to the quantity survey. For example, to calculate floor areas, one traces the tree downward to the apartment level, and picks up unit areas stored on these nodes. We are currently working on heat and cooling load and schedule reports. To generate finish or door schedules, we will move across the tree at the apartment level, tracing down at each node to locate the desired items.

During testing, we watched the reactions of users with some concern. The tree representation exposes the user rather directly to the data structure inside the computer. It requires that the map design information from sketches and drawings into a hierarchical representation quite different in appearance. Further, he must keep the tree constantly in mind as the design progresses, editing it each time drawings are changed. We were concerned that all this would be burdensome enough to make the system unattractive.

In practice, this fear proved unfounded. With some practice, the tree representation and editing commands proved quite easy to use. In fact, some of the more powerful techniques for using the tree structure developed only after some experience with the system.

More importantly, the tree structure had a positive effect beyond its use in the computer. It developed into a tool that helped the designer organize and control design information outside the machine. Figures 7 and 8 make this somewhat clearer. In Figure 7, graphic information has been organized in a hierarchical fashion exactly paralleling the tree structure in the computer. Individual components on the left are carried through successive levels of aggregation leading to buildings on the right. Output, taken directly from the computer, tabulates the contents of each grouping; a uniform nomenclature has been used on the drawings and in the computer. Figure 8 carries this one step further, to the level of the site plan for the whole project.

What these montages show is the beginnings of a cataloguing system that keeps track of building components and their various levels of assembly into complete buildings. In part, this catalog resides in standard details and assembly drawings. Information inside the computer augments the drawings, indexing and organizing them, and quantifying their contents.

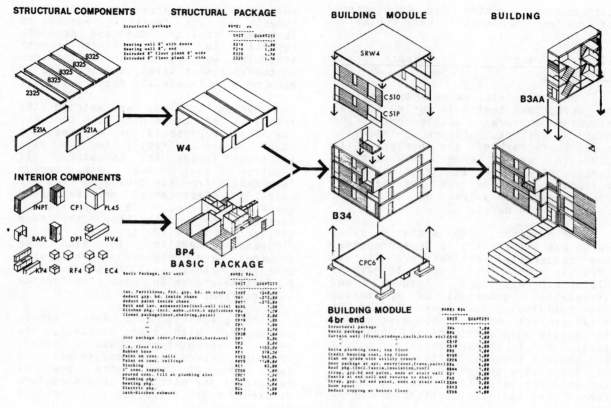

Figure 7

Although this "design catalog" was useful in the present project, it will be most valuable as a permanent control tool for Techcrete. Within the

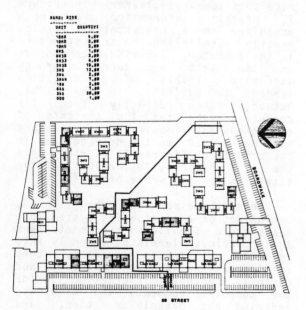

Figure 8

computer, this ongoing usage of design data has the effect of introducing a feedback loop, with completed design representations cycling back to become part of a pool of information upon which to draw in formulating new ones. This means several things. First, intuitively, it would seem to reflect rather naturally the evolving use of the building system in successive projects. The outcome of one project will influence the initial design of the next, and the feedback of design information in the computer reflects this quite directly.

Second, feedback will speed up the process of assembling tree representations. In this initial project, it was necessary to start from scratch, defining every node, and building up the tree level by level until it was complete. In the future, we will be able to call in more or less complete "chunks" of tree structure to formulate an initial representation.

Third, the ability to start off with a fully developed tree will give us a uniformly detailed basis for cost estimation throughout the life of a design project. This should overcome the discontinuity that occurs when a preliminary estimating basis (such as square footage) is dropped in favor of detailed quantity surveys (2). Figure 9 shows the system as extended to include additional report functions and the feedback of design information.

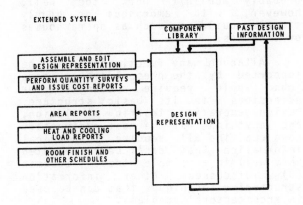

Figure 9

Inevitably, computer indexing of conventional drawings also suggested that we add a graphic capability to the system. In the beginning we had rejected this idea as jeopardizing our chances for practical results. However, by this time, we were pleased with how far we had got without graphics, and it seemed desirable to try some experiments.

Figures 10 and 11 show some preliminary results of this work. The material in these figures was assembled using an interactive display terminal,

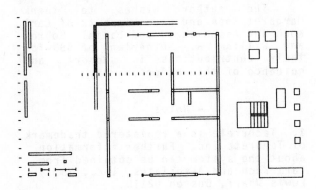

Figure 10

and then reproduced on a plotter. At the left in figure 11 we have created graphic symbols representing structural building components. In the center these have been grouped into the shell of a single apartment. At the right is a second group of components intended to form the apartment's interior contents.

Figure 11 shows a plan, at ground level, of a complete building. To get from figure 10 to figure 11, we combined the interior components with the structural shell to form a complete apartment. Then three of these were joined to form the building. The scales and tick marks in both figures are the computer equivalent of drafting tools; they help position picture elements as they are grouped together.

Internally, we used a tree structure similar to that in the initial system to store these drawings.

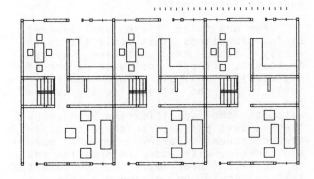

Figure 11

Individual components form the bottom level of the tree; groupings of these form nodes at successive levels above. Thus, figure 11 represents a single node at the top of the tree, containing three instances of the apartment node one level below plus an exterior wall. The only differences between this tree and the non-graphic one are 1) that component descriptions at the bottom level must contain graphic information describing their pictorial representations, and 2) that branches in the structure above must contain relative coordinates for the nodes they call out.

Externally, we exposed the user to the tree organization in much the same way as was done in the initial system. To produce figures 10 and 11, graphic symbols were first defined using a stylus device in conjunction with the display. Next, instances of these were called up onto the screen and grouped together into successive levels of hierarchy until the pictures were complete.

In doing these experiments, we were not seeking to perform basic graphics research. Thus, for example, we used graphics support programs already available at BBN. Our goal, rather, was to explore the possibility of incorporating graphics into the system we had built, using already established techniques. Although the work is still experimental, there appear to be few difficulties in the way of putting it into practice.

IV. Future Extensions

So far we have considered system features carried at least to the point of experimental testing. What follows are some thoughts on extensions to be added in future work.

For one thing, there are several useful functions that would fit quite easily within the existing system framework. These include a number of engineering analysis and reporting tools. Without stretching the system too much one could at least partially automate the specification process by linking text passages to the entries in the component library. Somewhat more ambitiously, with added information and appropriate programs, the component library could be expanded into a retrieval and analysis subsystem that would assist in component evaluation and support further engineering functions.

Viewing the full scope of component building - from manufacturing through construction - one can foresee further extensions. If extended into manufacturing the system could take on many functions of information systems currently in use in industry - inventory control and production scheduling, to name just two. In construction, it could assist in progress and cost monitoring, and job scheduling. As well as yielding a broader system, the manufacturing, design, and construction functions would mutually reinforce each other. For example, inventory control could utilize pooled quantity surveys of all current projects. Conversely, direct access to manufacturing data would

yield better unit costs and more accurate estimates.

Although developed for component building, we feel the system would also be effective with conventional structures such as housing, schools, and hospitals that are inherently hierarchical or repetitive. It probably wouldn't work too well, however, with amorphous or highly singular buildings such as opera houses or churches.

Although many functions could be supported by the present system, some jobs would require changes or extensions to its basic structure. Design generation, traffic simulation, and anything but the most rudimentary code checking all require topological information that can't be represented very well in a simple tree. Eastman (9) discusses other information structuring techniques that can be used in architectural problems.

V. Conclusion

This paper has explored the development of an information system for building design, focussing on its appearance to the user, and on the experience gained in using it. In this context, we feel the project demonstrates principally 1) the effectiveness with which simple tree structures can represent building projects, 2) the ease with which users can work directly with such structures, and 3) the extent to which a rather simple information system can assist in the design process.

Acknowledgement

The author wishes to thank Margaret Ross and Leon Lipshutz of Carl Koch and Associates, and Daniel Bobrow and William R. Sutherland of BBN for their contributions in support and guidance of this effort.

- Notes -

1. Techcrete is a registered trademark of Techrete Inc. Further information about the system can be obtained from Carl Koch and Associates, Inc., 35 Lewis Wharf, Boston 02110.

2. Myer, T. H., and R. I. Krauss, "Computer-Aided Cost Estimating

Techniques for Architects", Institute
for Applied Technology, National
Bureau of Standards, December 1965.

3. Krauss, R. I., and T. H. Myer,
"Computer-Aided Cost Estimating
Techniques" in Computer Applications in
Architecture and Engineering, N. Harper
Ed., New York: McGraw-Hill 1968.

4. Strictly speaking, we used a "semi-
tree", since downward pointing branches
can meet at nodes lower in the
structure.

5. Carr, C. S., "Geometric Modeling",
Computer Science Department, University
of Utah, 1969.

6. Newman, William M., "An Experiment-
al Program for Architectural Design",
The Computer Journal, Vol. 9 No. 1,
May 1966.

7. Cogswell, A. R., Werner Hausler,
and C. David Sides, "Integrated
Building Industry System", North
Carolina Fund, 1968.

8. Davis, Charles F., "An Architectural Data Management System", to be
published at this conference.

9. Eastman, Charles M., "Representa-
tions for Space Planning",
Communications of the ACM, Vol. 13
No. 4, April 1970.

Session Seven:

Environmental Disposition and Preferences

Chairman: Kenneth H. Craik

Department of Psychology, Clark University

An understanding of the dynamics of human response to the everyday physical environment will require the kind of diverse yet inter-related efforts illustrated by the papers prepared for this panel on environmental dispositions and preferences.

For environmental decision-makers, declared preferences for qualities and attributes of the physical environment represent noteworthy behavioral considerations. At the same time, they often express broader dispositions toward the environment that hold considerable interest for environmental psychologists. The present contributions include discussions of preferences for urban beaches (Peterson), preferences for house forms (Sanoff), and preferences for varied conditions of privacy (Marshall). In part, Peterson and Sanoff emphasize the linkage of preferences to descriptive environmental attributes, speaking to the question: Precisely what perceived aspects of the environment are operative in accounting for differential preference patterns? Marshall stresses the manner in which preferences constitute elements of a larger response structure or orientation, speaking to the question: What aspects of environmental personality are reflected in specific declared preferences?

If scales are to be constructed to assess individual differences in environmental dispositions, then the task of establishing the psychological meaning of the scale scores must

be undertaken, through scrutiny of their behavioral correlates, their relationships to other standard personality variables, and the way in which persons who score high and low on the scale are described by themselves and by individuals who know them well. Marshall, McKechnie, and Markman report upon efforts to clarify and delineate the psychological meaning of a variety of recently identified and assessed environmental dispositions.

A comprehensive description of an individual's environmental personality demands a multidimensional approach. The full taxonomy of environmental dispositions required to afford a differentiated account of any person's orientation to the everyday physical environment has not yet been developed. However, McKechnie and Marshall have begun to apply multivariate strategies to this problem.

In addition to exploring a broad array of environmental dispositions, each variable must be examined intensively from many vantage points. For example, the issue of sensation-seeking and sensation-avoiding arises in the presentations of Markman, McKechnie, and perhaps Marshall. Bringing to bear the functional perspective yielded by experimental studies of sensory deprivation and sensory overload, Wohlwill addresses himself directly to this recurrent theme.

Kenneth Craik

Sensation-Seeking and Environmental Preference

by Robert Markman

North Carolina State University

Abstract
The concept Sensation-Seeking (optimal level of stimulation, activation) is suggested as a possible vehicle for further understanding man's interaction with his physical environment. Utilizing two design student groups (Freshman Design (FD) and Upperclass Design (UD) and a non design student group (ND), the effect of sensation-seeking on environmental preference through visual perception of the physical environment was investigated. In addition the possible differences in sensation-seeking between design and non design student samples and its effect on the visual perception of the physical environment was also investigated. A chi square analysis found the UD group to be higher on the sensation-seeking dimension than either the FD or ND groups. The effect of this on environmental preference was still in the analysis stage.

Man's interaction with his physical environment, natural and man-made, his ability to transact with his environment, as well as the quality of that transaction for need fulfillment, and growth, is in large measure dependent on his character-istic mode of being in the world (personality, perception, life style, etc.) as well as the unique stimulus attributes of the environment at any given moment in time.

Craik (2) states that along with the intra-personal and interpersonal dimensions of personality "Individuals also seem to display fairly enduring styles of relating to the everyday physical environment."

One very important aspect of this environmental life style is our disposition towards and interaction with the designed environment. A great deal of one's time is spent in designed environments and this is likely to increase as our population and pollution problems increase. That man can adapt to this everchanging situation is fairly certain. Paradoxically, it is just this adaptability which necessitates an investigation into the consequences of interacting with designed environments. As Dubois (4) states, man can adapt to almost any condition from polluted air to concentration camps, however the adjustment to environments that sustain life but destroy human values is a poor and costly solution. In essence, the future quality of life will depend on our ability to create environments in which both human and biological life can co-exist. In the past, the task of designing was left to a group of experts who were not trained for or even made aware of the necessity to consider the behavioral consequences of their designs. "Designers have long been operating with a stock of principles from historic concerns of planning environments; and these principles predispose them to make certain assumptions about what people want and ought to want. The user has been taken for granted, his characteristics merely assumed as undifferentiated constants. Though the architect today may be dissatisfied with the appropriateness of his solutions, he is still unable to predict the consequences of his decisions with any degree of accuracy." (13)

One way in which the behavioral scientist can contribute to the current situation is to investigate those organismic variables which are believed to affect one's environmental life style. This life style can be effected by both the social and physical environment. This study deals essentially with the effect of the physical environment on one's life style.

The purpose of this study is to investigate the relation between sensation-seeking (activation, need for variation, optimal level of stimulation) and environmental preference. Originally postulated as a substitute for the more limited concept of drive reduction (10) the concept of optimal level of stimulation has been utilized to explain sensory deprivation results (8) and effects of early environment (7), it has also more recently been described as a dimension of personality (5,11). Zuckerman (15) comments that while the theory postulates an optimal level of stimulation, wide individual differences must exist in what is considered an optimal level of stimulation during a waking day. Maddi (11) in postulating a personality theory based on the concept of activation, utilizes this view of individual differences to delineate two major personality types; the High Activation (HA) type and the Low Activation (LA) type. Essentially the HA person is characterized by an approach tendency toward stimulation while the LA person exhibits an avoidance tendency. The theory emphasizes the importance of the information or emotional experience the person gets out of interacting with the external world. The assumption is that a particular kind of information or emotional experience is best for the person, (customary level of activation) and hence, he will develop a personality which increases the likelihood of his interacting with the world such as to get this kind of information or emotional experience. The personality is therefore determined much more by the feedback from interaction with the world than it is by inherent attributes of man.

Although other optimal level of stimulation theorists (1,3,7) do not postulate approach-avoidance motives as such, all agree that humans require some stimulus variability to function effectively and this optimal amount necessarily differs from person to person. It is from this basis that the investigation into the possible differences in perception of the physical environment of people with differing optimal stimulation needs begins. Not only is this of importance for the general population but the possibility that our future designers (design students) are greater seekers of stimulation is worth identifying. This possibility is enhanced by the findings of Barron & Welsh (1a) in which painters showed a marked preference for the more complex and asymmetrical figures of the Welsh Figure Preference Test while a sample of non-artists showed a marked preference for the simple and symmetrical drawings. This coupled with the findings of Berlyne (1)

that preference for complexity and asymmetry are indicative of a high need for stimulation, might lead one to predict a higher activation level for design students. This finding would perhaps isolate a contributing factor to the widespread general uneasiness with one's designed environment. The assumption being that with relatively high stimulus-seeking people designing our environments avoidance behavior is being engendered in users who are lower stimulus-seeking people and as such have an avoidance tendency toward stimulation. This situation might then relegate much of the relation between user and environment to a surface interaction geared toward survival instead of a more desirable transactional one which implies growth.

While Fiske & Maddi (5) propose the need for environmental variation as a necessary construct for personality theory, the major drawback of this concept as a dimension of personality has been the inability to assess the intensity of an individual's needs. One possible solution to this problem is an adjective check list developed by Thayer (14) which requires the subject to give some indication of his present activation level by selecting from a group of self-descriptive adjectives (e.g. from peppy to sleepy). This test purporst to measure four activation factors; 1) general activation, 2) high activation, 3) general de-activation, 4) de-activation sleep. Thayer views these factors as roughly constituting four points on a hypothetical activation continuum from sleep to anxious tension, thereby providing a seemingly simple measure of what Maddi (11) refers to as customary level of activation. Craik (2) lists several attempts to assess environmental dispositions by seeking to measure the inclination for varied experience: a test of Change-Seeking Behavior (9), the Change-Seeker Index (CSI) (6), the Sensation-Seeking Scale (SSS) (15), and the Stimulation-Variation Seeking Scale (SVS) (12). Of these the SSS appears to have the most utility for the present study. It has shown expected correlations with three of Maddi's activation personality types.(11) Also as a measure of sensation-seeking for situations outside of the experimental session it is a necessary compliment to the Activation De-activation-Adjective Check List (AD-ACL). The SSS is a forced choice type test which requires subjects to choose between paired items which indicate sensation-seeking needs (e.g. A. I often wish I could be a mountain climber, B. I can't understand people who risk their necks climbing mountains). The subject chooses one of the statements as indicative of his feelings, and his score is determined by the number of statements chosen in the sensation-seeking direction.

The hypothoses for this study are: 1. People with different sensation-seeking needs will display different environmental preferences, with high sensation-seeking individuals preferring the more complex and stimulating designs. 2. Design students will display higher sensation-seeking needs than non-designers.

Method
Subjects
One hundred and fifty male undergraduate students at North Carolina State University served as subjects. Forty subjects participated in order to fulfill a departmental requirement for introductory psychology students. Ten additional subjects were solicited at a campus dormitory in order to complete the non-design (ND) group. The remaining 100 subjects were students enrolled at the School of Design at NCSU. Fifty of these were from the Freshman class and were designated Freshman Design (FD) while the remaining fifty, Upperclass Design (UD), were students in their 3rd and 4th year of studying.

Testing Materials
The testing materials consisted of two sets of questionnaires. Set A contained two measures of the need for variation, the AD-ACL and the SSS. Set B was made up of four residential silhouette designs selected to encompass the dimensions of simplicity to complexity and commonness to novelty. (see Figure 1)

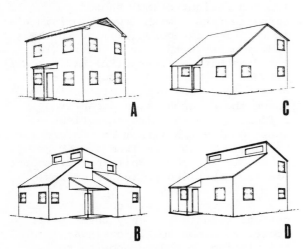

Figure 1. Residential silhouette designs

Prior to the administration to subjects Design A was judged the most simple and common, Design C was judged simple but more novel than A, Design D was judged more complex and novel than either A or C, and finally Design B was judged the most complex and novel. In addition, two photographs of actual buildings were also used with Building F being judged more complex and novel than Building E. (see Figure 2)

Figure 2. Photographs of actual buildings

Each of the six designs (A through F) was presented separately with an identical sixteen item semantic differential rated on a seven-point scale. (see Table 1)

Table 1. Semantic Differential

1. complex   to simple
2. stimulating   "   sedate
3. rough   "   smooth
4. asymmetrical   "   symmetrical
5. unobtrusive   "   bold
6. boring   "   interesting
7. individual   "   universal
8. common   "   novel
9. static   "   dynamic
10. tense   "   relaxed
11. dislike   "   like
12. Colorful   "   colorless
13. beautiful   "   ugly
14. warm   "   cold
15. impractical   "   practical
16. familiar   "   unknown

In addition to the semantic differentials each subject was asked to rank the four residential silhouette designs from best liked to least liked. The final questionnaire, the Environmental Stimulation Index (ESI), a short semantic differential, was administered so that each subject could rate the perceived stimulation effect of the experimental session.

Procedure

Subjects were tested in groups. All subjects were tested in familiar classroom surroundings, psychology students in the psychology department, dormitory subjects in their dormitory lounge and design students in the School of Design. All subjects were tested during the hours of 11:00 a.m. to 3:00 p.m. The following instructions were given before the testing packet was distributed. "This is a study to investigate some characteristics of an individual's perception of his physical environment. The study is intended to give us some insights into the factors which facilitate or impede one's interaction with his environment. During this hour you will be asked to fill out a number of questionnaires. It is of utmost importance that you answer all questions to the best of your ability, and in the order in which they appear in the packet. Are there any questions? If any questions arise during the session please raise your hand and I will try to

answer them. Thank you." Only questions of a procedural nature were answered. All others were handled in a way in which indicated that the subject was to answer according to his present feeling. Half of each group received set A of the questionnaire first, while the other half received set B first. In addition, four of the twenty-four possible arrangements of the residential silhouette designs were collated and randomly distributed within each group. Regardless of the order in which the subject received the two sets of the questionnaires, his final task was always the completion of the environmental stimulation index.

Results

A chi square (x^2) analysis was run for the two measures of sensation-seeking (AD-ACL, and SSS). No difference was found between groups for the AD-ACL scores. On the SSS scores the following distribution was obtained. (see Table 2)

Table 2. Chi square for SSS

		SSS		
Group	Low	Medium	High	Total
ND	12	26	12	50
FD	7	29	14	50
UD	2	22	26	50
Total	21	77	52	150

The upperclass designers (UD) had the most individuals in the high category on sensation-seeking (26) and the lowest number in the low category (2). The non designers (ND) showed an opposite result with fewest individuals in the high category (12) and the most individuals in the low category (12). The freshman designers (FD) had a result between the ND and UD groups on both dimensions. The chi square analysis shows the UD group significantly different (in the high sensation-seeking direction) from the FD group, $x^2 = 7.4 > .05$ and from the ND group, $x^2 = 12.6 > .01$. While no difference was found between FD and ND groups, $x^2 = 1.60 < .05$.

A factor analysis on the six designs resulted in only three pairs of concepts common to all designs; stimulating to sedate, boring to interesting, and dislike to like.

In addition the six designs were separated in essentially three groups; with designs B,C,D,E responded to similarly, design F somewhat differently responded to and design A the most uniquely responded to.

The analysis of environmental preference is still in progress at this time.

References

1. Berlyne, D. R. Conflict, arousal & curiosity. New York:McGraw-Hill, 1960.
1a. Barron, F. and Welsh, G.S. Artistic perception as a possible factor in personality style: its measurement by a figure preference test. Journal of Psychology, 33, 1952, 199-203.
2. Craik, K. H. Assessing environmental dispositions, a contribution to the symposium "Assessing environmental contexts of behavior", American Psychological Association, 1969, Washington, D.C.
3. Dember, W. N. The psychology of perception. New York:Holt, 1960.
4. Dubois, R. J. Man adapting: His limitations and potentialities. in Environment for Man, W. R. Ewald, Jr., ed., Indiana University Press, 1967, p. 11-26.
5. Fiske, D. W. and Maddi, S. R. (eds.) Functions of varied experience. The Dorcey Press, Homewood, Illinois, 1961.
6. Garlington, W. K. and Shimota, H. E. The change seeking index: a measure of the need for variable stimulus input. Psychological Reports, 14, 1964, 919-924.
7. Hebb, D. O. The motivating effects of extroceptive stimulation. American Psychologist, 13, 1958, 109-113.
8. Hebb, D. O. and Thompson, W. R. The social significance of animal studies in G. Lindzey (ed) Handbook of Social Psychology, Cambridge, Massachusetts, Addison-Wesley, 1959, 551-552.
9. Howard, K. I. A test of stimulus-seeking behavior. Perception and Motor Skills, 13, 1961, 416.
10. Leuba, C. Toward some integration of learning theories: the concept of optimal stimulation. Psychological Reports, 1, 1955, 27-33.
11. Maddi, S. R. Personality theories: a comparative analysis. Homewood, Illinois: the Dorcey Press, 1968.
12. Penny, R. K. and Reinher, R. C. Development of a stimulus variation seeking scale for adults. Psychological Reports, 18, 1966, 631-638.
13. Sanoff, H. Student Publication, School of Design, N. C. State University, Raleigh, N.C., 1969.
14. Thayer, R. E. Measurement of activation through self-report. Psychological Reports, 20, 1967 663-678.
15. Zuckerman, M., Kolin, E. A., Price, I. and Zoob, I. Development of a sensation seeking scale. Journal of Consulting Psychology, 28, 1964, 477-482.

Personality Correlates of Orientation toward Privacy

by Nancy J. Marshall

James Madison College and
Multidisciplinary Social Science Program, Michigan State University

Abstract. Six orientations toward privacy were
identified by means of the Privacy Preference
Scale, centering around preferences for non-
involvement with neighbors, seclusion of home,
solitude, privacy with intimates, anonymity,
and reserve. In junior college and university
samples, orientations were found to be related
to the personality dimensions Extraversion-
Introversion and Thinking-Feeling on the Myers-
Briggs Type Inventory and to Wanted and
Expressed Affection and Inclusion on FIRO-B.
Individual differences in privacy orientation
were found between adult and junior college
samples and between sexes, but not between
socioeconomic statuses. The developmental
sources and correlated environmental beliefs of
orientations were also assessed.

Privacy Preference as an Environmental Disposition. The value placed on privacy seems to
have varied greatly historically (1,2), offering little evidence that privacy is an innate
"need" or privacy-oriented behavior a function
merely of the immediate environment. Viewing
privacy orientations as dispositions toward the
environment, they can be defined as preferences
to control access to others, with features of
the physical environment either aiding or hin-
dering this control.

This study was concerned with answering
the following questions: (a) can a generalized
preference for privacy be subdivided into
distinct orientations, (b) do persons differing
in age, sex, or socioeconomic status also show
differences in orientation, (c) are there personality differences that are related to the
orientations, and (d) to what extent do persons
with differing orientations also differ in
their beliefs about the environment and about
legal protection of the right to privacy?

The Concept of Privacy. The concept of privacy
was explored using the Privacy Preference
Scale. This scale, developed first in a university setting, contained items tied to the
unique living experiences of the college
student (living in a dormitory, fraternity, or
apartment; studying). A revision to make it
applicable to a more general population

adapted the items to the living situation of
the family in a residential setting. A sample
of 149 junior college students living at home
and 101 of their parents responded to the
86-item final scale. Principal components
analysis of the responses for the adult and
student samples, and for the two combined,
revealed six factors that appeared in the
combined analysis and in both the adult and
student analyses. The six subscales formed
from these factors and their intercorrelations
with each other and with total score on the
privacy scale (PPS) were discussed in my
earlier paper (3) and will be mentioned only
briefly here.

Three of the factors could be generally
characterized as centering on control over
degree of self-disclosure to others, with the
Reserve factor dealing directly with preferences regarding self-disclosure. Both the
Neighboring and Anonymity factors can be
construed as means of controlling involvement
with and therefore disclosure to others by
limiting involvement with neighbors and
choosing the anonymity of city living, respectively.

Two of the factors, Solitude and Seclusion, are centered around physical barriers
(including distance between self and other)
as means of gaining privacy. These factors,
particularly Seclusion, reflect Seaton's (4)
concept of control over input and output,
both visual and auditory, but were not completely consistent with this interpretation,
since several items regarding input more
broadly defined (e.g., not answering the telephone, drawing the drapes, erecting fences)
were not included. The final factor, Intimacy, involves the size of the unit for which
privacy is desired, and was thus expected to
show the observed relationship with Solitude,
Seclusion, and Reserve.

Age, Sex, and Socioeconomic Status Differences
in Privacy Orientations. Age group (adult,
student) and sex classifications were placed
in a 2 x 2 multivariate analysis of variance
design, with the six privacy subscales as
dependent variables. This technique enables

one to test for significant mean differences between groups for several dependent variables simultaneously. It provides a test of the significance of the overall main and interaction effects, as well as indicating by means of step-down F coefficients and standardized discriminant function coefficients which of the dependent variables contributes most to differentiating the groups. The overall multivariate F-ratios for both age and sex were highly significant, with no significant interaction effect (multivariate Fs = 17.06 and 4.77; dfh = 6, dfe = 24, p ⋜ .0001). The mean scores by age group are graphed in Figure 1 as deviations from the midpoint of each scale, the midpoint being the score obtained if a subject chose the neutral response to all items. The means and mean differences on the subscales indicated that, while both adults and students favored reserve (R), solitude (So), seclusion (Se), and privacy for intimacy (I), and rejected non-involvement with neighbors (N) and anonymity (A) as means of gaining privacy, adults were significantly more oriented toward reserve and non-involvement with neighbors, and students toward solitude and privacy with intimates.

Analysis of the differences between sexes (see Figure 2) indicated that females were less self-disclosing than males and showed greater preference for solitude and for privacy with intimates, while males showed higher preference for seclusion. These findings, particularly the female preference for low self-disclosure, do not support the common stereotype about sex differences in this area, nor the finding of Jourard and Lasakow (5) that males disclosed less than females.

Placement of socioeconomic status and age in a similar 2 x 2 multivariate analysis of variance matrix with the six subscales as

dependent variables did not reveal significant differences in orientation between social classes (multivariate F = 1.20, df = 18 and 671, p = .26).

Personality Correlates of Privacy Orientations. Responses to two personality scales were correlated with privacy preferences, the FIRO-B (6) in the pilot study with university students (n=198) and the Myers-Briggs Type Inventory (6) with the junior college sample (students only). The six subscales of FIRO-B measure wanted and expressed affection, inclusion, and control in interpersonal relationships. It was expected that, since high scores on the first four FIRO-B scales reflect both the frequency (on a scale from "never" to "usually") and generality (from "no one" to "most people") of inclusion and affection preferences, high scorers on these four scales would have relatively low scores for at least those items of the Privacy Preference Scale concerning solitude and self-disclosure. Placing a high value on including others in activities and being included by others (Expressed and Wanted Inclusion) would almost necessarily preclude having a high level of solitude. Similarly, Jourard (8) suggested that developing a close friendship requires reciprocal disclosure by both parties. Thus, a high value on friendship as measured by the Wanted and Expressed Affection scales would require a willingness to disclose both more broadly and more deeply than otherwise. As hypothesized, these four of the six FIRO-B scales (Expressed Inclusion, Wanted Inclusion, Expressed Affection, Wanted Affection) were significantly correlated with total scores on the Privacy Preference Scale (rs = -.54, -.44, -.44, and -.49, respectively), but the FIRO-B Control scales were not significantly related. The subscales of PPS had not been developed at

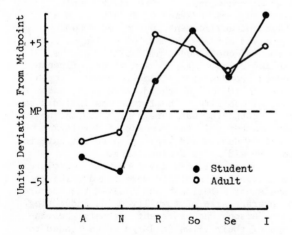

FIG. 1. Means of privacy subscale scores by age, shown as deviations from scale midpoints.

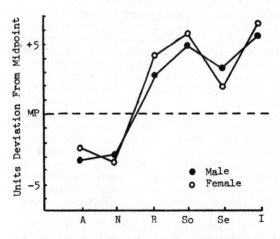

FIG. 2. Means of privacy subscale scores by sex, shown as deviations from scale midpoints.

this time, so more specific relationships with the orientations could not be explored.

The four bipolar scales of the Myers-Briggs Type Indicator (MBTI) are based on Jungian typology (7). The Extraversion-Introversion (E-I) dimension is designed to reflect whether perception and judgment are directed toward the outer world of people or the inner world of concepts and ideas; Sensing-Intuition reflects perceiving directly through the five senses or indirectly by way of the unconscious. Thinking-Feeling (T-F) reflects whether judgment is arrived at by impersonal and logical or by subjective processes, and the Judging-Perceiving (J-P) whether the judging or perceptive attitude is relied upon the majority of the time in dealing with the outer world.

Stricker and Ross (9) have suggested, based on the correlates of the dimensions, that the E-I dimension reflects more closely the conventional definition of introversion-extraversion as ease in and liking for interpersonal contact than it does interest in the inner world of ideas. Mendelsohn (10) has suggested that the S-N dimension reflects an orientation toward the practical, conventional, and realistic rather than toward ideas or theories. Legalistic, rationalistic as opposed to humanistic, sympathetic concerns seem to characterize the T-F dimension; the J-P dimension concentrates on order and planning versus spontaneity and novelty.

One hundred eighteen of the 149 student Ss in the junior college sample completed the MBTI. As hypothesized, the Extraversion-Introversion scale was significantly related to overall PPS (r = .30) and to the Neighboring, Seclusion, Reserve, and Anonymity subscales (rs = .22, .24, .24, and .17, respectively). The pattern of the correlations indicated that the major factor in the relationship between E-I and privacy preference was an emphasis on non-involvement with non-intimate others. Solitude, which was expected to correlate highly with E-I, was not significantly related in this sample. If one assumes that preference for solitude indicates a desire for time for thought and reflection, and thus an orientation toward ideas, these relationships support the Stricker and Ross (9) interpretation of the E-I scale as measuring "ease in and liking for interpersonal contact" more than Myers' (6) "perception and judgment directed upon the environment or upon the world of ideas." The highest privacy correlate of E-I was PPS total score, indicating that Introversion was related to privacy preferences in a variety of situations rather than being characteristic of a particular situation or means of obtaining privacy.

The Thinking-Feeling scale was significantly related to PPS (r = -.25) as well as to Neighboring and Reserve (rs = -.31 and -.22, respectively). The negative correlations indicated that persons scoring toward the Thinking

end of the dimension had high preference for privacy (PPS), and tended to prefer low involvement with neighbors and low levels of disclosure. The other significant correlation related preference for non-involvement with neighbors to preference for the judging rather than perceiving mode (J-P). In light of the preponderance of items on the Neighboring subscale dealing with having persons casually drop in rather than be more formally invited, this finding corroborates Mendelsohn's interpretation of J-P as differentiating dispositions toward order and planning from dispositions toward spontaneity. It is interesting to note that although high preference for privacy as measured by PPS was positively related to the Thinking rather than the Feeling disposition, the relationship was reversed with a measure of beliefs about a legal right to privacy. With the legal scale, the direction of the correlations indicated that persons scoring toward the Thinking end of the dimension tended to value public safety, the need to apprehend criminals, and company efficiency over the right of privacy, while persons toward the Feeling end tended to value the human dignity and privacy rights of the prisoner, suspected criminal, or employee over conflicting considerations. Thus, the relationship between PPS and T-F may indicate that the feeling person, being more oriented toward other persons, is less desirous of privacy or withdrawal from others; but at the same time, when privacy desires come into conflict with bureaucratic considerations, he is more sympathetic with personalistic needs.

Development of Preference for Privacy.
Central to a concern with individual differences in orientations toward privacy is an interest in the developmental source of these differences, including their relationship to past environments. In the adult sample, measures were obtained of density of the childhood environment (perceived crowding, perceived privacy, number of siblings, having a room of one's own), amicability of the sibling relationship (which might influence judged crowding or privacy), amount of open space in the neighborhood, town size, and spatial mobility. The latter was included on the hypothesis that more mobile persons would be constantly in the process of developing new friendships and might as a result have to be more widely self-disclosing.

In general, few developmental correlates of privacy orientations were found. The most consistent relationships involved the measure of average size of town lived in, indicating that persons who had spent a greater percentage of their lives in large towns tended to have higher overall preferences for privacy and to be oriented toward Intimacy and Anonymity. The causal direction of the latter relationship is uncertain; since Anonymity reflects a liking for city living as a means of gaining privacy, persons may have chosen or been open to city living as a result of privacy preferences as well as the reverse. Persons with high perceived crowding during childhood tended to be open to the anonymity of city living and be reserved, as indicated by the positive correlations with these subscales. The hypothesized negative correlation based on adaptation level theory of perceived crowding with Solitude appeared but was not significant (r = -.12). The hypothesized relationship of high mobility to high levels of disclosure also was not substantiated.

Beliefs about Privacy and the Environment. With the concern expressed from many sources that crowding and cities are "bad" or unhealthy and the natural environment "good," it is of interest to assess beliefs about the value of various parts of the everyday physical environment and about the effects of the environment on humans. Responses to several items dealing with beliefs about privacy and the environment by the adult and student samples are presented here as a small step in that direction. Three of the seven items showed substantial differences between adult and student samples; adults were more likely than students to say that "one ought to be allowed a private life and a public one, completely separate," and that "the stress of living in crowded cities is psychologically damaging." Adults were more likely than students to disagree with an item reading "I wouldn't mind living in an apartment building holding hundreds of people." Both samples felt that "children need open space, lawns, and gardens in order to develop naturally," and disagreed with items reading "people in general are very adaptable--they can adjust to almost any amount of crowding with no ill effects," and "Americans put too much emphasis on the value of privacy."

Answers to the opinion items were consistently predictable from the scores on orientation toward seclusion, "seclusives" indicating positive evaluations of open space and privacy and negative evaluations of crowding. Overall scores on the PPS also tended to be consistently related to environmental beliefs. Two items were strongly related to several of the orientations. The item reading "one ought to be allowed a private life and a public one, completely separate" showed 11 significant correlations out of 14 possible correlations for the two samples, and was particularly closely associated with scores on PPS, Solitude, and Intimacy for the adult sample. The item "A decay of 'inner life,' of concern for secluded and inward qualities, is common today" was highly correlated with Seclusion, Reserve, and Intimacy in both samples and with PPS in the adult sample. Comparing this to responses on the item dealing with the emphasis Americans put on privacy reveals a belief that

Americans, rather than placing too much emphasis on privacy, may in fact not place enough emphasis on it.

Conclusion. Further information about characteristics of these orientations toward privacy can be found in my companion paper (3), particularly their correlates in the current physical environments and behavior of the adult sample; many additional aspects remain to be explored. One of the major discoveries I have made in attempting to assess individual differences in privacy preferences is the usefulness of multivariate techniques which allow comparison of sets of variables rather than limiting comparisons to single variables. These techniques are still being developed and many of them have not been used enough in the social sciences to produce an extensive literature on accurate interpretation of the results, but they are nevertheless invaluable in the analysis of complex data.

Notes

1. Reubhausen, Oscar, & Brim, Orville. Privacy and behavioral research. American Psychologist, 1966, 21, 423-437.

2. Aries, Philippe. Centuries of childhood. New York: Knopf, 1960.

3. See "Environmental components of privacy preferences," also prepared for this conference.

4. Seaton, Richard. Personal communication, January, 1969.

5. Jourard, Sidney, & Lasakow, Paul. Some factors in self-disclosure. Journal of Abnormal and Social Psychology, 1958, 56, 91-98.

6. Schutz, William. FIRO: a three-dimensional theory of interpersonal behavior. New York: Rinehart, 1958.

7. Myers, Isabel. Manual, Myers-Briggs Type Indicator. Princeton, N. J.: Educational Testing Service, 1962.

8. Jourard, Sidney. The transparent self: self-disclosure and well-being. New York: Van Nostrand, 1964.

9. Stricker, L., & Ross, J. Some correlates of a Jungian personality inventory. Psychological Reports, 1964, 14, 623-643.

10. Mendelsohn, Gerald. The Myers-Briggs Type Indicator. In O. Buros (Ed.), The sixth mental measurements yearbook. Highland Park, N. J.: Gryphon Press, 1965. Pp. 321-322.

Measuring Environmental Dispositions with the Environmental Response Inventory

by George E. McKechnie

Institute of Personality Assessment and Research,
University of California, Berkeley

Abstract

The notion of environmental dispositions is offered as a means of tapping significant environment-related personality dimensions. The Environmental Response Inventory (ERI) is presented as a research instrument to measure a number of these dispositions. Development of the ERI is discussed, as well as the process of conceptual analysis by which the validity, personological meaning, and real-life utility of personality variables are appraised. Suggestions for potential research applications are made.

The Study of Environmental Dispositions

People differ greatly in the ways they comprehend and make use of the environment. Leisure recreation behavior provides an unusually good display of these differences: While some people enjoy backpacking in the Sierra wilderness, others prefer the excitement of water sports or the leisurely quiet of boating. Still others choose the security and comfort of their own home or back yard for leisure activity. Even within a rather narrow recreational category--such as boating --substantial stylistic differences exist among enthusiasts. Fisherman boaters, sailers, speed boat racers, and cruiser owners each interact in unique ways with their chosen segment of the environment. Differences undoubtedly exist also in the attitudes, preferences, and beliefs with which these groups approach their favorite leisure activity, and in the ways in which aspects of their recreational interludes are incorporated into their non-leisure lives. It is clear that research in environmental psychology must take into consideration the environmental dispositions-- the configurations of attitudes, beliefs, values, and sentiments--of the people whose environmental behavior are being studied and whose future environmental responses are being predicted.

The need for reliable methods of distinguishing among people along environment-related dimensions has been recognized recently both by psychologists and by designers and managers of the environment. The environmental dispo-

sitions of special user groups and of observers generally have been acknowledged as theoretically important variables in both Peterson and Neumann's (1969) conceptual model for predicting human response to the visual recreation environment and in Craik's (1970) general process model for the assessment of environments. In research practice, (Sonnenfeld 1966; Lowenthal, 1967; Hendee, et al, 1968; Craik, 1969; Peterson and Neumann, 1969) personal characteristics of the observer have taken on increasing importance. This trend promises to make available to environmental managers and other specialists useful procedures for assessing the motivations, moods, and preferences of the environmental observer, be he special user, environmental specialist, or everyman. To date, however, research in this area--misleadingly described by the rubric 'environmental perception'--has typically related subject preference differences to demographic subject variables (e.g., sex, age, or familiarity of the observer) or to analytic environmental vaiables (e.g. intensity of vegetation), leaving the individual observer essentially undescribed. The approach presented in this report, in contrast, searches for meaningful configurations of attitudes, sentiments, beliefs, and values which cut across demographic variables and which possess deeper personological meaning and predictive validity than the variables employed to date in this research area.

Recently, I have conducted research to discover environmental dispositions which are personologically meaningful and which possess predictive utility in forecasting significant environment-related behavior. I have developed the Environmental Response Inventory (ERI) for the assessment of these dispositions. The rationale underlying the development of the ERI is drawn from the psychology of personality: that people relate to the everyday physical environment in stable, characteristic ways, just as they relate to themselves and to others according to enduring patterns. While psychologists have long considered it reasonable and useful to study and describe persons in terms of intra-psychic (e.g., self-punishing, self-accepting) and inter-personal (e.g., dominant, nurturant) dispositions, the study of environmental dispositions, with perhaps the exception of Hendee's (Hendee, et. al., 1968) Wildernism scale and several measures of the stimulus-seeking disposition (Howard, 1961; Zuckerman, et. al., 1964; Penny and Rienher, 1966), is an essentially new enterprise. This is so even though the historical anticedents for the latter run throughout the American intellectual tradition (Marx, 1964) and can be traced back to the astrology and physical philosophy of the Greeks (Glacken, 1967).

Currently, the ERI consists of 218 True-False items (e.g., I like to explore unfamiliar places,) tapping a number of environment-related themes, such as urban life, environmental memories, and geographic preferences. In completing the ERI, the respondent simply indicates whether each item is descriptive of his views or of his typical behavior. Some of the configurations identified through preliminary research with the ERI have been labeled Urbanism, Pastoralism, Stimulus-seeking, and Environmental Security. A generally successful effort was made to develop scales which would be statistically independent of each other. Moreover, preliminary research has revealed that the ERI scales do have interesting and significant patterns of correlations with numerous traditional personality measures, with such environment-related behaviors as membership in conservation and agricultural organizations, and with such demographic variables as length of residence in urban areas and population of the community of current residence.

Development of the ERI: Methodological prelude

Interest in describing the personality of an individual--in comprehending the full complexity of his unique and enduring character--may be traced back through centuries of eulogists, diplomats, and men of letters to the Greek writers Suetonius and Theophrastus. Yet is is only within the last thirty-five years that psychologists have begun systematic and comprehensive study of lives (Murray, 1937.) A problem that has endured throughout this brief history is that of description: how does the psychologist find out what a person is really like? One solution to this problem has been to ask subject a series of questions designed to reveal important information about his enduring psychological orientations. If a number of such questions dealt with a single theme, e.g. dominance vs. submission, a scale could be constructed to measure people along this dimension. This was achieved by assigning different values to different responses, and by computing a score for each person on the dimension. Questionaires designed to measure comprehensively a number of such dimensions have become known as inventories.

A number of different strtegies have evolved for constructing the scales of psychological inventories. In the rational approach, the psychologist decides a priori that a given question (hereafter referred to as inventory item) belongs on a certain scale, and will be scored in a given direction (e.g. one point for dominance if answered true.) The success of this approach depends--of course--on the ability of the psychologist to make correct a priori inferences about both the manifestations of underlying psychological dispositions and the subtleties of verbal self-report. Not surprisingly, its success has been modest.

Numerous empirical strategies of scale construction have also evolved. Two of these, the criterion group method and factor analysis, deserve special mention. In the criterion group approach, as with the rational approach, the test constructor decides a priori which dimension he wishes to scale. Here, however, instead of deciding a priori which item should be scored on which scale and in what direction, the psychologist chooses criterion groups-- either naturally occurring or formed by nomination or rating--which he believes ought to score high and low on the dimension being scaled. Thus, for example, a dominance scale could be constructed using highly successful salesmen vs. filing clerks or using people rated by their friends as dominant vs. those rated submissive. Responses of these groups are obtained for a large pool of items, which is then analyzed to determine which items reliably distinguish between the high and low dominance groups. The advantage of this approach is that items are scaled on a dimension only after they have been shown to relate to one or more meaningful personological criteria external to the item-pool itself. The disadvantages are several. First, a set of scales constructed in this manner often are significantly intercorrelated, and thus provide information about the individual that is redundant, i.e. already partially tapped by other scales. The second major disadvantage is that individual scales often contain unwanted variance--surplus meaning due to the fact that criterion groups may differ in ways other than (or in addition to) those intended by the psychologist. In spite of these limitations, the criterion group method has yielded several of the most successful psychological inventories, among them the Strong Vocational Interest Blank (Strong, 1966), the Minnesota Multiphasic Psychological Inventory(Hathaway and McKinley, 1968) and the California Psychological Inventory (Gough, 1964).

With the method of factor analysis (Harmon, 1967), the psychologist need not make a priori assumptions about what his dimensions ought to be. Instead, he administers his item pool to a large--and hopefully representative--group of subjects, and then performs an item (fator) analysis to determine which items have similar patterns of covariance (i.e., which items cluster together in the sense that people tend to respond to them in a similar way.) These items will load highly on a factor, and can be grouped together to form a scale measuring the dimension represented by the factor. Items with high negative loadings are included in the scale, but are scored for an opposite (e.g. false) response. Thus both the selection of dimensions and the keying of items on these dimensions is empirical. Notice that the scaling criterion employed with this method is an internal one. Scales are formed on the basis of patterns of interrelationships that are found among items within the item-pool. The advantages claimed for this method are that the scale constructor need not make a priori judgments about which dimensions should be tapped by his item-pool, and that the dimensions that are obtained are usually orthogonal (i.e. independent) and thus non-redundant. The potential disadvantage is that the factor solution reflects patterns of covariance among all items, good and bad. Thus the factor analysis of an item-pool containing a large proportion of items which fail to tap meaningful aspects of personality may yield scales of limited utility, while the criterion group method more successfully selects out the good items, scaling them on more powerful, though perhaps more arbitrary, dimensions.

Factor Analysis of the ERI Item Pool

The factor analytic method was employed in the development of the ERI. This choice reflects the fact that in a new area of investigation such as environmental dispositions, there is precious little research to consult in choosing dimensions to be scales. Moreover even if good concepts were available, so little is known about individual differences along these dimensions that there would be little basis for selecting criterion groups. Under these conditions, the factor analysis of a pool of items sufficiently broad to cover the field is a much more reasonable approach than selecting a priori an arbitrary number of dimensions of undetermined utility and sufficiency.

While no single theory was considered rich or explicit enough to supply criterion group dimensions, the many themes which run throughout the history of environmental theory were of heuristic value in writing items. Items were written to tap the following themes: pastoralism, conservation, science and technology, urban life, rural life, stimulus preferences, cultural life, leisure activities, the outdoors, geographic and architectural preferences, and environmental memories and knowledge. The item-pool was administered to a group of approximately 800 subjects (400 males, 400 females), including students from the Berkeley and Davis campuses of the University of California, Corning Community College, New York, and Wesleyan

University, Middletown, Connecticut, faculty members of the College of Environmental Design, Berkeley, a group of local registered nurses, and several other smaller samples. Separate analyses were performed for males and females. Factors were tentatively identified by examining the content of the items having the highest loadings for each factor. The following factors were found:

Male Factors
1. Pastoralism
2. Urbanism
3. Environmental Adaptation
4. Stimulus Seeking
5. Environmental Well-Being

Female Factors
1. Pastoralism
2. Environmental Security
3. Environmental Stimulation
4. Abstract Conservationism
5. Modernism
6. Urbanism

Factors were tentatively identified by examining the contents of the items having high loading for each factor. Descriptions of the scales follow:

Description of Male Factors
Pastoralism (scale 1) contains items which reveal a deeply personal orientation toward the natural environment, including those which affirm basic environmental experiences (e.g., I occasionally take a walk in the rain just for the experience; I would be content living by myself in the wilderness), items expressing concern over the deterioration of the natural environment (e.g., In our society, silence has become a luxury that too few people can obtain; Nuclear power station should be closed until the long-term effects of radiation on human genetics has been studied sufficiently,) and items expressing a dislike of urban life (e.g. I would enjoy living in a modern high-rise apartment, [scored in reverse direction]; The stress of city life distorts man's spirit; Whenever I enter a large city, I think of death.)

Urbanism (scale 2) expresses a personal orientation toward all of the civilized aspects of city life, including those which affirm the joys or pleasures of city life (e.g., Every child should have the opportunity to enjoy the excitement of a large city; I enjoy the excitement of Christmas shopping in a large city; I enjoy the random sound of the city street,) express an esthetic responsiveness to the nam-made environment (e.g., I understand the architectural maxim that form follows function; I often have strong emotional reactions to building; I like oriental carpets), and express a distaste for the day-to-day rural life (e.g., Life in a small town is too slow for me; I would be very unhappy if

I had to live the rest of my life in a rural community; I prefer to live in a small town where I know everyone by name [reversed]).

Environmental adaptation (scale 3) expresses a "Man over Nature" (Kluckhohn & Strodtbeck, 1961) value orientation, which suggests that the environment be adapted to accomodate personal comforts and desires (e.g. Our national parks would better serve the public if motels and other vacation facilities were made available along the main access roads; I would like the physical environment to be much more responsive to my wishes and intentions; The information value of highway billboards outweighs the artificiality they impose on our landscape), express a faith in technology (e.g., The technological advances of the twentieth century will soon make man's utopian dreams a reality; Man's increasing control over the physical environment will ultimately lead to solutions for many of our pressing social problems), and endorse an environmental restrictiveness or territoriality (e.g., The trespassing laws of this country should be more carefully enforced; The more I see of other regions, the more I love my own; A person should have a private "territory" in his home which is off limits to everyone else)

Stimulus-seeking (scale 4) includes items which suggest stimulus seeking activity, (e.g. I would enjoy riding a motorcycle on a clear spring day; On a weekend, I would rather travel somewhere than putter around the house; I like to listen to music while working.)

Environmental Well-Being (scale 5) includes items which refer to childhood environmental memories, (e.g., As a child, I spent most of my free time playing outdoors; I have vivid memories of the house I grew up in: As a child, I often watched my father repair things around the house), and which are probably related to childhood environmental experiences, (e.g., I like to explore unfamiliar places; I consider myself an adventuresome person.) It also contains items which deny the threat of technology and modern living to human psychological well-being (e.g., I worry about the effects of a complex industrial society on our psychological well-being [reversed]; Our complex technological society increasingly isolates us from the life-giving forces of the natural environment [reversed]).

Descriptions of Female Factors

Pastoralism (scale 1) shares 29 items with the male pastoralism scale, and taps essentially the same themes.

Environmental Security (scale 2) contains items which call for an environmental restrictiveness and which express a fear of potentially dangerous environments (e.g., The trespassing laws of this country should be more carefully enforced; There ought to be a law against people attempting risky mountain climbs; I often vary my route to everyday des-

tinations [reversed]), as well as items which express a dislike of the city, not for esthetic reasons but perhaps out of fear (e.g., The stress of city life distorts man's spirit; I like the constant flow of diverse stimulation that only a city can offer [reversed]; City slums, although ugly and depressing, possess an intrinsic interest and excitement [reversed]). The underlying theme here seems to be fear of unfamiliar environments, especially urban ones.

Environmental Stimulation (scale 3) contains a number of items similar to those scored on the male stimulus seeking scale, and also contains items which affirm the psychic importance of space (e.g., The physical surrounding often play an important role in my dreams; I sometimes feel that the space around me is a part of me; I would like the physical environment to be much more responsive to my wishes and intentions; I remember the places I went to as a child when I wanted to be alone).

Abstract Conservationism (scale 4) includes items which express a doctrinaire anti-technological, conservationist stance (e.g., The industrial revolution has undermined the human spirit and the human community; I worry about the effects of a complex industrial society on our psychological well-being; Our complex technological society increasingly isolates us from the life-giving forces of the natural environment), but also includes items which affirm a preference for urban life over the pastoral (e.g., I would feel more comfortable living in a palace than in a cottage; I enjoy hiking [reversed]; I like the constant flow of diverse stimulation that only a city can offer). The pattern which emerges is thus one of an intellectualezed--and thus perhaps superficial--conservationist stance.

Modernism (scale 5) contains items which express a preference for the new and man-made rather than the old and natural (e.g., I like the modern architectural style better than most of the older styles; I would rather travel to Europe by jet than by ocean liner; I would prefer to live in a modern, planned community than in an old, historic one), and also items which implicitly deny the psychological significance of the environment (e.g. I often have nostalgic memories of the neighborhood I grew up in [reversed]; I sometimes feel that the space around me is a part of me [reversed]; I have vivid memories of the house I grew up in [reversed]).

Urbanism (scale 6), somewhat similar conceptually to the male Urbanism scale, scores items which extol the benefits of urban life (e.g., City slums, although ugly and depressing, possess an intrinsic interest and excitement; Every child should have the opportunity to enjoy the excitement of a large city; I enjoy riding on crowded subways) and which deny that technology is dehumanizing (e.g., Man's increasing control over the physical environment will ultimately lead to solutions for many of our pressing social problems; Despite the mechanical ease and increasing leisure of our technological society, we are more restricted and compartmentalized in our everyday life than we would like to admit[reversed])

Scales were constructed by assigning unit weights to the items with the highest factor loadings for each factor. In some cases, items loaded highly on two or more factors, and were thus scored on more than one scale. Scale intercorrelations for male and female samples appear in Table 1. For the male sample, the scoring procedures yielded scales that were generally independent of each other, with the exception of correlations of .45 between Stimulus-seeking and Environmental Well-Being. Intercorrelations among the female scales were somewhat higher, with an r of -.69 between Pastoralism and Modernism, and somewhat smaller but significant correlations between Urbanism and the first three female scales.

Conceptual Analysis of the ERI

Identifying the meaning of a psychological dimension solely on the basis of the content of scaled items is often psychologically unsound for two reasons. Not only does it assume that the respondent reports honestly his true preferences, but it also fails to recognize that people interpret inventory items in subjective--and perhaps ideocyncratic--ways. Moreover, for many items (e.g., The physical surroundings often play an important role in my dreams), it is difficult to imagine how the psychologist might go about confirming that a respondent actually holds a belief which he claims.

Paul Meehl (1945) dealt with this thorny problem in a classic paper. According to Meehl's Dictum, the subtleties of the language of self-report are such that the psychologist should treat item responses not as direct and unambiguous expressions of truly held beliefs and sentiments, but rather as bits of verbal behavior. Thus the question of interest is not whether, e.g. persons who answer true to the item 'The physical surroundings often play an important role in my dreams,' actually do have dreams in which the physical surroundings often play an important role. Rather, the vital question is,what are the significant non-test correlates of this item (i.e., what are people like who answer true [or false] to this item, or more generally, what are people like who score high [or low] on the scale upon which this item is keyed?) Thus Meehl's Dictum provides a throughly empirical basis for analyzing the psychological meaning of inventory scales.

Gough (1965) has expanded Meehl's approach into a three-phase model of conceptual analysis which explores the full meaning of inventory scale scores. The first phase, primary evaluation, involves such basic determinations as criteria relevant to the variable as well as its concurrent and predictive validity. The question of interest is: Does the variable (scale) actually measure what it purports to measure? For example, are Pastoralism scale scores significantly related to such pastoral behaviors as membership in conservation organizations, participation in rural or wilderness activities, or enjoyment of such basic everyday environmental experiences as walking in the rain or watching the sun set? Secondary evaluation seeks to clarify the personological meaning of the scale, i.e., to specify what the scale is getting at psychodynamically. In finding out what people who score high on the Urbanism scale are like, for example, we would probably want to interview them on attitudes toward the city, obtain their scores on a number of psychological tests of recognised usefulness, and perhaps obtain biographical information with regard to their residence history. Tertiary evaluation involves the justification of the scale beyond the usefulness demonstrated in the first two phases through an examination of the scale's real-life implications and utility. The utility of the ERI scales could be demonstrated at this level of conceptual analysis through a case study in which the scales could be shown to predict interesting and important environment-related behavioral outcomes. An example of this sort of study is one which attempts to predict the success of adjustment to new geographic and demographic conditions of Appalachian migrants to northern cities.

The ERI has already undergone substantial conceptual analysis at the first two levels, as described in a technical report (McKechnie, 1969). Brief descriptions of the personal characteristics of high scorers on the ERI scales will serve to illustrate the psychodynamic significance of the scales. These sketches are based upon correlations of the ERI scales with a biographical questionaire, and with such well-known personality tests as the California Psychological Inventory (Gough, 1964), the Myers-Briggs Type Indicator (Myers, 1962), and the Study of Values (Allport, Vernon, and Lindzey, 1960).

The person scoring high on the male Pastoralism scale is impatient, critical, and outspoken. He is the sort of person who chooses not to engage in the pleasantries of social intercourse, but rather prefers to speak his mind on that which he believes is right--regardless of what people might think. He is not anti-social but rather a-social. He holds the natural environment in almost religious reverence, and places aesthetic values high above economic ones. In conservation matters he is bluntly assertive.

The male Urbanism scale appears to be positively related to social ascendancy, flexibility and resourcefulness. The high-urban male likes the city and knows how to enjoy it. He is a dominant person but not pushy. His ascendancy is mediated by tact and considertion for others. He is, in a word, charming.

The person who scores high on the Environmental Adaptation scale is dependable, methodical, and cautious. He seems to be somewhat preoccupied with obligations to other people and would prefer to take the environment for granted, adapting it to his personal needs as they arise.

The high scorer on the Stimulus-seeking scale is ascendant, poised, and self-confident, but in a somewhat more rugged than polished manner. He is not as responsible as he might want to be, perhaps due to his considerable impulsiveness. He is extroverted and intuitive (in a Jungian sense), and thus possesses great imagination and initiative in seeking out novel experiences and is easily bored by routine.

The Environmental Well-Being scale is positively related to the personal characteristics of spontaneity, poise, and resourcefulness. The person who scores high on this scale seems to have a rich interpersonal life. He takes the environment for granted only in the sense that he considers it a benevolent resource for an equally benevolent technology.

The female Pastoralism scale, not unlike the male counterpart, appears to identify the person who is somewhat outspoken, idealistic, and cynical. She cares deeply about environmental matters, and is willing to speak up for what she believes to be right. In most matters, however, she is rather retiring. A somewhat artistic person, she is most often guided by aesthetic--rather than economic--considerations.

The person d fined by a high score on the Environmental Security scale appears to have had an environmentally restricted biographical history. She more likely than not comes from a rural, non-professional background. She scores generally low on measures of ascendancy, poise, and self-assurance. She is somewhat conventional, unambitious, unassuming, and lacking in self-confidence.

Personologically, Environmental Stimulation measures social extroversion. The woman who scores high on Environmental Stimulation is likely to be seen as outgoing, active, robust, and self-confident--perhaps even aggressive. In this sense, the Environmental Stimulation scale is somewhat like the Male Urbanism scale. The present scale, however, measures little of the psychological-mindedness and self-insight characteristic of the Male Urbanism scale.

A high score on Abstract Conservationism appears to identify the woman who is shrewd, dissatisfied, self-centered, impatient, and self-pitying. She is critical of plans and projects, but seldom does anything constructive herself. She talks about conservation rather than actually participating in projects.

A high score on the Modernism scale identifies the person who is dull, unoriginal, methodical, shallow, and rigid, whose interests are narrow, and who approaches life and interpersonal relationships in a mechanical way.

The female Urbanism scale appears to be related to the same constellation of social skills and attitudes which the male Urbanism and Environmental Stimulation scales share. The present scale resembles the male Urbanism scale insofar as the ascendancy of both is tempered by a conformity and non-aggressiveness which are missing in the Environmental Stimulation scale.

These sketches reflect a substantial attempt at secondary conceptual analysis of the ERI scales. While data collected on the Biographical Questionaire provides concurrent validity for relevant scales, full primary and tertiary evaluation is just now beginning in several research projects. Since a psychological inventory is of little more than academic interest unless its real-life implications and utility have been demonstrated, it is perhaps fitting to conclude this introduction to the ERI with some suggested research designs in which its full value might be revealed.

In one type of study, individual scales of the ERI would be shown to correlate with important environmental behaviors, such as frequency of wilderness use (Pastoralism) or adjustment to urban migration (Urbanism). A more sophisticated design predicts behavioral outcomes from combinations of scales. Stepwise multiple regression analysis could be utilized to determine the optimal combination and weightings of ERI scales to predict, e.g., preferences for alternative regional planning options and architectural solutions.

Another approach is to use the ERI scales, individually or in combination, to identify different environmental types of people. For example, differences in aesthetic response to environmental arrays (such as color landscape slides) may be found for high and low scores on, e.g. the Environmental Adaptation or Modernism scales. Alternatively, an inverse factor analysis (or 'O' Typology) may be performed to identify different naturally occurring environmental types. This procedure groups people together who have similar overall ERI profiles (e.g., high Pastoralism, low Urbanism, medium Environmental Adaptation, and very high Stimulus-seeking, with the Environmental Well-Being scale unrelated.) It would then be possible to relate these environmental types to different recreation preferences. Information on typical profiles of skiiers, racetrack fans, and sailors would not only be of value in understanding the psychology of recreation and leisure, but would also serve as important data inputs to the policy decisions made by recreation specialists.

The notion of environmental dispositions, while still in its infancy, is now beginning to receive the research attention it deserves. The ERI promises to yield significant developments in this new area. Its full value as

an assessment instrument, however, can be
appraised only as its practical utility is
explored and research findings accumulate.

Table 1
Male Scale Intercorrelations

	1	2	3	4	5
1	1.000	-.041	.008	.090	-.119
2		1.000	.045	-.101	.205
3			1.000	.092	.059
4				1.000	.446
5					1.000

Female Scale Intercorrlations

	1	2	3	4	5	6
1	1.000	.055	-.180	-.087	-.695	-.406
2		1.000	-.176	-.166	.157	-.450
3			1.000	-.008	-.206	.569
4				1.000	.082	-.148
5					1.000	.123
6						1.000

References

Allport, G.W., P.E. Vernon, and G. Lindzey, Manual for the Study of Values. Boston: Houghton Mifflin Co., 1960.

Craik, K.H., Environmental Psychology, In Craik, K.H. et al. New Directions in Psychology IV. New York: Holt, Rinehart, and Winston, 1970.

Craik, K.H., Forest Landscape Perception: Final Report. Berkeley: Institute of Personality Assessment and Research, 1969.

Glacken, Clarence. Traces on the Rhodian Shore . Berkeley, California: University of California Press, 1967.

Gough, H.G. Conceptual analysis of psychological test scores and other diagnostic variables. Journal of Abnormal Psychology, 1965, 70, pp.294-302.

Gough, H.G. Manual for the California Psychological Inventory. Palo Alto, California: Consulting Psychologists Press, 1964.

Harmon, H.H. Modern Factor Analysis. Chicago: University of Chicago Press. 1967.

Hathaway, S.R., & McKinley, J.C. Manual for the Minnesota Multiphasic Personality Inventory. New York: Psychological Corporation, 1943. (Rev. 1968.)

Hendee, J.C., Catton, W.R., Jr., Marlow, L.D., and Brockman, C.G. Wilderness Users in the Pacific Northwest--their Characteristics, Values, and Maaagement Preferences. USDA Forest Service Research Paper PNW-61. Portland, Oregon: Pacific Norhtwest forest and Range Experiment Station, 1968.

Howard, K.I. A test of Stimulus-seeking behavior. Perceptual and Motor Skills, 1965, 21, p. 655.

Kluckhohn,F.R. & F.L. Strodtbeck. Variations in Value Orientations. Evnaston, Illinois, Row, Peterson, 1961.

Lowenthal, D. et al. An Analysis of Environmental Perception. Interem Report. Washington, D.C.: Resources for the Future, Ind. , 1967.

Marx, Leo. The Machine in the Garden. New York: Oxford University Press, 1964.

McKechnie, G.E., The environme tal Response Inventory: Preliminary Development. Unpublished report. Berkeley: Department of Psychology, University of California, 1969.

Meehl, P.E. The dynamics of "Structured" Personality Tests. Journal of Clinical Psychology, 1,1945,pp. 296-303.

Murray, H.A. , et al. Explorations in Personality. New York, Oxford University Press, 1938.

Myers, I.B. Manual for the Myers-Briggs Type Indicator. Princeton, New Jersy: Educational Testing Service, 1962.

Penny, R.K. and R.C. Reinher. Development of a stimulus-variation seeking scale for adults. Psychological Reports, 1966, 18, pp.631-638.

Peterson, G.L. and Newmann, E.S. , Modeling and Predicting Human Response to the visual Recreation Environment. Journal of Leisure Research, 1969, 1, pp. 219-237.

Sonnenfeld, J. Variable values in space and landscape: An inquiry into the nature of environmental necessity. Journal of Social Issues, 1966, 22, pp. 71-82.

Strong , E.K., Jr., Manual for the Strong Vocational Interest Blank. Stanford, California: Stanford University Press, 1966.

Zuckerman, M. ,Kolin, E.A., Price, I. , & Zoob, I.Development of a Sensation-Seeking scale. Journal of Consulting Psychology, 1964, 28, pp.477-482.

Perception and Use of Urban Beaches[1]

by Edward S. Neumann[2]
and George L. Peterson[3]

Abstract

An examination is made of the relationships between the appearance of the urban recreation environment, user attitudes toward appearances and demand. A model of attitudes hypothesizes that the subjective appealingness of an environment is a function of its visible characteristics and the magnitude of the positive or negative feelings that the individual associates with the characteristics. Attitudes toward the appearance of swimming beaches are classified along a continuum according to whether they favor crowded, urban appearing beaches, or empty, rural appearing beaches.

Analyses indicate that a majority of the subjects have attitudes which favor rural appearances, but this attitude does not seem to influence their use of urban beaches. Use of urban beach environments does not seem to be sensitive to the visual amenities of the environments; instead, demand is more strongly influenced by accessibility and habit. Despite this, it was tentatively determined that people who favor rural appearances may tend to obtain a different recreation experience from an urban beach than people who favor urban appearances. Preference for rural appearances is correlated slightly with age and education.

Introduction

The research described in this paper sought to determine how people tend to react to the appearance of the urban recreation environment. Can the visible characteristics of the recreation environment influence recreation demand by influencing satisfactions received, or is demand more dependent on other factors, such as the accessibility and activity-potential of the environment, and the socio-economic characteristics of the individual? This was the research question.

During 1967 and 1968, research was conducted to determine attitudes toward the appearance of urban swimming beaches. Research was based on interviews with a sample of two-hundred thirty-seven Chicago-area individuals who represented urban beach-goers with a variety of socio-economic characteristics and participation habits. All interviews were conducted on urban beaches in the Chicago area; thus, a sample of actively participating recreationists was obtained. Results indicate that attitudes toward appearances varied significantly within the sample, but individuals' attitudes toward the appearance of an urban facility do not seem to bear a direct relationship to the frequency with which they use it.

Model of Attitudes

Attitudes toward appearances were analyzed in the context of modern theories on attitudes and consumer behavior. An approach was taken in which attitudes on facility appearances were modelled using mathematical relationships which are conceptually akin to models proposed by others recently to explain consumer behavior and attitudes (4,5). In the model used in the study, individuals' attitudes on appearance are modelled as a simple linear function of two variables--the amounts of specific visible characteristics which are present in the environment, and the relative magnitude of the positive or negative feelings that the individual associates with the characteristics (6). It is hypothesized that each independently perceived visible characteristic has a "marginal value" to the individual and is capable of evoking some magnitude of either positive or negative feeling within him. As the individual perceives an environment, he subjectively values each visible characteristic according to its "marginal value" to him. The individual determines his overall attitude toward the appearance of the environment by subconsciously summing the values of its individual characteristics(7). In mathematical notation the model of attitudes may be expressed as

$$Y_{sk} = \sum_i B_{si} \cdot X_{ski} \text{, where}$$

Y_{sk} = the amount of overall positive or negative feeling (attitude) that individual s has for the appearance of facility k,

X_{ski} = the amount of characteristic i that individual s perceives facility k to have, and

B_{si} = the relative amount of positive or negative feeling ("marginal value") that individual s has for characteristic i.

The variables in the model represent subjective phenomena which can be measured using techniques of psychological measurement.

To obtain data for the model, individuals are shown a series of photographs of different environments and are asked to indicate how much of each visible characteristic is perceived to be present in each photo. Then, the individual is asked to give his overall feeling about the appealingness of each environment. By proper transformation of the data, it is possible to assign numerical values to the responses and fit the data to the model. Information about the magnitude of the feelings toward each characteristic, that is, information about the B_{si}, is not asked for during the interview. Instead, the B_{si} are entered into the model as unknowns and may be estimated using linear regression techniques. For reasons explained elsewhere, (9) all variables in the model are standardized to have zero mean and variance equal to one; hence, the B_{si} represent the statistical correlation between variations in overall attitude toward the environment, Y_{sk}, and variations in the amount of a perceived characteristic, X_{ski}. Varying between +1 and -1 value, the relative magnitudes of the B_{si} indicate the relative strength of the positive or negative feelings that the individual has for the characteristic in question.

Measurement of Attitudes

The photos used in the study are shown in Figure 1. The photos depict beaches offering different degrees of opportunity for a rural or urban experience. Each person in the interview sample was asked to evaluate each photo in the series by means of the following scales (10):

How Do You Find the Beach in the Photo with Respect to the Beach in General?
Unappealing ------------- Appealing
Small ---------------------- Large
Empty -------------------- Crowded

The Sand?
Littered -------------------- Clean
Smooth -------------------- Pebbly

The Trees and Natural Growth Around the Beach?
Small Amount --------- Large Amount
Unattractive ----------- Attractive

The Buildings in the Background?
Unattractive ----------- Attractive

Each scale offered five categories.

Overall attitude or preference for the environment was measured by the "appealingness" dimension. The other differentials were used to describe the physical appearance of the scenes. Analysis of responses along the appealingness dimension revealed that people generally tended to have attitudes favoring one end or the other of the rural-urban continuum. That is, people who rated the photos of rural beaches appealing (as depicted by photos 2, 5, 7) often described the urban beaches as unappealing (as depicted by photos 1, 3, 4, 6, 8), and people who rated the urban beaches appealing generally rated the rural beaches unappealing. On the basis of their attitudes on the relative appealingness of the photos, the individuals in the sample were divided into two groups for further analyses: one group included the individuals who favored rural appearances (67% of the total sample); the other group consisted of individuals who favored urban appearances (33% of the total sample).

The B_{si}, or the magnitude of the positive or negative feelings of the individuals toward each visible characteristic, were calculated and compared using each major group's central tendencies (see Table 1). Among the people who found the photos of rural beaches most appealing, overall attitude was best "explained" by strong positive

TABLE 1

B_{si}, or Strength of Feeling Toward Visible Characteristics Among People Having Attitudes Favoring:

Characteristic, i	Rural Appearances B_{si}	Urban Appearances B_{si}
1. Sand Texture	--	--
2. Sand Quality	--	+ .748
3. Intensity of Use	- .878	--
4. Attractiveness of buildings	--	+ .506
5. Greenery	+ .467	--
% of attitude toward appearance explained by feelings toward visible characteristics	98.8%	93.7%
Number of people in group as a per cent of total sample (237)	67%	33%

The numerical values of the B_{si} indicate the central tendencies of each group, as estimated by the relationship

$Y_{sk} = \Sigma_i B_{si} \cdot X_{ski}$, where Y_{sk} = the amount of overall "appealingness" of environment k, B_{si} = the magnitude of positive or negative feeling toward characteristic i, and X_{ski} = the perceived amount of characteristic i present in environment k.

FIGURE 1

Photographs Used in the Study

feelings for low intensity of use ($B_{1,2}$ = -.878) and somewhat less strong positive feelings toward attractive trees and natural growth ($B_{1,4}$ = .467). The fact that these values are statistically significant implies that people who prefer rural appearances may find crowds to be a source of dissatisfaction and natural growth a source of satisfaction. Among the group of people who most preferred photos of the urban beaches, increasing appealingness correlated significantly with perception of increasing sand quality ($B_{2,1}$ = .748) and increasing attractiveness of the buildings surrounding the beach ($B_{2,3}$ = .506). The attitudes of this latter group toward overall appearance did not seem influenced by greenery or intensity of use, according to the data. One possible explanation for a variation in attitude among individuals along the rural-urban continuum could be that their feelings toward such characteristics as intensity of use, greenery, the presence of buildings, and sand quality vary from person to person (11).

Relationships Between Attitudes and Demand

Generally, other studies have indicated significant relationships between socio-economic characteristics and recreation demand. In this study, relationships between attitudes toward appearances, frequency of beach use, and selected socio-economic characteristics were found to be weak or lacking, however. The beaches on which the interviews were conducted are often crowded and lack the naturalness of the rural beaches depicted in the photos. They are similar in appearance to the urban beaches in photos 1, 3, 4, 6 and 8. It could be expected that as individual preferences for the photos of rural beaches increased, the appealingness of the urban-type beaches being used would decrease. The data indicated that this was, in fact, the case, although the relationship was weak. During the interviews individuals were asked to evaluate the urban beaches they used by means of the same scales employed for the photos. Because the sample had been drawn from a number of beaches having different intensities of use at different times of the day and on different days of the week, and because amounts of greenery, etc., varied among the beaches, some variation in perceived characteristics was obtained. A correlation of .1724 existed between increasing preferences for photos of rural beaches and decreasing perceived appealingness of the beaches on which the interviews were conducted (a correlation of this magnitude, though significantly different from zero at the .05 level, is too small to be of predictive value). Interestingly, it was found that a correlation of .2319 existed between increasing preference for photos of rural beaches and decreasing perceived crowding on the beaches sampled. It is possible that

some of the people who disliked crowding went to crowded beaches anyway, but tended to seek less-crowded areas within the beaches. Increasing preference for photos of rural beaches was also weakly correlated with a decrease in the perceived attractiveness of the greenery around the beaches (r = .1363) and a decrease in the perceived attractiveness of the buildings near the beaches (r = .1294).

However, people generally judged the beaches they used in a favorable manner regardless of their attitudes toward the photos. This may have been one reason why those who preferred photos of rural beaches went to the urban-type beaches just as frequently as those who preferred photos of urban beaches. No significant correlation was found between the perceived appealingness (as measured by the semantic differential) of the beaches on which interviews were conducted and the frequency with which the beaches were used by the people in the sample.

Demand Relevant Variables

The satisfactions derived from the visible characteristics of the urban beaches sampled in the survey were found to be of lesser importance to users than other satisfactions derived from the beach environment. The individuals in the survey were asked to rank a list of nine activities in the order in which they were most enjoyed at the beach. The responses, presented in Table 2, indicate that those activities most highly dependent on visible characteristics -- being near the Lake for its scenic

TABLE 2

Responses to the Question "Please Rank the Following Activities in the Order in Which You Enjoy Them ... At the Beach."

| Activity | Average Rank Among People Having Attitudes Favoring the Appearances Of | |
	Rural Beaches	Urban Beaches
Being out in the Sun	1.75	1.86
Relaxing and Resting	3.14	3.32
Cooling off in the Water	4.03	3.65
Seeing Interesting Activity and People	5.01	4.46
Being Near the Lake for its Scenic Quality	4.65	5.71
Swimming for Exercise or Practice	5.38	5.72
Cooling off in the Breeze	5.47	5.71
Wading and Splashing Around	5.84	5.67
Finding Solitude	5.38	7.18

quality, and finding solitude -- were ranked lower in relative enjoyment than such activities as being out in the sun, relaxing, and cooling off in the water. It is possible that use was so strongly oriented toward these latter activities that attitudes on facility appearance had only a small influence on behavior. Furthermore, the data suggest that facility accessibility and the habits of the individual may exert the strongest influence on demand. The people in the survey were asked, "In addition to the beach you use, there are a number of other beaches along the Lake ... Why do you prefer the beach you are using?" The answers people gave are tabulated by per-cent in Table 3. The largest proportion of people, 47.7%, gave the reason "this beach is closest to my home." Reasons more related to facility appearance, such as "I prefer the characteristics of this beach," or "this beach is more scenic" were mentioned by fewer numbers of people.

TABLE 3

Reasons That People Gave for Preferring the Beach They Use to Other Beaches in the Area

Reason	Per Cent of Sample (237)
This beach is closest to my home	47.7%
My friends usually use this beach	33.8%
I prefer the characteristics of this beach	27.4%
I prefer the kind of people who use this beach	26.2%
This beach is more scenic	17.7%
Parking is better here	12.7%
No reason, I just happen to use it	10.1%
I am not sure what the other beaches would be like	3.8%

Attitudes and Other Aspects of Use

Despite the lack of correlation between attitudes and demand, there was a slight correlation between attitudes and the relative enjoyment obtained from two of the nine activities listed in Table 2. There were correlations of .2737 and .2930 between increasing preference for photos of rural beaches and an increasing relative amount of enjoyment obtained from finding scenery and privacy in an urban beach environment. Similarly, there were correlations of .1449 and .1311, respectively, between increasing preference for photos of urban beaches and an increasing relative enjoyment obtained from seeing interesting activity and people, and cooling off in the water. Thus, people who

found the photos of rural beaches appealing may have tended to place a higher value on scenery and solitude than people who preferred the photos of urban beaches, and vice-versa. Also, the rural-oriented group of users went to the beach with a significantly smaller number of friends and relatives, generally in groups of two, than did the urban-oriented users, who generally attended in groups of four or five (Table 4).

TABLE 4

Sizes of User Groups

Size of User Group	Per cent of Rural-Favoring People In Group This Size	Per cent of Urban-Favoring People In Group This Size
One person	7.8%	6.6%
Two people	42.2%	26.3%
Three people	29.2%	31.6%
Four or five people	14.9%	32.9%
Six or more people	5.9%	2.6%
Total	100.0%	100.0%

Only two of the socio-economic characteristics measured, age and education, had any relation to attitudes on facility appearance. Increasing age and education were correlated with increasing preference for a rural appearance (r = .1355 and r = .1703,

TABLE 5

Summary of the Most Significant Correlations Between 1) Preferences for Urban-rural Characteristics of the Photos and 2) Other Aspects of Attitude, Perception and Socio-economic Status.

An increase in attitude favoring rural appearances is correlated with:

A decrease in perceived	Appealingness (.1724) Crowding (.2319) Attractiveness of Buildings (.1294) Attractiveness of Greenery (.1363)	With respect to the urban beaches where the interviews were conducted.
An increase in the enjoyment of	Being near the Lake for its scenic qualities (.2737) Finding solitude at the beach (.2930)	--
A decrease in the enjoyment of	Seeing interesting activity and people (-.1449) Cooling off in the water (-.1311)	
An increase in	Age (.1355) Education (.1703)	

respectively)(12). An increase in age was also correlated with an increase in the enjoyment obtained from being near the Lake for its scenic qualities (r = .3342), cooling off in the breeze (r = .2827), relaxing and resting (r = .1697), and swimming for exercise or practice (r = .1416). Similarly, increasing education was correlated with increasing enjoyment of being near the Lake for its scenic quality (r = .2966), cooling off in the breeze (r = .1703), and finding solitude at the beach (r = .1297).

Summary and Conclusions

It can be hypothesized tentatively that there exists an urban-rural continuum of recreation needs. At one end of the continuum is the need for an "urban experience" obtained from recreating in a carnival-like atmosphere among buildings and crowds of people. In this environment, privacy may be difficult to find. At the other extreme on the continuum is the need for a "rural experience" obtained from being in a natural environment and isolated from other individuals. Here, there is greater opportunity for people to be alone.

The typical urban beach can be conceptualized as a point on this spectrum lying closer to the end defined as the "urban experience" than to the end defined as the "rural experience". Thus, urban beaches are capable of providing opportunities to satisfy only a narrow range of needs along this continuum. The relationships found in this study between attitudes toward rural versus urban appearances, perception of the visual quality of urban facilities, and the relative enjoyment of different activities suggest that many, perhaps a majority of the subjects, desire a rural experience. Only a smaller number of the subjects actively seek an urban environment, per se, to enhance their recreation experience. If this is true, then public recreation planning could accomodate a wider range of tastes by providing greater variety in the appearance of facilities near urban areas. In particular, facilities having rural appearances could be planned, within economic constraints and a beach, being a major open space, can be made symbolic of a "rural experience" even though located near dense urban development. Methods for enhancing rural appearances might consist of controlling the location and heights of surrounding buildings, effective utilization of vegetation for screening as well as scenic value, and, possibly, controlling density of use. Although a facility having an urban appearance may provide satisfactions for a great number of people, a facility possessing rural characteristics might produce greater satisfactions and provide an experience of higher value. Both kinds should be available.

Clearly, the research described in this report has only scratched the surface of the problem. Response to the appearance of only one type of facility has been studied. Further research should be directed toward a wider variety of facilities--parks, picnic areas, bicycle trails, etc. It is recognized that the recreation experience is multi-dimensional. The urban-rural continuum of experience discussed in this paper is only a simplified conceptualization of a very complicated phenomenon. What has been termed a continuum may actually consist of a number of factors working in combination and responses biased toward urban versus rural appearances may reflect moods or social contexts, rather than stable preferences. The lack of correlation between responses and socio-economic characteristics raises the important question of whether socio-economic status bears any relationship to attitudes towards facility appearance. The possibility that socio-economic variables could not be used to identify groups of people who would receive benefits or to predict satisfactions would pose serious problems in evaluating the consequences of visual design. Such possibilities deserve further investigation.

By devoting more effort to the identification and clarification of what is loosely referred to in this paper as the "recreation experience", planning might be able to provide the public with facilities more in harmony with individual needs and desires. In order to do this, a clearer understanding of recreation needs, particularly at the level of the subjective, is needed. A quantitative approach, like the one taken in this paper, is beneficial when it encourages a careful examination of the problem, raises basic questions, and provides a rigorous framework for analysis.

Notes

1. The study resulting in this publication was made under a fellowship granted by Resources for the Future, Inc., and a traineeship granted by the Public Health Service. It was also supported in part by research grants from the Public Health Service (5 R01 EC 00301) and the National Science Foundation (GS 1729).
2. Edward S. Neumann is currently serving as Captain with the U.S. Army Corps of Engineers at the Waterways Experiment Station, Vicksburg, Mississippi, where he is involved with environmental research for military purposes. He also teaches advanced statistics as an Adjunct Assistant Professor of the Mississippi State University Extension School. Following his tour of duty, he will be employed as an Assistant Professor in the Department of Civil Engineering at West Virginia University. His doctoral

research was at Northwestern University and was concerned with analysis of intangible recreation values.

3. George L. Peterson is Associate Professor of Civil Engineering at Northwestern University.

4. A modern theory of consumer behavior is presented in "A New Approach to Consumer Theory", by Kelvin Lancaster in the Journal of Political Economy, LXXIV, April, 1966, pp. 132-157.

5. Modern theories about attitudes and behavior are described by M. Fishbein in "A Behavior Theory Approach to the Relations Between Beliefs About an Object and Attitudes Toward the Object," in Attitude Theory and Measurement, M. Fishbein, editor, Wiley, New York, 1967, pp. 389-400. The reader is also referred to "The Behavior of Attitudes," by L. W. Doob, in Attitude Theory and Measurement, op. cit., pp. 42-59.

6. Although this may be an oversimplification, it serves an heuristic purpose by isolating, quantifying, and relating attitudes, or preferences, and aspects of the physical environment.

7. This model of visual preferences is stated in "A Model of Preference: Quantitative Analysis of the Perception of the Visual Appearance of Residential Neighborhoods," by G. L. Peterson, in the Journal of Regional Science, Vol. 7, No. 1, Summer 1967, pp. 19-32.

8. Theories and techniques of psychological measurement are described in Theory and Methods of Scaling, by W. S. Torgerson, Wiley, New York, 1958.

9. Detailed explanations of methodology are presented in "Evaluating Subjective Response to the Recreation Environment--A Quantitative Analysis to Dissimilar Preferences for the Visual Characteristics of Beaches," by Edward S. Neumann, in an unpublished doctoral dissertation submitted to the Graduate School, Northwestern University, Evanston, Illinois, June 1969.

10. Previous research indicated that users were most sensitive to these characteristics. This is described in the reference cited in note 9 above.

11. It is also possible that the individuals were responding differently to more abstract qualities of the scenes, such as simplicity or complexity. However, this was beyond the scope of the study.

12. This may be due to the fact that people who were older or more educated may have had more exposure to rural beaches and, thus, were more aware of the satisfactions obtainable from a rural experience.

House Form and Preference

by Henry Sanoff

Associate Professor of Architecture, School of Design,
North Carolina State University, Raleigh

Abstract

In response to the need for understanding the "connotative" meaning of a house, an attempt was made to seek responses to existing and hypothetical house forms through the use of a semantic differential scale. Low income Negro and middle income white respondents were requested to assess visual displays of designed and non-designed house silhouettes in an effort to compare the variability of responses.

The findings indicated that both respondent groups agree to their descriptions of an "ideal" house, but vary considerably in their assessment of the visual displays; this suggests that background and environmental experiences influence preferences which are at variance within groups as well as between groups.

Introduction

The variety of dwelling forms that exist in the world today are in response to people's different attitudes and ideals which vary cross-cultura-ly and are impinged upon by numerous external forces. The house is not just a structure, nor a shelter, but an institution influenced by the cultural milieu to which it belongs (1).

Therefore, the definition of the image and meaning of the house is of great importance to all people in our culture, especially for low income people. Recently, Mexican-American farm workers in the Central Valley of California constructed "self-help" houses based on the popular "house magazine" image symbolizing middle class America a decade ago. These people were not confident enough to express their differences and traditions or even respond to the needs of the region. It may well be that the expression of sub-cultural traditions is more likely in Latin America, Asia or Africa where the cultural traditions are stronger, especially when our socio-cultural ethos is towards assimilation. This ethos inhibits the individualistic expression of the various ethnic groups in their house form.

Through cross-cultural investigations, it is evident that house image is a reflection of ideas, attitudes and needs of its occupants. Vernacular architecture, however, was free of stylistic interests or symbolic connotations and oriented primarily towards utility. Today, inferential cues or symbolic meaning are directly associated with users' aspirations and preferences. The house is symbolic of a perceived set of values or life style and as such an important consideration for designers.

In primitive or preliterate societies, people had a diffuse knowledge of everything and every aspect of tribal life was everybody's business (2). Since the average member of the tribal group builds his own house, he understands his needs and requirements perfectly, especially since there were prescribed ways of building and commonly accepted building forms. This phenomenon explains the persistence of many building forms over long periods of time as well as the close relation between form and culture.

Today with the loss of common-shared values there is a greater disparity between the goals of the user and that of the designer. In order to minimize the gap, investigations are necessary to provide the designer with better insights into the difference between people and their responses to the built environment.

This research focuses on the direct responsiveness to the physical environment. It is assumed that reacting directly to specific environments, a person's form of responsiveness is likely to be influenced by his more enduring environmental disposition. The visual field is charged with meaning from individual to individual; to some degree independent of background as well as environmentally experienced. This meaning and perception are inextricably linked.

Previous research in personality dispositions has been interpersonal and intrapersonal and only recently has disposition toward the environment been undertaken. This recent work has been oriented towards the individual's need for varied experience through exploratory or change-seeking behavior (3), as well as activation and sensation seeking (4). A better understanding of the response patterns that a person brings to designed environments can contribute to and explain the nature of different responses to the physical environment.

Research Design
The research design held constant the observer groups, the media of presentations and the respondent formats, but varied the visual environment displays. The visual displays·

Visual Display (VD)1

required descriptive and evaluative assessments from two subgroups characterized by their different socio-economic status. The displays were photographs of models representing prototypical tract housing (VD2) and housing designed for low income families (VD1).

Quantification of the descriptive responses from the observers were obtained through ratings. Systematically selected sets of bi-polar rating scales, such as the Semantic Differential (5) were employed in the descriptive assessments of the visual displays.

The groups were requested to rate each of two visual displays using a bi-polar scale, as well as their assessment of the most ideal house type. The arithmetic mean distribution for each set of responses is described on Figures 1 and 2. Comparisons were made between two sets of responses both within the sample groups (VD1 and VD2) and between sample groups (aVD1 and bVD1). Based on the arithmetic mean scores, the greatest polarization occurred when groups "a" and "b" are internally compared. For example, aVD1, aVD2 and bVD1, bVD2 have the largest variance when compared with aVD1, bVD1, and aVD2, bVD2.

The Sample
Respondents were selected from two geographic areas of Raleigh, that have been classified by realtors as

Visual Display (VD)2

having substantially differing property values, associated with low and middle incomes. Respondents from the low income group were recent purchasers of Turnkey III housing who were former residents of condemned and dilapidated housing in the area. Those respondents from the middle income group had been homeowners for many more years while presently occupying houses with a similar visual appearance to the Turnkey Housing, with substantially varying site characteristics and size. There were 25 randomly selected subjects from each group.

Hypothesis

It was hypothesized that there would be a close correlation between the descriptions of the "preferred" or "ideal" dwelling for the two sample groups.

While each of the descriptive adjective sets have both positive and negative associations, it was assumed that they are culturally based (rather than sub-culturally) and that the respondents' preferences would be linked to societal norms.

It was also hypothesized that there would be a closer correlation between responses to VD2 and 1 for group "a" (low income) than for group "b" (middle income).

Responses to specific visual displays, especially housing silhouettes, are culture laden and are influenced by the respondents' previous experiences and current expectations. The low income respondents have had either direct or indirect contact with the

rural environment where the barn is a dominant, functional component of the environment. Therefore, the "barn form" (similar to VD1) is a symbol laden with sub-cultural implications and would affect the group's responses. Furthermore, recent entry into homeownership is a major fulfillment of a long standing aspiration which may further affect responses to VD2.

Analysis of Data

The concept "modern-old fashioned" tended to polarize responses to all displays (Figures 1, 2, 3, 4 and 5). Group "b" (middle income respondents) tended to prefer old-fashioned and assessed VD2 similar to their ideal where VD1 was more modern (.01) (Figure 6).

Group "a" (low income respondents) preferred a more "modern" looking dwelling than group "b" and assessed VD2 as more "modern" than VD1 (Figure 1). VD1 appeared to be too modern for group "b" and too old-fashioned for group "a"; however, group "b" preferred a slightly "old-fashioned" dwelling which corresponded with their assessment of VD2 (Figure 2).

On the "simplicity-complexity" continuum both groups tended to prefer a slightly complex form and assessed VD2 as moderately "simple" and VD1 identical to their ideal (Figure 1 and 2).

Both respondent groups agreed that their preferred image of the dwelling was very "relaxed" as opposed to "tense" (Figure 5). The low

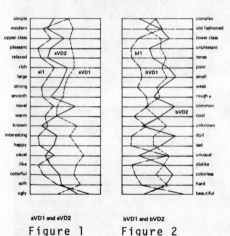

aVD1 and aVD2

Figure 1

bVD1 and bVD2

Figure 2

COMPARISONS WITHIN GROUP "a" AND GROUP "b"

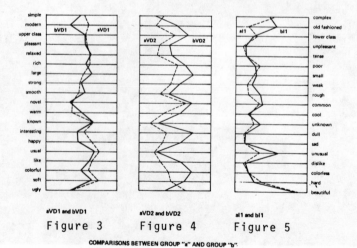

aVD1 and bVD1

Figure 3

aVD2 and bVD2

Figure 4

al1 and bl1

Figure 5

COMPARISONS BETWEEN GROUP "a" AND GROUP "b".

income respondents tended to associate VD2 with moderately "relaxed" and VD1 with slightly "tense" (Figure 1). The middle income respondents responded similarly, but less so (Figure 2). The two groups again tended to rate VD2 slightly "novelty" in their dwelling thought they both tended to rate VD2 slightly "common" and VD1 slightly "novel" corresponding with their ideal (Figure 1 and 2).

While the sample groups differed along the "usual-unusual" continuum, the respondents from group "b" tended to favor the more unusual. VD2 was slightly more "usual" for the group "a" and very usual for the group "b", while both groups tended to agree that VD1 was more unusual than preferred (Figure 3 and 4).

When comparing responses to the "upper class-lower class" continuum, both groups rated VD1 slightly "lower class", though group "b" preferred a more "upper class" dwelling than group "a" (Figure 3). Group "a", however, rated VD2 more "upper class" dwelling than group "b" (Figure 4). These responses were consistent with the ratings of both groups along the "rich-poor" continuum.

Both respondent groups rated their ideal dwelling as extremely "interest-

ing" than VD2 (Figure 2) while group "a" favored VD2 (Figure 1). Again, the ideal ratings along the "colorful-colorless" continuum were identical for both groups but differed in their assessment of the visual displays (Figure 5). While group "a" rated VD2 more "colorful" than group "b" (Figure 4), the latter groups' responses to VD1 were slightly more colorful (Figure 3).

The middle income respondents (group "b") believed VD1 to be "happier" than VD2 (Figure 2), though the low income respondents (group "a") rated VD2 considerably "happier" than VD1 (Figure 1). Both groups concur that their ideal dwelling should be extremely "happy" (Figure 5).

Both groups also indicated a preference for a visual form that was slightly "familiar" (Figure 5) and indicated that while VD2 was more "familiar" than their ideal, VD1 was too "unknown" (Figure 1 and 2).

The frequency distribution of responses to VD1 do indicate intragroup polarity while responses to the VD2 appear to be less variant and the ideal even less so. Respondents from group "a" differed in their assessment of VD1 in the following adjectives:
simple   complex

Figure 6.
Analysis of Variance: Levels of Significance Between Visual Displays

	Group "a" (Low Income) Visual Display Comparisons			Group "b" (Middle Income) Visual Display Comparisons		
Attributes	VD1&2	VD1&Ia$_1$	VD2&Ia$_1$	VD1&2	VD1&Ib$_1$	VD2&Ib$_1$
1. Simple-Complex	.01	--	--	.01	--	.01
2. Modern-Old Fashioned	.01	.01	--	.05	.01	--
3. Upper Class-Lower Class	--	.01	.01	.01	.01	.01
4. Pleasant-Unpleasant	.01	.01	.01	.05	.01	.01
5. Relaxed-Tense	.01	.01	.05	.01	.01	.01
6. Rich-Poor	--	.01	.01	.05	.01	.01
7. Large-Small	--	.01	.01	.05	.01	.01
8. Strong-Weak	--	.01	.01	--	.01	.01
9. Smooth-Rough	.05	.01	.05	--	.01	--
10. Novel-Common	.01	--	.01	.01	--	--
11. Warm-Cool	--	.01	.05	--	.01	.01
12. Familiar-Unknown	.01	.05	--	.01	.01	.01
13. Interesting-Dull	--	.01	.01	.01	.01	--
14. Happy-Sad	.01	.01	.01	.05	.01	.01
15. Usual-Unusual	.01	.01	.05	.01	--	.01
16. Like-Dislike	.01	.01	.01	--	.01	.01
17. Colorful-Colorless	.01	.01	.01	.01	.01	.01
18. Soft-Hard	.01	.01	--	--	.01	.01
19. Ugly-Beautiful	.01	.01	.01	--	.01	.01

Figure 7.
Analysis of Variance: Levels of Significance between Visual Displays
(Combined scores of Groups "a" and "b")

	VD1 and VD2	VD1 and I_1	VD2 and I_1
1. Simple-Complex	--	.01	.01
2. Modern-Old Fashioned	--	--	--
3. Upper Class-Lower Class	--	.01	.01
4. Pleasant-Unpleasant	.01	.01	.01
5. Relaxed-Tense	.01	.01	.01
6. Rich-Poor	--	.01	.01
7. Large-Small	--	.01	.01
8. Strong-Weak	--	.01	.01
9. Smooth-Rough	.05	.01	--
10. Novel-Common	.01	--	.01
11. Warm-Cool	--	.01	.01
12. Familiar-Unknown	.01	.01	--
13. Interesting-Dull	--	.01	.01
14. Happy-Sad	--	.01	.01
15. Usual-Unusual	.01	.01	.01
16. Like-Dislike	.01	.01	.01
17. Colorful-Colorless	--	.01	.01
18. Soft-Hard	.01	.01	.01
19. Ugly-Beautiful	.01	.01	.01

modern	old-fashioned
pleasant	unpleasant
rough	smooth
novel	common
familiar	unfamiliar
interesting	dull
colorful	colorless

This suggests that there are differing dispositions towards environmental displays or house forms within what is generally described as homogeneous groups.

Conclusion

While the sample size is relatively small, the significance test of the data supports the hypotheses and further suggests that the instrument is sufficiently sensitive to discriminate differences.

These data suggest that there are commonly accepted attributes that describe an individual's preferred dwelling, while crossing socio-economic differences. Clearly, then, the connotations of the polar adjectives seem to have different associative meanings to different people based on their background and experiences.

It is also evident that assessments of the dwelling forms vary considerably when the respondents draw upon their own experiences and perceptions than when they are requested to respond to hypothetical questions. Though group "a" rated their "ideal" dwelling as extremely modern, their meaning of this attribute and its associations may be at variance with other groups, especially designers (6). This is evidenced by the minor variance of their assessment of VD2 to their stated ideal which was opposite to group "b's" assessment of VD2.

Since the comprehension of real and imaginary environments are not entirely the domain of designers, but users as well, comparative investigations of physical environments can provide useful clues to designers creating new environments. It is becoming increasingly clear that there are differences between people's needs beyond functional requirements. These differences have gone unattended for too long, thus creating a visual poverty in the designed environment. This study is but an exploratory probe in the man-environment interface in an attempt to stress the importance of the visual impact of the physical environment.

Notes
1. Rapoport, Amos, House Form and Culture, Prentice-Hall, New Jersey, 1969.

2. Wagner, Philip, The Human Use of the Earth, Free Press, 1960.

3. Howard, K.I., "A Test of Stimulus Seeking Behavior", Perceptual and Motor Skills, 1961, 13.

4. Zuckerman, M., E.A. Kolin, I. Price, and I. Zoob, "Development of a Sensation Seeking Scale", J. of Consulting Psychology, 1961, 25. Domino, G., "A Validation of Howard's Test of Change Seeking Behavior", Education and Psychological Measurement, 1965, 24.

5. Osgood, C., G. Suci, and P. Tannenbaum, The Measurement of Meaning, University of Illinois Press, Urbana, 1957.

6. Sanoff, Henry, "Visual Attributes of the Physical Environment" in Response to Environment, Coates, G. and Moffett, K. (eds.), Student Publication, North Carolina State University, 1969.

Frequency Distribution of Responses to Visual Displays: A Graphic Output

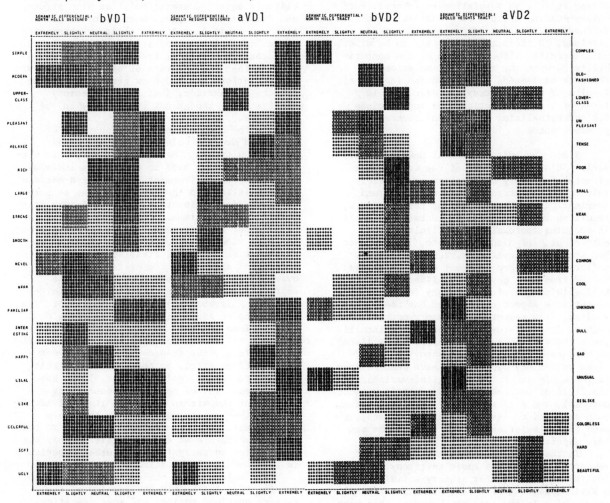

The Concept of Sensory Overload

by Joachim F. Wohlwill

Division of Man-Environment Relations, The Pennsylvania State University

Abstract

Little evidence exists on the psychological effects of extreme amounts of stimulation, in spite of the obvious relevance of this condition for environmental problems such as those of urban life. The results reported by Zuckerman, et al., on effects of overstimulation are contrasted with the findings of Glass, et al., on adaptation to intermittent noise, leading up to a differentiation between diffuse and specific components of sensory overload. Diffuse effects appear to be minor, while specific effects depend on the compatibility between the type of stimulation and the task or demands imposed on the individual. Results of a pilot study are discussed in terms of this distinction, and implications for conceptualizing certain environmental problems noted.

Since the initial work at McGill in the early '50's showing some of the dramatic effects of sensory deprivation on behavior, this topic has attracted the attention and imagination of a small army of psychologists, resulting in a profusion of research which it is becoming increasingly difficult to keep abreast of, let alone integrate,(1). We have had studies of sophomores, schizophrenics, sailors, and prison inmates; deprivation has varied from mere physical confinement to virtual elimination of all sensory input; every conceivable aspect of behavior has been studied, from measures of sensory mechanisms such as critical-fusion frequency, to intelligence tests, from somatic symptom check lists to elaborate Personality Inventories. Reactions to sensory deprivation have been related to the whole gamut of nosological variables in the field of personality study (mostly without success), and a large variety of stimuli have been employed to assess the extent of subject's need for stimulation aroused through the sensory deprivation experience.

In the aggregate, this massive body of research has provided ample testimony to the reality of the need for sensory stimulation as a basic condition of human, as well as animal existence. In the process, however, this work has implicitly fostered a "the more the merrier" view of the effects of stimulation, with a resultant virtually total neglect of the effects of overstimulation, or sensory overload, as it has been called on occasion. Thus, we find Fiske and Maddi (2), in their general introduction to their volume on the motivational role of level and diversity of stimulation, blithely equating overstimulation with stress, and dismissing the problem as of no interest to them - this in spite of their incorporation of an "optimal level of stimulation" concept into their theoretical framework, which would suggest that high degrees of stimulation should impair performance and show generally adverse effects on behavior, just as does sensory deprivation - though not necessarily in the same ways.

In the decade since the appearance of Fiske and Maddi's volume, the picture has scarcely altered. There has, as yet, been virtually no attempt made to expose the individual to a stimulus environment containing a maximum of stimulation, in the sense that the sensory deprivation experiments have reduced such stimulation to a minimum. Yet, a strong case can be made for the argument that in order to come to grips with the effects of the physical environment on behavior, it is more pertinent to understand effects at the overstimulation or overload end of the continuum than at the deprivation end. This view underlies, for example, Milgram's (3) recent analysis of "the experience of living in cities" in terms of the overload concept. While Milgram's primary interest is in behavior directed at other individuals (e.g., assistance-giving, bystander intervention, etc.), so that his use of this concept remains largely inferential, he has formulated a set of postulates concerning the effects of the strain placed on the individual's information-processing powers by the urban environment, and his mode of adaptation to this strain, which are at the very least highly suggestive for an analysis of the urban experience in terms of levels of stimulation.

The major aim of the present paper is to examine more thoroughly the meaning of the sensory overload notion, and more specifically to bring into relief the major dimensions or components that need to be considered in looking at the effects of high levels or amounts of stimulation on the individual. With this purpose in mind, we will examine the meager evidence available from past research on this problem, focusing in some detail on two significant studies. Hopefully, the results of this research, together with findings from a recently completed pilot study devoted to the same problem, will lead us to a revised and sharpened view of the overload problem, and to a reassessment of the overstimulation present in our physical environment.

Let us consider, first of all, a study by Zuckerman, Persky, Miller, and Levin (4), on sensory deprivation into the overstimulation realm. It is of particular interest since it compares effects of sensory deprivation and overstimulation on the same subjects, and with respect to the same set of response measures. The latter included Zuckerman and Lubin's "Multiple Affect Adjective Check List," an "Isolation Symptom Questionnaire," as well as heart rate, breathing rate and Galvanic Skin Response data. Subjects were also asked to rate the degree of their overall satisfaction with their experience.

The sensory deprivation condition was a standard one, consisting of an 8-hr. period spent under conditions "of total darkness and silence, lying on a bed in a soundproof cubicle, wearing gauntlet type gloves to reduce tactual stimulation." (p. 319). The overstimulation condition, on the other hand, was clearly designed to provide the subject with a veritable feast of stimulation for a similar 8-hr. period spent in the same cubicle as that used under sensory deprivation. The conditions are described as follows: "Stimulation was provided by two slide projectors; one filmstrip projector; one movie projector; two tape recorders playing three separate channels of sound rotating around four speakers in the cubicle; and a strobe light programmed for three different rates of flash. A programmer with 80 steps, set to move from step to step at 5-sec. intervals, controlled the advance or reverse of slide and filmstrip projectors, the on-off or pulsing of bulbs in all projectors, the 5-sec. on of the strobe and its rate, and the rotation of the speaker sources . . . The 1,280 slides used for the two slide projectors were quite varied, consisting of travel scenes, people, art, designs, close-ups of common objects, foods, flowers, and a small number (21) of scenes of heterosexual activity or female nudes . . . The filmstrip consisted of a variety of subject matter (e.g., cartoons, old movies, travel shots, newsreels, some semi-nude females, etc.), with no particular theme persisting for any length of time . . . The recorded sounds consisted of music, voices, and sounds. As with the visual stimuli, no one theme persisted for any length of time and change was frequent . . . The strobe light was programmed to go on

at irregular intervals averaging about a fifth of the entire time. Random methods were used in the programming of the simultaneous events for each 5-sec. period. The programmer advanced automatically changing the particular combination of events about 12 times each minute." (p. 319).

The remarkable aspect of the results of this study is its failure to reveal any very marked effects of overstimulation, in spite of the evident attempt by the investigators to create a stimulus environment characterized by an extreme of quantity and diversity. Not surprisingly, "most" Ss (no specific figures are reported) gave more favorable ratings to the overstimulation than to the deprivation condition, in terms of how well they liked each, and how interesting they found it. Similarly, measures of physiological activation, i.e., heart and breathing rate and GSR fluctuations were significantly higher during overstimulation than during deprivation, though apparently neither differed significantly from the baseline control measures. On two very different types of measures, on the other hand, both experimental conditions were significantly raised over the control measures, with the two conditions not differing from one another. These were measures of hostility, obtained from the adjective check list, and physiological measures of adrenocortical arousal known to be responsive to a variety of psychological stressors.

Zuckerman, et al.'s pioneering attempt inevitably leaves many questions unanswered. Above all, they report no behavioral measures that might reveal the subject's ability to adapt to the situation, in terms of the efficiency or quality of his response to a task, such as a problem-solving, reasoning, or linguistic task, for instance. Nor do we have any other information of the kinds of behavior in which the subjects engaged while exposed to the situation that might allow us to form a better picture of their adaptation to the situation.

In this respect, a study by Glass, Singer, and Friedman (4) is considerably more enlightening, even though it deals with sensory overload, if at all, only in a highly restricted sense. It is actually an investigation of response and more particularly adaptation to repeatedly presented noise, presented at intensities at which it is experienced as aversive. The noises utilized were created by superimposing several different sounds on one another and taping the resultant mixture, in which the component sounds were no longer distinguishable. Glass, et al., varied the presentation of these noises in two different ways: in terms of intensity (56 vs. 110 db.), and in terms of the regularity of their occurrence (under one condition the schedule provided for 9-second bursts of noise regularly every minute; under the other, both the lengths of the bursts and the intervals between them varied randomly). Glass, et al.'s interest in adaptation processes (as expressed succinctly in the title of their paper: "Psychic Cost of Adaptation to an Environmental Stressor," led them to obtain a variety of response measures, both during the course of the 23-minute period during which the noise was presented, and following the termination of this period. Measures of GSR adaptation were recorded at every occurrence of the noise; the subject's performance on simple arithmetic tasks on which he worked during the period of exposure to noise was likewise monitored, yielding two measures of efficiency of performance, one for each half of the exposure period. Finally, two response measures were obtained following the end of this period, one consisting of a proof-reading task, while the other represented a measure of tolerance for frustration, as indexed by the number of trials the subject took on each of two insoluble puzzles before abandoning it.

The results indicated considerable adaptation occurring over the 23-minute exposure period, as shown at the physiological level in terms of a marked reduction in the magnitude of the GSR response over the course of the period, and at the behavioral level in terms of a consistent decrease in number of errors from the first to the second half of the period. Neither of the two stimulus variables, intensity or regularity, exerted a significant effect on the arithmetic-task measures. The GSR's were considerably higher under the high – as opposed to the low – intensity condition, but this difference too tended to become attenuated as the period progressed. But by far the most interesting results were obtained on the post-adaptation measures, especially on the frustration-tolerance task. Here, it was found that subjects who had been exposed to irregular bursts of noise devoted an average of 6.3 and 9.2 trials to the first and second puzzles, respectively, before quitting; in contrast, those who had been exposed to noise at regular intervals "lasted" for an average of 19.2 and 26.3 trials, respectively. As for intensity, it exerted an effect only under the random presentation condition, with subjects from the low-intensity condition persevering for a significantly more trials than those from the high-intensity condition.

In a further experiment, Glass, et al., showed that providing the subjects with a feeling of control over the occurrence of the noise, by presenting them with a button which they could push in order to keep the noise bursts from being heard for the remainder of the session, dramatically affected both of the above-mentioned post-adaptation measures: it resulted in greatly heightened resistance to frustration, as well as increased efficiency of performance on the proofreading task following the end of the noise-exposure period. (None of the subjects actually exercised their option to terminate the noise.)

But the reason for presenting this study at such length here is not primarily to dwell on the significance of the findings themselves, interesting though they are. As noted at the outset, this was not in effect a study of overload or overstimulation, in the usual sense, but rather a study of the effects of a very particular kind of noxious stimulus, i.e., noise. (This feature, incidentally, should not make it any the less relevant to the environmental psychologist or designer.) Of greater significance for us is the conception of the research - the inclusion of a number of different response measures, both physiological and behavioral, and above all the monitoring of the response to the stimulus conditions over the course of the exposure period, as well as following its termination, so as to provide a direct indication of the individual's adaptation to the conditions, as well as the "cost", to use Glass, et al's own aptly chosen phrase, of the experience, as shown in the post-adaptation measures.

But the study of Glass, et al., raises at the same time a much more substantive question: Were the marked effects shown on the post-adaptation measures a result of the exposure of the noise per se, or rather of the disruptive effects of the noise on the task performance demanded of the subject during the adaptation period? The design of the study does not allow us to answer this question, although one would guess that in the absence of these imposed tasks the follow-up effects would have been much less severe. The main point, however, is that the effects of a set of stimulus conditions thought to constitute sensory overload must be considered in both a general and a particular sense, i.e., in terms of its diffuse effects on the individual's overall psychological state, and in terms of its specific effect on the behavior in which the individual is engaged. In this latter sense, the role exerted by these conditions is obviously a function of their compatibility with the ongoing behavior - or, to put it in the negative form, of their intrusiveness, i.e., of the extent to which the subject is unable to shut them off while carrying out a particular task. Note that this specific aspect of the overload situation does not have any counterpart in the case of sensory deprivation, since where stimulation is absent there obviously can be no distinction between intrusive and non-intrusive aspects of the stimulus environment.

The study of effects of overload is thus inevitably linked to that of selective attention, as studied by Broadbent, Maccoby, and others, though the latter have generally employed highly specific and limited channels of stimulation, which would probably not be considered as overload. It seems thus important to approach this problem in rather more controlled fashion, allowing us to assess the contribution of various aspects of the stimulation provided to the behavioral measures obtained. For instance, if Zuckerman, et al.'s subjects had been given a test of intellectual performance, much of the stimulus input these investigators utilized (especially the visual portion) might have contributed only minimally to the effects produced, if any, since such information is relatively easy to shut off from awareness.

The above considerations provide the basis for an exploratory study recently carried out by Nancy Saplikoski, working under my direction at Clark University. Miss Saplikoski investigated the effects of an environment in which the subject, sitting in an otherwise dimly illuminated room, was exposed to patterns of auditory and visual stimuli varying randomly over time; specifically, sequences of tones and other sounds were presented at irregular intervals over a 20-minute period simultaneously with sequences of flashes of variously colored lights, interspersed with occasional bursts of a strobe light. The effects of this type of stimulation were compared with those of a mild-deprivation group which was exposed only to the same dim illumination.

The plan of the study combines certain features of both of the previously presented studies: More particularly it was intended to reveal the effects of conditions of relative sensory overload, deriving from the use of overlapping and unpatterned, random sources of auditory and visual stimulation, which individually would not be considered noxious in terms of either quality or intensity (e.g., as Glass, et al.'s noises clearly were intended to be), but which, in the aggregate, could be assumed to approximate, though certainly far from duplicate, the overload conditions employed by Zuckerman, et al. The hypothesis was that, upon initial exposure to the situation, performance on cognitive tasks would be impaired while affect and measures of preference for complexity might show no effects, or possibly even some positive, potentiating effect of stimulation in increasing preference for complexity and heightening positive mood states. But over the course of exposure to the situation, as the individual becomes adapted to it, the impairment of performance would be expected to decrease, while at the same time, according to Glass et al.'s notions of the "psychic cost" of adaptation, the affective responses should change in the opposite direction.

With these aims in mind, measures of task performance consisting of the number of anagrams solved in a 3-min. period, and speed and efficiency of proofreading, were obtained on four occasions during the experimental session: before the onset of the stimulation period, after five minutes' exposure to it; near the end of the period, and after the stimulation had ceased. In addition, ratings of degree of liking (on a seven-point scale) of a set of slides needed for complexity were obtained before and after the stimulation period, and an adjective check-list was administered at the very beginning and end of the period.

The statistical analysis of the results is not as yet completed; in certain respects they appear to provide partial evidence for the hypothesis, but the overall impression they convey is that both in their task performance and affective and aesthetic-preference responses individuals are, by and large, impervious to the effects of the limited degree and duration of the "overstimulation" conditions utilized in this study. Thus, there was little positive evidence of adaptation processes, except on the measure of speed of proofreading, where the experimental group increased steadily from the pre- to the post test, whereas the control group, though initially superior to the experimental, changed little over the four successive trials. The results from the mood check-list, on the other hand, indicated for both experimental and control groups a marked decrease in the percentage of positively toned mood-adjectives checked (from 78% to 63% for both groups combined); the negatively toned mood-adjectives checked likewise showed a drop, but a much smaller one (from 46% to 40%). There was little overall difference between the two groups, suggesting that the cumulative effect of the low illumination condition of the control group may have been as aversive as that of the intermittent visual and auditory stimulation of the experimental. There was an intriguing hint of an interaction with sex in this respect, however: females tended to shift towards a more strongly negative response in the experimental condition, whereas the males showed a similar shift only in the control condition. It must be emphasized, however, that the statistical significance of these differences remains to be established.

The overall absence of any marked effects of the condition of stimulation employed in Miss Sapliski's study, however disappointing it may seem, is in fact generally consistent with the findings of Zuckerman, et al; together, the two studies provide eloquent testimony of the ability of the human individual to tolerate such conditions of overlapping stimulation amounting, one would have thought, to sensory overload, and even to respond adaptively under such conditions to tasks imposed on them. Thus, for the conditions of this particular study, the distinction between specific and generalized effects of overstimulation did not find support. The fact that the much more potent negative effects obtained by Glass, et al., for similarly intermittent stimuli were not replicated indicates that the stimuli must contain an outright aversive component, preventing the individual from shutting them off from his attention, if evidence of behavioral disruption is to appear.

Before overgeneralizing from the results of these studies, and particularly from the predominantly negative findings in Miss Saplikoski's work, it should be remembered that the period of duration of the stimulation condition was quite brief, and that only meaningless stimuli - which for that very reason were probably easier to "tune out" - were employed. Note, also that her subjects - college students - have grown up in a culture and especially a subculture, as teenagers, which all but prides itself on providing high levels of intensity and amount of stimulation as a normal background for much of daily life. We can only guess as to the reactions of a subject population with a very different history in this respect - such as a group of monks, for example.

In closing, let us consider briefly the relevance of the problem of overstimulation to the study of the role of the physical environment. As noted earlier, Milgram, among others, has stressed the overload concept as it applies to our contemporary urban environment. The question is, what features of that environment account for the presumed effects he has discussed. To begin with, many of the particular effects on social-responsibility measures are most likely attributable to either specific sociogenic fears originating in our urban areas - fears of attack, of theft, of robbery, and the like - as well as the role of crowding in producing goal-blocking, i.e., in interfering with sheer locomotion and attainment of specific goals. These effects must be differentiated both from the diffuse, generalized effects of amount and lack of patterning of stimulation and from their specific effects in interfering with the maintenance of task-directed attention. Thus, for a by-stander passively watching a downtown scene at rush hour, for instance, or the activity surrounding the building of a new subway, it is likely that no dramatic effects of sensory overload would be observable, though such conditions would still be expected to play a role in disrupting ongoing performance - as anyone trying to lecture to a class over the din of the ubiquitous bulldozer outside of his classroom window can attest. This particular example relates more properly to the question of the human tolerance for levels of intensity of stimulation, which likewise is only slowly attracting the attention of researchers (as in the studies of the problem of noise around airports, etc.); similarly for work on the effects of crowding and congestion, viewed in terms of tolerance for interference with goal-directed behavior. But these problems, as noted above, should be distinguished from the overload problem per se.

Finally, the importance of further work on this problem for the environmental designer should be apparent. The control of noise levels, e.g., around airports, the separation of vehicular from pedestrian traffic, the provision for visual order in the environment, which underlies most of the ideas for the planning of civic centers, new towns, etc., all these are predicated on knowledge about the individual's response to stimulation of different degrees of predictability, and different degrees of meaningfulness, as well as his tolerance for prolonged exposure to goal-blocking stimuli. Thus, the problem of sensory overload is seen as only one among several which jointly provide an opposite pole to the sensory deprivation problem, at least as far as the environmental psychologist is concerned.

Notes

1. A fairly recent, non-annotated bibliography of the sensory-deprivation literature runs to some 44 pages of small print! See Weinstein, S., Fisher, L., Richlin, M., and Weisinger, M. Bibliography of sensory and perceptual deprivation, isolation and related areas. Perceptual and Motor Skills, 1968, 26, 1119-1163.

2. Fiske, D. W., and Maddi, S. R. The forms of varied experience. In Fiske, D. W. and Maddi, S. R. Functions of Varied Experience. Homewood, Ill.: Dorsey Press, 1961.

3. Milgram, S. The experience of living in the cities. Science, 1970, 167, 1461-1568.

4. Zuckerman, M., Persky, H., Miller, L., and Levin, B. Contrasting effects of understimulation (sensory deprivation) and overstimulation (high stimulus variety). Proceedings, 77th Annual Convention, American Psychological Association, 1969, 319-320.

5. Glass, D. C., Singer, J. E., and Friedman, L. N. Psychic costs of adaptation to an environmental stressor. Journal of Personality and Social Psychology, 1969, 12, 200-210.

Session Eight:

Constructs for Human Adaptation

Chairman: Aristide Henry Esser

M.D., Letchworth Village, Thiells, New York

This session will elicit the bases of cultural designs whereby man relates to his physical environment and his fellowmen. The written contributions refer to the two guiding principles for the discussion:

(1) How the individual adapts to structural designs accommodating groups.
(2) The importance of designing intelligent environments which will serve as functional pros-theses for human groups.

The papers by Barrie Greenbie, Robert Bechtel, and M. Powell Lawton deal with the importance of adaptive behaviors in human settings of decreasing magnitude.

The paper by Alton Delong will attempt an overview of the role of culture in resolving conflicts between different levels of human adaptation.

Aristide Esser

A Behavioral Comparison of Urban and Small Town Environments

by Robert B. Bechtel

Ph.D., Epidemiological Field Station, Kansas City, Missouri

Abstract

A comparison was made between the residential areas of a small town and two residential city blocks using Barker's behavior setting survey technique. The main finding was that the setting survey method can be used in the urban area but with necessary modification. The behavior settings available to city block residents are nearly three times as many as those available to town residents. Yet the town residents have control over their settings while the city block residents are mostly on-lookers or audience. Based on past research this means the city environment is largely over-manned and fosters passivity and apathy. A suggested restructuring to make city life more demanding is made. Other differences show the town residents have a life style more characterized by residential social life while the city block residents are exposed more to activities of a service or functional nature.

Introduction-The Ecological Approach To Psychological Studies

In the current wide usage of the word "ecology" with all the assumptions that this is something new on the academic scene and in popular jargon it may be a surprise to learn that a branch of psychological study called ecological psychology is 23 years old and has produced five hard-cover books, about a dozen paper-back research reports and countless numbers of articles in journals, not to mention masters' theses, Ph.D. dissertations and chapters in many current textbooks.

Still, ecological psychology remains largely unfamiliar to many, despite the prolific output of its followers and the recognition given the founder, Roger Barker, by the American Psychological Association in naming him distinguished scientist. The discipline of ecological psychology is probably new to most of the audience, or if not exactly new, little understood.

The reasons for the failure of ecological psychology to gain more immediate popular attention are probably two[1]: The fact that it has concentrated on the small town rather than urban areas, and that most psychologists have career investments in the study of personality as the true explanation of human behavior.

Ecological psychology does not attack the study of personality or the use of personality variables as an explanation of human behavior. It presents no evidence that personality studies are invalid or inadequate. It simply deals with an area of measurement that requires no inference about personality or individual psychological differences.

The last statement requires a gigantic intellectual step: to imagine a psychology that does not deal with the individual but with only groups of individuals; that treats the environment as a part of behavior not separate from the pattern of behavior; and that makes no measurement of those processes that go on inside the individual person.

Consider that such an approach seems to violate most of the basic assumptions about behavior that now exist not only in the behavioral science professions but among architects, engineers, and others in the design professions as well. Ask any person why he does things or why people in general behave the way they do and the response is likely to be that the cause is found in some internal impulse, some factor of personality, some individual quirk or trait.

Without necessarily attacking this position[2] the ecological psychologist would simply bypass all of these assumptions and begin by saying that a profitable way to answer why people behave as they do is to begin by examining a unit of measure that is larger than the individual person, i.e., the behavior setting.

The behavior setting is a natural unit. If one looks out on the wide ocean of human behavior with its currents and eddies he notices behavior settings as natural occurring "nodes" which are as easily recognized by the persons who take part in them as by the behavioral scientist. In a community, the people who inhabit the buildings of the community sort themselves out into behavior settings in order to get the business of living done. The behavior settings are the office meetings, the school classes, the stores, the streets and sidewalks, the athletic games, the church services, the ladies aide society meetings, the bridge club parties, the boy scout hikes, the swimming pool party, and all the myriad of human activities that are tied to a particular place and time.

A behavior setting has a specific geographical location that it is tied to, a specific and regular time for which it begins and ends and a standing pattern of behavior which is understood by its participants. There are particular physical parts of the setting that are necessary to it, merchandise, bottles, chairs, tables, whatever objects are necessary for setting performance. And the geography, the physical objects, the time limits and the pattern of behavior are all tied together and inseparable. They form a behavior setting unit.

Barker and Wright[3] observed that the town of Midwest, population 750, sorted itself out into 2030 settings during the year July 1, 1951 to June 30, 1952 in order to get all their living done. The technique of counting these settings is called a behavior setting survey.

Once one knows the behavior settings of the community it is possible to predict in very extensive and intricate detail the global behavior of any individual or group in that community. No other known technique of behavioral science can make this claim. The issue is not whether even more detail could be predicted by personality theory but that it has so far been impossible to amass enough data in personality theory to even begin approaching this level of measureably describing human behavior.

Therefore, I submit that at the present time and in the current state of knowledge in the behavioral sciences ecological psychology, with its unit of the behavior setting and the technique of the behavior setting survey is the most promising approach to measure the effect of environments on behavior, and measuring the effects that changes in the environment have on the daily lives of persons in any community. The behavior setting techniques are especially pertinent to the goals of the design professions for these professions build for ordinary, everyday behavior and ecological psychology studies daily behavior.

Now let's return to the first reason given by Kenneth Little as to why ecological psychology has not gained more popular acceptance - its over-emphasis in the past on the rural or small town environment. This paper describes what constitutes the first attempt to translate the methods of ecological psychology into the urban environment.

Background of Research - The Setting-Size Hypothesis

In their volume, Big School, Small School, Barker and Gump[4] expound their discovery of the relationship between the size of the institution, the size of the behavior settings and behavior. Essentially, this relationship is that larger institutions create larger settings, while smaller institutions naturally form smaller settings. The important ingredient is the manpower available and since the larger institution has more manpower it simply allots more persons per setting to produce an over-manned situation in each setting. The smaller institution, by contrast, has under-manned settings. The effect on behavior is easily observed. Since the under-manned settings have fewer people to do the job, they require more of each person in the way of performance to get the job done. The result is that in the under-manned setting the average person has a greater amount of participation in the setting and consequently, a greater degree of satisfaction and a sense of greater obligation to the setting[5].

Wicker[6] discovered that it was not the actual size of the setting that determined the greater satisfaction and sense of obligation, but the experiences of participation themselves. Even the larger institutions had persons in over-manned settings who experienced greater involvement. The conclusion seems to be that it is the experience of parti-cipation or involvement in the working operations of the setting that produce the feelings of greater satisfaction and obligation. Larger institutions simply have fewer experiences to hand out per member than do smaller institu-tions.

The greater distribution of pos-itive experiences among smaller insti-tutions was as important as the greater range of marginal or non-involved behavior in the larger institutions. It was found by Willems[6] that the marginal members of under-manned settings had a greater sense of obligation than the central members of the over-manned settings. Thus, the larger institution is composed of over-manned settings where one would expect more un-involved persons, greater numbers of drop-outs, and a greater degree of passive as opposed to active participants in the behavior of the institution.

These findings correspond to many common sense aphorisms that one hears about education. For example, one can obtain a better education at the small college as opposed to the impersonal environment of the multiversity.

Barker[7] provides a quantitative scale for measuring the degree of par-ticipation central to the standing pattern of behavior in the setting. This scale is called the penetration level scale and it provides a number from 1 to 6 for the level of penetration for each person taking part in the setting. Level one is the on-looker who is not a member, but merely an ob-server in the sense of a person watching a construction gang. Level two is that of an audience such as the audience at a play. Level three is the role of a member of the organization, such as a

member of the rotary club. Level four is being an officer of the organization, such as secretary or treasurer or sergeant-at-arms. Level five is a shared leadership role; the president of an organization is the leader but he is not always present and shares some of his leadership with a vice-president or others. Level six is that relatively rare phenomenon of the single leader without whom the setting could not take place; a person gets a rating of six if his presence in the setting is such that without him the setting could not go on. A one man radio station might be an example but so would the only TV repairman in a small town.

Now the setting-size hypothesis can be expressed in penetration level terms. Larger institutions have fewer percentages in the levels 4 - 6 and greater percentages of people at levels 1 - 3 in all their settings than do smaller institutions.

This hypothesis suggests that per-haps one of the greatest sources of social problems in the city is the fact that the city as a large community simply has too many over-manned settings and the result is too many marginal, non-involved people. This would seem to be intuitively correct as well. We tend to think of the city as the place where unemployment is highest, where city schools have the highest number of dropouts, and where virtually all settings seem to be over-crowded. But the city is so complex that one cannot tell whether this is a fact that touches all social strata of life there or whether this is only true at certain levels. In the midst of over-crowding are many examples of under-manned settings such as professional services.

Study Methods - The Urban Ecology Project

The research project undertaken by the Epidemiological Field Station at the Greater Kansas City Mental Health Foundation was not able to handle the formiddable task of doing a behavior setting survey of an entire city. It was decided, therefore, to attempt to adapt the behavior setting survey tech-nique to the urban area, recognizing that this would involve accepting many limitations on generalizability of the data and on comparability between the small town data already collected and the urban data to be collected in the project.

Recognizing the limitations of time and money, it was decided to select two residential blocks and conduct a behavior setting survey on those blocks in the fall of 1969. No attempt was made to be random in selecting these blocks. They were chosen on the basis of their external appearance of typicality. It also must be recognized that there are far-reaching limitations involved in comparing only two city blocks with an entire small town community. Detailed descriptions of the blocks and the resident composition are contained in the larger report (Bechtel, Achelpohl, and Binding). Briefly, one block, the Westside contained 91 caucasion persons; 30% of whom were Mexican-American. Mean age was 27.4. The second block was composed of 39 persons, all Negro whose mean age was 40.2. Both blocks were in poor neighborhoods with several residents in each on welfare.

The behavioral observations lasted for one month from October 15, to November 15, 1969. Three residents in each block were hired and trained as observers. Their schedules of observation were staggered to cover the 24 hour period of the day. Observers would write in prose the continual observations. These observations would be checked by the researchers, vague and partial observations were explicated by re-observing certain settings and/or questioning participants after the fact. The observations would then be classified into settings and a list of settings was made up for each block. An attempt was made to account for all the local neighborhood-activity of each person in the block outside of his house. In some cases when activity in the house was public, such as a party or meeting, this was, of course, included; the invited observer-resident would report on the party or meeting just as he did for external street activities. This is essentially the same technique as described in Barker's[7] chapter four and would make the urban data as nearly comparable in range if not in time considering the shortened time of one month as compared to Barker's full year.

The researchers then calculated the various behavior scales listed in Barker's[7] manual. This was done with frequent consultation with the observers.

Finally, the research was written up in detail and published (Bechtel, Achelpol, Binding,[8]).

Comparisons of the various behavior scales were made between Barker's[7] findings of Midwest, a small Kansas town, and the data from the two city blocks.

Findings - Content

In comparing the small town to the city environments studies it was discovered that some difficulties reported in East Side, West Side and Midwest could be overcome by re-analyzing the Midwest data by residences rather than taking the entire community data from Barker's (1968) report. This re-analysis brought out further problems that were generally overcome. The following data constitute a more refined methodology and supercede the results in East Side West Side and Midwest.

In the city blocks combined there are 46 families while the small town had 320. Looking at the amount of time each person spent in the out-of-house settings (265 hours) for the city compared to 176 hours for the small town, it would appear that residents of the city spend more time in the out-of-house settings, than do small town residents. However, when one removes the amount of time accounted for by out-of-block persons, that is, persons entering the city block who do not live there, most of the differences disappear. The result is a roughly comparable amount of time spent in out-of-house settings for both the city and small town residents.

On the other hand, if one looks at the number of settings that occur per person, there are 2.9 in the city blocks and 1.2 in the small town, indicating more settings occur per unit of population in the city than in the small town.

The really important data to look at, however, are those that tell something about participation. Although there are more settings per person in the city, the important dimension to consider is at what level the city residents take part in these settings.

Of the 96 residential settings discovered in Midwest, Figure I shows (see below) that most of these are at the maximal penetration level of 5 and 6.

Figure 1

MAXIMAL PENETRATION LEVELS OF MIDWEST

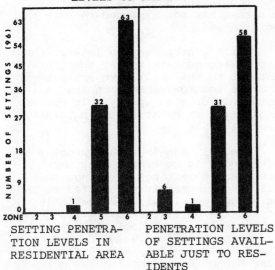

SETTING PENETRA-
TION LEVELS IN
RESIDENTIAL AREA

PENETRATION LEVELS
OF SETTINGS AVAIL-
ABLE JUST TO RES-
IDENTS

This means that residents largely run the settings. The second half of Table I shows that if the penetration level is adjusted to account for the six settings that intrude into the residential area but originate outside, then there is a slight change to show six at the three or member participation level.

There is a marked contrast when one looks at the city blocks. In Figure 2, East side settings show a majority have maximum penetration levels at 5 and 6, with some at three.

Figure 2

MAXIMAL PENETRATION LEVELS OF EASTSIDE

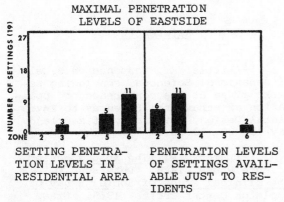

SETTING PENETRA-
TION LEVELS IN
RESIDENTIAL AREA

PENETRATION LEVELS
OF SETTINGS AVAIL-
ABLE JUST TO RES-
IDENTS

This is not too dissimilar from the

profile for Midwest settings in the left half of Figure I. However, when one accounts for the settings that originate outside of the residential area, one finds a radical shift of the majority of settings to the audience onlooker levels of penetration. What this means is that the majority of settings in East side are not run by the residents but by persons outside the residential area.

The same holds true for the West side data in Figure 3.

Figure 3

MAXIMAL PENETRATION LEVELS OF WESTSIDE

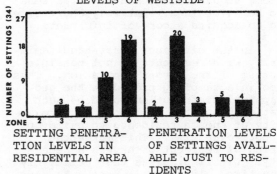

SETTING PENETRA-
TION LEVELS IN
RESIDENTIAL AREA

PENETRATION LEVELS
OF SETTINGS AVAIL-
ABLE JUST TO RES-
IDENTS

Here the majority of settings have maximum penetration levels at five and six but when settings originating outside the residences are taken into account, the people who live in the houses run very few of their settings.

To summarize these findings, although the kinds of behavior available to people in the city may be as much as three times greater than the kinds of behavior available to the townspeople, the striking contrast is that most of the people in the small town have contol over their own activities while in the city most of the people are followers or onlockers.

Some further remarks are necessary on the quality or flavor of the settings in Midwest as compared to those of the two city blocks. In looking at the small town settings one discovers settings of a truly social nature in the residential area such as bridge clubs, ladies aide society, etc. The city blocks, by contrast have settings of a more functional or service nature such as street repair, deliveries, police check, etc.

Findings - Methodology

Perhaps the most significant finding of this study was that the behavior setting survey technique, used so successfully in small towns, could be adapted to the city with relatively minor modifications. The modifications that were necessary are detailed in the full report (Bechtel, Achelpohl, Binding[9]). Some of these included a much stronger emphasis in selecting observers. Barker[8] and Barker and Wright[9] were able to live with the residents of Midwest and become a part of the community. In a small town of less than 1,000 persons, it is then possible to become acquainted with all the persons and behavior in a relatively short time and to acquire a core of informants.

In the city such first-hand familiarity with residents is not possible because of the larger population. Thus, even in a sampling procedure the geographical distribution would be such that a researcher could not get proximity of enough residents to build up rapport over time. This makes the hiring of resident observers a necessity. Our finding was that relatively long-time, older female residents made the best observers and this did not limit coverage of young people's behavior or male settings since many informants were in those categories.

The use of resident observers is the largest deviation from the Barker (1968) technique but there are other modifications that need to be made. For example, the greater variety of dress in the city requires modification of Barker's[9] clothing scale to determine more precisely which forms of dress are to be classified as "dressed up" in a city environment. Generally, however, the finding is that the technique can be applied with relatively little modification.

Conclusion

The problems of the urban area today seem to involve large numbers of people. The numbers of people in poverty are in the millions. It seems that dropouts, delinquents, and other behavior problems are also very large. Yet one level on understanding some of these problems seems to be a relatively simple one - to study them in terms of behavior setting participation levels in an environment rather than as individuals in a system. When one uses the behavior setting technique he sees many of these problems in terms of an overall environment which has provided too many people to perform only a limited number of all behavior tasks available. It is not just a question of over population but of a social structure that has not expanded to suit the social needs.

Still another way to look at the city environment is to say that in contrast to the small town environment it makes too few demands on the residents. It creates apathy. It fosters marginality in behavior and passivity in attitude.

The solution, once this problem is understood, is to create many more under-manned settings, settings that will be deliberately constucted so that not enough people will be available to get all the daily task of living done without effort. The solution is to change the city from a low demand, over-manned environment to a high demand, under-manned environment. The solution is simple to propose but not simple to enact. It means decentralization, fragmentation of many efforts, and a new value system that replaces mechanical efficiency of social structure as the highest goal with the necessity of participation of members as the highest good.

Notes

[2] There is considerable evidence that the clinical inference system based on personality theory is breaking down as witnessed by clinician Peterson's (1969) attack as well as those of Szasz (1965) and Dumont (1969)

References

[1] Little, K., Response on Behalf of Behavioral Sciences, concluding remarks given at the conference on Application of Behavioral Sciences to Environmental Design, University of Maryland, May 18, 20, 1970.

[2] Dumont, M., The Absurd Healer, Science House, 1969. Peterson, D., The Clinical Study of Social Behavior, Appleton-Centur-Crofts, 1969. Szasz, T., The Myth of Mental Illness, Hoebes-

Harper, 1964.

[3] Barker, R., and Wright, H., Midwest and It's Children, Row, Peterson, 1955.

[4] Barker, R. and Gump, P., Big School, Small School, Stanford U. Press, 1964.

[5] Willems, E., Planning a Rationale for Naturalistic Research, in Willems, E., and Rausch, H. (eds.), Naturalistic Viewpoints in Psychological Research, Holt-Rinehart, 1969, pages 44-71.

[6] Wicker, A., "Size of Church Membership and Members' Support of Church Behavior Settings", Journal of Personality and Social Psychology, Volume 13, 1969, pages 278-288.

[7] Barker, R., Ecological Psychology, Stanford University Press, 1968.

[8] Bechtel, R., Achelpohl, C., and Binding, F., East Side, West Side, and Midwest: A Behavioral Comparison of these Environments. Epidemiological Field Station, 1970.

Coding Behavior and Levels of Cultural Integration:
Synchronic and Diachronic
Adaptive Mechanisms in Human Organization

by Alton J. De Long
Pennsylvania State University

Abstract

Constancy and change are fundamental and inter-dependent concepts underlying human organization. In order to cope with a complex environment, every organism requires a mechanism which will simplify environmental complexity and introduce a degree of constancy. At the same time, it must also possess a mechanism capable of making temporal adjustments to a variable environment. Coding behavior is seen as a synchronic adaptive mechanism which insures constancy. The levels of cultural integration function as a diachronic adaptive mechanism producing change. Western Man's emphasis on science and technology may be destroying the balance required between the two mechanisms and jeopardizing Man's symboling behavior as a basis of human organization.

Introduction

In traditional terminology, the East and West have often been compared by considering the primary relationship between Man and environment. The East, as exemplified by early Indian philosophy (1, 2), can be characterized by the deep-rooted belief that the environment is the prime variable, controlling the destiny of Man. The West, by contrast, lays prime emphasis on Man's control of the environment. To the Easterner, the environment is the omnipotent force which requires of Man the most harmonious adjustment he can effect. But the Westerner has traditionally viewed the relationship in reverse: Man is the omnipotent force who adjusts the environment to his personal and collective desires. The two macro-cultures operate according to different clocks. Environmental rhythms are paramount to the Easterner whereas Western Man gives primary allegiance to "extensional" rhythms (3). While Eastern Man internalizes temporal criteria based essentially on the gradual emergance and disappearance of natural environmental phenomena, Western Man is continually extending himself in order to subjugate the environment to his own arbitrarily determined temporal requirements (4).

Man's extensions are known as technology. It has been through technology that Western Man has dreamed his utopias and anti-utopias (5, 6, 7), has thought of the salvation of Mankind from all that has been considered unacceptable (e.g., hunger, pestilence, and war), and has forseen the doom of the species (8, 9, 10). In essence, Western Man has lived a psycho-neurotic existence, seeing himself via his extensions as the source of hope on the one hand, while recognizing that he also carries the embodiment of disaster on the other. No sooner do we uncover nuclear fission, a milestone in Man's intellectual history, than we bemoan its terrible destructive potential. We discover the gene as the basis of life and then worry about the possibility of fiendish genetic engineering. The fact that such concerns are irrelevant does not seem to provide any comfort to a culture whose existence depends upon science and technology.

The era of the optimistic "we-can-do-anything-we-set-our-rational-minds-to" seems finally to be coming to an end, but its terribly sarcastic antithesis is no less discomforting. What is encouraging, however, is that at a time when an entire younger generation is turning inward in much the same way that Eastern Man turned inward centuries ago to shut out an overwhelming environment, meta-technology, the study of the "...integration of technology in the total culture," (11) is finally becoming a serious academic pursuit by anthropologists, a discipline heretofore content with avoiding problems inherent in technological cultures. And the central question is not whether we are pro or anti-technology. Given the constraint of culture these stances are irrelevant. The important question is how technology functions as a socio-cultural phenomenon and how it is integrated with other equally fundamental aspects of culture.

Culture, Man's primary mode of adaptation, consists of complex, highly interrelated mechanisms. It appears to be a unique phenomenon in the animal kingdom and is generally recognized as Man's prized possession. A careful consideration of its characteristics may throw into contrast some of the more important features underlying how perfectly natural adaptive mechanisms can lead to dilemmas of the magnitude we are now facing. Hopefully, such an elaboration will lead to the appreciation that the problem is somewhat more than we have generally considered it to be.

The conceptual organization of this paper will revolve around three interrelated topics. First, a micro behavioral system considered uniquely human, Language, will be examined in simplified structural terms in order to evaluate its synchronic and diachronic adaptive power. Second, coding behavior as a synchronic adaptive mechanism necessary for human organization will be elaborated. Third, the interplay between the levels of cultural integration as originally outlined by Hall and Trager (12) will be examined as a diachronic adaptive mechanism necessary for human existence. Finally, the interaction of the synchronic and diachronic mechanisms will be considered in order to underscore the concept of culture as a medium by which Man continually effects a balance between constancy and change. The impact of science and technology appears to be weakening the delicate balance culture has established.

Language as a Micro-Behavioral System

If Man is faced with any paradox, it might be most appropriately labelled the paradox of consciousness. Being aware of ourselves and our behavior seems to be an evolutionary luxury not afforded many species other than our own. Yet our self-awareness turns out to be as much mirage as reality, for we have drawn the erroneous conclusion that Man is fundamentally a rational animal (13). While we are a species characterized in part by self-awareness, the awareness of our awareness or, negatively, the realization that there exists aspects of our behavior of which we are not aware, required a man of the stature of Freud for enunciation (14). It was Freud's contribution to the study of Man that much of what underlies his behavior lies beyond his conscious awareness and therefore beyond his control. Psycho-analysis rests on the observation that a person's behavior cannot be understood or adjusted to within what are deemed tolerable limits unless that portion of behavior characterized by awareness is appropriately related to those portions which occur out-of-awareness: a simple but nonetheless profound working assumption.

Within the environmental context a parallel process emerges. For the most part our environment is the product of decisions based on the rational capacity of Man. Economists, politicians, planners, and designers ultimately shape our environment by making

decisions related to aspects of our behavior of which we are aware. Rational decision making based upon expectant rational behavior or upon behavior characterized by awareness is not alone sufficient or even adequate to guarantee a reasonable fit between Man and his environment. The ice-berg analogy is not altogether inappropriate here, for like the naive captain who charts the course of his ship on the basis of the visible portions of the ice-berg, we may well be on a collision course unless we seriously begin to take account of the "invisible" portions of Man's behavior. Like the ice-berg, there is much in the cultural matrix of Man that lies beneath the superficial surface of the immediately observable.

Aspects of Behavior

The development of structuralism in linguistics (15) reaffirmed the essence of Freud's observations. As the analysis of verbal behavior became formalistic and acquired the status of science it soon became clear that linguistic behavior was manifested on several levels of awareness simultaneously. People were aware of what they were saying, the content, but quite unaware of how they were saying it, the structure.

Teaching someone to speak a second language, programming him to reorganize and reperceive the phonic universe, in many ways parallels the process of therapy. As linguists devoted more attention to the area of language learning, it soon became apparent that an efficient program required the mapping of out-of-awareness linguistic behavior with behavioral aspects which were in awareness. The process of teaching a second language then became one of breaking down the existing patterns of the speaker's native language and introducing the new patterns of the second language through pattern drills (16).

These developments led to the recognition of three distinct but interrelated aspects of linguistic behavior, the etic, the emic, and the tactic (17). The etic, coined from the term phonetic, refers to behavior as it is actually and objectively manifested. It is what Barker (18) has referred to as the "stream of behavior." The emic aspect of behavior, from the term phonemic, refers to how people "view" the stream of behavior as being manifested, not in a conscious manner but behaviorally, based upon what portions of the behavioral stream they consistently monitor. Put another way, the etic is a continuum, a line. It is all of the things that constitute behavior. The emic is how the events on that line are organized into a finite number of discrete classes, or points. As there are always fewer emic classes than etic events, the emic aspect of behavior represents a simplification of the etic continuum. Emics, therefore, is essentially concerned with similarities between objectively different events as a basis for establishing classes of behavioral events. Thus, while the etic refers to the manifestation of behavior, the emic refers to the organization of behavior, its structure. The analytical determination of the particular classes, or emes, employed by a given language is possible through the use of distributional logic (19). There exists another important structural feature in linguistic behavior, however, in addition to the emic. This is known as tactics.

The emic classes function as the elements of the system. Their combinations, however, are subject to numerous restrictions which results in the use of only a small portion of actually possible combinations. Tactics might be thought of as the rules to which the elements of the system must conform if their combinations are to be legitimate expressions of the system. Expressions not conforming to the tactical patterns are reacted to as being "foreign."

There are, then, three aspects to linguistic behavior: the way it is actually manifested, the etic; the internal organization of the behavior, the emic; and the permissable patterns of the behavior, the tactic. As Hall (20) has discussed, and as Pike (21) has outlined in detail, these three aspects apply to all facets of cultural behavior.

Hierarchical Levels of Behavior

The etic, emic, and tactic aspects of behavior exist at every hierarchical level of behavior. Language, for example, is composed of many hierarchical levels ranging from the sound-base (phonemics) to the ways in which words are constructed (morphemics) and grammatical categories organized into utterances (syntax) (22). Despite the vast differences in complexity and organization between these levels, there is a degree of continuity from one level to another. Such continuity is possible because of the way in which etics, emics, and tactics are integrated with one another. At the phonic level, the etic refers to the actual sounds a speaker utters. The emic refers to how the speakers of the language organize the phonic continuum into a set of discrete sound-classes which function as the underlying units in the language. In English, for example, we use around 46 different classes (phonemes) even though the number of different sounds we utter is much greater (23). This means that we consistently ignore certain differences between sounds and treat objectively different phones as being equivalent on the basis of some shared characteristic. Further, of the sound-classes we recognize as being discrete units, only certain clusters are permissable. The combination of phonemes, via the tactical patterns of English, yields larger, more complex forms. But this large number of new forms is

merely the basis for another level of the language. These forms are also reduced by a process of classification into a smaller number of discrete classes called morphemes which are in turn subject to tactical (i.e., combinatorial) restrictions. What this means is that what is emic at a given level becomes the etic basis, via the tactical patterns, at the next higher level of behavioral organization. In other words, a line (etic) is transformed into a set of discrete points (emic) which via tactics yields yet another line (etic) which in turn is transformed into another set of discrete points (emic) subject to other tactic restrictions. This process is continued until all hierarchical levels of the system are exhausted. While linguists are still debating the characteristics and boundaries for such hierarchical levels (24), there is no question that the levels do exist.

The implications of the concept of hierarchical levels of behavior with etic, emic, and tactic aspects for each level are mutlifarious, but one deserves particular attention. The emic transformation of the etic continuum is a process of simplification since it reduces a potentially infinitely complex line of behavior to a finite series of discrete points (25). These points (emes) are characterized by redundancy since each point can be manifested in a variety of equivalent ways: any event which exhibits a class' characteristic can, by definition, represent the class. Being characterized by redundancy, such reference points can be internalized. But internalization results in a lack of awareness. One maintains an awareness of the class but loses all awareness of the class constituents. Their individual identity is lost as they become mutually equivalent (26). The selection of a particular event to represent a class in a given situation is relatively automatic, being conditioned by the distribution of other events or what might be referred to as context (27). Hence only the classes (emes) retain their identity as contrastive elements in the system -- one's awareness at the emic level is limited to an awareness of whether or not an event is contrastive or non-contrastive.

Tactics, the introduction of combinatorial restrictions on the elements of the system, also serves as a simplification process by limiting the number of permissable combinations of elements. Of the permissable combinations delineated by the tactics, it is unlikely that all will have currency. Some permissable combinations, therefore, remain unused. This feature is important for it provides a mechanism for change within the system without really affecting the boundaries of the system (28). It thus becomes possible to produce previously unused forms which are immediately recognized as belonging to the system. The recently introduced term "un-cola", for example, gained immediate acceptance and has wide appeal whereas the even more recent "cigar-lette", meaning small cigar, will probably fail. The correct form for "small cigar" is cigarette, but it has already been used and has connotations which the advertisers want to avoid. The tactic aspect is characterized by relatively more awareness than either the etic or the emic aspects, if for no other reason than people can deliberately coin new terms. People tend to be more aware, then, of the combinations of elements than they are of the elements themselves.

The simplified review of Language as a micro-behavioral system reveals that behavior occurs on numerous hierarchical levels simultaneously. Each level, in turn, is characterized by aspects which are completely automatic and beyond our awareness (etic), by aspects having a binary quality and the limited awareness of contrastive/non-contrastive (emic), and by aspects accompanied by considerably more awareness involving how elements can be combined (tactics). Two adaptive mechanisms are implicit in the existence of a behavioral hierarchy characterized by etics, emics, and tactics. First, a mechanism is provided for the simplification of complexity which operates in two ways. At any given level the raw behavioral continuum is reduced to a set of points (emes) which are subject to overriding combinatorial restrictions (tactics). The end result (emics + tactics) generates the raw behavioral continuum providing the basis for the next higher level. The value of this process in terms of information handling capacity has been outlined by Miller (29) and constitutes what he refers to as "re-coding." The second adaptive mechanism deals with the need for change. The tactic aspect allows for flexibility within the system while at the same time insuring that the degree of change will not exceed certain limits. This feature of language has been referred to as its "productivity" (30). In other words, the system has flexibility because it recognizes the need for change. At the same time, however, severely disruptive change is avoided because any change not occurring within the boundaries of the tactical patterns will be reacted to as "foreign" to the system. Continuity in the face of change is thus assured.

Two fundamental adaptive mechanisms required for human organization have been identified through the consideration of Language as a micro-behavioral system. The first permits Man to efficiently cope with an inordinately complex environment at any given point in time. This constitutes a synchronic mechanism. The second permits Man to construct a degree of temporal continuity by which he can successfully integrate his developmental existence. This constitutes a diachronic mechanism.

Coding Behavior as a Synchronic Adaptive Mechanism

The adaptive value of coding behavior as a synchronic mechanism can be best illuminated by outlining general characteristics of the environment in conjunction with basic requirements of organisms if they are to adequately negotiate their environments.

A prime characteristic of the environment is its inherent complexity. Depending upon how closely we examine the environment, there are probably no two events which are identical. Consequently, the environment is information-rich, being endemically variable. To be able to appreciate the full range of environmental complexity, however, would require an organism with extremely powerful sensory equipment. We know that all organisms have limited sensory capacities. But even given such limitations, the sensory capacity of most organisms still remains most incredible(31). The properties of the human eye alone are astounding (32), and the human ear under ideal conditions can detect up to 340,000 pure tones (33). The thermal sensitivity of the rattlesnake permits it to make differentiations in thermal variation approaching 1/1000 of a degree Farenheit. While most organisms are indeed equipped with rather remarkable sensory equipment, the full range of their sensitivity is not exhausted in their environmental transactions. And for good reason. Were an organism to treat every detectably different event within the ranges of its sensory capacities as being a different event, the organism would be dealing with a "perfect" information system. The occurrence of particular events would be approaching equiprobability (34), since as fineness of discrimination increases the likelihood of a particular event occurring decreases due to the fact that the number of alternatives has expanded. But general requirements of organisms are in direct conflict with the maximization of sensory discrimination. Organisms require some degree of predictability in their relationship to their environment. An organism could not tolerate a different Universe every moment of its existence. It would suffer from information-overload. Predictability in the environment implies regularity, a degree of constancy despite inherent environmental variability. In order to accomplish this, the organism must be able to significantly reduce the complexity of the environment.

The very survival of organisms in the face of a complex, variable environment, therefore, demands an adaptive mechanism to serve as mediator between the organism and its environment. Such a mechanism functions to de-sensitize the organism, to protect it from engaging in an overfine involvement with the environment. And such a mechanism distorts and collapses the temporal continuum through the introduction of constancy.

There are two primary modes of de-sensitizing the organism to its environment: genetic programming and cultural programming. In genetic programming the organism's perception of the environment is restricted by building into its biological structure a propensity to react to specific stimuli or sets of stimuli (signals). The genetic mode is of primary importance in pre-cocial species where the survival of the organism at birth is dependent upon being able to react quickly and with accuracy to the environment. Cultural programming can be employed only when the organism can be assured protection after birth and is effected through learning. Through this mode the organism learns to reduce the complexity of the environment by constructing classes which are then used to categorize the environment. Such classes can be referred to as symbols (35). While Man has generally been viewed as the sole possessor of culture, in the technical sense of the term, it is conceptually convenient to employ the term in reference to infra-human organisms to highlight its functional similarity to genetic programming in adapting organisms to their environments by restricting perceptual sensitivity. Obviously, one cannot preclude the possibility of learning as being adaptive in other species (36),nor can one preclude the possibility of a genetic basis for aspects of cultural behavior (37). The interaction between the two modes is considerable and complex (38).

Genetic programming, then, is of primary value in precocial species and restricts the organism's involvement with the environment by building into it a propensity to respond to specific stimuli which can be termed signals. Cultural programming assumes primary importance in altricial species and serves to restrict the organism's involvement with the environment by teachning it to react to the environment through the use of arbitrary classes, generally referred to as symbols.

While it has been customary to highlight basic differences between animal and human behavior in the context of the communication process(39,40,41,42) and to point out dissimilarities between signal and symbol (43), it would seem a valuable exercise to reinstate the biological continuity between Man and Animal (44, 45). Moles (46) suggests this can be done by equating communication with perception. But since there are many who would reject this notion, a more generic concept -- coding behavior -- may be more effective, encompassing as it does both signal and symbol with its emphasis on how organisms introduce and retrieve information from their environments.

Classification as Coding Behavior

Human beings operate on the basis of perceived characteristics which have a differential function (47,48). This is achieved through the process of classification. Levi-Strauss (49) unequivocally presents the issue when he states, "Classifying, as opposed to not classifying, has a value of its own, whatever form the classification may take." The process of classification had generally been considered by anthropologists to be functionally related to the survival needs of a given population. But Levi-Strauss' enviously careful examination of classification in cultures around the world led him to the conclusion that classification "...meets intellectual requirements rather than or instead of satisfying needs" (50). He then goes on to say,

> Examined superficially and from the outside,
> the refinements of ritual can appear pointless.
> They are explicable by a concern for what
> one might call 'micro-adjustment' -- the concern to assign every single creature, object
> or feature to a place within a class.

> For it seems to be the case that man began by
> applying himself to the most difficult task, that
> of systematizing what is immediately presented
> to the senses...(51)

Classification has the adaptive value of imposing on the environment an order, of introducing a systematic organization into the nature of things so that the organism can attend to them. Class characteristics, then, become the primary means by which organisms obtain information about their environments. The functioning of classification systems as codes can best be outlined by considering how codes relate to an organism's information processing.

It is obvious, as was suggested earlier, that even given the somewhat narrowed ranges of sensitivity to the environment of most organisms, they cannot make full use of their discriminatory powers and function efficiently. Every objectively different event would have to be treated and reacted to as a clearly individual entity. The organism would be unable to make a decision. He would inhabit a Universe with a sample of only one. Certain mental disorders, most notably catatonic schizophrenia, underscore this very clearly. Schizophrenics are extremely sensitive to their environments. Catatonics, of course, are completely immobilized and will remain in the same position for hours on end. In the presence of a catatonic one gets the distinct impression that nothing taking place in the immediate environment registers since there is no visible feedback that he is taking anything in. Yet the administration of a drug which temporarily eliminates the catatonic state reveals that the catatonic can describe in great detail events and their order of transactions witnessed several weeks prior. Contrary to the impression, the catatonic observes in micro-detail (52). It is also interesting to point out that schizophrenics in general have two closely related characteristics: they use language idiosyncratically, and they are notoriously poor at pattern recognition. Inordinate sensitivity, inability to recognize pattern, and idiosyncratic use of a pattern integrated medium all suggest the value of an adaptive mechanism which curtails an organism's sensitivity to its environment. Classification, and therefore coding behavior, can only exist if one is able to see similarities in quite obviously different events. Coding systems operate through the continual process of simplification. From a perfect informational environment the organism must reduce the complexity by constructing a significantly smaller number of classes (emes) which can represent the entire environmental continuum (etic). Survival absolutely depends on this ability. The establishment of classes functions to reduce complexity and variability by introducing redundancy, predictability, regularity, and constancy. This is possible since once a class is established one need only be aware of the class characteristic, the criterion for class membership. One need not take into account any other characteristics a class member might have since, by definition, they are irrelevant to the class. Therefore, the organism is not aware of the individual identity of any class constituent, but only of that constituent as manifesting the class characteristic.

The environment becomes transformed from something filled with infinitely variable properties into a discrete set of characteristics. Being able to identify such characteristics throughout the environment imparts to it a constancy. Decisions can be made with greater speed since the evaluation of an event is based upon only one relevant feature rather than all attributes of the event.

A basic feature of codes, therefore, is the reduction of variability. A particularly interesting study in this connection has been reported regarding imprinting in turkey chicks (53). Schulman found that imprinted birds displayed less behavioral variability when confronted with the imprinting stimulus than non-imprinted birds. Further, they also displayed less behavioral variability when presented with novel stimuli. Even more interesting, however, was the related finding that, "...in addition to a restriction of behavioral variability as a result of imprinting, there occurs a concomitant restriction of cardiac variability." This might suggest within the somewhat broader framework of information theory and coding behavior, that a reduction of behavioral (response) variability, which

implies a reduction of perceptual variability (i.e., classing) insuring that the amount of information present in the environment is automatically reduced, is also accompanied by a reduction of physiological variability in the organism. The striking thing is that when the chicks imprinted, de-sensitizing themselves to their environment by selecting a stimulus with particular characteristics to pay attention to, their heart rates decreased. Not only to the imprinting stimulus, but all others as well.

A well known laboratory phenomenon, "experimental neurosis," seems pertinent here also. While there are complicating factors of reinforcement and punishment involved, the noteworthy aspect of experimental neurosis is that it represents the deliberate breakdown of a previously learned classification system. What were previously coded "ellipses" and "circles" now become a continuum ranging from one to the other. When forced to make finer and finer discriminations, the organism becomes non-functional and breaks down entirely.

Classification systems which have evolved naturally (i.e., they have not been artificially imposed upon the organism) satisfy one aspect of coding behavior: they simplify a continuum into a relatively small number of classes. These classes then become the structure points by which the organism retrieves information from his environment. An organism's code thus becomes his unique key to the Universe and molds his perception of it, a point made with some virtuosity by Whorf (54). In order to be assured a stable referencing system the organism must relinquish a goodly portion of his discriminatory potential. He becomes the victim of his own ingenuity, a point well appreciated by Whitehead (55) with regard to Man's relationship to his symbols. Survival within the synchronic context thus appears to be as much a function of ignorance as it does of knowledge.

As we saw in our review of Language, there is another important aspect involved in coding behavior. It is not sufficient to merely possess a code (i.e., classes functioning as reference points). The use of a code in either reception or transmission always occurs in a medium which has some noise. Tactics, through combinatorial restrictions, functions to simplify the use of the code by introducing redundancy. Redundancy is effective in the presence of noise simply because not all combinations of code elements are permissable and hence some predictability is possible. Even if part of the sequence is missed the organism can narrow down rather successfully what the missing part must have been. By way of example, English has 24 consonant phonemes. Restricting the number of consonants before a vowel to three, the number of permutations and combinations is 24^3 or 13,824. Due to tactic restrictions operating in the language, however, the number that actually occurs is only 9 (56). While emics (the establishment of classes) can be seen to function as an error-reducing mechanism which operates by forcing the organism to limit his perceptual focus to a restricted range of environmental features, tactics can also be seen as functioning as an error-reduction mechanism which insures that the code itself will not be jumbled in the presence of noise. In other words, tactics prevents the classification system itself from becoming distorted.

Tactics as discussed above relates primarily to human coding systems. Animal systems have what appear to be functionally equivalent mechanisms which are built-in genetically. It would be as disastrous for lower animals to make coding mistakes as it would be for humans. In lower organisms tactics seem to be expressed through the importance of order and sequence. Marler (57) observes that play in animals can generally be discerned from serious encounters containing the same behavioral elements by the lack of sequencing. Play may have all of the behavioral manifestations of the serious counterpart, but they are not in any particular order. The crucial importance of appropriate event sequence in courting and reproductive behavior is well known (58). The sequence of events and their timing have been found to be critical to the relative effectiveness of auditory communication in birds (59). And, equally important, the short-circuiting of certain behavioral sequences is known to trigger aggression (60,61). The requirement that code elements be bound together in relatively invariant sequences interlaced with timing factors thus provides the animal with a significant degree of predictability. Misinterpretation is prevented because if any element in the sequence is missing the entire chain of behavior terminates.

In addition to rigid order, actual signal structure as a function of the environmental attributes of habitat seems to add stability to the signal in the presence of noise. The evolution of signals employed in code behavior in many species is apparently intimately related to ecological factors in such a way as to maximize the contrast between signal and background.

Given the etic, emic, and tactic aspects of coding behavior and their functional importance in terms of making an organization of the environment possible, it should be clear that it is quite impossible to achieve any scale of organization in the animal kingdom, let alone human organization, without the use of such an adaptive mechanism. Not so obvious, perhaps, are the implications pertaining to scientific thought and technology. Many have remarked that science and art are more closely related than we generally realize. McLuhan (62) emphasizes the similarity by pointing

out that one era's technology often becomes another's art forms. Barnett's classic work, Innovation: The Basis of Cultural Change, emphasizes that innovative processes whether essentially artistic or fundamentally scientific in orientation are characterized by the ability to pull apart existing arrangements and configurations and reassemble the components in unique forms. Levi-Strauss (63) reaffirms this point when he says,

> ... scientific explanation is always the discovery of an 'arrangement,' any attempt of this type, even one inspired by non-scientific principles, can hit on true arrangements.
>
> It is therefore better, instead of contrasting magic and science, to compare them as two parallel modes of acquiring knowledge.

These observations all emphasize what we have discussed under the rubric, tactics -- the rules of element combination. But the determination of the elements used is independent of tactic considerations. In other words, given the elements, tactical patterns prescribe how they can be configured. Tactical aspects are also those of which people are the most aware. Science is a process which might be characterized by "full awareness." It is also a process which overtly recognizes that its major goal is the determination of relationships. Science, therefore, is almost exclusively concerned with tactics. Art is essentially concerned with the same thing, only artists have never made explicit their methods of discovery. The implications are worth pondering. For in its determination to make explicit the tactical aspects of behavior and foster the innovative combination of the elements involved, science has tended to neglect a careful scrutiny of the elements themselves. In other words, our coding systems are taken for granted, in part because we tend to be unaware of them, but also because we feel they are outside the domain of scientific pursuit. Duncan (64) appropriately outlines the scientific community's skepticism of studying symbols because of their inherent subjectivity. Of course symbols are subjective in the sense that any culture's classification systems are arbitrarily determined. The fact that human coding systems are learned means that human organization is inherently variable from culture to culture. But this is hardly justification for not examining in detail a culture's classification systems. As de Saussure (65) pointed out, Man's symbols tend to become immutable precisely because they are arbitrary. But as Whitehead (66) observed, this does not mean his symbols are infallible for Man's troubles as well as his achievements equally spring from the same source, his symbols.

The alternative to studying our symbol systems is to

continue to pursue their tactical organization and to change their arrangements innovatively(67). While this might appear to yield dynamic change, the same elemental structure underlies our existence and if for any reason it is our classification system that is the source of our troubles merely rearranging the elements will not substantially alter our predicament. This is the reason why raising the question as to whether technology is good or bad is totally irrelevant: technology merely reintroduces us to ourselves, which enables McLuhan (68) following Innis (69) to correctly conclude the "medium is the message" and to be almost totally misunderstood by the scientific community. Science and its most overt manifestation, technology, is limited in its productive power because it tends to continually present us with unique expressions of our classification systems. It is the code that must be examined. The code is the synchronic adaptive mechanism and it is the basis for Man's relationship to his environment.

Levels of Cultural Integration as a Diachronic Adaptive Mechanism

Culture as a whole is integrated in three ways which parallel the aspects of behavior uncovered in our consideration of Language (70). These have been termed the Formal, Informal, and Technical. All systemic aspects of culture have Formal, Informal, and Technical elaborations (71). Since this terminology diverges sharply from the popular connotations, it will be necessary to describe briefly what they entail. The levels of integration are characterized by the ways in which they are learned, the amount of affect involved, and the degree to which the participants of the culture are aware of them.

Formal learning is by precept and admonition. It is a two-way process: people make mistakes and are corrected. Consequently there is a "right" way and a "wrong" way to do things. Other alternatives are not possible. Imitation characterizes Informal learning. One selects a model and copies it. There aren't merely "good" and "bad" models, but many depending upon the situation. Technical learning involves a one-way flow of information, from teacher to student. All rules can be made explicit and can, therefore, be verbalized and codified.

Formal affect is extremely intense, and the violation of a Formal norm causes severe frustration. The removal of a Formal underpinning can easily jeopardize the sanity of the individual since it constitutes a part of the very core of culture. The entire realm of the Formal is typified by deep-running emotional currents. Informal affect is almost non-existent until a norm is violated which results in anxiety. One knows Informal behavior is involved when he feels something has

gone wrong in his relationship with someone, but he can't quite put his finger on what it was. The elimination of all affect is the hallmark of the technical. Feelings are suppressed to the highest degree when dealing with Technically integrated aspects of culture.

Formal awareness is sharply delimited, involving almost exclusively an awareness of tradition. We are aware only of the "natural" and the "unnatural" so that Formal awareness functions as a binary opposition. Since nearly everything Informal occurs out-of-awareness, the term Informal awareness is a non-sequitur. Much of what happens on this level is completely internalized so that it remains background for us until we experience a different culture which serves to throw our own into relief. On the Technical level of culture we are dealing with its most conscious aspects and accordingly we can be rather precise.

In terms of programming, the Formal aspects of culture are programmed the earliest through the use of the customary binary formulas of "right and wrong," and "good and bad." The Formal level of culture is pervasive for two reasons. First, it is learned the earliest and unquestioningly. Second, because it is learned so early it becomes internalized and forms the background of a person's existence. Once internalized the individual and the culture are inseparable and a threat to the Formal level of the culture is a threat to the individual. It should also be noted that the Formal realm of culture has relatively greater currency, and all members are programmed more or less the same way.

Informal programming is a function of one's situation. Informal learning takes place through the process of imitation and therefore peer-group influences are paramount. Informal aspects of culture are also internalized and participants are completely unaware of Informal processes. Two features, however, distinguish Informally internalized behavior from that which has been internalized Formally. First, peer groups are demonstrably more influential with respect to the content of what gets internalized. A child, for example, will learn the dialect of his peer group rather than that of his parents, and once firmly established the dialect will remain with him the rest of his life. Second, the individual is completely unaware of the Informal level of culture (as opposed to the binary awareness of the Formal) because of the imitative process. He is unaware that he is being programmed. This means that people with different reference groups internalize slightly different Informal norms. Culture, by programming its participants situationally, builds into itself a degree of variability which provides a potential for change.

Technical programming is the most explicit of the

three. Technical aspects of culture are not internalized. Because very little affect is connected with the Technical, an individual's identity is not intimately involved as it is with either the Formal or the Informal. Consequently, Technical activity is not bounded by binary formulas or by situationally defined parameters. As a result, many alternatives can be generated at the Technical level of culture since there exist no inherent restrictions. The Technical level of culture, therefore, is inherently variable and functions to increase the content of culture through continual generation of alternatives.

Cultural change results from the interaction of the three levels of cultural integration (72). The Technical level functions to increase the content of culture and is essentially complexity-inducing. The Formal level serves to provide a classificational network for cultural activity. It, therefore, functions to reduce complexity. Change is initiated when Informal activity is made Technical. It is relatively easy to become Technical about Informal culture because people are unaware of it and have relatively little emotional involvement with it as compared to the Formal. The cycle of change, then, begins by getting Technical about previously Informal culture. But this increases the content base of the culture. If left unchecked the culture would soon become a mass of unsynthesized detail. The proliferation of content by the Technical level, then, must be re-indexed into the Formal level where it can be classified, synthesized, and simplified. But in so doing, the Formal level itself changes. Cultural activity previously Formal is then relegated to the Informal level and the primary responsibility for enculturation is relinquished by the parents and other authority figures to the peer group.

Functionally, the Formal level forms the Core of the culture around which all else is articulated. It is the code, simplifying cultural complexity to the point where people can handle it. Informal culture is Situational, adapting behavior to varying contexts. In this respect, the Informal level of integration seems to be roughly equivalent to Esser's concept of the "prosthetic brain" (73). Finally, the Technical level insures that there will be an adequate baseline of newly generated content which the culture can draw upon in its continual adjustment to a variable environment. Functionally, it can be termed Eco-Adaptive (74).

The interaction of the levels of cultural integration, then, results in a naturally adaptive process of change; and one which all levels of culture are affected by. Culture might be likened to a gigantic, intricately balanced mobile in which any force impinging on one part soon has ramifications on all others. Western Man, however, through his science and technological proliferation may have thrown the interrelationships between the synchronic and diachronic mechanisms out of balance.

Meta-Technology and Human Organization

The study of the relationships between the synchronic and diachronic mechanisms in human organization is the study of meta-technology: the impact of technology and science on the rest of culture. In general terms, the impact can be put quite simply -- an overemphasis on the Technical aspects of culture severely stresses the functioning of the synchronic adaptive mechanism. Science and technology are increasing the generation of cultural content exponentially. Unless this new content can be re-indexed into the Formal level of culture it cannot be handled efficiently. People must slow down their environmental transactions and make finer and finer distinctions. If the process continues unabated, the final result is similar to the unfortunate organism trying to deal with his environment without the benefit of a code. Human organization depends on the synchronic adaptive mechanism, and Man becomes the victim of his code. Once learned codes are not easily changed. Human beings are abundantly plastic until they acquire a culture. Thereafter the matter is considerably different.

The continual increase of cultural complexity places pressure on the Formal level of culture, a pressure so incessant that Esser (75) refers to it as "social pollution". There are several ways the synchronic mechanism can adjust. First, it can ignore the new content, but when the newly generated content is in the form of technology the organism is increasingly out of touch with larger and larger segments of his environment. Second, codes can change at somewhat faster rates, but this taxes temporal continuity which is so crucial to the enculturation process. Third, each person can be left on his own to develop his own esoteric code. But this is recognized as mental illness and, by definition, culture could not perpetuate itself. Finally, a higher level of structure which could accomodate the increasing complexity of the culture could evolve. But increased structure as a response to increased complexity means ultimately increased conformity and rigidification, perhaps as portrayed by Orwell in 1984.

Of these alternatives only the latter, the development of a higher context (76), can be considered truly adaptive. Yet this possibility appears to be compromised as science becomes increasingly Formal, for the delineation of a higher level of structure relies on the ability to recognize broad patterns between obviously disparate events and processes. The scientific attitude, insofar as science remains a technical process, emphasizes the generation of new data, making finer and finer observations, and high-lighting differences. While it acknowledges a primary interest in uncovering order and pattern (77), science still remains the road to specialization. In his quest for knowledge the scientist is driven into deeper and more refined study,eventually becoming a super-specialist who works at such a minute level of detail he cannot possibly hope to relate his findings to a con-siderably larger framework. Constantly being enmesh-ed within a discipline which demands that each bit of data be evaluated in terms of its specific context, the scientist becomes overly skeptical of any attempt to identify his data with a broader pattern. For while the data may be congruent on the basis of one characteris-tic, he is quick to point out that they fail to conform on many others. Generalization, an explicit goal of science, is thus viewed by the scientist himself as being dangerous. Pattern recognition is viewed as being arbitrary and subjective. Human behavior viewed through the prism of science is inherently vari-able and requires extremely careful study. Yet, cul-ture and communication are possible only on the pre-mise that human behavior is fundamentally regular and predictable.

The formalization of the scientific attitude would appear to be antithetical to the proper functioning of the Formal level of culture. For science has the ten-dency to eliminate arbitrary, non-rational systems of classification, and equally important,an inveterate reluctance to replace them with anything of equal simplicity. Our preoccupation with the Technical aspects of culture and with Man's rational capacity seems to have induced an unwillingness to examine Man's symbolic nature (78). The rapid proliferation of technology is drastically affecting the rate of change. Ultimately, it may eliminate the experience of change altogether. When Man loses grip of his symbols and when his classification power becomes stressed too heavily for effective functioning, he has no alterna-but to let his technology classify for him. And his technology will impose a classification system far finer than that of the stupefied catatonic.

Culture is Man's medium. During its evolutionary history it has developed mechanisms which give Man the experience of constancy in the face of change.His rational capacity guarantees him gradual and perpetu-al change. His symbols provide stability and constancy. Symbols, as irrational as they might be, are as neces-sary for human organization as the capacity for ration-al thought. Thus, the subjective and the objective attributes of Man intersect in a crucial way, resulting in an organizational matrix (79).To continue to ignore the symbolic -- to continue to disregard Man's cultur-al programming -- would seem roughly equivalent to expecting a precocial species to survive without

the benefit of its genetic heritage.

What seems to be needed, not wanted as Stover (80) suggests, is a "new myth for technology."

-Notes-

1. Zimmer, H. Philosophies of India, New York: Meridian Books, 1956.
2. Zimmer, H. Myths and Symbols in Indian Art and Civilization, New York: Harper& Brothers, 1956.
3. McLuhan, M. Understanding Media: The Exten-sions of Man, New York: McGraw-Hill, 1966.
4. LaBarre, W. The Human Animal, Chicago:Univ. of Chicago Press, 1954.
5. Feuer, L.(ed.) Marx & Engels, Garden City: Doubleday & Company, 1959.
6. Huxley, A. Brave New World, New York: Bantam, 1962.
7. Skinner, B.F. Walden Two, New York: Macmil-lan Company, 1948.
8. Carson, R. The Silent Spring, New York: Crest, 1969.
9. Ehrlich, P. The Population Bomb, New York: Ballantine Books, 1968.
10. Asimov, I. Dreaming is a Private Thing, In: J.Blish New Dreams This Morning, Ballantine, 1966.
11. Austin, W.M. Technology and Prediction, Tech-nology and Human Affairs, Vol. I, No. 2, pp. 14-15, Summer 1969.
12. Hall, E.T. & Trager, G.L. The Analysis of Culture,Washington, D.C.: American Council of Learned Societies, (prepublication ed.),1953.
13. LaBarre, op. cit., pp. 187-207.
14. Freud, S. New Introductory Lectures on Psycho-analysis, New York: Norton, 1923.
15. Waterman, J. Perspectives in Linguistics, Chicago: University of Chicago Press, 1963.
16. Whorf, B. Linguistics as an Exact Science, In: J.B. Carroll, ed., Language, Thought & Reality, Cambridge, Mass.: MIT Press, 1964.
17. Pike,K. Language in Relation to a Unified Theory of the Structure of Human Behavior, The Hague: Mouton & Company, 1967.
18. Barker, R.G. (ed.) The Stream of Behavior, New York: Appleton-Century-Crofts, 1963.
19. Harris, Z. Structural Linguistics, Chicago: University of Chicago Press, 1961.
20. Hall, E.T. The Silent Language, Garden City: Doubleday & Company, 1959.
21. Pike, op. cit.
22. Implicit in this discussion is a concern for the formal, expressional aspects of language rather than the contential, or semantic, aspects.

23. Gleason, H.A. An Introduction to Descriptive Linguistics, New York: Holt, Rinehart & Winston, 1955.

24. Lamb, S. Outline of Stratificational Grammar, Washington, D.C.: Georgetown University Press, 1966.

25. The use of the term 'transformation' in this context has no relationship to the use of the term in transformational linguistics.

26. Austin, W.M. Phonotactics and the Identity Theorem, Studies in Linguistics, Vol. 15, Nos. 1-2, pp. 14-18, 1960.

27. Gleason, op. cit., pp. 214-216.

28. This statement is not meant to imply there exists only one mechanism of change, nor that the boundaries of a system always remain intact.

29. Miller, G.A. The Magical Number Seven Plus or Minus Two: Some Limits on Our Capacity for Processing Information, In: The Psychology of Communication, Baltimore: Pelican, 1969.

30. Hockett, C. The Origin of Speech, Scientific American, pp. 1-10, September 1960.

31. Gerardin, L. Bionics, New York: McGraw-Hill, 1968.

32. Gregory, R.L. Eye and Brain, New York: McGraw-Hill, 1966.

33. Miller, G.A. Language and Communication, New York: McGraw-Hill, 1963.

34. Singh, J. Information Theory, Language, and Cybernetics, New York: Dover, 1966.

35. Symbols are here operationally defined as the elements of naturally evolved systems which have etic, emic, and tactic aspects. This definition still permits a distinction between symbol and signal but the arguments are too lengthy for inclusion here.

36. Hall, E.T. & Trager, G.L., op. cit.

37. Lenneberg, E.H. A Biological Perspective of Language, In: New Directions in the Study of Language, Cambridge, Mass.: MIT Press, 1964.

38. Ardrey, R. The Territorial Imperative, New York: Delta, 1966.

39. Hockett, op. cit.

40. Hockett, C. & Altmann, S. A Note on Design Features, In: T.A. Sebeok, (ed.), Animal Communication, Bloomington: Indiana University Press, 1968.

41. Sebeok, T.A. Goals and Limitations of the Study of Animal Communication, In: Animal Communication, Bloomington: Indiana University Press, 1968.

42. Ploog, D. & Melnechuk, T. Primate Communication, Neurosciences Research Program Bulletin, Vol. 7, No. 5, November 1969.

43. White, L.A. The Science of Culture, New York: Farrar, Straus & Company, 1949.

44. Hall, op. cit.

45. Diebold, A.R. Anthropological Perspectives, In: T.A. Sebeok, (ed.), Animal Communication, Bloomington: Indiana University Press, 1968.

46. Moles, A. Perspectives for Communication Theory, In: T.A. Sebeok, (ed.), Animal Communication, Bloomington: Indiana University Press, 1968.

47. Bloomfield, L. Language, New York: Holt, Rinehart & Winston, 1933.

48. Dinneen, F.P. An Introduction to General Linguistics, New York: Holt, Rinehart & Winston, 1967.

49. Levi-Strauss, C. The Savage Mind, Chicago: University of Chicago Press, 1966, p. 9.

50. ibid., p. 9.

51. Levi-Strauss, op. cit., pp. 11-13.

52. Esser, A.H. (personal communication).

53. Schulman, A. Imprinting Training Effects on Hyperstriatal EEG and on Heart Rate in Young Chicks and Turkeys, Doctoral Dissertation, Pennsylvania State University, 1969.

54. Whorf, B. The Relation of Habitual Thought and Behavior to Language, In: J.B. Carroll, (ed.), Language, Thought and Reality, Cambridge, Mass.: MIT Press, 1964.

55. Whitehead, A.N. Symbolism, New York: Capricorn Books, 1959.

56. Hill, A.A. An Introduction to Linguistic Structures, New York: Harcourt, Brace & World, 1958.

57. Marler, P. & Hamilton, W. Mechanisms of Animal Behavior, New York: John Wiley & Sons, 1966.

58. Tinbergen, N. The Curious Behavior of the Stickleback, Scientific American, pp. 22-26, December 1952.

59. Marler & Hamilton, op. cit., pp. 442-467.

60. Lorenz, K. On Aggression, New York: Bantam, 1966.

61. Hall, E.T. Adumbration as a Feature of Intercultural Communication, American Anthropologist, Vol. 66, No. 5, Part 2, pp. 154-163, 1964.

62. McLuhan, op. cit.

63. Levi-Strauss, op. cit., pp. 11-13.

64. Duncan, H.D. Symbols in Society, New York: Oxford University Press, 1968.

65. de Saussure, F. Course in General Linguistics, New York: McGraw-Hill, 1966.

66. Whitehead, op. cit.

67. Strictly speaking, science has only approached the problem quasi-tactically as a legitimate tactic analysis requires a prior emic analysis. Nonetheless, of the three aspects, science deals more closely with what we have been discussing as tactics.

68. McLuhan, op. cit.
69. Innis, H.A. The Bias of Communication, Toronto: University of Toronto Press, 1951.
70. Hall, E.T. & Trager, G.L., op. cit.
71. Hall, (1959), op. cit.
72. Hall, (1959), op. cit.
73. Esser, A.H. Social Pollution in the Evolution of Man, Presented at the Centennial Symposium, Man and His New Life Environment, St. John's University, New York, 1970.
74. In addition to the cycle of change outlined here, it is also possible to derive the existence of a non-systemic source of cultural change. This has been discussed in an unpublished paper, "A High-Context Consideration of Cultural Change." The importance of a source of change which is independent of the one discussed in this paper resides in the need to break the circularity inherent in the levels of integration.
75. Esser, A.H. From Territorial Image to Cultural Environment, Geloof en Wetenschap, 68: 81-98, Amsterdam, the Netherlands, 1970.
76. I am indebted to Edward T. Hall for the concepts of high and low contexts as they relate to structure.
77. Bronowski, J. Science and Human Values, New York: Harper & Row, 1956.
78. Duncan, op. cit.
79. Berger, P.L. & Luckmann, T. The Social Construction of Reality, Garden City: Doubleday & Company, 1967.
80. Stover, L. Wanted: A New Myth for Technology, Technology and Human Affairs, Vol. 1, No. 2, pp. 11-12, Summer 1969.

Some Implications for Urban Design from Studies of Animal Behavior

by Barrie Barstow Greenbie

Visiting Associate Professor, Department of Landscape Architecture,
University of Massachusetts, Amherst, Massachusetts

Abstract

Ethology, the study of animal behavior in the natural habitat, may have significance for the understanding of human behavior in the natural habitat of modern man, cities. Of particular interest is the territorial behavior of animals. There is reason to believe that humans also exhibit territorial behavior, and that a better understanding of the symbols by which human cultures establish boundaries may enable designers and planners to improve the urban environment and reduce some of the stresses in urban society. Extrapolation from animal to human behavior is difficult, and a comprehensive theory applicable both to man and other animals is needed.

A Biological Basis for Design

The "urban crisis" which built up like a thunder cloud over the past decade, and the "environmental crisis" that hangs like smog over the present one, has brought the planning professions up against what might be called a "design crisis". It is becoming increasingly clear that the methods and techniques by which contemporary human beings relate to their environment and to each other are not working satisfactorily.

This is particularly true in the United States where a melting pot of many cultures has emerged almost entirely without the unifying influence of traditions inherited from pre-industrial societies. In older more homogeneous cultures there will tend to be implicit and often unconscious agreement as to the way things should be done and how things should look based on generations of trial-and-error. In a pluralistic society such as ours, formal values, on which the design professions have so long relied, cannot solve contemporary urban problems - social, physical, or even esthetic - except perhaps for small enclaves of like minded people educated under the same value system. As a result designers today find themselves targets of outright hostility from many directions, and rightly so. Much of what we are producing, or what we are sometimes unfairly credited with producing, is merely adding to the general chaos and the general dissatisfaction with urban life.

If formal value systems cannot provide the answer to contemporary design problems, what can? One answer, possibly the only answer, may lie in biology. Despite the vast cultural differences between various human societies, and even within given societies, we are all one species. Scientists seem to be in unanimous agreement that the physical differences between races are very superficial when compared with the total human organism; there is every reason to believe that our physical similarities include the basic neurological equipment with which we perceive our environment and position ourselves in relation to it and to our fellow beings within it. Recent discoveries in anthropology indicate that in our fundamental responses to stimuli we homosapiens have changed little in 100,000 years (1). Our cultural identity as civilized beings is thus only one-twentieth as old as the physical identity on which all human culture in all its diversity depends. If there is a common denominator that unites all men in brotherhood it is in common needs and common responses to certain aspects of our physical environment. It is surprising, therefore, that so little is known, and so little effort has been made until quite recently, to find out what these common needs and common responses are. In testimony before a congressional committee on the environment, ecologists Hugh Iltis and Orie Loucks last year noted an almost total lack of information as to what constitutes a biologically satisfactory environment (2).

Fortunately, as this conference indicates, there has recently been a shift in focus among the design fields from purely formal values to fundamental psycho-physical relationships. The initiative for this change in thinking has come generally not from designers, but from scientists who have made a most laudable effort to establish a dialogue between what C.P. Snow named "Two Cultures" (3). Dubos has eloquently examined the biological basis for all culture and especially its expression in the way modern man designs his environment (4). Anthropologist Edward T. Hall has stressed the biological foundations of the complex and varied ways that human beings perceive space (5). Psychologist Robert Sommer has made extensive empirical studies of the way people occupy space in relation to one another (6).

Potentially one of the most promising, but presently one of the least understood, areas of investigation is the relatively new science of ethology, the study of animal behavior in the natural environment. Behavioral psychology in general has based its investigations on subjects confined in the artificial environments of laboratories and zoos, where various phenomena can be studied in isolation, where suitable controls can be set up, and where findings may be verified by repeated experiments. Ethology requires a very different method; it relies heavily on gestalt perception of total processes, in place of statistical analysis of separate aspects of behavior, and its findings are somewhat harder to substantiate, or at least to repeat on order, since nature conducts the "experiments" on its own time schedule in its own way.

While ethologists by definition study animals in the natural habitat, many of them have not hesitated to extrapolate their findings to man, and they have produced some theories which, if they are in fact applicable, have considerable significance for the understanding of human behavior in the "natural habitat" of modern man: cities. Prominent among ethological concepts are those pertaining to an animal's instinctive attachment to territory which have been widely popularized by Robert Ardrey (7). According to these concepts territoriality is, among other things, a device for distributing species over the available food supply, and it also has an interesting implication in terms of guiding species development by limiting mating possibilities. Corollary theories, especially those advanced by Konrad Lorenz (8), pertain to the role of intra-species aggression in the maintenance of territories, and the function of ritualized behavior in limiting the destructive effects of such aggression.

Popular interest in the subject has most recently been given further impetus by Zoologist Desmond Morris (9). He has noted that there is a major exception to the ethological view that aggression in animals rarely results in violence as it so often does among men. Only in captivity, Morris says, do animals "mutilate themselves, masturbate, attack their offspring, develop stomach ulcers, become fet-

ishists, suffer from obesity, form homo-sexual pair bonds, or commit murder"(10). Similar conclusions have been reached by many experimenters with animals in captivity. Calhoun's studies show that when rats are sufficiently crowded, social behavior patterns, including mating and care of offspring, break down completely, in what is called the "Behavioral Sink" (11).

As might be expected, these theories are highly controversial, and as so often happens, the controversy itself tends to obscure what is actually being said. The complexity of human life makes specific conclusions based on animal studies difficult to substantiate and difficult to apply to human affairs. For instance, Calhoun's studies of the behavior of rats under conditions of intense crowding strongly suggest that the high crime rate in dense urban areas may be at least partly the result of crowding. Such studies are useful as a warning to planners that increased residential densities without proper understanding of the effect on human behavior may be dangerous; however, they do not "prove" it, and furthermore, they cannot tell us specifically how to arrange human communities in a satisfactory manner. For that purpose it is essential that we observe the behavior of human beings. Nevertheless, observation of rats and other animals can help us in establishing a fresh conceptual base from which to do the viewing. The potential value of ethological studies to urban designers and planners is not that they will likely tell us how to arrange our cities but rather that they will give us a better understanding of the thresholds beyond which our biological natures will not permit us to go without serious consequences, and also suggest means by which we might establish certain relationships which are essential to our psychological well being.

Empirical research in this area is presently hampered by the lack of a cohesive theory which will enable researchers to correlate observations of human behavior with those of animals. The development of such a theory will require the synthesis of at least four scientific disciplines, and its testing will require exhaustive study of a wide range of human settlements. Not only does there seem to be no such theory at present, but there are few, if any, clear working hypotheses. The first step in a construction of an hypothesis, especially in uncharted fields, is pure speculation. Such speculation has characterized some of the writings of Lorenz on aggression, and to a lesser extent those of Morris; it abounds in the writings of Ardrey. All three have been attacked at one time or another for making unsubstantiated judgments and arriving at conclusions not corroborated by empirical evidence. Yet, they have succeeded in stirring up fresh ways of looking at ancient problems and this is a major contribution. The fact that some ideas are not "proved" or even "provable" in a laboratory sense does not always bar their usefulness. Urban and regional planners of necessity make use of theories which are at best probability. Designers traditionally lean heavily, often too heavily, on intuition. Most of the urban environment we all move in has been constructed without even an effort to make a good guess at psycho-biological needs.

The Meaning of Ethological "Territoriality."

It is, therefore, appropriate that we ask in what specific ways an ethological view of human behavior, particularly territorial behavior, might influence the design and planning of urban areas. But first, it would be well to clarify the meaning of "territory" in the ethological sense. It is not synonymous with "ownership of private property". As used here territory means the perceived space that surrounds an individual or group which serves to identify it as distinct within a larger group of the same species. It may be a fixed space on the ground into or out of which the animal may move, or the distance around a moving animal (or vehicle in the case of humans), and it may be defined in an infinite variety of ways. All that matters is that the boundaries are recognizable to members of a given species. Among human beings in some cultures, especially our own, legal "ownership" of land may be one convention by which territorial boundaries are defined, but possession, and not legality, is the key. People "possess territory" in a countless variety of ways on land which they do not "own", as indicated by the studies of Sommer (12). On the other hand, legal title to land which is not owner-occupied, such as that of absentee landlords, can not be considered territory in a biological sense. Biological territory, at least among most animals, apparently cannot be given up without important psychological consequences. Territory is not a "thing", and other kinds of property, including vehicles or buildings, are territorial only to the extent that they are symbols that define boundaries.

Territory and Self Identity

Comparative ethology suggests that animals exist in a continuum between the need for individual identity and the need for social cooperation. Different species vary considerably in their position on the continuum. The ant is way over at the social pole, the jaguar on the individual pole. Man is both more individual and more social than any of them; whatever the arguments among behaviorists, there

will certainly be agreement that man is the most complex of earthly creatures.

Everyday experience and most psychological research indicates that human beings also have a strong need to identify themselves as individuals, (a) within a group, and (b) as members of a group vis a vis other groups. In many, if not most, animal species, at least at certain times, the individual distinguishes himself from the group by maintaining or "defending" a territory or space against, or at least apart from, other members of the group, while the group also distinguishes itself from other groups in its species by maintaining a territory for the group. It is hard to know how "conscious" animals are of anything, including their own individuality; it depends in part on how consciousness is defined. Nevertheless, individuality of the animal, both personal and social, appears to be related to its territory.

Allowing for the immensely greater variety of behavior exhibited by the human species there does appear to exist in man a strong relationship between individuality, both personal and social, and relationship to territory. It is not necessary for our purposes that this characteristic is directly linked to animal behavior through instinct. Human history is replete with evidence that most human beings, when they are able to make choices in the matter at all, will identify themselves with a particular territory, whether possessed as an individual, a family, or a tribe; usually all three types of identification appear to be present, certain primitive societies notwithstanding. "Where are you from?", is nearly always closely related to "Who are you?", apparently even among nomadic people.

Because of the ever-increasing size, complexity, and impersonality of modern man's social institutions, his personal and local-group, (i.e., "village", "neighborhood", or "family") identity is seriously threatened. The consequences of loss of self-identity have been well documented by psychologists and they are not happy ones. It hardly is coincidence that the same forces that have depersonalized social institutions for large numbers of people are also dispossessing larger numbers of people from traditional relationship to territory. There may be a very specific relationship between the perception of self in a rural village and problems of self-identity in a street full of tenements or a public housing tower. Jeffersonian Democracy, which is the standard of culture by which middle class Americans tend to measure the welfare of our cities, was based on village life, not big city life.

While the effects of the abrupt change

from one social pattern to another on migrating peoples have been noted in studies by anthropologists and sociologists; less attention has been given to the effects of changing territorial patterns. It is time to investigate in detail the relationship between social stability and territorial possession and territorial identity. At least one study (13), indicates that urban neighborhood stability is related to clearly definable neighborhood boundaries.

Symbols and Boundaries

If the study of territoriality in man is immensely more difficult than the study of territoriality in animals, it is probably partly because of the human capacity to create abstract symbols of desires and needs. Territoriality in man may be more conceptual than otherwise, but that would not make it less territorial. I am inclined to think this is the case. For example, the distinction between possession of a leased apartment and "ownership" of a mortgaged home is primarily in the legal symbol of a "deed". As a practical matter occupants of either type of dwelling can be evicted with equal ease if they run out of money; ordinarily neither have much land or spatial privacy. But the psychological difference often is immense, and it will be manifest, in all probability, in the emotions which accompany crossing the boundary which separates private and public territory. That boundary itself is a symbol, i.e., a twenty-five foot set-back of cropped grass sans dandelions, a low white picket fence, or a tree enclosed patio.

Among the propertyless inhabitants of urban ghettos territory would appear to become more, rather than less, symbolic--more collective, but no less territorial. The boundary that separates the turf of one gang from another may be quite invisible to those not a party to the conventions that establish it, but it is no less firmly rooted in space than the picket fence.

If the healthy citizen is in fact a man with a clear-cut image of his own identity, if self-identity is in fact significantly related to territorial boundaries, it is obviously important for urban designers and planners to be aware of the fact. How these boundaries are established should be a major subject for research.

Territory as a Basic Human Right

In general, current planning and design processes rely heavily on economic considerations. Closely related are transportation considerations, which involve not so much the possession of territory as the right to move through it. With important exceptions, public rights tend to be rights of access rather than rights of occupation, so that it cannot be said that public agencies possess territory in quite the same way that private individuals or groups possess it. This is implicitly recognized in planning theory in our culture, by distinctions between the "public sector" and the "private sector". It must be stressed that the rights of public access and the rights of the public to the benefits of land-based resources are important considerations in planning, and it is not suggested that any of the ideas proposed here will minimize that importance.

On the other hand, if research supports this new concept of the role of territoriality in man conceivably some new components might overlap into areas traditionally considered strictly the private sector. These could lead to recognition of rights to territorial exclusiveness which are independent of conventional property rights with their economic emphasis; rather they would be fundamental rights equal to food, shelter, education, and health, and would be closely related to the latter. They might be termed the "right to privacy", but a better description should be found, since there is a kind of privacy which is not territorial, such as protection against self-incrimination, or of the privacy of mail and personal possessions. Most importantly, there are also territories which are not private in a personal sense, such as clubs, communities, and neighborhoods.

The right to private property is, of course, a fundamental element in our culture. The psychological importance of territory in the ethological sense is also recognized, particularly as regards the territory of the individual family, the home; it is protected, at least in principle, against search and seizure without due process, and in social attitudes such as "a man's home is his castle". What is new in this concept as far as the planning profession is concerned is the right of both individuals and constellations of individuals in various kinds of social groups to territorial identity independent of legal property ownership. The right to determine their life style within a given area and to resist invasion of other life styles by outsiders would be guaranteed to renters as well as house owners, to poor as well as the affluent, as a basic human right. Such an approach would have to accept as socially valid a certain amount of exclusiveness on all sides; so long as no one group infringed on another group's equal rights to its own territory on terms satisfactory to it, and so long as all maintained their obligations to mutually needed public territory.

One possible result of such an approach would be not only a greater emphasis on the neighborhood as a design unit, but a much better understanding of the way neighborhood boundaries are established. It would not be enough for a neighborhood to be quiet (it would be noisy if most of its inhabitants preferred), well served with utilities and schools accessible to transportation, and so forth. It would be necessary that the neighborhood be clearly identified as a community by means of the symbols understood in and acceptable to the culture of its inhabitants. Boundaries would be located where the residents felt they should be, not merely in terms of efficient street systems, school districts, tax districts, or natural topography. It would be the task of designers and planners to identify the desired characteristics and symbols through an understanding of the culture of the particular group involved, to develop physical and symbolic means of establishing psychologically acceptable boundaries, and to reconcile, as fully as possible, conflicts between the boundaries of one group and those of another. This would presumably apply also on a regional level; in fact, with modern high speed transportation, regional boundaries and regional differencies become increasingly significant.

Directions for Future Research.

If the concepts loosely postulated here can be reduced to firm working hypotheses, empirical research may conceivably turn up important new design tools. Designers may be in a position for the first time since the advent of the industrial revolution to offer diverse, mobile, synthetic modern man a renewed sense of his place in a scheme of nature. If, as suggested, man is truly a territorial animal, and if, as seems probable, he conceptualizes his territories through a complex of material forms and abstract symbols, the designer should be peculiarly fitted to assist in bringing natural order out of urban chaos. The designer's stock-in-trade is physical form; so is that of the engineer and the mechanic. Unlike the latter, the designer is concerned primarily with the symbolic and emotional attributes of form. Lacking the constraints which tradition once imposed on art and any objective knowledge of how human beings perceived their world, the designer can hardly be blamed for imposing his own emotional responses, i.e., his cultural value system, on the form he handles. Modern designers have been accused of arrogance and indifference to human needs. Perhaps it is not insensitivity and callousness of which we are guilty, so much as lack of curiosity. This may of course amount to the same thing.

The empirical work demanded to be carried out in this area is unlimited. The essential problem might be formulated in three questions as follows:
(1) Is some form of territorial identification common to all human cultures, or at least enough cultures to justify the conclusion that it is a basic human impulse and a basic human need?
(2) What are the common elements, or perceptual thresholds, in human delineation of territory, what are the impulses behind them, and how best can a common recognition of these be accomplished to minimize stress in human societies, especially under conditions of crowding?
(3) What device for observation and communication might be evolved which would assist the designer in giving form to the territorial concepts of diverse cultures to enable them to coexist most comfortably with other cultures and with least harm to the natural environment?

These are broad questions applicable on every scale from the layout of a private bedroom to the boundaries of nations. Other papers at this conference, and in this session of it, will present attempts to investigate such problems in much more specific terms. This paper is intended only to suggest new directions and frames of reference; its author is still in the process of attempting to make an hypothesis out of a hunch.

But one thing seems indisputable. Man's belief in his ability to override nature with his own culture must come to an end, or nature's conquest over man will soon be total and irrevocable. It is not enough for us to re-examine our relationship to the external environment; nature is not only around us but inside us. And the decisions which can save the environment will ultimately depend, not on man's control of nature, but on his control over himself. War -- national war, religious war, class war, and race war -- is still the ultimate pollutant and territory seems to be so closely related to war of all kinds that it deserves a much closer look than we have given it.

Notes

1 Dubos, Rene, So Human an Animal, New York: Scribners, 1968, chapter 2.

2 Iltis, H.H., O.L. Loucks, and P. Andrews, "Criteria for Judging an Optimum Environment - Cultural Views on an Optimum Environment Reformulated on Biological Bases," in National Environmental Policy, Hearing before the Committee on Interior

and Insular Affairs, United States
Senate. (91st Congress, 1st Session,
April 16, 1969) Washington D.C., Govern-
ment Printing Office, 1969, pp. 162-169.

3   Snow, C.P., *The Two Cultures and the Scientific Revolution*, New York: Cambridge
University Press, 1959.

4   Dubos, *op.cit*.

5   Hall, Edward T., *The Hidden Dimension*, New
York: Doubleday, 1966.

6   Sommer, Robert, *Personal Space*, Englewood,
N.J.: Prentice-Hall, 1969.

7   Ardrey, Robert, *The Territorial Imperative*,
New York: Delta, 1966.

8   Lorenz, Konrad, *On Aggression*, New York:
Harcourt, Brace & World, 1966.

9   Morris, Desmond, *The Naked Ape*, New York:
McGraw-Hill, 1969, and *The Human Zoo*,
1969.

10 Ibid, *Human Zoo*, p. 8.

11 Calhoun, John B., "A Behavioral Sink," in
E.L. Bliss, ed., *Roots of Behavior*, New
York: Harper Bros., 1962.

12 Sommer, *op.cit*.

13 Jakobson, Leo, "A Report on the Chicago
Experience in Community Change," in
Aspects of Environmental Design, Chicago:
Jack Meltzer Associates, October, 1960.

Public Behavior of Older People in Congregate Housing[1,2]

by M. Powell Lawton

Ph.D., Philadelphia Geriatric Center

Abstract. The behavior of tenants in the common spaces of 12 housing environments for the elderly was observed. The paper discusses, primarily in "clinical" fashion, the differences among the 12 environments in the way they were used by tenants. Variations in tenants' behavior are considered in the light of known environmental features that might account for the behavior variation. Hypotheses are generated for later testing, though a few statistical analyses were possible (supported by Grant MH 14923 from the National Institute of Mental Health).

One major focus of the present concern with the environment is the establishment of links between the structure of the physical environment and the behavior of individuals within it. Even with this surge of interest in environment and behavior, productions in the new field have been high in thought content, perhaps, but low in empirical data. The present report sits in the middle ground between pure thought and pure empiricism. The situation is somewhat analogous to the clinical psychologist's personality test assessment, which is based on data, but interpreted freely, with the aid of non-test data from the clinician's previous experience. Briefly, the ecological transactions between older people and their congregate housing environments were observed. Differences among environments in the behavior of their occupants will be considered in the light of structural and social characteristics of the environments. While the data are objective, the patterns of association between behavior and environment are frequently too complex to allow statistical treatment when our N is only 12 environments.

The study of congregate housing

The larger research project of which this report is a part aimed to study the impact of new high-rise, age-segregated congregate housing on older people formerly living in housing scattered through the community. An important aspect of the project is the place of on-site services in the life of elderly tenants. In order to study how such services were involved in the adjustment of the tenants our housing sites were chosen so as to contrast sites offering services and those not offering them. Structural aspects of the housing were not a basis for selection of research sites. Thus, the physical characteristics of sites occurred randomly, rather than being selected so as to vary systematically. While purposeful sampling of physical characteristics might have allowed a better chance to explore statistical associations, it is hoped that the semi-quantitative ideas gained from this study may afford a basis for later hypothesis testing.

Approximately 100 tenants from each of of 15 housing sites were interviewed; tenants from five of the sites were interviewed prior to moving in and again one year following occupancy. In addition, five groups of community residents not applying for congregate housing were interviewed. The interview, lasting 60-90 minutes, obtained information on social background, housing history, social relationships, activities, health, attitudes, adjustment, and evaluation of their current environment.

Method. The behavioral data were obtained by a trained observer's making complete tours of all the halls and indoor and outdoor common spaces of 12 of the housing environments. Varying numbers of tours, ranging from 10 to 27, median number 21, were done in each building, representing times of day proportionately (8:00-10:00 AM; 10:00-12 noon; 12:00-2:00 PM; 2:00-4:00 PM; 4:00-6:00 PM; 6:00-9:00 PM), and insofar as possible an equal sampling of days of the week. An effort was made to observe only when the weather was suitable for sitting outdoors, although this was not always possible; in these latter instances, account of this fact will be taken in the interpretation.

The observer's task was to count the

number of people (tenants, employees, and visitors) in a given area and note briefly their behavior at a given moment. This method can be compared to a motion picture camera's moving steadily from place to place, lingering on a given area (or person) only long enough to register it. Specifically, the following were noted:

1. The number of people seen in the hall of each floor (including those standing in their apartment threshold, but not those standing further back in their apartments.)

2. Brief words or phrases noting the behavior of those counted.

3. The number of tenants conversing, or appearing to be in a group where either conversation or a mutually dependent activity was in progress.

4. The room numbers of apartments whose doors were open or ajar (but not on chain latch.)

5. The number of people, and their behavior, in each of the following common spaces:

a. Lobby (the area into which the main entrance led, including the front desk)

b. Functional spaces (area by elevators; by mailboxes; laundry rooms; clinics; offices; stores; beauty parlor.)

c. Activity spaces (any room for tenant use that is neither lobby nor functional space.)

d. Outdoor space (usually limited to the area clearly on the property of the housing site; in some multibuilding projects arbitrary borders were drawn between buildings to delineate the relevant area.)

Some characteristics of the sites and the tenants are shown in Table 1. Since the number of tenants in each building is different, and the number of observation tours varies, the data have been reduced to the same base by (a) obtaining a mean number of people observed in each location in each building (over the tours on all days of week and times of day); (b) expressing the mean number observed as a percentage of all tenants living in the building. Table 2 shows in columns 2 through 7 the percentages of each building's total population observed in the various areas - referred to as occupancy percentages.

Another index of interest is called the distribution percentage (shown in columns 10 through 14 of Table 2.) The distribution

percentage uses as a base the mean total number of people observed in common spaces per tour in each building, and calculates how this number is distributed over the major common space categories for that building.

Results. For the most part, results will be discussed using the material in Tables 1 and 2 in an informal way. A limited number of Spearman rank-difference correlations were computed when there seemed to be a logical reason to expect an overall cross-environment relationship.

All common spaces. In column 2 of Table 2 are shown the occupancy percentages for all common spaces -- the most general indicator of total visibility of a building's tenants. There seems to be rather wide variation, from the almost 18 percent of the Van Winkle population that is visible during the average tour, down to the less than three percent of the Golden Years population. In overall terms, there is no relationship between the total amount of common space available (Column 1, Table 2) and the occupancy percentage of all common spaces (rho= .30, n.s.). Within the sizes of buildings we have studied (all large) it thus seems to make no difference whether there is a single area for gathering or whether there are many; in either case, the probability of pulling in tenants is the same.

Golden Years is located one block from the boardwalk of a populous resort; it is very clear that the center of the summer's social life is the boardwalk. Informal observation also made it clear that the situation is totally different in the winter, where the building teems with activity. Thus, one may suggest that the pull of nearby competing spaces is one major determinant of space utilization. A similar phenomenon is illustrated by the low all-spaces occupancy rate in Samuel Gompers Gardens. This site is the only one with a near-ideal center-city location; in addition, it is a couple of blocks removed from the health center and senior adult center operated by the union that sponsors the project. It is easy to speculate that the combined pull of proximity to urban resources and pre-housing centers of activity lessens the tendency of occupants to use the within-site common space areas.

The relatively high visibility of Riverlake and Van Winkle tenants is partially attributable to the existence of on-site senior centers, staffed by several salaried workers. Tenants in both Gotham Houses also have relatively high total visibility. Other work has indicated that people with limited physical capacity tend to sit in public places to watch ongoing activity more than do the physically able. This may have been the situation in the Gotham Houses, whose populations are in somewhat poorer health than others. For the eleven sites on which health data are available, the rank-order correlation between mean health status and all common-space occupancy percentage was .60, significant at the .05 level. Subject to future checking, one may infer that adequate provision of common space becomes increasingly important as the population to be housed becomes less physically well.

Halls. The institution for the elderly is noted for the high population of its hallways. Chairs are frequently located there and staff often find it more convenient to have residents visible there rather than less readily observable in their rooms. The situation is quite different in these housing projects for the elderly, where the health of tenants is relatively good and there is much less of an institutional atmosphere. It was a very rare sight to see anyone locate himself in the hall for any purpose other than to go somewhere. About one-third of all people seen in the hall were conversing, but these conversations were usually conducted by people passing each other in the hall or walking to or from the elevator. Nevertheless, some structural feature is at hand that might explain the relatively high hall occupancy percentages (Column 3, Table 2) of the three highest sites. Riverlake was the only site that had an exterior gallery serving as hallway (for one wing, or about half the apartments in the building). The building was not air-conditioned, and many people sat on the gallery, although they could choose to sit behind locked screen doors in their apartments, with almost equal cooling effect. More than half of all those observed in the galleries were engaged in social interaction, as contrasted to the one-third so engaged (in halls) over all sites. Luther Lodge is built in a circular cross-section with a totally unobstructed central hall area. While the small number of observations here limits how much one can make of its somewhat higher hall occupancy, staff corroborate the impression that there tends to be much incidental conversation as people pass through the halls. Certainly, the open circular pattern is "sociopetal" (Osmond, 1960); people are more likely to make physical and visual contact in this setting. What is particularly interesting, however, is that all these central areas in Luther Lodge have chairs and other homelike furnishings. They were designed as they were partly in the hope that they would serve as small social centers for the occupants of the floor, or for a floor occupant to use for small parties for family

or friends. Despite the physical adaptability of the space for these purposes, 132 visits to these central spaces revealed not one instance of people sitting down there to converse. Despite the general esthetic appeal of the space, it is socially unfriendly because of the ring of doors around the circumference, and the low proportion of wall space as compared to door space. Three of the four buildings where hall occupancy is lowest share the feature of being public housing sites, and three of them are located in slum neighborhoods. Conceivably, there may be some tendency for people in slum-located buildings to use hallways infrequently, as a matter of safety. However, the hall occupancy percentage is not associated with a ranking of the safety of the neighborhoods (rho= .35, n.s.).

The lobby. In our experience, the lobby is one of the most important areas of housing for the elderly. One lobby that we studied is totally open to the sidewalk and to whatever malevolent wind, temperature, or person chooses to cross the threshold. There is no place to sit, to talk, or to watch from, and there is no monitoring of access to the apartment floors.

Our housing varied widely in the extent and type of lobbies provided. All 12 of the sites shown in Table 2 had an entrance space beyond the front door, from which staff offices and elevators opened. However, four of the five sites with lowest lobby occupancy percentage (Column 4, Table 2) had no chairs or benches provided, though there was ample space for furniture. Thus, the only people counted in these lobbies were those passing through, waiting for someone, or choosing to stand. We have found a great aversion among gerontologists, housing managers, policy makers, and people in general to the sight of old people "just sitting." The thought of inactivity seems to make active people very anxious; the intensity of this kind of reaction goes far beyond a reasonable wish to provide activity for those who wish it. Thus, our "space managers," to use Robert Sommer's term, have at least passively tolerated the absence of seating in the potentially busiest area of the building, and in a number of cases have actively forbidden tenants to place their own portable chairs in the lobby.

The six sites with relatively high lobby occupancy percentages have hotel-style lobbies with comfortable seating where traffic is highly visible. The importance of both seating and traffic functions is underlined by contrasting the entrance lobby occupancy of these six buildings with the occupancy of other comfortably furnished, but peripherally located, sitting rooms in the same buildings.

For all six buildings combined, the mean number of people observed in the entrance lobbies was almost five times greater than the mean number in the peripheral sitting rooms (4.62 and .96, respectively; p <.02, sign test). The halls are usually also quite devoid of action to watch, as compared to the coming and going of insiders and outsiders in the lobby--perhaps one important reason for people's being uninterested in sitting in the halls.

Activity space. The category of activity space is not as clearly homogeneous as are other spaces. Three of the sites with seat-less lobbies used a general-purpose room in lieu of a lobby. In other sites there were as many as seven separate rooms in addition to the lobby. Thus, the three highest activity room occupancy rates were in public housing sites with minimal lobbies (Riverlake, Van Winkle, and President House -- Column 5 of Table 2). The first two contained senior centers that were open most of the time. The activity room at President House was the single most populated room in our 12 sites. While comfortably furnished, it had the disadvantage of having no visual connection with the lobby, and only two small doors leading to the main floor hall. Its one great advantage, however, was a wall of windows looking onto the main outdoor entrance to the building, and beyond that, a moderately busy small city street. This opportunity to sit and watch was used lavishly by a regular contingent who were both very sociable with one another and greatly interested in who came and went. The fact that this activity room was both isolated from the usual business of the lobby, but at the same time a center for minding one's brother's affairs, seemed to encourage clique formation among the users, and a certain amount of resentment by other tenants of the users' nosiness.

All of the non-central activity areas contrasted in the section above with lobby occupancy were included in the activity space totals of Table 2. Only three sites that have ample lobby plus other activity space (the Gotham Houses and Sholom Aleichem House) attain even an average of one percent of its occupants using these auxiliary spaces. Most such use reflected in our observations was informal use by individual tenants, for unplanned activities. On the other hand, these areas almost all have organized and scheduled times of peak use, which occur relatively infrequently. Thus, an auditorium may be used twice a week, with a large proportion of the building population attending at these times.

Functional space. Every housing site contained an elevator area, mailbox area, and laundry area. Not all had an administrative office within the particular building -- from our point of view, a very bad omission, though not backed up with data. The "optional" functional spaces were medical clinic, hairdresser, store, soda fountain, etc. (Dining rooms were not included, since these involved, by administrative decision, almost all tenants, and would therefore not reflect variation in tenant behavior). The occupancy percentage in functional spaces (Column 6, Table 2) was a fairly direct function of the total amount of common space in the building (rho= .65, p <.05), which in turn is a function of the number of functional spaces. Provision of space for performing functional roles probably has some value in maintaining meaningful behavior. Therefore, this statistical relationship suggests that to some extent the provision of resources within the housing environment can heighten the probability of effective role maintenance.

Outdoor space. The outdoor spaces of these housing environments frequently seem so bad as to defy any probability of their having simply occurred by chance. One site has a formal paved rectangle facing the blank side of the building, with a wall to an adjoining property on the opposite side of the rectangle. The only seats are regularly-spaced, fixed, flat concrete benches with no backs. Thus, there is nothing to look at, no conversational grouping possible, and active physical discomfort involved in using the benches. Another building has an ample grassy area planted with attractive fruit trees, but only one outdoor bench, which is rarely used because it stands in the path of a shortcut used by neighborhood children. Our most ideal sitting area was a resort boardwalk.

Column 7 of Table 2 shows the occupancy percentages of outdoor space. Two sites (Sholom Aleichem House and Samuel Gompers Gardens) cannot be compared numerically with the others because a number of observations were done in rainy or cold weather. Variation in use of outdoor space among sites is relatively wide, the two lowest being a site where there are no seats outdoors, and the other a center-city location with no street-side sitting. The next lowest occurred in a very hot climate (Luther Lodge) and in the next lowest (Golden Years) the boardwalk siphoned off possible users. The highest use occurred, surprisingly, in the building located in the worst neighborhood, in a building for the elderly imbedded in a large complex of other high-rise buildings for families (Van Winkle). Factors working in favor of these tenants using their outdoor space include (a) the space's having the protection of two sides of the building; (b) staff's opportunity to monitor the behavior of outsiders through the windows of the senior center, and the fairly easy access from the center to the sitting area; (c) the opportunity to choose between right-angle oriented conversational groupings or street-oriented watching; (d) the existence of a boundary divider that is not too much like a prison fence. Another major factor in this high use of outdoor space may be the direct negative result of the slum neighborhood: Van Winkle tenants have no other way of experiencing the outdoors. The Van Winkle tenants have the lowest rates of off-site activity participation, and of neighborhood and city mobility; they may feel safe moving around only very close to home. Their utilization of the outdoors may thus be compensatory. To a lesser extent, many of these features characterize the sitting area at Riverlake, also.

Blueberry Acres shows a different type of compensatory use of the outdoors. This site has no seats in the lobby, and during the summer we were there, the only activity room was frequently locked during the day. Thus, these tenants literally had no place to go. There were only a few outdoor seats. There were a few seats near the clotheslines in back of the building, where the women gathered to talk; the men congregated in front of the building, commanding an interesting view of a working-class white neighborhood and small business district. Seating was very limited, but a number of tenants interacted while standing. The Gotham Houses, with relatively high use of the outdoors, have some of the best all-around outdoor seating. Their grounds are ample, the neighborhood is middle-class, there are a large number of employees and visitors constantly traversing the grounds, there are many benches, and one group of them is oriented so as to facilitate conversation (circular form) while still allowing a view of activity in a relatively wide area.

Social interaction. Social interaction is the only content category of behavior analyzed here. Column 8 of Table 2 shows the percentage of each building's tenants observed interacting in all building areas. An alternative indicator of social interaction as it occurs among buildings is the percentage of all those observed who were interacting; in other words, considering only those who were visible, what proportion were interacting (Column 9, Table 2)? The two vantage points reveal somewhat different findings.

At any given time, one can expect to find that somewhat less than six percent of a building's population will be interacting socially within the common spaces of the buildings (median from Column 8 is 5.8 percent). On the other hand, of all those observed in the common spaces of the buildings,

about 55 percent will be interacting (median of Column 9). Comparing Columns 2 (percentage of population observed in all common spaces) and Column 8 (percentage of building population observed interacting socially), we see that common space occupancy implies interaction -- the rank-order correlation between the two is .96. Despite the clarity of the relationship between being visible and engaging in social behavior, the proportion of such "visibilities" being converted into social interactions among the buildings is not at all related to the buildings' percentages who are visible. Statistically speaking, the rank-order correlation between Column 2 (percentage of building population observed in common spaces) and Column 9 (percentage of observed common space occupants who are interacting) is .08. The meaning of this set of findings is that common space occupants of some buildings are more likely to sit or go about the building without interacting than are occupants of other buildings. Further, this relative proportion of involvement-noninvolvement is independent of the actual percentage of the buildings' populations that are visible. Conversely, however, an increment in the number that are visible produces more who interact, even though the proportion of interactors so recruited varies widely among buildings.

Does the amount of common space available determine the amount of interaction? At first glance there seems to be a negative relationship -- a large amount of common space (Column 1, Table 2) is associated with a lower proportion of interactors among the occupants of common spaces (Column 9; rho= -.62, p∠.05). However, small amounts of common space occur primarily in public housing. When housing is divided according to whether it is 202 (lower-middle income) or public housing, the association between high proportion of interactors and public housing is significant at the .05 level (Fisher exact test). We can thus state the alternative hypotheses that (a) small amounts of common space result in greater density of individuals and therefore a higher proportion of interactors or (b) the lower the socioeconomic level of people using common spaces, the more likely they are to interact socially. Certainly our data cannot choose between these two explanations, nor can they in either case offer support for a causative relationship. However, the results do suggest that it may be worthwhile to investigate more thoroughly, in an experimental manner, whether there is a point beyond which the provision of extra common space actually reduces the probability of a social interchange.

Looking at the individual sites, one sees that Van Winkle has both the highest proportion of its population in observable interaction and also the highest rate of interaction among common space occupants. The favorably located outdoor space and the organized senior center no doubt brought people out; once exposed to each other either the spatial factors or personal characteristics of the tenants led them to interact, rather than to remain isolated. Ebenezer Towers showed a very low percentage of its population engaging in social behavior and a very low proportion of visible occupants interacting. This adds up to a characterization of this environment as being relatively impoverished socially, with no apparent structural explanation. It is the only environment sponsored by a black group, and it contains a mixture of middle-class financially self-sufficient tenants and a group of tenants from the welfare rolls. Whether this socioeconomic mix is related to the tendency of their tenants to stay out of common spaces is uncertain.

Open doors. We have presented extensive material elsewhere on the meaning and empirical correlates of leaving one's apartment door open (Lawton and Simon, 1968). Briefly, there is evidence that one meaning of the open door is to announce one's availability for socializing. Column 15 of Table 2 shows the percentage of each building's population leaving doors open or partially open. It is of interest to note that there was no relationship between the percentage of open doors and the presence of air conditioning. The relationship between percentage of open doors and percentage of building observed in social interaction was .54, significant at the .05 level. For the ten sites for which we have individual interviews, the incidence of open doors is positively associated with the number of within-building friends named by tenants (rho= .72). Further, the occupancy percentage in halls is highly correlated with percentage of open doors (rho= .76), and the correlation of hall occupancy with number of within-building friends just misses significance (rho= .53, N= 10, p .05= .56). Thus, social interaction within the building, and particularly on one's own floor is partially indexed by occupancy of hall space and the leaving of an apartment door open.

Security considerations probably underlay the low incidence of open doors in Flower Towers and Van Winkle though the neighborhood of Riverlake is just as crime-ridden. The low number of open doors in Golden Years and Samuel Gompers Gardens probably reflects, among other things, the fact that many tenants are out of the building during the day. The very high number in Riverlake and in President House reflects the open social attitude in these two sites. Riverlake is an active community in every way; the President House occupants are less active than other groups generally, but they maintain a high concentration of social relationships on their own

building floors (Lawton and Simon, 1968).

What is meaningful public behavior? The fact that space population, social interaction, and open doors are easy to count certainly is no guarantee that they will be the best indicators of differential behavioral effects of the physical environment. However, they do seem basic, the kind of indicator that will provide a baseline for a more searching look at how an environment works. Acknowledging the usefulness of such bread-and-butter kinds of data, let us consider what a more refined look at behavior in public places might indicate about the human use of the physical environment.

The function of visual scanning for older people has not been studied empirically. The prevalence of what I have called the "sitting and watching syndrome" (Lawton,1970) is well known. Most of us, anxiously denying the possibility that we too may age, look upon lobby-sitting as the zero point of behavior. It is clear, however, that watching the ongoing scene represents something very active for many older people, perhaps the most active substitute for muscular energy output that some people can manage. We have vague knowledge that activity in parks, or the coming and going of people in building lobbies attract elderly watchers, but we have no idea exactly which activities, under what conditions, in what physical settings, evoke greater or lesser interest. It is possible to take a fine-grained look at the facial and postural indicators of interest as unobtrusively as we did in our gross observations. The orientation of the body and head, the length of time a general area is fixated, the content of activity that makes a person redirect his gaze, are all capable of objective notation. Unlike many other indicators of reaction to space and structure, visual scanning behavior is amenable to experimental investigation, rather than being limited to naturalistic observation. It is possible to put older people in different physical locations or at different distances, or to vary the activity being observed.

A related question would be the activity or passivity of behavior occurring as function of the surroundings. Some aspects of this question would be self-evident: activity is probably greatest in the halls of apartment buildings, since they are used mainly for transit. The importance of the setting is underlined by my previous observation that the same is not necessarily true of the halls of homes for the aged. Sufficient attention to these relationships might eventually establish guidelines for the design of rooms, or room interrelationships, that maximize, minimize, or optimize the amount of energy expenditure demanded of the user.

Microsocial behavior as it occurs naturally or in response to an experimentally arranged environment shows great promise of revealing person-environment transactions. Ample evidence is at hand to indicate that chair arrangement and body orientation influence the content of social behavior, and that the perceived social demands of the situation in turn influence the arrangement of people in space (Hall, 1966; Sommer, 1969). Only in the unusual situation of the mental hospital ward have such variables been formally studied among older people (Sommer and Ross, 1958). Observation of the extent to which older people sitting side-by-side (the way most seating in public places is arranged) turn to orient themselves to each other, and the effect of varied seating orientations on the frequency and content of social interaction would be worthy of study. Somewhat more difficult to deal with unobtrusively, but still possible, are such variables as interaction distance, touching, eye contact, and approach-avoidance body pointing as indicators of differential reaction to the physical environment.

The differential environmental pull of particular structures on particular individuals is a very accessible area, provided the situation is one where it is possible to identify the users and their characteristics. Important questions involving mixed-age, mixed-sex, or mixed-race interaction can be answered even without more intimate knowledge of the people involved. Beyond that, there is every reason to think that decor, structure, siting, or neighborhood, would appeal differently to people with different backgrounds or attitudes. The best index of this appeal would be their use of the area under conditions of free choice.

Finally, a different type of look at behavior would be obtained from observing the "stream of behavior", rather than the discrete events focused on in our camera-eye view. Barker (1965) has made much of the idea that the meaning of behavior and its interaction with the environment can be investigated only in its complete time dimension, rather than in terms of behavior "tesserae" -- time samplings of discrete events. We have done some of this at our center, where the full day of several residents of our home for aged have been mapped. Certainly, these have revealed more starkly than the behavior tesserae method could how grossly impoverished the environment is for these people. Observing the same person over long periods and as he goes from setting to setting is necessary to give a complete picture of a living person. However, these kinds of data are much more expensive to gather and difficult to treat empirically, and would certainly have to be obtained on few people and in fewer environments than our method allows.

Summary. The results of many hours' observation of many older people behaving in 12 housing environments for the elderly have been reported. The data on occupancy of different types of space, the frequency of social interaction, and the incidence of open doors should be useful as baselines of ecological transactions, in the same way that basic demographic information is useful in the design of any program for people.

Beyond this point, I hope that the systematic, though basically qualitative, look at congregate housing for the elderly in action may provide some ideas for future empirical testing. Some of the more promising ideas are:

1. The degree to which activities are centered within a building varies with the building's proximity to resources in the larger environment within which the building is embedded.

2. Within-building centeredness of life is also a function of the types of spaces available within the housing environment, and the activities conducted within those spaces.

3. Use of common space increases up to a point as the average health of a building's tenants becomes poorer.

4. Halls are primarily transit spaces, though structural variations and the characteristics of the users may modify this use to a certain extent.

5. Safety from intrusion by outsiders is a major determinant of the population of many common spaces, but this factor may be greatly moderated by proper environmental and administrative engineering.

6. The entrance lobby is the most important common space. At its best (roomy, attractive, ample seating) it serves as a social, traffic, and visual stimulation center.

7. Common spaces located away from the center of activity serve a real social purpose for a small number of people, but are grossly underused. Adequate use of these areas depends on their having organized activities at scheduled times. Further investigation of the positive and negative features of "all-purpose" rooms is indicated.

8. Provision of spaces where functional activities can be maintained (laundry, stores, hairdresser, soda fountain) may result in better exercise and preservation of the older person's competence.

9. Ideal outdoor space demands adequate seating, physical protection, visibility by behavior-monitoring personnel, and a view of ongoing action.

10. The greater the population of common spaces, the more likely is social interaction. However, many factors may determine the proportion of a building's common space occupants who interact. Possible determinants of high interaction rate are low

socioeconomic level of tenants or small
amount of common space.

   11. The incidence of open doors is related to the amount of social life in a building. An open door is, among other things, a
social invitation.

   Some other possible behavioral indices
of person-environment transactions are discussed, with some suggestions for future research.

References

   Barker, R.G. Explorations in ecological psychology. American Psychologist,
1965, 20, 1-14.

   Hall, E.T. The hidden dimension. Garden City, N.Y.: Doubleday, 1966.

   Lawton, M.P. Environments for the
elderly. Journal of the American Institute
of Planners, 1970, 36, 124-129.

   Lawton, M.P. & Simon, B. The ecology
of social relationships in housing for the
elderly. The Gerontologist, 8, 108-15.

   Sommer, R. Personal space. Englewood
Cliffs, N.J.: Prentic-Hall, 1969.

   Sommer, R. & Ross, H. Social interaction in a geriatrics ward. International
Journal of Social Psychiatry, 1958, 4,
128-33.

Footnotes

   1. This research was wholly supported
by Grant MH 14923, from the National Institute of Mental Health.

   2. A large number of people participated in the gathering of data for this
research. Particular assistance from
Patricia Nash, Bonnie Simon, Sally DeSilva,
Jeanne Bader, Mark Fulcomer, Diana Rosen-
kaimer, Susan Singer, and Maurice Singer is
gratefully acckowledged. The managers,
staff, and tenants of our housing sites were
extremely helpful. We cannot name them
since, as the careful reader will discover,
we have chosen to disguise the names of the
sites. We nevertheless are very grateful
for the work and tolerance they have expended for us.

TABLE 2

Site	1 No. of common spaces	2 All spaces	3 Halls	4 Lobby spaces	5 Activity Functional spaces	6 Out-door space action	7 Social inter-action space	8 Social inter-action action	9 All spaces	10 Halls	11 Lobby spaces	12 Activity Functional spaces	13 Out-door doors	14 Open doors	15 %
		Percentage of tenants observed in							Percentage of common space occupants in						Open doors
Blueberry Acres	2	9.6	1.9	0.5	0.6	1.3	5.2	6.0	64	20	6	6	13	55	7.9
Ebenezer Towers	3	6.7	1.8	2.9	0.4	1.6	0.0	3.3	48	27	43	6	24	0	1.4
Flower Tower	4	7.1	1.1	1.6	0.5	0.5	3.4	4.9	69	15	7	22	7	48	0.1
Golden Years	4	5.1	2.2	0.5	1.6	0.7	2.9	2.9	57	41	10	14	14	34	1.1
Luther Lodge	8	10.9	4.2	2.6	0.8	1.8	1.5	5.7	52	38	2	17	17	14	7.1
New Gotham House	8	15.2	3.9	3.8	2.1	1.6	3.8	8.2	54	25	25	11	11	25	5.8
Old Gotham House	8	14.4	2.5	3.1	0.9	1.7	6.3	7.2	52	17	21	6	43	43	2.6
President House	2	13.2	3.6	0.3	7.3	1.3	0.8	8.9	66	27	2	12	10	6	21.0
Riverlake	7	15.1	5.7	1.1	4.1	1.1	3.1	9.1	60	7	55	7	21	21	17.5
Samuel Gompers Gardens	6	6.9	2.3	0.8	0.8	1.6	0.4	3.7	55	34	22	12	8	8	1.3
Sholom Aleichem House	10	10.5	2.3	3.0	1.4	2.2	1.6	5.6	54	28	13	21	16	16	2.5
Van Winkle Homes	4	17.7	1.5	0.4	6.5	1.1	8.2	12.9	71	8	3	37	6	46	0.9

TABLE 1

Characteristics of Housing Sites

Site	Loca-tion	Type of location	Neighborhood*	Type housing**	No. units	No. people	No. floors	Services†	Ethnic, relig., social
Blueberry Acres	NE	City	W, m-c, r.	PH	156	210	13	None	W, w-c
Ebenezer Towers	NE	Large city	B, low, m-c,w-c,r.	202-PH	140	155	11	Med.	B, m-c, & w-c
Flower Tower	NE	Large city	B, & PR,w-c r.	PH	160	210	16	None	Mixed w-c
Golden Years	South	Resort city	Boardwalk area	202	202	280	14	S.C., lunch	Jewish m-c
Luther Lodge	South	Large city	Suburb,up,m-c r.	202	200	251	13	Med., Meals	Prot, m-c
New Gotham House	NE	Large city	W, m-c r.	231	240	251	12	Med., Meals	Jewish, m-c
Old Gotham House	NE	Large city	W, m-c r.	231	220	264	11	Med., Meals	Jewish, m-c
President House	NE	Small city	W, w-c r.	PH	143	160	8	None	Prot, w-c
Riverlake	MW	Large city	B, w-c r.	PH	247	319	16	SC,Lunch, Med.	Mixed, w-c
Samuel Gompers Gardens	NE	Large city	Center city, bus.	202	278	308	17	SC, Med.	W, w-c, m-c
Sholom Aleichem House	NE	Large city	W, up, m-c r.	202	310	350	11	Meals, Nurse	Jewish, m-c
Van Winkle Homes	NE	Large city	B, PR, w-c r.	PH	112	167	14	SC, Lunch	Mixed, w-c

*m-c = middle-class
w-c = working-class
r = residential
W = White
B = Black
PR = Puerto Rican

**PH = Public housing

†SC = Senior center

Session Nine:

Computer-Aided Design

Chairman: Weldon E. Clark

Sonder, Clark, Griffin and Associates, Inc., Tarzana, California

Four papers are presented in this section labelled as Computer-Aided Design. Many other papers of the Conference, might equally well fit this label, for the computer can be utilized to aid design efforts in many ways: to explore relationships or patterns, to search for precedents, to calculate implications, to present alternatives for comparison, to analyze and optimize mathematical models, to simulate complex systems, and even just to store facts and account for efforts.

The papers by Mitchell and Kamnitzer/Hoffman describe actual computer work, although aspirations for further expanded program systems are clear. The Steadman and Willoughby papers describe techniques designed for computer application, but not computer results.

The paper by Steadman applies graph theory to provide analytical solutions for arrangement of defined spaces in two dimensions. The Willoughby paper describes a heuristic approach that would provide solutions in three dimensions.

The Mitchell paper illustrates application of cluster analysis to explore the spatial configurations resulting from locational relationships. Mitchell states that the technique is concerned with conflict, compromise, and ambiguity and useful in an early stage of the design process.

The Kamnitzer and Hoffman paper explores an approach to design more than a particular technique. The authors are concerned with interactive computer-graphic media as an interface between designer and computer program aids.

Welden E. Clark

INTUVAL: An Interactive Computer Graphic Aid
for Design and Decision Making In Urban Planning

by Peter Kamnitzer

Associate Professor

and Stan Hoffman

Research Assistant

School of Architecture and Urban Planning,
University of California, Los Angeles

ABSTRACT

INTUVAL (Intuition and Evaluation) is a computer graphic program under development utilizing interactive computer graphics (IBM 360/91 and 2250 display scope) for systematic evaluation and iterative refinements of intuitively conceived design proposals. Presently INTUVAL uses a simple transportation model for evaluating some of the physical and socio-economic repercussions of alternative freeway routes. Evaluations for six parameters and several subcomponents each are displayed on-line in bar chart form. A simplified impact model generates before-after land value maps on-line. Trade-offs between major parameters are not internally performed but are left to the decision makers. The program is intended for designers and for non-expert user-participants.

INTRODUCTION AND SUMMARY

Urban Planners and decision-makers are limited in their ability to explore alternative design concepts for the urban environment because of inadequate tools for assessing the consequences of various design options in terms of evaluative criteria. It is therefore urgent to develop techniques which can: (1) channel knowledge continuously from research to urban decision-makers; (2) translate this knowledge into forms which are easily comprehensible, usable for the creation of new solutions as well as for analysis, and which supplement rather than replace judgment, intuition and experience.

An ideal tool would be a manipulable and faithful analogue of the city. This is neither economically nor technologically feasible. Mathematical models are an available alternative, but their output is in forms that do not directly tie into the design and decision-making processes. Intermediate steps of translation by the designer or intervening experts are therefore necessary.

The raw or translated outputs are usually in the form of reports and monographs; computer print-outs; maps, charts or graphs. Although these may be comprehensible and useful after attentive study, they necessitate lengthy turn-around times when fed back into the iterative design and evaluation process. Thus the quali-

ties of immediacy and simultaneity are sacrificed. INTUVAL, on the other hand, practically eliminates turn-around time. It generates directly visual and manipulable outputs thus eliminating interruptions in the design process.

INTUVAL is an evaluative device combined with an information retrieval system. It serves as an aid (not a substitute) for the intuition and judgment of the planner or decision maker. When fully developed, INTUVAL will channel pertinent and usable information (existing and continuously emerging) into the urban design process. It will enable the planner or decision-maker to: (a) use this information to develop tentative plans or designs for the urban area; (b) test these without delay in terms of evaluative criteria (established or proposed); (c) react to this evaluation and generate improved designs; (d) develop several alternatives with costs and effects made explicit, immediately and graphically.

INTUVAL makes no attempt to internally perform trade-offs between the various categories, because in a real situation these trade-offs are determined by the interests of the various political forces in a pluralistic society and a single set of scale factors will neither satisfy all of the decision-makers at a given time, nor satisfy any single decision-maker for all situations which could arise in a given problem. The responsibility of making trade-offs thus remains with the decision-makers.

At present INTUVAL uses a simple transportation model for evaluating some of the physical and non-physical repercussions of the intuitively conceived designs, or decisions of planners of policy makers. A region of varied characteristics is displayed on the output cathode ray tube (IBM 2250). Using a light pen or other graphic input device, the user sketches the route for a proposed freeway directly on the cathode ray tube on any one of the following nine maps: contour, geology, water, road pattern, land use, land values, community composition, conservation, and visual interest.

Once the route is located to the initial satisfaction of the user-participants, access points and necessary bridges are added. Then

INTUVAL can be commanded to evaluate six physical and non-physical repercussions of constructing the freeway along this route. The evaluations are displayed visually in bar chart
form, in such terms as driving time, cost,
safety, visual interest, conservation, and community service. As the purpose of the evaluation is not merely to make a statement post
facto, but to aid in the design process, the
user-participant will want to know what precisely determined the rating in any of the categories. Upon request, INTUVAL produces a
breakdown of the factors and a graphic analysis
of how the proposed route rated in each one of
these. Responding to this analysis, the user
can modify the original design by iteration, or
he can design any number of different routes,
and receive new evaluations without delay. At
the present time, up to ten evaluations can be
compared simultaneously.

INTUVAL also shows graphically, on-line,
the impact of alternative freeway routes on the
community in the future. At present, a growth
model is incorporated which demonstrates graphically the predicted change in land values
under the impact of alternative freeway designs.

In future, growth models should show predicted change at regular time intervals and
should include such factors as land use, population distribution, voting patterns, and
others. Future capabilities should also include the enlargement of any section of the
source maps for greater detail and finer grain
information. In addition, evaluative criteria
will be made graphically explicit and subject
to individual adjustments. Ultimately, the
program aims to be so general in nature that it
could accept any task once all necessary parameters for the evaluative criteria and its needed models are determined.

BACKGROUND AND DISCUSSION

"The unmeasurable is strictly the province
of the mind. If measure is accepted only when
absolute, how could one measure realization,
concept, truth, desire, silence?...The machine
can communicate measure, but the machine cannot create, cannot judge, cannot design. These
belong to the mind." Louis Kahn

Most professions, in modern times, require
a combination of science and art. After the
Second World War, and particularly after Sput-
nik, an overwhelmingly strong movement asserted
itself in the direction of the "scientization
of the professions". In the fierce enthusiasm
which often characterizes strong reactions
to a previously deplorable state of affairs,
the baby was nearly thrown out with the bath
water. In the attempt to be scientific at all
costs, most valuable aspects of intuition and
judgment were in danger of being lost, particularly in such fields as urban design and decision-making.

As we convert intangibles into tangibles,
the greater our awareness of new intangibles.
It is obvious that we will never be able to

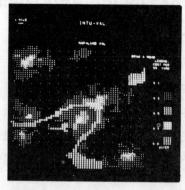

Fig. 1

LAND VALUE
MAP

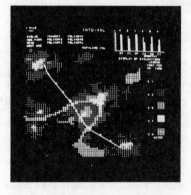

Fig. 2

LAND VALUE
MAP
WITH FREEWAY
AND EVALUATIONS

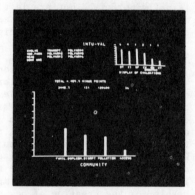

Fig. 3

DETAILED
"COMMUNITY"
BAR CHART
AFTER FIRST
EVALUATION

Fig. 4

DETAILED
"COMMUNITY"
BAR CHART
AFTER SECOND
EVALUATION

make everything explicit or, even more so, to make everything quantifiable. It is equally obvious that decisions will always be a mixture of the explicit and of experience, intuition, hunches, and idiosyncracies. The challenge, it appears to us, is to develop methods which will make possible the optimal utilization of the rational as well as of the intuitive.

Mathematical models have contributed greatly toward more scientific and rigorous description of a system. In complex systems, however, the fact is inescapable that the more elegant the model the greater its failure to encompass the totality of the problem. In urban planning, one of the most complex large systems we know of, this weakness, seen realistically, will be with us for a long time and, conceptually, may well be an eternal one. A simplified representation of reality, no matter how elegant, cannot be justified as the predominant basis for decisions affecting the lives of large numbers of people.

Values. Particularly in the field of urban planning, decision-making is intimately intertwined with varying perceptions of reality and highly divergent value systems. Optimization presupposes pure statements of goals and objectives. In matters affecting society, agreement is very difficult to achieve, unless the goals are stated in such broad terms that they become "motherhood statements". It is only when hard choices in trade-off situations have to be made from case to case that the value system of the people affected will truly emerge.[1] In fact, we submit that it is impossible to quantify such value systems in the abstract, and even if it were possible, that the resultant world would be frighteningly reminiscent of 1984. Especially in the urban field, where the "client" is society as represented by its political system, it is questioned whether the "client" is capable of predetermining his value structure and express it quantitively without having been exposed to a number of alternatives which force him into a value decision. What price beauty, what price safety, what price community cohesion, can only be faced in each case within the context of a given problem for a given community.

In the urban field value decisions cannot be made by the "designer" or "planner". They are made through the complex, and often mysterious, political process of our society. Unfortunately, the present chasm between "experts", "decision-makers", and "the people", is ever widening and steps must be taken to open up the planning process to include all those affected by the decisions under consideration. This requires decision aids which permit the non-expert to participate actively in the planning process. City councilmen, representatives of the community, politicians, should be exposed to a number of alternative proposals with costs and effects made visible, and should have an opportunity to react to these, add their own

suggestions, test the costs and effects of their own proposals without delay, and gradually arrive at a mutually acceptable solution. INTUVAL will offer a man-machine supported planning process which will expose the participants to the constant need for trade-offs. At the very least, INTUVAL will help to structure meaningful debate underlying conflicting points of view by offering immediate access to a demonstration of the costs and benefits of each proposal. As INTUVAL is being used with the participation of representatives of the community and real-life decision-makers it will soon become apparent that the original list of parameters is insufficient and that the list will grow in response to the values expressed by the participants.

INTUVAL, in the future, will offer various kinds of evaluations: (1) evaluation for the total planning area under consideration; (2) evaluation for a given portion of the planning area.

How will a specific proposal affect a specific community? The ratings for a proposal might be highly favorable on a metropolitan scale. Yet the impact on a specific community within this larger area could be altogether different. Separate evaluations will be obtained for all communities affected by the proposal, offering a significant indication of the degree of its probable acceptability.

Each of the above two categories (1) and (2) will be available for evaluation in two different ways: (a) Preprogrammed Evaluations and (b) Individually Determined Evaluations. INTUVAL will make explicit the rating system stored in the computer and will offer a format to guide the user in substituting his own criteria. The computer will record the identity of the user and his preferred rating system for future research and for a gradual updating of the stored evaluation system.

In real-life situations decision-makers utilize information which varies greatly in degree of reliability, from well-documented research to expert opinion, and even expert hunches. The decision-maker must proceed with his task with the full awareness that the information available to him is severely limited. INTUVAL accepts this fact of life and will utilize models of varying degrees of reliability reflecting the state of the art at a given moment. INTUVAL, however, will make explicit in graphic form the degree of reliability of the information used in a given instance. This will be expressed by graphic symbols and bar graphs informing the user of the source and quality of the information used.

INTUVAL is a pragmatic tool that attempts to put the best knowledge available at a given time at the disposal of the designer. (The word "designer" throughout this paper is meant to include the user-participants-decision-makers.) Knowledge from many sources and many quarters will be translated into evaluative models and, thus, will be available in a form truly responsive to the needs of the designer. INTUVAL will offer the designer the equivalent of the best experts in all relevant fields looking over his shoulder during the very act of design. Each "built-in" expert in a given field will first give an overall judgment as to the quality of the tentative proposal in terms of his area of expertise. He may describe it as "poor", "fair", "good", or "excellent". The designer will wish to know the reason for the expert's judgment whereupon the expert proceeds to explain what factors entered into his judgment and what the effects of the tentative proposal were in each one of these. The designer, now better educated than before, will modify his proposal to improve his design...whereupon the "expert" in another field may now complain that the quality of the modified proposal has significantly decreased in his area of expertise. Again, a point-by-point analysis of the factors determining his judgment will follow... etc., etc., etc. The designer will proceed in this manner until he cannot improve his design any further within the framework of his value system.

This process seems, indeed, reminiscent of the old method of trial and error, or trial and human judgment. However, it is now immeasurably strengthened by the availability of instant information of the effects and costs of the design proposal, and of an overall evaluation in terms of the major "areas of concern". Beyond this, the "expert comments" will evoke new sets of stored knowledge and will provide the stimulus for the next "creative leap" sending the designer off in new directions.

"In the field of design, it is the function of all design aids to heighten the understanding and perception of the designer so as to provoke the next creative leap in a continuing process. It is the creative leap that has been the major driving force in all innovative work, be it in the sciences or the arts. The fundamental shortcoming of this intuitive process, however, has been the lack of an immediate systematic evaluation of the intuitively arrived at solutions.

"What is needed is a method which would permit the designer the free reign of his intuitive and creative powers (subconscious as well as conscious), yet would provide him with an immediate evaluation of the cost and effect of his tentative design proposals. By iteration he can improve his designs until he has arrived at the highest evaluations in the greatest number of factors.

"The immediate availability of this evaluation is of paramount importance. It is in the nature of the creative process that an evaluation, however precise, which is available only at a "later" time is of limited value. Rather than being an aid, it is most often experienced as an unpleasant interference with the creative process. By that "later" time, the designer is committed to his design. It is frozen, not open any more."

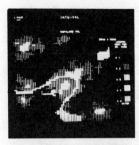
COMMUNITY PATTERN

CONTOUR OVERLAY

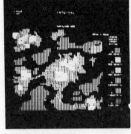
LAND USE

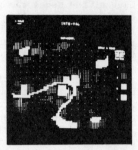
LAND VALUE

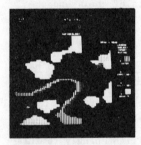
GEOLOGY

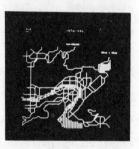
ROAD PATTERN

CONSERVATION

VISUAL INTEREST

Fig. 5

BASE MAPS APPEARING ON CRT

This early description of the INTUVAL concept[2] now needs to be expanded to include other, more sophisticated analytical methods.

The use of optimization within each "area of concern" for calibration and for guidance of the designer is presently being incorporated in the program.

Observation of design opportunities opening up at various levels of sub-optimization could further act as a source of inspiration during the design process.

Porter's "Discourse" with its flexible data structure that combines the assets of associative and matrix organizations, attribute and geometric searches[3] can further educate and guide the designer-decision-maker in his search for viable solutions.

Ultimately, the computer's ability to enlarge our horizon by showing us totally unexpected and new combinations and patterns (both intellectually and graphically) must be utilized for a true man-machine partnership.

The emphasis here, however, is on the incorporation of many techniques into a method of "design and evaluation", in contrast to passive reliance on any of these analytical techniques for providing "the" solution.

The ability within the INTUVAL concept to evaluate and modify any proposed solution--no matter what methods helped to generate them--and the ability to provide instant feedback for a continuing creative problem solving process.. remains the guiding principle of the INTUVAL concept.

THE INTUVAL SYSTEM

A demonstration of the INTUVAL process has been implemented, using as a first example, the planning and design of a freeway in a metropolitan area. INTUVAL, however, is not restricted only to this particular use. Provisions have been made in the program to incorporate, in the future, many other models to deal with such systems as rapid transit, allocation of public facilities, or selection of alternate redevelopment projects.

The INTUVAL program is written in FORTRAN IV and the GRAF (Graphical Additions to FORTRAN) language. The GRAF language was developed by the UCLA, Health Science Computer Facility, and is an interactive computer graphics language for the IBM 2250, MOD II, display scope. The scope is connected to an IBM 360/91 computer, but INTUVAL could run on a smaller IBM system, such as a 360/40, because the largest core requirement by the program is 180K bytes.

An independent part of the INTUVAL system is the preprocessor program (non-interactive) which is used for data handling and manipulation prior to the start of the interactive portion. Presently, the preprocessor is used to precalculate information for use during program operation. It is also being expanded to handle data, such as census tapes.

The INTUVAL process, using a transportation example will now be described:

The Transportation Example

The user is seated facing the 2250 console and has available: a light-pen (Graphic input device), a function keyboard (with 32 programmable keys), and an alphameric keyboard. After the program has been started, the first user action is required at the "CROSSROADS" (Pt.1). At present, only the transportation policy variable is available, but provisions have been made to include the addition of up to six policy variables.

Upon entering the transportation mode (Pt. 2), the user selects the particular map (Pt. 3) upon which to design the freeway. Any of the maps, shown in Figure 5, can be displayed individually on the screen base or linear feature maps (contour and road pattern). The linear feature maps can be overlayed on any of the base maps, as shown by the contour map over the community. (All pts. refer to Figure 6.)

The maps constitute part of the data base and describe an imaginary region, the County of Intuville, which is a virtual obstacle course of mountains, cities, rivers, and roads. The maps are composed of 60 x 60 characters, with each representing half a mile square, describing a region of 30 miles square. The maps at present are:

NATURAL   1. Contour (linear); 2. Geology;
                3. Water
SOCIO-   4. Road Pattern (linear);
ECONOMIC 5. Land Use; 6. Land Values;
                7. Community Patterns

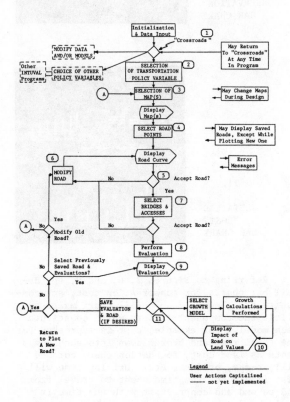

Fig. 6
Flow Diagram

ELEMENTS   8. Conservation; 9. Visual Interest
OF VALUE

Building a Road

After selecting a particular base map,
with or without an overlay, the user begins to
plot the points (Pt. 4) which mark the freeway
route, with the aid of the light-pen. When all
the desired points are specified, pressing one
of the programmable function key commands the
computer to plot the road. The line is displayed superimposed on the particular map(s)
being displayed (Figure 7). Any of the maps can
be interchanged. In the future, a better curve
plotting device will be used, such as a RAND
tablet.

At this point, the user can either accept
the route (Pt. 5) or continue to modify it (Pt.
6), by adding or deleting points. The modified
route is then requested to be plotted. If accepted, the bridges and accesses are selected
(Pt. 7) by indicating the location with the
light-pen and by pressing the appropriate function key. The bridges and accesses can also be
modified before proceeding.

Evaluation

After the tentative design is complete,
the evaluations are requested (Pt. 8) by pressing the appropriate function key. During the
"STAND BY" phase, while the evaluations are
performed, the user must not interact with IN-
TUVAL. The wait is usually 5-20 seconds.

There are two methods for displaying the
evaluations: the overview and detail bar
charts. The overview bar chart (Figure 2)
gives the user a GESTALT, or overall feeling,
for the strength and weakness of the major parameters (to be described), while the detail bar
charts (Figures 3, 8, 9) display objective
facts, such as: dollars spent, time travelled,
as well as bonus and penalty points accumulated.
It should be noted that overview bar chart always remains in the upper right hand corner of
the screen whether the detail displays or map(s)
are being viewed. This provides the user with
a constant overview of the total route evaluation.

The evaluations displayed (Pt. 9) on the
overview bar chart (see Figure 2), also titled
"DISPLAY OF EVALUATIONS", are:
1. Driving Time (DT); 2. Visual Interest
(VI); 3. Safety (SF); 4. Conservation (CV);
5. Community Patterns (CP); 6. Cost (CT).

These ratings are presently based on assumed transportation models with intuitive
weightings given to the several components within a particular parameter. The models represent the first approximation of the kinds of
models that will have to be carefully structured by experts in their respective areas of
knowledge, and serve as a basis for futher research needs. Each of the six models is a sum
of linearly weighted factors of the form:

$$P_n = W_1F_1 + W_2F_2 ------- + W_mF_m$$

where: P_n = Parameter (1-6); F_m = Factors;
       W_m = Weightings.

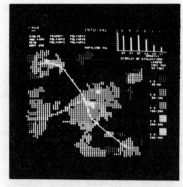

Fig. 7

FREEWAY
DESIGNED ON
LAND USE MAP

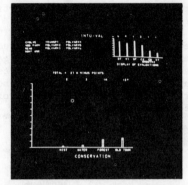

Fig. 8

DETAILED
"CONSERVATION"
BAR CHART

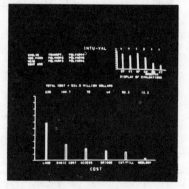

Fig. 9

DETAILED
"COST"
BAR CHART

Referring to Figures 3, 8, and 9, the detail bar charts for conservation cost, and community are shown. Each detail chart makes explicit the component factors which constitute
each model. For example, cost is expressed for
the total road and broken down into such components as land cost, foundation cost, cut and
fill, ramps, bridges, etc. Driving time will
list in minutes the time spent to travel from
end to end and contrast it with the time it
would have taken to travel on surface streets
instead. Community patterns lists the penalty
points accumulated for families displaced,
neighborhoods dissected, families deprived of
adequate access to transportation. Safety

lists penalty points for unsafe conditions such as dangerous curves and spacing of freeway accesses.

The height of the bars on the overview bar chart indicates a rating from excellent to poor on a scale from 0 to 10. The calibration of these bars is temporarily based on an empirical method. In the future, optimization techniques within each parameter will be used for calibration. The optimum rating for the freeway, within a defined corridor will set the standards.

In the overview bar chart, a number above each bar indicates the road section which accumulated the lowest score in that particular parameter. Generally an inspection of the road, in the segment cited, will reveal the cause for the low rating. The road has been divided into 10 sections. At present, the detailed charts are for the total road, but in the future, similar detailed charts will be available for each section. This will allow the user to alternate between the regional and the community scale. An overview bar chart could also be displayed for that particular section alongside the one for the total road. Future display of evaluations will include the display of information in the form of curves, statistics, and tabulations.

When a modified or new route is evaluated it is displayed on the charts (both overview and detail) along side the previous evaluations (Figure 10), with up to 10 possible. This allows parameter by parameter inspection and modification, both in the overview and detailed bar charts (Figures 4, 11, 12).

The most recent evaluations is displayed as a bar, with the previous evaluations shifted to the left, in sequence, by a special routine, and represented by straight lines.

Revising the Design (The Iterative Process)

As tentative designs are studied, the user can investigate all of the evaluations to determine where improvement is needed. The process is one of using "instantaneous" feedback as an intuitive guide, which allows for rapid testing and comparison of various designs.

In Figure 9, the overview bar chart for the first evaluation shows that cost and community received low ratings. After investigating the detail charts and the road on different maps, a modification was made. Figure 11 shows the results. In the overview chart it can be seen that both the community and cost rating improved, while the conservation and visual interest ratings decreased. The ratings for driving time and safety remained about the same.

This illustrate the constant trade-offs that must be made during the INTUVAL process. The essence of INTUVAL is that it operates in a value laden situation where the decision-makers must chose between competing alternatives. Yet, the value judgments remain with the user. This process continues until a route, or set of alternatives, have been achieved that are satisfactory to the user-decision-makers.

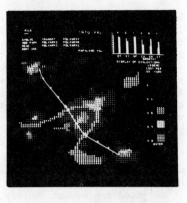

Fig. 10

EVALUATION OF TWO DESIGN ATTEMPTS SHOWN IN OVERVIEW BAR CHART

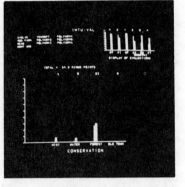

Fig. 11

DETAILED "CONSERVATION" BAR CHART FOR TWO DESIGN ATTEMPTS

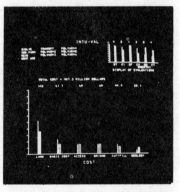

Fig. 12

DETAILED "COST" BAR CHART FOR TWO DESIGN ATTEMPTS

Growth Model

The effect of the freeway on the environment in the future is an important consideration. In the process of developing a growth model, INTUVAL has begun with an elementary land value change model based on change in accessibility to employment centers (six in the region). For this model, time is held constant for comparison of land values before and after the freeway.

In the study, "The Effects of Public Investments and Urban Land Values", Czamanski[4] calculated the accessibility potentials of three hundred lots in Baltimore and found them highly correlated with actual prices of urban land. Regressions were run by Czamanski and two more dependent variables were found to be significant for variations in the land values: (1) zoning; and (2) age of structures. A simplified Czamanski model has been implemented in the INTUVAL program, which temporarily is exclusively based on accessibility. The land value at point i, is:

$$Value_i = C_1 + C_2 \sum_{j=1}^{N} \frac{E_j}{1+d_{ij}}$$

where: C_1, C_2 = constants adjusted to region; d_{ij} = distance from point i to j. N = number of weighted employment centers, E = employment center$_j$.

After the user is satisfied with a particular route, the impact of the freeway on the region can be studied on a new land value map (Pt. 10). The changes in land value that have occurred are visually highlighted. This before/after growth pattern (shown in Figures 13 and 14) now becomes another basis for judging the desirability of the particular road, and can be compared with the growth patterns which other roads have generated.

At present, the growth model displays the effects only at one point in time over the future. The growth patterns can be saved along with their corresponding roads. The time required for the model to calculate and display the results is about 10 seconds.

Output

Upon termination of the program, a hardcopy is generated on the printer. This report can be filed by the user for further study and includes the following listing: (1) all user decisions; (2) the various decision sets (i.e. road descriptions); (3) a plot of each road; (4) all evaluations, including section by section; and (5) a plot of the resultant growth patterns. In the present absence of a plotting device such as a cal-comp plotter, the road patterns are represented by alphanumeric characters.

Conclusion

INTUVAL has reached a second level in its development. Following the original phase of demonstrating the feasibility of the concept INTUVAL has now begun to incorporate growth models, however, simple, and is proceeding to test some of its capabilities in a real rather than imaginary metropolitan region (Los Angeles see Figure 15). The full impact of this new attempt will soon be felt, and will give an indication of the large scope of the task ahead.

ACKNOWLEDGEMENTS

We wish to thank the following persons and organizations who have given us invaluable help with our work:
Owen Podger and Bernt Capra, Research Assistants; Robin Liggett and John Rouse, Programmers; Eric Andresen, Photographer. The UCLA Health Science Computing Facility sponsored by NIH Grant RR-3, the Rockefel-

ler Bros. Fund; The Urban Transportation Institutional Grant for Research and Training; U.S. Department of Transportation; and School of Architecture and Urban Planning, UCLA.

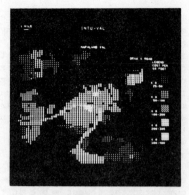

Fig. 13

LAND VALUES BEFORE IMPACT OF FREEWAY

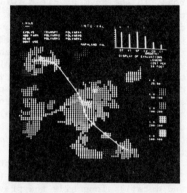

Fig. 14

LAND VALUES AFTER IMPACT OF FREEWAY

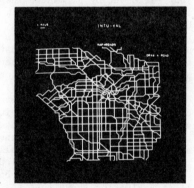

Fig. 15

GREATER LOS ANGELES ROAD NETWORK

Notes

(1) The Goals Programs of Los Angeles and other cities have visibly suffered from this "motherhood" syndrome.
(2) "Computer Aid to Design", P. Kamnitzer. Architectural Design (AD), September 1969.
(3) As described by N. Negroponte, "The Architecture Machine".
(4) Czamanski, J. "Effects of Public Investments on Urban Land Values". AIP Journal, 7/66.

A Computer-Aided Approach
to Complex Building Layout Problems

by William J. Mitchell

Assistant Professor, School of Architecture and Urban Planning,
University of California, Los Angeles

Abstract

This paper discusses the relations between locational objectives for activities and the result-ant arrangements of built spaces to satisfy these objectives. In particular it is concerned with object-ives which are complex, ill-defined, incomplete, and contradictory It describes the logic, and the uses, of an experimental interactive computer pro-gram, CLUMP 3, which enables a designer to test the effects on the spatial structure of a built environ-ment of adopting different locational objectives, and alternative resolutions of conflict amongst object-ives.

(1) Locational Objectives and Spatial Order

The notion of ordered, organized spatial re-lationships is central to architecture. In designing, we attempt to relate each space in the built environ-ment to other spaces, and to the external environ-ment, in accordance with some set of locational objectives which we have explicitly or implicitly adopted.

When the locational objectives are clear and simple, the relationship between objectives and form may be direct and obvious. Consider for instance, the following configuration of dots dis-posed at randomly selected locations in a plane (figure 1)... that is, their arrangement is not de-termined in relation to any particular objectives, and there is no discernible order in the form.

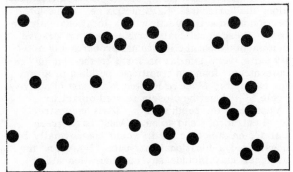

Figure 1

If we now introduce the locational objective "any dot is better adjacent to another dot than to empty space", it is easy to rearrange the dots into a configuration which satisfies this objective, and which as a consequence, displays a clearly evident system of order (figure 2).

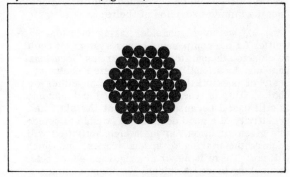

Figure 2

But architecture is rarely so simple. The set of locational objectives which we wish to satisfy will usually be quite large and complex, ill-defined, and riddled with all kinds of conflicts and contra-dictions. The systems of spatial order which we develop in response need to be much more com-plicated and subtle than our circle of dots. Further-more, where incomplete data, ambiguity, conflict, and compromise are involved, there is no clear separation between the processes of definition of objectives and synthesis of form. The information and insights gained as we grope towards synthesis result continually in redefinition and clarification of objectives. We do not always know what we want until we have it.

This paper is concerned with the process of generating spatial configurations in response to such complex objectives. It demonstrates how al-ternative formulations of locational goals for a set of spaces imply groupings of those spaces together in different ways, and describes an experimental interactive computer program, CLUMP 3, which enables a designer to test the effects on the group-ing structure of adopting different locational object-ives, and alternative resolutions of conflicts amongst objectives.

391

(2) Modelling the Spatial System

In order to model problems of spatial grouping in architecture, we must develop some satisfactory definition of the basic spatial components of the built environment, and find a suitable method for describing relevant relationships between these components.

When the Beatles sang "Let's Do It In The Road" they brought into focus the distinction which we draw in our lives between "locational" and "non-locational" activities. Some activities can take place anywhere, whilst some require a specific, definable physical space or facility, with various special properties. Often, an activity will be locational because it requires a more or less immovable piece of hardware (e.g. taking a bath), but as the Beatles knew well, the reasons are often much more subtle, and depend on particular cultural assumptions. We are greatly concerned, in architecture, with identifying those activities which are locational, and building special places for them. Indeed, without the phenomenon of locational activity to consider, architecture would be concerned with little more than the simple provision of shelter.

So, we might consider taking locational activities as the components of our system. It could be objected though, that the properties "locational" and "non-locational" are the extreme points of a scale of possibilities, rather than an either-or choice. This is true of course, but the dichotomy is still useful because it is part of the skill and sensitivity of a good designer to be able to decide, in a given situation, on just which activities will require the making of special places, and which will not. There is never any rigorous set of rules for making these decisions. We must commence building our model, then, at a point where the set of locational activities has already been defined.

The definition of components is still incomplete though, because we have not as yet considered the question of level of aggregation. "Activities" can be endlessly subdivided into component activities, or aggregated into more general activities, so we must select an appropriate scale at which to work. This brings us to the concept of "room". An aggregate of locational activities implies an actual, physical aggregate of built spaces. Thus a "kitchen" is a space and set of facilities to accommodate a set of closely interrelated locational activities. We might accept this object as an indivisible component of our system, considering it to be an aggregate of appropriate size, and identify it equally well either with a description of the locational activities, or the name "kitchen". Acceptance of such an entity obviously implies the acceptance of a whole set of spatial relationships which may or may not be valid. If we have a lot of time, money, information, and patience, we can afford to work with a very fine-grained model. If the economic constraints are more severe, then we must work with larger units, and accept more conventional assumptions.

The components of our system can now be defined as "activity units", arbitrarily sized places made with specific properties to accommodate specific activities, identified either by the name of the place or by a description of the activities. "Activity Units", in a specific situation, either may or may not correspond to "rooms" as they are conventionally defined. (1)

Having defined a set of activity units, the next step in modelling a system of spatially related activities is to make some statements of spatial relationship between them in a way that is rigorous enough to be useful. The simplest and most obvious way of doing this is to set up a square matrix, with activity units ranged along both axes. Each cell can be used to represent a potential spatial relation between a pair of activity units. In each, we can enter some information defining the character of that relation (or non-relation). We could for instance, collect and enter measures or estimates of the cost of flow of people or materials between the various activity units. Such studies have often been carried out (2), but circulation cost data alone is insufficient for our purposes, for we want to simultaneously consider many different reasons for spatial aggregation, not simply minimization of circulation costs.

Another approach would be to enter "measures of relationship" made on some appropriate kind of scale, based on any relevant data or criteria whatsoever. We have a wide variety of different types of scales open to us (3), ranging in strength from simple binary choices of "related" or "not related" to a scale of real numbers. The problem with the weaker scales is that they form very insensitive coding devices, whilst conversely, with the stronger scales, it becomes increasingly difficult to define precisely enough what we mean by "strength of relationship", or to frame exact rules for computing its value, so that we are left with no logical way of making decisions.

A further disadvantage of the square matrix is that there may be a multitude of different reasons for relating spaces, but it does not allow us to record date concerning the particular bases of each decision.

Fortunately we can overcome these difficulties, to a large extent, by use of a rectangular matrix, with the activity units arranged along the vertical axis, and a string of "locational attributes" along the horizontal. Each matrix cell is the intersection of an activity unit with a locational attribute. These locational attributes are imperative statements about the locational properties of activity units, very similar in form to the list of "requirements" found in traditional building programs, for example, "Must be located to be part of activity cycle X", "Must be closely related to facility Y", "Must be on the south wall", "Must have street-level entrance", and so on. "Must have green walls", on the other hand, would not normally be considered a locational attribute. However, the designer may include any consideration at all which he wishes to influence the location of activity units. In each matrix cell, we can enter a decision as to whether that particular activity unit should or should not, in the built environment that we are considering, possess that particular locational attribute. The conjunction of all positive entries in the matrix row now becomes a statement defining all the required locational properties of the corresponding activity unit. From data recorded in this format (through a series of simple binary choices) we are able, as we shall see, to generate useful descriptions of the strength and character of the spatial interrelationships amongst activity units.

Obviously, the selection of our appropriate string of locational attributes is a crucial step in coding data in this fashion. Very precise expression, and a careful thinking through of the implications of each statement are required. A definite coding problem is still with us ... there are rela-

tions too subtle to be captured in this format, and it is easy to be trapped by ambiguities, but we can do amazingly well, and I have not found a better way. The following working rules have proved to be useful guides for making good locational attribute strings:

1. Each locational attribute should be in some sense elemental. This can be tested by asking, first, whether it can be usefully subdivided into two or more simpler locational attributes, and second, if the making of an interaction decision contributes more than one piece of data.
2. Two locational attributes which will have identical interaction profiles should not

A TYPICAL SET

OF DECISIONS

FOR

A SMALL

SUBURBAN HOUSE

ACTIVITY UNITS	LOCATIONAL ATTRIBUTES
1 Bathroom 1 (related to bedrooms)	
2 Bathroom 2 (related to living areas	
3 Breakfast/informal eating	
4 Carport	
5 Child bedroom	
6 Child study	
7 Entry area	
8 Family room	
9 Formal dining	
10 Garbage disposal	
11 General storage space	
12 Guest bedroom	
13 Informal entry	
14 Kitchen	
15 Laundry	
16 Library/study	
17 Outdoor eating	
18 Parent bedroom	
19 Parent private courtyard	
20 Small child outdoor play	

KEY TO ATTRIBUTES

1 Part of group linked by food preparation/serving/disposal activities
2 Part of group linked by visitor/guest reception/entertainment activities
3 Part of group around main plumbing/sewerage/exhaust vent access point
4 Face east for morning sunlight
5 Part of area supervisable by mother whilst working
6 Oriented towards street
7 Part of activity oriented zone
8 Part of quiet/retire oriented zone
9 Parents' private territory
10 Child's private territory

Figure 3
A Typical Set of Decisions for a Small Suburban House

both be included. One or the other should
be selected.

3. Locational attributes which will not serve
to distinguish between the locations of
different activity units should not be included.

It could be argued that we should make weighted, rather than binary decisions, since some locational attributes will clearly be more important
than others. However, the binary nature of the data
does not derive from an assumption of equal importance of locational attributes, but from the consideration that if any one locational attribute of an
activity unit is unfulfilled, then we must regard the
location of that activity unit as unsatisfactory. This
in turn derives from the assumption that we do not
consider degrees of possession of a locational attribute. A built space either is regarded as having
a locational attribute, or not. Some locational attributes can clearly only be of this nature, e.g.,"Must
be on the south wall". Others, like "Must be closely
related to facility X", can be dealt with by use of
the notion of "simple pay-off function"... proximi-
ties up to a certain threshold level of distance are
considered to be satisfactory, whilst anything beyond is not (4).

Typical activity units, locational attributes,
and decisions for a small problem are shown in
figure 3.

(3) The Discovery of Groupings

Spatial groups, or clusters are defined by the
possession of common locational attributes. If we
scan down any column of the matrix in figure 3, we
can see that the "yes" decisions in that column define a spatially related group of activity units.
From column 4, for instance, we see that breakfast/
informal eating, child's bedroom, guest bedroom,
informal entry, kitchen, parents' bedroom, and
small children's outdoor play area form together a
spatially related group by virtue of possession of
the locational attribute "face east for morning sunlight". By taking numbers of columns together, it
is possible to form clusters defined by possession
of two or more common locational attributes. It is
obvious that there are many different ways of
grouping activity units together according to common locational attributes. The question is, "Which
of the many logically possible grouping strategies
will give results that are most useful for design
purposes?"

There are two ways of describing the locational attributes of a cluster We can describe each
locational attribute of each activity unit, or we can
generalize... describing only those locational attributes common to all members. Unless all members of the cluster have identical locational attributes, we "lose" some data in making this generalized description. Thus the data content of a cluster
may be defined as :

$$D = \frac{(n \times q)}{p} \times 100\%$$

n = number of activity units in the cluster
q = number of common locational attributes
p = total number of locational attributes
    possessed by members of the cluster.

The more "common", and the fewer "exceptional"
locational attributes, the higher the data content.
It can be seen that clusters having low data content
have comparatively little spatial meaning; their
members will be more "different" than "alike" in
their locational attributes. On the other hand,
clusters of high data content imply coherent spatial
groupings. We are interested then, in a grouping
strategy which yields clusters having the highest
possible data content.

Now, in forming clusters, we are transform-
ing our initial representation of our locational objectives, which was useless for design purposes,
into another representation... which is considerably more useful because it is simpler. The simplicity of our representation may be defined as :

$$S = \frac{(a - b)}{(a - 1)} \times 100\%$$

a = total number of activity units
b = total number of clusters existing
    (including one-member clusters)

If no clustering takes place, simplicity is zero, and
if all activity units are grouped into one cluster,
simplicity is 100%. Other things being equal, the
greater the simplicity, the more comprehensible
and useful the representation.

But unfortunately, due to the diversity of
locational attributes of the various activity units,
we can normally only gain in simplicity at the cost
of reducing the data content of the clusters. There
are two ways of dealing with this. Firstly, we
could simply define either the range of sizes or the
range of data contents which were of interest to us.
The more satisfactory alternative is to generate a
hierarchy of clusters in which, as we move up the
levels, the clusters are fewer and contain more
members, representation is consequently more
economical, but more of the richness and complexity in our initial description of the data is lost. At
the lowest level, 100% of the initial data is retained,
but no simplification is achieved... each cluster
consists simply of one activity unit. At the highest
level, the simplest possible representation, one
big cluster of all the activity units, is achieved at
the cost of disregarding most, if not all, of our
initial data. If we adopt this approach to forming
clusters, the technical problem is to find the best
strategy that we can for gradually trading off loss
in data against gain in simplicity, so that clusters
at any level in the hierarchy are in accord with the
principle of maximum possible data content...that
is, have as many common, and as few exceptional
locational attributes as possible.

The essential operation performed by CLUMP 3
is to generate such a hierarchy of clusters. I have
described the details of the algorithm elsewhere (5).
The principle of trading off data loss and simplicity

gain is illustrated in figure 4. This shows a rather typical pattern for real data.

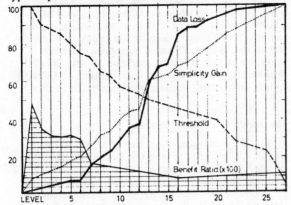

Figure 4
Data Loss and Simplicity Gain

Initially, a number of well-defined, distinctly separate clusters are discovered. Considerable simplification is achieved at the cost of comparatively little data. But it becomes progressively more difficult to achieve further simplification without heavy losses of data. It should be noted though, that even at high levels in the hierarchy, where most clusters are fairly meaningless (and the overall data content is quite low), there may still exist some individual clusters with high data content.

Output from CLUMP 3 is in the form of verbal descriptions of each cluster discovered, in a format designed to be easily comprehensible to a non-specialist user. Figure 5 shows a typical piece of output... a cluster discovered at hier-

archy level 2 in the data in figure 3. In addition to the lists of cluster members and common attributes, various numerical measures of the clusters' internal structure and reliability are given. The meaning and importance of these measures is discussed in the following section.

(4) The Structure, Meaning, and Reliability of Clusters Discovered by CLUMP 3

Clusters are generated through a process of "linking together" activity units which have "similar" strings of activity units. The numerical value of similarity between any two activity units is computed as:

$$R_{AB} = \frac{2c}{a+b}$$

c = number of pairs of matched locational attributes
a = number of locational attributes of activity unit A
b = number of locational attributes of activity unit B

At low levels in the hierarchy, the minimum value of R to define a link is high, links are consequently few, and clusters small. As we move up the hierarchy, more links form, and clusters grow larger.

Any cluster, at any level, may be drawn as a graph, in which nodes represent activity units, and every activity unit is connected, either directly or indirectly, to every other. Figure 6 shows two such clusters, each containing four activity units, but structured rather differently. We can see intuitively that their meaning may be rather different, as a consequence.

```
********************************************************************

     CLUSTER  NUMBER   2.1

     MEMBERS                              LINKS        CONNECTED TO
          3 BREAKFAST/INFORMAL EAT          2           14, 13
         13 INFORMAL ENTRY                  1           3,
         14 KITCHEN                         1           3,

     ATTRIBUTE LIST  (ATTRIBUTES POSSESSED BY 100.000 PERCENT OF MEMBERS)

     PART OF GROUP LINKED BY FOOD PREPARATION/SERVING/DISPOSAL ACTIVITIES
     FACE EAST FOR MORNING SUNLIGHT
     PART OF AREA SUPERVISABLE BY MOTHER WHILST WORKING
     PART OF ACTIVITY-ORIENTED ZONE

     PARAMETERS...IAT  15,ASF  3,APR  80.000,LIN  2,PLN  3,ALN  2,
     PCN  66.667,PRD  0.0 ,MOA  3
     NEXT PAIRS TO JOIN WILL BE...
     ( 14, 15) ( 3, 20) ( 3, 17) (                   NEW CLUSTER


********************************************************************
```

Figure 5
Typical Cluster Description Output by CLUMP 3

Figure 6
Comparison of Cluster Structures

Potential Links	6	6
Actual Links	6	3
Connectivity	100%	50%
Connection Redundancy	100%	0%
Data Content	Probably High	Probably Low
Stability	Probably High	Probably Low

Linearly structured clusters generally have a rather low data content, and tend to be quite sensitive to small alterations in the input data, whereas tightly interconnected clusters have higher data contents, and tend to be much more robust.

In order to assist in the interpretation of clusters, CLUMP 3 prints out a considerable amount of description of the data content and structure of each cluster discovered. It is not always necessary to take account of this, when interpreting output, but it can be of considerable assistance in some situations. The following data is printed out:

IAT ... Number of locational attributes possessed by cluster members.

ASF ... Number of attribute statements sacrificed to form the cluster.

APR ... Data content.

LIN ... Level of hierarchy at which cluster initially formed.

PLN ... Number of potential links in a cluster of this size.

ALN ... Number of links actually formed.

PCN ... Connectivity, $\frac{ALN}{PLN}$ x 100%

PRD ... Connection redundancy $\frac{ALN-(n-1)}{PLN-(n-1)}$ x 100%

MOA ... A measure of the isolation of the cluster from the next most closely related activity unit outside the cluster, $(R_1 - R_2)$, where R_1 is the threshold value of the relationship coefficient at which the cluster formed, and R_2 is the threshold value at which the next new member joins.

A table of all links formed is also given.

As we reach the higher levels in the hierarchy, clusters begin to appear in which the data content, as we have defined it, is zero... that is, there are no locational attributes common to all members. Such clusters are no longer "classes" in the Aristotelean sense (classes defined by sets of characters, the members of which are severally necessary and jointly sufficient, or alternatively severally sufficient and at least one necessary), but they are in the sense that Wittgenstein used when he spoke of classes defined by a kind of "family resemblance". We can still describe the properties of the class quite satisfactorily in statistical terms... x% of members possess attribute A, y% possess attribute B, etc. (6). Where clusters have zero data content, CLUMP 3 prints out a brief statistical description of this type.

(5) Use in the Design Process

The technique which has been described enables a designer to see the spatial implications of adopting a particular set of locational objectives, and test the effects of making alterations in these objectives. Its aim is to facilitate a better understanding of the structure of a spatial planning problem, and the relations between possible alternative solutions, rather than to generate some allegedly optimum configuration. Over the past year, it has been used for this purpose, with considerable success, in case studies carried out at Yale, U.C.L.A., and Rice Universities. It has rarely produced many surprises for competent, experienced building planners, but there is no reason to expect that it should... any more than we would expect the results of structural computations to surprise a good structural engineer.

In its present form, it is not really an economical proposition in most design situations. It is generally far quicker and cheaper to rely on known prototypes and past experience, since input to CLUMP 3 is fairly slow and cumbersome, and output is only in the form of the most rudimentary spatial description... verbal descriptions of clusters. However, it is certainly possible both to make input very much quicker and simpler, and to write heuristic routines to produce output in the form of graphic displays of spatial configurations. Work is now proceeding on both these aspects, and I expect this to result in the development of a very practical working technique.

NOTES

(1) For alternative approaches to this problem, see:
(a) Alexander, Christopher, and Poyner, Barry, The Atoms of Environmental Structure, Center for Planning and Development Research, Berkeley, 1966.
(b) Haviland, David S., The Activity Space: A Least Common Denominator for Architectural Programming. Paper presented at the 1967 A.I.A. Architect-Researchers' Conference.

(2) For an early, and excellent, formulation of spatial planning problems in these terms, see: Koopmans, T.C., and Beckmann, M., Assignment Problems and the Location of Economic Activities, in Econometrica, Volume 25, Number 1, January 1957.

(3) Coombs, C. H, Raiffa, H. and Thrall, R.M.
Some Views on Mathematical Models and
Measurement Theory. Chapter II, Decision
Process. Wiley, N.Y. 1954. Edited by
Coombs, C.H., Thrall, R.M., and Davis,
R.L.

(4) Simon, Herbert, Models of Man, pages
246-248

(5) Mitchell, William J., Computer-Aided Spatial
Synthesis, in Proceedings of the Association
for Computing Machinery Symposium on the
Application of Computers to Urban Problems,
New York, August 1970

(6) Hull, David L, The Effect of Essentialism on
Taxonomy, Part I, The British Journal for the
Philosophy of Science, Volume 15, pages
321-326.

A Generative Approach
To Computer-Aided Planning

by Tom Willoughby

Land Use and Built Form Studies, University of Cambridge
School of Architecture, 16 Brooklands Avenue, Cambridge, England

Abstract

The paper discusses the method of constructing a computer program which lays out
the elements of a building to generate a
coherent three dimensional form.

A building is considered as a number of
departmental units linked by complex relationships to each other and to the external
environment created by the site. The interaction between departmental requirements and
the limitations of the site is accommodated
by the use of a scoring mechanism which combines the criteria concerned, indicating the
relative positioning for the departments,
within a three dimensional context

Summary

This paper describes a mathematical
method of approaching the problems arising in
the planning of a building at a departmental
scale It is the basis for a computer program that allows the architect, client and
consultant to understand and investigate the
planning implications of specified relationships between the departments of a building.
The method considers the planning process in
two and three dimensions, identifying contradictory requirements in the brief and taking
into account the physical properties necessary
in the departments. The architect will be
able to explore the consequences of the decisions made, to understand the results of
alterations in the brief, and to investigate
different solution types.

The method is a tool for design to assist
in decision making and point the direction of
a solution. If the method is properly utilised
it will allow the architect to explore several
directions simultaneously minimising time loss
and increasing the creative time available for
the development of the final design. It is
the objective to provide for the designer an
instrument that will add to his role rather
than detract from it.

The architect and client specify the
needs of the building in subjective and
objective terms. The approach requires a
detailed examination of the conditions of the
site, with a resulting quantification of the
conditions. By the use of a scoring mechanism these criteria interact to produce a
suggested building form. The architect has
a "conversational" role with the computer
program, enabling him to explore the consequences of modifying decisions in the light
of the results produced. Thus the criteria
on which the layout of the building are
based on are continually being adjusted.
There is no unique solution to a given design
problem by this method The interpretation
of the objective and subjective needs and
the relationship between the two, will
diverge between differing architects. Given
the same brief, two architects would not
produce an identical building with this
approach.

The evaluation of the building produced
by the computer method is not within the
scope of this paper; however, important work
in this sphere has been carried out by
D. Hawkes and R. Stibbs (see LUBFS Working
Paper 15: Environmental Evaluation of Buildings). The method for generation is used to
its fullest in association with an evaluative
model.

The computer method is able to examine
the building process on three scales, (a)
the site scale (b) the departmental scale
and (c) the room scale The criteria to be
considered are scored and weighted within a
common range, and by this means they are
processed into the mechanism of the computer
method to develop the building form.

This paper deals with the application
of the model to the departmental scale. A
building is considered as a number of departmental units for this purpose. The departments have relationships to each other and
to the physical conditions of the site.

Each will have particular needs, requiring it to be placed adjacent, or in close proximity to another department. Alternatively, departments may require to be at a distance from others. In addition the departments will demand physical conditions in terms of lighting, orientation, shape and size, i.e. departments have a relation both to the external environment and the internal environment. By interrelating these factors the relative positions of the departments to each other and to the site are indicated.

The computer utilizes a combination of scores for various constraints. The departments are located where the summation of the scores reaches a maximum. Taken into account are a) the physical constraints of the site, b) the degree of association or disassociation between the departments, and c) the physical constraints of each department.

a) The site conditions are considered by placing a grid over the proposed site. Numbers are placed in each cell of the grid reflecting the degree of amenity to building of that portion of the site. A set of grids are independantly constructed, each grid reflecting one criterion.

b) The association between the departments is expressed in association charts. A number of charts are used, each reflecting a different criterion, e.g. association might be considered in terms of service need, work efficiency, social contact and other factors.

c) The physical constraints are expressed in terms of orientation, number of cells occupied by the department, shape and lighting conditions.

The building is planned by floors, however the method considers each department in a three dimensional context, i e. if it became desirable for a department to be on another floor the method would recognize this and move the department to that floor. A series of experimental circulation routes, horizontal and vertical, are used to investigate their effect on the building form.

The departments are placed progressively to form a plan. The order in which departments are located has an influence on the final solution. If the initial sequence of placing leads to the point where all the physical demands of a department cannot be met, the order of placing is automatically altered to gain a solution where possible. Thus a type of advanced search mechanism avoids cul-de-sac situations. If a solution is impossible because the design requirements are in contradiction, the program will determine where the contradiction occurs and print out the plan as far as possible, thus pointing out the

difficulty. The matter is then in the hands of the architect and client who must decide their priority of requirements.

The output produced by the method is in the form of departmental layouts of the floors of a building. From these, three dimensional building forms are demonstrated. Also the horizontal and vertical circulation routes can be identified. These results enable the architect and client to examine the consequences of his decisions and to modify elements or criteria for a re-run of the program.

Summarizing the method:

1   The architect, client and specialist prepare the information in terms of departmental asso iation, site conditions and physical requirements of the departments.

2   For each departmental placing, the association charts are weighted and summed. The site grids are weighted and summed.

3   Limits on storey heights are imposed.

4   The association charts are summed (unweighted) and from this the initial sequence of placing departments is obtained

5   An experimental circulation route is positioned.

6   The departments are positioned (by the computer program) in plan, floor by floor.

7   The plans are output.

8   Alterations are made, the program is re-run.